ADVANCED JAVA™: INTERNET APPLICATIONS

SECOND EDITION

Art Gittleman

California State University, Long Beach

Scott/Jones Inc.
P.O. Box 696,
El Granada, California 94018
Voice: **650-726-2436**
Facsimile: 650-726-4693
e-mail: **marketing@scottjonespub.com**
Web page: //www.scottjonespub.com

ISBN 1-57676-096-0

Advanced Java™ : Internet Applications

Art Gittleman
California State University, Long Beach

Copyright 2002 by Art Gittleman

YXW   321

ISBN: 1-57676-096-0

Composition: Stephen Adams
Book Manufacturing: Von Hoffmann Graphics

Scott/Jones Publishing Company

Publisher: Richard Jones
Editorial Group: Richard Jones, Michelle Windell, Denise Simon, Mike Needham, Natascha Hoffmeyer, and Patricia Miyaki
Production Management: Heather Bennett
Marketing and Sales: Viskie Judy, Hazel Dunlap, Donna Cross, Page Mead, and Michelle Windell
Business Operations: Michelle Robelet and Cathy Glenn

A Word About Trademarks
All product names identified in this book are trademarks or registered trademarks of their respective companies. We have used the names in an editorial fashion only, and to the benefit of the trademark owner, with no intention of infringing the trademark.

Additional Titles of Interest from Scott/Jones

From Objects to Components with the Java™ Platform
Computing with Java™, Second Edition
Computing with Java™, Alternate Edition
  by Art Gittleman

Starting Out with Visual Basic
Standard Version of Starting Out with C++, Third Edition
Brief Version of Starting Out with C++, Third Edition
Alternate Version of Starting Out with C++, Second Edition
  by Tony Gaddis

Modern Fortran 77/90/2000, Third Edition
Introduction to Programming with Visual Basic 6, Second Edition
  by Gary Bronson

C by Discovery, Third Edition
  by L.S. and Dusty Foster

Assembly Language for the IBM PC Family, Third Edition
  by William Jones

The Visual Basic 6 Coursebook, Fourth Edition
QuickStart to JavaScript
ShortCourse in HTML
QuickStart to DOS for Windows 9X
  by Forest Lin

Advanced Visual Basic 6, Second Edition
  by Kip Irvine

HTML for WebDevelopers
Server-Side Programming for Web Developers
  by John Avila

The Complete Computer Repair Textbook, Third Edition
  by Cheryl Schmidt

Windows 2000 Professional Step-by-Step
  by Debby Tice and Leslie Hardin

The Windows 2000 Professional Textbook
A Prelude to Programming
  by Stewart Venit

The Windows 2000 Server Lab Manual
  by Gerard Morris

Contents

CHAPTER 10   *Enterprise JavaBeans™*   387

CHAPTER 11   *Collections*   421

CHAPTER 12   *Security and the Java Virtual Machine*   457

CHAPTER 13   *XML*   497

Preface

When I need information, I go to the Internet first. I buy books and running shoes, and make airline reservations online. I register for 5K events online and get the results that way too. But I am only standing at the gate to the Internet revolution, which includes entertainment, mobile devices, appliances, and transportation in ways that will dramatically change our lives.

Java and the Internet are growing together. Java works behind the scenes to power Internet applications. Students and professionals who accept the challenge of rapid change and exciting technology need a book that introduces them in a friendly way to the latest advanced Internet applications using Java.

This book is for those who have programmed in Java at the level of a first course and are familiar with its basic constructs. I include a combination of client-side and server-side techniques and the very latest Java technology. The second edition expands the first to include five additional chapters to cover emerging areas that Java developers need to know.

The book is advanced but I have tried to present concepts clearly, illustrating them with many programming examples, so readers will get sound introductions to all the important topics. Readers will be able to continue with advanced courses in specialized areas or enter rewarding career paths.

I made the chapters as independent as possible so that readers may pursue different paths through the book without difficulty. The following graph shows the dependencies among the chapters.

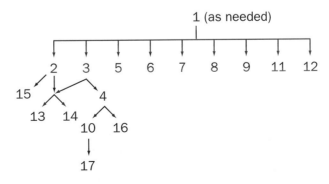

Features
· · · · · · · · · · ·

Content

This text covers state-of-the-art material on Internet applications with Java™ technology, including Enterprise JavaBeans™, JavaServer™ Pages, Security, JDBC™, Swing™, Networking, Servlets, Java 2D™, Java 3D™, JavaBeans™, Internationalization, Concurrent Programming, RMI, Java Media Framework™, Collections, the Java Virtual Machine, XML, SOAP, the J2ME™ and Mobile Devices, Jini™ and JavaSpaces™, JSP™ Tags, Messaging, and Naming

Annotated Example Programs

Examples facilitate learning. Almost two hundred complete programs are annotated with informative notes. These notes appear after the program, separated from the textual sections, which explain the concepts. Readers do not have to search through the text to find an explanation of a line of code. The notes also eliminate the need for detailed embedded comments which make the Java code hard to read.

Exercises

The many varied exercises allow the learner to assimilate concepts and techniques actively.

Test Your Understanding exercises provide an immediate opportunity to use the ideas presented. By putting exercises in each section I target each new idea as it occurs. Answers to many of these appear at the end of the text and the answers to most of the rest can be found on the disk included with the text. Some, labeled **Try It Yourself** encourage the learner to experiment with the examples, modifying them to better understand the principles involved.

Much of a professional programmer's work involves modifying existing code, so I believe in providing practice using **Program Modification Exercises**. Marked **Putting It All Together Exercises** revisit examples from previous chapters in the light of the new ideas in the current chapter.

Program Design Exercises appear in quantity to provide a variety of assignments at varying levels of difficulty to enable students to gain hands-on experience with the concepts covered

The Big Picture

Big Picture boxes, at the end of each section, help readers to synthesize the material into a coherent whole, so they can use the concepts effectively.

Chapter Survey

· · · · · · · · · · ·

Startup

Chapter 1, **Preliminaries**, includes material, which may be postponed until needed in later chapters. It starts with exception handling, which is required for I/O, which in turn is required for networking. The event-handling section may be review. I include mouse and key events in Appendix A, because I do not use them in other chapters. I cover threads, used in networking and animation, and concurrent programming. The gridbag layout occurs in a few examples including the GUI for database access. I use vectors in a few places, and they provide an introduction and contrast to the Collections chapter.

Using Servers

Java has become very popular on the server side. The next chapters show how to make network connections to web servers, connect to databases, and use servlets.

Chapter 2, **Networking**, starts with URLs, which hide the details of the protocols. I explain the HTTP protocol, and use a URLConnection to customize the connection. At a lower level, sockets handle the protocol directly to communicate. I use sockets to develop rudimentary browsers and web servers. The last section covers RMI, a high-level basis for distributed computing.

Chapter 3, **Java Database Connectivity (JDBC)**, contains a thorough guide to databases using Java. To make it self-contained, I cover the basic SQL commands. The examples use Microsoft Access, but will work with any database that has a JDBC driver, and many will work with text files. The chapter covers SQL, connecting, creating tables, queries, metadata, prepared statements, and transactions. It concludes with an extended example of a GUI to query a database.

Chapter 4, **Servlets and JavaServer™ Pages**, shows how to add functionality to a web server. I use the JRun™ application server (found on the included CD). The chapter starts with HTML forms on web clients that call servlets to handle processing on the server. I discuss server-side includes and the new JavaServer™ Pages which are superceding them. The last three sections are essential for web applications. I illustrate a three-tiered architecture by connecting to a servlet, which in turn connects to a database. Session tracking enables the server to maintain client information. The new JavaServer™ Pages technology makes it easier to separate content and presentation.

Enhancing the Client

Java provides many facilities for building better client applications. The next few chapters turn to client-side development.

Chapter 5, **Swing**, presents the Swing components for building graphical user interfaces including text, images, buttons, borders, lists, toggle buttons, menus, dialogs, tabs, and tables. Swing has much to offer. This introduction will enable readers to use Swing effectively with the understanding that there is much more than could be covered here.

Chapter 6, Java 2D™, provides the tools to make fabulous presentations incorporating text and graphics. It covers geometric shapes, the rendering of graphics and text, and printing.

The World Wide Web is worldwide. Internationalization enables applications to adapt to the customs of the user's locale. **Chapter 7, Internationalization**, treats number, currency, date and time formatting, collation, localizing user interfaces, and message formatting. A few examples use simple Spanish words and phrases that could be replaced by ENGLISH, which is English with all upper-case letters, if desired.

As bandwidth increases, multimedia applications are becoming more prevalent. **Chapter 8, Multimedia**, covers animation and sound, and introduces the Java Media Framework™, which can play and capture audio and video in many formats. Two sections delve into the powerful Java 3D API.

Component Technology

The next two chapters present component technology. JavaBeans™ are primarily a client-side technology, while Enterprise JavaBeans™ are a key server-side platform.

Chapter 9, Java Beans, covers JavaBeans™, components that can be configured and combined using a visual application building tool. I use the bean box included with the Beans Development Kit . After using predefined beans in the bean box, I show how to write and deploy a bean, and use BeanInfo to make a bean more user friendly. The chapter concludes by showing how to use beans in a program rather than a visual tool.

Chapter 10, Enterprise JavaBeans™, treats the new and popular Enterprise JavaBeans™, using the J2EE reference implementation from Sun. Enterprise Java-Beans™ are server components that allow developers to build applications focusing on the business problems while the server handles the low-level details of concurrency, transactions, and scaling. This chapter covers entity and session beans, and uses standalone as well as servlet and JavaServer™ Page clients.

Tools

The next two chapters cover useful tools. Data structures are essential in storing data in memory, and security protects against unwanted access. The Java Virtual Machine is the core support for Java execution.

The Collections hierarchy provides data structures and algorithms. **Chapter 11, Collections**, covers collections, sets, lists, maps, and iterators. It shows how to handle ordered data, and introduces algorithms.

Each Java release enhances the security features. **Chapter 12, Security and the Java Virtual Machine**, discusses the use of a security manager, policy files, and digital signatures. It concludes with a survey of the instruction set for the Java Virtual Machine and the structure of Java class files.

Hot Topics

The remaining chapters cover hot topics that are providing great excitement now.

Just as Java provides code that can run anywhere, XML provides a platform independent data representation useful in communicating from one application to another. **Chapter 13, XML (Extendible Markup Language)**, covers this extremely important area including SAX and DOM parsing, XSLT stylesheets, and the easy SOAP approach for web services.

Using Java on mobile devices provides a uniform platform for developers. The device market for cell phones and personal digital assistants will grow beyond that for personal computers. **Chapter 14, Programming Mobile Devices)**, uses the Java™ 2 Micro Edition to program cell phone applications including user interfaces, networking, data storage, and graphics and low-level events.

As more and more devices interact over networks new technologies will be necessary to enable all these devices to locate each other without massive configuration overhead. Jini™ technology is a Java approach to plug-and-play connectivity for software and hardware that will become more important as network use increases. JavaSpaces™ is an easy and powerful facility for distributed computed built on Jini™. **Chapter 15, Jini™ and JavaSpaces™**, provides simple examples to illustrate these innovative technologies.

Web services are becoming the dominant application model. **Chapter 16, JSP Tags**, covers JavaServer™ Page (JSP) tag libraries. These libraries help enable web designers to concentrate on the page design while Java developers encapsulate Java methods inside custom tags. Using such tags provides an easy and effective way to create dynamic web pages.

Finally, **Chapter 17, Messaging and Naming**, discusses finding and sending messages to other resources. Messaging using the Java Messaging Service allows asynchronous communication in both publish-and-subscribe and point-to-point forms. The Java Naming and Directory Interface supports various frequently used naming and directory services.

Software

The programs will run in any environment that supports the Java 2 Platform. (In the Java numbering scheme the version must be 1.2 or higher.) The following table shows the software that I used for each of the chapters.

Program	Chapter(s)
Java™ 2 SDK Standard Edition v. 1.2 (or higher)	All
JRun™ 3.0 (or Tomcat)	4, 16
Java Media Framework™ 2.1	8
Java 3D™	8
Beans Development Kit™	9
Java™ 2 SDK Enterprise Edition v. 1.2.1	10
Java™ 2 SDK Enterprise Edition v. 1.3	17
Java™ 2 Micro Edition, MIDP and CLDC	14
Jini™ Technology Starter Kit	15
Java™ API for XML Processing (JAXP)	13
SOAP	13

The included CD contains the first two items. All may be downloaded (except for JRun, SOAP, and Tomcat) from Sun at `http://java.sun.com`. JRun may be downloaded from Macromedia at `http://www.macromedia.com`. SOAP may be downloaded from `xml.apache.org`. Tomcat is available from `jakarta.apache.org`.

To Instructors

Because there are few dependencies, instructors have a great deal of flexibility in choosing appropriate content. The amount one can cover depends on the background of the students. Students should have programmed in Java before, and will benefit from any additional maturity in computer science.

The CD included with the book contains all the programs and the answers to the even numbered Test Your Understanding questions. A disk available to instructors teaching from this book contains solutions to most of the odd numbered programming exercises.

Other Options

Instructors who would like a text that includes both elementary and advanced material may use my *Computing with Java*™: *Programs, Objects, Graphics, Alternate Second Edition*, Scott/Jones, Inc., 2002. That text contains twelve chapters of introductory Java, object-oriented programming, event-driven programming, and data structures. In addition it contains chapters 1, 2, 3, 4, 5, 9, 11, and 13 from this text.

A brief comparison of my series of Java texts with Scott/Jones Publishing is given on the next page.

Acknowledgments

. . . .

Thanks go especially to my wife, Charlotte, and daughter, Amanda, for their patience. My one book project has become a trilogy. My students keep me thinking. They have helped greatly with preliminary versions, and found many typographical errors. Heather Bennett, Stephen Adams, Victoria Judy, Michelle Windell and the entire Scott/Jones team provide their usual fabulous support. I thank Richard Jones for giving me the go ahead to proceed to the bleeding edge of an exciting technology. I appreciate the helpful critiques of the excellent reviewers.

I have been using Java since it appeared in 1995. I thank the Java people at Sun and their partners for providing the language and the libraries that make developing Internet applications successful and fun.

Computing with Java™: Programs, Objects, Graphics, Second Edition	Computing with Java™: Programs, Objects, Graphics, Alternate Second Edition	Advanced Java™ Internet Applications, Second Edition
Introductory: Control structures before objects 1. Computing with Java 2. Java Programming Basics 3. Software Engineering with Control Structures 4. More Control Structures and Types 5. Getting Started with Object-Oriented Programming	Introductory: Objects before control structures 1. Computing with Java 2. Programming with Objects 3. Software Engineering with Control Structures 4. More Control Structures and Types 5. Object-Oriented Design and Programming	Advanced course with an introductory Java prerequisite Reviewed in 1 1. and Appendix A Reviewed in 1 5. Swing Components 11. Collections 8. Multimedia
Chapter 6–15 are identical 6. Event-Driven Programming 7. User Interfaces 8. Arrays 9. Inheritance 10. Window, Mouse, and Key Events 11. Exception Handling and Input/Output 12. Swing Components 13. Data Structures 14. Collections 15. Multimedia and Networking		2. Networking 3. JDBC 4. Servlets and JSP 9. JavaBeans 13. XML This text also contains Java 2D™, Java 3D™, Concurrent Programming, Internationalization, Enterprise JavaBeans™, Security and the Java Virtual Machine, Programming Mobile Devices, Jini™ and JavaSpaces™. JSP Tags, Messaging, and Naming
	Chapters 16–20 available only in Alternate Edition 16. Networking 17. JDBC 18. Servlets and JSP 19. JavaBeans 20. XML	

Web Site

My web site specifically for this book is

`http://www.cecs.csulb.edu/~artg/internet`

Check this site for updates including a revision of Chapter 10 to use version 1.3 of the J2EE reference implementation.

Errata

Check my web site for the most current list. I would very much appreciate receiving any corrections, which may be emailed to me at `artg@csulb.edu`.

1

Preliminaries

OBJECTIVES

This chapter presents material that may not have been covered in a prior Java course that will be useful in succeeding chapters.

- Handle standard exceptions: Exception handling is essential for input and output, which in turn is essential for networking.

- Read and write binary, text, and object data: Input and output forms the basis for network communication.

- Understand the Java event model: We review event-driven programming, which is useful in implementing client interfaces.

- Create threads and synchronize access to data: Concurrent programming using threads supports large enterprise applications.

- Use the gridbag layout to create a user interface: The gridbag layout provides more flexibility for user-interface design.

- Utilize vectors and enumerations: Vectors are useful in concurrent applications and will be contrasted with the new Collection classes.

1.1 Exception Handling

Java provides an exception handling facility to allow the programmer to insert code to handle unexpected errors and allow the program to recover and continue executing, or to terminate gracefully, whichever is appropriate. An **exception** signals that a condition such as an error has occurred. We **throw** an exception as a signal, and **catch** it to handle it and take appropriate action.

Exception Classes

In Java, exceptions are instances of a class derived from `Throwable`. Figure 1.1 shows the exception classes that we discuss in this chapter (the ... indicates a class that we do not use and has been omitted from the display.)

Figure 1.1 Classes of Exceptions

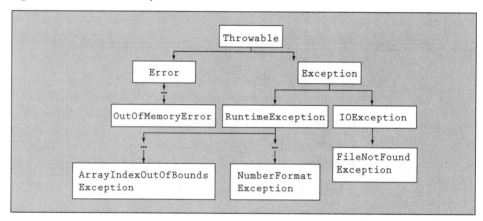

In this section we consider **array index out of bounds** and **number format** exceptions, leaving the IO exceptions to the next section. Java allows us to handle array index out of bounds and number format exceptions, but does not require us to handle them. Java requires that we handle IO errors, usually beyond our control, which would otherwise cause our program to abort.

The Array Index Out of Bounds Exception

The array

```java
int[] a = {4,5,6};
```

has three elements which we can access using the indices 0, 1, and 2. If we try to use an index other than these three, as for example in the expression `i=a[3]`, Java will throw an array index out of bounds exception. Each exception is an instance of a class. We can write our own classes to define new types of exceptions, but in this text we use the Java exception classes.

Throwing an exception interrupts the program, transferring control to a user-defined `catch` clause, if any, which specifies how to handle the exception, or aborting if no `catch` clause is found

Java does not require the programmer to handle the array index out of bounds exception, but it allows the programmer to do so. To handle an exception, we put the code that could cause that exception to occur in a `try` block followed by a `catch` clause to handle the exception, as in:

```
try {
  // some code that might generate an out of bounds exception
} catch(ArrayIndexOutOfBoundsException e) {
  // some code to execute when that exception occurs
}
```

`ArrayIndexOutOfBoundsException` is the type of exception we are trying to catch. Java passes an instance, `e`, of this exception, which contains information about the array index out of bounds exception that occurred, to the `catch` clause.

If an exception occurs in the try block, Java looks for a `catch` clause that handles that exception. If it finds one, it jumps immediately to execute that code, never returning to any code in the `try` block after that which caused the exception. If Java does not find such a `catch` clause, it will abort the program with an error message.

In Example 1.1 we put our use of the array index into a `try` block, and when Java throws the array index out of bounds exception, we catch it and display an error message. Our program does not abort, and execution continues after the `catch` clause. With a little more effort, we could use a loop to give the user another chance to input a correct value after making an error. We leave this enhancement to the exercises.

EXAMPLE 1.1   **TryException.java**

```java
/* Puts the array code in a try block
 * and catches the array index out of bounds exception
 * if it occurs.
 */

public class TryException{
  public static void main(String [] args) {
    int value;
    try {
      int [ ] anArray = {5,6,7};
      int index = Integer.parseInt(args[0]);              // Note 1
      value = anArray[index];                             // Note 2
      System.out.println("Execution does not get here if index is bad");
    }catch (ArrayIndexOutOfBoundsException e) {           // Note 3
      System.out.println("Stick with 0, 1, or 2");
    }
    System.out.println("This is the end of the program");  // Note 4
  }
}
```

Output (from `java TryException 2`**)**

```
Execution does not get here if index is bad
This is the end of the program
```

Output (from `java TryException 89`**)**

```
Stick with 0, 1, or 2
This is the end of the program
```

....

Note 1: The `parseInt` method converts the string that we pass as a program argument to an integer.

Note 2: Java will throw an array index out of bounds exception if index < 0 or if index > 2.

Note 3: After throwing an array index out of bounds exception, Java jumps here to the handler, skipping any code remaining in the try block.

Note 4: After executing the code in the `catch` clause, Java continues executing here. Handling the array index out of bounds exception allows the program to continue executing whether or not Java throws this exception.

If there is no `catch` clause for an exception immediately following the try block, then, when that exception occurs, Java looks for the `catch` clause in the caller of the method in which the `try` block is contained.

In Example 1.2, we use an out of bounds array index in the `getSquare` method, but do not include a `catch` clause in that method. When Java encounters the invalid index during execution it throws an array index out of bounds exception and looks for a `catch` clause which handles that exception. Not finding one in `getSquare`, Java looks in the caller of the `getSquare` method, the `main` method, which does have a clause that catches the exception. Java jumps to the `catch` clause in the `main` method in which we call `e.printStackTrace()`, where e is the array index out of bounds exception which Java passes to the `catch` clause.

An important use of stacks is in implementing method calls in programming languages. We stack up local variables and arguments passed to the method. When starting to execute the `main` method, Java pushes the data that `main` needs onto the stack. When the `main` method calls the `getSquare` method, Java pushes the data that `getSquare` needs onto the top of the previous data on the stack. In Example 1.2, we have only two methods, but in larger examples we could have half a dozen or more methods using the stack, many of them from the Java library packages.

The data for the method that Java is currently executing is on the top of the stack. When Java throws an array index out of bounds exception it passes an object of that exception type to the `catch` clause for that exception. This object contains a list of all the methods whose data is on the stack when the exception occurred. To see this list, we call the `printStackTrace()` method, which outputs[1]

```
java.lang.ArrayIndexOutOfBoundsException: 98
  at TryExceptionTrace.getSquare(TryExceptionTrace.java:10)
  at TryExceptionTrace.main(TryExceptionTrace.java:15)
```

The first line names the exception that occurred and displays the invalid value, 98. The next two lines are the stack entries. TryExceptionTrace is the class name for Example 1.2. The data for getSquare is on the top of the stack and the exception occurred at line 10 of the program. By printing the stack trace we can find the line at which the exception occurred. The second stack entry says that the bottom of the stack contains the data for the main method, and that the main method called the getSquare method at line 15 of the program.

By reading the stack trace, we can follow the sequence of method calls that culminated in the throwing of the exception. After executing the code in the catch clause, Java continues execution with the code following the catch clause. Had we omitted the catch clause, Java would have aborted the program with an error message. Handling the exception allows us to recover from the error and continue executing the remainder of the program.

EXAMPLE 1.2   **TryExceptionTrace.java**

```
/* Shows the use of the printStackTrace method
 * to obtain the sequence of method calls that
 * culminated in the throwing of the array index
 * out of bounds exception.
 */

public class TryExceptionTrace{
  public static int getSquare(int index) {
    int [ ] anArray = {5,6,7};
    return anArray[index]*anArray[index];                        // Note 1
  }
  public static void main(String [ ] args) {
    int value;
    try {
      value = getSquare(Integer.parseInt(args[0]));             // Note 2
      System.out.println("Execution does not get here if the index is bad");
    }catch (ArrayIndexOutOfBoundsException e) {
      e.printStackTrace();
    }
    System.out.println("This is the end of the program");
  }
}
```

---

1. We need to disable the Just in Time compiler (JIT) to view the line numbers in a stack trace. To disable the JIT in Java 1.1, use the command `java -nojit TryExceptionTrace`. To disable it in the Java 2 platform use the command
   `java -Djava.compiler=NONE TryExceptionTrace`.

Output (from `java TryExceptionTrace 98`)

```
java.lang.ArrayIndexOutOfBoundsException: 98
    at TryExceptionTrace.getSquare(TryExceptionTrace.java:10)
    at TryExceptionTrace.main(TryExceptionTrace.java:15)
This is the end of the program
```

Note 1:   This is line 10 which causes the exception.

Note 2:   This is line 15, where the `main` method calls the `getSquare` method that produces the exception.

The Number Format Exception

Java allows us to construct an `Integer` object from a string, as in:

```
Integer i = new Integer("375");
```

If we provide a string that is not a valid integer constant, as in:

```
Integer j = new Integer("3.75");
```

Java will throw a number format exception. If we do not handle the exception in a `catch` clause, Java will abort the program with an error message.

Example 1.3 shows both valid and invalid attempts to construct `Integer` and `Double` objects from strings. As in Example 1.2, we call the `printStackTrace` method to determine the exception and where it occurred. In this example the stack of method calls shows three entries, the bottom from our `main` method and the top two from the `Integer` class of the Java library. Java uses `<init>` to denote a constructor.

EXAMPLE 1.3   **StringToNumber.java**

```
/* Illustrates wrapper classes used to convert
 * a string to an int or a double, and the number format
 * exception when the string has an invalid format.
 */

public class StringToNumber {
  public static void main(String [] args) {
    try {
    int i = new Integer("435").intValue();           // Note 1
    System.out.println("i = " + i);
    int j = new Integer("45.2").intValue();          // Note 2
    System.out.println("j = " + j);
    }catch(NumberFormatException e) {
      e.printStackTrace();                            // Note 3
    }
    double d = new Double("3.14").doubleValue();     // Note 4
    System.out.println("d = " + d);
  }
}
```

Output

```
i = 435
java.lang.NumberFormatException: 45.2
    at java.lang.Integer.parseInt(Integer.java:238)
    at java.lang.Integer.<init>(Integer.java:342)
    at StringToNumber.main(StringToNumber.java:11)
d = 3.14
```

Note 1: We construct an `Integer` object from the string "435" which represents an integer literal. The `intValue` method returns a value, 435, of type **int**.

Note 2: Passing the string "45.2" to the `Integer` constructor causes Java to throw a number format exception, as 45.2 is not a valid integer literal.

Note 3: The stack trace shows two methods from the `Integer` class. The bottom line of the trace shows that line 11 of our program caused Java to throw the exception.

Note 4: After handling the exception, we wrap a valid **double** value as a `Double`.

THE BIG PICTURE

Enclosing code that can throw an exception in a `try` block allows us to handle that exception in a `catch` clause. When Java throws an exception it will jump to a `catch` clause for that exception in the same method if there is one, and continue searching for a `catch` clause in the calling method, otherwise. Printing the stack trace shows the methods that were in progress when the exception occurred.

TEST YOUR UNDERSTANDING

TRY IT YOURSELF

1. Run Examples 1.1 and 1.2, entering a negative value for the index to see that Java throws an exception in this case.

TRY IT YOURSELF

2. Revise Example 1.3 to remove the `try` statement and the `catch` clause for the `NumberFormatException`. Rerun the revised code and note what happens and what code gets executed.

3. Which of the following will cause Java to throw a `NumberFormatException`?

   a. `Integer i = new Integer("-7200");`
   b. `Double d = new Double("PI");`
   c. `String s = new String("PI");`
   d. `String s = new String("64000");`
   e. `Double d = new Double(".123");`

1.2   Input and Output

. . . .

Java distinguishes between binary and character I/O. Binary data consists of 8-bit bytes. Java uses input and output streams to read and write binary data. A stream is an ordered sequence of bytes. We think of input flowing in and output flowing out, so the term *stream* evokes the right image.

Internally, Java character data consists of 16-bit Unicode characters. Java uses readers and writers to read and write character data. Readers convert from various character encodings to Unicode and writers reverse that process.

Java reads and writes values of the various primitive types, and provides object serialization to read and write objects properly. When reading and writing objects, we must be very careful in dealing with shared objects. Fortunately the Java object serialization facilities handle these details automatically, allowing us to easily store and retrieve objects.

The File Class

The File class has several methods that return properties of the file. Example 1.4 uses some of these methods, whose names nicely signify their functions.

EXAMPLE 1.4   **FileProperties.java**

```
/* Creates a file and returns some of its properties.
 */

import java.io.*;
public class FileProperties {
  public static void main(String [ ] args) {
  File f = new File(args[0]);
  System.out.println("Name: "+f.getName());
  System.out.println("Path: "+f.getPath());
  System.out.println("Can write: "+f.canWrite());
  System.out.println("Is directory: "+f.isDirectory());
  System.out.println("Length: "+f.length());
  System.out.println("Parent directory: "+f.getParent());
  }
}
```

....

Output (from java FileProperties \book3\prelim\FileProperties.java**)**

```
Name: FileProperties.java
Path: \book3\prelim\FileProperties.java
Can write: true
Is directory: false
Length: 635
Parent directory: \book3\prelim
```

Reading and Writing Bytes

The abstract `InputStream` class contains three read methods. The method

```
public native int read( ) throws IOException;
```

where the modifier `native` indicates that Java implements this method in a platform-dependent manner, reads a single byte. The `int` return type guarantees that the return value will be positive. The `byte` type represents values from −128 to 127. Character codes use unsigned values better represented using the `int` type where a single byte will have a value between 0 and 255.

The method

```
public int read(byte[ ] b) throws IOException;
```

reads into a byte array. It may not fill the array if not enough input bytes are available. The three-argument version of read,

```
public int read(byte[] b, int off, int len)
                               throws IOException;
```

reads into an array of bytes, with the second argument specifying the starting offset in the file, and the third giving the number of bytes to read. The last two `read` methods return the number of bytes read, or −1 if at the end of the file.

Because files represent external resources there is always a possibility of hardware failure or corruption or deletion by other users, so Java requires that we catch the `IOException` that would be thrown when such an error occurs. Omitting the `try-catch` code in Example 1.5 will cause a compiler error.

In Example 1.5, we read and display bytes from standard input by default, but can read from a file by entering its name on the command line. Java declares the standard input stream, `System.in`, usually the keyboard, as an `InputStream`. The `FileInputStream` class lets us read from a file.

EXAMPLE 1.5   **ReadBytes.java**

```
/* Reads and displays bytes until end-of-file. Reads from the keyboard
 * or from a file name entered as a program argument.
 */

import java.io.*;
public class ReadBytes {
  public static void main(String[] args) {
    InputStream input;
    try {
      if (args.length == 1)
        input = new FileInputStream(args[0]);
      else
        input = System.in;
      int i;
```

```
      while((i = input.read()) != -1)
        System.out.print(i + " ");
      input.close();
    }catch(IOException e) {
      e.printStackTrace();
    }
  }
}
```

Output (from `java ReadBytes`)

```
a big car
97 32 98 105 103 32 99 97 114 13 10 ^Z                                    // Note 1
```

Output (from `java ReadBytes test.data` where `test.data` contains á big car)

```
225 32 98 105 103 32 99 97 114                                            // Note 2
```

Note 1:   The program outputs the ASCII values for the characters. The last two values, 13 and 10, represent carriage return and newline generated in Windows by pressing the Enter key. Java buffers the standard input so that the user can backspace and make changes. Hitting the Enter key signals that the user is satisfied with the input. To signal the end of the input, the user enters Control Z on a separate line of input.

Note 2:   We added an accented character, á, to show a value, 225, that would be negative if the return type was byte.

We can make reading from a file much more efficient by buffering the input. Buffering involves reading a block, say 2048 bytes, from the disk to an internal memory buffer. The next reads will take bytes from the buffer rather than having to make inefficient disk accesses. When the buffer is empty, the next read will grab another block to fill it. We could have buffered the file input in Example 1.5 using the constructor

```
new BufferedInputStream(new FileInputStream(args[0]))
```

Example 1.6 uses a read statement to read a file, and copies it to a new location with the write method of FileOutputStream. We can copy either text files or binary files this way. The FileOutputStream class has three versions of the write method: write one byte, write an array of bytes, or write a given length of an array of bytes from a starting offset in the file.

We close the file in a finally clause, which is an extra exception handling option to ensure proper clean up. Java executes the finally clause whether or not an exception was thrown.

EXAMPLE 1.6

FileCopy.java

```java
/* Copies a file using read and write statements.
 * Pass source and target file names as program arguments.
 */

import java.io.*;
public class FileCopy {
    public static void main(String [] args) {
      FileInputStream input = null;
      FileOutputStream output = null;
      try {
        File f = new File(args[0]);
        input = new FileInputStream(f);                     // Note 1
        int length = (int)f.length();                       // Note 2
        byte [] data = new byte[length];                    // Note 3
        input.read(data);                                   // Note 4
        output = new FileOutputStream(args[1]);             // Note 5
        output.write(data);
      }catch (IOException e) {
      e.printStackTrace();
      }finally {
        try {
          input.close();                                    // Note 6
          output.close();
      } catch(IOException ex) {
        ex.printStackTrace();
      }
    }
  }
}
```

....

Output

The command `java FileCopy FileCopy.java NewFileCopy.java` copies `FileCopy.java` to `NewFileCopy.java`

....

Note 1:   We create a File object, f, and pass it rather than the file name, because we need a `File` object to get the file's length. We leave the buffering of the input as an exercise.

Note 2:   The `length` method returns a value of type `long`, which we must cast to an `int` because the new operator creates an array with size given by a value of type `int`.

Note 3:   We create an array large enough to hold the entire file.

Note 4:   We created the data array to have the size of the file, so we use the `read` method that fills the entire array. This is equivalent to `read(data,0,length)`.

Note 5:   We do not need a `File` object for the output file, so we just pass the file name directly to the constructor.

Note 6:   We close each file to release any operating system resources used. Closing them in the `finally` clause means that Java will close the files whether or not an exception occurs. The `close` statements may throw an exception and need to be in a `try-catch` block.

For greater efficiency, we could have buffered the output using the constructor.

```
new BufferedOutputStream(new FileOutputStream(target))
```

We leave the buffering of the output as an exercise.

Reading and Writing Primitive Types

The `DataOutputStream` class has methods for writing each of the primitive types in binary form, including `writeBoolean`, `writeChar`, `writeDouble`, `writeFloat`, `writeInt`, and `writeLong`, while `DataInputStream` has methods for reading these types including `readBoolean`, `readChar`, `readDouble`, `readFloat`, `readInt`, and `readLong`.

To create a `DataOutputStream`, we first create a `FileOutputStream`

```
new FileOutputStream(args[0])
```

where `args[0]` is the name of the file to which we write. We pass this `FileOutput-Stream` to a `BufferedOutputStream`

```
new BufferedOutputStream(new FileOutputStream(args[0]))
```

so that each `write` statement does not force an expensive write to external storage, but rather writes to a buffer which, when filled, is written to the disk. Finally, we construct the `DataOutputStream` from the `BufferedOutputStream`

```
new DataOutputStream(new BufferedOutputStream(new FileOutputStream(args[0])))
```

In Example 1.7, we use the `writeDouble` method to write the integers 0 through 9 and the decimals from 0.0 through 9.0 to a file. The binary format, used internally, is not suitable for human reading. We use the `readDouble` method to read from the newly created file, displaying the values on the screen using the `System.out.print` method to verify the file was written correctly.

EXAMPLE 1.7   Binary.java

```
/* Illustrates the DataOutputStream and DataInputStream
 * classes for primitive type IO using int and double.
 */

import java.io.*;

public class Binary {
  public static void main(String [] args) {
```

```
try {
   DataOutputStream output = new DataOutputStream
                              (new BufferedOutputStream
                              (new FileOutputStream(args[0])));
   for (int i = 0; i < 10; i++) output.writeInt(i);
   for (double d=0.0; d < 10.0; d++) output.writeDouble(d);     // Note 1
   output.close();
   DataInputStream input = new DataInputStream
                            (new BufferedInputStream
                            (new FileInputStream(args[0])));
   for (int i=0; i<10; i++)
     System.out.print(input.readInt() + " ");
   for (int i=0; i<10; i++)
     System.out.print(input.readDouble() + " ");
   input.close();
  }catch (IOException e) {
   e.printStackTrace();
  }
 }
}
```

....

Output (from java Binary primitive.data)

0 1 2 3 4 5 6 7 8 9 0.0 1.0 2.0 3.0 4.0 5.0 6.0 7.0 8.0 9.0

....

Note 1:   Although **for** loops usually use integer indices, using a **double** index suits this example well. We illustrate the DataOutputStream and DataInputStream classes using types **double** and **int**, leaving the use of other primitive types for the exercises.

Example 1.7 writes the **int** and **double** values in binary form, using four bytes for each **int** and eight for each **double**. Running Example 1.5 to inspect this representation, using the command

```
java ReadBytes primitive.data
```

produces

```
0 0 0 0   0 0 0 1   0 0 0 2   0 0 0 3   0 0 0 4   0 0 0 5
0 0 0 6   0 0 0 7   0 0 0 8   0 0 0 9
0 0 0 0 0 0 0 0    63 240 0 0 0 0 0 0 64 0 0 0 0 0 0 0
64 8 0 0 0 0 0 0   64 16 0 0 0 0 0 0   64 20 0 0 0 0 0 0
64 24 0 0 0 0 0 0 64 28 0 0 0 0 0 0   64 32 0 0 0 0 0 0
64 34 0 0 0 0 0 0
```

The first ten entries show the four-byte integer values, while the second ten show eight-byte doubles. The **double** format is not obvious, and not meant for human reading. It separates each number into a fraction part and an exponent, and includes a sign bit.

Reading and Writing Text

Example 1.5 works well for ASCII characters, but is not satisfactory for the 16-bit Unicode characters needed to handle most of the world's languages. Java provides `Reader` and `Writer` classes for 16-bit character input. The three `Reader` read methods are `int read()`, `int read(char[] chars)`, and `int read(char[] chars, int offset, int length)`. The `Writer` class contains analogous `write` methods.

We often use the subclasses `InputStreamReader`, `BufferedReader`, `FileReader` for input and `PrintWriter`, `BufferedWriter`, `FileWriter`, and `OutputStreamWriter` for output. The `BufferedReader` class has a `readLine` method that returns the next line of input as a `String`, returning **null** at end-of-file. `PrintWriter`, which is buffered, includes `print` and `println` methods for strings and for each primitive type.

The `PrintWriter` constructor

```
public PrintWriter(OutputStream out, boolean autoFlush)
```

includes a second argument which, if **true**, causes Java to flush the output when executing a `println` statement. This automatic flushing helps to see each line of output immediately when writing to the screen. Otherwise, we would have to wait until the buffer fills before seeing the output.

Example 1.8 writes a string and a decimal to a file. We use the `readLine` method to read each string from the file. We could easily display each line as a string. However, in order to compute with the decimal, we need to convert the decimal string to a binary representation for a **double** value. We try to convert each string we read to a double. A string, such as 123.4567, which has the proper format will convert properly, but a character string, such as "Bottles of glue," will cause Java to throw a number format exception. In the `catch` clause we display the original string instead.

EXAMPLE 1.8   **TextIO.java**

```java
/* Writes a string and a double to a file. Reads each, from text.data
 * containing the lines
 *        Bottles of glue
 *        123.4567
 * and tries to convert it to a double. Displays the original
 * string if conversion fails.
 */
import java.io.*;
public class TextIO {
  public static void main(String [] args) {
    String line;
    try {
      PrintWriter writer =
        new PrintWriter(new FileWriter(args[0]));
      writer.println("Bottles of glue");
      double d = 123.4567;
      writer.println(d);
      writer.close();
```

```
BufferedReader reader =
    new BufferedReader(new FileReader(args[0]));
while((line=reader.readLine()) != null)
  try {
    double convert = new Double(line).doubleValue();     // Note 1
    System.out.println(convert*convert);                 // Note 2
  }catch(NumberFormatException e) {
    System.out.println(line);                            // Note 3
  }
reader.close();
}catch(IOException e) {
  e.printStackTrace();
}
}
}
```

Output (from `java TextIO text.data`**)**

```
Bottles of glue
15241.55677489
```

Note 1:   To convert a string to a **double**, we construct a `Double` object from the string and use the `doubleValue` method to retrieve the value of type **double**.

Note 2:   We convert the input string to a double so that we can compute its square, for example.

Note 3:   If the conversion fails, because the string did not have the proper format, we catch the exception and display the unconverted input string. The conversion code is in a **while** loop that reads the whole file, no mater what the outcome of each attempted conversion.

The text.data file used in Example 1.8 contains one value on each line. We can use a `StreamTokenizer` object to parse a line containing multiple fields.[1]

Random Access Files

We access `FileInputStream`, `FileOutputStream`, `DataInputStream`, and `DataOutputStream` objects sequentially. We read one item after another, going forward in the file, but cannot go back to data before the current file position. Similarly, when writing data, we cannot return to an earlier position in the file. By contrast, the **random access file**, which we can use for both reading and writing, allows us to read or write at any position in the file.

[1.] See *Computing with Java™: Programs, Object, and Graphics,* Art Gittleman, Scott/ Jones, Inc., 1998, pp. 422–424, or *Object to Components with the Java™ Platform,* Art Gittleman, Scott/Jones, Inc., 2000, pp. 324–326 for examples.

A random access file implements the methods to write primitive types that a
`DataOutputStream` does, and provides the same methods to read primitive types as
found in a `DataInputStream`. The `seek` method locates a position in the file. Calling
`seek(20)` sets the position at the twentieth byte in the file, at which position we can
either read or write. After completing a read or write operation, we can use `seek(4)` to
move the position to the location further back in the file at byte 4.

When creating a random access file, we use the second argument in its constructor
to specify the access mode, "r" for read-only or "rw" for read-write access. For example,

```
new RandomAccessFile("random.dat", "rw");
```

creates a random access file with read and write capabilities on the file `random.dat`.
The system will create `random.dat` if it does not exist.

EXAMPLE 1.9   **RandomAccess.java**

```
/* Seek forward and back to write and read
 * in a random access file.
 */

import java.io.*;
public class RandomAccess {
  public static void main(String [ ] args) {
    try {
      RandomAccessFile raf = new RandomAccessFile("random.dat", "rw");
      for (int i = 0; i < 10; i++)
        raf.writeInt(i);
      raf.seek(20);                                                    // Note 1
      int number = raf.readInt();
      System.out.println("The number starting at byte 20 is " + number);
      raf.seek(4);                                                     // Note 2
      number = raf.readInt();
      System.out.println("The number starting at byte 4 is " + number);
      raf.close();
    }catch (IOException e) {
      e.printStackTrace();
    }
  }
}
```

....

Output

```
The number starting at byte 20 is 5
The number starting at byte 4 is 1
```

....

Note 1:   Each integer is 32 bits or 4 bytes, so the position at byte 20 will bypass the
first five integers, 0, 1, 2, 3, and 4, in the file. (The bytes are numbered 0,
1, …, 19.) Reading at byte 20 should result in reading the integer 5.

Note 2:   Going back to byte 4 will position the file after the first integer, 0, so reading an integer at this position should return the value 1.

Reading and Writing Objects

Java provides object persistence, the ability to write objects to and read them from external files. Each class whose objects we wish to store must implement the Serializable interface, which has no methods. Implementing Serializable shows we intend to write objects of that class to disk. For security reasons, Java did not make the capability for persistence the default, but requires programmers to explicitly permit persistence by implementing the Serializable interface.

Transparently to the programmer, Java writes an object's type information to the file. Reading the object will automatically recover its type.

Sharing objects could cause problems.

- References are memory addresses that would be meaningless when we reload the objects.

- Saving a copy of a shared object each time it is referenced may result in the maintenance of several copies of the formerly shared object.

Java solves these problems by automatically numbering objects and using these numbers to refer to shared objects which need to be saved only once. This process of coding objects so they can be written to external storage and recovered properly is called **object serialization**.

Example 1.10 illustrates the saving and restoring of objects. An Account, general, and a SavingsAccount, savings, share an account holder, fred, of type Person.

Figure 1.2   Two accounts share an account holder

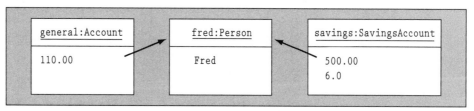

To show that Java handles types correctly, we declare both accounts as Account and create an ObjectOutputStream, calling writeObject to serialize these objects to a file. The classes, Account, SavingsAccount, and Person all implement Serializable.

We cast the objects to their compile-time type, Account. ObjectInputStream provides the readObject method to read these objects, allowing us to verify that Java restored the types correctly. The aGeneral object should be just a plain Account, not an instance of the subclass SavingsAccount, while the aSavings object should be a SavingsAccount. We also check that both the aGeneral and the aSavings accounts have the identical account holder, fred, which shows that Java restored the shared object correctly. Using object serialization, Java saves all the type information and does the object numbering automatically.

EXAMPLE 1.10   **ObjectIO.java**

```java
/* Illustrates object persistence.
 */

import java.io.*;
public class ObjectIO {
  public static void main(String [] args) {
    try {
      Person fred = new Person("Fred");
      Account general = new Account(fred, 110.0);
      Account savings = new SavingsAccount(fred, 500.0, 6.0);       // Note 1
      ObjectOutputStream oos = new ObjectOutputStream(
                       new FileOutputStream("Objects.dat"));
      oos.writeObject(general);                                     // Note 2
      oos.writeObject(savings);
      oos.close();
      ObjectInputStream ois = new ObjectInputStream(
                       new FileInputStream("Objects.dat"));
      Account aGeneral = (Account)ois.readObject();
      Account aSavings = (Account)ois.readObject();                // Note 3
      if (aGeneral instanceof SavingsAccount)
        System.out.println("aGeneral account is a SavingsAccount");
      else if (aGeneral instanceof Account)
        System.out.println("aGeneral account is an Account");      // Note 4
      if (aSavings instanceof SavingsAccount)
        System.out.println("aSavings account is a SavingsAccount");
      else if (aSavings instanceof Account)
        System.out.println("aSavings account is an Account");      // Note 5
      if (aGeneral.holder == aSavings.holder)                      // Note 6
        System.out.println("The account holder, fred, is shared");
      else
        System.out.println("The account holder, fred, has been duplicated");
      ois.close();
    }catch (IOException ioe) {
      ioe.printStackTrace();

    }catch (ClassNotFoundException cnfe) {                         // Note 7
        cnfe.printStackTrace();
    }
  }
}
class Person implements Serializable {                             // Note 8
  String name;
  Person (String name) { this.name = name; }
}
class Account implements Serializable {
  Person holder;
  double balance;
  Account(Person p, double amount) {
    holder = p;
```

```
      balance = amount;
    }
  }
  class SavingsAccount extends Account implements Serializable {
    double rate;
    SavingsAccount(Person p, double amount, double r) {
      super(p,amount);
      rate = r;
    }
  }
```

Output

```
aGeneral account is an Account
aSavings account is a SavingsAccount
The account holder, fred, is shared
```

Note 1: We declare savings to have type Account, but assign it an instance of the SavingsAccount subclass to check that writeObject saves the object's actual type correctly.

Note 2: Besides the writeObject method, ObjectOutputStream provides the primitive type output methods such as writeDouble and writeInt. The object written, general, is of type Account which implements the Serializable interface.

Note 3: The second object written had type SavingsAccount. Reading it should create an object of type SavingsAccount. The readObject method returns type Object, so we cast the return value to type Account and assign it to an Account reference, but will check later that its original SavingsAccount type has been preserved.

Note 4: The object aGeneral was read from the first object written, general, so it should be an Account object.

Note 5: The object aSavings was read from the second object written, savings, so it should be a SavingsAccount.

Note 6: `if (aGeneral.holder == aSavings.holder)`
We check that these references are equal, meaning they point to the identical object. The structure of the objects has been preserved due to the object serialization facility. Objects shared before writing are still shared after being read again. In our example both accounts have the identical account holder, fred.

Note 7: `}catch (ClassNotFoundException cnfe) {`
The readObject method may throw a ClassNotFoundException.

Note 8:   `class Person implements Serializable {`
The `Person`, `Account`, and `SavingsAccount` classes are simplified versions of these classes which we use to illustrate object serialization. Each must implement the `Serializable` interface.

THE BIG PICTURE

The `File` class allows us to get file properties. To read binary files we can use one of the three `read` methods of a `FileInputStream`. To read primitive types we construct a `DataInputStream` from the basic `FileInputStream`, and use the `readInt` and other similar methods. To read objects we construct an `ObjectInputStream` and use the `readObject` method. Such objects must implement the `Serializable` interface. Analogous classes and methods exist for writing. A random access file, used for both input and output, allows us to seek specific locations without having to process the file sequentially.

TEST YOUR UNDERSTANDING

TRY IT YOURSELF   4.   Modify Example 1.6 to add buffering using the `BufferedInputStream` and `BufferedOutputStream` classes.

TRY IT YOURSELF   5.   Modify Example 1.10 so that class `Person` does not implement the `Serializable` interface. Describe the result.

TRY IT YOURSELF   6.   Modify Example 1.7 to use the `readLong` and `writeLong` methods instead of `readDouble` and `writeDouble`.

TRY IT YOURSELF   7.   Modify Example 1.9 to write the same values using type **double** instead of **int**. Seek the position of 5.0, and then the position of 1.0.

1.3   Event-Driven Programming

· · · · · · · · · ·

Interactive programs respond to user-generated events. When the user enters text in a field or presses a button the program responds. Much of the code of such a program handles these events and responds appropriately. Possible responses include getting information, placing an order, or updating a database, for example. We assume readers have had some exposure to event-driven programming in Java. This section serves as a brief review.

The Java Event Model

Each event has a source and a target action. For example, when the user presses a button, we may wish to display a message. The button is the source of the event, and displaying the message is the target action. Java uses an adapter class to connect the target action with the event source. At runtime

■   the user presses a button

■   the button generates an event object

- the button calls a method of the adapter class, passing it the event object. We call this method the event handler method.

- the event handler method of the adapter class executes the target action.

In order for these event-handling steps to work, Java provides

- an event class, for each event type, to describe the properties of the event that an event handler needs to implement the target action.

- a listener interface, for each event type, to specify the methods that the adapter class must implement to handle events of that type.

- an add*EventName*Listener method in the source class, so the source knows which adapters are listening for source events.

For the example of a button press displaying a message, Java provides

- the ActionEvent class to describe events including button presses and text field entries. It contains the methods
  getSource returns the button object pressed
  getActionCommand by default, returns the button's label

- the ActionListener interface which the adapter implements. It contains the method

  ```
  public void actionPerformed(ActionEvent e)
  ```

  that performs the target action.

- the addActionListener(ActionListener listener) method of the Button class which informs the button about an adapter which is listening for action events generated by presses of that button.

  Java event handling uses a callback approach, in which the adapter registers as an event listener with the event source. When the event occurs, the source calls the appropriate method of the listener interface implemented by the adapter. In our example,

- the adapter class implements the ActionListener interface, providing a definition of the actionPerformed method to display the message.

- the startup code calls the button's addActionListener method, to inform the button that the adapter is listening.

- when the user presses the button, the button calls the adapter's actionPerformed method to display the message.

Four Types of Adapters

The adapter class can be any of the following:

- the same as the user interface class
  (Takes the least thought, but combines the user interface code with the program logic, which is often not a good design.)

- a separate class
  (Separates interface code from program logic. Adds another class name to the global space.)

- an inner class
  (Class name is local, but may only be needed once.)

- an anonymous inner class
  (Defined where needed)

We illustrate each of these four types of adapters using an example in which pressing a Print button displays the button's label, while pressing the Clear button erases the display. The UIAdapter applet serves also as the adapter. To run it, we use the applet viewer or a browser with the HTML file

```
<applet code = UIAdapter.class width=300 height=200>
</applet>
```

Figure 1.3 shows the resulting user interface after the user has pressed the Print button.

Figure 1.3   The user interface for the four examples

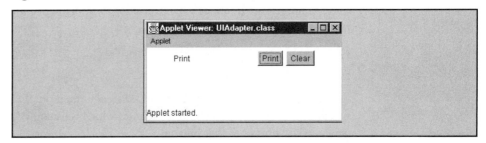

EXAMPLE 1.11   UIAdapter.java

```
/* A print button prints a message. A clear button erases
 * the message. We use a Label component to hold the
 * message. The applet is also the adapter.
 */

import java.awt.*;
import java.awt.event.*;
import java.applet.Applet;

public class UIAdapter extends Applet
                          implements ActionListener {          // Note 1
   private Button print = new Button("Print");
   private Button clear = new Button("Clear");
   private Label message = new Label("Message goes here");

   public void init() {
```

```
      add(message);
      add(print);
      add(clear);
      print.addActionListener(this);                              // Note 2
      clear.addActionListener(this);
    }
  public void actionPerformed(ActionEvent event) {               // Note 3
    Object source = event.getSource(); // Note 4
    if (source == print)
      message.setText(event.getActionCommand());                 // Note 5
    else if (source == clear)
      message.setText("");
    }
  }
}
```

Note 1: The applet is also the adapter class. It implements the `ActionListener` interface.

Note 2: We pass `this` to each button, representing the adapter object whose `actionPerformed` method the button will call when pressed by the user.

Note 3: The `actionPerformed` method implements the desired action, which is to display a message when the `Print` button is pressed, and to erase the message when the user presses the `Clear` button.

Note 4: The `getSource` method returns the button that the user pressed. We choose the action depending on which button was pressed.

Note 5: The `getActionCommand` method returns the command name set using the `setActionCommand` method, or, by default, the button's label.

In Example 1.12, the adapter class is separate from the user interface class. The class `Separate` defines the user interface, while the class `SeparateAdapter` implements `ActionListener` to handle action events.

EXAMPLE 1.12   Separate.java

```
/* Uses a separate adapter class.
*/

import java.awt.*;
import java.awt.event.*;
import java.applet.Applet;

public class Separate extends Applet {
  private Button print = new Button("Print");
  private Button clear = new Button("Clear");
  private Label message = new Label("Message goes here");
  private SeparateAdapter adapter =
                          new SeparateAdapter(message);         // Note 1
```

```
      public void init() {
        add(message);
        add(print);
        add(clear);
        print.addActionListener(adapter);                        // Note 2
        clear.addActionListener(adapter);
      }
    }
    class SeparateAdapter implements ActionListener {             // Note 3
      private Label message;

      public SeparateAdapter(Label 1) {                          // Note 4
        message = 1;
      }
      public void actionPerformed(ActionEvent event) {
      String command = event.getActionCommand();
      if (command.equals("Print"))                               // Note 5
        message.setText(command);
      else
        message.setText("");
      }
    }
```

....

Note 1:   We create an adapter object, passing it the label in which to display the message. Because the adapter class is separate, it does not have access to the user interface fields.

Note 2:   We pass the adapter object to each button.

Note 3:   The adapter class for a button must implement the ActionListener interface to handle action events generated by the button. This adapter handles action events generated by both the Print and the Clear buttons. We could have defined an adapter class for each button.

Note 4:   The constructor saves the applet's label to use to display the message.

Note 5:   Since the adapter class does not have access to the button fields in the applet, using the getSource method to get the source object for the event is not helpful. Instead we check the action command to see which button was pressed. We could have avoided this problem by using a separate adapter class for each button. We leave this modification as an exercise.

When compiling Separate.java, the compiler also produces a class file, Separate-Adapter.class, for the adapter class. The name, SeparaterAdapter, would conflict with any use of that name. This is not a problem for small examples which use few names, but could present problems in larger applications.

Example 1.13 uses a named inner adapter class. We define InnerAdapter inside the class Outer. We call such classes inner classes.

EXAMPLE 1.13   Outer.java

```java
/* Uses an inner adapter class.
 */

import java.awt.*;
import java.awt.event.*;
import java.applet.Applet;

public class Outer extends Applet {
  private Button print = new Button("Print");
  private Button clear = new Button("Clear");
  private Label message = new Label("Message goes here");
  private InnerAdapter adapter = new InnerAdapter();

  public void init() {
    add(message);
    add(print);
    add(clear);
    print.addActionListener(adapter);
    clear.addActionListener(adapter);
  }
  public class InnerAdapter implements ActionListener {          // Note 1
    public void actionPerformed(ActionEvent event) {
      Object source = event.getSource();
      if (source == print)
        message.setText(event.getActionCommand());
      else if (source == clear)
        message.setText("");
    }
  }
}
```

Note 1:   We define the `InnerAdapter` class inside the applet. It has access to the applet's fields so we can use the same code we used when the applet was the adapter class. We could have defined a separate inner adapter class for each button.

When compiling `Outer.java`, the compiler also creates a file, `Outer$InnerAdapter.class`, for the adapter class. Because the adapter is an inner class its name, `InnerAdapter`, is prefixed by the outer class name, `Outer`, followed by a dollar sign.

    We can avoid naming an inner class by defining it, without a name, where it is to be used. The only use we make of an adapter class is to pass an instance of it to the `addActionListener` method to let the button know whom to notify when a button press occurs. The syntax "`new ActionListener()`" means that we will create a new, unnamed class that implements the `ActionListener` interface. The definition of that class follows. In this example it consists of an `actionPerformed` method, but in general could have several constructors, fields, and methods. Example 1.14 uses an anonymous inner adapter class.

EXAMPLE 1.14   **Anonymous.java**

```java
/* Uses an anonymous inner adapter class.
 */

import java.awt.*;
import java.awt.event.*;
import java.applet.Applet;

public class Anonymous extends Applet {
  private Button print = new Button("Print");
  private Button clear = new Button("Clear");
  private Label message = new Label("Message goes here");

  public void init() {
    add(message);
    add(print);
    add(clear);
    print.addActionListener(new ActionListener() {          // Note 1
      public void actionPerformed(ActionEvent event) {
        message.setText(event.getActionCommand());
      }
    });
    clear.addActionListener(new ActionListener() {           // Note 2
      public void actionPerformed(ActionEvent event) {
        message.setText("");
      }
    });
  }
}
```

Note 1:   We define an anonymous class that implements the `ActionListener` interface. The class contains the definition of the `actionPerformed` method. We define the class at the place we use it. Here we pass it to the `addActionListener` method of the `Print` button.

Note 2:   Using anonymous classes, we define a separate adapter for each button.

When compiling `Anonymous.java`, the compiler produces two additional class files, `Anonymous$1.class` and `Anonymous$2.class`. Because they have no names, the compiler uses the numbers 1 and 2 to label them.

Window Events

The Java event model applies to high-level events generated by user interface components and to low-level events generated by the mouse and keyboard. Appendix A lists some of these event types and their corresponding listener interfaces. We look briefly at window events so that we can close our standalone windows.

The `WindowListener` interface has seven methods to handle each of the window events.

`windowActivated`	The window gets the focus.
`windowDeactivated`	The window loses the focus.
`windowOpened`	The window is opened.
`windowClosed`	The window is closed.
`windowClosing`	The user asks to close the window.
`windowIconified`	The window is minimized as an icon.
`windowDeiconified`	The window is restored from an icon.

An adapter class must implement all seven methods so it can handle any of the window events that might occur. We only care about the `WINDOW_CLOSING` event that occurs when the user closes the window.

Fortunately, Java provides a `WindowAdapter` class that implements each of the seven `WindowListener` methods with empty bodies. For example,

```
public void windowActivated(WindowEvent e) {
}
```

We create our window adapter class by extending `WindowAdapter` and overriding methods for window events we wish to handle. To close a top-level window, we override the `windowClosing` method to dispose of any resources used and terminate the program. We use the `addWindowListener` method to inform a window of an adapter that wishes to be notified when a window events occurs.

Example 1.15 simply creates a window, shown in Figure 1.4, and responds to the user's request to close it, made by clicking the **x** in the upper-right corner, or by selecting the `Close` item from the menu in the upper-left corner.

Figure 1.4   A top-level closeable window.

EXAMPLE 1.15   CloseIt.java

```java
/* Creates a top-level window and allows the
 * user to close it.
 */

import java.awt.*;
import java.awt.event.*;

  public class CloseIt extends Frame {                          // Note 1
    public CloseIt(String title) {
    super(title);                                               // Note 2
    addWindowListener(new WindowClose());                       // Note 3
  }
  public static void main(String[] args) {
    CloseIt f = new CloseIt("Close this frame");                // Note 4
    f.setSize(300,200);                                         // Note 5
    f.setVisible(true);                                         // Note 6
  }
  class WindowClose extends WindowAdapter {                     // Note 7
    public void windowClosing(WindowEvent e) {
        System.exit(0);                                        // Note 8
    }
  }
}
```

....

Note 1:   The Frame class represents a top-level window with a title bar.

Note 2:   We pass the title to the Frame constructor.

Note 3:   The CloseIt class define the frame that we want to close. Thus we add the window listener to the this object, which we omit because it is understood.

Note 4:   Creates the frame, passing it the title.

Note 5:   Defines the size of the frame in pixels.

Note 6:   f.setVisible(true);
Makes the frame visible.

Note 7:   class WindowClose extends WindowAdapter
The WindowAdapter class implements the WindowListener interface. We need only override the methods for the window events we wish to handle.

Note 8:   System.exit(0);
We terminate the program when we close the frame.

THE BIG PICTURE

An event-driven program responds to events such as button presses and text field entries. When an event occurs, the event source notifies an adapter, which implements the desired action. The source passes the adapter an event object describing the event. The adapter implements an event listener interface, and the source calls one of the interface methods when an event occurs. Often adapters are anonymous inner classes.

TEST YOUR UNDERSTANDING

TRY IT YOURSELF   8.   What happens in Example 1.11 if we omit the call to the `Print` button's `addActionListener` method?

TRY IT YOURSELF   9.   In Example 1.12, the `SeparateAdapter` class handled presses from both buttons. Replace it with adapter classes, `PrintAdapter` and `ClearAdapter`, for each button.

1.4   Introduction to Threads

The term **thread** is short for thread of control. Someone who can read a book and watch television at the same time is processing two threads. For awhile she concentrates on the book, perhaps during a commercial, but then devotes her attention to a segment of the TV program. Because the TV program does not require her undivided attention, she reads a few more lines every now and then. Each thread gets some of her attention. Perhaps she can concentrate on both threads simultaneously, like musicians who are able to follow the different parts of the harmony.

If we have only one thread of control, then we have to wait whenever that thread gets delayed. For example, suppose our thread is downloading a picture from the Internet. It may have to wait while the system transfers all the pixels of the picture from some remote site. If our program can create a second thread to wait for the input from the remote site, it can go with other processing while the new thread is waiting. When some new data comes in from the remote site, the new thread can receive it while the first thread waits for awhile. The two threads share the processor. Figure 1.5 illustrates this sharing.

Figure 1.5   Two threads sharing the processor

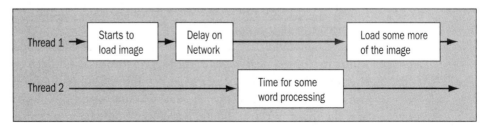

The Thread Class

Java allows us to use threads in our program. Our program can define two or more threads, and the processor will divide its attention among the active threads. Each thread that we define executes a run method when it gets the processor. We can define a thread by extending the Thread class, overriding the run method to specify what our thread will do when it has control, as in

```
public class MyThread extends Thread {
    ...
  public void run () {
    // put code here for thread to run
    // when it gets control
  }
}
```

To make a thread, we can create a new thread and call its start method, as in

```
MyThread t = new MyThread();
t.start();
```

This will make the thread ready, and when it gets scheduled, it will execute its run method. When another thread gets a turn, the thread, t, will stop executing the code in its run method, but will continue from where it left off, when it gets another turn.

Optionally, we can name our thread, passing the name to the constructor which in turn passes it to the Thread superclass constructor, as in:

```
public MyThread(String name) {
  super(name);
  ...
}
```

The Thread class has a static method, sleep(int milliseconds), which will cause its caller to **sleep** (be blocked from using the processor) for the specified number of milliseconds. While one thread sleeps, another will get a turn. We call the sleep method in a try block, as in:

```
try {
  Thread.sleep(1000);
}catch(InterruptedException e) { return;}
```

where we have to catch the InterruptedException which would occur if another thread interrupted this one. We will not consider interruption or other more advanced thread concepts in this text.

In Example 1.16 we create two threads, Bonnie and Clyde, and let them write their names five times, sleeping after each writing. Bonnie will sleep for 1000 milliseconds after each writing, while Clyde will sleep for 700 milliseconds. Processors are so fast that a thread could do a large amount of output while it has its turn. We sleep here to slow the thread down to human scale, so we only have to read a few lines of output. The main method runs in a thread, different from the two we create, so we will actually have three threads sharing the processor, writing their names when they get their turns. We let main sleep for 1100 milliseconds after it writes.

EXAMPLE 1.16   **NameThread.java**

```java
/* Creates two threads that write their names and
 * sleep. The main thread also writes its name
 * and sleeps.
 */

import java.io.*;

public class NameThread extends Thread {
  int time;     // time in milliseconds to sleep

  public NameThread(String n, int t) {
    super(n);
    time = t;
  }
  public void run() {
    for (int i = 1;i <= 5;i++) {                        // Note 1
      System.out.println(getName() + " " + i);          // Note 2
      try {
        Thread.sleep(time);
      } catch (InterruptedException e) {return;}
    }
  }

  public static void main(String argv[]) {              // Note 3
    NameThread bonnie = new NameThread("Bonnie",1000);
    bonnie.start();
    NameThread clyde = new NameThread("Clyde",700);
    clyde.start();
    for (int i = 1; i <= 5; i++) {                       // Note 4
      System.out.println(Thread.currentThread().getName() + " " + i);
      try {
        Thread.sleep(1100);
      } catch (InterruptedException e) {return;}
    }
  }
}
```

....

Output

```
main 1
Bonnie 1
```

```
Clyde 1
Clyde 2
Bonnie 2
main 2
Clyde 3
Bonnie 3
Clyde 4
main 3
Clyde 5
Bonnie 4
main 4
Bonnie 5
main 5
```

Note 1: Each thread will print its name five times and sleep after each time, returning where it left off when it gets the processor again. We can see in the output that after Bonnie prints her name the first time, Clyde gets a turn and manages to print his name twice before Bonnie returns printing her name the second time. Main started first because it had the processor first, at the start of the program.

Note 2: The getName method of the Thread class returns the thread's name.

Note 3: We put the main method in the NameThread class for simplicity. We could have created another class, say TryNameThread, with a main method to create the threads.

Note 4: The main method also writes its name five times. Because we did not create this thread in our program we get it using the static currentThread method of the Thread class.

Figure 1.6 helps us to understand the order in which the three threads execute in Example 1.16. Each thread spends most of its time sleeping; printing its name takes a mere fraction of the time it sleeps. By graphing the sleep times we can get a good idea of when each thread will be ready to run.

Figure 1.6

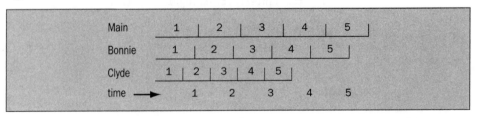

Main prints its name first and then sleeps for 1.1 seconds. Bonnie starts next, printing her name and sleeping for 1 second. Clyde prints his name and sleeps for .7 second. When he wakes up the other two threads are still sleeping so he prints his name again (#2). Because Bonnie woke up before main, she prints her name (#2) first, followed by main (#2). (Picking the thread that becomes ready first is a choice made by the thread scheduler.) When main finishes both Bonnie and Clyde are awake, but Clyde woke up first and executes first (#3). We leave it to the reader to continue following the diagram in Figure 1.6 to explain the results of Example 1.16.

The Runnable Interface

In Example 1.16 we extended the Thread class, creating a NameThread subclass which overrode the run method to provide the code for a NameThread object to execute in its thread of control. The Runnable interface provides an alternate method to use threads. In this approach we use an interface to perform a callback as we have been doing with the various listener interfaces used in event handling.

The Runnable interface contains just the one run method.

```
public interface Runnable {
   public void run();
}
```

A concrete class that implements the Runnable interface must implement the run method. An object of this class must pass itself to a thread so that when that thread gets the processor it will execute the object's run method. In Example 1.17 we rewrite the last example, creating a class that implements the Runnable interface rather than extending Thread.

EXAMPLE 1.17   NameUsingThread.java

```
/* Revises Example 1.16 to implement the Runnable
 * interface rather than extending Thread.
 */

import java.io.*;

public class NameUsingThread implements Runnable {
   private int time;
   private Thread thread; // the thread to execute the run method

   public NameUsingThread(String n, int t) {
      time = t;
      thread = new Thread(this,n);                            // Note 1
      thread.start();
   }
   public void run() {                                        // Note 2
      for (int i = 1;i <= 5;i++) {
         System.out.println(thread.getName() + " " + i);
         try {
            Thread.sleep(time);
         } catch (InterruptedException e) {return;}
      }
   }
}
```

```
public static void main(String argv[ ]) {
  NameUsingThread bonnie = new NameUsingThread("Bonnie",1000);
  NameUsingThread clyde = new NameUsingThread("Clyde",700);
  for (int i = 1;i <= 5; i++) {
    System.out.println(Thread.currentThread().getName() + " " + i);
    try {
      Thread.sleep(1100);
    } catch (InterruptedException e) {return;}
  }
 }
}
```

Output (same as that from Example 1.16.)

Note 1: We create a new thread, passing it the current object of type NameUsingThread, which implements the run method that the thread will run when it gets the processor, and the name of the thread. The next line starts the thread, making it ready to run when it gets its turn.

Note 2: The NameUsingThread class implements the run method which the thread will call when it gets the processor.

Either Example 1.15 or 1.16 works fine; there is no reason to prefer one approach. When a class already extends a class, it cannot extend the Thread class, therefore only the approach of Example 1.16, implementing the Runnable interface, would work.

THE BIG PICTURE

Threads appear to execute simultaneously. When a thread gets the processor it executes the code in a run method. A thread which extends the Thread class has its own run method. Alternatively a thread may execute the run method of a class which implements the Runnable interface. In either case, the start method makes the thread ready to run. Threads that are ready to run share the processor in a manner determined by a scheduler. We use the sleep method to pause a thread for a specified period of time.

TEST YOUR UNDERSTANDING

TRY IT YOURSELF 10. In Example 16, change the sleep amounts for threads Bonnie, and Clyde to 300 and 200 milliseconds respectively. How does the output change when you rerun the example?

TRY IT YOURSELF 11. In Example 1.17, change the sleep times for the main thread to 200 milliseconds. How does the output change when you rerun the example?

TRY IT YOURSELF 12. What do you predict the output would be if you omit all the sleep statements from Example 1.16? Rerun the program with these changes, and see if your supposition is correct.

1.5 Concurrent Programming

Having seen threads running independently in the last section, we take up the interesting and difficult problem of threads which share data and need to cooperate with each other to operate correctly.

An Example without Synchronization

To illustrate the problem, suppose that two threads are depositing to an account, and that a deposit involves two steps:

1. computing the new balance

2. recording the change in a log

We assume each thread computes the balance separately, but shares the log to enter the result.

A thread runs for a certain time period, and then another thread gets its turn. If each thread completes both steps when it has its turn, the balance and the log will be consistent, but perhaps thread1 loses its turn after completing step 1.

Figure 1.7   A problem with threads

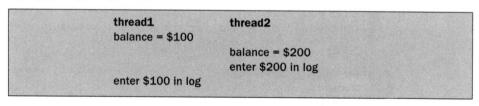

The execution sequence of Figure 1.7 shows that after thread1 computes a balance of $100 it loses its turn to thread2 which computes a balance of $200 and records the new balance in the log. When thread1 gets its turn again it finishes where it left off, entering $100 in the log, which is now incorrect.

To create a simple program to illustrate this phenomenon, we use a buffer that contains an integer, number, which two threads share. The increment method adds 1 to number and reports its new value, while the decrement method subtracts 1 and reports the new value. When the threads operate correctly, successive reports will display values that differ by one. For example, starting with number at 5, two increments give

```
thread1 increments to 6
thread1 reports 6
                thread2 increments to 7
                thread2 reports 7
```

while an increment followed by a decrement results in

```
thread1 increments to 6
thread1 reports 6
                thread2 decrements to 5
                thread2 reports 5
```

Only when the threads operate incorrectly do we get the same value on successive reports. For example, again starting at 5,

```
thread1 increments to 6
                    thread2 decrements to 5
                    thread2 reports 5
thread1 reports 5
```

Example 1.18 shows this behavior, but not very often. The `increment` and `decrement` methods are so short they are rarely interrupted before completion. For larger methods, this error would occur more often.

EXAMPLE 1.18   **TallyWrong.java**

```java
/* Two threads occasionally err in reporting
 * values because they get interrupted before
 * finishing to execute a method.
 */

public class TallyWrong {
  class Buffer {
    int number = 0; // the number to increase or decrease
    int previous = 0;
    int total = 0; // total number of operations performed
    int errors = 0; // number of errors

  public void increment() {
    number++;
    report(number);
  }
  public void decrement() {
    number--;
    report(number);
  }
  public void report(int n) {
    total++;
    if (n == previous)                                        // Note 1
      System.out.println(++errors + "\t" + total );
    previous = n;
   }
  }
  class Plus extends Thread {
    Buffer buf;
    Plus(Buffer b) {
      buf = b;
    }
    public void run() {
      while (true)                                            // Note 2
        buf.increment();
   }
  }
```

```
class Minus extends Thread {
  Buffer buf;
  Minus(Buffer b) {
    buf = b;
  }
  public void run() {
  while (true)
    buf.decrement();
  }
}
public static void main(String[ ] argv) {
  TallyWrong tw = new TallyWrong();
  Buffer b = tw.new Buffer();                              // Note 3
  Plus p = tw.new Plus(b);
  Minus m = tw.new Minus(b);
  p.start();
  m.start();
 }
}
```

....

Output

1	456250
2	4649634
3	7245105
4	12916833
5	14452346
6	23241347
7	24257947
8	29420248
9	30436644
10	36110307

....

Note 1:   When the current and previous values of number agree, an error has occurred, and we output the number of errors and the total number of operations performed. We illustrated the error when a thread loses its turn after changing number but before reporting. It could also lose its turn while executing the report method. The point is that errors can occur due to the interleaving of execution of various threads.

Note 2:   This thread keeps incrementing number in an unending loop. We need to abort execution manually.

Note 3:   We used inner classes to make the class names local to theTallyWrong class. To access these classes we use an instance of TallyWrong.

Synchronization

To correct the problem exhibited by Example 1.18, we need to enable the `increment` and `decrement` methods to execute completely once they have begun. Java provides the **synchronized** keyword to enforce this behavior. We declare the `increment` method as

```
public synchronized void increment() {
  number++;
  report(number);
}
```

For example, when thread1 calls this method of the `buf` object,

```
buf.increment();
```

if no other thread is executing any method of `buf`, thread1 gets a **lock** for the object. Therefore no other thread can use `buf` until thread1 has finished executing the `increment` method. If another thread is executing a method of `buf`, then thread1 must wait until that operation completes. If several threads are waiting to get a lock on an object, the thread scheduler determines who will get it when it becomes available.

Figure 1.8   thread1 locks `buf` while thread2 waits

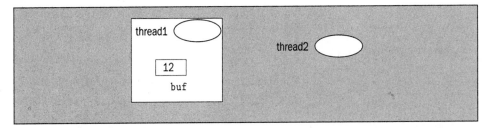

We only need make the `increment` and `decrement` methods in Example 1.18 synchronized to ensure that they work correctly when accessed by multiple threads. With synchronized methods, behavior like that shown in Figure 1.7 cannot occur because once a thread starts executing a synchronized method it is allowed to finish.

EXAMPLE 1.19   TallyRight.java

```
/* Uses synchronized methods to correct the
 * error in Example 1.18.
 */

public class TallyRight {

  // The rest of the code is the same as Example 1.18.

  public synchronized void increment() {
    number++;
    report(number);
  }
```

```
public synchronized void decrement() {
  number--;
  report(number);
}
}
```

Output

There is none, because no errors occur.

A LITTLE EXTRA Synchronizing methods exacts a performance penalty. If only a portion of the code of a large method is critical, we can improve performance by only synchronizing that portion of the code. Schematically,

```
public returnType someMethod(someParameters) {
  // some code not synchronized

  synchronized(this) {
    // synchronize the critical code here
  }

  // more non-synchronized code
}
```

When a thread calls this method it will only lock the object while executing the synchronized block.

Communication

Synchronization allows threads to complete portions of code without interruption. Sometimes threads also need to communicate with one another to signal the occurrence of a condition that may affect their ability to proceed. For our example, we look at the classic **producer-consumer problem**, in which both producer threads and consumer threads access a data buffer. Producers add data to the buffer, while consumers remove it.

Assuming a fixed-size buffer, a producer cannot add more than the buffer can hold, while a consumer cannot retrieve data from an empty buffer. Each Java object has wait and notify methods which are useful in this situation.

When a producer has a lock on the buffer, and cannot add data because the buffer is full, it executes the wait method causing it to release the lock and wait to be notified the state of the buffer has changed. When a consumer removes an item from a full buffer, it executes the notify method to notify a waiting thread that the buffer is no longer full.

Similarly, when a consumer has a lock on the buffer, and cannot remove data because the buffer is empty, it executes the wait method causing it to release the lock and wait to be notified that the state of the buffer has changed. When a producer puts an item into an empty buffer, it executes the notify method to notify a waiting thread that the buffer is no longer empty.

Example 1.20 solves this producer-consumer problem. We input sleep times for each thread to see how the behavior varies depending on which thread has more time. We use one producer and one consumer thread.

EXAMPLE 1.20   PutGet.java

```java
/* Uses wait and notify to enable
 * producer and consumer threads to
 * cooperate in using a buffer.
 */

public class PutGet {
  public static final int size = 3;
  class Buffer {
    int[ ] buffer = new int [size];         // the data
    int putpos = 0;                         // next position to put a value
    int getpos = 0;                         // next position to get a value
    int number = 0;                         // number of items in the buffer

    public synchronized void put(int value)
                         throws InterruptedException {        // Note 1
      if (number == size) {
        System.out.println("Cannot put -- Buffer full");
        wait();                                               // Note 2
      }
      number++;
      buffer[putpos] = value;
      System.out.println("Put "+value);
      putpos = (putpos + 1) % size;                          // Note 3
      if (number == 1) notify();                             // Note 4
    }
    public synchronized int get() throws InterruptedException {
      if (number == 0) {
        System.out.println("Cannot get -- Buffer empty");
        wait();
      }
      number--;
      int n = buffer[getpos];
      System.out.println("Get "+n);
      getpos = (getpos + 1) % size;
      if (number == size - 1) notify();                      // Note 5
      return n;
    }
  }
  class Producer extends Thread {
    Buffer buf;
    int time;
    Producer(Buffer b, int t) {
```

```
          buf = b;
          time = t;
        }
      public void run() {
        for(int i = 1; i <= 10; i++)                           // Note 6
          try {
            buf.put(i);
            sleep(time);                                       // Note 7
          }catch (InterruptedException e){
            e.printStackTrace();
          }
      }
    }
  class Consumer extends Thread {
    Buffer buf;
    int time;
    Consumer(Buffer b, int t) {
      buf = b;
      time = t;
    }
    public void run() {
      for (int i = 1; i <= 10;i++)
        try {
          buf.get();
          sleep(time);
        }catch (InterruptedException e) {
          e.printStackTrace();
        }
    }
  }
  public static void main(String[ ] args) {
    PutGet pg = new PutGet();
    Buffer b = pg.new Buffer();
    Producer p = pg.new Producer(b,Integer.parseInt(args[0]));
    Consumer c = pg.new Consumer(b,Integer.parseInt(args[1]));
    p.start();
    c.start();
  }
}
```

....

Output – from java PutGet 300 500

```
Put 1
Get 1
Put 2
Get 2
Put 3
Put 4
Get 3
Put 5
```

```
Put 6
Get 4
Put 7
Get 5
Put 8
Cannot put -- Buffer full
Get 6
Put 9
Cannot put -- Buffer full
Get 7
Put 10
Get 8
Get 9
Get 10
```

Note 1: The `wait` method may throw an `InterruptedException`, which we declare here to pass it on to the caller of the `put` method who will handle it.

Note 2: The `wait` method is a member of the `Object` class, so any object, such as a buffer in this example, may invoke it. `wait` must be invoked in a synchronized method so the thread invoking it has a lock on the object.

Note 3: We use a circular buffer. Visualizing the array as a circle shows that after filling position 2, we move to position 0 again. This formula computes indices in this way: 0, 1, 2, 0, 1, 2, ... and so on.

Note 4: After putting an item into an empty buffer, we call `notify`. The scheduler will notify one thread, making it ready to run. In our example, we have at most one thread waiting, so if it is waiting it will be notified that the buffer is non-empty. When more than one thread may be waiting, calling `notify-All` will wake them all up.

Note 5: By removing an item from a full buffer, the consumer has just made it possible for a waiting producer to add an item. Calling `notify` will wake up a waiting producer.

Note 6: `for(int i = 1; i <= 10; i++)`
We let the producer produce 10 numbers, and the consumer consume these 10. We could have run these threads in an unending loop, and aborted the program manually.

Note 7: `sleep(time);`
Typically there will be some extended computation to produce the value to put in the buffer. For simplicity we sleep to simulate some computational time.

Deadlock

When threads wait for locks to be freed that cannot be freed we have **deadlock**. We can easily modify Example 1.20 to produce deadlock. If we change the condition for the producer to put only when the buffer is empty and the consumer to get only when the buffer is full we reach a deadlocked state almost immediately. The buffer starts out empty so the producer can put one item into it, but no more until the consumer removes that item, making the buffer empty again. The consumer cannot remove the one item in the buffer until the producer adds two more items to fill the buffer. Both the producer and consumer are stuck, each waiting an action by the other that can never occur.

Good programming is the only prevention for deadlock. In more complicated situations it can be very difficult to determine if deadlock can occur.

EXAMPLE 1.21   **Deadlock.java**

```java
/* Modifies Example 1.20 to illustrate deadlock.
 */

public class Deadlock {

  // the rest of the code is the same as Example 1.20

  public synchronized void put(int value) throws InterruptedException {
    if (number != 0) {
      System.out.println("Cannot put -- Buffer not empty");
      wait();
    }
    ......
  }
  public synchronized int get() throws InterruptedException {
  if (number != size) {
    System.out.println("Cannot get -- Buffer not full");
      wait();
    }
    ......
  }
}
```

Output
```
Put 1
Cannot get -- Buffer not full
Cannot put -- Buffer not empty
```

(At this point the program hangs up because neither the producer nor the consumer can proceed.)

THE BIG PICTURE

Concurrent programming coordinates multiple threads. When threads share data we can synchronize access so that a thread using the data will be able to complete its operation before another thread gets access to that data. A thread gets a lock on the object which contains the data until it finishes the synchronized method or block.

Threads can wait on a condition, to be notified by other threads when changes occur that may make the condition satisfied. Deadlock occurs when threads wait for locks that can never be freed and no thread can proceed.

TEST YOUR UNDERSTANDING

TRY IT YOURSELF   13. Vary the sleep times when running Example 1.20, and determine how that affects the results.

TRY IT YOURSELF   14. Modify Example 1.20 to start two producers and two consumers, and explain the resulting behavior.

1.6   Gridbag Layout

· · · · · · · · · · ·

The gridbag layout provides a grid of variable-sized cells, giving more flexibility than the flow, border, or grid layouts, but is more complex and difficult to learn. The best way to understand its features is through experimentation with simple examples. Figure 1.9 shows a form designed using a gridbag layout whose code appears as Example 1.27.

Default GridBag Constraints

A `GridBagConstraints` object holds the values which customize the location and appearance of each component. Setting the values of these constraint variables determines how the layout manager will display a component. The `GridBagConstraints` variables, with their default values and uses, are:

Variable	Default value	Use
gridx, gridy	RELATIVE	Upper-left corner of display area
gridwidth	1	Number of cells used for width
gridheight	1	Number of cells used for height
fill	NONE	Resizing behavior
ipadx, ipady	0	Internal padding
insets	new Insets(0,0,0,0)	External padding
anchor	CENTER	Placement
weightx	0.0	Distribute row space
weighty	0.0	Distribute column space

As we experiment, we will come to understand the meaning of these default values.

Figure 1.9   A form with a gridbag layout

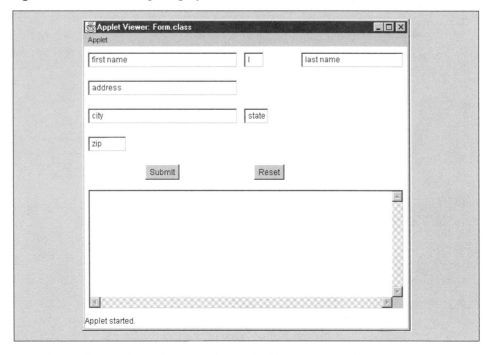

The applet of Example 1.22, shown in Figure 1.10, adds two buttons to an applet using all default settings for the `GridBagConstraints`. We do not activate the buttons; our purpose is to discuss the layout.

Figure 1.10   Using the `GridBagConstraints` defaults in Example 1.22

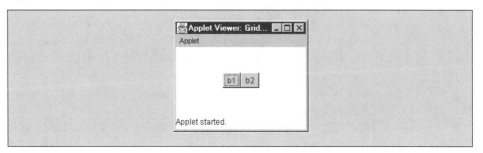

`gridx` and `gridy` each start out at 0, indicating column 0 and row 0. The default of `GridBagConstraints.RELATIVE` positions the component just to the right of the previous component (or below if placing it in a column). Thus `b2` is just to the right of `b1`. Because `gridwidth` and `gridheight` are 1, they each use one row and one column. Because `weightx` and `weighty` are each 0.0, the extra space in the applet is outside the layout of the two components, which are clustered in the center. The `fill` constraint has no effect as there is no extra space to fill.

EXAMPLE 1.22   **GridBag1.java**

```
/* Uses default settings for GridBagConstraints.
 */

import java.awt.*;
import java.applet.*;
public class GridBag1 extends Applet {
    private Button b1 = new Button("b1");
    private Button b2 = new Button("b2");
    public void init() {
    GridBagLayout gbl = new GridBagLayout();
    setLayout(gbl);
    GridBagConstraints c = new GridBagConstraints();          // Note 1
    gbl.setConstraints(b1, c);                                // Note 2
    add(b1);
    gbl.setConstraints(b2, c);
    add(b2);
  }
}
```

Note 1:   We only need one `GridBagConstraints` object, c, which we can reuse for each component. In this example, we do not change any values of its variables, using the default settings.

Note 2:   Before adding a component to the applet, we call the `setConstraints` method to associate the current constraint settings with the component to be added.

Setting Weight and Fill

The weight and the fill determine how a component uses the available space. `weightx` and `weighty` distribute the space and `fill` specifies how a component uses it.

In Example 1.23, we set `weightx` to .7 for button `b1` and `weightx` to .3 for `b2`. We see, in Figure 1.11, that `b1` is centered in the left 70 percent of the applet while `b2` is centered in the right 30 percent. Had we left the default `fill` of NONE, the buttons would have remained their normal size as in Figure 1.10. By giving `b1` VERTICAL fill, it expands to fill its space vertically. Button `b2`, with HORIZONTAL fill, expands horizontally. Had we chosen BOTH for `fill` the button would have expanded to fill its entire area. Had we left `weightx` and `weighty` at the default of 0.0, no additional area would have been allocated to each component and the setting `fill` would have no effect. Had we left `weighty` at 0.0, specifying VERTICAL fill would have no effect.

EXAMPLE 1.23   **GridBag2.java**

```
/* Sets weightx, weighty, and fill.
 */
```

Figure 1.11   Using `weightx`, `weighty`, and `fill` in Example 1.23

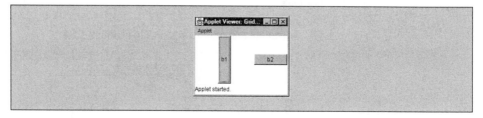

```
import java.awt.*;
import java.applet.*;
public class GridBag2 extends Applet {
  private Button b1 = new Button("b1");
  private Button b2 = new Button("b2");
  public void init() {
    GridBagLayout gbl = new GridBagLayout();
    setLayout(gbl);
    GridBagConstraints c = new GridBagConstraints();
    c.weightx = .7;                                       // Note 1
    c.fill = GridBagConstraints.VERTICAL;
    gbl.setConstraints(b1, c);
    add(b1);
    c.weightx = .3;
    c.weighty = 1.0;                                      // Note 2
    c.fill = GridBagConstraints.HORIZONTAL;
    gbl.setConstraints(b2, c);
    add(b2);
  }
}
```

Note 1:   The `weightx` setting applies to the whole column of components. In this case we have only `b1` in the first column, but with more components the layout manager takes `weightx` for the column to be the maximum of `weightx` for each component.

Note 2:   The `weighty` setting applies to the whole row of components. The layout manager takes `weighty` for the row to be the maximum of `weighty` for each component. Thus `b1` expands vertically even though its `weighty` setting is 0.0, because the `weighty` setting for the entire row is 1.0.

Anchoring and Internal Padding

Example 1.24 illustrates anchoring and internal padding. We use the anchor field to position a component that is smaller than its display area. Its possible values are CENTER, NORTH, NORTHEAST, EAST, SOUTHEAST, SOUTH, SOUTH-WEST, WEST, and NORTHWEST. Internal padding adds to the dimensions of the component. Setting `ipadx` to 25 causes the buttons in Figure 1.12 to have 25 pixels of internal padding on both the left and the right. Similarly, setting `ipady` to 25 causes the buttons to have 25 pixels of top and bottom padding. We anchor `b1` to the

WEST of its area and b2 to the NORTH. In this example, we return to the default NONE for fill.

Figure 1.12   Anchoring and internal padding in Example 1.24

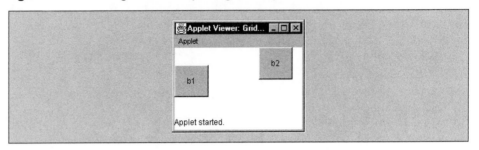

EXAMPLE 1.24   **GridBag3.java**

```
/*Illustrates anchoring and internal padding
 */

import java.awt.*;
import java.applet.*;
public class GridBag3 extends Applet {
  private Button b1 = new Button("b1");
  private Button b2 = new Button("b2");
  public void init() {
    GridBagLayout gbl = new GridBagLayout();
    setLayout(gbl);
    GridBagConstraints c = new GridBagConstraints();
    c.weightx = .7;
    c.anchor = GridBagConstraints.WEST;
    c.ipadx = 25;
    c.ipady = 25;
    gbl.setConstraints(b1, c);
    add(b1);
    c.weightx = .3;
    c.weighty = 1.0;
    c.anchor = GridBagConstraints.NORTH;
    gbl.setConstraints(b2, c);
    add(b2);
  }
}
```

....

Insets

The insets determine the external padding around a component. In Example 1.25, we set fill to BOTH so the buttons expand to fill their display areas. However, we set the external padding for b2 to provide a border of 10 pixels around it. The type of the insets variable is Insets, a class used to specify the four values for the border in each direction., top, left, bottom, and right.

Figure 1.13   Insets and fill.BOTH in Example 1.25

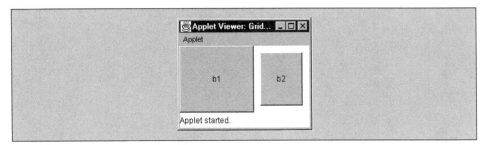

EXAMPLE 1.25   **GridBag4.java**

```
/* Illustrates Insets and fill BOTH
 */

import java.awt.*;
import java.applet.*;
public class GridBag4 extends Applet {
  private Button b1 = new Button("b1");
  private Button b2 = new Button("b2");
  public void init() {
    GridBagLayout gbl = new GridBagLayout();
    setLayout(gbl);
    GridBagConstraints c = new GridBagConstraints();
    c.weightx = .7;
    c.fill = GridBagConstraints.BOTH;
    gbl.setConstraints(b1, c);
    add(b1);
    c.weightx = .3;
    c.weighty = 1.0;
    c.insets = new Insets(10,10,10,10);
    gbl.setConstraints(b2, c);
    add(b2);
  }
}
```

Positioning Constraints

By setting gridx and gridy we can locate a component at a specific row and column, while setting gridwidth and gridheight defines the number of cells for a component. The constant GridBagConstraints.REMAINDER specifies the remaining space in the row or column, while GridBagConstraints.RELATIVE indicates a position next to the preceding component.

In Example 1.26, shown in Figure 1.14, we use six buttons to illustrate the use of positioning constraints.

Figure 1.14   The applet of Example 1.26

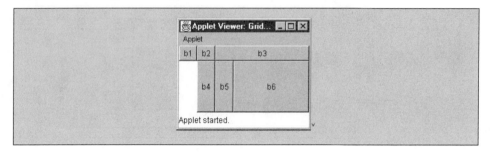

EXAMPLE 1.26   **GridBag5.java**

```java
/* Illustrates positioning constraints
 */

import java.awt.*;
import java.applet.*;
public class GridBag5 extends Applet {
  private void makebutton(String name,                              // Note 1
      GridBagLayout gridbag, GridBagConstraints c) {
    Button button = new Button(name);
    gridbag.setConstraints(button, c);
    add(button);
  }
  public void init() {
    GridBagLayout gbl = new GridBagLayout();
    setLayout(gbl);
    GridBagConstraints c = new GridBagConstraints();
    c.fill=GridBagConstraints.BOTH;
    makebutton("b1",gbl,c);
    makebutton("b2",gbl,c);
    c.gridwidth = GridBagConstraints.REMAINDER;                     // Note 2
    makebutton("b3",gbl,c);
    c.gridwidth = 1;                                                // Note 3
    c.gridx = 1;                                                    // Note 4
    makebutton("b4",gbl,c);
    c.gridx = GridBagConstraints.RELATIVE;                          // Note 5
    makebutton("b5",gbl,c);
    c.weightx = 1.0;                                                // Note 6
    c.weighty = 1.0;
    makebutton("b6",gbl,c);
  }
}
```

....

Note 1:   Because we are using six buttons, we use a method to create each button, set its constraints, and add it to the applet.

Note 2:   Using REMAINDER for `gridwidth` specifies that it is the last component in its row.

Note 3:   We set `gridwidth` back to its default value of 1. Had we not done that, buttons b5 and b6 would appear under b4, each filling an entire row.

Note 4:   Setting `gridx` to 1 positions b4 in the second column, because a value of 0 represents the first column.

Note 5:   Returning to the default RELATIVE for `gridx` keeps b5 and b6 in the same row as b4; otherwise they would each be positioned with `gridx` equal to 1, underneath b4.

Note 6:   `c.weightx = 1.0;`
The other buttons in the second row, b4 and b5, have `weightx` equal to 0.0, so b6, with `weightx` equal to 1.0, gets all the extra space. Because b3 occupies the remainder of the first row, it gets stretched along with b6.

The Form Applet

Finally, Example 1.27 contains the code for the `Form` applet shown in Figure 1.9. Typically, the user would be filling out the form to buy a product or register for access to a restricted site. The information would go to a web site server which would return a response. In this example, since we do not really submit the data anywhere, we just display the information the user enters in a text area.

A text area provides a rectangular area in which to display information. We can specify initial text and the number of rows and columns of the display using the constructor

```
public TextArea(String initialText, int rows, int cols);
```

or use the default constructor

```
public TextArea();
```

to get a blank text area with a default size. The text area comes with scroll bars to see the text that is not visible.

We want this form to look good when the applet is resized, so we keep the `fill` HORIZONTAL for all text fields except those with a small fixed size, which along with the buttons have `fill` NONE. The text area for messages expands in both directions.

EXAMPLE 1.27   **Form.java**

```
/* Illustrates creating a form with a GridBagLayout.
 */

import java.awt.*;
import java.applet.*;
public class Form extends Applet implements ActionListener {
  private TextField first = new TextField("first name",12);
  private TextField middle = new TextField("I",1);
  private TextField last = new TextField("last name",15);
  private TextField address = new TextField("address",25);
  private TextField city = new TextField("city",20);
```

```
      private TextField state = new TextField("state",2);
      private TextField zip = new TextField("zip",5);
      private Button submit = new Button("Submit");
      private Button reset = new Button("Reset");
      private TextArea message = new TextArea();

      public void init() {
        GridBagLayout gbl = new GridBagLayout();
        setLayout(gbl);
        GridBagConstraints c = new GridBagConstraints();
        c.anchor = GridBagConstraints.WEST;
        c.weightx=1.0;
        c.weighty=1.0;
        c.fill=GridBagConstraints.HORIZONTAL;
        c.insets = new Insets(5,5,5,5);
        gbl.setConstraints(first,c);           add(first);
        c.fill=GridBagConstraints.NONE;
        gbl.setConstraints(middle,c);          add(middle);
        c.fill=GridBagConstraints.HORIZONTAL;
        gbl.setConstraints(last,c);            add(last);
        c.gridy=1;
        gbl.setConstraints(address,c);         add(address);
        c.gridy=2;
        gbl.setConstraints(city,c);            add(city);
        c.fill=GridBagConstraints.NONE;
        gbl.setConstraints(state,c);           add(state);
        c.gridy=3;
        gbl.setConstraints(zip,c);             add(zip);
        c.gridy=4;
        c.anchor = GridBagConstraints.CENTER;
        gbl.setConstraints(submit,c);          add(submit);
        gbl.setConstraints(reset,c);           add(reset);
        c.gridy=5;
        c.gridwidth=3;
        c.fill=GridBagConstraints.BOTH;
        gbl.setConstraints(message,c);         add(message);
        submit.addActionListener(this);
        reset.addActionListener(this);
      }
    public void actionPerformed(ActionEvent event) {
      Object source = event.getSource();
      if (source == submit){
        String initial = middle.getText();
          if (initial != null)
            initial += ". ";
        message.setText(first.getText() + ' ' + initial + last.getText());
        message.append('\n' + address.getText());
        message.append('\n' + city.getText() + ", " + state.getText());
        message.append(' ' + zip.getText());
      }
```

```
        else if (source == reset) {
          message.setText("");
          first.setText("");
          middle.setText("");
          last.setText("");
          address.setText("");
          city.setText("");
          state.setText("");
          zip.setText("");
        }
      }
    }
```

THE BIG PICTURE

The gridbag layout gives us the most flexibility in arranging components. The various gridbag constraints allow us to specify the starting position of a component, the number of rows and columns it takes, internal padding, anchoring, external padding, the direction(s) in which it will fill up its allocated cell, and its weighting relative to other components which determines how much screen space it gets relative to them. The gridbag layout manager uses the largest weight in a row or column to determine how to allocate space to that row or column. The fill for a component determines how it will appear within its allocated space. Experimenting, as we did in Examples 1.22–1.27, helps to understand the effect of the different constraints.

TEST YOUR UNDERSTANDING

TRY IT YOURSELF   15. Modify Example 1.23 so b1 has a `weighty` of `1.0` and b2 has a `weighty` of `0.0`. Explain the result.

TRY IT YOURSELF   16. Modify Example 1.26 to omit the line `c.gridwidth = 1`. Explain the result.

TRY IT YOURSELF   17. Modify Example 1.26 to omit the line `c.gridx = GridBagConstraints.RELATIVE;` Explain the result.

TRY IT YOURSELF   18. Modify Example 1.26 to omit the line `c.gridwidth = GridBagConstraints.REMAINDER;` Explain the result.

1.7 Vectors and Enumerations

A **vector** is like an array that can grow in size. The cost of this flexibility is a decrease in performance compared to arrays. Vectors are useful in multithreaded applications as they are designed for safe access from concurrent threads.

The Vector class, in the java.util package, has three constructors. We can specify the initial size of the vector and the amount to increase its size when it becomes full. Using the default

```
new Vector();
```

will give us a vector of capacity 10 which doubles in size when more space is needed. The constructor

```
new Vector(20);
```

creates a vector with the capacity to hold 20 elements, which doubles in size when necessary. Finally,

```
new Vector(15,5);
```

starts out with a capacity of 15 which increases by 5 when necessary.

To add an element to the end of a vector, we use the addElement method which has a parameter of type Object. Because every class is, directly or indirectly, a subclass of Object, we can add any object to a vector. The code

```
Vector v = new Vector();
String s = "Happy days";
v.addElement(s);
```

creates a vector and a string and adds the string to the vector. We can only add objects to a vector. To add primitive types we must use the wrapper classes such as Integer and Double.

Using the addElement method, as in

```
v.addElement("A big car");
v.addElement("Less is more");
```

adds the strings at the end of the vector

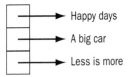

We could use the insertElementAt method to insert an item at a given index in the vector, but that is less efficient than adding at the end. For example,

```
v.insertElementAt("Candy and cake",1);
```

changes v to

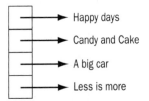

requiring the moving of two elements. In a large vector, insertion might require moving a large number of elements.

The `elementAt` method lets us get the element at a given index. For example,

```
String atTwo = (String)v.elementAt(2);
```

assigns "`A big car`" to `atTwo`. Because `elementAt` returns a value of type `Object`, we must cast it to `String` to assign it to a string variable. The vector v contains only string elements so we know casting to a string will not cause an error.

The `Vector` class provides several methods to locate elements in a vector. The contains method returns **true** if its argument is an element of the vector and **false** otherwise. Thus

```
v.contains("A big car");
```

returns **true**, while

```
v.contains("Sweet dreams");
```

returns **false**. If we need the exact location of an element, the `indexOf` method returns the index of its first occurrence in the vector, or –1 if it does not occur. For example,

```
v.indexOf("A big car");
```

would return 2, while

```
v.indexOf("Sweet dreams");
```

returns –1. The call

```
v.indexOf("Happy days",1);
```

returns –1, because there is no occurrence, in v, of "`Happy days`" starting at index 1.

The `capacity` method returns the number of elements allocated for the vector, while the `size` method returns the number of its elements. Thus

```
v.capacity();
```

returns 10, while

```
v.size();
```

returns 4.
    Either

```
v.removeElement("Candy and cake");
```

or

```
v.removeElementAt(1);
```

would remove the element at index 1 from v.

The `elements` method returns an enumeration which allows us to get all the elements of a vector. The `Enumeration` interface is a general facility for retrieving the elements of a container. It has two methods, `nextElement`, which returns the next element in an arbitrary order, and `hasMoreElements` which returns **true** if there are more elements not yet returned. We can use the method

```
public void listAll(Enumeration e) {
  while(e.hasMoreElements())
    System.out.println(e.nextElement());
}
```

to list the elements of any enumeration. This `listAll` method applies to any container that has an enumeration, completely separating the details of the container type, `Vector`, `Stack`, `List`, or other container, from the listing process. We could list the elements of v with

```
Enumeration e = v.elements();
listAll(e);
```

To illustrate `Vector` objects, we create a vector of the first 1000 Fibonacci numbers. The Fibonacci sequence starts with its first two elements, `f1 = f2 = 1`, and the remaining computed by

$$f_{i+1} = f_i + f_{i-1}$$

so the first 10 Fibonacci numbers are 1, 1, 2, 3, 5, 8, 13, 21, 34, and 55. The Fibonacci numbers have useful applications in numerical analysis and occur in nature, but here we use them solely to illustrate vectors.

We use the `BigInteger` class, in the `java.math` package, to handle large Fibonacci numbers. We create big integers from strings as for example,

```
BigInteger twentyDigits = new BigInteger("12345678909876543210");
```

and add them using the `add` method, as in

```
BigInteger stillTwentyDigits = twentyDigits.add(twentyDigits);
```

EXAMPLE 1.28   **Fibonacci.java**

```
/* Uses the Fibonacci sequence to illustrate vectors.
 */

import java.util.*;
import java.math.BigInteger;

public class Fibonacci {
  public static void main(String[] args) {
    Vector fib = new Vector(1000);
    BigInteger previous = new BigInteger("1");
    BigInteger current = previous;
    fib.addElement(previous);
    fib.addElement(current);
    BigInteger temp;
```

```
for(int i=2; i<fib.capacity(); i++) {                           // Note 1
  temp = current;
  current = previous.add(current);
  previous = temp;
  fib.addElement(current);
}
System.out.println
      ("The fifth Fibonacci number is " + fib.elementAt(4));     // Note 2
System.out.println("The one-thousandth Fibonacci number is "
                + fib.elementAt(999));
Vector prime = new Vector();
for (int i = 0; i < 100; i++) {
  BigInteger aFib = (BigInteger)fib.elementAt(i);
  if (aFib.isProbablePrime(10))                                  // Note 3
    prime.addElement(aFib);
}
System.out.println
      ("The probable primes in the first 100 Fibonacci numbers are:");
Enumeration e = prime.elements();                                // Note 4
while(e.hasMoreElements())
System.out.println("\t" + e.nextElement());
System.out.println("Vector prime's capacity is "
                                    + prime.capacity());         // Note 5
System.out.println("Vector prime's size is " + prime.size());
System.out.println("The ninth probable prime is the "
                + (fib.indexOf(new BigInteger("514229")) + 1)    // Note 6
                + "th Fibonacci number");
int count = 0;
BigInteger random100;
do {
  random100 = new BigInteger
      (String.valueOf((int)(100*Math.random()) + 1));            // Note 7
  count++;
}while (!fib.contains(random100));                               // Note 8
System.out.println("It took " + count
    + " tries to find a Fibonacci number randomly");
  }
}
```

....

Output

```
The fifth Fibonacci number is 5
The one-thousandth Fibonacci number is
434665576869374564356885276750406258025646605173717804024817290895365554179490518904038798400792551692959225930803226347752096896232398733224711616429964409065331879382989696499285160037044761377795166849228875
The probable primes in the first 100 Fibonacci numbers are:
2
3
5
```

```
13
89
233
1597
28657
514229
433494437
2971215073
99194853094755497
Vector prime's capacity is 20
Vector prime's size is 12
The ninth probable prime is the 29th Fibonacci number
It took 12 tries to find a Fibonacci number randomly
```

....

Note 1: We fill `fib` to its capacity of 1000. We use two variables, `previous` and current to represent the last two Fibonacci numbers computed. Each time through the loop we save the current number, add it to the previous number to get the updated `current`, and then copy the saved old `current` to get the new `previous`.

Note 2: It is always a good practice to check a computation with a known value, which we do here, checking that the fifth Fibonacci number is 5.

Note 3: We create a new vector containing those of the first 100 Fibonacci numbers that are probably prime. Determining whether a number is prime (has no divisors other than itself and 1) can be time consuming for large numbers. The `BigInteger` class has a method, `isProbablyPrime`, that determines with a certain probability that a number is prime. Making the probability higher, makes the computation longer. This method uses the probability $1 - (1/2)^n$ where n is its argument. We pass the argument `10`, so it uses the probability $1 - 1/1024$, which means there is greater than a `99.9%` chance that the number is prime.

Note 4: Because we are using the `Vector` class, from the `java.util` package, we can use the `elements` method to get an enumeration. When creating our own container, we can implement an enumeration by implementing the `hasMoreElements` and `nextElement` methods.

Note 5: There turned out to be 12 probable primes in the first 100 Fibonaaci numbers, so the vector, `prime`, automatically grew to capacity 20 from its initial capacity of 10.

Note 6: We check which Fibonacci number happens to be the ninth probable prime.

Note 7: We get a random number between 1 and 100 and then convert it to a string, using the `valueOf` method, so we can construct a `BigInteger` from that random number.

Note 8:   We keep computing random numbers from 1 to 100 as long as they are not Fibonacci numbers. Because there are 11 Fibonacci numbers between 1 and 100, we expect about $100/11$ = 9.09 trials, on the average, until we find a Fibonacci number.

THE BIG PICTURE

A vector grows automatically to accommodate more data. We add values of type `Object`, or any of its subtypes, to a vector. An `Enumeration`, with `hasMoreElements` and `nextElement` methods, lets us iterate through the elements of a vector.

TEST YOUR UNDERSTANDING

19. Declare a vector that initially can hold 25 elements, and grows by seven when it becomes full.

20. Explain the difference between the `capacity` and the `size` methods for the `Vector` class.

SUMMARY

- We put code that might throw an exception in a `try` block, and use a `catch` clause to include code to handle the exception. A Java class represents each exception. Java passes an exception object to the `catch` clause when it throws an exception. We often use that object's `printStackTrace` method to find out where the exception was thrown. Java requires that we handle exceptions thrown that are subclasses of `Exception`, other than `RuntimeException` and its subclasses. Thus we do not need to include code that generates a `NumberFormatException` in a try-catch block, but do need to include code that generates an `IOException` in such a block.

- The `File` class encapsulates file properties. Java provides input and output stream classes for reading and writing binary data, and reader and writer classes for reading and writing text data. For binary data, the basic `read` method returns the **int** value of a single byte, while two other `read` methods fill byte arrays. The `FileInputStream`, `DataInputStream`, `BufferedInputStream`, and `ObjectInputStream` classes let us read from a file, read primitive types, buffer the input for efficiency, and read serializable objects. Corresponding classes exist for writing.

- For text data, the basic `read` method returns the **int** value of a single character, while two other `read` methods fill character arrays. We use the `FileReader` class to read from a file, and `BufferedReader` to buffer the input. The `readLine` method, for buffered input, lets us read lines from a text file. The `PrintWriter` class includes buffering. It overloads the `print` and `println` methods to write each primitive type in a text format. The `FileWriter` class lets us write to a file. Random access files support reading and writing, and let us seek a particular position in the file.

- Java event-handling uses a callback approach. An adapter class prepares to listen for an event by implementing a listener interface for that event. The event source has a method to add listeners, so it knows whom to notify when an event occurs. When an event occurs, the event source notifies each adapter by calling one of the listener interface methods that it implemented.

- For button presses, an adapter implements the `ActionListener` interface. The `addActionListener` method registers an adapter with a button source. An `ActionEvent` describes the event. When the user presses the button, the button calls the `actionPerformed` method for each registered adapter.

- The `WindowListener` interface includes methods to handle each of the seven window events. For window events, the adapter often overrides `WindowAdapter`, which provides a default implementation of the `WindowListener` interface.

- The user interface class can also serve as the adapter, or the adapter can be a separate class. Defining the adapter class an inner class, inside the user interface class, allows it easier access to the user interface fields. Anonymous inner classes are especially useful because they are unnamed and defined where they are used.

- Java allows several threads of control to proceed simultaneously, sharing the processor. Each thread executes the code in a `run` method when it gets the processor. We can extend the `Thread` class to override the default `run` method, or another class can declare that it implements the `Runnable` interface. Such a class must implement the `run` method and pass itself to a thread that will execute its `run` method.

- Calling the `start` method of a thread makes it ready to run. When it gets the processor it will execute either its `run` method, if it is an extension of the `Thread` class, or the `run` method that a `Runnable` object passed to it. An applet often starts a thread in its `start` method, which is called by the browser or applet viewer whenever the user returns to the web page containing the applet. To stop the thread, we set a flag and have the thread check the flag periodically during the execution of its `run` method. If the flag becomes **true** the thread returns from the `run` method, terminating itself.

- A thread can sleep for a specified number of milliseconds. A call to the static `sleep` method occurs in a try block with a catch clause to handle the `InterruptedException` that might be generated.

- When threads share data we must be careful to ensure correct access. Using the keyword **synchronized** locks an object either for the duration of a method or block of code. The thread holding the lock may complete the method or block of code without interruption.

- The `wait` and `notify` methods help threads communicate. The `wait` method signals a condition is not satisfied, so the thread executing it must wait. The `notify` method wakes up one thread, signaling a condition has been satisfied. Concurrent programming requires great care to avoid problems such as deadlock where threads are unable to proceed, halting the system.

- The gridbag layout flexibly positions components by appropriately setting the `gridx`, `gridy`, `gridwidth`, `gridheight`, `fill`, `ipadx`, `ipady`, `insets`, `anchor`, `weightx`, and `weighty` constraint variables.

- A vector is like an array, but it can grow in size. The `addElement` method adds an element, of type `Object` or a subtype, to the end of a vector, causing the vector to grow in size to accommodate it, if necessary. We retrieve an element using the `elementAt` method. Other methods help us find an element in a vector. The `elements` method returns an `Enumeration` object with which we can list the elements of an array using the `hasMoreElements` and `nextElement` methods. Enumerations are useful for listing object from many types of containers.

Program Modification Exercises

· · · · · · · · · · ·

1. Modify Example 1.1 to give the user another chance to enter a correct value after Java throws an exception.

2. Modify Example 1.9 to close the files in a `finally` clause so the files will be closed even if an exception is thrown.

3. Modify Example 1.13 to define an adapter class for each button, rather than one adapter which handles presses from both the `Print` and `Clear` buttons.

4. Modify Example 1.15 to use an anonymous inner adapter class rather than `WindowClose`.

5. Modify Example 1.15 to let the `CloseIt` class be the adapter class instead of using the `WindowClose` adapter.

6. Modify Example 1.11 to be a standalone application instead of an applet. The user should be able to close the window.

7. Modify Example 1.14 to be a standalone application instead of an applet. The user should be able to close the window.

Program Design Exercises

· · · · · · · · · · ·

8. Write a Java standalone application that presents data read from a file in a bar chart. Enter the file name as a program argument.

9. Write a Java program that searches a file for a string. Pass the string and the file name as program arguments.

10. Write a Java program that reads a text file, removing any extra spaces between words, and writes the output to a file. Enter the file names to read from and write to as program arguments.

11. Write a Java program with a button which closes the top-level window when pressed.

12. Write a Java program which provides a GUI to copy Java programs to the screen or to another file. List the Java programs in a choice box. Use checkboxes in a checkbox group to indicate whether to copy the file to the console window or to another file. Use a text box to enter the name of the file receiving the copy.

13. Write a Java program that uses a thread to flash a message every second. Alternate the colors between black and red.

14. Write a Java program that displays a digital clock which shows the correct time. To get the current time, use the `getInstance()` method of the `Calendar` class, in the `java.util` package, to get a `Calendar` object, c. Then use the `Calendar` get method to get the hours, minutes, and seconds, as in:

```
int hour = c.get(Calendar.HOUR);
int minute = c.get(Calendar.MINUTE);
int second = c.get(Calendar.SECOND);
```

Use a thread to allow the clock to keep the correct time.

15. Using a gridbag layout, design a form for a program to send email. Include such items as text fields to enter the sender's name, the addresses of the recipient(s), a text area to enter the message, and a checkbox to indicate whether to save the message. Rather than actually sending email, save the message to a file if the checkbox is check, and display it on standard output otherwise.

16. Write a program that adds each word on a file to a `Vector`. Use an `Enumeration` to list all the words of the `Vector` that do not contain the letter 'e'.

2 Networking

Introduction

Java makes it easy to connect to other computers, using classes from the `java.net` package. We first write client programs that connect to a server, which is a program that performs a task useful to its clients, and then write our own servers. A web server provides files such as web pages, Java applets, and images.

To write client programs, we first use Java classes that enable us to hide the details of the interaction between client and server. We then try classes that let us customize the connection, and present classes that give us full control of the communication, but require us then to know the details of the request and response commands.

The simplest clients connect to a server using a `URL` object, or for more flexibility, a `URLConnection` object. The `URLConnection` talks to a server using a specific protocol. We introduce HTTP, the Hypertext Transfer Protocol used to connect to a web server. Understanding HTTP allows us to customize a connection using `URLConnection` methods, and to write our own simple web client and web server using `Socket` and `ServerSocket` objects. This will enable us to develop and use our own protocols for clients and servers to communicate.

On a higher level, Remote Method Invocation (RMI) allows us to invoke objects on remote machines, introducing powerful distributed computing using Java.

OBJECTIVES:
- Use a URL to connect to a remote site from an applet or an application.
- Introduce HTTP to understand how web clients and servers communicate.
- Use `URLConnection` to customize a connection.
- Use `Socket` and `ServerSocket` objects to have full control over the communication.
- Write a very simple browser and a very simple web server.
- Use threads to enable a server to handle multiple clients.
- Introduce distributed computing using RMI.

2.1   Using a URL to Connect

· · · · · · · · · ·

Computers use **protocols** to communicate. A **client** sends requests using the commands provided by the protocol in the order specified in the protocol, and the **server** responds similarly. The URL class encapsulates several popular protocols, handling their details thereby making it easier for Java programmers to make network **connections** to display a page, retrieve a file, or get mail, for example.

We will describe a URL, then show how to use an applet to display a resource downloaded from a remote site. Finally we use a standalone application to make a connection using a URL.

The Uniform Resource Locator (URL)

A **URL** has four parts: the protocol name, the host address, the port, and the path to the resource file. The **port** number specifies a specific communication link between computers. For example, the full URL for Sun's Java home page is

```
http://java.sun.com:80/index.html
```

where HTTP is the protocol, `java.sun.com` is the host address, `80` is the port, and `index.html` is the path to the resource. Because `80` is the default port for the HTTP service, and `index.html` is the default file name, we can write the same URL more concisely as

```
http://java.sun.com/
```

Using the URL for Sun's Java home page, our Java client connects our machine to the web server on Sun's host machine. This server program must understand HTTP, which we will introduce in the next section. Using a URL and a `URLConnection` to write our client programs, we let Java handle the details of the messages specified by the HTTP protocol to communicate with a **web server**.

Connecting from an Applet

We can use the URL class in a Java applet to have the browser get and display a resource for us. We pass a string specifying a URL to the URL constructor, as in:

```
URL url = new URL("http://java.sun.com/");
```

for Sun's Java home page, or

```
URL myURL = new URL("http://www.cecs.csulb.edu/~artg/");
```

for the author's home page.

Each applet has a `getAppletContext()` method which returns an object that implements the `AppletContext` interface. The **applet context** is the **browser** or applet viewer that started the applet. Each object that implements the `AppletContext` interface has a `showDocument` method which will display the document specified by the `URL` object, if it is able to do so. We can use the applet context to display the resource using the `showDocument` method, as in:

```
getAppletContext().showDocument(url);
```

TIP

If the applet context is a browser, then the `showDocument` method will cause the browser to display the page requested in the `URL`. However, if the applet context is an applet viewer, then the `showDocument` method will only display the applets contained in the document, and not the rest of the page, as the applet viewer just runs applets and does not interpret HTML.

Example 2.1 shows how an applet can get the browser to display a document. We input the URL as a parameter in the HTML file to make it easier to change. The HTML file we use to run the applet of Example 2.1 is:

```
<applet code = ShowURL.class width=300 height=400>
<param name = url value = http://www.cecs.csulb.edu/~artg/>
</applet>
```

Naturally, when requesting a resource from a remote site, we must be connected to the Internet.

EXAMPLE 2.1   **ShowURL.java**

```
/* Running this applet in a browser will cause
 * the browser to display the resource specified
 * in the URL parameter in the HTML file used to run
 * the applet. The applet viewer cannot
 * show a document.
 */

import java.net.*;
import java.applet.Applet;

public class ShowURL extends Applet {
  public void init() {
    try {                                              // Note 1
      URL url = new URL(getParameter("url"));
      getAppletContext().showDocument(url);
```

```
      }catch(MalformedURLException e) {
        e.printStackTrace();
      }
    }
}
```

Note 1:   Java will throw a `MalformedURLException` if the argument to the constructor does not have the correct form for a URL.

Figure 2.1   Example 2.1 displaying a web site

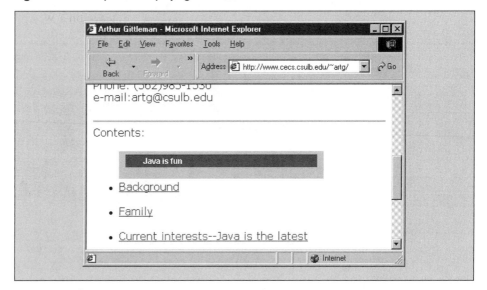

Connecting from a Standalone Application

We can use a URL object in a standalone program, reading characters from the resource specified by the URL. The URL class has a method, `openStream`, which opens a connection to the server, and allows us to read its responses to our client's request. The `openStream` method returns an `InputStream` that we pass to an `InputStreamReader` to convert the bytes to characters, and then pass the `InputStreamReader` to a `BufferedReader` to buffer the input so we can read one line at a time.

```
BufferedReader input = new BufferedReader
                (new InputStreamReader(url.openStream()));
```

Example 2.2 reads one line at a time from the URL specified on the command line, writing each line to the screen. Our Java program is not a browser, so when we read HTML files we get output with the embedded HTML tags. Passing the program argument

```
http://java.sun.com/
```

will list the HTML file for Sun's Java home page.[*] Most files that we access on web servers are HTML files, but we can get other types of files too. Passing the program argument

```
http://www.cecs.csulb.edu/~artg/TryURL.java/
```

will connect to the web server at the California State University Long Beach, Engineering and Computer Science department, retrieving the source code file, TryURL.java. We could read a file from the local machine passing a file URL as a program argument, as in:

```
file:///java/TryURL.java/
```

where the file TryURL.java is in the directory c:\java on a Windows system.[†] Leaving the host name empty defaults to **localhost**, which is the user's machine rather than a remote host. Including localhost, as in,

```
file://localhost/java/TryURL.java/
```

gives the same URL.

TIP ☛ Use forward slashes in writing URLs, even on Windows machines for which the default separator is the backslash.

EXAMPLE 2.2   **TryURL.java**

```java
/* Displays the resource specified by the URL
 * entered on the command line.
 */

import java.net.*;
import java.io.*;

public class TryURL {
  public static void main(String[] args) {
    BufferedReader input;
    try {
      URL url = new URL(args[0]);
      input = new BufferedReader
        (new InputStreamReader(url.openStream()));
      String s;
      while ((s = input.readLine()) != null)
        System.out.println(s);

      input.close();
```

```
    }catch(Exception e) {                                    // Note 1
      e.printStackTrace();
    }
  }
}
```

Output

(The output will display the contents of any file we pass as the program argument. Passing

`http://www.cecs.csulb.edu/~artg/TryURL.java/`

will display the code for this example.)

Note 1:   The URL constructor may throw a `MalformedURLException`, and the `readLine` method may throw an `IOException`. We could write a catch clause for each, but we are not taking the trouble to do anything special for these exceptions so we just catch the superclass `Exception` which is the parent of both of these exceptions. If Java throws either a `MalformedURLException` or an `IOException`, control will jump here to print the stack trace and the message indicating which exception occurred.

THE BIG PICTURE

Network clients and servers communicate using protocols. The URL class hides the details of some popular protocols, letting us make connections more easily. An applet can ask its context, the browser, to show a document. A standalone client uses streams to send data to the servers and receive its response. A URL consists of a protocol, a server address, a port, and a path to the resource.

TEST YOUR UNDERSTANDING

TRY IT YOURSELF   1.   Try using an applet viewer, rather than a browser, to run Example 2.1. What is the result?

TRY IT YOURSELF   2.   Use Example 2.2 to display the file `TryURL.java`. Use a file URL to get the program from the local disk. For example, using Windows, if the file is in the directory `c:\java`, use the URL `file:///c:/java/TryURL.java`

TRY IT YOURSELF   3.   Use Example 2.2 to connect to the author's home page, `http://www.cecs.csulb.edu/~artg/`. Explain the result.

2.2   Protocols with a URLConnection

The URLConnection class makes a connection using a URL, but it adds methods for us to customize the connection and get its properties. It still hides the details of the protocol, while giving the programmer more control.

The Hypertext Transfer Protocol (HTTP)[*]

We used the **HTTP** protocol for our URL in Example 2.1, and suggested the HTTP or file protocols for the URL in Example 2.2. Java supports other protocols, including FTP (File Transfer Protocol) and mailto, when connecting using a URL, but here we concentrate on HTTP. Each protocol allows a formal exchange of messages using well-specified formats. Before going further with networking we describe HTTP, which we will use when customizing a URLConnection, and when writing our own HTTP client and server.

An HTTP client sends a **request** to the server in which the first line has the form

```
Method used      Identifier for the resource     Protocol version
```

The following lines of the request are various request headers which provide information about the capabilities of the client. After the request headers comes the data (if any) to be sent to the server. Figure 2.2, obtained using the HeaderServer program of Example 2.7, shows the request sent by the Java client of Example 2.2 when we pass it the argument

```
http://www.cecs.csulb.edu/~artg/TryURL.java
```

Figure 2.2   The HTTP client request from Example 2.2

```
GET /~artg/TryURL.java HTTP/1.0
User-Agent: Java1.3.0
Host: www.cecs.csulb.edu:80
Accept: text/html, image/gif, image/jpeg, *; q=.2, */*; q=.2
Connection: keep-alive
```

In the first line of Figure 2.2, GET is the method used; we are asking the server to get us a file. The path to that file is the second part of that first line, while the protocol, HTTP/1.0, is the third.

The next four lines of Figure 2.2 are request headers of the form

```
name: value
```

---

[*] See http://www.w3.org/ for the complete HTTP specification.

They are:

Field	Description
User-Agent	Indicates that Java 1.3.0 is running our client.
Host	Identifies the server.
Accept	Specifies the types of files that the client is prepared to accept. Each type has a preference associated with it given by the value of q (for "quality"). This value ranges from a low of 0 to the default of 1. The three types* text/html, image/gif, and image/jpeg have the highest preference (the default of q=1 is not shown). If the server cannot send these types, then the client will accept any type, denoted by *, or any subtype of any type, denoted by */*. These latter generic types have preferences of q=.2.
Connection	Specifies the type of connection. Here keep-alive expresses the client's wish to keep the connection alive for multiple requests.

* The type names are MIME (Multipurpose Internet Mail Extensions) types.

Our Java client has sent a request followed by four request headers selected from various header types available. We will see in the next section how to determine the client's request, and will see that different clients such as Netscape and Internet Explorer send different request headers to the server.

An HTTP server responds to a request with a **status line** followed by various **response headers**. The status line has the form

```
HTTP Version     Status Code     Reason
```

We will use Example 2.3 to find the server's response to a request. Figure 2.3 shows the server's response to the client request of Figure 2.2.

Figure 2.3   The HTTP server response

```
          Status line:
             HTTP/1.0 200 Document follows
          Response headers:
             Date: Mon, 07 Dec 1998 21:12:05 GMT
             Server: NCSA/1.4.2
             Content-type: text/plain
             Last-modified: Wed, 11 Feb 1998 19:19:01 GMT
             Content-length: 439
```

The server sends a status line showing the HTTP version, 1.0 in this example, a code, 200, and the reason for the code, `Document follows`.

The response headers are:

Field	Description
Date	Gives the day and Greenwich Mean Time.
Server	Names the web server used.
Content-type	Describes the content. (Here `text/plain` for a Java program.)
Content-length	Number of bytes in the file.

As we shall see in Example 2.3, other servers use different response headers.

A LITTLE EXTRA

⇨

Status codes have five types, distinguished by their first digit. Some are:

Success	200	OK
Redirection	301	Moved Permanently
Client Error	400	Bad Request
	404	Not Found
	406	Not Acceptable

Using a URLConnection

Using a URL we can download a file. For more flexibility, we can use a `URLConnection` to set some capabilities of a connection, including the client request header fields, and to retrieve the server response status and headers.

We implicitly used a `URLConnection` in Example 2.2 because the URL `openStream` method is supplied by Java as a convenient shorthand for

```
openConnection().getInputStream()
```

where `openConnection` is a URL method that returns a `URLConnection` whose `getInput-Stream` method returns an `InputStream` to the caller. By using `URLConnection` explicitly, we can use the other `URLConnection` methods.

To get the names of the response header fields that the server sends, we use the `getHeaderFieldKey` method, and to get the field value we use `getHeaderField`. The first field returned is the status line.

EXAMPLE 2.3   GetResponses.java

```
/* Uses a URLConnection to find the response status
 * and headers sent by the server.
 */

import java.net.*;
import java.io.*;


public class GetResponses {
  public static void main(String[] args) {
    try {
      URL url = new URL(args[0]);
      URLConnection c = url.openConnection();                    // Note 1
      System.out.println("Status line: ");
      System.out.println('\t' + c.getHeaderField(0));           // Note 2
      System.out.println("Response headers:");
      String value = "";
      int n = 1;
      while (true){ // Note 3
        value = c.getHeaderField(n);
        if (value == null) break;
        System.out.println('\t' + c.getHeaderFieldKey(n++) + ": " + value);
      }
    }catch(Exception e) {
      e.printStackTrace();
    }
  }
}
```

Output – Connecting to http://www.cecs.csulb.edu/~artg/TryURL.java
See Figure 2.3

Output – Connecting to http://java.sun.com/

```
Status line:
  HTTP/1.1 200 OK
Response headers:
  Date: Mon, 07 Dec 1998 21:14:55 GMT
  Server: Apache/1.3.3 (Unix)
  Connection: close
  Content-Type: text/html
```

Output – Connecting to http://ibm.com/

```
Status line:
  HTTP/1.0 200 IBM-Planetwide Document OK
Response headers:
  MIME-Version: 1.0
  Server: Domino-Go-Webserver/4.6
  Title: IBM Corporation
  Date: Mon, 07 Dec 1998 21:17:45 GMT
  Last-modified: Mon, 07 Dec 1998 21:17:45 GMT
  Connection: keep-alive
  Expires: Tue, 08 Dec 1998 01:17:45 GMT
  Window-target: _top
  Vary: User-agent
  Reply-to: webmaste@us.ibm.com
  Content-type: text/html
  Content-Language: en-us
  Content-Length: 9919
```

Note 1: In contrast to Examples 2.1 and 2.2, we explicitly open a URLConnection. With its various methods we can customize a connection as we shall see in Example 2.4.

Note 2: We use the getHeaderField method that takes an integer argument which is the number of the header in the order sent by the server. Given the argument 0, getHeaderField returns the status line sent by the server.

Note 3: The loop continues indefinitely until getHeaderField returns a **null** value, which it does when there is no header with number n.

In the output from the second run of Example 2.3 we see that the Sun server sends a Connection: close response header meaning that it closes the connection after each response. It sends Content-type: text/html because we have requested its Java home page which is an HTML file.

The IBM server, in the third run, includes an Expires response with an expiration date. This is to aid the client in using a **cache** to store the response. If we connect again to IBM's home page, we can save the time and effort of downloading that HTML file again by using the file that we saved in the cache the last time we browsed IBM's site. However when reading the cache, the client should connect with IBM's web server again if the date is later than the expiration date. By including an Expires response header, the server advises the client when it might be necessary to download a fresh copy of the file.

The Vary response header states the file the server returns may vary based on the fields indicated, in this case User-agent. IBM might have versions customized for particular browsers which do not always display HTML files in the same way.

The `Content-Language` header describes the language for the intended audience for the response, using first a language abbreviation such as "en" for English, and then a country code such as us for United States, to represent a dialect of the language.

A LITTLE EXTRA	The language abbreviations are registered with the International Standards Organization (ISO-639). Some abbreviations are:

⇨

Chinese	zh
French	fr
German	de
Greek	el
Spanish	sp

The country codes follow ISO-3166. Some country codes are:

Canada	CA
China	CN
Germany	DE
Great Britain	GB
Greece	GR
Spain	ES
Switzerland	CH
Taiwan	TW

In Example 2.3, we used the generic `getHeaderField` method to list all the response headers sent by the server. We can also get response headers using their names, as in

```
getHeaderField("Content-length")
```

The `URLConnection` class has separate methods for the most common header requests, so we could also get the content length using

```
getContentLength()
```

which returns -1 if the server does not send a Content-length response.

We can use the `setRequestProperty` method to customize the request headers sent by the client. For example,

```
setRequestProperty("Accept", "text/plain");
```

would indicate a client preference for a plain text file. The server should send a 406 (not acceptable) status code if it cannot supply an entity of that type for the request, but it is not required to do so.

Example 2.4 modifies Example 2.2 to use a `URLConnection` explicitly, using some of the `URL` methods to customize the connection and get information about the response.

TIP
☞

When requesting a large file, the response will scroll out of the command window. In many operating systems we can redirect the output to a file. For example, the command

```
java TryURLConnect http://java.sun.com/ text/html
```

causes the output of the response to scroll out of the window, but

```
java TryURLConnect http://java.sun.com/ text/html >out
```

writes the output to a file named out which we can read using a text editor. In Windows, we can use the MSDOS, Properties menu to increase the height of the command window.

EXAMPLE 2.4   **TryURLConnect.java**

```java
/* Displays the resource specified by the URL passed as the
 * first program argument, with the MIME types acceptable for
 * the response passed as the second program argument.
 * Uses URLConnection methods.
 */
import java.net.*;
import java.io.*;
import java.util.*;

public class TryURLConnect {
  public static void main(String[] args) {
    BufferedReader input;
    try {
      URL url = new URL(args[0]);
      URLConnection c = url.openConnection();
      c.setRequestProperty("Accept", args[1]);                    // Note 1
      input = new BufferedReader
          (new InputStreamReader(c.getInputStream()));
      String s;
      while ((s = input.readLine()) != null)
        System.out.println(s);
      input.close();
      System.out.println();
      System.out.println("Content type: " + c.getContentType());
      System.out.println("Content length: " + c.getContentLength()); // Note 2
      System.out.println("Length using getHeaderField: "
                         + c.getHeaderField("Content-length"));    // Note 3
    }catch(Exception e) {
      e.printStackTrace();
    }
  }
}
```

Output – arguments http://www.cecs.csulb.edu/~artg/TryURL.java   text/plain
(The file of Example 2, not shown)

```
Content type: text/plain
Content length: 439
Length using getHeaderField: 439
```

Output—arguments http://www.cecs.csulb.edu/~artg/ShowURL.java   text/plain
(The file of Example 1, not shown)

```
Content type: text/plain
Content length: 305
Length using getHeaderField: 305
```

Output—arguments http://java.sun.com/   text/html
(Sun's HTML file for its Java home page, not shown)

```
Content type: text/html
Content length: -1
Length using getHeaderField: null
```

Output—arguments http://ibm.com/   text/html
(IBM's HTML file for its home page, not shown)

```
Content type: text/html
Content length: 9924
Length using getHeaderField: 9924
```

Note 1:   Passing text/plain as a program argument will change the client's default Accept request header to request text/plain. We could use the setRequest-Property method to set any of the client's request headers.

Note 2:   In Example 2.3 we listed the response headers actually sent by the server. Here when we ask for the content length, the server may not have sent it, in which case the method returns -1.

Note 3:   This version of the getHeaderField returns a response header for the field name passed as its argument. Its return value has type String so if the server has not sent any header for that field, it returns **null**.

THE BIG PICTURE

Using HTTP to communicate with a web server, the client sends a request followed by various request headers giving information about the client. The server responds with a status line and various response headers describing the server and the response. The URLConnection class still hides the details of the protocol, but allows us to customize the request and inquire about the response.

4. For the `Accept` request header given by

    `Accept: text/plain; q=0.5, text/html, application/zip; q=0.8, image/gif`

    which two file types are most preferred, which is next, and which is least preferred.

TRY IT YOURSELF 5. Rewrite Example 2.2 to explicitly use `URLConnection` rather than implicitly using it via the `openStream` method.

TRY IT YOURSELF 6. Use Example 2.3 to connect to five different web sites, in addition to those tried in the text.

TRY IT YOURSELF 7. In Example 2.4 use the `getHeaderField` method to get the content type instead of `getContentType`.

2.3   Clients and Servers Using Sockets

The `URL` and `URLConnection` classes hide the details of a few common protocols, most importantly HTTP, so we can easily write programs to connect to a web server, for example. With the `Socket` and `ServerSocket` classes, we can write clients and servers using existing protocols, and develop our own protocols for communicating between client and server. After introducing ports, through which we connect, we use our own protocol, writing both a server and a client to illustrate the use of **sockets**. Finally, we use the HTTP protocol to write a server which echoes the requests sent by the client.

Server Ports

Each server listens on a numbered port. The system servers use port numbers below 1024; we can use higher numbered ports for our servers. The familiar services use standard port numbers. For example web servers usually use port 80, **SMTP** servers (Simple Mail Transfer Protocol) for sending mail use port 25, and **POP3** servers (Post Office Protocol-version3) for receiving mail use port 110.

We could use Java to write a client to connect to a system server. For example we could get our email by writing a client for a POP3 server. In writing such a client we would have to follow the Post Office Protocol-version 3 which specifies the form of the communication between the client and the server. Figure 2.4 shows sample interaction between a client and a POP3 server.

Figure 2.4   Interacting with the POP3 server

```
Server:    +OK POP3 server ready,        // server responds welcome
Client:    USER username                 // client sends user's name
Server:    +OK                           // server responds OK
Client:    PASS password                 // client sends the password
Server:    +OK 23 messages 3040 octets   // server sends message info
Client:    RETR 23                        // asks for message 23
Server:    text of message 23, ending
           with a '.' alone on a line
Client:    QUIT
```

A Client-Server Example

If we write our own server we can use our own protocol for communicating with a client. We write a very simple server which reverses the text that the client sends it. Figure 2.5 shows the client window and the server window.

Figure 2.5   `ReverseClient` and `ReverseServer`

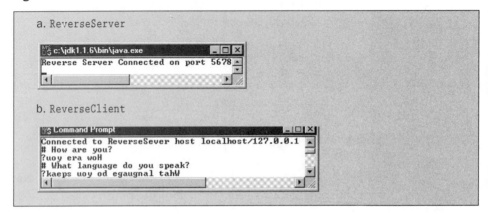

Java provides a `Socket` class for the client to connect to a server on a specific port, and a `ServerSocket` class for the server to listen for clients who wish to make a connection. Once the client connects with the server, they use the reader and writer classes to send and receive data to and from one another. Example 2.5 shows the code for a server that reverses whatever the client sends it.

We choose an arbitrary port number, 5678, on which our server will listen. The `accept` method waits for a client to make a connection. When a client connects, the `accept` method returns a client socket and our server prints a message announcing the connection. The client socket has a `getInputStream` method which the server uses to create a `BufferedReader` to read from the client. The server uses the client's `getOuput-Stream` method to create a `PrintWriter` to write to the client. The server reads one line at a time from the client, reversing it and sending it back.

EXAMPLE 2.5   **ReverseServer.java**

```
/* Listens on port 5678. When a client connects, the server
 * reverses whatever the client sends, and sends it back.
 */

import java.net.*;
import java.io.*;


public class ReverseServer {
  public static void main(String [] args) {
    String s;   // the string to reverse
```

```
int size;   // the length of the string
char[] c;   // the reversed characters
try {
  ServerSocket server = new ServerSocket(5678);            // Note 1
  Socket client = server.accept();                         // Note 2
  BufferedReader input = new BufferedReader
      (new InputStreamReader(client.getInputStream()));
  PrintWriter output = new PrintWriter
      (client.getOutputStream(),true);                     // Note 3
  while ((s = input.readLine()) != null){
    size = s.length();
    c = new char[size];                                    // Note 4
    for (int i = 0; i < size; i++)
      c[i] = s.charAt(size - 1 - i);                       // Note 5
    output.println(c);                                     // Note 6
  }
  input.close();
  output.close();
  client.close();
}catch(Exception e) {
  e.printStackTrace();
  }
 }
}
```

....

Note 1:   We create a server to listen for connections on port 5678.

Note 2:   The accept statement blocks any further progress in the program until a client connects; it then returns the client socket.

Note 3:   We set the second argument to the PrintWriter constructor to **true** so println statements will flush the output, rather than waiting until the buffer fills up.

Note 4:   We cannot change a String object, so we create an array of characters to hold the reverse of the line the client inputs. We could also have used a StringBuffer object which is like a String but allows changes.

Note 5:   We use the charAt method to get the character which is i positions from the right end of the string and copy it into element i of the char array.

Note 6:   output.println(c);
           The array c contains the reversed characters of the string sent by the client. We send these reversed characters back to the client.

We can run the server on the same machine as the client or on a different machine.[*] The server does not terminate until we abort it, so we should run it in the back-

---

[*] When running a server on the same machine as the client in Windows, the machine does not need to be connected to the Internet, but the TCP/IP protocol should be installed. (Click on the *Start* button, *Settings*, *Control Panel*, *Network* icons, then *Protocol* tab to check the installed protocols.)

ground in its own thread, and we can do other things while it is waiting for clients to connect.* Figure 2.5 shows the client and server running on the same machine. The client connects using the address of the host which we pass as a program argument. The name localhost denotes the local machine so the client connects to the server on the same machine with the command

```
java ReverseClient localhost
```

Using two machines, we would have started the server on one machine and let the client connect to it using the server's name or its **IP address**†. We usually refer to machines by their names, as for example, www.cecs.csulb.edu, but underlying each name is a four byte IP (Internet Protocol) address, as for example 134.139.67.68. (The local machine, named localhost, has the IP address 127.0.0.1.) In connecting in a small lab, whose computers are linked to the Internet, we may just use these basic IP addresses. If we start ReverseServer on machine 134.139.67.68, we would connect to the server from another machine using the command

```
java ReverseClient 134.139.67.68.
```

The client creates a socket using the port, 5678, on which the server is listening. The client uses the getInetAddress method of the socket to display the address of the host to which it is connected. As in the server of Example 2.5, the client and the server use readers and writers to communicate with each other. The client uses the getInput-Stream method of the socket to create a BufferedReader to read from the server, and uses the getOutputStream method of the socket to create a PrintWriter to write to the server. The client also creates a BufferedReader to get the input from the user.

The client enters a loop printing a prompt, getting a line from the user, sending it to the server, getting the reversed line from the server, and displaying it on the screen, exiting when the user signals the end of input (Control + Z in Windows). Example 2.6 shows the client program which connects to a server that reverses its input.

EXAMPLE 2.6   **ReverseClient.java**

```
/* Connects to a server which reverses whatever
 * the user inputs. Specifies the host of the
 * server on the command line.
 */

import java.net.*;
import java.io.*;
```

---

* Using the JDK, in Windows systems, use the start command to run the server in the background: start java ReverseServer. On Unix systems, run in the background using the command java ReverseServer &. If using an integrated development environment, use separate projects for the server and client, running the server first.

† The IP address is actually associated with a network interface card.

```
public class ReverseClient {
  public static void main(String[] args) {
    String s; // the string to reverse
    if (args.length != 1){                                       // Note 1
      System.out.println("Pass the server's address");
      System.exit(1);
    }


    try {
      Socket server = new Socket(args[0],5678);                  // Note 2
      System.out.println("Connected to ReverseServer host "
                         + server.getInetAddress());

      BufferedReader fromServer = new BufferedReader
              (new InputStreamReader(server.getInputStream()));
      PrintWriter toServer = new PrintWriter
              (server.getOutputStream(),true);
      BufferedReader input = new BufferedReader(
              new InputStreamReader(System.in));
      while (true) {
        System.out.print("# ");
        System.out.flush();
        if ((s=input.readLine()) == null)
          break;
        toServer.println(s);
        System.out.println(fromServer.readLine());
      }
      fromServer.close();
      toServer.close();
      input.close();
      server.close();
    }catch(Exception e) {
      e.printStackTrace();
    }
  }
}
```

....

Note 1:   We check that the user passed the address of the server's host machine as a
program argument. If not, we abort the program with a message indicating the omission.

Note 2:   The client creates a socket connection to the server on port 5678, the port
on which the server is listening.

A Request Header Server

While ReverseServer (Example 2.5) works fine when connected to by ReverseClient
(Example 2.6), we will see it does not respond properly to an HTTP client such as
our TryURL program of Example 2.2. ReverseServer does not respond properly to

TryURL because it does not follow HTTP. We modify it, producing a server, `Header-Server`, that echoes the lines sent by the client.

We used `ReverseClient` to connect to `ReverseServer`, but we can use other clients to connect to `ReverseServer`. Using our `TryURL` client using the command

```
java TryURL http://localhost:5678/~artg/TryURL.java
```

gives the result shown in Figure 2.6.

Figure 2.6   Connecting to ReverseServer using `TryURL`

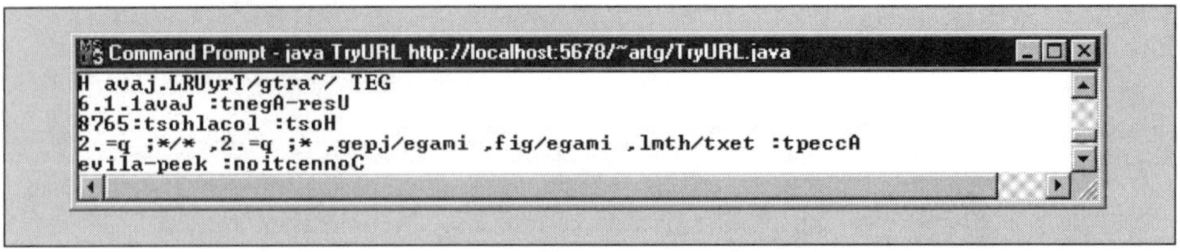

```
Command Prompt - java TryURL http://localhost:5678/~artg/TryURL.java
H avaj.LRUyrT/gtra~/ TEG
6.1.1avaJ :tnegA-resU
8765:tsohlacol :tsoH
2.=q ;*/* ,2.=q ;* ,gepj/egami ,fig/egami ,lmth/txet :tpeccA
evila-peek :noitcennoC
```

We wrote the `TryURL` program to connect to a server and request it to send us a file. `TryURL` does not send any user data to the server; it only sends its request headers. `ReverseServer` reverses those headers and sends them back to the client which displays them as if they were the sought after file. Thus Figure 2.6 looks almost like Figure 2.2, except in reverse, of course, because `ReverseServer` dutifully reverses everything sent to it before sending it back.

One difference is minor. Line 3 (reversed so that we can read it) shows the host as localhost:5678 because we connected to our `ReverseServer` on the local machine rather than to a web server at a remote site. The important difference is in the first line which is shortened in Figure 2.6 to

```
H avaj.LRUyrT/gtra~/ TEG
```

which reversed is `GET /~artg/TryURL.java H`.

The explanation for this mysterious shortening is that the client, `TryURL`, is using HTTP, and expects the server to follow that protocol. A web server should send the status line, any response headers, and then a blank line to signal the beginning of file to the client. The browser, or other web client, such as `TryURL`, uses the response headers internally but does not display them. It waits for the blank line, using the header information it received to appropriately display what follows the blank line.

`ReverseServer`, not using HTTP, does not send a blank line. This confuses `TryURL` which discards the first seven characters of the first line of data sent by `ReverseServer`. The first line that `TryURL` sent was the request, and we see in the result that the first seven characters, 0.1/PTT, of the reversed request line are missing from Figure 2.6.

By modifying `ReverseServer`, we can make a very simple server to show us the request and headers that an HTTP client sends. We send a status line

```
HTTP/1.0 200 OK
```

and the single response header

```
Content-type: text/plain
```

then send a blank line before sending any data to the client. We no longer want to reverse what the client sends, so we can remove the code from `ReverseServer` that does the reversing. Rather than trying to satisfy the client's request, our server will return to the client whatever it sent. An HTTP client sends a request and perhaps some request headers, so this is what the server will return.

Figure 2.7   A Netscape client connected to `HeaderServer`[*]

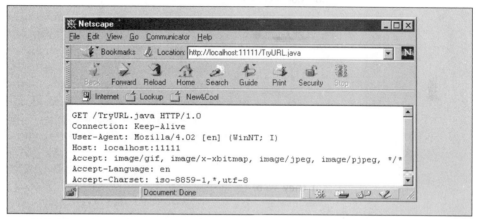

> [*] Use the command `start java HeaderServer 11111`, where 11111 is the port number, to start header server running in the background in Windows. This server will terminate after one client connects.

Because the server indicates that every file has type `text/plain`, Internet Explorer, when connecting to `HeaderServer`, pops up a Notepad editor window, shown in Figure 2.8, to display the text.

Figure 2.8   An Internet Explorer client connected to `HeaderServer`

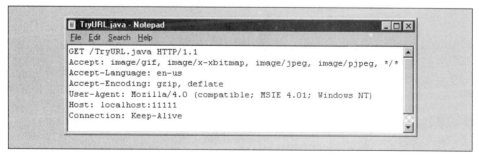

We see that each client has its own variants of the request headers that it sends to the server.

EXAMPLE 2.7   **HeaderServer.java**

```
/* When an HTTP client connects, the server sends
 * the client's request and its request headers back to it.
 */

import java.net.*;
import java.io.*;


public class HeaderServer {
  public static void main(String[] args) {
    String s;
    try {
      ServerSocket server = new ServerSocket(Integer.parseInt(args[0]));
      Socket client = server.accept();
      System.out.println("Header Server Connected on port " + args[0]);
      BufferedReader fromClient = new BufferedReader
          (new InputStreamReader(client.getInputStream()));
      PrintWriter toClient = new PrintWriter
          (client.getOutputStream(), true);
      toClient.println("HTTP/1.0 200 OK");                    // Note 1
      toClient.println("Content-type: text/plain");           // Note 2
      toClient.println();
      while (!(s = fromClient.readLine()) .equals("")){       // Note 3
        toClient.println(s);
      }
      fromClient.close();
      toClient.close();
      client.close();
    }catch(Exception e) {
      e.printStackTrace();
    }
  }
}
```

....

Output from `java TryURL http://localhost:11111/TryURL.java.`
(See also Figures 7 and 8)

```
GET /TryURL.java HTTP/1.0
User-Agent: Java1.3.0
Host: localhost:11111
Accept: text/html, image/gif, image/jpeg, *; q=.2, */*; q=.2
Connection: keep-alive
```

....

Note 1:   A web server must send a status line to the client which reflects the status
of the request. For simplicity, we always send the code 200 meaning OK
even though we make no attempt to serve the file requested. We leave

improvements to the server to the exercises. Were we to omit sending the status line, HTTP clients would drop some characters from the response.

Note 2:   If we do not send this header to the client, then both Netscape and Internet Explorer run all the headers together in a long line rather than displaying each header on a separate line as we see in Figures 2.7 and 2.8. This shows that HTTP clients use the response headers sent by the server to display the requested resource.

Note 3:   We check for the empty string instead of **null**. The ReverseClient user sends an end-of-file which terminates ReverseServer. TryURL sends a request and then request headers terminated by an empty line, but not an end-of-file.

THE BIG PICTURE

Using a Socket to connect gives the most flexibility, but both client and server must follow the appropriate protocol. When writing our own server, we can define the protocol by which client and server communicate. The server creates a ServerSocket and uses an accept statement to wait for a client to connect.

TEST YOUR UNDERSTANDING

TRY IT YOURSELF   8.   Start the ReverseServer of Example 2.5. Connect to it with a client. After sending some strings for the server to reverse, send an end-of-file to the server. What happens to the client and the server programs? In the Exercises we will suggest modifications to the ReverseServer to change this behavior.

TRY IT YOURSELF   9.   Revise Example 2.7 to omit sending the status line to the client. What error occurs in the result?

TRY IT YOURSELF   10. Revise Example 2.7 to omit the Content-type response header. How does the output change when using either Netscape or Internet Explorer as the client?

2.4   Browsers and Web Servers

· · · · · · · · · ·

A browser is an HTTP client, which may use other protocols, while a web server is an HTTP server. In this section we write a very simple browser and a very simple web server, leaving to the exercises many improvements to make them more functional. We conclude with a threaded web server, which can handle multiple clients connected simultaneously.

A Very Simple Browser

An HTTP client sends a request to the server followed by request headers and a blank line. It then reads the status line, response headers, and the requested file from the server. A browser typically can handle several types of files, the most important being HTML files which define web pages. The browser has to interpret the HTML tags to guide it in displaying the page. With so many file types to handle, and such intricate processing necessary for web pages, a useful browser is not a small or simple undertaking. Our very simple browser just handles plain text files.

Figure 2.9 shows `VerySimpleBrowser` connecting to the author's web site to download a file using the command

```
java VerySimpleBrowser www.cecs.csulb.edu 80 /~artg/TryURL.java
```

where 80 is the standard HTTP port on which the server is running. An alternative approach would pass a URL, as in the command

```
java VerySimpleBrowser http://www.cecs.csulb.edu/~artg/TryURL.java
```

and use the URL methods `getFile`, `getHost`, and `getProtocol`, which each return a `String`, and `getPort`, which returns an **int**, to break the URL into the parts needed in Example 2.8.

Figure 2.9 `VerySimpleBrowser` **downloads a file**

```
Command Prompt                                                    _ □ ×
D:\book3\gittleman\ch2>java VerySimpleBrowser www.cecs.csulb.edu 80 /~artg/TryUR
L.java
Connected to host www.cecs.csulb.edu/134.139.4.17
import java.net.*;
import java.io.*;

public class TryURL {
  public static void main(String [] args) {
    BufferedReader input;
    try {
      URL url = new URL(args[0]);
      input = new BufferedReader(new InputStreamReader(url.openStream()));
      String s;
      while ((s=input.readLine())!= null)
        System.out.println(s);
    }catch(Exception e) {
        e.printStackTrace();
    }
  }
}
```

`VerySimpleBrowser` always sends a `GET` request, and a `Host` request header. It ignores the status line and response headers sent by the server, rather than trying to use them to get information that would help it to display the requested resource.

EXAMPLE 2.8   **VerySimpleBrowser**

```
/* Connects to a web server to download a text file.
 * Exercises suggest extensions to handle other file types.
 */

import java.net.*;
import java.io.*;

public class VerySimpleBrowser {
  public static void main(String[] args) {
    String s;
    if (args.length != 3){
```

```
        System.out.println("Usage: java VerySimpleBrowser host port file");
        System.exit(1);
      }
      try {
        int port = Integer.parseInt(args[1]);                        // Note 1
        Socket server = new Socket(args[0],port);
        System.out.println("Connected to host "
            + server.getInetAddress());
        BufferedReader fromServer = new BufferedReader
            (new InputStreamReader(server.getInputStream()));
        PrintWriter toServer = new PrintWriter
            (server.getOutputStream(),true);
        toServer.println("GET " + args[2] + " HTTP/1.0");            // Note 2
        toServer.println("Host: " + args[0]+ ':' + args[1]);
        toServer.println();
        while (!(s = fromServer.readLine()).equals(""));            // Note 3
        while ((s = fromServer.readLine()) != null)                 // Note 4
          System.out.println(s);
        fromServer.close();
        toServer.close();
        server.close();
      }catch(Exception e) {
        e.printStackTrace();
      }
    }
  }
}
```

....

Note 1:   The standard HTTP port is 80, but some servers use 8080. We run our
              simple web server on port 11111. The user should pass the server port
              number as the second program argument.

Note 2:   We use the path to the resource, /~artg/TryURL.java in Figure 2.9, sending
              the host address and port in a separate Host header. Alternatively, we could
              have sent the GET command
              GET www.cecs.csulb.edu:80/~artg/TryURL.java HTTP/1.0

Note 3:   We read and ignore the status line and headers sent by the server, looking
              for the blank line that signals the end of the headers and the start of the file
              we requested. We leave it to the exercises to improve the browser to make
              use of this information.

Note 4:   This loop reads the file we requested from the server, displaying it in the
              command window. Extending this very simple browser to display HTML
              would use graphics extensively.

A Very Simple Web Server

An HTTP server reads the request from the client, any headers, and in some cases
additional data. It sends a status line followed by headers and the requested resource, if
any. Web servers often transmit data from the client to other programs for processing

before returning results to the client. Our very simple web server only responds to GET requests, and only serves text files. We leave it to the exercises to add features to make this server more functional.

To start VerySimpleWebServer, we use the command

```
start java VerySimpleWebServer 11111
```

which, on Windows systems, starts the server in a new window. Figure 2.10 shows Netscape connecting to VerySimpleWebServer to download a file. We could also have used VerySimpleBrowser as the client.

Figure 2.10   **A Netscape client connecting to** VerySimpleWebServer

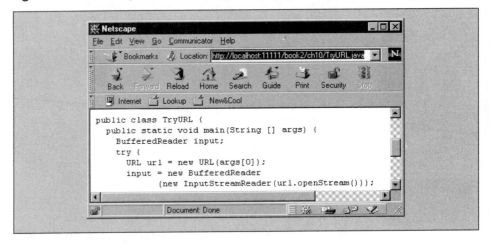

EXAMPLE 2.9   **VerySimpleWebServer.java**

```java
/* Serves a text file to an HTTP client submitting a GET
 * request. Exercises suggest extensions to make the
 * server more functional.
 */

import java.net.*;
import java.io.*;
import java.util.StringTokenizer;

public class VerySimpleWebServer {
  public static void main(String[] args) {
    String s;
    try {
      ServerSocket server = new ServerSocket(Integer.parseInt(args[0]));
      Socket client = server.accept();
        System.out.println
            ("VerySimpleWebServer Connected on port " + args[0]);
      BufferedReader fromClient = new BufferedReader
          (new InputStreamReader(client.getInputStream()));
```

```
          PrintWriter toClient = new PrintWriter
              (client.getOutputStream(), true);
          s = fromClient.readLine();                            // Note 1
          StringTokenizer tokens = new StringTokenizer(s);      // Note 2
          if (!(tokens.nextToken()).equals("GET")) {            // Note 3
            toClient.println("HTTP/1.0 501 Not Implemented");
            toClient.println();
          }
          else {
            String filename = tokens.nextToken();               // Note 4
            while (!(s = fromClient.readLine()) .equals(""));    // Note 5

            BufferedReader file =
                new BufferedReader(new FileReader(filename));    // Note 6
            toClient.println("HTTP/1.0 200 OK");                 // Note 7
            toClient.println("Content-type: text/plain");
            toClient.println();
            while ((s = file.readLine()) != null)               // Note 8
              toClient.println(s);
            file.close();
          }
          fromClient.close();
          toClient.close();
          client.close();
        }catch(Exception e) {
          e.printStackTrace();
        }
    }
}
```

....

Note 1:   We read the first line from the client to find the method and the identifier for the resource.

Note 2:   Blanks separate each item of the request. We use a StringTokenizer to get the method and identifier parts of the request.

Note 3:   If the request method is anything other than GET, the server sends a status line with a code of 501 to indicate the method is not implemented.

Note 4:   The file name comes after GET, separated by a blank, in the request from the client. We save it here before we read the next line from the client which will overwrite the string s.

Note 5:   We read and ignore any request headers sent by the client, looking for the blank line that separates the request and headers from any data the client might send.

Note 6:   `BufferedReader file = new BufferedReader(new FileReader(filename));`
If file cannot be found or another error occurs, the exception thrown will cause control to jump to the catch clause and the server to terminate.

We leave to the exercises the improvement of the server to handle the error and send an error message to the client.

Note 7: `toClient.println("HTTP/1.0 200 OK");`
Having created the file to send, the server sends a status line with code 200 meaning OK, and follows with one header describing the content type to help the client to display it.

Note 8: `while ((s = file.readLine()) != null)`
This loop sends the file to the client.

A Threaded Web Server

Our `VerySimpleWebServer` has the very unusual behavior for a server in that it serves one request and terminates. We can easily modify Example 2.9 to put the server code in a loop. After it responds to one request, it can respond to another, and keep serving clients one at a time. Each client has to wait until the server finishes with the preceding client before being served.

Web servers may get requests from many clients at many dispersed locations. Using threads would allow the server to serve many clients simultaneously. The server interacts with one client while others are preparing their requests or displaying responses. It divides its attention among all connected clients so that they share the server. Large web sites may have a number of servers sharing the load of serving many, many clients.

Our `ThreadedWebServer` runs in an unending loop. Each time a client connects, the server creates a thread to handle its processing with that client. The client thread creates the files needed to communicate with the server in its constructor and starts itself running. Its `run` method contains the code from Example 2.9 in which the server responds to the client.

A good test for a threaded server would check how it handles simultaneous requests. We can make a step in that direction by starting two `VerySimpleBrowser` clients, each requesting a large file so the server will give each request some of its attention. We will see both browser windows scrolling the text of the file. The server will alternate, sending some of the first file to the first browser, then some of the second file to the second browser, then returning to the first, and so on until it has satisfied both requests.

We start `ThreadedWebServer` using the command

```
start java ThreadedWebServer 11111
```

on Windows systems, and

```
java ThreadedWebServer 11111 &
```

on Unix systems. Once the server is running, we start the two clients. Figure 2.11 shows both clients receiving the text of this chapter from a `ThreadedWebServer`.

Figure 2.11   Two browsers receiving text from `ThreadedWebServer`

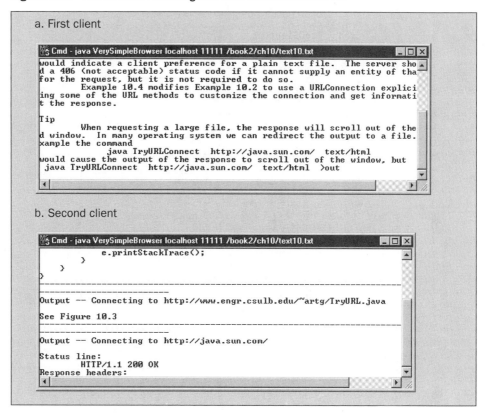

EXAMPLE 2.10   **ThreadedWebServer.java**

```
/* When an HTTP client connects, the server creates a thread
 * to respond to the client's request, so that multiple clients
 * can be connected simultaneously.
 */

import java.net.*;
import java.io.*;
import java.util.StringTokenizer;

public class ThreadedWebServer {
  public static void main(String [] args) {
    try {
      ServerSocket server = new ServerSocket(Integer.parseInt(args[0]));
      ThreadedWebServer web = new ThreadedWebServer();           // Note 1
      while(true) {                                              // Note 2
        Socket client = server.accept();
        web.new ClientThread(client);                           // Note 3
        System.out.println("ThreadedWebServer Connected to "
                  + client.getInetAddress());
      }
```

```
      }catch(Exception e) {
        e.printStackTrace();
      }
    }
class ClientThread extends Thread {
  Socket client;
  BufferedReader fromClient;
  PrintWriter toClient;
  public ClientThread(Socket c) {
    try {
      client = c;
      fromClient = new BufferedReader
          (new InputStreamReader(client.getInputStream()));
      toClient = new PrintWriter
          (client.getOutputStream(), true);
      start();                                            // Note 4
    }catch(Exception e) {
      e.printStackTrace();
    }
  }
  public void run() {                                     // Note 5
    try {
      String s;
      s = fromClient.readLine();
      StringTokenizer tokens = new StringTokenizer(s);
      if (!(tokens.nextToken()).equals("GET")) {
        toClient.println("HTTP/1.0 501 Not Implemented");
        toClient.println();
      }
      else {
        String filename = tokens.nextToken();
          while (!(s = fromClient.readLine()) .equals(""));
          BufferedReader file =
              new BufferedReader(new FileReader(filename));
          toClient.println("HTTP/1.0 200 OK");
          toClient.println("Content-type: text/plain");
          toClient.println();
          while ((s=file.readLine()) != null)
            toClient.println(s);
          file.close();
        }
        fromClient.close();
        client.close();
        toClient.close();
      }catch(Exception e) {
        e.printStackTrace();
      }
    }
  }
}
```

Note 1: We need an instance of `ThreadedWebServer` to create the client thread to run each client. `ClientThread` is an inner class and must be created using a reference to its containing class, `ThreadedWebServer`.

Note 2: The server runs in an unending loop, until aborted, continuing to serve clients as they connect.

Note 3: By making `ClientThread` an inner class, we avoid conflicts in the global namespace. `ClientThread` has the full name `ThreadedWebServer$Client`, so the name `ClientThread` may be used in other contexts without conflict. Because `ClientThread` is an inner class of `ThreadedWebServer`, we create a `ClientThread` instance using the instance, `web`, of `ThreadedWebServer`. We leave the alternative, defining `Client` outside of `ThreadedWebServer`, as an exercise.

Note 4: This makes this thread runnable, so when it gets scheduled, Java will execute its `run` method.

Note 5: The `run` method contains the code from Example 2.9 by which the server and client communicate. If several threads are active, then the server will be communicating with several clients who are all connected simultaneously.

THE BIG PICTURE

Browsers and web servers use HTTP to communicate. Our `ThreadedWebServer` spawns a new thread to handle a connection from a client, so many clients may be connected to this server simultaneously. Rather than terminating after a client connects, `ThreadedWebServer` remains in a loop waiting for the next client.

TEST YOUR UNDERSTANDING

TRY IT YOURSELF

11. Modify Example 2.8 to use the HEAD method which just sends headers and does not ask for a resource in response. Connect with the very simple web server of Example 2.9. What happens?

TRY IT YOURSELF

12. Put the server of Example 2.9 into a loop so instead of terminating after each connection, it waits for another client to connect. Make the loop unending, so the server will have to be aborted to terminate it.

TRY IT YOURSELF

13. Test the threaded web server of Example 2.10 by connecting to it from two simple web browser clients at close to the same time. Find long text files to request so both clients will be connected to the server at the same time while downloading the requested files. Describe what you observe.

2.5   Remote Method Invocation (RMI)

· · · · · · · · · · ·

Remote Method Invocation (**RMI**) takes networking to a higher level, providing distributed computing for Java programs. In distributed computing a program can be composed of parts located on more than one computer. So far we have used input and output streams to communicate between a client and server. These streams transfer data from one machine to another. Using RMI we can distribute our objects on various machines, invoking methods of objects located on remote sites.

Distributed Computing: The RMI Solution

We use a very simple example, a fortune server, to show how RMI works without introducing the extra complications of an involved example. The fortune server may be running on one machine. Clients, from remote sites, can request a fortune. In making these requests, clients will invoke a method of an object on the server. A **distributed computing** system must provide the following capabilities:

1. Clients must know what services the fortune server provides.
    RMI Solution: A `Fortune` interface lists the methods available to remote clients.

2. Clients must find a `Fortune` object on the server.
    RMI Solution: The fortune server registers an object with a special server, called the **rmiregistry**, so that clients can look it up by name.

3. Clients must be able to pass arguments to, and invoke a method of the `Fortune` object located on the server.
    RMI Solution: A special compiler, called **rmic**, creates a `stub` class for use on the client, and a `skeleton` class for use on the server. The stub takes the request from the client, passes the arguments to the skeleton which invokes the `Fortune` method and sends the return value back to the stub which passes it to the client.

Figure 2.12 shows how RMI operates.

Figure 2.12 The parts of RMI illustrated

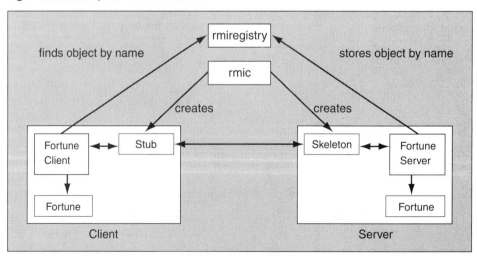

For our example which provides a fortune server that will enable clients to request fortunes (the fortune cookie kind, not the billionaire kind), we need to write the following programs:

Fortune   The interface that shows the client what remote methods it can invoke, the getFortune method in this example.

FortuneServer   The implementation of the Fortune interface to provide the remote object which is served to clients who wish to use its method to get a fortune.

FortuneClient   A client that gets a reference to a Fortune object and invokes its getFortune method remotely.

We run this example on one machine but use two directories, one for the client and one for the server, to simulate the use of a remote site. To compile and run our example we follow these steps:

In the server directory

1.   Compile Fortune.java and FortuneServer.java.

2.   Create the stub and skeleton classes using the command* rmic FortuneServer

3.   Copy FortuneServer_Stub.class to the client directory.

4.   Start the registry server using the command start rmiregistry on Windows systems, or rmiregistry & on Unix systems.

5.   Start FortuneServer using the command† start java FortuneServer localhost on Windows systems, or java FortuneServer localhost & on Unix systems.

In the client directory

6.   Compile Fortune.java and FortuneClient.java.

7.   Run FortuneClient using the command† java FortuneClient localhost

---

TIP
☞

To run using two machines, follow the above steps, changing localhost, in steps 5 and 6, to the address of the server.

---

* If this command generates an error, it may be necessary to set the classpath.
† When using the Java™ 2 Platform, due to changes in the security model, we need to specify a security policy on the command line, so the command would be
   start java -Djava.security.policy=d:\policy FortuneServer localhost
   where d:\policy is the file containing the security policy. For testing RMI, the policy file
   grant { permission java.security.AllPermission; }; will work.

Figure 2.13 An RMI example

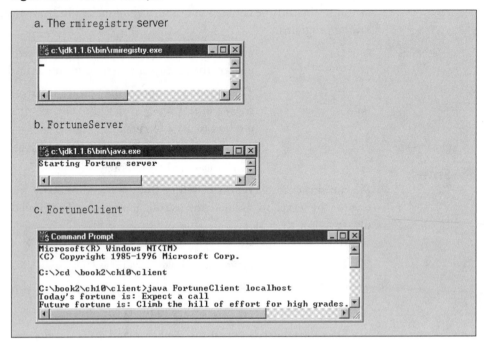

a. The rmiregistry server

b. FortuneServer

c. FortuneClient

The Interface

Let us build each part of this example RMI application. The Fortune interface specifies the getFortune method. We ensure that objects that implement the Fortune interface can be used remotely by making Fortune extend the Remote interface. Because any network communication may fail, every method used remotely must declare that it may throw a RemoteException.

EXAMPLE 2.11   **Fortune.java**

```
/* The server implements this interface and clients call
 * its method remotely. Clients get a fortune from the server.
 */

import java.rmi.*;                                              // Note 1
public interface Fortune extends Remote {
   public static final String NOW = "Now";                     // Note 2
   public static final String LATER = "Later";
   public String getFortune(String when) throws RemoteException; // Note 3
}
```

....

Note 1:   The `java.rmi` package contains the basic classes and interfaces needed for RMI, such as `Remote` and `RemoteException` in this example.

Note 2:   In addition to methods, we can declare constants in an interface. We declare two `String` constants here to show clients the choices they have for arguments to the `getFortune` method. They can either request a fortune for NOW or for LATER.

Note 3:   Using RMI, Java passes arguments and return values across the network using object serialization. Objects passed must have a type, such as `String`, that implements the `Serializable` interface.

The Server

On the server, the `FortuneServer` class implements the `Fortune` interface. Figure 2.12 shows the client uses the `Fortune` interface, and only sees that part of the `FortuneServer` object declared in the interface. The client only sees the `getFortune` method, and cannot access any other methods of the `FortuneServer` object. The `getFortune` method, which returns a message of good fortune to the client, must declare that it throws `RemoteException` because it will be called from a remote site. By contrast, the `find` method, used only within the `FortuneServer` class and declared as private, does not throw `RemoteException`.

We declare the `getFortune` method as synchronized because many clients may try to access the server simultaneously. Although our example is so simple it is really not necessary to synchronize access, in many cases we want a client to have exclusive access to the server object so any changes made will be completed before another client gets access.

The `java.rmi.server` package contains the classes needed for implementing servers of objects accessed remotely using RMI. Our `FortuneServer` class directly extends `UnicastRemoteObject`, a remote object sent to one destination at each request.

In the `main` method, we set up a server for a `FortuneServer` object, so remote clients can call its `getFortune` method to get a fortune. When using RMI, we may need to load class files from a remote site and need a security manager to ensure the safety of such operations. Java provides the `RMISecurityManager` class for this purpose, which we install using the `setSecurityManager` method of the `System` class.

The server and the client use the URL syntax with the RMI protocol to refer to remote objects. The server gives the object a name and places it, using that name, in the registry server, using the form

```
rmi://host:port/name
```

which the client also uses to locate that object. The `Naming` class handles interactions with the registry. Here the server uses the `rebind` method which registers the object with the rmiregistry server, replacing an earlier object of that name if any in the registry. In our example, the server binds a `FortuneServer` object in the registry under the name *Seer*.

EXAMPLE 2.12   FortuneServer.java

```java
/* Implements the Fortune interface. Establishes a server
 * for remote clients to use a FortuneServer object.
 */

import java.rmi.*;
import java.rmi.server.UnicastRemoteObject;
import java.util.Vector;

public class FortuneServer extends UnicastRemoteObject
                            implements Fortune {
  public static final int SIZE = 3;
  private Vector now = new Vector(SIZE); // Fortunes for NOW
  private Vector later = new Vector(SIZE); // Fortunes for LATER
  public FortuneServer() throws RemoteException {
    now.addElement("A friend is near");
    now.addElement("Expect a call");
    now.addElement("Someone misses you");
    later.addElement("Wealth awaits -- if you desire it.");
    later.addElement("Climb the hill of effort for high grades.");
    later.addElement("The door to success is open to you.");
  }
  private Vector find(String when) {                      // Note 1
    if (when.equals(Fortune.NOW))
      return now;
    else return later;
  }
  public synchronized String getFortune(String when)
                              throws RemoteException {
    int number = (int)(SIZE*Math.random());              // Note 2
    Vector fortunes = find(when);
    return (String)fortunes.elementAt(number);           // Note 3
  }
  public static void main(String[] args) {
    System.setSecurityManager(new RMISecurityManager());
    try {
      Fortune fortune = new FortuneServer();
      String url = "rmi://" + args[0] + "/Seer";         // Note 4
      Naming.rebind(url,fortune);                         // Note 5
      System.out.println("Starting Fortune server");
    }catch(Exception e) {
      e.printStackTrace();
    }
  }
}
```

....

Note 1:   We only use the find method within FortuneServer to select a vector of fortunes based on the argument passed by the client. Just in case the client passes something other than NOW or LATER, we do not put a condition in the **else** clause and return LATER if the client passes anything but NOW.

Note 2:   We get a random number between 0 and SIZE-1 to choose one of the fortunes to return to the client.

Note 3:   Because `elementAt` returns type `Object`, we must cast the return value to type `String`. We know the elements of the vector have type `String` because we created them that way.

Note 4:   We use the name `Seer` for the `fortune` object. The client uses the same name when looking up a reference to this object on the rmiregistry server. We pass the host and port as a program argument so that we can run our server on different machines without having to recompile the program. By default the rmiregistry server runs on port 1099; if we do not wish to change the port, we may omit it from the URL, just passing the host name as the program argument. Note that although we use the URL syntax, we do not declare a URL object, but rather a string.

Note 5:   We associate the `fortune` object with the `Seer` URL when binding to the registry, so client can find it.

The Client

`FortuneClient` is the last program we need to complete our RMI example. It sets `RMISecurityManager`, just as the server does, and looks up a reference to the `Seer` object in the rmiregistry server. When the client calls the `getFortune` method of this remote object, it receives a fortune as the return value. From the client's point of view there is no difference between calling a method of a remote object and a method of a local object. RMI handles the details of the remote method call, using the `stub` and `skeleton` classes to pass arguments to the server and return values to the client.

EXAMPLE 2.13   **FortuneClient.java**

```
/* Looks up a Fortune object in the registry.
 * Invokes its getFortune method remotely to
 * get a fortune for now and for later.
 */

import java.rmi.*;

public class FortuneClient {
  public static void main(String[] args) {
    System.setSecurityManager(new RMISecurityManager());
    try {
      String url = "rmi://" + args[0] + "/Seer";              // Note 1
      Fortune fortuneTeller = (Fortune)Naming.lookup(url);    // Note 2
      String fortune = fortuneTeller.getFortune(Fortune.NOW); // Note 3
      System.out.println("Today's fortune is: " + fortune);
      fortune = fortuneTeller.getFortune(Fortune.LATER);
```

```
        System.out.println("Future fortune is: " + fortune);
    }catch(Exception e) {
      e.printStackTrace();
    }
  }
}
```

....

Note 1:   We pass the host name of the server as a program argument, omitting the port number, because we have no need to change the default port of 1099 used by the rmiregistry server.

Note 2:   The lookup method returns a reference, obtained from the rmiregistry server, to an object of type Remote, meaning it implements the Remote inter-face. We need to cast this reference to type Fortune to invoke the getFor-tune method.

Note 3:   This remote method invocation looks like a method call of a local method, but the fortuneTeller object is actually on the server, which may be at a remote site. The FortuneServer_Stub sends the argument to FortuneServer_Skel on the host which invokes the getFortune method of the fortuneTeller object on the host. FortuneServer_Skel gets the return value from the getFortune method and sends it to the FortuneServer_Stub back on the client which returns it to the caller here to display. Fortu-nately, RMI handles all these details of communication using object serial-ization to transfer values.

THE BIG PICTURE

RMI lets us distribute our program across the network. We can bind an object in the rmiregistry server, so an object on another machine can look it up, and invoke its methods. The rmic compiler creates the skeleton and stub needed to call remote methods. Remote objects use interfaces to declare their remote methods.

TEST YOUR UNDERSTANDING

14. In Example 2.12 which classes from the java.rmi package are we using?

TRY IT YOURSELF   15. Run the RMI example of this section using port 3000 for the rmiregistry server. Start the registry with the command start rmiregistry 3000. Change the local-host program argument to localhost:3000.

SUMMARY

- Java makes it easy to connect to other computers. The `URL` class encapsulates some of the common communication protocols, such as HTTP (Hypertext Transfer Protocol) and FTP (File Transfer Protocol). Its four parts are the protocol name, the host name, port, and path to the resource. In an applet, we can use the `showDocument` method of the applet context to display a resource specified by a URL. The `openStream` method allows us to download the object referred to by a URL.

- The Hypertext Transfer Protocol specifies the messages by which browsers and web servers communicate. A browser or other web client sends a request, then some request headers, and a blank line to the server. The server sends a status line, followed by response headers, a blank line, and the requested resource. The examples show web clients and servers vary in the headers they choose to send.

- The `URLConnection` class has methods which allow us to set properties of the connection to customize it, or to get information about the connection. The `getHeaderField` method lets us determine the response headers sent by the server. The `setRequestProperty` method allows us to set request headers to send to the server. Special methods such as `getContentLength` return the value of specific headers.

- Sockets allow us to communicate using standard protocols, or to devise protocols of our own for use with clients and servers. A `ServerSocket` accepts connections on a numbered port. Standard services have default ports such as 80 for web servers, 25 for sending mail, and 110 for receiving it. Once we make a connection, we use input and output streams to send data back and forth between the client and the server. The `ReverseClient` example sends strings to the `ReverseServer` which sends them reversed back to the client. Modifying the `ReverseServer` produces `HeaderServer`, which just sends back to a web client the headers that it sent.

- To display a web page, a browser must interpret all the HTML tags embedded in that page. Our `VerySimpleBrowser` uses HTTP to communicate with web servers. It is a bare outline of a browser, following HTTP but ignoring the response headers and only displaying plain text, not HTML or images. Similarly our `VerySimpleWebServer` ignores any headers the client sends, and puts no effort into accurately sending response headers. Nevertheless our browser can connect and download files from various web servers and our web server can respond to plain text request from browsers. The exercises suggest many improvements. Our `ThreadedWebServer` permits several clients to be connected at the same time, each served in its own thread.

- Remote Method Invocation (RMI) takes networking to a higher level in which a client can invoke methods of a remote object on the server. The `rmiregistry` server allows the client to find a reference to a remote object. The `rmic` compiler creates the `stub` and `skeleton` files used to pass arguments and return values across the network. An interface, implemented on the server, specifies the remote methods available to the client.

Program Modification Exercises

. . . .

1. Modify Example 2.3 to use a `String` argument to `getHeaderField` instead of an **int**. User `getHeaderFieldKey` to find the names of the headers.

2. Example 2.4 uses two program arguments. Add a check that the user passed two arguments and if not, print a message showing the proper usage and exit the program.

3. Modify Example 2.8 to pass a URL such as
   `http://www.cecs.csulb.edu/TryURL.java`
   rather than passing the host, port, and resource path program arguments. The `URL` methods `getHost`, `getPort`, `getHost`, and `getProtocol` will be helpful.

4. Modify Example 2.9 to send a status line with code 404 and reason Not Found when the file requested is not available on the server.

5. Modify Example 2.9 so when the server has responded to one client it can accept a request from another.

6. Modify Example 2.10 to avoid using any inner classes.

7. Modify Example 2.9 to send a Content-length header giving the length of the file in bytes.

8. Modify Examples 2.5 and 2.6 to pass the port number as a program argument.

9. Modify Example 2.5 to put the `accept` statement and the code following it into a nonterminating loop, so the server can accept another client as soon as the current client finishes.

10. Modify Example 2.5 so the server can handle several clients simultaneously. After the server accepts a connection from the client, the server should create a separate thread to handle the communication with that client and loop back to the `accept` statement waiting for another client to connect.

11. Modify Example 2.13 to ask if the user wants another fortune. When testing, let two clients stay connected at the same time.

12. Modify Examples 2.11, 2.12, and 2.13 to allow the client to request a lucky number. The server will return a number from 1 to 10 at random.

Program Design Exercises

. . . .

13. Write an applet which lists URLs in a choice box. When the user selects a URL, use the `showDocument` method to display the page to which it refers.

14. Write a multithreaded server which will pass whatever message line it receives from a client to all the other clients that are connected. Write a client program to connect to this server, which sends its lines and receives the lines sent by the other clients.

15. Write a mail client which will connect to a POP3 server (find the address of your server) and retrieve the first message. Specify the server address, user name, and password as program arguments. The protocol of Figure 2.4 may be helpful.

16. Write a browser that displays a plain text file in a text area, rather than in the command window as `VerySimpleBrowser` does.

17. Write a piece of a browser which will display HTML files. This piece will only display text within header tags, `<h1>` ... `<h6>`. Use the largest point size for text between `<h1>` and `</h1>` tags, and the smallest for text between `<h6>` and `</h6>` tags.

18. Add to the browser of Exercise 2.17 the capability to handle `<em>` and `<strong>` tags.

19. Write a new version of `ReverseClient` in which the user enters the text to be reversed in a text field.

20. Use RMI to allow clients to connect to a broker to get the price of a stock, or to buy and sell some stock. Use just three stocks, StockA, StockB, and StockC, each with a price that varies randomly within a range. Assume two accounts numbered 1111 and 2222.

    a. For simplicity, do not maintain account information, so no records are kept about buy and sell orders.

    b. Add account information, so each account keeps a record of how many of each stock it contains.

21. Improve the very simple browser of Example 2.8. The browser should properly interpret HTML tags `<h1>`, ..., `<h6>`, `<em>`, `<strong>`, `<ul>`, `<li>`, `<br>`, `<p>`, `<a>`, and `<img>`.

22. Improve the very simple web server of Example 2.9. Use the status codes 200, 301, 400, 404, 406, and 501 appropriately. Send `Date`, `Last-modified`, `Content-type`, and `Content-length` response headers.

23. Implement a chess game in which the server relays moves from one player to the other. Two clients play against one another, with each showing the board and the moves as they are made. Players will use the mouse to drag a piece to its new position. (Alternatively, substitute another game for chess. For example, checkers would be simpler.)

24. Make a user interface for the mail-reading client of Exercise 2.15. The screen will show the message headers and allow the user to choose which message to read. For additional information on the POP3 protocol, search the Internet for RFC 1939 which contains its specification.

25. Implement an SMTP client to send email. Provide a user interface to compose and send the message. Testing requires access to an SMTP server. An example session is:

```
Server:   220 charlotte.cecs.csulb.edu ESMTP Sendmail 8.8.4/8.8.4;
              Thu, 11 Feb 1999 15:31:27 -0800 (PST)
Client:   HELO gordian.com                                  // sent from

Server:   250 charlotte.cecs.csulb.edu Hello ppool3.gordian.com
              [207.211.232.196], pleased to meet you
Client:   MAIL FROM:artg@csulb.edu                          // email address
Server:   250 <artg@csulb.edu>... Sender ok
Client:   RCPT TO: artg@csulb.edu                           // recipient
Server:   250 <artg@csulb.edu>... Recipient ok
Client:   DATA                                              // signals message
Server:   354 Enter mail, end with "." on a line by itself
Client:   This is                                           // message
          a test.
              .                                             // signals end
Server:   250 PAA27651 Message accepted for delivery
Client:   QUIT
Server:    221 Closing connection.
```

3

Java Database Connectivity (JDBC)

Introduction

For small applications, we can use files to store data, but as the amount of data that we need to save gets larger the services of a database system become invaluable. A database system allows us to model the information we need while it handles the details of inserting, removing, and retrieving data from individual files in response to our requests.

Of course each database vendor provides its own procedures for performing database operations. The Java Database Connectivity (JDBC) programming interface hides the details of different databases; our programs can work with many different databases on many different platforms. JDBC can be used as part of large scale enterprise applications. In this chapter we cover the JDBC concepts using a small example which allows many extensions, some of which we pursue in the exercises.

The example programs illustrate JDBC concepts using console applications so as not to obscure them with the details involved in building a GUI. In the last section our extended case study develops a graphical user interface to a database.

3.1   Database Tables and SQL Queries

Database design is best left to other texts and courses. We introduce a few database concepts here to provide an example with which to illustrate the Java Database Connectivity techniques for working with databases using Java. Relational databases provide an implementation-independent way for users to view data. The Structured Query Language (SQL) lets us create, update, and query a database using standard commands that hide the details of any particular vendor's **database system**.

Relational Database Tables

When designing a **database** we need to identify the entities in our system. For example, a company might use a database to keep track of its sales and associated information. In our example company, an order has one customer who can order several items. A salesperson may take several orders from the same customer, but each order is taken by exactly one salesperson.

Using a **relational database**, we keep our data in **tables**. In our example, we might have a Customer table with fields for the customer id, name, address, and balance due as shown in Figure 3.1.

Figure 3.1   The Customer table

CustomerID	CustomerName	Address	BalanceDue
1234	Fred Flynn	22 First St.	1667.00
5678	Darnell Davis	33 Second St.	130.95
4321	Marla Martinez	44 Third St.	0
8765	Carla Kahn	55 Fourth St.	0

Each row of the table represents the information needed for one customer. We assign each customer a unique customer ID number. Customer names are not unique; moreover they may change. CustomerID is a **key** that identifies the data in the row. Knowing the CustomerID we can retrieve the other information about that customer.

TIP
☛

Do not embed spaces in field names. Use CustomerID rather than Customer ID.

Figures 3.2 and 3.3 show the Salesperson and Item tables which we define in a similar manner. A more realistic example would have additional fields, but our purpose here is only to illustrate JDBC.

Figure 3.2   The Salesperson table

SalespersonID	SalespersonName	Address
12	Peter Patterson	66 Fifth St.
98	Donna Dubarian	77 Sixth St.

Figure 3.3   The Item table

ItemNumber	Description	Quantity
222222	radio	32
333333	television	14
444444	computer	9

The SalepersonID serves as the key for the Salesperson table, while we use the ItemNumber to identify an item in the Item table. We have to be more careful in designing the Orders table, as an order can have multiple items. We use a second table, the Order-Item table, to list the items in each order. Figure 3.4 shows the Orders table with the fields OrderNumber, CustomerID, SalespersonID, and OrderDate. The OrderNumber is the key. CustomerID and SalespersonID are **foreign keys** that allow us to avoid redundancy by referring to data in other tables. For example, including the CustomerID lets us find the customer's name and address from the Customer table rather than repeating it in the Orders table.

Figure 3.4   The Orders table

OrderNumber	CustomerID	SalespersonID	OrderDate
1	1234	12	4/3/99
2	5678	12	3/22/99
3	8765	98	2/19/99
4	1234	12	4/5/99
5	8765	98	2/28/99

TIP
☞

When choosing field names, avoid names like `Number`, `Value`, `Order`, `Name`, or `Date` that might conflict with reserved names in the database system.

The `OrderItem` table uses a **compound key** consisting of both the `OrderNumber` and the `ItemNumber` to identify a specific item that is part of an order. Figure 3.5 shows that each pair (`OrderNumber`, `ItemNumber`) occurs only once, identifying a row containing the data for a specific item in a particular order. For example, the first row shows that for order number one, and item 222222, four units were ordered at a price of $27 each.

Figure 3.5

OrderNumber	ItemNumber	Quantity	UnitPrice
1	222222	4	27.00
1	333333	2	210.50
1	444444	1	569.00
2	333333	2	230.95
3	222222	3	27.00
3	333333	1	230.95
4	444444	1	569.00
5	222222	2	27.00
5	444444	1	725.00

Now that we have defined our `Sales` database, we want to see how to get information from it, and how to make changes as needed.

Structured Query Language (SQL)

The Structured Query Language (SQL) is a standard language with which to get information from or make changes to a database. We can execute SQL statements from within Java. The SQL statements we shall use are `CREATE`, `SELECT`, `INSERT`, `DELETE`, and `UPDATE`. We illustrate these statements using the `Sales` database defined above. The names for the data types may depend on the actual database system used. Our examples work with Microsoft Access.

We could use the `CREATE` statement

```
CREATE TABLE Customer (CustomerID CHAR(4), CustomerName
  VARCHAR(25), Address VARCHAR(25), BalanceDue CURRENCY)
```

to create the `Customer` table, the statement

```
CREATE TABLE Orders (OrderNumber VARCHAR(4), CustomerID
    CHAR(4), SalepersonID CHAR(2), OrderDate DATE)
```

to create the `Orders` table, and the statement

```
CREATE TABLE OrderItem (OrderNumber VARCHAR(4), ItemNumber
    CHAR(6), Quantity INTEGER, UnitPrice CURRENCY)
```

to create the `OrderItem` table. We use character fields for `CustomerID`, `OrderNumber`, `SalepersonID`, and `ItemNumber`, even though they use numerical characters, because we have no need to do arithmetic using these values. By contrast, we use the type `INTEGER` for the `Quantity` field because we may wish to compute with it.

Standard SQL uses various types which are not all supported in every database system. Figure 3.6 shows the SQL types we use in this text.

Figure 3.6   SQL types

Type	Standard SQL	Description
CHAR(N)	Yes	Fixed size string of length N
VARCHAR(N)	Yes	Variable size string up to length N
INTEGER	Yes	32-bit integer
DATE	Yes	year, month, and day
CURRENCY	No	dollars and cents

The type `DECIMAL(M,N)`, where `M` is the maximum number of digits and `N` is the maximum number of digits after the decimal point, is standard SQL, but is not supported in Access.

To insert the first row in the `Customer` table, we could use the `INSERT` statement

```
INSERT INTO Customer VALUES (1234,'Fred Flynn','22 First St.',1667.00)
```

TIP
☞

Use the single quote, ', to enclose strings within an SQL statement.

The statement

```
INSERT INTO Orders VALUES (1,1234,12,'Apr 3, 1999')
```

inserts the first row into the `Order` table. We write dates in the form

```
Month Day, Year
```

to avoid confusion among date formats used in various locales and to indicate the century explicitly. The database system translates this form to its internal representation, and can present dates in various formats in its tables.

The `DELETE` statement

```
DELETE FROM OrderItem WHERE OrderNumber = '1'
```

will delete the first three rows of the `OrderItem` table in Figure 3.5. These rows contain the data for the three items comprising the order with an `OrderNumber` of 1.

TIP ☞	Use the single equality sign, =, in the equality test, OrderNumber = 1, instead of the Java equality symbol, ==.

To delete just the televisions from that order and leave the order for radios and a computer, we could use the statement

```
DELETE FROM OrderItem
WHERE OrderNumber = '1' AND ItemNumber = '333333'
```

To update an existing row we use the UPDATE statement. For example, to reduce the number of radios in order number 1 to 3, we can use the statement

```
UPDATE OrderItem SET Quantity = 3
WHERE OrderNumber = '1' AND ItemNumber = '222222'
```

When we change an order we will also want to change the balance due in the Customer table, which we can do using

```
UPDATE Customer SET BalanceDue = 1640.00
WHERE CustomerID = '1234'
```

TIP ☞	Because the OrderItem table uses a compound key (OrderNumber, ItemNumber) to identify a row, we needed to specify values for both in the WHERE clause. In updating the Customer table we only needed to specify the value of the single CustomerID key to identify a row.

The CREATE statement creates a table, and the INSERT, DELETE, and UPDATE statements make changes in a table. In many applications, we retrieve information from the database more frequently than we create a table or make changes to a table. To retrieve information we use the SELECT statement.

The simplest **query** we can make is to retrieve the entire table. For example, the statement

```
SELECT * FROM Customer
```

retrieves the entire Customer table. We use the star symbol, *, which matches every row. To retrieve the names and addresses of the customers we use the statement

```
SELECT CustomerName, Address FROM Customer
```

If we do not want data from the entire table, we can use a WHERE clause to specify a condition that the data of interest satisfy. For example, to retrieve all orders for radios we could use the statement

```
SELECT * FROM OrderItems
WHERE ItemNumber = '222222'
```

The power of database systems becomes evident when we use SQL to get information combined from several tables. For example, suppose we would like to know the names of all customers who placed orders on March 22, 1999. We can find that information using the statement

```
SELECT CustomerName FROM Customer, Orders
WHERE Customer.CustomerID = Orders.CustomerID
AND OrderDate = {d '1999-03-22'}
```

where {d '1999-03-22'} is an escape sequence.

Date formats vary among database systems. To make programs general Java uses a generic string format yyyy-mm-dd with a four-digit year, a two-digit month, and a two digit day. The curly braces, {}, enclose the escape sequence which tells the driver to translate it to the specific form used by the database system. The keyword, d, signifies that a date follows. The date format for the Access database we are using is #3/22/99#, which we could have used, but the escape sequence makes the code more general.

TIP
☛

When a field such as Address occurs in more than one table, prefix the field name with the table name, as in Customer.Address, to state precisely which Address field you desire. Similarly, use the prefixes Customer and Orders to refer to the CustomerID fields in each of these tables.

In finding the names of customers who placed orders on March 22, 1999, the database joins two tables. Customer names occur in the Customer table, while we find order dates in the Orders table, so we list both the Customer and the Orders tables in the FROM part of the query. We want to find which orders each customer placed. CustomerID, the primary key of the Customer table, is also a foreign key of the Orders table. For each CustomerID in the Customer table we only want to inspect the rows of the Orders table which have the same CustomerID, so we include the condition

```
Customer.CustomerID = Orders.CustomerID
```

in our query.

The first row of the Customer table has a CustomerID of 1234. The first and fourth rows of the Orders table have the same CustomerID of 1234 but neither of the OrderDate fields equals 3/22/99. The second row of the Customer table has CustomerID 5678 as does the second row of the Orders table and the OrderDate is 3/22/99 so the system adds 'Darnell Davis' to the result set of customers placing orders on March 22, 1999. Continuing the search turns up no further matches. A three-line SQL statement can cause many steps to occur in the process of retrieving the requested information. The database handles all the details. We will use other interesting examples of SELECT statements when we develop our Java programs later in this chapter.

Figure 3.7 shows the general pattern for the SQL statements we have introduced so far.

Figure 3.7   Some patterns for SQL statements

```
CREATE TABLE tablename
(fieldname1 TYPE1, fieldname2 TYPE2, ... , fieldnameN TYPEn)

INSERT INTO tablename
VALUES (field1value,field2value, ..., fieldNvalue)

DELETE FROM tablename
WHERE fieldname1 = value1 ... AND fieldnameN = valueN

UPDATE tablename SET fieldnameToSet = newValue
WHERE fieldname1ToCheck = value1ToCheck

SELECT fieldname1, ..., fieldnameN FROM table1, ..., tableM
WHERE condition1 ... AND conditionN
```

THE BIG PICTURE

In a relational database, we keep our data in tables, making sure not to enter information redundantly. Using SQL, we can write statements to create a table, insert, delete, and update elements, and query the database. Generally SQL is standardized so queries do not reflect implementation details of specific database systems.

TEST YOUR UNDERSTANDING

1. Why is it a good idea to use SalespersonID as the key in the Salesperson table, rather than the salesperson's name?

2. Write an SQL statement to create the Salesperson table with the fields shown in Figure 3.2.

3. Write SQL statements to insert the data shown in Figure 3.2 into the Salesperson table.

4. Write an SQL statement to add a new salesman, Paul Sanchez, who lives at 88 Seventh St., and has an ID of 54, to the Salesperson table of Figure 3.2.

5. Write an SQL statement to delete Carla Kahn's order of a computer from the Sales database.

6. Write an SQL statement to find the names of all salespersons in the Sales database.

7. Write an SQL statement to find the order numbers of all orders taken by Peter Patterson.

3.2   Connecting to a Database

After an overview contrasting two-tiered with three-tiered architectures for software systems, we show how to connect to a database using the Java Database Connectivity programming interface.

Database and Application Servers

In building large systems, a **database server** may reside on one machine to which various clients connect when they need to access the stored data.

Figure 3.8   Client-server database access

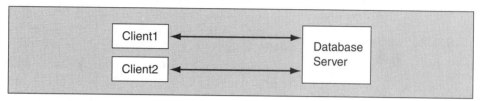

In a three-tiered design, business logic resides in a middle machine, sometimes called an **application server**, which acts as a server to various application clients. These clients provide user interfaces to the business applications on the middle machine which is itself a client of the database server.

Figure 3.9   A three-tiered system architecture

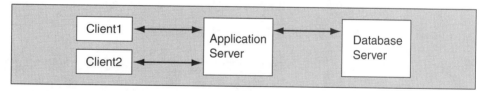

For example, a business may have an accounting department that runs a payroll client providing a user interface to the payroll application on the middle machine which itself is a client of the database server. The marketing department might have several client programs running in their sales offices enabling salespersons to get necessary information. Rather than configuring each salesperson's machine to process all the details of the application, the company just allows the sales staff to interact with the sales application on the middle machine. This sales program gets data from the database server as needed.

Java Database Connectivity (**JDBC**) allows us to write Java programs that will work no matter which database system we use. We can work entirely on one machine or use a two-tier, three-tier, or even more complex architecture for our system. What we need for any database system we wish to use is a JDBC driver. The driver provides a uniform interface to our Java programs. Many database vendors provide JDBC drivers for use with their products.

A JDBC Driver

A **driver** translates JDBC statements to the specific commands of a particular database system. Several different categories of drivers exist, but in this text we use the JDBC to ODBC bridge to allow JDBC to work with Microsoft Access which has an existing **ODBC** driver (for an earlier technology, Open Database Connectivity, that is still used). To connect to our database using Java, we need only specify our JDBC driver and the URL for the database.

Creating an ODBC Data Source

Before using Java we need to register our database as an ODBC data source. The Microsoft Open Database Connectivity (ODBC) interface, introduced prior to the development of Java, provides an interface to many databases. Sun makes a JDBC to ODBC bridge available, so if a database has an ODBC driver, we can access it using the JDBC to ODBC bridge as our JDBC driver.

In this chapter, our examples will use Microsoft Access databases on Windows. Only the driver name and the data source URL need to be changed to use another database system.

The first step is to register the database we will be creating as an ODBC data source. The steps we use are:

1. Click on the My Computer icon and the Control Panel icon to open the Control Panel.

2. Click on the ODBC icon in the Control Panel, which pops up the ODBC Data Source Administrator window shown in Figure 3.10.

Figure 3.10   ODBC Data Source Administrator

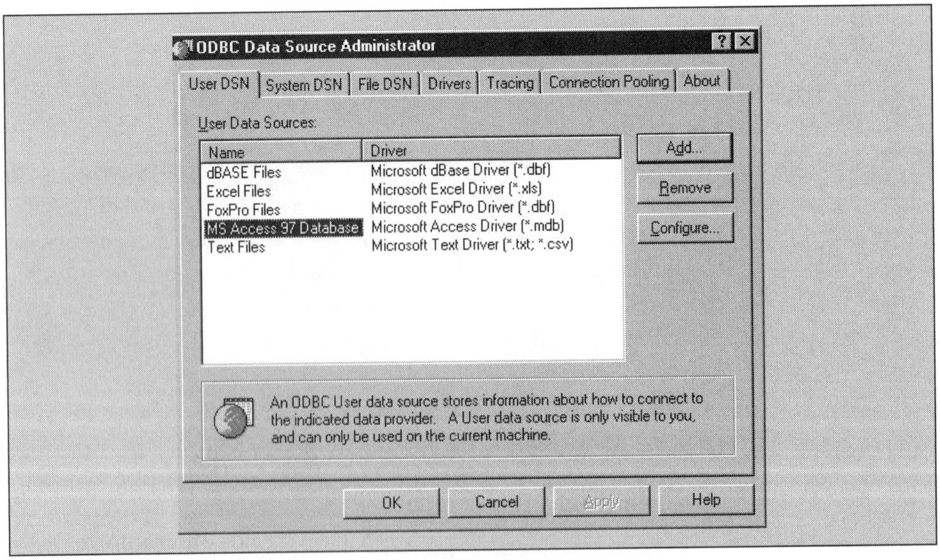

3. Select MS Access Database.

4. Click Add, which pops up the Create New Data Source window shown in Figure 3.11.

Figure 3.11   Create New Data Source

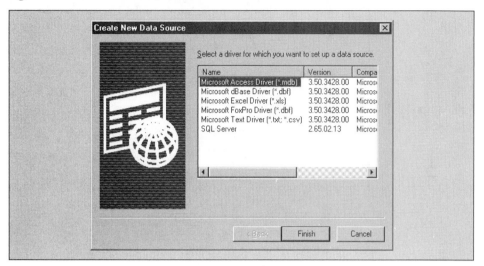

5. Select Microsoft Access Driver and click Finish, which pops up the ODBC Microsoft Access Setup window shown in Figure 3.12.

Figure 3.12   ODBC Microsoft Access Setup

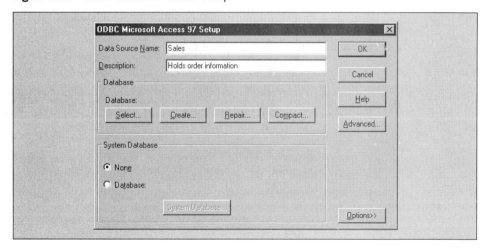

6. Fill in the Data Source Name. We use this name to refer to this database in our Java programs. We use the name `Sales` for our example.

7. Fill in a short description, such as "Holds order information" in the Description field.

8. Click Create, as we are creating a new database.

Figure 3.13 New Database

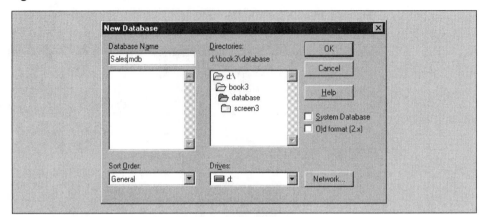

9. In the New Database window, shown in Figure 3.13, navigate to the directory in which to place the new database, give it a name, such as Sales.mdb, and click OK.

10. If all went well, a message that the database was successfully created will appear.

TIP
☛

On a Windows system without Microsoft Access, much of what we do in this chapter can be done with ordinary text files. The steps for using text files are:

1. Click on the My Computer icon and the Control Panel icon to open the Control Panel.

2. Click on the ODBC icon in the Control Panel, which pops up the ODBC Data Source Administrator window.

3. Click on Text Files.

4. Click Add, which pops up the Create New Data Source window.

5. Select Microsoft Text Driver and click Finish, which pops up the ODBC Text Setup window.

6. Fill in the Data Source Name. We use this name to refer to this database in our Java programs. We use the name Sales for our example.

7. Fill in a short description, such as "Record sales orders" in the Description field.

8. Deselect the UseCurrentDirectory box, click Select Directory, navigate to the desired directory for the files, and click OK in all the open windows.

Connecting from Java

We want our Sales database to contain the five tables with the data shown in Figures 3.1–3.5. We could create these tables and populate them within Access, but prefer to show how to do this using Java.

Every Java program that uses JDBC to access a database must load the driver that it will use and connect to the desired database. To load the driver we create a new driver object. Sun provides the JDBC classes in the `java.sql` package and the JdbcOdbcDriver in the `sun.jdbc.odbc` package. The core Java packages all start with the java prefix. Sun includes the `JdbcOdbcDriver` with the JDK but it is not one of the core Java classes. Sun also includes the helper file, `JdbcOdbc.dll`, with the JDK.

The statement

```
new JdbcOdbcDriver();
```

will load a new driver object, calling its constructor. The drawback of using the **new** operator to load `JdbcOdbcDriver` is that if we want to use a different driver, we have to modify the program. Java has the ability to load classes while the program is running so that we could pass a class name in as a program argument and let Java load whichever driver we decide to use. We use the `forName` method of the class `Class` in the `java.lang` package

```
Class.forName("JdbcOdbcDriver");
```

to load `JdbcOdbcDriver`. To make the loading dynamic we could use

```
Class.forName(args[0]);
```

which would load the class whose name we pass as the first program argument.

TIP
☞

Each class loaded into the JVM has a Class object associated with it. This object has various methods that give information about the structure of the class. We do not use any of these methods, but use only the static `forName` method which loads the class whose full name is passed as the argument.

Once we load the driver, it registers with the `DriverManager` that keeps a vector of drivers to use when making a connection to a database. We connect to a database using the static `getConnection` method of the `DriverManager` class that returns a connection representing our session with the database.

We use a URL to locate the database to which we wish to connect. We could use a database server which would require a remote connection in which case the URL would include the Internet address of the server. The URL has the form

```
jdbc:<subprotocol>:<subname>
```

where the **subprotocol** is the name of the driver or a database connectivity mechanism such as **odbc** which is what we will use. The **subname** identifies the database. For the case of ODBC drivers we just need the name of the database that we registered with the ODBC Data Source Administrator, which is `Sales` for our example. Thus the URL we will use is

```
jdbc:odbc:Sales
```

The developer of the JDBC driver defines the URL needed.

Example 3.1 will just connect to the Sales database. The code we use will occur at the beginning of all of our examples in this chapter.

EXAMPLE 3.1   **Connect.java**

```
/* Connects to a Microsoft Access database
 * using the JDBC-ODBC bridge
 */

import java.sql.*;                                              // Note 1
import java.io.*;
import sun.jdbc.odbc.*;                                         // Note 2

class Connect {
  public static void main (String args[]) {
    try{
      new JdbcOdbcDriver();                                     // Note 3
      String url = "jdbc:odbc:Sales";                           // Note 4
      String user = "";                                         // Note 5
      String password = "";
      Connection con =
      DriverManager.getConnection(url, user, password);         // Note 6
      System.out.println("Made the connection to the Sales database");
    }catch (Exception e) {e.printStackTrace();}                 // Note 7
  }
}
```

Output

Made the connection to the Sales database

Note 1:   The java.sql package contains the JDBC classes.

Note 2:   The sun.jdbc.odbc package contains the JdbcOdbcDriver we use to access our ODBC data source, a Microsoft Access database.

Note 3:   We create a new JdbcOdbcDriver which registers itself with the DriverMan-ager which stores a vector of all the registered drivers. The driver hides the details of the specific database. We use JDBC generic methods which the driver translates to the specific procedures provided by the database vendor. By changing the driver, the same program can work with data on a different database system. We do not need to assign the driver to a variable, because we will not refer to it again explicitly.

Note 4:   The supplier of the driver defines the URL needed. If we change the driver then we also need to change the URL. Making these changes will allow our program to work with another database system. Our programs would be more flexible, if rather than hard coding the driver and URL we pass them as program arguments. We leave this modification to the exercises.

Note 5: For the Access database we are using we do not need a user name or a password. For other databases we may need to log in to the server. For generality we left the user and password fields in the program and set them both to empty strings.

Note 6: `Connection con =`
`DriverManager.getConnection(url, user, password);`
This static method looks through the vector of registered drivers to find a driver that can connect to this database, and throws an exception if one is not found. If it finds a suitable driver, it attempts to make the connection. In this example, we could have used the method
`DriverManager.getConnection(url);`
which omits the user and password arguments.

Note 7: `catch (Exception e) {e.printStackTrace();}`
We catch all exceptions here. We could have used the `SQLException` class to catch exceptions relating to SQL.

Building the Database

Once we have a connection to the database we can execute SQL statements to create and **populate** our database. The `createStatement` method returns a `Statement` object that we use to send SQL statements to the database.

Some SQL statements, such as those used to create tables and insert values in a table, change the database but do not return any values to the program. To execute SQL `CREATE` and `INSERT` statements we use the `executeUpdate` method. The argument to `executeUpdate` is a `String`, which will be sent to the database. The string argument should represent an SQL statement in a form understandable by the database system. If not, Java will throw an exception. As an example,

```
stmt.executeUpdate
("INSERT INTO Item VALUES ('555555','CD player',10)");
```

would insert a fourth row into the `Item` table.

Example 3.2 uses Java to create and populate the `Sales` database. We create the five tables shown in Figures 3.1–3.5, using a `CREATE` statement to create each table, and `INSERT` statements to add the rows. Figure 3.14 shows the resulting Access `Sales` database and Figure 3.15 shows the `Customer` table that results from executing Example 3.2.

TIP
☛
After running this program, the database contains the five tables. Therefore running the program again will cause an error, unless the tables are first deleted from the database.

Figure 3.14   The Access `Sales` database created by Example 3.2

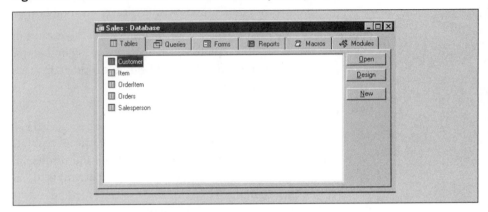

Figure 3.15   The `Customer` table created by Example 3.2

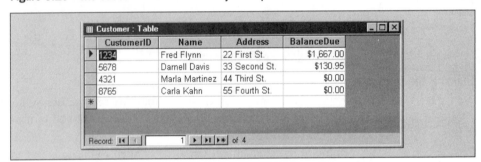

EXAMPLE 3.2   Create.java

```
/* Creates and populates the Sales database.
 */

import java.sql.*;
import java.io.*;
import sun.jdbc.odbc.*;

public class Create {
  public static void main (String args[]) {
    try{
      new JdbcOdbcDriver();
      String url = "jdbc:odbc:Sales";
      String user = "";
      String password = "";
      Connection con = DriverManager.getConnection(url, user, password);
      Statement stmt = con.createStatement();

      stmt.executeUpdate ("CREATE TABLE Customer (CustomerID "
          + "VARCHAR(4), CustomerName VARCHAR(25), Address "
          + "VARCHAR(25), BalanceDue CURRENCY)");                   // Note 1
```

```
stmt.executeUpdate ("INSERT INTO Customer "
    + " VALUES (1234,'Fred Flynn','22 First St.',1667.00)");   // Note 2
stmt.executeUpdate ("INSERT INTO Customer "
    + " VALUES (5678,'Darnell Davis','33 Second St.',130.95)");
stmt.executeUpdate ("INSERT INTO Customer"
    + " VALUES (4321,'Marla Martinez','44 Third St.',0)");
stmt.executeUpdate ("INSERT INTO Customer "
    + " VALUES (8765,'Carla Kahn','55 Fourth St.', 0)");

stmt.executeUpdate("CREATE TABLE Salesperson (SalespersonID "
    + " VARCHAR(2), SalespersonName VARCHAR(25), "
    + " Address VARCHAR(25))");
stmt.executeUpdate ("INSERT INTO Salesperson "
    + " VALUES (12,'Peter Patterson','66 Fifth St.')");
stmt.executeUpdate ("INSERT INTO Salesperson "
    + " VALUES (98,'Donna Dubarian','77 Sixth St.')");

stmt.executeUpdate("CREATE TABLE Item (ItemNumber VARCHAR(6),"
    + "Description VARCHAR(20), Quantity INTEGER)");
stmt.executeUpdate("INSERT INTO Item VALUES (222222,'radio',32)");
stmt.executeUpdate("INSERT INTO Item VALUES (333333,'television',14)");
stmt.executeUpdate("INSERT INTO Item VALUES (444444,'computer',9)");

stmt.executeUpdate("CREATE TABLE Orders (OrderNumber VARCHAR(4),"
    + " CustomerID VARCHAR(4), SalespersonID VARCHAR(2),"
    + " OrderDate DATE)");
stmt.executeUpdate
    ("INSERT INTO Orders VALUES (1,1234,12,'Apr 3, 1999')");
stmt.executeUpdate
    ("INSERT INTO Orders VALUES (2,5678,12,'Mar 22, 1999')");
stmt.executeUpdate
    ("INSERT INTO Orders VALUES (3,8765,98,'Feb 19, 1999')");
stmt.executeUpdate
    ("INSERT INTO Orders VALUES (4,1234,12,'Apr 5, 1999')");
stmt.executeUpdate
    ("INSERT INTO Orders VALUES (5,8765,98,'Feb 28, 1999')");

stmt.executeUpdate("CREATE TABLE OrderItem (OrderNumber CHAR(4),"
    + " ItemNumber CHAR(6), Quantity INTEGER, UnitPrice CURRENCY)");
stmt.executeUpdate("INSERT INTO OrderItem "                        // Note 3
    + " VALUES (1,222222,4,27.00)");
stmt.executeUpdate("INSERT INTO OrderItem "
    + " VALUES (1,333333,2,210.50)");
stmt.executeUpdate("INSERT INTO OrderItem "
    + " VALUES (1,444444,1,569.00)");
stmt.executeUpdate("INSERT INTO OrderItem "
    + " VALUES (2,333333,2,230.95)");
stmt.executeUpdate("INSERT INTO OrderItem "
    + " VALUES (3,222222,3,27.00)");
stmt.executeUpdate("INSERT INTO OrderItem "
    + " VALUES (3,333333,1,230.95)");
```

```
        stmt.executeUpdate("INSERT INTO OrderItem "
            + " VALUES (4,444444,1,569.00)");
        stmt.executeUpdate("INSERT INTO OrderItem "
            + " VALUES (5,222222,2,27.00)");
        stmt.executeUpdate("INSERT INTO "
            + " OrderItem VALUES (5,444444,1,725.00)");

        stmt.close();                                      // Note 4
      }catch (Exception e) {e.printStackTrace();}
    }
  }
```

Note 1: Just as with any string, we need to split the SQL statement over multiple lines using the concatenation operator so that each string constant fits on one line.

Note 2: When splitting the SQL statement over multiple lines we must be sure to add spaces to separate identifiers. Without the spaces either after `Customer` or before `VALUES`, then the juxtaposition of `CustomerVALUES` would cause an error.

Note 3: Using nine statements to insert the nine rows into the `OrderItem` table is cumbersome, and would be more so if the table were larger. A better method is to read the data to enter from a file. We leave this improvement to the exercises.

Note 4: The `Statement` object, `stmt`, is closed automatically by the garbage collector and its resources freed, but it is good programming practice to close it explicitly.

THE BIG PICTURE

JDBC uses a driver to translate its platform-independent interface to work in a specific database system. We use the JDBC to ODBC bridge to connect to Access or a text file which have ODBC drivers. A URL, specific to the database system, locates the database. Once connected to the database, we can create tables and insert data into them from a Java program. Optionally we could have created the tables outside of Java.

TEST YOUR UNDERSTANDING

TRY IT YOURSELF 8. Register a new `Sales` database as an ODBC data source.

TRY IT YOURSELF 9. Modify Example 3.1 to input the JDBC driver and the database URL as program arguments.

TRY IT YOURSELF 10. Modify Example 3.2, as described in Note 2, to omit the spaces after `Customer` and before `VALUES`. What is the effect of this change?

3.3 Retrieving Information

Now that we have created the `Sales` database, we can use JDBC to extract information from it. When executing an SQL statement that returns results, we use the `executeQuery` method which returns a `ResultSet` containing the rows of data that satisfy the query. Executing

```
ResultSet rs = stmt.executeQuery
  ("SELECT CustomerName, Address FROM Customer");
```

returns the rows containing the names and address of all entries in the `Customer` table.

Viewing Query Results

To view the results, the `ResultSet` has `getXXX` methods where `XXX` is the Java type corresponding to the SQL type of the data field we are retrieving. Because `CustomerName` and `Address` both have the `VARCHAR` SQL type, we use the `getString` method to retrieve these fields. We can retrieve fields by name or by field number. The loop

```
while(rs.next())
  System.out.println(rs.getString(1) + '\t' + rs.getString("Address"))
```

will list the rows of names and addresses from the `Customer` table. We retrieve the `CustomerName` field using its column number 1 and the `Address` field using its name. The `next()` method returns **true** when another row is available and **false** otherwise. Figure 3.16 shows the Java methods corresponding to the SQL types we use.

Figure 3.16 Java methods for SQL types

Java method	SQL type
getInt	INTEGER
getString	VARCHAR
getBigDecimal	CURRENCY
getDate	DATE

SELECT Statement Options

The `SELECT` statement has additional options. The `ORDER` clause allows us to display the results sorted with respect to one or more columns. The query

```
SELECT CustomerName, Address FROM Customer ORDER BY CustomerName
```
returns the result set by name in alphabetical order. We could use

```
SELECT CustomerName, Address FROM Customer ORDER BY 1
```
to achieve the same result using the column number in the `ORDER` clause.

Sometimes a query may return duplicate rows. For example, in selecting customers who ordered computers we would get the result

```
Fred Flynn
Fred Flynn
Carla Kahn
```

because Fred Flynn bought computers in orders 1 and 4. We can remove duplicates by using the SELECT DISTINCT variant of the SELECT statement.

This query

```
SELECT DISTINCT CustomerName
FROM Customer, Item, Orders, OrderItem
WHERE Customer.CustomerID = Orders.CustomerID
AND Orders.OrderNumber = OrderItem.OrderNumber
AND OrderItem.ItemNumber = Item.ItemNumber
AND Description = 'computer'
```

joins rows from four tables to produce the result.

The UPDATE and DELETE statements change the database, but do not return results, so we use the executeUpdate method to execute them.

EXAMPLE 3.3   ExtractInfo.java

```java
/* Demonstrates the use of SQL queries from
 * a Java program.
 */

import java.sql.*;
import java.io.*;
import sun.jdbc.odbc.*;
import java.text.*;

public class ExtractInfo {
  public static void main (String args[]) {
    try{
      new JdbcOdbcDriver();
      String url = "jdbc:odbc:Sales";
      String user = "";
      String password = "";
      Connection con = DriverManager.getConnection(url, user, password);
      Statement stmt = con.createStatement();

      String query = "SELECT CustomerName, Address FROM Customer "
          + "ORDER BY CustomerName";
      ResultSet rs = stmt.executeQuery(query);                        // Note 1
      System.out.println(" Names and Addresses of Customers");
      System.out.println("Name\t\tAddress");                         // Note 2
      while (rs.next())
        System.out.println(rs.getString("CustomerName") + '\t'
                          + rs.getString(2));

      query = "SELECT * FROM OrderItem "
          + "WHERE ItemNumber = '222222'";
      rs = stmt.executeQuery(query);
      System.out.println();
      System.out.println(" Order items for radios");
      System.out.println("OrderNumber\tQuantity\tUnitPrice");
```

```
NumberFormat cf = NumberFormat.getCurrencyInstance();
while (rs.next())
  System.out.println(rs.getString(1) + "\t\t"
    + rs.getInt(3) + "\t\t" + cf.format(rs.getBigDecimal(4))); // Note 3

query = "SELECT CustomerName FROM Customer, Orders "
+ "WHERE Customer.CustomerID = Orders.CustomerID "
+ "AND OrderDate = {d '1999-03-22'}";
rs = stmt.executeQuery(query);
System.out.println();
System.out.println(" Customer placing orders on Mar 22, 1999");
while(rs.next())
  System.out.println(rs.getString("CustomerName"));

query = "SELECT DISTINCT CustomerName "
    + "FROM Customer, Item, Orders, OrderItem "
    + "WHERE Customer.CustomerID = Orders.CustomerID "
    + "AND Orders.OrderNumber = OrderItem.OrderNumber "
    + "AND OrderItem.ItemNumber = Item.ItemNumber "
    + "AND Description = 'computer'";
rs = stmt.executeQuery(query);
System.out.println();
System.out.println(" Customers ordering computers");
while(rs.next())
  System.out.println(rs.getString(1));                       // Note 4

query = "SELECT OrderNumber FROM Orders "
    + "WHERE OrderDate "
    + "BETWEEN {d '1999-04-01'} AND {d '1999-04-30'}";
rs = stmt.executeQuery(query);
System.out.println();
System.out.println(" Order numbers of orders from 4/1/99 to 4/30/99");
while(rs.next())
  System.out.println(rs.getString("OrderNumber"));

String sql;
sql = "INSERT INTO Item VALUES (555555,'CD player',10)";     // Note 5
stmt.executeUpdate(sql);
sql = "UPDATE Item SET Quantity = 12 "
    + "WHERE Description = 'CD player'";
stmt.executeUpdate(sql);                                     // Note 6
System.out.println();
System.out.println(" Added and updated a new item");

System.out.println("Description");
query = "SELECT Description FROM Item";
rs = stmt.executeQuery(query);
while(rs.next())
  System.out.println(rs.getString(1));

sql = "DELETE FROM Item WHERE Description = 'CD player'";
stmt.executeUpdate(sql);
```

```
            query = "SELECT Description FROM Item";
            rs = stmt.executeQuery(query);
            System.out.println();
            System.out.println(" Deleted the new item");
            System.out.println("Description");
            while(rs.next())
               System.out.println(rs.getString(1));

            stmt.close();
          }catch (Exception e) {e.printStackTrace();}
        }
}
```

Output

```
Names and Addresses of Customers
Name             Address
Carla Kahn       55 Fourth St.
Darnell Davis    33 Second St.
Fred Flynn       22 First St.
Marla Martinez   44 Third St.

Order items for radios
OrderNumber   Quantity    UnitPrice
1             4           $27.00
3             3           $27.00
5             2           $27.00

  Customer placing orders on Mar 22, 1999
Darnell Davis

Customers ordering computers
Carla Kahn
Fred Flynn

  Order numbers of orders from 4/1/99 to 4/30/99
1
4

  Added and updated a new item
Description
radio
television
computer
CD player

  Deleted the new item
Description
radio
television
computer
```

Note 1:   The SQL SELECT statement returns the selected rows in a ResultSet. We use the executeQuery method to execute SELECT statements.

Note 2:   We embed tab characters, \t, in the string to space the data horizontally.

Note 3:   We omitted field 2, ItemNumber, from the display because we selected all results to have ItemNumber = 222222. We could insert a single tab character using single quotes, '\t', but inserting two characters requires the double-quoted string, "\t\t". We use the getInt method because field 3, Quantity, has SQL type INTEGER. We use getBigDecimal to display a currency value, and we format it. This UnitPrice field has type Currency in the database.

Note 4:   We used the field number, 1, but could have used the field name, CustomerName, as the argument to getString. We will see in the next section how to get the number of fields and their names from the database if we do not know them.

Note 5:   We add a new row to illustrate the UPDATE and DELETE statements which change the database. We update the new row, and then delete it, leaving the database unchanged when we exit the program. This is nice while learning JDBC because we can try various SELECT statements running the same program repeatedly without changing the data.

Note 6:   stmt.executeUpdate(sql);
Because the UPDATE and DELETE statements do not return values, we use the executeUpdate method to execute them.

THE BIG PICTURE

When querying the database, a result set contains the selected rows. We use methods such as getString to display a value from a row of the result set. The SQL types have corresponding Java methods, so the Java getInt method retrieves INTEGER values, for example. We can write our SQL queries to order the results or to eliminate duplicate rows. A query may have to join several tables on common fields to obtain the desired information.

TEST YOUR UNDERSTANDING

11. Write an SQL statement to find names of salespersons and the customers that have placed orders with them. Be sure to eliminate duplicates.

TRY IT YOURSELF   12. Modify Example 3.3 to use only field names in the getString, getInt, and getBigDecimal methods.

TRY IT YOURSELF   13. Modify Example 3.3 to use only field numbers in the getString, getInt, and getBigDecimal methods.

TRY IT YOURSELF   14. Modify Example 3.3 to list CustomerID in addition to CustomerName and Address. Arrange the output rows so that the CustomerID numbers appear in numerical order.

15. Write a SELECT statement to find the names and addresses of customers who placed orders with Peter Patterson. Be sure to eliminate duplicates.

3.4   Metadata and Aggregate Functions

· · · · · · · · · · ·

Java, with JDBC, allows us to get information about the database (**metadata**) with which we are working, and about any result sets we obtain. We can use SQL functions to compute with the data.

Database Metadata

The `DatabaseMetaData` methods return information about the database to which we are connected. To use these methods we first execute

```
DatabaseMetaData dbMetaData = con.getMetaData();
```

where `con` is the connection to the database. We can ask what level of SQL the database system supports by using the three methods

```
dbMetaData.supportsANSI92EntryLevelSQL();
dbMetaData.supportsANSI92IntermediateSQL();
dbMetaData.supportsANSI92FullSQL();
```

where ANSI (pronounced an´-see) stands for the American National Standards Institute. Java requires that JDBC drivers support ANSI92 entry level SQL so the first method must always return **true**. The Microsoft Access version 7.0 that we use supports ANSI89 but does not support ANSI92 intermediate or full SQL.

The method

```
dbMetaData.getIdentifierQuoteString();
```

returns the character used to delimit strings; in our database that is the single quote, '. Executing

```
ResultSet rs = dbMetaData.getTypeInfo();
```

gives us the type names used in the database itself, which may be different from the standard SQL types, or Java types. For example Microsoft Access uses the CURRENCY type and internally uses TEXT for the SQL VARCHAR type. We can list the type names from the result set using the loop

```
while(rs.next())
  System.out.println(rs.getString("TYPE_NAME"));
```

The very handy `getTables` method lets us obtain the names of the tables in our database. For example,

```
dbMetaData.getTables(null,null,"%",tables);
```

will return the names of the five tables in the `Sales` database. The first two arguments represent the catalog and schema facilities. Our application is not so elaborate, and here we pass **null** for these arguments.

The third argument to `getTables` is a string representing a search pattern for the tables we are seeking. In a large database with many tables, we might search for all tables starting with "Payroll" by using the string "Payroll%" where the % character matches zero or more characters. Because we want all tables, we use the string "%" which matches any string. To match a single character we could use the string "_", so "Payroll_" would match strings such as Payroll1, Payroll2, and so on.

The fourth argument to `getTables` uses an array of strings to specify the types of table for which to search. In addition to the tables that we created, there are various system tables in the database in which we are not interested. To limit our search we declare the fourth argument as

```
String[] tables = {"TABLE"};
```

which restricts the search to user-defined data tables.

We can also use database metadata to find the column names and types for each table. The method call

```
ResultSet rs = dbMetaData.getColumns(null,null,"Customer","%");
```

returns information about each column of the `Customer` table. As with the `getTables` methods we pass **null** arguments for the catalog and schema which we do not use. The third argument is a pattern for the tables to search; we pass the name `Customer` to get its columns. The fourth argument allows a string pattern to select the columns. We pass "%" to retrieve all columns. The details of interest about each column are its name and type which we access using

```
rs.getString("COLUMN_NAME");
```

and

```
rs.getString("TYPE_NAME");
```

Result Set Metadata

JDBC allows us to get information about each result set. We use

```
ResultSetMetaData rsMetaData = rs.getMetaData();
```

to get the `rsMetaData` object, and then use the methods

```
rsMetaData.getColumnCount();
```

to return the number of columns in the result set,

```
rsMetaData.getColumnLabel(i);
```

to return the name of column `i`, and

```
rsMetaData.getColumnTypeName(i);
```

to return its type.

Using the `getColumns` method, we suggested just listing the `COLUMN_NAME` and `TYPE_NAME` fields of the result set returned. In Example 3.4 we use result set metadata to list all the fields of the result set describing each column of the database. Perhaps not surprisingly, we found these result set fields differ from those described in the documentation included with the JDK, using versions 1.1.6 and 1.3.0.

The `colNamesTypes` method in Example 3.4 uses the `getColumnLabel` and `getColumnTypeName` methods to return the names and types of each of the columns of its result set argument. We can use it with any result set. For example, using it with the result set returned by

```
stmt.executeQuery("SELECT * FROM Item");
```

would list the all columns, with their types, from the Item table, because using the star, `*`, in the `SELECT` clause returns all the columns of the table.

Aggregate Functions

Aggregate functions compute values from the table data, using all the rows to produce the result. For example, the query

```
SELECT SUM(BalanceDue),
       AVG(BalanceDue),
       MAX(BalanceDue)
FROM Customer
```

returns the sum, average, and maximum of all the balances due in the customer table. These functions operate on the `BalanceDue` column for all rows in the `Customer` table. Using a `WHERE` clause, as in

```
SELECT COUNT(*), MIN(Quantity) FROM OrderItem
WHERE ItemNumber = '222222'
```

will limit the computation to the rows of the `OrderItem` table which correspond to orders for radios. The function `COUNT(*)` will return the total number of rows satisfying this condition. `MIN(Quantity)` returns the minimum quantity of radios ordered in one of the three rows of the `OrderItem` table which represent orders for radios (item number 222222).

EXAMPLE 3.4   DatabaseInfo.java

```java
/* Illustrate DatabaseMetaData, ResultSetMetaData
 * and SQL aggregate functions.
 */

import java.sql.*;
import java.io.*;
import java.text.*;

class DatabaseInfo {
  public static void main (String args[]) {
    try{
      ResultSet rs;
      Class.forName("sun.jdbc.odbc.JdbcOdbcDriver");        // Note 1
      String url = "jdbc:odbc:Sales";
      Connection con = DriverManager.getConnection(url);    // Note 2

      DatabaseMetaData dbMetaData = con.getMetaData();
```

```
System.out.println("Supports entry level SQL: " +
        dbMetaData.supportsANSI92EntryLevelSQL());
System.out.println("Supports intermediate SQL: " +
        dbMetaData.supportsANSI92IntermediateSQL());
System.out.println("Supports full SQL: " +
        dbMetaData.supportsANSI92FullSQL());
System.out.println("Supports stored procedures: "+
        dbMetaData.supportsStoredProcedures());
System.out.println("Quote string: " +
        dbMetaData.getIdentifierQuoteString());
System.out.println("Types used in the database:");
System.out.print('\t');

rs = dbMetaData.getTypeInfo();
while (rs.next())
  System.out.print(rs.getString("TYPE_NAME") + " ");        // Note 3
System.out.println();

String[] tables ={"TABLE"};
rs = dbMetaData.getTables(null,null,"%",tables);
System.out.println("Tables in the Sales database:");
System.out.print('\t');
while(rs.next())
  System.out.print(rs.getString("TABLE_NAME") + " ");       // Note 4
System.out.println();

rs = dbMetaData.getColumns(null,null,"Customer","%");
System.out.println("Columns in the Customer table");
while(rs.next())
  System.out.println('\t'+rs.getString("COLUMN_NAME")+"      // Note 5
      "+rs.getString("TYPE_NAME"));
displayStrings("Fields describing each column",
                                  colNamesTypes(rs));        // Note 6
String query;
query = "SELECT * FROM Item";
Statement stmt = con.createStatement();
rs = stmt.executeQuery(query);
displayStrings("Item Columns",colNamesTypes(rs));           // Note 7

query = "SELECT SUM(BalanceDue),AVG(BalanceDue), "
      + "MAX(BalanceDue) FROM Customer";
rs = stmt.executeQuery(query);
displayStrings("Function columns",colNamesTypes(rs));       // Note 8
System.out.println("Sum, average, and maximum balance due");
NumberFormat cf = NumberFormat.getCurrencyInstance();
while(rs.next())
  System.out.println(cf.format(rs.getBigDecimal(1)) + " "
      + cf.format(rs.getBigDecimal(2)) + " "
                      + cf.format(rs.getBigDecimal(3)));
```

```
      query = "SELECT COUNT(*), MIN(Quantity) FROM OrderItem "
              + "WHERE ItemNumber = '222222' ";
      rs = stmt.executeQuery(query);
      while(rs.next()){
        System.out.println("Number of radio order items: " + rs.getInt(1));
        System.out.println
            ("Minimum quantity of radios ordered in any order item: "
              + rs.getInt(2));
      }

      stmt.close();
    }catch (Exception e) {e.printStackTrace();}
  }
  public static String[] colNamesTypes(ResultSet rs) throws SQLException {
    ResultSetMetaData rsMetaData = rs.getMetaData();
    int cols = rsMetaData.getColumnCount();
    String[] s = new String[cols];                              // Note 9
    String label, tab;
    for (int i =1; i <= cols; i++) {
      label = rsMetaData.getColumnLabel(i);
      if (label.length() < 8) tab = "\t\t"; else tab = "\t";    // Note 10
      s[i - 1] = '\t' + label + tab
            + rsMetaData.getColumnTypeName(i);                  // Note 11
    }
    return s;
  }
  public static void displayStrings(String description, String[]s) { // Note 12
    System.out.println(description);
    for(int i = 0; i < s.length; i++)
    System.out.println(s[i]);
  }
}
```

....

Output

```
Supports entry level SQL: true
Supports intermediate SQL: false
Supports full SQL: false
Supports stored procedures: true
Quote string: `
Types used in the database:
    BIT BYTE LONGBINARY VARBINARY BINARY LONGTEXT CHAR
CURRENCY LONG COUNTER SHORT SINGLE DOUBLE DATETIME TEXT
Tables in the Sales database:
    Customer Item OrderItem Orders Salesperson
Columns in the Customer table
    CustomerID TEXT
    CustomerName TEXT
    Address TEXT
    BalanceDue CURRENCY
```

```
Fields describing each column
    TABLE_QUALIFIER TEXT
    TABLE_OWNER     TEXT
    TABLE_NAME      TEXT
    COLUMN_NAME     TEXT
    DATA_TYPE       SHORT
  TYPE_NAME     TEXT
  PRECISION     LONG
  LENGTH        LONG
  SCALE         SHORT
  RADIX         SHORT
  NULLABLE      SHORT
  REMARKS       TEXT
  ORDINAL       LONG
Item Columns
  ItemNumber    TEXT
  Description   TEXT
  Quantity      LONG
Function columns
  Expr1000      CURRENCY
  Expr1001      CURRENCY
  Expr1002      CURRENCY
Sum, average, and maximum balance due
$1797.95 $449.49 $1667.00
Number of radio order items: 3
Minimum quantity of radios ordered in any order item: 2
```

Note 1: To show how it works, we use the `forName` method to load the JDBC driver. The advantage of this approach is we could easily modify this program to pass the driver name as a program argument. We have no need to do that here but it might be useful in writing a general application designed to work with different databases.

Note 2: We use the form of the `getConnection` method that does not require a user name or a password because these are not needed for the Microsoft Access database system we are using.

Note 3: According to the JDK documentation, the `getTypeInfo` method returns 18 columns of information for each type provided by the database system. We only list one, TYPE_NAME, leaving as an exercise the use of the `colNamesTypes` to list the names and types of all columns of this result set to see if they correspond to the 18 listed in the documentation.

Note 4: According to the JDK documentation, the `getTables` method returns five columns of information for each table in the database. We list only TABLE_NAME. It is column 3 so we could have used `getString(3)` to retrieve it, but using the column name is much more helpful.

Note 5: According to the JDK documentation, the `getColumns` method returns 18 fields to describe each column. (However, see Note 6.) We list `COLUMN_NAME` and `COLUMN_TYPE`.

Note 6: `displayStrings ("Fields describing each column",colNamesTypes(rs));`
Using the `colNamesTypes` method to list the names and types of the columns in the result set returned by the `getColumns` method we see that the result set actually contains 13 columns, some of which are named differently than the columns listed in the JDK documentation.

Note 7: `displayStrings("Item Columns",colNamesTypes(rs));`
This shows that we can use the `colNamesTypes` method to display the names and types of the columns of any result set, in this case the one which selects all columns from the `Item` table.

Note 8: `displayStrings("Function columns",colNamesTypes(rs));`
The result set gives the values of the `SUM`, `AVG`, and `MAX` functions. These are not columns of the `Customer` tables, but rather they are values computed from the `BalanceDue` column. We use the `colNamesTypes` method to list the names and types of the columns in the result set. Because these columns have no names Java creates the names Expr1000, Expr1001, and Expr1003 for them. They have internal database types of `CURRENCY` which does not correspond to a SQL type. The Java `getBigDecimal` method will return the value of each function.

Note 9: `String[] s = new String[cols];`
We use a string array to hold the name and type of each column in the result set argument to this method.

Note 10: To keep the type column aligned we use two tab characters as a separator when the column name is less than eight characters in length, but one tab character otherwise.

Note 11: `s[i-1] = '\t' + label + tab +`
`rsMetaData.getColumnTypeName(i);`
Column numbers start at 1, while array indices start at 0, so we store column `i` in array component `i-1`.

Note 12: The `displayStrings` method displays a description and a list of the elements of its `String` array argument.

THE BIG PICTURE

Database metadata tells us properties of the database such as the names of its tables, and the names and types of the columns in a table. Result set metadata lets us find properties of a result set. We can find the number of columns in the result set and the label and type of each column. We can use result set metadata on a result set from a database metadata method or on a result set from an SQL query. Aggregate functions compute values from the rows of a table.

TEST YOUR UNDERSTANDING

TRY IT YOURSELF   16. Modify Example 3.4 to pass **null** as the fourth argument to the `getTables` method, instead of the `tables` array. This will list all tables in the database, including the system tables.

TRY IT YOURSELF   17. Modify Example 3.4 to change the third argument to the `getTables` method to find the tables in the `Sales` database which start with `Order`.

TRY IT YOURSELF   18. Modify Example 3.4 to use the `colNamesTypes` method to list all the fields of the result set returned by the `getTypeInfo` method. Compare these fields to those listed in the JDK documentation, if available.

TRY IT YOURSELF   19. Modify Example 3.4 to use the `colNamesTypes` method to list all the fields of the result set returned by the `getTables` method. Compare these fields to those listed in the JDK documentation, if available.

3.5 Prepared Statements and Transactions*

· · · · · · · · · ·

A **prepared statement** lets us translate a statement to low-level database commands once, and execute it many times, thus avoiding the inefficient repetition of the translation process.

When making changes to a database we must be very careful that we complete all steps of the transaction. It would not do to withdraw funds from one account, but not have it deposited in another. **Transaction processing** allows us to explicitly control when changes become final, so that we only **commit** changes when all those desired have completed correctly.

Using Prepared Statements

Often we may wish to execute a query repeatedly using different conditions each time. The query

```
SELECT * FROM OrderItem
WHERE ItemNumber = '222222'
```

selects all order items with number 222222. To execute this query for each item, we could use a loop such as

```
String[] numbers = {"222222","333333","444444"}
ResultSet rs;
for (int i = 0; i < numbers.length; i++) {
  rs = stmt.executeQuery("SELECT * FROM OrderItem "
            + "WHERE ItemNumber = '" + numbers[i] + '\'');
  // process results
}
```

---

* The ODBC text driver does not handle prepared statements or transactions.

We have only three products in our database, but we might have had many more. For each product, the database system must process the SQL query analyzing how to find the requested data from the database in the most efficient way possible. Our query is quite simple, but it could have been much more complex. Each time we call `execute-Query`, we have to process the query, spending the time over and over again to find the best way to find the results that satisfy it.

The prepared statement allows the database system to process an SQL query once, determining the best way to get the results. We can then use this prepared statement over and over again with different data but without the overhead of translating it again.

We use the question mark, ?, to denote the arguments to query that we wish to change from one execution to the next. To make a prepared statement from our previous query, we write it as

```
String query = "SELECT * FROM OrderItem "
  + "WHERE ItemNumber = ?";
```

where the question mark stands for the item number that we will pass in. Next we create a prepared statement using

```
PreparedStatement pStmt = con.prepareStatement(query);
```

where `con` is the connection to the database.

To pass arguments to a query we use `setXXX` methods where `XXX` stands for the type of the argument. In our example, `ItemNumber` has type `VARCHAR` which corresponds to the string type in Java, so we use the `setString` method, as in

```
pStmt.setString(1,"222222");
```

where we enclose the item number in double quotes because we are inside Java and not writing an SQL statement for this database system. The first argument to `set-String` is the number of the argument to which we want to pass the value specified. We number the arguments in the order they appear in the query, with the first argument having number 1. The statement

```
rs = pStmt.executeQuery();
```

executes the prepared query with the argument 222222.

TIP ☛ The `executeQuery` method takes no arguments when used with a prepared statement because we have already passed the query to the `prepareStatement` method.

....

We process the result set as we did with simple statements. The code

```
System.out.println("OrderNumber\tQuantity\tUnitPrice");
NumberFormat cf = NumberFormat.getCurrencyInstance();
while (rs.next())
  System.out.println(rs.getString(1) + "\t\t" + rs.getInt(3)
    + "\t\t" + cf.format(rs.getBigDecimal(4)));
```

extracted from Example 3.3 will return the other columns of all rows in the OrderItem table having the specified item number.

After closing the result set with

```
rs.close();
```

we could pass another argument to the query and execute the query again as in

```
pStmt.setString(1,"333333");
rs = pStmt.executeQuery();
```

which would find the rows of the OrderItem table whose item number is 333333, representing a television order.

To pass multiple arguments we use additional question marks in the query. In the query

```
query = "SELECT OrderNumber FROM Orders "
       + "WHERE OrderDate BETWEEN ? AND ?";
```

the arguments represent the starting and ending dates of orders. After creating the prepared statement, we pass the arguments using the setDate method as in

```
pStmt.setDate(1, Date.valueOf("1999-04-01"));
```

which replaces the first question mark with April 1, 1999, and

```
pStmt.setDate(2, Date.valueOf("1999-04-30"));
```

which replaces the second question mark with April 30, 1999. The Date class, in the java.sql package, extends java.util.Date. The valueOf method translates a string representing the date to a Date that can be used in the database system.

In preparing a statement to which we pass an argument that is a currency amount, we use the setBigDecimal method to pass the currency value. For example, the query

```
SELECT CustomerName FROM Customer
WHERE BalanceDue > ?
```

has an argument for the BalanceDue value. To pass such a value to the prepared statement created from this query, we use

```
pStmt.setBigDecimal(1, new java.math.BigDecimal(0.0));
```

The BigDecimal, created from the double 0.0, will represent the amount $0.00, so our query will return the names of all customers with a non-zero balance.

Transaction Processing

Often when using a database we need to execute several statements to perform the desired transaction. For example, if a customer places a new order we will update the Order table with another order, the OrderItem table with the items ordered, and the Customer table with a new BalanceDue. We would be unhappy if an error occurred after some, but not all of these changes were made. Java allows us to manage transactions so we only commit the changes to the database when they complete without error.

The JDBC default is to commit the change as soon as we execute the update. The statement

```
con.setAutoCommit(false);
```

changes from the default behavior to require that we explicitly commit changes using

```
con.commit();
```

If we have already executed some updates and decide we do not want to commit them, we can roll back to the point when we executed the last commit, undoing these changes using

```
con.rollback();
```

For example, if we have removed the auto commit default, after executing the queries

```
INSERT INTO Item VALUES (555555,'CD player',10)
```

and

```
UPDATE Item SET Quantity = 12
WHERE Description = 'CD player'
```

we can either commit them, making the changes permanent, using the `commit` method, or undo them using the `rollback` method.

EXAMPLE 3.5   **Prepare.java**

```
/* Illustrates prepared statements
 * and transaction processing.
 */

import java.sql.*;
import java.io.*;

class Prepare {
  public static void main (String args[]) {
    try {
      ResultSet rs;
      Class.forName("sun.jdbc.odbc.JdbcOdbcDriver");
      String url = "jdbc:odbc:Sales";
      Connection con = DriverManager.getConnection(url);
      con.setAutoCommit(false);                                    // Note 1

      String query;
      query = "SELECT Quantity FROM Item "
          + "WHERE Description = ?";                               // Note 2
      PreparedStatement pStmt = con.prepareStatement(query);
      pStmt.setString(1, "radio");
      rs = pStmt.executeQuery();
```

```
System.out.println
            (" Using a prepared statement to find quantity of radios");
while(rs.next())
  System.out.println(rs.getInt("Quantity"));
rs.close();                                                          // Note 3

pStmt.setString(1, "computer");
rs = pStmt.executeQuery();
System.out.println
        (" Using a prepared statement to find quantity of computers");
while(rs.next())
  System.out.println(rs.getInt("Quantity"));
rs.close();

query = "SELECT OrderNumber FROM Orders "
      + "WHERE OrderDate BETWEEN ? AND ?";
pStmt =con.prepareStatement(query);
pStmt.setDate(1, Date.valueOf("1999-04-01"));                        // Note 4
pStmt.setDate(2, Date.valueOf("1999-04-30"));
rs = pStmt.executeQuery();
System.out.println(" Using a prepared statement to find orders in April");
while(rs.next())
  System.out.println(rs.getInt("OrderNumber"));
rs.close();

query = "SELECT CustomerName FROM Customer "
      + "WHERE BalanceDue > ?";
pStmt = con.prepareStatement(query);
pStmt.setBigDecimal(1, new java.math.BigDecimal(0.0));
rs = pStmt.executeQuery();
System.out.println(" Using a prepared statement to find customers "
      + "with non-zero balance");
while(rs.next())
  System.out.println(rs.getString("CustomerName"));
pStmt.close();                                                       // Note 5

Statement stmt = con.createStatement();
String sql;
sql = "INSERT INTO Item VALUES (555555,'CD player',10)";
stmt.executeUpdate(sql);

sql = "UPDATE Item SET Quantity = 12 "
    + "WHERE Description = 'CD player'";
stmt.executeUpdate(sql);
System.out.println();
System.out.println
        (" Before commit or rollback -- table changed, but can rollback");
System.out.println("Description");
query = "SELECT Description FROM Item";
rs = stmt.executeQuery(query);
while(rs.next())
  System.out.println(rs.getString(1));                              // Note 6
```

```
        con.rollback();                                            // Note 7
        System.out.println();
        System.out.println(" Rolled back insert and update -- table unchanged");
        System.out.println("Description");
        query = "SELECT Description FROM Item";
        rs = stmt.executeQuery(query);
        while(rs.next())
          System.out.println(rs.getString(1));

        sql = "INSERT INTO Item VALUES (555555,'CD player',10)";    // Note 8
        stmt.executeUpdate(sql);
        sql = "UPDATE Item SET Quantity = 12 "
            + "WHERE Description = 'CD player'";
        stmt.executeUpdate(sql);
        con.commit();                                              // Note 9
        System.out.println();
        System.out.println(" Committed insert and update -- table changed");
        System.out.println("Description");
        query = "SELECT Description FROM Item";
        rs = stmt.executeQuery(query);
        while(rs.next())
          System.out.println(rs.getString(1));

        sql = "DELETE FROM Item WHERE Description = 'CD player'";   // Note 10
        stmt.executeUpdate(sql);
        con.commit();                                              // Note 11
        query = "SELECT Description FROM Item";
        rs = stmt.executeQuery(query);
        System.out.println();
        System.out.println(" Deleted the new item");
        System.out.println("Description");
        while(rs.next())
          System.out.println(rs.getString(1));

        stmt.close();
      }catch (Exception e) {e.printStackTrace();}
    }
}
```

....

Output

```
Using a prepared statement to find quantity of radios
32
  Using a prepared statement to find quantity of computers
9
  Using a prepared statement to find orders in April
1
4
  Using a prepared statement to find customers with non-zero balance
Fred Flynn
```

```
Darnell Davis

  Before commit or rollback -- table changed, but can rollback
Description
radio
television
computer
CD player

  Rolled back insert and update -- table unchanged
Description
radio
television
computer

  Committed insert and update -- table changed
Description
radio
television
computer
CD player

  Deleted the new item
Description
radio
television
computer
```

....

Note 1: With auto commit off, we must execute the commit statement in order to make our updates permanent.

Note 2: The question mark indicates where we can substitute one of the descriptions, radio, television, or computer.

Note 3: With simple statements we do not need to close the result set after each query. The stmt.close method also closes the result set when we are done with the statement, stmt. For prepared statements we need to close the result set after each query.

Note 4: The Date class, in the java.sql package, extends java.util.Date.

Note 5: Closing the prepared statement, pStmt, automatically closes the last result set too.

Note 6: `while(rs.next()) System.out.println(rs.getString(1));`
Outputting the descriptions of the items in the database shows that the database system has entered the item CD player (with the updated quantity of 12 not shown). We have not yet executed the commit statement so we still have a chance to rollback this change.

Note 7:   `con.rollback();`

After we rollback the updates we find only the original three items in the `Item` table.

Note 8:   `sql = "INSERT INTO Item VALUES (555555,'CD player',10)";`

Now we make the same updates, this time actually committing them to the database.

Note 9:   `con.commit();`

This will commit the previous updates to the database and prevent further rollbacks of them. Only updates executed after this can be rolled back.

Note 10:   `sql = "DELETE FROM Item WHERE Description = 'CD player'";`

We delete the new row from the database, to leave it as we found it in this pedagogical example.

Note 11:   `con.commit();`

We must commit the DELETE transaction for it to take effect.

THE BIG PICTURE

A prepared statement lets us translate a query once and substitute values for its parameters to execute it repeatedly. By deciding explicitly when to commit changes to the database, we reserve the option to rollback some changes if the entire transaction cannot be completed.

TEST YOUR UNDERSTANDING

20. Write a SELECT statement to return the names of customers who ordered an item given by its description in the Item table, which we pass in as an argument, so we can create a prepared statement from the query.

TRY IT YOURSELF   21. Modify Example 3.5 to omit the first `rs.close()` statement. Does any error result? If so, which?

TRY IT YOURSELF   22. Modify Example 3.5 to find the order numbers of orders placed in March. Use the same prepared statement.

TRY IT YOURSELF   23. Modify Example 3.5 to omit the last `commit` statement. Run the modified program and check the database afterward to see that the new row has not been deleted; it must be deleted manually.

3.6 A GUI for Database Queries

Our case study builds a graphical user interface for querying our `Sales` database. This example illustrates the JDBC techniques covered in this chapter, adding the user interface concepts studied earlier. Even as presented here it is large for an introductory example. It would need many extensions and much polishing to make it a really useful application. Some of these extensions are left to the exercises.

The SearchSales program allows the user to create a SELECT query, and executes it, displaying the resulting rows. We use the gridbag layout to arrange the components. Figure 3.17 shows the initial screen.

Figure 3.17 The SearchSales **initial screen**

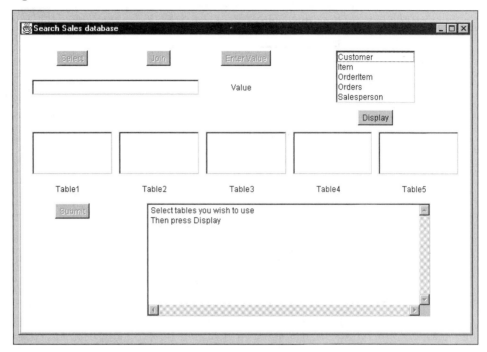

The List (we cover the List component below) at the upper-right shows the five tables of the Sales database. The user selects the tables to search. The names of these tables will appear after FROM in the query. The text area at the bottom gives instructions to the user, and displays the final results of the search. We disable all buttons, except Display, until we are ready to use them.

Figures 3.18-3.22 show the steps in the creation and execution of the query

```
SELECT CustomerName FROM Customer, Orders
WHERE Customer.CustomerID = Orders.CustomerID
AND OrderDate = {d '1999-03-22'}
```

Figure 3.18 shows the screen after the user has selected the Customer and Orders tables, and pressed the Display button. We have disabled the Display button because the user has already chosen the tables. The column names for the Customer table appear in the leftmost List, while those for the Orders table appear in the fourth List. The labels underneath now show the table names. Thus far our query is

```
SELECT ... FROM Customer, Order.
```

The user now selects the columns to be part of the result set, in this example choosing CustomerName and pressing the Select button. The partially constructed query is now

Figure 3.18   Screen to choose columns for the result

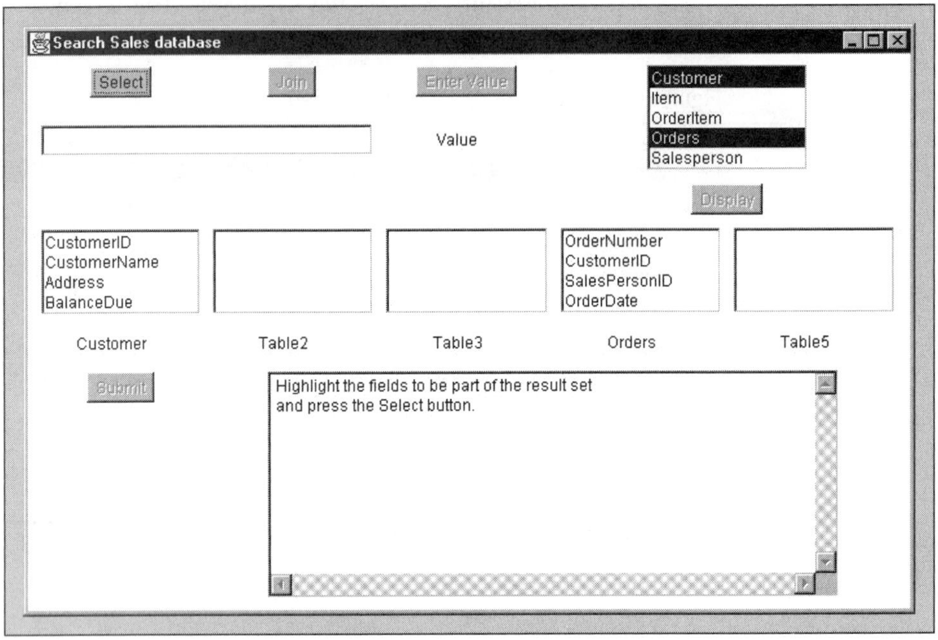

```
SELECT CustomerName FROM Customer, Order
```

Figure 3.19 shows the next screen in which we disabled the Select button, because we only select the fields of the result once. We deselect all fields so that the user will not have to deselect the fields before going on to the next step. At this point we enable the *Join*, *Enter Value*, and *Submit* buttons. The user would be ready to execute queries without conditions, such as

```
SELECT CustomerName FROM Customer,
```

so we enable the Submit button. The Join and Enter Value buttons allow us to add conditions that restrict the scope of the query.

In our example query we join the Customer and the Orders tables, requiring the condition

```
Customer.CustomerID = Orders.CustomerID.
```

We impose this condition to join the information from the two tables properly, and also impose the condition

```
OrderDate = {d '1999-03-22'}
```

to select orders placed on March 22, 1999.

Figure 3.20 indicates the user has selected the CustomerID field in the Customer table and the CustomerID field in the Orders table.

Figure 3.19   After pressing the `Select` button

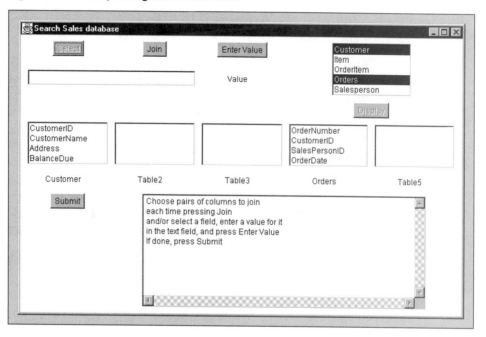

Figure 3.20   Adding a `Join` condition

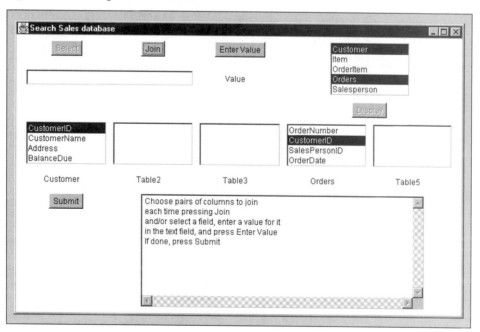

After pressing the Join button the partially completed query will be

```
SELECT CustomerName FROM Customer, Order
WHERE Customer.CustomerID = Orders.CustomerID
```

The next screen, Figure 3.21 has the same options as in Figure 3.20, because we can add conditions or submit the completed query. We choose the OrderDate column from the Orders table and enter the value {d '1999-03-22} in the text field. Pressing the Enter Value button will add to our query the condition that the order date be March 22, 1999. We only use the equality relation in our conditions leaving the extension to less than and greater than to the exercises.

Figure 3.21   Entering the OrderDate condition

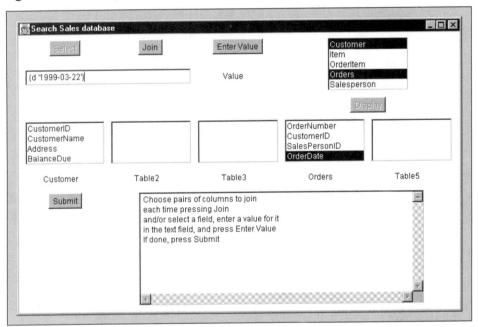

We could add more conditions, but this completes our query, so we press the Submit button. Figure 3.22, shows the resulting list (of only one customer, Darnell Davis) displayed in the text area. We disable all buttons, leaving for the exercises the option to continue executing additional queries.

The List Component

The List component we use in Example 3.6 differs from a choice box in that we can specify how many entries to display and select multiple entries.

The constructor

```
List(5,true)
```

specifies a box that will show five entries, providing a scroll bar if the list contains more than five items. A second argument of **true** permits multiple selections.

Figure 3.22 The query result

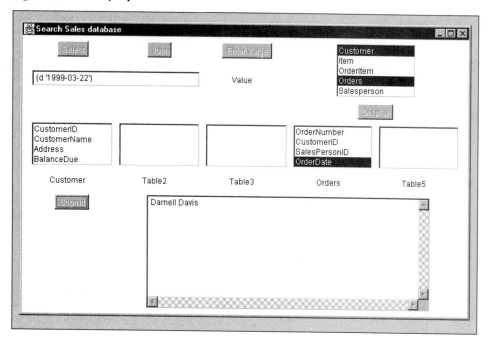

We add items to a List using the add method, as in

```
tables.add("Customer");
```

Single-clicking the mouse on a list item generates an ItemEvent, while double-clicking on an item generates an ActionEvent. We do not handle these events in this example, because we prefer to wait until the user selects all the desired items and presses the appropriate button to ask us to process the selections.

EXAMPLE 3.6   **SearchSales.java**

```java
/* Provides a GUI to execute an SQL query
 * on the Sales database.
 */

import java.awt.*;
import java.awt.event.*;
import java.sql.*;
import java.net.*;

public class SearchSales extends Frame implements ActionListener{
  public static final int SIZE = 5;
  List tables = new List(SIZE,true);          // tables in Sales database
  List[] columns = new List[SIZE];            // columns in each table
  Label[] colLabel = new Label[SIZE];         // label for each table's col list
  Label value = new Label("Value");
  TextField fieldValue = new TextField(12);   // enter a value in a condition
```

```
Button submit = new Button("Submit");      // submit the query
Button join = new Button("Join");          // choose common columns in a
                                           //   condition
Button enter = new Button("Enter Value");  // enter the value for the
                                           //   condition
Button select = new Button("Select");      // choose the columns for result
                                           //   set
Button display = new Button("Display");    // display the selected tables'
                                           //   columns
TextArea result = new TextArea();          // display prompts and final
                                           //   result


Connection con;
Statement stmt;
DatabaseMetaData dbMetaData;
String[] tableName = new String[SIZE];     // names of the selected Sales
                                           //   tables
int[] indices = null;                      // indices of Sales tables
                                           //   selected
String resultCols = "";                    // result set columns, after
                                           //   SELECT
boolean firstJoin = true;                  // first time for join
String joinClauses = "";                   // clauses to be joined, after
                                           //   WHERE or AND
String condition = "";                     // condition clauses, after WHERE
                                           //   or AND
String fromTables = "";                    // tables used, for FROM part of
                                           //   query
String query = "SELECT ";                  // the query to be executed
int count = 0;                             // number of cols in result set

public SearchSales(String title) {
  setTitle(title);
  for(int i = 0; i < SIZE; i++)                                    // Note 1
    columns[i] = new List(4,true);
  for(int i = 0; i < SIZE; i++)                                    // Note 2
    colLabel[i] = new Label("Table" + (i+1));
  GridBagLayout gbl = new GridBagLayout();
  setLayout(gbl);
  GridBagConstraints c = new GridBagConstraints();
  c.insets = new Insets(5,5,5,5);                                  // Note 3
  gbl.setConstraints(select,c); add(select);
  gbl.setConstraints(join,c); add(join);
  gbl.setConstraints(enter,c); add(enter);

  c.gridwidth = GridBagConstraints.REMAINDER;                      // Note 4
  c.gridheight = 2;
  gbl.setConstraints(tables,c);add(tables);

  c.gridx = 0;
  c.gridy = 1;
```

```
c.gridwidth = 2;
c.gridheight = 1;
c.fill = GridBagConstraints.HORIZONTAL;                      // Note 5
gbl.setConstraints(fieldValue,c); add(fieldValue);

c.fill = GridBagConstraints.NONE;
c.gridwidth = 1;
c.gridx = 2;
gbl.setConstraints(value,c);              add(value);

c.gridx = 3;
c.gridy = 2;
c.gridwidth = GridBagConstraints.REMAINDER;
gbl.setConstraints(display,c);            add(display);

c.gridy = 3;
c.gridwidth = 1;
c.gridheight = 2;
for(int i = 0; i < SIZE; i++) {                              // Note 6
  c.gridx = i;
  gbl.setConstraints(columns[i],c);
  add(columns[i]);
}

c.gridheight = 1;
c.gridy = 5;
for(int i=0; i<SIZE; i++) {
  c.gridx = i;
  gbl.setConstraints(colLabel[i],c);
  add(colLabel[i]);
}
c.gridx = 0;
c.gridy = 6;
gbl.setConstraints(submit,c);             add(submit);

c.gridx = 1;
c.gridheight = 2;
c.gridwidth = GridBagConstraints.REMAINDER;
gbl.setConstraints(result,c);             add(result);

addWindowListener(new WindowClose());
display.addActionListener(this);
select.addActionListener(this);
select.setEnabled(false);
join.addActionListener(this);
join.setEnabled(false);
submit.addActionListener(this);
submit.setEnabled(false);
enter.addActionListener(this);
enter.setEnabled(false);
```

```
try {
  Class.forName("sun.jdbc.odbc.JdbcOdbcDriver");
  String url = "jdbc:odbc:Sales";
  con = DriverManager.getConnection(url);
  stmt = con.createStatement();
  result.setText("Select tables you wish to use\nThen press Display");
  dbMetaData = con.getMetaData();
  String[] tableTypes ={"TABLE"};
  ResultSet rs = dbMetaData.getTables(null,null,"%",tableTypes);
  int i = 0;
  while(rs.next())
    tables.add(tableName[i++] = rs.getString("TABLE_NAME"));     // Note 7
}catch (Exception e) {e.printStackTrace();}
}

public void actionPerformed(ActionEvent event) {
  Object source = event.getSource();
  if (source == display) {
    indices = tables.getSelectedIndexes();                       // Note 8
    for(int i = 0; i < indices.length; i++){
      colLabel[indices[i]].setText(tableName[indices[i]]);       // Note 9
      colLabel[indices[i]].invalidate();                         // Note 10
      fromTables += tableName[indices[i]] +',';                  // Note 11
    }

    fromTables = fromTables.substring(0,fromTables.length() - 1);  // Note 12
    display.setEnabled(false);
    result.setText("Highlight the fields to be part of the result set\n"
    + "and press the Select button.");

    for(int i = 0; i < indices.length; i++) {
      try {
        ResultSet rs =
          dbMetaData.getColumns(null,null,tableName[indices[i]],"%");
                                                                 // Note 13
        while(rs.next())
          columns[indices[i]].add(rs.getString("COLUMN_NAME"));  // Note 14
      }catch(SQLException e) {e.printStackTrace();}
    }
    select.setEnabled(true);
    validate();                                                  // Note 15
  }

  else if (source == select) {
    for(int i = 0; i < indices.length; i++)
      count += columns[indices[i]].getSelectedIndexes().length;  // Note 16
    resultCols = build("",',');                                  // Note 17
    resultCols = resultCols.substring(0,resultCols.length() - 1);
    result.setText("Choose pairs of columns to join\n"
            + "each time pressing Join\n"
            + "and/or select a field, enter a value for it\n"
```

```
                    + "in the text field, and press Enter Value\n"
                    + "If done, press Submit");
      join.setEnabled(true);
      enter.setEnabled(true);
      select.setEnabled(false);
      deselectAll(columns,indices);                          // Note 18
      query += resultCols + " FROM " + fromTables;           // Note 19
      submit.setEnabled(true);
    }

else if (source == join) {
  String keyword = "";
  if (firstJoin) {                                           // Note 20
    keyword = " WHERE ";
    firstJoin = false;
  }

  else
    keyword = " AND ";
  joinClauses = build(keyword,'=');
  joinClauses = joinClauses.substring(0,joinClauses.length()-1);
  deselectAll(columns,indices);
  query += joinClauses;
}

  else if (source == enter){
  String keyword = "";
  if (firstJoin) {
    keyword = " WHERE ";
    firstJoin = false;
  }

  else
    keyword = " AND ";
  condition = build(keyword,'=');
  condition += fieldValue.getText();
  query += condition;
}

  else if (source == submit) {
    try {
      ResultSet rs = stmt.executeQuery(query);
      result.setText("");
      while(rs.next()) {
        String s = "";
        for(int i = 1; i <= count; i++)
        s += rs.getString(i) + ' ';                          // Note 21
        s += '\n';
        result.append(s);
      }
    }catch(Exception e) {
```

```
            e.printStackTrace();
        }
        submit.setEnabled(false);
        join.setEnabled(false);
        enter.setEnabled(false);
      }
    }

    public String build(String start, char c ) {              // Note 22
      String s = start;
      String[] colNames;
      for(int i = 0; i < indices.length; i++) {
        colNames = columns[indices[i]].getSelectedItems();
        for (int j = 0; j < colNames.length; j++) {
          s += tableName[indices[i]]+ '.' + colNames[j] + c;
        }
      }
      return s;
    }

    public void deselectAll(List[] columns, int[] indices) {   // Note 23
      for(int i = 0; i < indices.length; i++)
        for(int j = 0; j < columns[indices[i]].getItemCount(); j++)
          columns[indices[i]].deselect(j);
    }

    public static void main(String[] args) {
      SearchSales search = new SearchSales("Search Sales database");
      Toolkit toolkit = Toolkit.getDefaultToolkit();           // Note 24
      Dimension d = toolkit.getScreenSize();                   // Note 25
      search.setSize(d.width,d.height - 30);
      search.setLocation(0,30);                                // Note 26
      search.setVisible(true);
    }

    public class WindowClose extends WindowAdapter {
      public void windowClosing(WindowEvent e) {
        System.exit(0);
      }
    }
  }
```

....

Note 1:   We create a `List` box to hold the columns in each of the five tables in the `Sales` database.

Note 2:   We create the `Label` objects to which the `Label` array, `colLabel`, refers. The constructor for `colLabel` initialized these references to **null**.

Note 3:   Except for setting the insets to provide a border of five pixels around each component, we use the default values for the gridbag constraints.

Note 4:   Setting the `gridwidth` to `GridBagConstraints.REMAINDER` lets the list of tables use the remainder of the row. Because the `List` has a default width of 1, it is centered in the remaining two columns.

Note 5:   We want the text field to fill two columns, so we set the `gridwidth` to 2 and the `fill` to `GridBagConstraints.HORIZONTAL` so it will expand horizontally to fill the two-column space available.

Note 6:   `for(int i = 0; i < SIZE; i++) {`
This loop adds the five `List` boxes, one for each table of the `Sales` database.

Note 7:   `tables.add(tableName[i++]=rs.getString("TABLE_NAME"));`
This statement concisely achieves several objectives. It gets the next table name from the result set, assigns it to the `tableName` array for use later, increments the index i, and finally adds the table name to the tables list.

Note 8:   `indices = tables.getSelectedIndexes();`
We constructed the tables list to allow the user to select multiple items. The `getSelectedIndexes` method returns the array of index numbers corresponding to selected items.

Note 9:   `colLabel[indices[i]].setText(tableName[indices[i]]);`
Initially, we labeled the five tables, `Table1,...,  Table5`. We change the labels underneath the selected tables to their actual table names. We could have labeled all five tables correctly, but chose this to differentiate those tables the user selected from the unselected ones.

Note 10:   `colLabel[indices[i]].invalidate();`
Because the new label may have a different length, we later invoke the `val-idate` method to get the layout manager to redo the layout. Each changed label calls `invalidate` here so the layout manager will know that it needs to be laid out with its new size.

Note 11:   `fromTables += tableName[indices[i]] +',';`
We save the names of the selected tables in a string, separated by commas, to use after `FROM` when we construct the SQL `SELECT` query.

Note 12:   `fromTables = fromTables.substring(0,fromTables.length()-1);`
This removes the last comma.

Note 13:   `ResultSet rs = dbMetaData.getColumns`
`    (null,null,tableName[indices[i]],"%");`
For each table the user selected, we get the names of its columns.

Note 14:   `columns[indices[i]].add(rs.getString("COLUMN_NAME"));`
We add each column name to the `List` box representing the selected table.

Note 15:   `validate();`
The gridbag layout manager will redo the layout, so components whose size has changed will be laid out properly.

Note 16:   `count += columns[indices[i]].getSelectedIndexes().length;`

We save the total number of columns in the result set for the query, obtaining it by adding up the number of columns selected in each `List` box. After executing the query, we use `count` to list the results.

Note 17:   `resultCols = build("",',');`

The `build` method combines the selected item into a string, using the second argument as the separator. The first argument is the initial value of the string.

Note 18:   `deselectAll(columns,indices);`

The `deselectAll` method deselects each of the selected items so the user does not have to manually deselect the previous choices before making selections at the next step toward building the query.

Note 19:   `query += resultCols + " FROM " + fromTables;`

We continue to build the query we wish to execute, adding the pieces we have constructed so far.

Note 20:   `if (firstJoin) {`

The first condition, if any, in the query follows WHERE, while the remaining conditions follow AND. We use the **boolean** variable `firstJoin` to specify whether or not this is the first condition.

Note 21:   `s += rs.getString(i) + ' ';`

For simplicity, we have not dealt with the types of each table column. Knowing the column type would allow us to use a more specific method than `getString`. For example, knowing the column has type INTEGER would allow us to use the `getInt` method, but the `getString` method will also work for every type, although sometimes the formatting will not be as nice.

Note 22:   `public String build(String start, char c ) {`

The `build` method combines the selected `List` items into a string. The `start` argument is the initial value of the string, while the argument `c` is the character used to separate the selected items.

Note 23:   `public void deselectAll (List[] columns, int[] indices) {`

For simplicity, this method deselects every column, even those the user had not selected. The arguments are the array of `List` boxes, one for each table, and the array of indices specifying which tables the user selected.

Note 24:   `Toolkit toolkit = Toolkit.getDefaultToolkit();`

The `Toolkit` class allows us to access some properties of the host platform.

Note 25:   `Dimension d = toolkit.getScreenSize();`

We get the screen size of the user's machine so we can size the frame to fill the screen. Setting the size using a fixed number of pixels, such as 500 by 300, as we have done in previous examples, will cause the frame to appear smaller on a higher resolution screen, and may make the frame too large for a low resolution screen.

Note 26:   `search.setLocation(0,30);`

The `setLocation` method allows us to position the frame; otherwise we get the default of (0,0) for its upper-left corner.

THE BIG PICTURE

A graphical user interface lets the user compose a query. At each stage the user presses a button which causes some actions to occur and instructions to appear in the text area. The user first selects the tables to be used, then the fields to be displayed. The user may add conditions by joining tables or requiring a field have a specific value. After pressing the `Submit` button, the user sees the results in the text area.

TEST YOUR UNDERSTANDING

TRY IT YOURSELF   24. Run Example 3.6 to execute the query which returns the customer names who placed orders on March 22, 1999, but this time add the condition that the `OrderDate` is March 22, 1999 before the join condition that `Customer.CustomerID = Orders.CustomerID`. This shows we can enter conditions in any order.

TRY IT YOURSELF   25. Modify Example 3.6 to remove the call to the `validate` method. Run the modified program and describe any changes from the original version.

TRY IT YOURSELF   26. Modify Example 3.6 to omit setting `gridwidth` to `REMAINDER` for the tables list. Run the modified program and describe any changes from the original version.

TRY IT YOURSELF   27. Modify Example 3.6 to omit setting the `fill` for the `fieldValue` text field to `HORIZONTAL`. Run the modified program and describe any changes from the original version.

SUMMARY

- Java Database Connectivity (JDBC), in the `java.sql` package, allows us to create database tables, insert, update, and delete data, and query a database from a Java program. Relational databases store data in tables, and each table has a key that uniquely identifies each row. As our example, we use the `Sales` database with five tables. The `Customer` table has `CustomerID` as its key. The `Orders` table has `OrderNumber` as its key, but also includes the foreign keys `CustomerId` and `SalespersonID` which refer to entries in the `Customer` and `Salesperson` tables so the information does not have to be duplicated in the `Orders` table. The `OrderItem` table has a compound key (`OrderNumber`, `ItemNumber`); we need both values to identify an order item.

- Structured Query Language (SQL) provides an interface to database systems from different vendors. Users can write statements that each database will translate to process the desired request. In this text, we use the `CREATE`, `INSERT`, `UPDATE`, `DELETE`, and `SELECT` statements. The `CREATE` statement defines data in a table. This statement may use data types that are valid in a particular database system. In this text, we use `VARCHAR(N)`, a variable size character string of maximum size N, `INTEGER`, and `DATE`, all of which are standard, and `CURRENCY` which is used in Microsoft Access.

- To use the JDBC we need a driver to translate from the JDBC interface to the commands used by the database system, which may reside on the user's machine or at a remote site. Loading the driver, using the **new** operator, or the `forName` method, causes it to register with `DriverManager`. The `getConnection` method connects to the database using a URL to specify the location of the database. In this text we use the `jdbc:odbc:Sales` URL because we use the `JdbcOdbcDriver` to translate to the older ODBC commands, which then use the ODBC driver for the Microsoft Access database system. `Sales` is the name of our ODBC database. Other database system will provide the URL's needed to access them. In this text, we do not discuss the other types of JDBC drivers available.

- Once connected to the database, we use the `createStatement` method to create a statement, whose `executeUpdate` method we can use to execute SQL statements to create a new table or to insert values into a table. We could also create and populate tables using the database system, outside of Java.

- To retrieve information from the database, we use the `executeQuery` method, which returns a `ResultSet`, to execute SQL `SELECT` statements. The `ResultSet` contains the rows that satisfy the query. To get the fields in a row, we use the `getXXX` method, where `XXX` is the type of the data, so we use `getInt` for an `INTEGER` field and `getString` for a `VARCHAR` field. We pass either the column number of the field or its name, so we could use `getString(1)` or `getString("CustomerName")` if `CustomerName` is the first column of the result set.

- The `SELECT` statement has various options, including a `WHERE` clause to add conditions, `SELECT DISTINCT` to remove duplicates, and `ORDER BY` to sort the result. A `SELECT` statement may refer to one table or may join information from several tables.

- Metadata describes data. The `DatabaseMetaData` class provides many methods which give information about the database. We can find the data types in uses, the names of its tables, and the names and types of the columns of each table. We use the `ResultSetMetaData` class to find the number of columns in a result set and the names and types of each column.

- Aggregate functions compute values using all the rows of the table. We use `SUM`, `MAX`, `MIN`, `AVG`, and `COUNT` in our examples. Prepared statements allow us to pass arguments to a statement to reuse it without having to repeat its translation to an efficient implementation in the database system. Transactions permit us to rollback SQL commands in the event the whole sequence did not complete successfully. The default is to commit each command as soon as it is executed, but we can change the default and use the `commit` statement to make the changes permanent only when appropriate.

- Our case study builds a graphical user interface for the `Sales` database, allowing users to specify various parts of a `SELECT` statement and execute it.

Program Modification Exercises

....

1. Modify Example 3.3 to pass the JDBC driver and the database URL as program arguments.

2. Modify Example 3.4 to pass the JDBC driver and the database URL as program arguments.

3. Modify Example 3.2 to read the data from a file to insert into the tables.

4. Modify Example 3.6 to use the most appropriate getXXX method rather than the getString method referred to in Note 21.

5. Modify Example 3.6 to allow >=, <=, >, and < operators in addition to =.

6. Modify Example 3.6 to check that exactly two columns, from different tables, have been selected when the user presses the Join button.

7. Modify Example 3.6 to add a checkbox to require that the query remove duplicates from the result.

8. Modify Example 3.6 to check that exactly one column has been selected when the user presses the Enter Value button.

9. Modify Example 3.6 to add column headings in the output.

10. Modify Example 3.6 to allow the user to keep executing queries.

11. Modify Example 3.2 to create a Sales1 database that is like Sales except it has LastName and FirstName fields, instead of CustomerName, in the Customer table.

Program Design Exercises

....

12. Write a graphical user interface for the Sales database which lists all customer names in one Choice box and all products in another. When the user selects a customer name and a product, and presses the Submit button, display a list with the customer name, product, quantity, and date of orders by customers with that name for that product. Use prepared statements wherever possible.

13. Write a graphical user interface for a salesperson using the Sales database. The salesperson should be able to enter new orders. Rollback the order, if, after part of an order has been entered, a part of the order cannot be filled because of insufficient quantity of a product.

14. Develop an Account database to use with an electronic banking system. provide a user interface for a client to transfer funds from one account to another. The user should be able to select the source and target accounts, and enter an amount to transfer.

15. Design and populate a database for a car rental system. Allow the client to check availability of a category of car, and to make reservations.

16. Design and populate a database for a record collection. Provide a screen for the collection's owner to add and remove items, to change entries, and to search.

17. Design and populate a database for sports records. Use an almanac or search the Web for sample data. Provide a screen for the user to add and remove items, to change entries, and to search.

4

Servlets and JavaServer Pages™

Introduction

Servlets add functionality to web servers. In contrast to applets, which we download and execute on the client, servlets execute on the server where they may connect to database servers and process information returning results in a web page to the client. Some web servers are able to include servlets, while others use a third-party tool to run them. We use the JRun tool, free from www.allaire.com, which includes a web server that we will use to test our servlets.*

HTML forms can pass information to servlets which process it and send results back to the client. In this approach the servlet includes sends a web page back to the client which includes presentation and content. By using server-side includes or JavaServer Pages the web page designer can focus on the presentation while the programmer handles the content.

---

* The free Apache web server for Unix or NT is available from www.apache.org. Setting up a web server is beyond the scope of this text.

With a three-tiered architecture, the client communicates with a servlet on the middle-tier which in turn connects with a database server on the third-tier. In this way clients do not have to connect directly to a database.

HTML connections are stateless, meaning that when a client connects again there is no record of previous connections. Session-tracking allows servers to maintain client information from one connection to the next, an essential feature needed for many web applications including web commerce.

OBJECTIVES:

- Use JRun to test servlets and JavaServer Pages
- Interact with servlets from HTML forms
- Use server-side includes to embed servlets in web pages
- Send the output of one servlet to another in a servlet chain
- Add database connectivity in a three-tiered architecture
- Use session-tracking to maintain user information
- Use JavaServer Pages to separate content from presentation

4.1 A First Servlet

We start with a simple servlet that just prints a welcome message, testing our servlet engine installation.

Servlets with the JSWDK or JRun

The servlet API (Application Programming Interface) is not part of the core Java packages, but rather one of the standard extensions using the package prefix, javax. We find it in the packages javax.servlet, javax.servlet.http, and javax.servlet.jsp. We obtain the servlet API with the JavaServer™ Web Development Kit (JSWDK) from Sun Microsystems, http://java.sun.com/products/jsp/download.html, or with JRun from Allaire Corp., http://www.allaire.com/. Both products include a web server to handle client requests and a servlet engine to run the servlets, but only JRun handles all the examples in this chapter. We use JRun, but will indicate how to use the JSWDK.

The simplest way to get started is to add our servlets in the default directory containing the tool's sample servlets. For the JSWDK the default directory is JSWDK_HOME\examples\Web-inf\servlets where JSWDK_HOME is the directory in which the JSWDK is installed. On Windows systems, executing startserver.bat in the JSWDK_HOME directory will start the JSWDK server and its servlet engine. (The startserver file works for Unix systems.)

For JRun, the default location for servlets is

```
JRUN_HOME\servers\default\default-app\web-inf\classes
```

where JRUN_HOME is the directory in which JRun is installed. Clicking *Start, JRun 3.0, Default server* the *Start* menu will start the JRun web server, which runs on port 8100, and the servlet engine.

Web server configurations specify the URL for servlet access. For example, in Example 4.1 we create a servlet, Welcome.java, compile it, and put Welcome.class in the default servlet directory for the tool we are using. Using the JSWDK web server, the URL to access the Welcome servlet is

```
http://localhost:8080/examples/servlet/Welcome
```

while using JRun the correct URL is

```
http://localhost:8100/servlet/Welcome
```

Generic Servlets

The GenericServlet class, in javax.servlet, defines a protocol-independent servlet. It handles the starting, stopping, and configuration of a servlet. The only method we need to override is

```
public abstract void service(ServletRequest req, ServletResponse res)
  throws ServletException, java.io.IOException
```

which handles a request from a client. The ServletRequest interface encapsulates the parameters sent from the client, while ServletResponse includes methods to access the properties of the server's response. The service method throws exceptions of types ServletException and IOException to its caller, so that we do not need to handle them inside the service body.

Our first servlet example, Welcome, just displays a welcome message, not processing any data from the client. Figure 4.1 shows the result when connecting from a browser using the JRun web server with the URL

```
http://localhost:8100/servlet/Welcome
```

Naturally, if the server were on another machine we would have used its IP address instead of localhost. The JRun web server by default invokes a servlet when we specify the /servlet path in the URL. This configuration is independent of the directory

Figure 4.1 The Welcome servlet

name where the servlet is stored. The servlet is a Java program, `Welcome.java`, which we compile in the usual way.

TIP

To make the servlet library available to the compiler we can include the JAR files in the classpath. Using JRun, we could add

```
JRUN_HOME\lib\ext\servlet.jar
```

to the classpath or compile and run using the option

```
-classpath .;JRUN_HOME\lib\ext\servlet.jar.
```

We could also connect to the server using another client such as our `VerySimple-Browser` with the command

```
java VerySimpleBrowser localhost 8100 /servlet/Welcome
```

which returns the uninterpreted HTML file, since our browser is very feeble.

EXAMPLE 4.1   **Welcome.java**

```java
/* A simple servlet which uses no data from the client */

import java.io.*;
import javax.servlet.*;

public class Welcome extends GenericServlet {
  public void service(ServletRequest req, ServletResponse resp)
                                throws ServletException, IOException {
    resp.setContentType("text/html");                           // Note 1
    PrintWriter out = resp.getWriter();                         // Note 2
    String message = "Welcome to Servlets";
    out.println("<html>");                                      // Note 3
    out.println("<head><title>Welcome Servlet</title></head>");
    out.println("<body><h1><strong>"+message+"</strong></h1></body>");
    out.println("</html>");
    out.close();
  }
}
```

Output using Internet Explorer (See Figure 4.1)

Output using java VerySimpleBrowser localhost 8100 /servlet/Welcome

```
<html>
<head><title>Welcome Servlet</title></head>
<body><h1><strong>Welcome to Servlets</strong></h1></body>
</html>
```

Note 1: We use the `setContentType` method to indicate the MIME type for the response. We could have also used the `setContentLength` method to specify the length of the response.

Note 2: The `getWriter` method conveniently encapsulates the details of creating a `PrintWriter`.

Note 3: We send several lines encoded with HTML, containing the response, to the client.

Using the Web Server

While we use the JSWDK and the JRun web servers in conjunction with their corresponding servlet engines to execute servlets, they can serve other files. Using JRun

```
JRUN_HOME\servers\default\default-app
```

is the default directory for the JRun web server. If we copy `jrunlogo.gif` from `JRUN.HOME\servers\default\demo-app` to this directory, browsing with the URL

```
http://localhost:8100/jrunlogo.gif
```

will return the image for JRun's logo. Using JSWDK the default directory for the web server is

```
JSWDK_HOME\webpages
```

Browsing with the URL

```
http://localhost:8080/FAQ.html
```

returns a frequently asked questions page for the JSWDK.

TIP
☞

Instead of entering the servlet URL in our browser, we can enter it in an anchor tag in an HTML file. For example, pointing a browser to `TryServlet.html` given by

```
<html>
<head><title>Try a Servlet</title></head>
<body><h3>The Welcome servlet displays a message</h3>
<p><h5><a href="http://localhost:8100/servlet/Welcome">
Try a servlet </a></h5>
</body></html>
```

will show a link to the Welcome servlet. Clicking on the link produces the result shown in Figure 4.1.

THE BIG PICTURE
Servlets add the power of Java programming to a web server. The servlet API is a standard Java extension, but not part of the core. Tools such as JRun enable web servers to use servlets and have their own servers for testing servlets. The generic servlet defines a protocol-independent servlet which we can use if we do not use details specific to HTTP requests and responses.

TEST YOUR UNDERSTANDING

TRY IT YOURSELF   1.   Put `Welcome.class` in the default servlet directory and enter the appropriate URL in a browser to execute the `Welcome` servlet.

TRY IT YOURSELF   2.   Point any browser to `TryServlet.html` and click on the link to execute the `Welcome` servlet. If not using `JRun`, modify the URL in `TryServlet` to the one need for the web server used.

TRY IT YOURSELF   3.   Put a file in the default directory for the web server you are using. Enter the appropriate URL for that file in a browser to see that the web server does serve files.

4.2   HTML Forms

The easy to use HTML has helped the World Wide Web to become a primary computing platform. HTML forms let the user submit information to a remote site. The HTTP protocol defines how web servers and clients communicate. A client sends GET and POST requests which may include data entered in forms. In fulfilling requests the server may have the servlet engine execute servlets. With GET we send any data as part of the GET command, while with POST we send the data separately. GET is useful for small amounts of data, while POST is more suitable when we need to send more data.

GET Requests

Extending the `HttpServlet` class, in the `javax.servlet.http` package, allows a servlet to use properties specific to HTTP requests and responses. To handle a GET request the `HttpServlet` class provides a `doGet` method

```
public void doGet (HttpServletRequest req, HttpServletResponse resp)
  throws ServletException, IOException;
```

to handle GET requests from a client. The first argument, an `HttpServletRequest` object, encapsulates the data sent by the client, while the second argument, of type `HttpServletResponse`, encapsulates the response information from the server. The `doGet` method throws exceptions of types `ServletException` and `IOException` to its caller, so that we do not need to handle them inside the `doGet` body.

When sending data in a GET request we can either append it to the URL or include it in the HTML file, letting the browser append it to the URL. In Example 4.2, we will send an order to the server, which will invoke our `GetOrder` servlet to respond. The first way to send our order when, for example, requesting food and drink, is:

```
http://localhost:8100/servlet/GetOrder?Order=Food and Drink
```

which gives the response shown in Figure 4.2. We use a question mark, ?, to begin the data. Since HTTP does not allow spaces in a GET request, the browser replaces the space by its ASCII value, hexadecimal 20, prefixed by the escape character, %, so that the GET request becomes

```
http://localhost:8100/servlet/GetOrder?Order=Food%20and%20Drink
```

We send GET data in the form of parameter values. In this example, we use an Order parameter, giving its value as Food and Drink. A variant of this approach includes the servlet URL in an anchor tag

```
<a href= "http://localhost:8100/servlet/GetOrder?Order=Food+and+Drink">
```

Figure 4.2   The GetOrder servlet

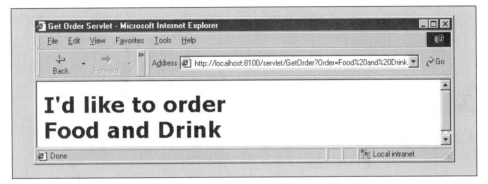

To explicitly use the GET command in our HTML file we use the form tag. Figure 4.3 shows an HTML file we can use for our GetOrder example.

Figure 4.3   GetOrder.html

```
<html>
<head><title>Get Order</title></head>
<body>
<h3>Enter an order</h3>
<form action="http://localhost:8100/servlet/GetOrder" method=GET>
Order: <input type=text name=Order size=20>
</form></body></html>
```

In the form tag we indicate the action we wish the server to apply to our data; in this example, the action is the URL for the GetOrder servlet. We fill in GET as the request method to use in the method attribute of the form tag. To make the form we can use input tags of various types. Here we use one input tag of type text, meaning a text field input, for the user to enter the order. We name it Order, by which the servlet will find it, and give it a size of 20 characters. Pointing our browser to GetOrder.html gives the web page of Figure 4.4. Filling in Food and Drink in the text field and hitting Enter will result in the same response as in Figure 4.2, except that Communicator replaces the spaces with + characters, using the URL

```
http://localhost:8100/servlet/GetOrder?Order=Food+and+Drink
```

Figure 4.4   An HTML form

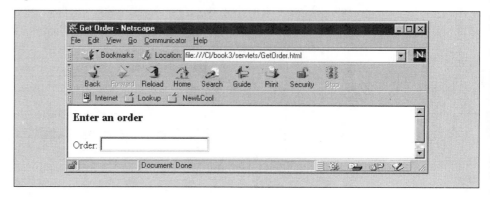

EXAMPLE 4.2   **GetOrder.java**

```
/* Echoes the user's order made in a GET request */

import java.io.*;
import javax.servlet.*;
import javax.servlet.http.*;

public class GetOrder extends HttpServlet {
    public void doGet(HttpServletRequest req, HttpServletResponse resp)
                throws ServletException, IOException {
        resp.setContentType("text/html");
        PrintWriter out = resp.getWriter();
        String message = req.getParameter("Order");                    // Note 1
        out.println("<html>");
        out.println("<head><title>Get Order Servlet</title></head>");
        out.println("<body><h1><strong>I'd like to order<br>");
        out.println(message+"</strong></h1></body>");                  // Note 2
        out.println("</html>");
        out.close();
    }
}
```

....

Note 1:   The getParameter method returns the parameter entered in an HTML form or appended directly to a URL.

Note 2:   Here we just echo the order back to the user.

POST requests

To include more data in our request we use the POST request, making a more extensive form for user input. Before going on we revise Example 4.2 to allow the user to submit an order either with a GET or a POST request. To use a POST request, we create PostOrGetOrder.html by changing the method in the GetOrder.html file of Figure 4.3 to POST. The HttpServlet class has a doPost method to handle POST requests. Since we are simply recreating Example 4.2, we delegate any POST requests to the doGet method, as shown in Example 4.3.

EXAMPLE 4.3   **PostOrGetOrder.java**

```java
/* Revises Example 4.2 to allow the user to order with
 * a POST request as well as a GET request
 */

import java.io.*;
import javax.servlet.*;
import javax.servlet.http.*;

public class PostOrGetOrder extends HttpServlet {

  // the doGet method is the same as in Example 2


  public void doPost(HttpServletRequest req, HttpServletResponse resp)
                    throws ServletException, IOException {
    doGet(req,resp);
  }
}
```

In Figure 4.5 we see that the browser does not include the data with the POST request. Thus using POST rather than GET is essential to keep the data sent private. Data set with a GET request is appended to the URL and displayed in the browser's address field.

Figure 4.5   PostOrGetOrder.html

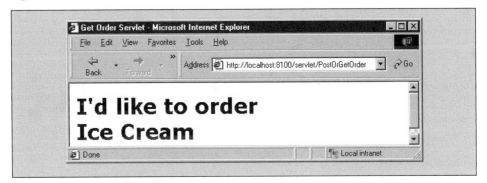

To send a more detailed order for an ice cream sundae, we add additional elements to an HTML form. Figure 4.6 shows the HTML file, while Figure 4.7 shows the form in a browser.

Figure 4.6 The `PostOrder.html` file

```html
<html>
<head><title>Post Order</title></head>
<body>
<form action="http://localhost:8100/servlet/PostOrder" method=POST>
  <strong>Name:</strong>
    <input type=text name=name size=20><br>
  <strong>Password:</strong>
    <input type=password name=password size=12><p>
  <strong>Flavor:</strong>
    <select name=flavor size=3>
      <option>Vanilla
      <option>Chocolate
      <option>Strawberry
    </select><p>
  <strong>Toppings:</strong>
    <input type=checkbox name=toppings value="Hot Fudge">  Hot Fudge
    <input type=checkbox name=toppings value="Butterscotch"> Butterscotch
    <input type=checkbox name=toppings value="Nuts">     Nuts
    <input type=checkbox name=toppings
      value="Whipped Cream">Whipped Cream <p>
    <input type=radio name=place value="Eat here"> Eat here
    <input type=radio name=place value="Take out"> Take out<p>
    <input type=submit value="Order">
    <input type=reset>
</form></body></html>
```

This form uses a text field to enter the customer's name. An `input` tag of type `password` is like a text field, but it hides the input. We use the `select` tag to get the list box for the ice cream flavors. Each `option` tag within the `select` tag specifies an item in the list. We can only select one flavor from the list. To enable multiple selections we could add the attribute `multiple` to the `select` tag.

We use the `input` tag of type `checkbox` to allow multiple selections for toppings. We use the `radio` type to allow only one choice of where to eat. The `submit` type creates a button to allow the user to submit the data to the server. The `value` attribute allows us to choose a name for the button. The `reset` type provides a button to allow the user to reset the form.

Figure 4.7 `PostOrder.html` displayed in a browser

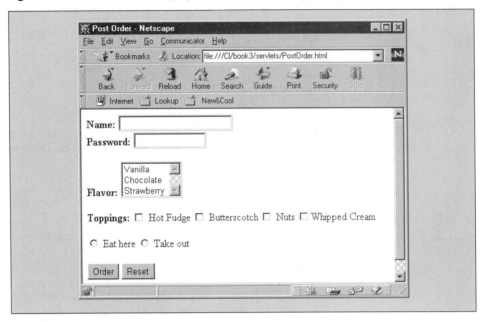

Filling in the form and pressing the *Order* button produces the result shown in Figure 4.8.

Figure 4.8 The `PostOrder` servlet

In the `PostOrder` servlet we get the values of the parameters submitted by the customer and send that information back to the client.

EXAMPLE 4.4   **PostOrder.java**

```
/* Echoes the user's order made in a POST request. */

import java.io.*;
import javax.servlet.*;
import javax.servlet.http.*;

public class PostOrder extends HttpServlet {
  public void doPost(HttpServletRequest req, HttpServletResponse resp)
                            throws ServletException, IOException{
    resp.setContentType("text/html");
    PrintWriter out = resp.getWriter();
    String message = req.getParameter("name");
    String result = req.getParameter("password");              // Note 1
    out.println("<html>");
    out.println("<head><title>Ice Cream Servlet</title></head>");
    out.println("<body><h1><strong>Hi " + message);
    out.println("</strong></h1><h3>");
    result = req.getParameter("flavor");
    out.println("Got your order for "+result+" ice cream<br>");
    String[] kinds = req.getParameterValues("toppings");       // Note 2
    if (kinds==null) out.println("with no toppings");
    else {
      out.println("with <ul>");
      for(int i=0; i<kinds.length; i++)
        out.println("<li>" + kinds[i]);
      out.println("</ul>");
    }
    result = req.getParameter("place");
    if (result.equals("Eat here"))
      out.println("to eat here.");
    else
      out.println("to go");
    out.println("</h3></body></html>");
    out.close();
  }
}
```

Note 1:   We get the password but make no use of it in this example.

Note 2: Whenever a parameter can have more than one value we use the getParameter-Values method which returns an array of String. We could use it instead of the getParameter method even when a parameter has only one value.

THE BIG PICTURE

HTML forms let users communicate with a web server. A GET request appends data to the URL, while a POST request sends data separately. The form tag has an action attribute that specifies the program on the server that will handle the form data, and a method attribute to specify the type of request. A form may include various input tags including text, password, checkbox, radio, submit, and reset types. We use the select tag to add a list. Servlets use the getParameter method to obtain the form data, and respond by sending an HTML page to the client.

TEST YOUR UNDERSTANDING

4. What change to Example 4.2 would we have to make if we change the name attribute in the HTML file of Figure 4.3 from Order to Choices?

5. In addition to modifying the HTML file of Figure 4.3 to use a POST request instead of GET, what other change do we need to make to it in order to use the servlet of Example 4.3?

TRY IT YOURSELF   6. Omit the value attribute of the submit type in the input tag of the HTML file of Figure 4.6. How will Figure 4.7 change as a consequence of this change?

4.3   Server-Side Includes and Servlet Chaining*

. . . .

In our previous examples clients communicated with servlets which sent entire HTML pages back to them. Thus the servlet writer had to handle the application's content and the HTML presentation to return to the client. Using a server-side include, we can embed the servlet response in a web page, so the servlet can focus on content. Servlet chaining lets us send the output of one servlet to another before presenting the results to the client.

The JSWDK server does not support server-side includes or servlet chaining, but it does handle JavaServer Pages which we cover later in this chapter. JavaServer pages can replace server-side includes, so this section may be omitted.

Server-Side Includes

Using server-side includes (SSI) we can embed servlets in web pages using the <servlet> tag. The web server which handles server-side includes serves the file in the usual manner, and in addition calls a special servlet to process the <servlet> tag. To alert the server, we use a special file extension such as .shtml to denote an HTML file which contains the <servlet> tag.

---

* See http://www.cecs.csulb.edu/~artg/internet/ch4changes.txt for an update to this section.

The default configuration for the JRun server uses this .shtml extension for server-side includes. We put .shtml files in the directory

```
JRUN_HOME\servers\default\default-app
```

when using the default web server included with JRun, and users can request these files via the URL http://localhost:8100/*file_name*.shtml

The path /servlet/ indicates a call by the server to the invoker servlet to execute a servlet. We have been using this path in our examples.

As an example we use a server-side include to call a servlet that tallies how many times a user has requested pages with a given subject. Figure 4.9 shows the .shtml file

Figure 4.9   TallyTest.shtml

```
<html>
<head><title>Tally Test</title></head>
<body>
<h2>Testing the Tally servlet</h2>
<servlet code=Tally codebase="http://localhost:8100/servlet/">
<param name=size value=3>
<param name=subject value=Test>
This server does not support server side includes.
</servlet>
</body></html>
```

The <servlet> tag uses the code attribute to specify the servlet to execute and the codebase to specify its URL. The Tally servlet will use the size and subject parameters specified using the <param> tag as in applets. The size parameter represents the size of the heading used to output the message, while the subject parameter represents a subject reflecting a type of request. We add a message after the param tag that displays only if the server does not support server-side includes. Our servlet will keep a separate tally of connections for each subject from clients who connect with that subject value. Figure 4.10 shows a client connecting using the subject Test.

Figure 4.10   Using a server-side include

We can add a server-side include to any HTML file. Our tally servlet tells us the number of connections. We can have several pages active at once, and the servlet will report connections according to subject. For example, we add the code

```
<servlet code=Tally codebase="http://localhost:8100/servlet/">
<param name=size value=3>
<param name=subject value=Order>
This server does not support server side includes.
</servlet>
```

to the `PostOrder.html` file of Figure 4.6 to create the `TallyOrder.shtml` file. Pointing our browser to the URL

```
http://localhost:8100/TallyOrders.shtml
```

will return the form of Figure 4.7, with the additional line

```
There has been 1 connection for Order since this servlet started.
```

Repeated connections to this URL will increase the count for the subject `Order`, each time. This will be distinct from the count for the `Test` subject shown in Figure 4.10.

The `Tally` servlet extends `GenericServlet` rather than its subclass `HttpServlet`, since it is not responding to GET or POST requests. We use a hash table to keep track of the number of connections from a given subject. In contrast to an array, which uses integer indices to find its elements, a hash table uses the data itself. In our example, we have a simple table

Subject	Number of connections
Order	1
Test	3

Using additional subjects would add entries to the table.

We create a hash table using the constructor

```
Hashtable table = new Hashtable();
```

for the `Hashtable` class in the `java.util` package. To make an entry we call

```
table.put("Order", new Integer(1));
```

for example, where we wrap the value 1 as an `Integer` object.. To retrieve an entry we call

```
Object o = table.get("Order");
```

which returns the value associated with `Order`.

EXAMPLE 4.5   Tally.java

```java
/* Uses a hash table to keep track of the number of
 * connections regarding a particular subject.
 */

import java.io.*;
import javax.servlet.*;
import javax.servlet.http.*;
import java.util.*;

public class Tally extends GenericServlet {
  int count;
  Hashtable table = new Hashtable();

  public void service(ServletRequest req, ServletResponse resp)
                  throws ServletException, IOException {
    resp.setContentType("text/html");
    String subject = req.getParameter("subject");
    Object o = table.get(subject);
    if (o==null)                                              // Note 1
    count = 0;
    else
    count = ((Integer)o).intValue();
    table.put(subject, new Integer(++count));                // Note 2
    PrintWriter out = resp.getWriter();
    String size = req.getParameter("size");
    String have = count==1?"has":"have";                     // Note 3
    String suffix = count==1?"":"s";
    out.println("<h" + size + "> There " + have + " been " + count   // Note 4
        + " connection" + suffix + " for <em>" + subject
        + "</em> since this servlet started </h" + size + ">");
    out.close();
  }
}
```

....

Note 1:   A **null** value from the hash table for a given subject means that there is no entry for that subject and we set count to 0. Otherwise, we cast the value to Integer and use the intValue method to get the **int** value of count.

Note 2:   We update the hash table, increasing count to reflect the current connection. We must wrap the **int** value in an Integer object, since the put method uses Object values.

Note 3:   We use the Java conditional expression to help us with grammar. When count is 1 we want to use has and to use have otherwise. A conditional expression of the form

```
condition ? true_value : false_value
```

has the value `true_value` if the condition is **true**, and `false_value` if the condition is **false**. The conditional expression is a short form of the **if-else** statement.

Note 4:   We use the `size` parameter to specify the size of the header tag in the HTML response.

Servlet Chaining

We can use servlet chaining to pass the output of one servlet as the input to another. As an example, we devise our own HTML tag, `<lucky>`. When this tag occurs in an HTML file we want the user to receive six lucky numbers. Since the `<lucky>` tag is not part of standard HTML, we use the `LuckyTag` servlet to process an HTML file, replacing the `<lucky>` tag by the six lucky numbers.

Two different methods will allow us to implement servlet chaining. The first chains the servlets in the URL; for example

```
http://localhost:8100/servlet/LuckyWelcome,LuckyTag
```

Figure 4.11 shows this approach.

Figure 4.11 Servlet chaining in the URL

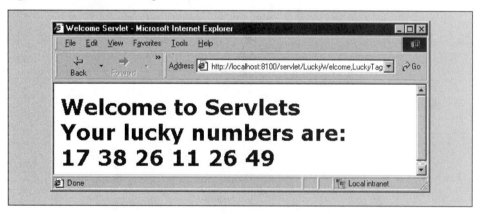

The second approach uses a MIME (Multipurpose Internet Mail Extensions) filter. We configure the web server to pass servlet output with a specified MIME content type to another servlet for further processing. We create a custom MIME type called `custom/lucky`. The LuckyWelcome servlet sets the content type to `lucky/welcome` to signify that it is sending output that contains the tag. In our example, we will configure the JRun default web server to pass output whose content is `custom/lucky` to the LuckyTag servlet, which will check for the tag.

To configure JRun, we use the JRun Management Console (JMC). We must first start the web server, which is different than the default server, by clicking on *Start, JRun Admin Server*. Entering the URL

```
http://localhost:8000
```

in the browser brings up the JMC. A user login box appears in which we enter the user name and password used during the JRun install. The default user name is `admin`.

Once logged in, we open the `JRun Default Server` entry in the left frame in the browser. Next, we open the `Web Applications` entry, and within that, the `Default User Application Entry`. Clicking on `MIME Type Chaining` brings up the frame of Figure 4.12

Figure 4.12 Using the `JRun` **Management Console**

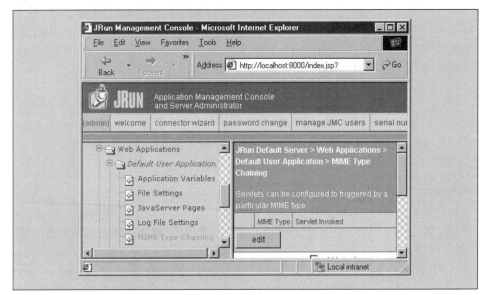

Clicking the `Edit` button brings up a window that allows us to associate the `LuckyTag` servlet with the MIME type `custom/lucky`. Any servlet whose output has content type `custom/lucky` will have that output filtered through the `LuckyTag` servlet. We enter `custom/lucky` as the MIME type and `LuckyTag` as the servlet invoked in Figure 4.13, and click on `Update`.

Figure 4.13 Configureing `JRun` **to use a MIME filter**

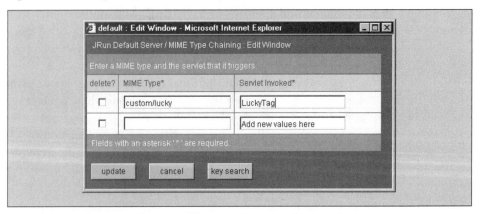

When we change the configuration, we must stop and restart the default server to use the new configuration. Since LuckyWelcome outputs an HTML file, the MIME filter will send it to the LuckyTag servlet to add the lucky numbers.

Figure 4.14 Using a MIME filter

EXAMPLE 4.6

LuckyWelcome.java

```
/* Includes the <lucky> tag which the LuckyTag servlet
 * interprets in a servlet chain or as a MIME filter
 */

import java.io.*;
import javax.servlet.*;
import javax.servlet.http.*;

public class LuckyWelcome extends HttpServlet {
  public void doGet(HttpServletRequest req, HttpServletResponse resp)
                         throws ServletException, IOException {
    resp.setContentType("custom/lucky");
    PrintWriter out = resp.getWriter();
    String message = "Welcome to Servlets";
    out.println("<html>");
    out.println("<head><title>Welcome Servlet</title></head>");
    out.println("<body><h1><strong>" + message + "<br>");
    out.println("<lucky></strong></h1></body>");                  // Note 1
    out.println("</html>");
    out.close();
  }
}
```

Note 1: The <lucky> tag is not standard HTML. The custom/lucky content must be sent to the LuckyTag servlet, either in a servlet chain, or using a MIME filter, to replace the <lucky> tag by a message with six random numbers.

EXAMPLE 4.7

LuckyTag.java

```
/* Replaces the <lucky> tag by a message
 * with six random numbers.
 */

import java.io.*;
import javax.servlet.*;
import javax.servlet.http.*;

public class LuckyTag extends GenericServlet {

  public void service(ServletRequest req, ServletResponse resp)
                            throws ServletException, IOException {
    resp.setContentType("text/html");
    BufferedReader in = req.getReader();
    PrintWriter out = resp.getWriter();
    String line;
    int index;
    while((line=in.readLine())!=null) {
      index = line.toUpperCase().indexOf("<LUCKY>");          // Note 1
      if(index == -1)                                         // Note 2
          out.println(line);
        else {
          out.println("<strong>Your lucky numbers are: <br>");
          for(int i=0; i<6; i++)
            out.println((int)(51*Math.random()+1)+ " ");
          out.println("<br>");
      }
    }
    in.close();
    out.close();
  }
}
```

Note 1:   Tags are not case sensitive, so we convert the line to upper-case before searching for the <lucky> tag.

Note 2:   We output lines unchanged which do not contain the <lucky> tag, but replace lines with the tag by a message with six random numbers. We leave it as an exercise to just replace the <lucky> tag by random number rather than the whole line containing it.

> ### THE BIG PICTURE
>
> Server-side includes use the `<servlet>` tag to include a call to a servlet in an HTML file. The servlet returns HTML lines which fit within the page rather than as a separate page.
>
> Using servlet chaining we can pipe the output of one servlet to another before sending results back to the client. One way to chain is to include both servlets in the URL. Another is to use a MIME filter. We configure the servlet engine to pipe the output of a servlet which outputs a particular MIME type, such as text/html, to another servlet. We use the second servlet to filter the output of the first before presenting it to the client.

TEST YOUR UNDERSTANDING

TRY IT YOURSELF   7. Browse `TallyTest.shtml` several times, either using different browsers, or pressing the *Reload* or *Refresh* button. Also browse `TallyOrders.shtml`. Describe the results.

8. Why do we need use the .shtml extension for HTML files which include the servlet tag?

TRY IT YOURSELF   9. Try to execute a servlet chain with the URL

   `http://localhost:8000/servlet/LuckyWelcome, LuckyTag`

   which includes a space between the two servlet names. Describe the result.

TRY IT YOURSELF   10. Write an HTML file with an anchor tag to use servlet chaining, rather than entering the URL directly in the browser.

4.4 Three-tiered Architectures

In a two-tiered client-server application, the client connects directly to a database server. The client handles the business logic, the code needed to implement the business model, as well as the presentation of the data. The inevitably frequent changes in business logic require changes to the programs running on each client. Adding a middle tier to handle business logic simplifies maintenance and does not require as much computational power on client machines.

Using a Database in a Three-tiered Architecture

We can use a servlet to access a database. In a three-tiered architecture, the client tier contains a user interface. The client connects to a middle-tier server that processes the client's request, accessing a database server in the third tier to store and receive information. In this way the business logic resides in middleware and can be changed without reconfiguring the various clients.

Our SalesServlet simply executes the client's SQL query. We leave it to the exercises to design a servlet to create a query from form information supplied by the client. In this example we provide a form with a text area for the user to enter a SQL query which the servlet executes.

Figure 4.15 Sales.html

```
<html>
<head><title>Sales</title></head>
<body>
<form action="http://localhost:8100/servlet/SalesServlet" method=POST>
  <strong>Select:</strong>
  <textarea cols=50 rows=8 name=select></textarea><p>
  <input type=submit value="Query">
  <input type=reset>
</form></body></html>
```

Figure 4.16 The Sales query form

In SalesServlet, we use the init method to connect to the database. Once we initialize the servlet, the connection to the database will remain while the servlet is active. Connecting to the database in the doGet method would require a new connection for each client request.

Figure 4.17   Result from the `Sales` query

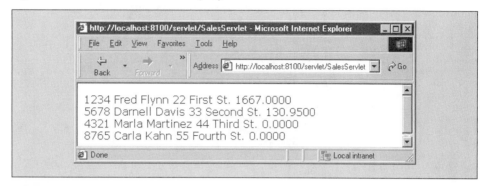

EXAMPLE 4.8   **SalesServlet.java**

```
/* Queries the Sales database. Needs to be modified
 * to use metadata to correctly output the result set.
 */

import java.io.*;
import javax.servlet.*;
import javax.servlet.http.*;
import java.sql.*;
import sun.jdbc.odbc.JdbcOdbcDriver;

public class SalesServlet extends HttpServlet {
  Connection con;
  Statement stmt;

  public void init(ServletConfig sc) throws ServletException {
    super.init(sc);                                               // Note 1
    try{
      new JdbcOdbcDriver();
      String url = "jdbc:odbc:Sales";
      String user = "";
      String password = "";
      con = DriverManager.getConnection(url, user, password);
      stmt = con.createStatement();
    }catch (Exception e) {
      e.printStackTrace();
      System.exit(1);
    }
  }
  public void doGet(HttpServletRequest req, HttpServletResponse resp)
                         throws ServletException, IOException {
    resp.setContentType("text/html");
    PrintWriter out = resp.getWriter();
    try{
      String query = req.getParameter("select");
      ResultSet rs = stmt.executeQuery(query);
```

```
        ResultSetMetaData rsMetaData = rs.getMetaData();
        int cols = rsMetaData.getColumnCount();
        while(rs.next()) {
          String s = "";
          for(int i=1; i<=cols; i++)
            s += rs.getString(i) + ' ';
          s += "<br>";
          out.println(s);
        }
      }catch(Exception e) {
        e.printStackTrace();
      }
      out.close();
    }
    public void doPost(HttpServletRequest req, HttpServletResponse resp)
                    throws ServletException, IOException {
      doGet(req,resp);
    }
}
```

....

Note 1: Always call the super.init method when overriding init.

THE BIG PICTURE
A three-tiered architecture configures business logic on a middle tier. The client handles the graphic presentation and communicates with the middle tier which handles the content. The middle tier stores and retrieves data from a database server on the third tier. This architecture keeps business logic in a central location making it easier and cheaper to perform updates. Powerful middle tier application servers can scale to meet the demands of serving many clients.

TEST YOUR UNDERSTANDING

TRY IT YOURSELF 11. Change the method in Sales.html in Figure 15 from POST to GET. Does the servlet still function properly? Why or why not?

TRY IT YOURSELF 12. Point a browser to Sales.html and enter a query to find the names of all the salespersons. Describe the result.

4.5 Session Tracking

Internet commerce will continue growing in importance. The HTTP protocol does not automatically maintain a connection, so that if a customer selects an item and moves to another page, perhaps for an additional item, the connection is lost. The vendor would like to keep the customer's information, including the items ordered, so that the customer can add items to the order and complete the purchase. The session tracking API lets a servlet keep track of clients from one connection to the next. Session tracking may be implemented using cookies which are bits of information sent by the web server to the client, which the client sends back to the browser when it accesses that page again. A cookie uniquely identifies a client.

We will use an `HttpSession` object to allow a servlet to maintain a session with each client. With an `HttpSession` object, we can store values using the `putValue` method and retrieve them using the `getValue` method. The HTML form of Figure 4.18 defines a form for the client to place an order.

Figure 4.18 `SessionOrder.html`

```html
<html>
<head><title>Session Order</title></head>
<body>
<form action="http://localhost:8100/servlet/SessionOrder" method=GET>
<strong><h3>Choose the items you would like to order.</h3></strong><p>
<input type=checkbox name=Order value="Java Book"> Java Book        <br>
<input type=checkbox name=Order value="Baseball">  Baseball         <br>
<input type=checkbox name=Order value="Bicycle">   Bicycle          <br>
<input type=checkbox name=Order value="Dress">     Dress            <br>
<input type=checkbox name=Order value="Shirt">     Shirt            <br>
<input type=checkbox name=Order value="Shoes">     Shoes            <br>
<input type=checkbox name=Order value="Theater tickets">
                                              Theater tickets <br>
<input type=checkbox name=Order value="Compact disk">
                                              Compact disk     <br>
<input type=checkbox name=Order value="Cellular phone">
                                              Cellular phone   <br>
<input type=checkbox name=Order value="Computer">  Computer         <p>
<input type=submit value="Order">
<input type=reset>
</form></body></html>
```

Figure 4.19 shows the order form. Submitting an order sends the user's choices to the `SessionOrder` servlet. The servlet sends back a list of all items ordered so far and the user's session id as Figure 4.20 shows.

Figure 4.19 An order form

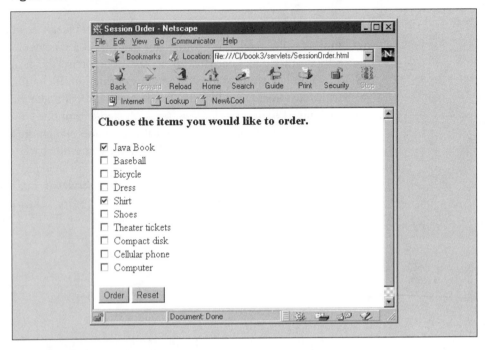

Figure 4.20 The response to an order

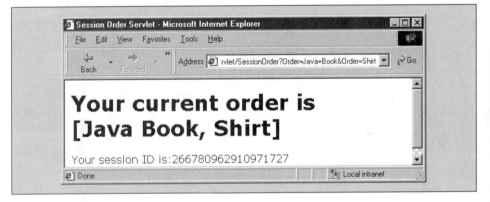

The SessionOrder servlet returns a list of the items ordered, and also displays the client's session ID. Since we use a GET request, the browser appends the items requested to the URL, in making the request.

Figure 4.21 shows the request from another customer and Figure 4.22 shows the servlet's response.

Figure 4.21 An order from another customer

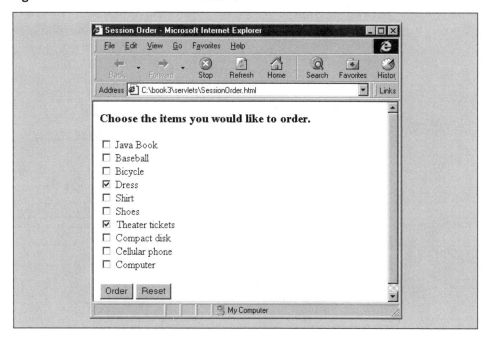

Figure 4.22 The servlet's response to the second customer

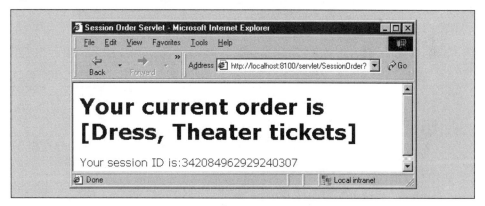

The servlet still remembers the order from the first customer. Figure 4.23 shows the response when that customer connects again, ordering shoes and a compact disk.

The SessionOrder servlet adds the new items maintaining all the items ordered by the first customer.

Figure 4.23 The response to an additional order

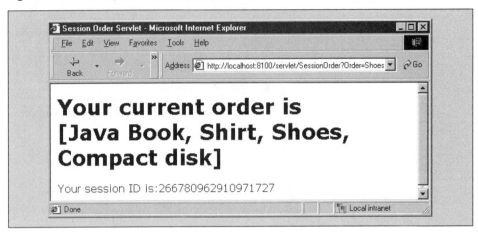

EXAMPLE 4.9   **SessionOrder.java**

```
/* Uses session tracking to maintain a customer's
 * information over multiple connections.
 */

import java.io.*;
import javax.servlet.*;
import javax.servlet.http.*;
import java.util.*;

public class SessionOrder extends HttpServlet {
  public void doGet(HttpServletRequest req, HttpServletResponse resp)
                         throws ServletException, IOException {
    resp.setContentType("text/html");
    PrintWriter out = resp.getWriter();
    HttpSession session = req.getSession(true);              // Note 1
    String[] newItems = req.getParameterValues("Order");
    Vector items = (Vector)session.getValue("items");        // Note 2
    if(items==null)                                          // Note 3
      items = new Vector();
    for(int i=0; i<newItems.length; i++)
      items.addElement(newItems[i]);                         // Note 4
    session.putValue("items",items);                         // Note 5
    out.println("<html>");
    out.println("<head><title>Session Order Servlet</title></head>");
    out.println("<body><h1><strong>Your current order is<br>");
    out.println(items + "</strong></h1><p>");
    out.println("Your session ID is:" + session.getId() + "<br>");
    out.println("</body></html>");
    out.close();
  }
}
```

Note 1:   The getSession method returns the current session. If the argument is **true**, it creates a new session if there is no current session.

Note 2:   The getValue method returns the Object associated with the argument "items". We cast it to a Vector which is what we are using in this example.

Note 3:   If items is **null** we have just begun a session and need to create a new Vector to hold the orders.

Note 4:   We add the newly chosen items to the Vector containing the previous choices.

Note 5:   Having updated items, we use the putValue method to save it, associated with the name "items".

THE BIG PICTURE

Session tracking allows the server to keep track of a client during multiple connections. Information the client sent will be saved so that the server can read it the next time the client connects. Using HTTP each client request requires a separate connection, so session tracking is essential for e-commerce applications. Session tracking may use cookies, bits of stored information, to save the data for later recall.

TEST YOUR UNDERSTANDING

TRY IT YOURSELF   13. Browse SessionOrder.html repeatedly, returning this page several times and making various choices of items. Describe the results.

TRY IT YOURSELF   14. Browse SessionOrder.html placing an order, and then open a new copy of the browser and browse SessionOrder.html again. Compare the results to those of Exercise 4.13.

4.6   JavaServer Pages (JSP)

JavaServer Pages make using servlets even simpler. JSP provides script tags to include Java code in a web page to create dynamic content. It automatically creates a servlet from the JSP page. We can call JavaBeans component methods to more cleanly separate application logic from web page presentation.

Getting Started with JSP

We use the JSP in place of the servlet of Example 4.2, in order to compare the two approaches to adding dynamic content to a web page. Using JSP, rather than writing a separate servlet class we add Java code directly in the web page returned to the client.

In writing a servlet we use an HttpServletRequest object to get parameters from the client and a PrintWriter to send a response. Both these objects are implicitly available in a JSP page, as request and out respectively.

JSP tags are case sensitive. In Example 4.10 we include a Java code fragment using

```
<% code fragment %>
```

In place of the servlet of Example 4.2, we write a JSP page, giving it a .jsp extension. We replace the action in the HTML file of Figure 4.3, which refers to the servlet of Example 4.2, by a reference to our JSP page. Figure 4.24 shows the revised HTML. We use a relative URL for the action, indicating that GetOrder.jsp can be found in the same directory as the HTML file. Browsing GetJspOrder.html will bring up the screen of Figure 4.4.

Figure 4.24 GetJspOrder.html

```
<html>
<head><title>Get Jsp Order</title></head>
<body>
<h3>Enter an order</h3>
<form action = GetOrder.jsp method=GET>
 Order: <input type=text name="Order" size=20>
    <input type=submit>
</form>
</body></html>
```

In Example 4.10 we write the web page we want to return in response to the client's request. We insert only one Java line in the response

```
<% out.println(" " + request.getParameter("Order")); %>
```

which says to echo the order the customer requested. When the user browses GetJspOrder.html and submits an order, the output will be the same as that of Figure 4.2 that resulted from using the servlet of Example 4.2.

EXAMPLE 4.10   **GetOrder.jsp**

```
<%-- JSP version of the servlet of Example 2 --%>                    // Note 1

<html>
<head><title>Get Jsp Order Results</title></head>
<body>
<h1><strong>

I'd like to order<br>

<%
 out.println(" " + request.getParameter("Order"));
%>

</strong></h1>
</body></html>
```

Note 1:   We use the `<%-- comment --%>` tag to insert a hidden comment that documents the file but is not sent to the client.

Comparing Example 4.10 to Example 4.2, we see how much simpler a JSP page can
be to write. We do not have to send HTML formatting from a servlet, but rather
augment the HTML page with Java code and let the servlet engine create the servlet.

To execute JavaServer Pages, we put the file `GetJspOrder.html` of Figure 4.24 and
GetOrder.jsp of Example 4.10 in the `JRUN_HOME\servers\default\default-app` direc-
tory, where `JRUN_HOME` is in the directory in which `JRUN` is installed. We browse the
URL

`http://localhost:8100/GetJspOrder.html`

when using a local machine, but replace localhost with the IP address of a remote site
if we are connecting to it.

Two stages occur in the processing. At HTML translation the JSP source file is
compiled to a servlet, using a Java compiler associated with the servlet engine. When
the client submits a request the servlet is executed.

A JSP Response to a Form

The simple form produced by the page of Figure 4.24 was easy to handle. For a more
complex example, we respond to the `POST` command of Figure 4.6, whose form is
shown in Figure 4.7, using JSP rather than the servlet of Example 4.4. The result of
processing the form by the JSP will be the same, shown in Figure 4.8. The
`PostJspOrder.html` file of Figure 4.25 is the same as the `PostOrder.html` file of Figure
4.6 except that the action is now a JSP rather than a servlet.

In the JSP of Example 4.11, we use an expression tag

`<%= expression %>`

where the expression can be any valid Java expression. We interleave Java code inside
scriptlet tags with HTML code. For example, the fragment

```
<% if (kinds==null) %>
with no toppings.
<% else { %>
with <ul>
<% for(i=0; i<kinds.length; i++) { %>
<li> <%= kinds[i] %>
<% } %>
</ul>
```

uses Java code to generate a web page. If the user did not choose any toppings, we
display "`with no toppings.`" Otherwise, we create an unordered list and display each
kind of topping as a list item. The Java code, including braces, goes in scriptlet tags,
`<%   %>`. We put the Java variable, `kinds[i]`, in an expression tag which we can insert
directly into the HTML.

Figure 4.25 PostJspOrder.html

```
<html>
<head><title>Post Order</title></head>
<body>
<form action="PostOrder.jsp" method=POST>
<strong>Name:</strong>    <input type=text name=name size=20><br>
<strong>Password:</strong> <input type=password name=password size=12><p>
<strong>Flavor:</strong>
<select name=flavor size=3>
<option>Vanilla
<option>Chocolate
<option>Strawberry
</select><p>
<strong>Toppings:</strong>
  <input type=checkbox name=toppings value="Hot Fudge">      Hot Fudge
  <input type=checkbox name=toppings value="Butterscotch"> Butterscotch
  <input type=checkbox name=toppings value="Nuts">            Nuts
  <input type=checkbox name=toppings value="Whipped Cream"> Whipped Cream<p>
  <input type=radio name=place value="Eat here"> Eat here
  <input type=radio name=place value="Take out"> Take out<p>
  <input type=submit value="Order">
  <input type=reset>
</form></body></html>
```

EXAMPLE 4.11   PostOrder.jsp

```
<!-- Echoes the user's order made in a POST request. -->       // Note 1
<% String message = request.getParameter("name");              // Note 2
String result = request.getParameter("flavor");
String[] kinds = request.getParameterValues("toppings");
int i;
%>
<html>
<head><title>Ice Cream Servlet</title></head>
<body><h1><strong>Hi <%= message %>                            // Note 3
</strong></h1><h3>

Got your order for <%= result %> ice cream<br>

<% if (kinds==null) %>
with no toppings.
<% else { %>
with <ul>
<% for(i=0; i<kinds.length; i++) { %>
<li> <%= kinds[i] %>
<% } %>                                                         // Note 4
</ul>
```

```
<% }
result = request.getParameter("place");
if (result.equals("Eat here"))
%>
to eat here.
<% else %>
to go.
</h3></body></html>
```

Note 1:   This comment is sent to the client in the page source, and not hidden.

Note 2:   The `request` object is implicitly available. It represent the POST request that the user made.

Note 3:   We use the `expression` tag to embed the value of the expression in the HTML file. In this case the `message` string represents the user's name entered in the form. The form includes a password field, but we do not use it to restrict access, leaving that improvement for the exercises.

Note 4:   The closing brace, }, is part of the Java code and not the HTML file, so we must enclose it in a scriptlet tag.

TIP   To import a package, use the page directive, as for example

☞   `<%@ page import="java.io.*" %>`

JSP and JavaBeans Components*

To further separate the content of a response from its presentation in HTML we can use the JavaBeans components that we will cover in a later chapter. For this section, all we need to know about JavaBeans is that they are Java programs which allow us to store and retrieve values using get and set methods. For example to store a name we use `setName("George")`, while to retrieve it we use `getName()`.

Example 4.12 shows the bean we will use. It contains methods to set and get the values associated with the sundae ordering of Example 4.11 which we will redo using this bean. We could add additional methods if desired.

EXAMPLE 4.12   **OrderBean.java**

```
/* A JavaBean to hold values from a form request
 */

package order;

  public class OrderBean {
  private String name = "Name";                              // Note 1
  private String password = "Password";
```

---

* See http://www.cecs.csulb.edu/~artg/internet/orderbean.txt for another example.

```
                    private String flavor = "Flavor" ;
                    private String[] toppings = {"Toppings"};
                    private String place = "Place";

                    public void setName(String n) {                              // Note 2
                      name = n;
                    }
                    public String getName() {                                    // Note 3
                      return name;
                    }
                    public void setPassword(String p) {
                      password = p;
                    }
                    public String getPassword() {
                      return password;
                    }
                    public void setToppings(String[] t) {
                      toppings = t;
                    }
                    public String[] getToppings() {
                      return toppings;
                    }
                    public void setFlavor(String f) {
                      flavor = f;
                    }
                    public String getFlavor() {
                      return flavor;
                    }
                    public void setPlace(String p) {
                      place = p;
                    }
                    public String getPlace() {
                      return place;
                    }
                  }
```

Note 1:   We declare one variable for each form value.

Note 2:   We declare one `set` method for each value we wish to set.

Note 3:   We declare one `get` method for each value we wish to retrieve. To retrieve a value there must be a corresponding `set` method to set the value.

The `PostJspOrderBean.html` file that we use to define our form is the same as Figure 4.25 except that the action is `PostOrderBean.jsp`. In that JSP file we introduce tags to use bean values.

To use a bean we use a `<jsp:useBean>` tag which may include various attributes. In our example we use the `id` attribute to refer to our bean, and the `class` attribute to specify its class file.

```
<jsp:useBean id="sundae" class="order.OrderBean" />
```

With the ⟨jsp:setProperty⟩ tag we can set some or all of the bean values sent by the client in the POST request. In our example, we set all the values using

```
<jsp:setProperty name="sundae" property="*" />
```

The name attribute gives the name of the bean, while the property attribute states which property to set. In this tag, the * value represents a wildcard that matches all properties, so all values sent by the client will be set in the bean.

We can retrieve bean values using the ⟨jsp:getProperty⟩ tag. For example, the tag

```
<jsp:getProperty name="sundae" property="name" />
```

retrieves the name property. We embed the returned value in the HTML code.

Inside the scriptlet tag we can call bean methods directly. In Example 4.13, we call

```
sundae.getToppings()
```

to retrieve the kinds of topping the client selected.

EXAMPLE 4.13   **PostOrderBean.jsp**

```
<!-- Echoes the user's order made in a POST request. -->

<jsp:useBean id="sundae" class="order.OrderBean" />
<jsp:setProperty name="sundae" property="*" />

<%
  String[] kinds;
  int i;
  %>
<html>
<head><title>Ice Cream Servlet</title></head>
<body><h1><strong>Hi <jsp:getProperty name="sundae" property="name" />
</strong></h1><h3>

Got your order for <jsp:getProperty name="sundae"
                                property="flavor" /> ice cream<br>
  <% kinds = sundae.getToppings();
  if (kinds==null) %>
with no toppings.
  <% else { %>
with <ul>
  <% for(i=0; i<kinds.length; i++) { %>
    <li> <%= kinds[i] %>
  <% } %>
</ul>
  <% }
    String result = sundae.getPlace();
    if (result.equals("Eat here"))
  %>
to eat here.
```

```
<% else %>
to go
</h3></body></html>
```

To execute this example using the JRUN

- Place `PostJspOrderBean.html` and `PostOrderBean.jsp` in the `JRUN_HOME\servers\default\default-app` directory.

- Create an `order` subdirectory of `JRUN_HOME\servers\default\default-app\web-inf\classes`.

- Compile `OrderBean.java` and place `OrderBean.class` in this directory.

- Browse `http://localhost:8100/PostJspOrderBean.html`.

THE BIG PICTURE

JSP allows the easy creation of server side HTML pages. JSP uses Java as a scripting language. Both JRun and the JSWDK have a server that handles JSP. JSP commands augment HTML to add dynamic content. A JSP page is compiled to a servlet which is executed when the client submits a request. JavaServer Pages can use JavaBeans components to respond to client requests.

TEST YOUR UNDERSTANDING

TRY IT YOURSELF   15. Modify `GetJspOrder` of Figure 4.24 to use a POST request instead of GET. What differences if any do you observe when sending an order?

TRY IT YOURSELF   16. What difference do you observe in effect of the comments between Example 4.10 and Example 4.11?

17. In Example 4.13, what is the difference in usage between a bean method call and the `<jsp:getProperty>` tag?

SUMMARY

- Servlets extend the functionality of a web server. They can respond to GET and POST requests from web clients. A servlet can extend `GenericServlet`, using the service method to handle request, or extend `HttpServlet` and use the `doGet` or `doPost` methods to handle requests. A servlet has access to request and response objects to communicate with the client. Servlets may output HTML code to the client. HTML forms include various types of input including text fields, lists, checkboxes, radio buttons, and buttons.

- Server-side includes allow us to embed a servlet in a web page using a `<servlet>` tag. The server-side include response will be included with the response to the rest of the page. For example, we could add a server-side include to each page to display the date and time and other current information.

- Servlet chaining lets us direct the output of one servlet to another servlet to filter the output before sending it back to the client. We can chain two servlets in a URL, or configure the server to use a MIME filter, sending every file of a certain type to the servlet filter.

- Three-tiered architecture allows the client to concentrate on presentation, connecting to a middle-tier executing a servlet to implement the business logic and connect to a database on the third tier.

- Session tracking lets the server keep track of a client who makes multiple requests. Since HTTP is a stateless protocol, not saving information about the client, session-tracking is essential to enable electronic commerce applications.

- JavaServer Pages (JSP) add dynamic content to web pages. They use scripting to enhance HTML code. The resulting JSP page gets compiled to a servlet which executes when the client submits a request.

Program Modification Exercises

1. Modify the servlet of Example 4.1 to extend `HttpServlet` and to handle a GET request.

2. Modify Examples 4.6 and 4.7, so that the `<lucky>` tag does not have to be on a separate line.

3. Modify Example 4.7 so that it always returns distinct random numbers.

4. Modify Figure 4.15 and Example 4.8 to pass the JDBC driver name and the database URL from the HTML form to the servlet.

5. Modify Example 4.9 to allow the customer to delete items from an order.

PUTTING IT ALL TOGETHER 6. Use the `SearchSales` program, Example 3.6, to create the query to send to the `SalesServlet` of Example 4.8.

7. Modify Example 4.8 to create an SQL query from a form the user fills in, rather than having the user enter the query directly.

8. Modify Example 4.6 to add a `doPost` method to handle POST requests.

9. Modify Example 4.9 to add a `doPost` method to handle POST requests. Modify `SessionOrder.html` and browse it to test the revised servlet.

10. Modify Example 4.10 to use a JavaBean.

Program Design Exercises

11. Write a server-side include that displays the current date. Use the `Date` class to get the date. Add it to `GetOrder.html` so the output from the server will show the date.

12. Write a servlet filter that outputs the date in place of a `<date>` tag. Create an HTML page which includes a `<date>` tag and use a servlet chain to let the filter process it to ouput the date in the web page.

PUTTING IT ALL TOGETHER   13. Write an HTML page with a form for the user to select a favorite food. Write a servlet to save the client's response in a database, and output the number of clients who prefer each food.

14. Write an HTML page with a form for the user to select a favorite sport. Write a servlet to save the client's response in a hashtable, and output the number of clients who prefer each sport.

15. Write an HTML page with a form for the user to order a pizza with either thick or thin crust and a choice of toppings. Write a JSP page to echo this request back to the client.

16. Write an HTML page with a form for the user to order a pizza with either thick or thin crust and a choice of toppings. Write a JSP page which uses a JavaBean to echo this request back to the client.

CHAPTER

5 Swing

Introduction

The **Abstract Windowing Toolkit** (AWT) uses native methods to create heavyweight components that use the platform's windowing system. This gives components a different look and feel on each platform, rather than appearing uniformly on all platforms. The peer classes that Java uses to access the native code require extra resources. The AWT has a limited set of components for user interface design; professional designers need a more powerful system.

Swing is such a more powerful set of user interface components, implemented in Java so the components have the same look and feel across platforms. The user can change the look and feel among several choices. With a separate download one can use Swing with the JDK 1.1. It is included in the Java™ 2 platform along with other parts of the Java Foundation Classes such as a greatly enhanced 2D API, accessibility support, printing, cut-and-paste, clipboard, and drag-and-drop capabilities.

The SwingSet demo, found in \JAVA_HOME\demo\jfc\SwingSet\, where JAVA_HOME is the directory in which the JDK is installed, shows all the components in a very impressive way. In the Java™ 2 release, the Swing classes are in packages

197

starting with the `javax` prefix, meaning they are not part of the core Java packages but are a standard extension. The Swing classes appeared in other packages in earlier Java versions.

OBJECTIVES

- Convert AWT applets and applications to Swing.

- Make look and feel choices.

- Use buttons with images and borders.

- Take advantage of double buffering.

- Use lists, checkboxes, radio buttons, and combo boxes.

- Use menus and dialogs.

- Use tabs and tables.

5.1   Getting Started with Swing

We explore the Swing hierarchy of classes, show how to convert AWT applets and applications to Swing, and learn to specify the desired look and feel from among the three choices Java currently provides.

The Swing Classes

Many of the Swing classes have the J prefix. The `JComponent` class is a subclass of the AWT `Container` class. It is lightweight, having no native code peer. Figure 5.1 shows some of the Swing classes we will use.

Figure 5.1   Some Swing subclasses of `JComponent`

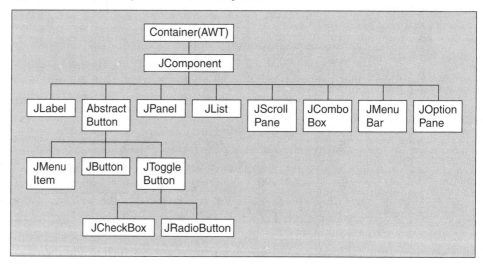

Converting an AWT Applet to Swing

Before Swing, applet writers used the AWT classes. We begin by converting an AWT applet to use Swing. Figure 5.2 shows the applet of Figure 5.3 that we will convert from AWT to Swing.

Figure 5.2   The applet of Figure 5.3

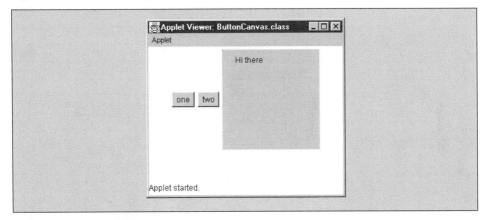

Figure 5.3   An AWT applet

```
import java.awt.*;
import java.applet.Applet;

public class ButtonCanvas extends Applet {
  public void init() {
    add(new Button("one"));
    add(new Button("two"));
    DrawOn canvas = new DrawOn();
    add(canvas);
    canvas.setBackground(Color.pink);
    canvas.setSize(150,150);
  }
  class DrawOn extends Canvas {
    public void paint(Graphics g) {
      g.drawString("Hi there",20,20);
    }
  }
}
```

To write an applet in Swing, we extend the JApplet class which is a subclass of Applet. We never add components directly to the outermost window, but rather call the get-ContentPane method to get a Container in which to add them.

Swing has no need for a `Canvas` class. We can subclass the `JComponent` or `JPanel` classes instead. Lightweight components can be transparent, taking on the color of their containing window in areas on which we do not draw. Extending `JComponent` always gives us transparency, but we can get a `JPanel` to paint its background, by calling its `paintComponent` method. For drawing in Swing, we use the `paintComponent` method rather than the `paint` method. To set the size we use the `setPreferredSize` method rather than the `setSize` method. Making these changes gives the applet of Example 5.1 shown in Figure 5.4. The **Metal** look and feel is the default in Swing. Later we will see how to change to another look and feel.

Figure 5.4 The Swing version of the applet

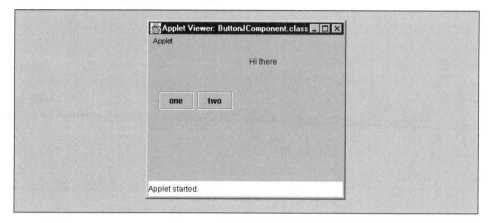

Example 5.1 overrides `JComponent` to draw on, so the drawing component is transparent and the background of the containing content pane shows through. It uses the Swing `JButton` class that we will discuss further in the next section.

EXAMPLE 5.1   **ButtonJComponent.java**

```
/* Converts the AWT applet of Figure 3 to Swing
 */

import javax.swing.*;                                          // Note 1
import java.awt.*;                                             // Note 2

public class ButtonJComponent extends JApplet {
  public void init() {
    Container c = getContentPane();
    c.setLayout(new FlowLayout());
    c.add(new JButton("one"));
    c.add(new JButton("two"));
    DrawOnJComponent canvas = new DrawOnJComponent();
//    canvas.setBackground(Color.pink);                        // Note 3
    canvas.setPreferredSize(new Dimension(150,150));          // Note 4
    c.add(canvas);
  }
```

```
class DrawOnJComponent extends JComponent {          // Note 5
   public void paintComponent(Graphics g) {
//      super.paintComponent(g);                     // Note 6
      g.setColor(Color.black);
      g.drawString("Hi there",20,20);
   }
  }
}
```

Note 1: The `javax.swing` package in Java 2 contains the basic Swing classes. Earlier releases used different package names.

Note 2: Even though it uses Swing components, this example also uses `Container`, `FlowLayout`, `Color`, `Dimension`, and `Graphics` classes from the AWT.

Note 3: We commented this line out because it would have no effect. A `JComponent` has no background.

Note 4: The `setPreferredSize` method takes an argument of type `Dimension`, rather than the `width` and `height` arguments used in `setSize`.

Note 5: We have no need for a `Canvas` class in Swing. We subclass `JComponent` here to draw on. In the next example we use a `JPanel`, which can have a background.

Note 6: `//super.paintComponent(g);`
The purpose of this line is to fill in the background. Because a `JComponent` has no background it has no effect and we comment it out. We will see it used with `JPanel` in the next example.

Figure 5.5   Using a `JPanel` to draw on

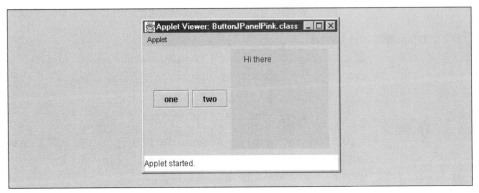

If we use a `JPanel` to draw on instead of a `JComponent`, we can fill in the background and make it pink, as in Figure 5.5. To do that we remove the two comments placed in the Example 5.1 code.

EXAMPLE 5.2 **ButtonJPanelPink.java**

```java
/* Converts Example 1 to draw on a JPanel instead of
 * JComponent and to fill in its background in pink.
 */

import javax.swing.*;
import java.awt.*;

public class ButtonJPanelPink extends JApplet {
  public void init() {
    Container c = getContentPane();
    c.setLayout(new FlowLayout());
    c.add(new JButton("one"));
    c.add(new JButton("two"));
    DrawOnJPanelPink canvas = new DrawOnJPanelPink();
    canvas.setBackground(Color.pink);
    canvas.setPreferredSize(new Dimension(150,150));
    c.add(canvas);
  }
  class DrawOnJPanelPink extends JPanel {
    public void paintComponent(Graphics g) {
      super.paintComponent(g);                              // Note 1
      g.setColor(Color.black);
      g.drawString("Hi there",20,20);
    }
  }
}
```

....

Note 1: Causes the JPanel to fill in its background. If we omit this line, the JPanel will be transparent and the applet will look like Figure 5.4.

Text Components and Labels

The JTextField class extends JTextComponent as does JTextArea, which we use in later examples. We use the constructors

```java
public JTextField(int columns)
public JTextArea(int rows, int columns)
```

and others are available. As with the corresponding AWT components, text fields hold a single line of text, while text areas can contain a number of rows. To access text we use the method

```java
public String getText()
```

while to replace it we use

```java
public void setText(String s)
```

We label a text component with a JLabel using the constructor

```
public JLabel(String label)
```

but we could also use

```
public JLabel(Icon icon)
```

which uses an icon for a label. We discuss the `Icon` interface in the next section. The `setText` and `setIcon` methods let us make changes to a label.

A Swing Application with Look and Feel Demo

A look and feel defines a consistent style for all components. Because the AWT uses the native windowing platform found on the host machine, AWT interfaces have the look and feel of the host windows. With Swing components we can choose the look and feel. The **Metal** look and feel is the default for Java, but we can also choose the **Windows** look and feel which will make our interfaces appear like those on Windows platforms, or the **Motif** look and feel which will cause them to look like Unix X-Windows applications.

Example 5.3 is a standalone application rather than an applet. A Swing application extends `JFrame` rather than `Frame`. As with a Swing applet, we enter components in the content pane rather than the frame itself, extend `JComponent` to draw rather than `Canvas`, and use `paintComponent` rather than `paint`.

To illustrate we develop an application in which the user enters an interest rate, an initial balance, and a number of years in text fields, and presses a button to see the final balance if the interest is compounded annually.[*]

We use the `UIManager.getInstalledLookAndFeels` method to show the choices for a look and feel, and the `UIManager.setLookAndFeel` method to dynamically install our choice. Figure 5.6 shows the **Metal** look and feel, while Figure 5.7 shows the one for **Motif**.

Figure 5.6 The **Metal** look and feel

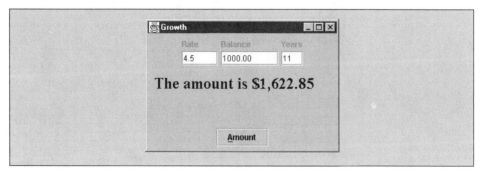

---

[*] Readers of *Computing with Java™: Programs, Objects, Graphics,* Art Gittleman, Scott/ Jones, Inc., 1998, will recognize this as a Swing version of Example 9.8, `Growth-Frame.java`.

Figure 5.7 The **Motif** look and feel

EXAMPLE 5.3   **GrowthFrameSwing.java**

```
/* Illustrate look and feel using a standalone application.
 */

import javax.swing.*;
import java.awt.*;
import java.awt.event.*;
import java.text.NumberFormat;
import java.util.Enumeration;

public class GrowthFrameSwing extends JFrame
                  implements ActionListener {
  private JTextField getRate = new JTextField(5);
  private JTextField getBalance = new JTextField(8);
  private JTextField getYears = new JTextField(3);
  private JLabel rate = new JLabel("Rate");
  private JLabel balance = new JLabel("Balance");
  private JLabel years = new JLabel("Years");
  private MyCanvas canvas = new MyCanvas();
  private JButton button = new JButton("Amount");
  private String amount = "Press button";
  private NumberFormat nf;

  public GrowthFrameSwing(String title, String[] args) {
    super(title);
    UIManager.LookAndFeelInfo[] info =
        UIManager.getInstalledLookAndFeels();                      // Note 1
    for(int i=0; i<info.length; i++)
      System.out.println(info[i]);
    try {
    UIManager.setLookAndFeel
        (info[Integer.parseInt(args[0])].getClassName());          // Note 2
    }catch(Exception e) {
      e.printStackTrace();
    }
```

```
      Container pane = getContentPane();
      JPanel p1 = new JPanel();
      p1.setLayout(new GridLayout(2,1));
      p1.add(rate);
      p1.add(getRate);
      JPanel p2 = new JPanel();
      p2.setLayout(new GridLayout(2,1));
      p2.add(balance);
      p2.add(getBalance);
      JPanel p3 = new JPanel();
      p3.setLayout(new GridLayout(2,1));
      p3.add(years);
      p3.add(getYears);
      JPanel p = new JPanel();
      p.add(p1);
      p.add(p2);
      p.add(p3);
      JPanel p4 = new JPanel();
      p4.add(button);
      pane.add(p,"North");
      pane.add(canvas,"Center");
      pane.add(p4,"South");
      addWindowListener(new CloseWindow());
      button.addActionListener(this);
      nf = NumberFormat.getCurrencyInstance();             // Note 3
   }
   public String computeGrowth() {
     double rate = new Double(getRate.getText()).doubleValue();
     double balance = new Double(getBalance.getText()).doubleValue();
     int years = new Integer(getYears.getText()).intValue();
     for (int i = 1; i <= years; i++)
       balance += balance * rate/100;
     return nf.format(balance);
   }
   public void actionPerformed(ActionEvent event) {
     amount = "The amount is " + computeGrowth();
     canvas.repaint();
   }
   public static void main(String [] args) {
     GrowthFrameSwing f = new GrowthFrameSwing("Growth",args);
     f.setSize(300,200);
     f.show();
   }
   class CloseWindow extends WindowAdapter {
     public void windowClosing(WindowEvent event) {
       System.exit(0);
     }
   }
```

```
class MyCanvas extends JComponent {
    public MyCanvas() {
    Font f = new Font("Serif",Font.BOLD,24);
    setFont(f);
    }
    public void paintComponent(Graphics g) {
      g.drawString(amount,10,30);
    }
  }
}
```

Output (java GrowthFrameSwing 0 produces Figure 5.6)
(java GrowthFrameSwing 1 produces Figure 5.7)

```
javax.swing.UIManager$LookAndFeelInfo
  [Metal javax.swing.plaf.metal.MetalLookAndFeel]
javax.swing.UIManager$LookAndFeelInfo
  [CDE/Motif com.sun.java.swing.plaf.motif.MotifLookAndFeel]
javax.swing.UIManager$LookAndFeelInfo
  [Windows com.sun.java.swing.plaf.windows.WindowsLookAndFeel]
```

Note 1:   The UIManager class keeps track of the current look and feel. The LookAnd-FeelInfo class is an inner class of UIManager. The getInstalledLookandFeels method returns a LookAndFeelInfo array. Each LookAndFeelInfo object displays two fields, the look and feel name and the name of the Java class that implements the look and feel.

Note 2:   The getClassName method of the LookAndFeelInfo class returns the class name of a class that implements this look and feel. The setLookAndFeel method uses this class name to set the look and feel. The integer 0 will generate the **Metal** look and feel because it is first in the look and feel array returned by the getInstalledLookAndFeels method. Similarly, index 1 generates **Motif**, and 2 generates the **Windows** look and feel.

Note 3:   We use the getCurrencyInstance() method of the NumberFormat class to output the resulting amount formatted in the local currency, dollars and cents in the United States.

THE BIG PICTURE

Swing provides many user interface components, greatly improving the limited selection in the AWT. We can easily convert AWT applets and applications to use Swing classes, and create transparent components. Look and feel classes let our windows conform to a desired style.

TEST YOUR UNDERSTANDING

TRY IT YOURSELF   1.   Uncomment the commented lines in Example 5.1 and rerun it. What can you say about the result?

TRY IT YOURSELF   2.   Comment the lines in Example 5.2 that are commented in Example 5.1 and rerun it. What can you say about the result?

TRY IT YOURSELF   3.   Figures 5.6 and 5.7 show Example 5.3 with the **Metal** and **Motif** look and feels. Run Example 5.3 with the **Windows** look and feel.

5.2   Images, Buttons and Borders

Using Swing we can add an image to a button or label, change the image when the mouse rolls over it or presses it, add a tool tip, and specify a keyboard mnemonic. We can add borders of various styles to our components. We start by looking at how Swing handles images so we can add images to our buttons.

Images

The `Icon` interface, for a small fixed-sized picture often used to decorate components, has three methods

```
int getIconHeight()
int getIconWidth()
void paintIcon(Component c, Graphics g, int x, int y)
```

The `paintIcon` method draws the icon at the location (x,y) and may use its `Component` argument to get properties such as the background color.

The `ImageIcon` class implements the `Icon` interface to paint icons from images. Images loaded from a URL automatically use a media tracker to wait for the images to load, so the programmer does not need to provide a media tracker explicitly. Two `ImageIcon` constructors are:

```
public ImageIcon(String filename)
public ImageIcon(URL location)
```

For example, for a local image file we can use

```
ImageIcon("images/gittleman.gif")
```

for the image `gittleman.gif` which is in the images subdirectory of the directory containing the `.class` and `.html` files. We use the forward slash separator on all systems because Java creates a URL to find the image. For a remote image of the Mona Lisa we can use

```
ImageIcon(new URL("http://www.paris.org"
  + "/Musees/Louvre/Treasures/gifs/MonaLisaa.gif"))
```

A general method of getting a URL from a file name uses the `getResource` method from the Class class, as in

```
ImageIcon(getClass().getResource("images/gittleman.gif"))
```

The `getClass` method gets the class of the applet and the `getResource` method uses the same class loader that loaded the applet to get the `.gif` file.

We can implement the `Icon` interface to get an icon that we can add to a button or a label. The `paintIcon` method specifies how to draw the icon. In Example 5.4 we create the `RoundIcon` class which implements the `Icon` interface to provide a round icon which we add to two buttons.

Buttons

From Figure 5.1, we see that the `JButton` class is a subclass of abstract button, along with `JMenuItem`, and `JToggleButton`, which itself has the`JRadioButton` and `JCheckbox` subclasses. We work with `JButton` in this section, leaving the other button types until later in the chapter.

We can add images to any of the button types. To add an image to a `JButton` we use the constructor

```
public JButton(String text, Icon icon)
```

The `setPressedIcon` method allows us to specify a different icon which appears when the user presses the button. The `setRolloverIcon` method sets an icon which appears when the user rolls the mouse over the button.

The `JButton` class has a `setMnemonic` method to allow users to push a button from the keyboard by holding down the Alt key while pressing the key passed as the argument to the method. Thus

```
print.setMnemonic('p')
```

enables `Alt + p` to activate the print button. The `setToolTipText` method displays the tip passed as its argument (and the mnemonic, if any) when the user holds the mouse over the button for a few seconds.

Borders

Swing border classes, from the `javax.swing.border` package, let us add a border to any Swing component. The types, with a constructor for each, are:

```
public BevelBorder(int bevelType)
```

The types `BevelBorder.RAISED` or `BevelBorder.LOWERED` determine if the border is raised or lowered.

```
public SoftBevelBorder(int bevelType)
```

Softens the corners of a bevel border.

`public CompoundBorder(Border outsideBorder, Border insideBorder)`
Combines an outside and an inside border.

`public EmptyBorder (int top, int left, int bottom, int right)`
Creates an empty border that takes up space.

`public MatteBorder(Icon tileIcon)`

Creates a matte border with the specified tile icon and default insets.

`public MatteBorder(int top, int left, int bottom, int right, Color color)`
Creates a matte border with the specified insets and color.

`public MatteBorder(int top, int left, int bottom, int right, Icon tileIcon)`
Creates a matte border with the specified insets and tile icon.

`public EtchedBorder(int etchType)`

The types `EtchedBorder.RAISED` or `EtchedBorder.LOWERED` determine if the border is etched-out or etched-in.

`public LineBorder(Color color, int thickness)`

Creates a line border with the specified color and thickness.

`public TitledBorder(Border border, String title)`

Creates a titled border with the specified border and title.

In Example 5.4, we use a titled border created from a matte border, and leave the experimentation with other types of borders to the exercises.

Figure 5.8 The `ButtonBorder` applet

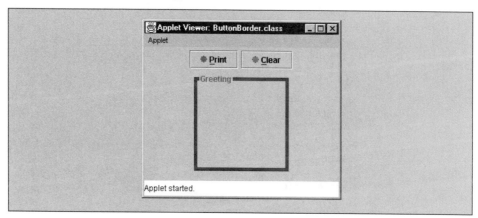

EXAMPLE 5.4   ButtonBorder.java

```java
/* Illustrates JButton with mnemonics, images, rollover images, and borders.
 */

import java.awt.*;
import java.awt.event.*;
import javax.swing.*;
import javax.swing.border.*;

public class ButtonBorder extends JApplet {
  private JButton print = new JButton("Print",
                          new RoundIcon(Color.yellow));          // Note 1
  private JButton clear =
                          new JButton("Clear",new RoundIcon(Color.red));
  private DrawOn canvas = new DrawOn();

  public void init() {
    Container c = getContentPane();
    c.setLayout(new FlowLayout());
    RoundIcon brightGreen = new RoundIcon(Color.green.brighter().brighter());
    RoundIcon white = new RoundIcon(Color.white);
    print.setPressedIcon(brightGreen);                          // Note 2
    print.setRolloverIcon(white);                               // Note 3
    print.setMnemonic('p');                                     // Note 4
    print.setToolTipText("Print a message");                    // Note 5
    clear.setPressedIcon(brightGreen);
    clear.setRolloverIcon(white);
    clear.setMnemonic('c');
    clear.setToolTipText("Erase the message");
    print.addActionListener(canvas);
    clear.addActionListener(canvas);
    c.add(print);
    c.add(clear);
    c.add(canvas);
    canvas.setPreferredSize(new Dimension(150,150));
    print.requestFocus();                                       // Note 6
  }
  class DrawOn extends JComponent implements ActionListener {
  String command = "";

  public DrawOn() {
    TitledBorder border = new TitledBorder(
                new MatteBorder(5,5,5,5,Color.blue),"Greeting");  // Note 7
    setBorder(border);                                          // Note 8
  }
```

```
  public void actionPerformed(ActionEvent event) {
    command = event.getActionCommand();
    repaint();
  }
  public void paintComponent(Graphics g) {
    if (command.equals("Print")){
      g.drawString("Hi there",20,60);
      g.drawString("You just pressed",20,80);
      g.drawString("the print button.",20,100);
    }
  }
}
class RoundIcon implements Icon {                       // Note 9
  public static final int SIZE = 10;
  Color color;
  public RoundIcon(Color c) {
    color = c;
  }
  public int getIconWidth() {
    return SIZE;
  }
  public int getIconHeight() {
    return SIZE;
    }
    public void paintIcon(Component c, Graphics g, int x, int y) {
      Color oldColor = g.getColor();
      g.setColor(color);
      g.fillOval(x,y,SIZE,SIZE);
      g.setColor(oldColor);
    }
  }
}
```

....

Note 1:   The second argument in this JButton constructor allows us to specify an image to place on the button.

Note 2:   We make the button image bright green when the user presses the button. We could also have used a different image.

Note 3:   We make the button image white when the mouse rolls over the button.

Note 4:   Keyboard users can press Alt+p to press this button.

Note 5:   When the mouse is over the button a tool tip pops up, explaining the effect of the button and giving the keyboard shortcut. The argument gives the text the tool tip displays.

Note 6:   We request the focus for the Print button, so the user can use the keyboard mnemonic to press it.

Note 7:   The first four arguments to the MatteBorder constructor give the insets from each direction. Other TitledBorder constructors create titles at various positions in the border.

Note 8:   The setBorder method installs the chosen border.

Note 9:   Implementing the Icon interface allows us to implement our own image to place on a button.

Automatic Double Buffering

Double buffering uses an offscreen image to do drawing, and then copies the offscreen image to the screen. This avoids the flicker that often occurs when drawing directly on the screen. The flicker results from clearing the screen between the drawing of successive frames of an animation. Using Swing automatically enables double buffering. The AnimateImage applet flickers using the AWT*, but does not when using Swing classes. We use the ImageIcon class to simplify the obtaining of an image.

EXAMPLE 5.5   AnimateImage.java

```java
/* Illustrate Swing's automatic double buffering.
 */

import java.awt.*;
import java.net.URL;
import javax.swing.*;

public class AnimateImage extends JApplet implements Runnable {
  private boolean done;
  private Image pic =
    new ImageIcon("images/gittleman.gif").getImage();      // Note 1
  private int imageWidth = pic.getWidth(null);
  private int imageHeight = pic.getHeight(null);

  public void init() {
    Container c = getContentPane();
    DrawOn canvas = new DrawOn();
    c.add(canvas);
  }
  public void start() {
    done = false;
    Thread t = new Thread(this);
    t.start();
  }
```

---

* For the AWT version of AnimateImage, see *Computing with Java: Programs, Objects, Graphics*, Art Gittleman, Scott/Jones Publishing, Inc., 1998, pp. 473–475.

```
public void stop() {
  done = true;
}
public void destroy() {
  done = true;

}
class DrawOn extends JComponent {
  public void paintComponent(Graphics g) {
    g.drawImage(pic,10,10,imageWidth,imageHeight,null);
  }
}
public void run() {
  int dx=20, dy=5;
    while (true) {
      for(int i=0; i<10; i++) {
      if (done) return;
      imageWidth += dx;
      imageHeight += dy;
      repaint();
      try {
        Thread.sleep(300);
      }catch(InterruptedException e) {
        e.printStackTrace();
      }
    }
    dx = -dx; dy = -dy;
  }
}
}
```

....

Note 1:   The getImage method returns the icon's image. It uses a media tracker so
the image will be fully loaded before we use it.

THE BIG PICTURE

The Swing image icon makes it easy to add an image to a button or a label. We can
draw our own icon to add to these components. Buttons may have a different
image when pressed as well as a rollover image. We may press the button from the
keyboard and a tool tip to remind users of its function. Borders decorate components. Swing includes several border styles. Swing provides automatic double buffering to avoid flicker in animations.

TEST YOUR UNDERSTANDING

TRY IT YOURSELF   4.   Remove the requestFocus call from Example 5.4. What happens when you rerun the modified example?

TRY IT YOURSELF   5.   Change the MatteBorder constructor used in Example 5.4 to MatteBorder(bright-Green). Describe the result. How does that compare with the result obtained from using MatteBorder(5,5,5,5,brightGreen)?

TRY IT YOURSELF   6.   Modify Example 5.5 to use the getResource method to get the image. If connected to the Internet, modify Example 5.5 to use the image of the Mona Lisa.

5.3   Lists and Toggle Buttons

· · · · · · · · · · ·

We discuss some useful Swing controls including JList, JScrollPane, JCheckbox, JRadioButton, and JComboBox. JRadioButton and JCheckbox, each a subclass of JToggleButton, have many similarities, as do JList and JComboBox which both hold lists of items.

Lists

Using an AWT List we have to add each element separately, but we can create a JList from an array or a Vector using the constructors

```
public JList(Object[] listData)
public JList(Vector listData)
```

Selecting an item from a JList generates a javax.swing.event.ListSelectionEvent. To handle such an event, we implement the ListSelectionListener interface, which has one method

```
public void valueChanged(ListSelectionEvent e)
```

and use the addListSelectionListener method to register with the JList.

We use the method

```
void setSelectionMode(int selectionMode)
```

to specify whether multiple selections are permitted. The selectionMode argument has three possible values

```
ListSelectionModel.MULTIPLE_INTERVAL_SELECTION
```
Select one or more contiguous ranges of indices at a time.

```
ListSelectionModel.SINGLE_INTERVAL_SELECTION
```
Select one contiguous range of indices at a time.

```
ListSelectionModel.SINGLE_SELECTION
```
Select one list index at a time.

The JList class uses an internal field that implements the ListSelectionModel to keep track of the list properties.

Scroll Panes

The JScrollPane class lets us add scroll bars to any component that implements the Scrollable interface, including JList and JTextComponent which is a superclass of JTextField and JTextArea. We use the constructor

```
public JScrollPane(Component view)
```

which passes the component which gets the scroll bars as an argument. We add the scroll pane to a container. In Example 5.6, we create a scroll pane from a list, giving the list vertical and horizontal scrollbars.

Checkboxes

In the AWT, the Checkbox class allowed the selection of multiple checkboxes, but adding checkboxes to a checkbox group would restrict the user to select exactly one of the group, making them behave like radio buttons. In Swing the JToggleButton class has two subclasses:

JCheckBox   usually allows multiple selections
JRadioButton   usually requires one and only one button to be selected
                       (as in the old-time radios).

The seven JCheckBox constructors allow us to specify some or all of the three arguments:

a String to identify the checkbox
an icon to add
whether the checkbox is selected initially

They are:

```
public JCheckBox()
public JCheckBox(Icon icon)
public JCheckBox(Icon icon, boolean selected)
public JCheckBox(String text)
public JCheckBox(String text, boolean selected)
public JCheckBox(String text, Icon icon)
public JCheckBox(String text, Icon icon, boolean selected)
```

In constructors without the boolean argument, the checkbox is initially unselected. These checkboxes generate an item event when their state changes. The ItemEvent class has a getStateChange method which returns SELECTED or DESELECTED. The getItem method returns an object which represents the item selected or deselected.

Example 5.6 uses JList, JScrollPane, and JCheckbox to produce the applet of Figure 5.9.

Figure 5.9   The `SelectMessage` applet

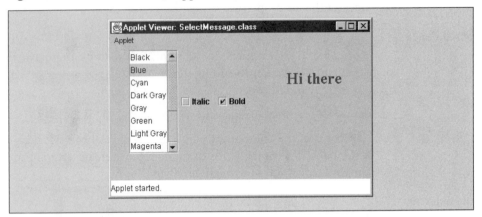

EXAMPLE 5.6   **SelectMessage.java**

```
/* Illustrates the use of JList, JScrollPane, and
 * JCheckbox components.
 */

import java.awt.*;
import java.awt.event.*;
import javax.swing.*;
import javax.swing.event.*;                                    // Note 1

public class SelectMessage extends JApplet {
  private DrawOn canvas = new DrawOn();
  private String [] colorName = {"Black","Blue","Cyan","Dark Gray","Gray",
    "Green","Light Gray","Magenta","Orange","Pink","Red","White","Yellow"};
  private JList names = new JList(colorName);                  // Note 2
  private JScrollPane color = new JScrollPane(names);          // Note 3
  private JCheckBox italic = new JCheckBox("Italic");          // Note 4
  private JCheckBox bold = new JCheckBox("Bold");
  private Color [] theColor = {Color.black,Color.blue,Color.cyan,
    Color.darkGray,Color.gray,Color.green,Color.lightGray,Color.magenta,
    Color.orange,Color.pink,Color.red,Color.white,Color.yellow};
  private String message = "Hi there";

  public void init() {
    Container c = getContentPane();
    c.setLayout(new FlowLayout());
    c.add(color);
    c.add(italic);
    c.add(bold);
      c.add(canvas);
      names.setSelectionMode(ListSelectionModel.SINGLE_SELECTION);
      names.setSelectedIndex(0);                               // Note 5
```

```
      names.addListSelectionListener(canvas);                      // Note 6
      canvas.setPreferredSize(new Dimension(150,150));
      italic.addItemListener(canvas);
      bold.addItemListener(canvas);
   }
   class DrawOn extends JPanel implements
                 ItemListener, ListSelectionListener {
      int style = Font.PLAIN;
      public void itemStateChanged(ItemEvent event) {
         Object source = event.getItem();
         int change = event.getStateChange();
         if (source == italic)
           if (change == ItemEvent.SELECTED)                        // Note 7
             style += Font.ITALIC;
           else
             style -= Font.ITALIC;
         if (source == bold)
           if (change == ItemEvent.SELECTED)
             style += Font.BOLD;
           else
             style -= Font.BOLD;
         repaint();
      }
      public void valueChanged(ListSelectionEvent e) {              // Note 8
         if (e.getValueIsAdjusting() == false)                      // Note 9
           repaint();
      }
      public void paintComponent(Graphics g) {
         super.paintComponent(g);
         g.setFont(new Font("Serif",style,24));
         g.setColor(theColor[names.getSelectedIndex()]);
         g.drawString(message, 50,50);
      }
   }
}
```

....

Note 1: The `javax.swing.event` package contains event classes such as `ListSelec-tionEvent` and `ListSelectionListener`.

Note 2: This `JList` constructor enters the strings from its array argument into the list.

Note 3: We pass the component to a `JScrollPane` to add scrollbars to it.

Note 4: We use the constructor that leaves the checkbox initially unchecked. To check it initially we could use the constructor

```
JCheckbox("Italic", true)
```

Note 5:   The `setSelectedIndex` initializes a `JList`, giving the index of the item initially selected.

Note 6:   `names.addListSelectionListener(canvas);`
A `ListSelectionListener` must implement the `valueChanged` method to respond to a `ListSelectionEvent`, which characterizes a change in the current selection.

Note 7:   `if (change == ItemEvent.SELECTED)`
We can select italic and/or bold styles. When we check the box, we select that style, and when we uncheck we deselect the style. When we select a style, we add its value to those selected, and when we deselect an item, we subtract its value.

Note 8:   `public void valueChanged(ListSelectionEvent e)`
We implement the `valueChanged` method to handle a `ListSelectionEvent`.

Note 9:   `if (e.getValueIsAdjusting() == false)`
Several changes occur when we make a selection. The previously selected item becomes deselected and the new item is selected. With multiple selections more changes occur. The `getValueIsAdjusting` method returns **false** only for the final event, at which point we repaint using the new selections.

Radio Buttons

A `JRadioButton`'s constructors are similar to those for `JCheckBox`.

```
public JRadioButton()
public JRadioButton(Icon icon)
public JRadioButton(Icon icon, boolean selected)
public JRadioButton(String text)
public JRadioButton(String text, boolean selected)
public JRadioButton(String text, Icon icon)
public JRadioButton(String text, Icon icon, boolean selected)
```
To insure the radio button property that exactly one button is selected, we add the radio buttons to a `ButtonGroup`. The user can select only one from the group. Radio buttons generate item events when selected or deselected.

Combo Boxes

The `JComboBox` is the Swing version of the AWT `Choice`. It is similar to a `JList` but displays only one item with the others displayed in a drop-down menu. We can construct it to hold an array or a vector of items using

```
public JComboBox(Object[] items)
public JComboBox(Vector items)
```

A combo box generates an item event when selected or deselected. The `getSelected-Index` method returns the index of the selected item.

Figure 5.10   The `SelectItem` applet

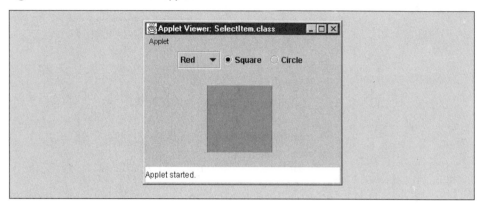

EXAMPLE 5.7   **SelectItem.java**

```
/* Illustrates JRadioButton and JComboBox.
 */

import java.awt.*;
import java.awt.event.*;
import javax.swing.*;

public class SelectItem extends JApplet {
  private DrawOn canvas = new DrawOn();
  private ButtonGroup group = new ButtonGroup();
  private JRadioButton square = new JRadioButton("Square");
  private JRadioButton circle = new JRadioButton("Circle", true);     // Note 1
  private Color [] theColor = {Color.red,Color.green,Color.blue};
  private String [] colorName = {"Red","Green","Blue"};
  private JComboBox color = new JComboBox(colorName);                  // Note 2

  public void init() {
    Container c = getContentPane();
    c.setLayout(new FlowLayout());
    c.add(color);
    group.add(square);                                                // Note 3
    group.add(circle);
    c.add(square);
    c.add(circle);
    c.add(canvas);
    canvas.setPreferredSize(new Dimension(150,150));
    color.addItemListener(canvas);
    square.addItemListener(canvas);
    circle.addItemListener(canvas);
  }
```

```
class DrawOn extends JPanel implements ItemListener {
  boolean isCircle = true;
  public void itemStateChanged(ItemEvent event) {          // Note 4
    Object source = event.getItem();
  if (source == circle)
    isCircle = true;
  else if (source == square)
    isCircle = false;
  repaint();
}
public void paintComponent(Graphics g) {
  super.paintComponent(g);
  g.setColor(theColor[color.getSelectedIndex()]);          // Note 5
  if (isCircle)
    g.fillOval(20,20,100,100);
  else
    g.fillRect(20,20,100,100);
  }
 }
}
```

....

Note 1:   Setting the second argument to **true** makes this button selected initially.

Note 2:   We construct the combo box to contain the color names in the array argument.

Note 3:   We add the square and circle radio buttons to a ButtonGroup to require that the user choose only one at a time.

Note 4:   The radio buttons and the combo box generate item events when their states change. When we select the radio button for a shape we set a flag and repaint so that shape will appear in the applet. When we select a color we just repaint, using the shape last selected.

Note 5:   We use the theColor array of colors to convert the string selected in the combo box to a Color.

THE BIG PICTURE

Swing has a number of user interface components. We can create a JList from an array or vector. Adding a JList to a JScrollPane will provide the list with scrollbars. Selecting a list item generates a list selection event. Both JCheckbox and JRadioButton extend JToggleButton. Each has seven constructors which let us choose to add a string, or an icon, or to initially select it. They generate an item event when the user makes a selection. We add radio buttons to a button group to require that exactly one radio button of the group is selected. A JComboBox may have multiple items, but only one is displayed. It also generates an item event to indicate a selection.

TEST YOUR UNDERSTANDING

TRY IT YOURSELF   7.   Omit the `setSelectionMode` statement from Example 5.6. Rerun the example and describe what happens.

TRY IT YOURSELF   8.   In Example 5.6, modify the constructor so that the *Italic* checkbox is selected initially. Rerun the example to see if the text is initially displayed in italics.

TRY IT YOURSELF   9.   Modify Example 5.7 to remove the button group. Rerun the example and describe what happens.

5.4   Menus and Dialogs
. . . .

The AWT had some classes for menus and dialogs, but Swing greatly extends Java's capabilities for these component types.

Menus

When using a menu, we create a `JMenuBar` and use the `setJMenuBar` method to install it in a `JFrame`. We create a `JMenu` for each menu, using the `add` method to place it on the `JMenuBar`, and create a `JMenuItem` for each item, adding it to its `JMenu`. We call the `addActionListener` method to provide a listener to respond to menu selections. In Example 5.8, we use menus to illustrate the various Swing dialog classes.

Dialogs

The `JOptionPane` class provides four types of dialogs, three of which, `Confirm`, `Option`, and `Input`, we illustrate in the *Feedback* menu shown as one of the menus in the menu bar of Figure 5.11. Each of these three provides feedback.

Figure 5.11   The *Feedback* menu of `MenuDialog`

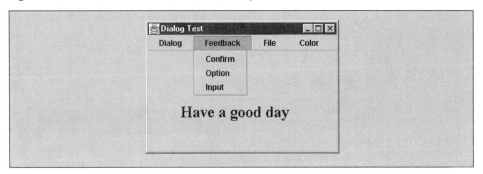

Pressing `Confirm` pops up the window of Figure 5.12, in which the user can choose `Yes`, `No`, or `Cancel`. The `showConfirmDialog` method returns the user's response to the program which in Example 5.8 responds with a message dialog saying `"Great!"`

Figure 5.12 A `Confirm` Dialog

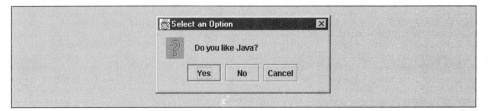

We can configure the `Option` dialog in many ways using the various parameters. Figure 5.13 shows the configuration in Example 5.8. Choosing `Quite well` causes the program to display a congratulatory message.

Figure 5.13 An `Option` dialog

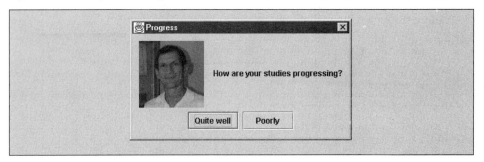

Pressing the *Input* menu item pops up an input dialog with a text field for user input and `OK` and `Cancel` buttons. In Example 5.8, we respond with a message echoing the user's input.

The `Message` dialog is the fourth type of dialog box provided by `JOptionPane`. The *Dialog* menu of Figure 5.14 shows the generic `Message` dialog, and then the five message dialog types, each of which includes a distinctive image and a message we have supplied as an argument. For example, Figure 5.15 shows the `Error` message, in which we specify both the title and the display message.

Figure 5.14 The *Dialog* menu

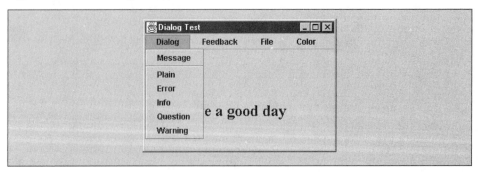

Figure 5.15 The `Error Message` dialog

The `File` menu in Example 5.8 has only one menu item, `Open`. When we press it a dialog pops up that lets us choose a file. We display the chosen file in a `JTextArea` of a new JFrame. The `Color` menu has one entry, `Choose`, which when pressed pops up the dialog of Figure 5.16. We repaint the text in the chosen color.

Figure 5.16   A Color dialog

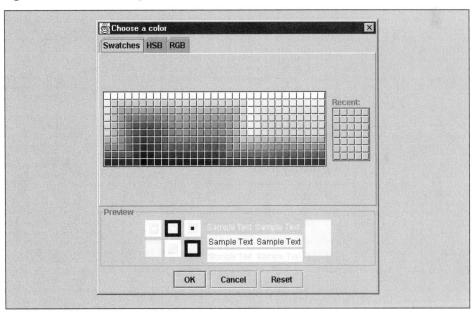

EXAMPLE 5.8   **MenuDialog.java**

```java
/* Illustrate some Swing menu and dialog features.
 */

import javax.swing.*;
import java.awt.*;
import java.awt.event.*;
import java.io.*;

public class MenuDialog extends JFrame
                        implements ActionListener {
```

```java
JMenuItem message = new JMenuItem("Message");
JMenuItem plain = new JMenuItem("Plain");
JMenuItem error = new JMenuItem("Error");
JMenuItem info = new JMenuItem("Info");
JMenuItem question = new JMenuItem("Question");
JMenuItem warning = new JMenuItem("Warning");
JMenuItem confirm = new JMenuItem("Confirm");
JMenuItem option = new JMenuItem("Option");
JMenuItem input = new JMenuItem("Input");
JMenuItem open = new JMenuItem("Open");
JMenuItem choose = new JMenuItem("Choose");
Color color = Color.black;
DrawOn canvas = new DrawOn();

public MenuDialog(String title) {
  super(title);
  Container c = getContentPane();
  c.add(canvas);
  JMenuBar bar = new JMenuBar();
  setJMenuBar(bar);

  JMenu dialogMenu = new JMenu("Dialog");
  bar.add(dialogMenu);
  dialogMenu.add(message);
  dialogMenu.addSeparator();
  dialogMenu.add(plain);
  dialogMenu.add(error);
  dialogMenu.add(info);
  dialogMenu.add(question);
  dialogMenu.add(warning);
  message.addActionListener(this);
  plain.addActionListener(this);
  error.addActionListener(this);
  info.addActionListener(this);
  question.addActionListener(this);
  warning.addActionListener(this);

  JMenu feedbackMenu = new JMenu("Feedback");
  bar.add(feedbackMenu);
  feedbackMenu.add(confirm);
  feedbackMenu.add(option);
  feedbackMenu.add(input);
  confirm.addActionListener(this);
  option.addActionListener(this);
  input.addActionListener(this);

  JMenu fileMenu = new JMenu("File");
  bar.add(fileMenu);
  fileMenu.add(open);
  open.addActionListener(this);
```

```java
    JMenu colorMenu = new JMenu("Color");
    bar.add(colorMenu);
    colorMenu.add(choose);
    choose.addActionListener(this);

    addWindowListener(new CloseWindow());
  }
  public void actionPerformed(ActionEvent event) {
    Object source = event.getSource();
    if (source == message)
      JOptionPane.showMessageDialog
                   (this,"Your message goes here");           // Note 1

    else if (source == plain)
      JOptionPane.showMessageDialog(this,"Very Plain",
        "Plain message", JOptionPane.PLAIN_MESSAGE);           // Note 2

    else if (source == error)
      JOptionPane.showMessageDialog(this,"Made an Error",
        "Error message", JOptionPane.ERROR_MESSAGE);

    else if (source == info)
      JOptionPane.showMessageDialog(this, "Information",
        "Some Info", JOptionPane.INFORMATION_MESSAGE);

    else if (source == question)
      JOptionPane.showMessageDialog(this, "?????????",
        "?????", JOptionPane.QUESTION_MESSAGE);

    else if (source == warning)
      JOptionPane.showMessageDialog(this, "This is a warning",
        "Uh-oh!!", JOptionPane.WARNING_MESSAGE);

    else if (source == confirm) {
    int answer =
      JOptionPane.showConfirmDialog(this,"Do you like Java?");
    if (answer == JOptionPane.YES_OPTION)
      JOptionPane.showMessageDialog(this,"Great!");
  }

    else if (source == option){
      int answer = JOptionPane.showOptionDialog(this,
        "How are your studies progressing?", "Progress",
        JOptionPane.DEFAULT_OPTION,
        JOptionPane.QUESTION_MESSAGE,
        new ImageIcon("images/gittleman.gif"),
        new String[] {"Quite well","Poorly"}, "Quite well");   // Note 3
      if (answer == 0)                                          // Note 4
        JOptionPane.showMessageDialog(this,"Great!");
    }
```

```
    else if (source == input){
      String name = JOptionPane.showInputDialog
                           (this,"Please enter your name");
      JOptionPane.showMessageDialog(this,"Hi " + name);
    }

    else if (source == open) {
      JFileChooser jfc = new JFileChooser();                      // Note 5
      int answer = jfc.showOpenDialog(this);
      if (answer == JFileChooser.APPROVE_OPTION) {                // Note 6
        File file = jfc.getSelectedFile();
        JFrame f = new JFrame(file.getName());
        Container c = f.getContentPane();
        JTextArea text = new JTextArea(10,50);
        JScrollPane scroll = new JScrollPane(text);               // Note 7
        c.add(scroll);
        int length = (int)file.length();
        char[] buffer = new char[length];
        try {
          BufferedReader br = new BufferedReader(new FileReader(file));
          br.read(buffer);                                        // Note 8
          text.setText(new String(buffer));                      // Note 9
          f.pack();
          f.setLocation(300,200);                                 // Note 10
          f.setVisible(true);
        }catch(IOException e) {
          e.printStackTrace();
        }
      }
    }
    else if (source == choose){
      color = JColorChooser.showDialog(this,"Choose a color",Color.yellow);
    }
    repaint();
  }
  class DrawOn extends JPanel {
    public void paintComponent(Graphics g) {
      super.paintComponent(g);
      Color oldColor = g.getColor();
      g.setColor(color);
      g.setFont(new Font("Serif",Font.BOLD,24));
      g.drawString("Have a good day",50,100);
      g.setColor(oldColor);
    }
  }
  public static void main(String [] args) {
    MenuDialog f = new MenuDialog ("Dialog Test");
    f.setSize(300,200);
    f.setVisible(true);
  }
```

```
class CloseWindow extends WindowAdapter {
  public void windowClosing(WindowEvent event) {
    System.exit(0);
  }
}
}
```

....

Note 1: The two arguments of the generic Message dialog, obtained using the show-MessageDialog method, are the component containing the dialog and the message.

Note 2: The additional two arguments for the special Message dialogs are the title and the message type.

Note 3: The eight arguments of the showOptionDialog method are:

parent Component
message
title
option type
  DEFAULT_OPTION
  YES_NO_OPTION
  YES_NO_CANCEL_OPTION
  OK_CANCEL_OPTION
message type
  ERROR_MESSAGE
  INFORMATION_MESSAGE
  WARNING_MESSAGE
  QUESTION_MESSAGE
  PLAIN_MESSAGE
icon
options
initial option

Note 4: The answer 0 represents the first option string, "Quite well."

Note 5: The JFileChooser class lets the user choose a file to open or save, using the showOpenDialog or showSaveDialog methods.

Note 6: `if (answer == JFileChooser.APPROVE_OPTION)`
The APPROVE_OPTION value represents a positive response such as clicking the OPEN button, while the CANCEL_OPTION represents a negative response such as clicking the CANCEL button.

Note 7: `JScrollPane scroll = new JScrollPane(text);`
As we did with the JList in Example 5.6, we add the JTextArea to a JScrollPane.

Note 8: `br.read(buffer);`
We read the entire file that we have selected.

Note 9: `text.setText(new String(buffer));`

We convert the character array to a string and enter it in the text area.

Note 10: `f.setLocation(300,200);`

Rather than accepting the default location of `(0,0)`, we position the frame at `(300,200)` so as not to cover the dialog.

THE BIG PICTURE

To use menus we create a menu bar, set it in a frame, and add menus with their menu items. Each menu choice generates an action event when the user presses it. `JOptionPane` provides `confirm`, `option`, `input`, and `message` dialogs. Types of `message` dialogs include `plain`, `error`, `information`, `question`, and `warning`. A file dialog lets the user choose a file, while a `color` dialog lets the user choose a color.

TEST YOUR UNDERSTANDING

TRY IT YOURSELF   10. Modify Example 5.8 to show a message dialog when the user presses the *No* button in the `Confirm` dialog.

TRY IT YOURSELF   11. Modify the option dialog of Example 5.8 to use `YES_NO_OPTION` for the option type, and **null** for the last three arguments. Describe how the resulting option dialog works.

TRY IT YOURSELF   12. Modify the option dialog of Example 5.8 to display a message when the user presses the *Poorly* button.

5.5   Tabs and Tables

. . . .

Tabbed components allow the user to select from multiple screens to provide more options without crowding a single screen. Swing tables can be configured to display data with great flexibility. We just introduce the basic table in this section.

Tabbed Panes

We construct a tabbed pane with the constructor

`JTabbedPane()`

which places the tabs on top. Using the constructor

`JTabbedPane(int tabPlacement)`

places the tabs at `SwingConstants.TOP`, `SwingConstants.BOTTOM`,`SwingConstants.LEFT`, or `SwingConstants.RIGHT`.

We use one of the methods

```
void addTab(String title, Component component)
void addTab(String title, Icon icon, Component component)
void addTab(String title, Icon icon, Component component, String tip)
```

to add a component as one of the tabs. The added components have indices 0, 1, 2, ..., determined in the order they were added. The `setSelectedIndex` method chooses the tab to display.

In Example 5.9 we illustrate a tabbed pane with two tabs, one for the `SelectItem` screen of Example 5.7 and one for the `SelectMessage` screen of Example 5.6.

Figure 5.17 The tabbed pane of Example 5.9

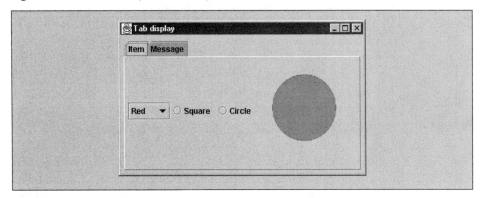

EXAMPLE 5.9   **Tabs.java**

```java
/* Illustrates a tabbed pane.
 */

import javax.swing.*;
import javax.swing.event.*;
import java.awt.*;
import java.awt.event.*;

public class Tabs extends JFrame {

  public Tabs(String title) {
    super(title);
    JTabbedPane tabPane = new JTabbedPane();
    Container c = getContentPane();
    c.add(tabPane);
    SelectItem item = new SelectItem();
    tabPane.addTab("Item",item);
    SelectMessage message = new SelectMessage();
    tabPane.addTab("Message",message);
    tabPane.setSelectedIndex(0);
    addWindowListener(new CloseWindow());
  }
  public static void main(String [] args) {
    Tabs t = new Tabs("Tab display");
    t.pack();// Note 1
    t.show();
  }
```

```
class CloseWindow extends WindowAdapter {
  public void windowClosing(WindowEvent event) {
    System.exit(0);
  }
}
class SelectItem extends JPanel {
  // same as SelectItem.java
}
class SelectMessage extends JPanel {
  // same as SelectMessage.java
}
}
```

....

Note 1:   The pack method arranges the components in the minimum space necessary.

Tables *

Swing provides a powerful table component JTable and a package, javax.swing.table, of utilities to help configure tables. A TableModel interface separates the data from views, so that we can display several different views of the same table, showing different columns or rearranging columns, for example. A TableColumnModel interface separates the column configuration from the data itself so that we can change columns without affecting the data model. A JTableHeader class manages table headers.

The methods of the TableModel interface are:

```
void addTableModelListener(TableModelListener 1)
```
Adds listener notified of changes to the data model.
```
Class getColumnClass(int columnIndex)
```
Returns the lowest common denominator Class in the column.
```
int getColumnCount()
String getColumnName(int columnIndex)
int getRowCount()
Object getValueAt(int rowIndex, int columnIndex)
boolean isCellEditable(int rowIndex, int columnIndex)
void removeTableModelListener(TableModelListener 1)
void setValueAt(Object aValue, int rowIndex,
                int columnIndex)
```

For simple tables, we do not need to use all of these capabilities. The AbstractTableModel class implements the TableModel interface, but the getRowCount, getColumnCount, and getValueAt methods are abstract. To use the AbstractTableModel class, we subclass it, implementing these three methods and optionally overriding others. In Example 5.10 we choose to also implement the getColumnName method to provide headings for each column. Otherwise Swing will create single-letter labels for each column.

Table entries must be objects, so we need to wrap primitive types in wrapper classes. The easiest way to provide data is to hardcode it into the program as an Object[][] array, and return these array values in the getValueAt method. We use a String[] array to specify the column names which we return in the getColumnName

---

* See http://www.cecs.csulb.edu/~artg/internet/TableDefault.java for another JTable example.

method. Using JDBC techniques we could present database tables in a `JTable`. We leave this enhancement for the exercises.

When we have created an instance of our subclass of `AbstractTableModel`, we pass it to the `JTable` constructor

```
JTable(TableModel dataModel)
```

Figure 5.18 The table of Example 5.10

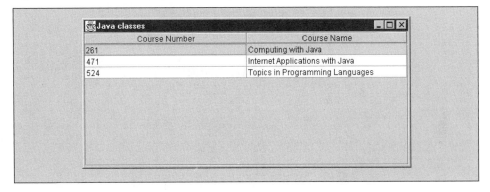

EXAMPLE 5.10   **Table.java**

```java
/* Illustrates a JTable.
 */

import javax.swing.*;
import javax.swing.table.*;
import java.awt.*;
import java.awt.event.*;

public class Table extends JFrame {
  public Table(String title) {
    super(title);
    Container c = getContentPane();
    JTable table = new JTable(new QuickModel());           // Note 1
    JScrollPane scrollpane = new JScrollPane(table);       // Note 2
    scrollpane.setPreferredSize(new Dimension(500,200));   // Note 3
    c.add(scrollpane);
    addWindowListener(new CloseWindow());
  }
  public static void main(String [] args) {
    Table t = new Table("Java classes");
    t.pack();
    t.show();
  }
  class QuickModel extends AbstractTableModel {
    Object[][] courses = { {"261", "Computing with Java"},
          {"471", "Internet Applications with Java"},
          {"524", "Topics in Programming Languages"} };
    String[] headings = { "Course Number", "Course Name" };
```

```
      public int getRowCount() {
        return courses.length;
      }
      public int getColumnCount() {
        return courses[0].length;
      }
      public Object getValueAt(int row, int col) {              // Note 4
        return courses[row][col];
      }
      public String getColumnName(int i) {                      // Note 5
        return headings[i];
      }
    }
  class CloseWindow extends WindowAdapter {
    public void windowClosing(WindowEvent event) {
      System.exit(0);
    }
  }
}
```

....

Note 1:   QuickModel is our subclass of `AbstractTableModel`.

Note 2:   We add our table to a scroll pane because in general it will not all fit in the display window.

Note 3:   Setting the preferred size reduces the amount of wasted space when the layout manager displays the table.

Note 4:   The `getValueAt` method uses the `courses` array to specify the data in the table.

Note 5:   The `getColumnName` method uses the `headings` array to specify the column headings.

The SwingSet provides much more than we are able to explore.

THE BIG PICTURE

Tabbed panes and tables help us to create professional looking user interfaces. Each tab provides a user interface for a facet of the application. Tables present data nicely in rows and columns without the need for the programmer to determine spacing. A table model separates the data from the views displayed.

TEST YOUR UNDERSTANDING

TRY IT YOURSELF   13. Modify Example 5.9 to make the *Message* tab appear on top initially.

TRY IT YOURSELF   14. Modify Example 5.10 to omit the `headings` array and the `getColumnName` method. Describe the changes to the table.

TRY IT YOURSELF   15. Modify Example 5.10 to add another row to the table. Make up your own course number and name.

SUMMARY

- Swing components allow us to develop professional looking user interfaces for applications and applets. Using Swing, we do not add components directly to the top level window or applet, but rather to a content pane container. For drawing we subclass `JComponent` or `JPanel` rather than the AWT Canvas class. Subclasses of `JComponent` always produce transparent components whose background shows through. When drawing on a `JPanel` we can use the `JPanel paintComponent` method to make it opaque.

- Because Swing uses lightweight components each component does not have a corresponding native object that uses the local windowing system. This reduces overhead and allows us to use different look and feels for our components. Swing provides a **Metal** look and feel, developed for Java, and **Windows** and **Motif** look and feels for Windows and Unix systems.

- Swing components have much more functionality than their AWT counterparts. We can easily add images, keyboard shortcuts, and tool tips to buttons, for example. Different images could appear when the user presses the button or when the user rolls the mouse over it. Borders decorate components in several possible styles.

- We can implement the `Icon` interface, for a small image to decorate components, to draw an icon, or we can use the `ImageIcon` to load a graphic image. The `ImageIcon` class uses a media tracker internally to fully load an image. The `getImage` method returns an `Image` object from an `ImageIcon`. Swing automatically uses double buffering to avoid flicker in animations.

- We construct a `JList` from an array of objects or a vector. Selecting a list item generates a list selection event which is handled by implementing the `valueChanged` method of the `ListSelectionListener` interface. A list may or may not allow multiple selections. Passing a list to the `JScrollPane` constructor will cause scrollbars to be added to view lists that do not fit in the available space.

- Check boxes and radio buttons may be labeled by text and/or icons and may or may not be selected initially. Typically, we put radio buttons in a button group so that exactly one will be selected. Check boxes and radio buttons generate item events. The `getItem` method returns an object that represents the item selected. The `getStateChange` method returns the type of item event, selection or deselection.

- We construct a combo box from an array of objects or a vector. A combo box differs from a list in that only one item shows and the other pop up. Selecting an item generates an item event. The `getSelectedIndex` method returns the index of the item selected.

- To use menus, we set a menu bar in a frame, adding menu items to menus which we add to the menu bar. Pressing a menu item generates an action event.

- Swing provides various dialogs to communicate with users. The JOptionPane class has methods to create message, confirm, input, and option dialogs. The message dialog can send a plain, error, information, question, or warning message. The constructor we used displays a default icon for each message type. Another constructor allow us to add our own icon. The confirm dialog allows the user to answer a question with choices like *Yes*, *No*, and *Cancel*. The input dialog prompts the user for input. The option dialog uses a constructor with eight arguments to allow us to customize the dialog messages, response buttons, and icon. A file dialog lets the user select a file, and a color dialog lets the user select a drawing color.

- Tabbed panes let us include more components than can fit on one screen. Tables display data in an attractive manner managing the details of its specific placement. A model separates the data from various presentations of it.

We do not have space to discuss all the many features of these and other Swing components.

Program Modification Exercises

. . . .

1. Modify Examples 5.1 and 5.2 to draw a happy face instead of printing a message. Rerun the examples and compare how they look.

2. Modify Example 5.6 to be able to change the look and feel. Run it with each of the three look and feel types and compare the results.

3. Modify Example 5.4 to pass the border type as a parameter. Run the applet with each of the Swing border types.

4. Modify Example 5.3 to add borders to each of the text fields, the button, and the canvas component.

5. Modify Example 5.6 to use a combo box instead of a list for the color names.

6. Modify Example 5.7 to use a JList instead of a JComboBox for the colors.

7. a. Convert Example 5.7 to a standalone application.

   b. Use menus for the colors and shapes instead of a combo box and radio buttons.

8. Modify Example 5.8 to draw an icon to display in the option dialog, rather than the image of the author.

9. Modify Example 5.9 to add a third tab for the GrowthFrameSwing component of Example 5.3.

10. Modify Example 5.10 to use Integer data for the course number rather than String.

PUTTING IT ALL TOGETHER 11. Modify the GetResponses class of Example 2.3 to present the responses in a Swing JTextArea. Let the user enter the URL in a JTextField.

PUTTING IT ALL TOGETHER 12. Modify the TryURLConnect class of Example 2.4 to present the responses in a Swing JTextArea. Let the user enter the URL and the strings to be reversed in a JTextField.

PUTTING IT ALL TOGETHER 13. Modify the ReverseClient class of Example 2.6 to present the server's responses in a Swing JTextArea. Let the user enter the URL and the lines to reverse in Swing JTextFields.

PUTTING IT ALL TOGETHER 14. Modify the VerySimpleBrowser class of Example 2.8 to present the responses in a Swing JTextArea. Let the user enter the URL in a JTextField.

PUTTING IT ALL TOGETHER 15. Modify the FortuneClient class of Example 2.13 to present the responses in a Swing JTextArea. Let the user enter the URL in a JTextField, and use Swing radio buttons to select a fortune for now or later.

PUTTING IT ALL TOGETHER 16. Modify the ExtractInfo class of Example 3.3 to present the responses in a Swing JTextArea.

PUTTING IT ALL TOGETHER 17. Modify the DatabaseInfo class of Example 3.4 to present the responses in a Swing JTextArea.

PUTTING IT ALL TOGETHER 18. Modify the Prepare class of Example 3.5 to present the responses in a Swing JTextArea.

PUTTING IT ALL TOGETHER 19. Convert the graphical user interface of Example 3.6 to use Swing components.

PUTTING IT ALL TOGETHER 20. Modify the SearchSales class of Example 3.6 to display the result of the query in a JTable.

Program Design Exercises
· · · · · · · · · · ·

PUTTING IT ALL TOGETHER 21. Write a Java program to enter an order in a Swing JTextField. Connect to a servlet which returns a message describing the order. Display the message in a JTextArea.

22. Write a Swing interface with menu items for an integrated development environment. Just implement the menu items to display a message, because we are not developing a programming environment tool, just the user interface.

23. Display sales figures for four items in each of five stores using a JTable.

24. Display sales figures for four items in each of five stores using a JTable. Add a menu with items for adding, inserting, and deleting a row. Add a row at the end of the table. Insert a row after the currently selected row. Use an input dialog to prompt for values. Before deleting the currently selected row, use a dialog to ask the user to confirm the deletion.

25. Use a button with an image of a square to trigger the drawing of a square, and a button with an image of a circle to draw a circle. Add a tip for each button and a mnemonic to allow it to be used from the keyboard. Include a `Color` menu item which pops up a color dialog to let the user choose the drawing color.

26. Use a `JTabbedPane`, providing one tab to input user data such as the name and address, and another to input information about a pizza order. Just echo the data submitted.

6

Java 2D™

Introduction

The Java 2D application programming interface provides for two-dimensional graphics and imaging, adding much to the original AWT to enable professional design. Java 2D requires the Java 2 platform and is being enhanced in new releases of that platform.

We cover geometry, rendering, text, and printing in this chapter.

OBJECTIVES

- Use the Shape interface
- Work with RectangularShape methods
- Combine shapes
- Transform shapes
- Paint using the solid, gradient, and texture styles
- Draw using Stroke styles
- Clip shapes and text
- Use text attributes
- Transform and Paint text
- Print graphics and files

6.1   Geometry

. . . .

The `java.awt.geom` package includes classes for defining and manipulating two-dimensional shapes. The simplest object is a point.

Points

The abstract `Point2D` class provides a common set of methods to operate on points. Inner classes `Point2D.Double` and `Point2D.Float` extend `Point2D`, each providing default constructors for a point at the origin,

```
Point2D pDOrigin = new Point2D.Double();
Point2F pFOrigin = new Point2F.Float();
```

and for a point at a specified position,

```
Point2D pDPlace = new Point2D.Double(3.5,4.7);
Point2D pFPlace = new Point2F.Float(3.5f,4.7f);
```

The `Point` class in `java.awt` provides points with integer coordinates.

Shapes

The `Shape` interface has been greatly enhanced in Java 2 and classes that implement it include

```
Polygon, RectangularShape, Rectangle, Line2D, CubicCurve2D,
Area, GeneralPath, QuadCurve2D.
```

The `RectangularShape` class has subclasses

```
Rectangle2D, RoundRectangle2D, Arc2D, Ellipse2D
```

Methods of the `Shape` interface include:

`boolean contains(double x, double y)`
    True if the shape contains the point (x,y).

`boolean contains(double x, double y, double w, double h)`
    True if the shape contains the rectangle with upper-left corner (x,y), width w, and height h.

`Rectangle getBounds()`
    Returns an integer rectangle that completely encloses the shape.

`Rectangle2D getBounds2D()`
    Returns a high-precision rectangle that bounds the shape.

`PathIterator getPathIterator(AffineTransform at)`
    Returns an iterator that provides access to the `Shape` boundary.

`boolean intersects(double x, double y, double w, double h)`
    True if the shape intersects the rectangle at (x,y) of width w and height h.

Figure 6.1 shows a rounded rectangle, its bounding box, a corner oval, and a rectangle that it intersects but does not contain, all produced in Example 6.1. We get a path iterator for the rounded rectangle that classifies each segment of the path. The notes explain the use of a path iterator.

Figure 6.1 Rounded rectangle, bounding box, corner oval, rectangle

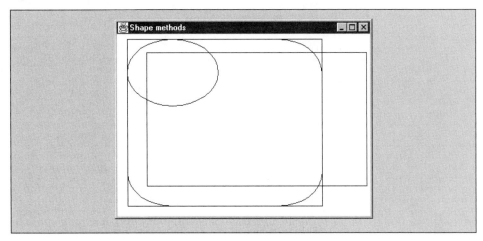

EXAMPLE 6.1   ShapeIt.java

```java
/* Illustrated the Shape interface methods.
 */

import java.awt.*;
import java.awt.geom.*;
import java.awt.event.*;
import java.text.*;

public class ShapeIt extends Frame {
  private RoundRectangle2D rounded =
    new RoundRectangle2D.Double(20.2,30.3,300.2,250.5,140.5,100);    // Note 1
  private Ellipse2D corner =
      new Ellipse2D.Double(20.2,30.3,140.5,100.0);                   // Note 2
  private PathIterator path = rounded.getPathIterator(null);        // Note 3

  public ShapeIt(String title) {
    super(title);
    addWindowListener(new WindowAdapter() {                         // Note 4
      public void windowClosing(WindowEvent e) {
        System.exit(0);
      }
    });
  }
  public void paint(Graphics g) {
  Graphics2D g2d = (Graphics2D)g;                                   // Note 5
  g2d.draw(rounded);
  g2d.draw(corner);                                                 // Note 6
  g2d.draw(rounded.getBounds2D());
  g2d.draw(new Rectangle2D.Double(50,50,340,200));
}
```

```
public void displayPath(PathIterator path) {
  NumberFormat nf = NumberFormat.getInstance();                    // Note 7
  nf.setMaximumFractionDigits(2);
  double[] p = new double[6];                                      // Note 8
  while (!path.isDone()) {                                         // Note 9
    int type = path.currentSegment(p);                            // Note 10
    switch(type) {
      case PathIterator.SEG_CLOSE:                                 // Note 11
          System.out.println("close");
      break;
          case PathIterator.SEG_CUBICTO:                          // Note 12
          System.out.println
            ("cubic to " + nf.format(p[4]) + ',' + nf.format(p[5]));
      break;
          case PathIterator.SEG_LINETO:                           // Note 13
          System.out.println
              ("line to " + nf.format(p[0]) + ',' + nf.format(p[1]));
      break;
          case PathIterator.SEG_MOVETO:                           // Note 14
          System.out.println
              ("move to " + nf.format(p[0]) + ',' + nf.format(p[1]));
      break;
          case PathIterator.SEG_QUADTO:                           // Note 15
          System.out.println
              ("quad to " + nf.format(p[2]) + ',' + nf.format(p[3]));
      break;
    }
    path.next();                                                  // Note 16
  }
}
public static void main(String[] args) {
  ShapeIt s = new ShapeIt("Shape methods");
  s.setSize(400,300);
  s.setVisible(true);
  System.out.println("Contains (300,200)? "
                + s.rounded.contains(300,200));                   // Note 17
  System.out.println("Contains 340x200 rectangle? "
                + s.rounded.contains(50,50,340,200));             // Note 18
  System.out.println("Intersects 340x200 rectangle? "
                + s.rounded.intersects(50,50,340,200));           // Note 19
    s.displayPath(s.path);                                        // Note 20
  }
}
```

....

Output (See Figure 6.1 for the graphical frame.)

```
Contains (300,200)? true
Contains 340x200 rectangle? false
Intersects 340x200 rectangle? true
```

```
move to 20.2,80.3
line to 20.2,230.8
cubic to 90.45,280.8
line to 250.15,280.8
cubic to 320.4,230.8
line to 320.4,80.3
cubic to 250.15,30.3
line to 90.45,30.3
cubic to 20.2,80.3
close
```

Note 1:   The abstract `RoundRectangle2D` class has two subclasses, the inner classes

```
RoundRectangle2D.Double
RoundRectangle2D.Float
```

The first four arguments give the dimensions of a rectangle with upper-left corner (20.2,30.3), width 300.2, and height 250.5. The last two arguments specify the width, 140.5, and height, 100, of the arc that rounds each corner. Figure 6.1 shows the full oval with width 140.5 and height 100. The actual corner size is half of these dimensions.

Note 2:   The abstract class `Ellipse2D` has two inner subclasses `Ellipse2D.Double`

```
Ellipse2D.Float
```

The arguments specify the dimensions of the bounding rectangle.

Note 3:   Passing **null** as the argument means that we do not transform the result. We consider affine transformations later in this section. The `PathIterator` interface includes methods

```
int currentSegment(double[] coords)
boolean isDone()
void next()
```

which we use in this example.

Note 4:   We use an anonymous inner class to provide the event handler to close the frame.

Note 5:   Java 2 passes a `Graphics2D` object to the `paint` method. We must cast `g` to `Graphics2D` to use the enhanced graphics context.

Note 6:   `g2d.draw(corner)`
Drawing this ellipse shows that the dimensions, 140.5 × 100, represent the whole oval even though only a portion of the oval is drawn as the rounded corner of the rounded rectangle.

Note 7:   `NumberFormat nf = NumberFormat.getInstance();`
We use a `NumberFormat` instance to output coordinates. After setting the maximum fraction digits to 2, the `format` method will display the numbers with two decimal places.

Note 8:   `double[] p = new double[6];`
Each segment of the path can be described by one or more points whose coordinates are stored in this array.

Note 9:   `while (!path.isDone()) {`
The `isDone` method returns **true** when there are no more segments to traverse in the path.

Note 10:   `int type = path.currentSegment(p);`
The `currentSegment` method returns the points describing the segment in the array `p` and the type of the segment as its return value. The segment types are `SEG_MOVETO`, `SEG_LINETO`, `SEG_QUADTO`, `SEG_CUBICTO`, or `SEG_CLOSE`.

Note 11:   `case PathIterator.SEG_CLOSE:`
The `CLOSE` segment closes the path by adding a line back to the most recent `MOVETO` which started that path.

Note 12:   `case PathIterator.SEG_CUBICTO:`
The `CUBICTO` segment represents a cubic curve (specified by a cubic equation). These mathematical curves can be very useful in scientific and graphics applications. The cubic segment uses all six elements of the array. Elements `p[4]` and `p[5]` represent the next point to which the segment is connecting. Points (`p[0]`,`p[1]`) and (`p[2]`,`p[3]`) are control points that we do not need to use. For the curious, a line from the first control point to the first endpoint of this segment will be tangent to the segment as will a line from the second control point to the second endpoint. We leave it to the exercises to show this graphically.

Note 13:   `case PathIterator.SEG_LINETO:`
The `LINETO` segment represents a line from the previous endpoint to (`p[0]`, `p[1]`).

Note 14:   `case PathIterator.SEG_MOVETO:`
The path iterator starts with a `MOVETO` segment to get to the starting point, (`p[0]`, `p[1]`), of the path.

Note 15:   `case PathIterator.SEG_QUADTO:`
The `QUADTO` segment represents a quadratic curve from the previous point to (`p[2]`, `p[3]`). Lines from the control point (`p[0]`, `p[1]`) to each of the endpoints of the segment will be tangent to the segment. We leave the illustration of this relationship to the exercises.

Note 16:   `path.next();`
The `next` method moves to the next segment of the path.

Note 17:   `s.rounded.contains(300,200)`
The `contains` method returns **true** if the shape, in this case the rounded rectangle, contains the given point.

Note 18: `s.rounded.contains(50,50,340,200)`

This version of the `contains` method returns **true** if the shape contains the specified rectangle, in this case with upper-left corner (50,50), width 340 and height 200.

Note 19: `s.rounded.intersects(50,50,340,200)`

The `intersects` method returns **true** if the shape has a non-empty overlap with the rectangle specified by the arguments.

Note 20: `s.displayPath(s.path);`

The `displayPath` method use its path iterator argument to describe the path. In this example, the iterator starts at the top of the line on the left and proceeds counterclockwise around the rounded rectangle.

Rectangular Shapes

We look at the `Rectangle2D`, `Ellipse2D`, and `Arc2D` abstract classes and their concrete subclasses for double values. Methods of the `Rectangle2D` class include:

```
abstract Rectangle2D createIntersection(Rectangle2D r)
```
Returns the largest rectangle contained in both rectangles.

```
abstract Rectangle2D createUnion(Rectangle2D r)
```
Returns the smallest rectangle containing both rectangles.

```
abstract int outcode(double x, double y)
```
Determines where the specified coordinates lie with respect to this `Rectangle2D`: top, bottom, left, right, or inside.

Figure 6.2 shows several rectangular shapes used in Example 6.2. Two `Rectangle2D.Double` objects colored green and blue, overlap. The `createUnion` method returns the smallest rectangle containing both which is the large rectangle in Figure 6.2, while the `createIntersection` method returns the largest rectangle contained in both, shown in white in Figure 6.2.

The three types of `Arc2D` objects appear in the bottom row of Figure 6.2, OPEN, PIE, and CHORD. The `Arc2D.Double` constructor we use takes seven arguments:

- the x- and y-coordinates of the upper-left corner of the bounding box
- the width of the bounding box
- the height of the bounding box
- the starting angle (in degrees, relative to the bounding box)
- the extent of the arc
  (in degrees, positive extending counterclockwise from the start)
- the type of arc, OPEN, PIE, or CHORD

For the pie arc we show the full ellipse of which it is a part and the bounding rectangle. Degree measure is relative to the bounding box. Our 45° starting angle is not a true 45° angle. It is defined to extend through the upper-right corner of the bounding rectangle. If the rectangle were a square, the angle would be true. For comparison, Figure 6.2 shows a line at a true 45° angle.

Figure 6.2   Rectangular shapes from Example 6.2

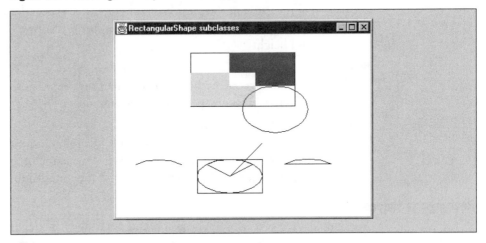

EXAMPLE 2   Rectangular.java

```java
/* Illustrates rectangular shapes.
 * (Subclasses of RectangularShape)
 */

import java.awt.*;
import java.awt.geom.*;
import java.awt.event.*;

public class Rectangular extends Frame {
  private Rectangle2D left =
    new Rectangle2D.Double(120.2,80.3,100.2,50.5);
  private Rectangle2D right =
    new Rectangle2D.Double(180.2,50.3,100.2,50.5);
  private Rectangle2D union = left.createUnion(right);
  private Rectangle2D intersect = left.createIntersection(right);
  private Ellipse2D oval = new Ellipse2D.Double(200.0,100.0,100,70);
  private Arc2D open =
        new Arc2D.Double(20,210,100,50,45,90,Arc2D.OPEN);      // Note 1
  private Arc2D pie =
        new Arc2D.Double(130,210,100,50,45,90,Arc2D.PIE);
  private Arc2D chord =
        new Arc2D.Double(250,210,100,50,45,90,Arc2D.CHORD);

  public Rectangular(String title) {
    super(title);
    addWindowListener(new WindowAdapter() {
      public void windowClosing(WindowEvent e) {
        System.exit(0);
      }
    });
  }
```

```
public void paint(Graphics g) {
  Graphics2D g2d = (Graphics2D)g;
  g2d.draw(union);                                              // Note 2
  g2d.setPaint(Color.green);
  g2d.fill(left);
  g2d.setPaint(Color.blue);
  g2d.fill(right);
  g2d.setPaint(Color.white);
  g2d.fill(intersect);                                          // Note 3
  g2d.setPaint(Color.black);
  g2d.draw(oval);
  g2d.draw(open);
  g2d.draw(pie);
  g2d.draw(chord);
  g2d.draw(new Line2D.Double(180,235,230,185));                 // Note 4
  g2d.draw(new Rectangle2D.Double(130,210,100,50));
  g2d.draw(new Ellipse2D.Double(130,210,100,50));
}
public void displayPosition(Rectangle2D r, double x, double y) {
  int position = r.outcode(x,y);                                // Note 5
  System.out.print(x + "," + y + " is ");
  if (position == 0) {                                          // Note 6
    System.out.println("Inside ");
    return;
  }
  if ((position & Rectangle2D.OUT_BOTTOM) != 0)                 // Note 7
    System.out.print("Below ");
  if ((position & Rectangle2D.OUT_LEFT) != 0)
    System.out.print("Left ");
  if ((position & Rectangle2D.OUT_RIGHT) != 0)
    System.out.print("Right ");
  if ((position & Rectangle2D.OUT_TOP) != 0)
    System.out.print("Above ");
    System.out.println();
}
  public static void main(String[] args) {
    Rectangular s = new Rectangular("Shape methods");
    s.setSize(400,300);
    s.setVisible(true);
    System.out.println("OUT_BOTTOM is " + Rectangle2D.OUT_BOTTOM);
    s.displayPosition(s.left,150,100);
    s.displayPosition(s.left,150,150);
    s.displayPosition(s.left,100,150);                          // Note 8
    System.out.println
        ("oval contains right: " + s.oval.contains(s.right));   // Note 9
  }
}
```

Output (See Figure 6.2)

```
OUT_BOTTOM is 8
150.0,100.0 is Inside
150.0,150.0 is Below
100.0,150.0 is Below Left
oval contains right: false
```

Note 1: This constructor creates an arc with bounding box upper-left corner (20,210), width 100, height 50, starting angle 45 degrees, extent 90 degrees swept out from the starting angle counterclockwise, and type `Arc2D.OPEN`.

Note 2: The `union` rectangle is the large rectangle in Figure 6.2 which contains both the `left` and the `right` rectangles.

Note 3: The `intersect` rectangle is the center white rectangle in Figure 6.2, common to both the `left` and `right` rectangles.

Note 4: This line is at a true 45° angle, which differs from the 45° starting angle of the arc which is measured relative to the bounding box.

Note 5: The `outcode` method returns the **logical or** of the constants `OUT_BOTTOM`, `OUT_TOP`, `OUT_LEFT`, or `OUT_RIGHT` of the `Rectangle2D` class to indicate the position (x,y) relative to the rectangle object.

Note 6: `if (position == 0)`
A value of 0 indicates that the point is inside the rectangle.

Note 7: `if ((position & Rectangle2D.OUT_BOTTOM) != 0)`
A point may have more than one location with respect to the rectangle. `Rectangle2d.OUT_BOTTOM` is 8 or 1000 in binary, meaning that bit 3 is set to 1. We check if bit 3 is set in `position` using the & operator which returns 1 only if the corresponding bit is set in both arguments. Because we know bit 3 is set in the right argument, the value of the & expression will be 1 if bit 3 is set in `position` and 0 otherwise.

Note 8: `s.displayPosition(s.left,100,150);`
The point (100,150) is both below and left of the rectangle s.left.

Note 9: `s.oval.contains(s.right)`
`Ellipse2D` inherits from `RectangularShape` this version of the `contains` method `boolean contains(Rectangle2D r)`

Combining Shapes

The `Area` class allows us to combine shapes, specifying an area using operations on previously defined areas, including `add`, `subtract`, `intersect`, and `exclusiveOr`. Methods of the `Area` class include:

```
Area()
```
Default constructor that creates an empty area.

```
Area(Shape g)
```
Creates an area geometry from the specified shape.

```
void add(Area rhs)
```
Adds the area to the current area.

```
void exclusiveOr(Area rhs)
```
The area becomes the area in either the current area or the argument, but not both.

```
void intersect(Area rhs)
```
The area becomes the intersection of the current shape and the shape of the specified area.

```
boolean isPolygonal()
```
Tests whether the area consists of straight edges.

```
boolean isRectangular()
```
Tests whether the area is rectangular in shape.

```
void subtract(Area rhs)
```
Subtracts the specified area from the current area.

Figure 6.3 shows the areas resulting from the add, subtract, intersect and exclusiveOr operations.

Figure 6.3   Combining areas

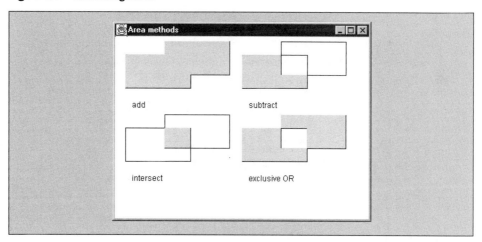

EXAMPLE 6.3   **Combining.java**

```
/* Combining area using the add, subtract, exclusive OR
 * and intersect operations.
 */
```

```java
import java.awt.*;
import java.awt.geom.*;
import java.awt.event.*;

public class Combining extends Frame {
  private Rectangle2D left1 = new Rectangle2D.Double(20,50,100,50);
  private Rectangle2D right1 = new Rectangle2D.Double(80,30,100,50);
  private Rectangle2D left2 = new Rectangle2D.Double(200,50,100,50);
  private Rectangle2D right2 = new Rectangle2D.Double(260,30,100,50);
  private Rectangle2D left3 = new Rectangle2D.Double(20,160,100,50);
  private Rectangle2D right3 = new Rectangle2D.Double(80,140,100,50);
  private Rectangle2D left4 = new Rectangle2D.Double(200,160,100,50);
  private Rectangle2D right4 = new Rectangle2D.Double(260,140,100,50);
  private Area area1 = new Area(left1);                     // Note1
  private Area area2 = new Area(right1);
  private Area area3 = new Area(left2);
  private Area area4 = new Area(right2);
  private Area area5 = new Area(left3);
  private Area area6 = new Area(right3);
  private Area area7 = new Area(left4);
  private Area area8 = new Area(right4);

  public Combining(String title) {
    super(title);
    area1.add(area2);                                        // Note 2
    area3.subtract(area4);
    area5.intersect(area6);
    area7.exclusiveOr(area8);
    addWindowListener(new WindowAdapter() {
      public void windowClosing(WindowEvent e) {
        System.exit(0);
      }
    });
  }
  public void paint(Graphics g) {
    Graphics2D g2d = (Graphics2D)g;
    g2d.draw(left1);                                         // Note 3
    g2d.draw(right1);
    g2d.draw(left2);
    g2d.draw(right2);
    g2d.draw(left3);
    g2d.draw(right3);
    g2d.draw(left4);
    g2d.draw(right4);
    g2d.setPaint(Color.green);
    g2d.fill(area1);                                         // Note 4
    g2d.fill(area3);
    g2d.fill(area5);
    g2d.fill(area7);
    g2d.setPaint(Color.black);
```

```
    g2d.drawString("add",30,130);
    g2d.drawString("subtract",210,130);
    g2d.drawString("intersect",30,240);
    g2d.drawString("exclusive OR",210,240);
  }
  public static void main(String[] args) {
    Combining s = new Combining("Area methods");
    s.setSize(400,300);
    s.setVisible(true);
  }
}
```

Note 1: We create eight areas from the eight rectangles to use the constructive area geometry operations, add, subtract, intersect, and exclusiveOr.

Note 2: We try each of the four operations, starting with add. The left argument changes as a result of the operation.

Note 3: We draw the rectangles to contrast them with the resulting areas.

Note 4: Each filled area shows the result of one of the constructive area geometry operations.

THE BIG PICTURE

The Shape interface includes methods, such as contains, useful to any shape. Classes such as RectangularShape implement Shape. Types of rectangular shapes such as Rectangle2D and Ellipse2D have inner classes that use double or float coordinates. A path iterator iterates through the segments of a shape, returning the parameters that define each segment. The Rectangle2D class has methods to find the intersection and union of two rectangles, and to find the relative position of a point. The Area class has add, subtract, intersect, and exclusiveOr operations for combining shapes.

TEST YOUR UNDERSTANDING

1. It would be simpler for the outcode method, used in Example 2, to return 0 if the point is above the rectangle, 1 if below, 2 if to the right, and 3 if left. Would this change be a good idea?

2. Write a statement to draw a pie-shaped quarter of a circle with center at (100,100). The endpoints of the boundary lines of the arc are (70,100) and (100,70).

TRY IT YOURSELF   3. Change the rectangles in Example 6.3 to ellipses. Describe the results of running the modified example.

TRY IT YOURSELF   4. Change the left rectangles in Example 6.3 to ellipses. Describe the results of running the modified example.

6.2 Rendering

· · · · · · · · · ·

The rendering process displays shapes, text, and images on output devices. We customize the rendering by setting `Transform`, `Stroke`, `Paint`, and `Clip` attributes.

Transformations

A transformation changes a shape to another shape. We use transformations in two ways in our examples. We can define a transformation and apply it to a single graphical object or add it to the `Graphics2D` context so it will apply to all objects displayed.

The `AffineTransform` class represents transformations of shapes that can be constructed using sequences of translations, rotations, shears, scales, and flips. `AffineTransform` methods include:

`AffineTransform()`
   Constructs the identity affine transformation that makes no changes.

`AffineTransform createInverse()`
   Returns the inverse transformation that undoes the transformation.

`Shape createTransformedShape(Shape pSrc)`
   Returns the shape which results from transforming the specified shape.

`void rotate(double theta, double x, double y)`
   Concatenates this transform with a transform that rotates coordinates around an anchor point.

`void scale(double sx, double sy)`
   Concatenates this transform with a scaling transformation.

`void shear(double shx, double shy)`
   Concatenates this transform with a shearing transformation.

`void translate(double tx, double ty)`
Concatenates this transform with a translation transformation.

Figure 6.4, created by the program of Example 6.4, shows both approaches. To transform the rectangle we create shapes that result from applying affine transformations to it. We only apply each transformation to a specific shape. We rotate a rectangle about its lower-left corner, specifying rotation angles in radians where 2π radians equal 360 degrees, or a full revolution around a circle.

After translating the rectangle to the right, we apply a shearing transformation to it. The first argument to the `shear` method is the multiplier by which coordinates are shifted in the positive x direction as a factor of their y-coordinate, while the second argument is the multiplier by which coordinates are shifted in the positive y direction as a factor of their x-coordinate. After translating down, we scale by a factor of 1.2, making the figure proportionally larger.

We use methods of the `Graphics2D` class to draw the ellipses in Figure 6.4. Adding a transformation to the `Graphics2D` context will cause it to be applied to all objects displayed. `Graphics2D` methods include:

Figure 6.4 Transforming shapes

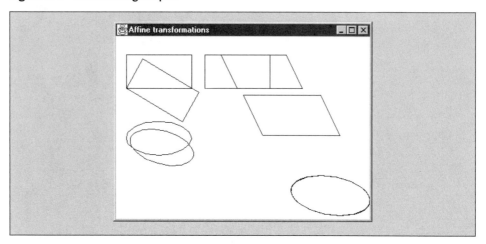

```
abstract void draw(Shape s)
```
Draws the outline of a shape using the current Graphics2D context.

```
abstract void fill(Shape s)
```
Fills the interior of a shape using the current Graphics2D context.

```
abstract void rotate(double theta, double x, double y)
```
Concatenates the current Graphics2D transform with a rotation about (x,y).

```
abstract void scale(double sx, double sy)
```
Concatenates the current Graphics2D transform with a scaling transformation.

```
abstract void setPaint(Paint paint)
```
Sets the Paint attribute for the Graphics2D context.

```
abstract void shear(double shx, double shy)
```
Concatenates the current Graphics2D transform with a shearing transform.

```
abstract void transform(AffineTransform Tx)
```
Composes the AffineTransform object with the current transform.

```
abstract void translate(double tx, double ty)
```
Concatenates the current Graphics2D transform with a translation.

To rotate the ellipse shown in Figure 6.4, we use the Graphics2D rotate method. After drawing the rotated ellipse, we undo the rotation and use the transform method to set the transform in the Graphics2D object to an affine transformation. This transform would then apply to any shapes drawn using that graphics context.

EXAMPLE 6.4   **Transform.java**

```
/* Illustrates affine trasformations: rotate, translate,
 * scale, and shear. Uses two methods to apply transformations,
 * first to each object, then to the graphics context.
 */
```

```
import java.awt.*;
import java.awt.geom.*;
import java.awt.event.*;

public class Transform extends Frame {
  private Rectangle2D rect = new Rectangle2D.Double(20,50,100,50);
  private Ellipse2D oval = new Ellipse2D.Double(20,150,100,50);
  AffineTransform affine = new AffineTransform();             // Note 1
  Shape rotated, translated, sheared, scaled;

  public Transform(String title) {
    super(title);
    affine.rotate(Math.PI/6, 20, 100);                        // Note 2
    rotated = affine.createTransformedShape(rect);            // Note 3
    affine.rotate(-Math.PI/6, 20, 100);                       // Note 4
    affine.translate(120, 0);
    translated = affine.createTransformedShape(rect);         // Note 5
    affine.shear(.5, 0);                                      // Note 6
    sheared = affine.createTransformedShape(rect);            // Note 7
    affine.translate(0,50);
    affine.scale(1.2,1.2);                                    // Note 8
    scaled = affine.createTransformedShape(rect);
    addWindowListener(new WindowAdapter() {
      public void windowClosing(WindowEvent e) {
        System.exit(0);
      }
    });
  }
  public void paint(Graphics g) {
    Graphics2D g2d = (Graphics2D)g;
    g2d.draw(rect);
    g2d.draw(rotated);                                        // Note 9
    g2d.draw(translated);
    g2d.draw(sheared);
    g2d.draw(scaled);
    g2d.draw(oval);
    g2d.rotate(Math.PI/12, 20, 200);                          // Note 10
    g2d.draw(oval);                                           // Note 11
    g2d.rotate(-Math.PI/12, 20, 200);
    g2d.transform(affine);                                    // Note 12
    g2d.draw(oval);                                           // Note 13
  }
  public static void main(String[] args) {
    Transform s = new Transform("Affine transformations");
    s.setSize(400,300);
    s.setVisible(true);
  }
}
```

Note 1: We create an `AffineTransform` representing the identity transformation that makes no change, and will compose it with other transforms.

Note 2: We add a rotation of π/6 radians (30 degrees) to the previous identity transform. The rotation is about the point (20,100), the lower-left corner of the rectangle.

Note 3: The `createTransformedShape` method applies the transform to the shape passed to it, returning the transformed shape. Using this method, we apply a transform to a specific shape rather than placing it in the graphics context to be applied by `Graphics2D` operations.

Note 4: We undo the previous rotation to return to the original identity transform.

Note 5: This translation moves every point of the rectangle 120 units to the right.

Note 6: `affine.shear(.5, 0);`
A shear with arguments (.5,0) will affect the x-direction only. Each point (x,y) of the rectangle will move to (x + .5y, y). Thus, for example, the upper-left corner of the original rectangle is (20,50) which will transform to (45,50), while the lower-left corner is (20,100) which will transform to (70,100).

Note 7: `sheared = affine.createTransformedShape(rect);`
When we compose transformations, the last transform added will be the first to be applied. The shear will apply to the original rectangle and the result will be translated. In this case, though not in general, the result will be the same if we apply the translation first and then the shear.

Note 8: `affine.scale(1.2,1.2);`
This scale transformation moves each point (x,y) to (1.2x, 1.2y).

Note 9: `g2d.draw(rotated);`
We draw each of the transformed shapes using the graphics context `g2d` with the default identity transform.

Note 10: `g2d.rotate(Math.PI/12, 20, 200);`
We illustrate the second approach to applying transforms by adding a rotation to the transform in the graphics context. Any shapes drawn with `g2d` will have this rotation applied to them.

Note 11: `g2d.draw(oval);`
The oval will be rotated using the transform attribute of the graphics context `g2d`.

Note 12: `g2d.transform(affine);`
After undoing the rotation, we set the transform in the graphics context to be the transform `affine` representing a rotation, another rotation undoing the first, a horizontal translation, a shear, a vertical translation, and a scale. Objects drawn using this graphics context will have this transformation applied to them. The graphics context composes the new transform with

the previous current transform, applying the newer transform first. Because the graphics context started with the identity transform and has not been changed prior to this line, the composition here will have no effect. We could have used the `setTransform` method to replace the previous transform.

Note 13:   The oval in the lower-right corner of Figure 6.4, is the result of the transform `affine`, described in Note 12, applied to the original `Ellipse2D` object. The transform `affine` is implicitly applied as part of the graphics context.

Painting

We can fill shapes with a solid color, a gradient, or a texture. The `Graphics2D` method

```
public void setPaint(Paint p);
```

sets the `paint` attribute in the graphics context to a class that implements the `Paint` interface.

Java provides three implementations: the classes `Color`, `GradientPaint`, and `TexturePaint`. We used the `Color` class in Examples 6.2 and 6.3, as for example,

```
g2d.setPaint(Color.green);
```

to fill a shape with a solid color.

A color gradient varies the color from color1 at point1 to color2 at point2. Painting continues beyond these two points in one of two modes. The default `acyclic` mode uses color1 beyond point1 and color2 beyond point2. The `cyclic` mode repeats the gradient over and over outward in each direction. The top rectangle in Figure 6.5 shows an `acyclic` paint while the oval uses a `cyclic` paint.

We can fill a shape with a texture which is specified as a `BufferedImage`, a class we will consider later in this chapter. A rectangle with the image is replicated to fill the shape. We can create a buffered image from an image or draw our own texture. The lower rectangle in Figure 6.5 is painted using a texture derived from an image of the Mona Lisa from the Louvre.[*]

EXAMPLE 6.5   Painting.java

```
/* Illustrates the acyclic and cyclic gradient paint
 * and texture paint replicating an image.
 */

import java.awt.*;
import java.awt.geom.*;
import java.awt.event.*;
import java.awt.image.BufferedImage;
```

---

[*] See http://www.paris.org/Musees/Louvre/Treasures/gifs/MonaLisaa.gif

Figure 6.5 `acyclic` and `cyclic` gradient, and texture paint

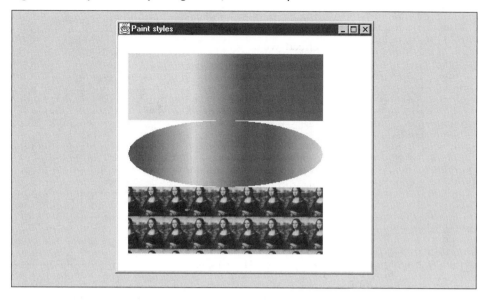

```
public class Painting extends Frame {
  private Rectangle2D rect = new Rectangle2D.Double(20,50,300,100);
  private Ellipse2D oval = new Ellipse2D.Double(20,150,300,100);
  private Rectangle2D rect1 = new Rectangle2D.Double(20,250,300,100);

  public Painting(String title) {
    super(title);
    addWindowListener(new WindowAdapter()      {
      public void windowClosing(WindowEvent e)      {
                             System.exit(0);
      }
    });
  }
  public void paint(Graphics g) {
    Graphics2D g2d = (Graphics2D)g;
    GradientPaint acyclic = new GradientPaint
              (120f,100f,Color.orange,220f,100f,Color.blue);       // Note 1
    g2d.setPaint(acyclic);                                         // Note 2
    g2d.fill(rect);
    GradientPaint cyclic = new GradientPaint
              (120f,200f,Color.orange,220f,200f,Color.blue,true);  // Note 3
    g2d.setPaint(cyclic);
    g2d.fill(oval);
    MediaTracker tracker = new MediaTracker(this);                 // Note 4
    Image lisa =
    Toolkit.getDefaultToolkit().getImage("MonaLisaa.gif");         // Note 5
    tracker.addImage(lisa,0);                                      // Note 6
    try {
      tracker.waitForID(0);                                        // Note 7
    }catch(InterruptedException e) {
```

```
        return;
    }
    BufferedImage mona = new BufferedImage(lisa.getWidth(null),
                lisa.getHeight(null), BufferedImage.TYPE_INT_RGB);  // Note 8
    Graphics2D graphMona = mona.createGraphics();                   // Note 9
    graphMona.drawImage(lisa,null,null);                           // Note 10
    Rectangle2D anchor = new Rectangle2D.Double
                (0,0,mona.getWidth()/2,mona.getHeight()/2);        // Note 11
    TexturePaint texture = new TexturePaint(mona, anchor);         // Note 12
    g2d.setPaint(texture);                                         // Note 13
    g2d.fill(rect1);                                               // Note 14
  }
  public static void main(String[] args) {
    Painting s = new Painting("Paint styles");
    s.setSize(400,380);
    s.setVisible(true);
  }
}
```

....

Note 1:   This constructor creates a `GradientPaint` which starts with orange at
            (120,100) and transitions to blue at (220,100). It is `acyclic` by default so
            the color to the right of (220,100) is blue, and the color to the left of
            (120,100) is orange.

Note 2:   We pass the `GradientPaint` to the `setPaint` method to add it to the graph-
            ics context so shapes will be filled with this gradient from orange to blue.

Note 3:   By adding an argument of **true** to the constructor we indicate a preference for
            a `cyclic` gradient, in which the gradient is repeated to the left and right of the
            given points, rather than solid colors. The oval in Figure 6.5 shows this effect.

Note 4:   The media tracker allows us to check when an image is completely loaded.

Note 5:   The `Toolkit` provides some implementation dependent methods such as
            `getImage`. The argument `MonaLisaa.gif` is an image file in the same direc-
            tory as the class file for this program.

Note 6:   `tracker.addImage(lisa,0);`
            We add an image with an arbitrary identifier and track all images with this
            identifier.

Note 7:   `tracker.waitForID(0);`
            Because we pass it the identifier 0, the `waitForID` method waits for images
            with an ID of 0 to load completely.

Note 8:   `new BufferedImage(lisa.getWidth(null),`
            `lisa.getHeight(null), BufferedImage.TYPE_INT_RGB);`
            We will discuss buffered images later in this chapter. We create a buffered
            image of the same size as the image we loaded. The `getWidth` and `getHeight`
            methods take a **null** argument because we know the image is loaded and
            do not need to pass an image observer. The last argument is an image type.

Note 9: `Graphics2D graphMona = mona.createGraphics();`
We create a graphics context to draw on the buffered image we created.

Note 10: `graphMona.drawImage(lisa,null,null);`
We draw the image we loaded on the buffered image. The last two arguments are an affine transform and an image observer, neither of which we use.

Note 11: `Rectangle2D anchor = new Rectangle2D.Double`
`    (0,0,mona.getWidth()/2,mona.getHeight()/2);`
This rectangle will be the basic tile of a texture that will repeat in identically sized rectangles throughout a shape. The point (0,0) refers to the upper-left corner of the frame, while the next two arguments give the width and height of the rectangle. We make the tile half the dimensions of the original image so we can fit more copies in the rectangle we will tile.

Note 12: `TexturePaint texture = new TexturePaint(mona, anchor);`
The `TexturePaint` constructor takes two arguments, a `BufferedImage` and a `Rectangle2D`. This texture tiles with an anchor rectangle filled with the `mona` image.

Note 13: `g2d.setPaint(texture);`
We pass a `TexturePaint` object to set the painting style in the graphics context.

Note 14: `g2d.fill(rect1);`
Filling the rectangle causes it to be painted with copies of the texture. The anchor rectangle starts in the upper-left corner of the frame so the upper-left corner of the rectangle occurs in the interior of a copy of the image.

Stroking

Stroking involves drawing a shape with a marking pen of the appropriate size. To set the stroke, we need to specify a line width, the style for drawing the end of a thick line, the style for joining lines, and the length and offset of dashes.

The three end styles for line segments are:

`CAP_BUTT`　　　　　No added decoration

`CAP_ROUND`　　　　Round decoration of radius half the width of the pen.

`CAP_SQUARE`　　　　Square decoration that extends beyond the end of the segment to a distance equal to half of the line width.

The three join styles for line segments are:

`JOIN_BEVEL`　　　　Connects the outer corners of their wide outlines with a straight segment.

`JOIN_MITER`　　　　Extends their outside edges until they meet.

`JOIN_ROUND`　　　　Rounds off the corner with an arc of radius half the line width.

Figure 6.6, generated by Example 6.6, illustrates each of these end and join styles.

Figure 6.6   Illustrating different strokes

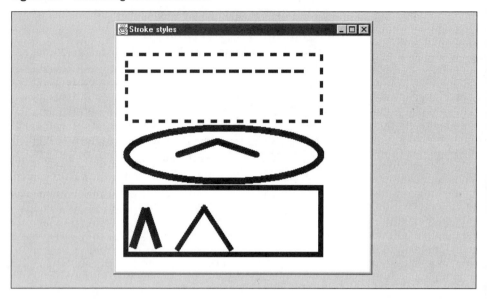

The ends of the leftmost angle inside the lower rectangle and the outer segments of the dashed rectangle use the CAP_BUTT style with no decoration. The ends of the angle inside the ellipse use the CAP_ROUND style, while the segments of the dashed line inside the dashed rectangle use the CAP_SQUARE style.

We join the corner of the left angle in the lower rectangle with the JOIN_BEVEL style. The corner of the angle to its right uses the JOIN_MITER style in which the outer edges of the segments extend until they meet, and the angle inside the ellipse joins segments using the JOIN_ROUND style.

Dashed lines use an array to specify the length of the dashes and spaces between the dashes. Using the {10, 10} array creates the dashed rectangle shown in Figure 6.6. The array {15, 5} would have made the dashes three times as long as the spaces between them. We could use a longer array to get a more varied pattern of dashes and spaces. The odd components represent widths of dashes while the even components represent widths of spaces. For example the array {10, 5, 5, 5} would produce alternating long and short dashes.

To set the stroke attributes in the graphics context, we call the setStroke method, passing it an implementation of the Stroke interface. Java provides the BasicStroke class which implements Stroke. We only use BasicStroke constructors in Example 6.6.

EXAMPLE 6.6   **Stroking.java**

```
/* Illustrates stroke styles.
 */

import java.awt.*;
import java.awt.geom.*;
```

```java
import java.awt.event.*;
import java.awt.image.BufferedImage;

public class Stroking extends Frame {
  private Rectangle2D rect = new Rectangle2D.Double(20,50,300,100);
  private Ellipse2D oval = new Ellipse2D.Double(20,160,300,80);
  private Rectangle2D rect1 = new Rectangle2D.Double(20,250,300,100);
  private Stroke buBeDa = new BasicStroke(5, BasicStroke.CAP_BUTT,
          BasicStroke.JOIN_BEVEL, 0, new float[] {10,10}, 0);      // Note 1
  private Stroke roRo = new BasicStroke
    (10, BasicStroke.CAP_ROUND, BasicStroke.JOIN_ROUND);           // Note 2
  private Stroke buBe = new BasicStroke
    (12, BasicStroke.CAP_BUTT, BasicStroke.JOIN_BEVEL);
  private Stroke sqMi = new BasicStroke(8);                        // Note 3
  private Stroke sqBeDa = new BasicStroke(5, BasicStroke.CAP_SQUARE,
          BasicStroke.JOIN_BEVEL, 0, new float[] {10,10}, 0);      // Note 4


  public Stroking(String title) {
    super(title);
    addWindowListener(new WindowAdapter() {
      public void windowClosing(WindowEvent e) {
        System.exit(0);
      }
    });
  }
  public void paint(Graphics g) {
    Graphics2D g2d = (Graphics2D)g;
    g2d.setStroke(buBeDa);                                         // Note 5
    g2d.draw(rect);
    g2d.setStroke(roRo);
    g2d.draw(oval);
    g2d.draw(new Line2D.Double(100,200,160,180));                 // Note 6
    g2d.draw(new Line2D.Double(160,180,220,200));
    g2d.setStroke(sqMi);
    g2d.draw(rect1);
    g2d.draw(new Line2D.Double(100,340,140,280));
    g2d.draw(new Line2D.Double(180,340,140,280));
    g2d.setStroke(buBe);
    g2d.draw(new Line2D.Double(30,340,50,280));
    g2d.draw(new Line2D.Double(70,340,50,280));
    g2d.setStroke(sqBeDa);
    g2d.draw(new Line2D.Double(20,75,300,75));                    // Note 7
  }
  public static void main(String[] args) {
    Stroking s = new Stroking("Stroke styles");
    s.setSize(400,380);
    s.setVisible(true);
  }
}
```

Note 1: The six arguments of this `BasicStroke` constructor specify

the width of the line (float)
the end style (one of the three integer constants)
the join style (one of the three integer constants)
the miter limit (a float, used if the join style is `JOIN_MITER`)
the dash array (float type)
the dash phase (float)

The miter limit guards against mitered joins of lines at a small angle to one another in which case the lines would extend for a long way before meeting, creating an undesirable shape. The dash phase specifies an offset for the start of the line. We use an offset of 0.0; an offset of 3.0 would cause the first dash to have length 7.

Note 2: This constructor specifies the line width, the end style, and the join style. For the `JOIN_MITER` style, the miter limit is 10.0. Another constructor allows a fourth argument to specify the miter limit.

Note 3: `CAP_SQUARE` is the default end style, `JOIN_MITER` is the default join style, and 10.0 is the default miter limit.

Note 4: This constructor for a dashed line stroke uses the `CAP_SQUARE` end style.

Note 5: We call the `setStroke` method to change the stroke attributes in the graphics context.

Note 6: `g2d.draw(new Line2D.Double(100,200,160,180));`
Draws the left side of the angle inside the oval.

Note 7: `g2d.draw(new Line2D.Double(20,75,300,75));`
Draws the dashed line inside the dashed rectangle. Using the `CAP_SQUARE` style makes the dashes extend out in either direction. Consequently they are longer than those defining the boundary of the rectangle which use the `CAP_BUTT` style.

Clipping

By clipping we can show only part of a shape. The `setClip` method sets the clipping shape in the graphics context, which then draws only those parts of figures that intersect that shape. Figure 6.7 shows the word CAT drawn above in full and below clipped to a rectangle that intersects only a portion of the word.

EXAMPLE 6.7 **Clipping.java**

```
/* Illustrates clipping.
 */

import java.awt.*;
import java.awt.geom.*;
```

Figure 6.7 Clipping a drawing to a rectangle

```
import java.awt.event.*;

public class Clipping extends Frame {
  private Font font = new Font("Serif",Font.BOLD,148);         // Note 1

  public Clipping(String title) {
    super(title);
    addWindowListener(new WindowAdapter() {
      public void windowClosing(WindowEvent e) {
        System.exit(0);
      }
    });
  }
  public void paint(Graphics g) {
    Graphics2D g2d = (Graphics2D)g;
    g2d.setFont(font);
    g2d.drawString("CAT",50,150);
    g2d.setClip(new Rectangle2D.Double(70,250,250,40));        // Note 2
    g2d.drawString("CAT",50,300);                              // Note 3
    g2d.drawString("CAT",70,150);                              // Note 4
  }
  public static void main(String[] args) {
    Clipping s = new Clipping("Clipping");
    s.setSize(400,320);
    s.setVisible(true);
  }
}
```

Note 1:   We create a font with font name Serif, bold style, and 148 points in
height.

Note 2: The rectangle defines the region we will be able to view. The `setClip` method sets the graphics context to clip drawings to this rectangle. We could have used any `Shape`.

Note 3: We only see the part of the word that fits within the clipping shape.

Note 4: We see nothing of this word because it does not intersect the clipping rectangle.

THE BG PICTURE

The rendering process displays shapes, text, and images. We can transform figures either by creating a transform which we apply to a figure, or by setting a transform in the graphics context which will then be applied to all figures. We can paint in a solid color, using a gradient, `cyclic` or `acyclic`, or a texture. The stroke defines the line width, the end and join styles for segments, and the size and spacing for dashed lines. Clipping shows the part of a figure contained in the clipping region.

TEST YOUR UNDERSTANDING

5. In Example 6.4 we define a horizontal shear, affecting only the x-coordinate. Had we passed .5 for the second argument to the shear, instead of 0, so the shear applies vertically also, what would be the coordinates of the endpoints of the upper sheared rectangle?

6. Why does the image of the Mona Lisa not start in the upper-left corner of the rectangle in Figure 6.5? How could you modify Example 6.5 to make the upper-left corner of the image coincide with the upper-left corner of the rectangle?

TRY IT YOURSELF 7. Modify Example 6.6 to draw the dashed rectangle with an alternating pattern of long and short dashes.

TRY IT YOURSELF 8. Modify Example 6.6 to draw the solid rectangle using a `JOIN_ROUND` style. How does the appearance of the rectangle change?

TRY IT YOURSELF 9. Modify Example 6.7 to clip to an ellipse rather than a rectangle. How does Figure 6.7 change?

6.3 Text

With Java2D we can embed graphics or shapes within text, and associate attributes with different portions of a string to style it differently. We can transform text and draw it with textures. Advanced text layout features provide awesome design capabilities beyond the scope of this chapter.

Attributes

The `java.awt.font.TextAttribute` class includes a number of attributes that we can apply to text. In Example 6.8 we will illustrate the following text attributes:

```
BACKGROUND
CHAR_REPLACEMENT
FONT
FOREGROUND
UNDERLINE
```

To apply attributes we first create an attributed string, as for example,

```
java.text.AttributedString atString =
                new java.text.AttributedString("Java is fun");
```

We use the `addAttribute` method to associate attributes with an attributed string. For example we can associate a foreground color with the entire string using

```
atString.addAttribute(TextAttribute.FOREGROUND, Color.red);
```
or with a portion using

```
atString.addAttribute(TextAttribute.FOREGROUND, Color.blue, 8, 11);
```
which would draw the word "fun," at position 8, 9, and 10 in the string "Java is fun," in blue.

The `CHAR_REPLACEMENT` attribute allows us to replace a single character with an image or a shape. The `addAttribute` method takes as its second argument a `Graphic-Attribute` which can be either an `ImageGraphicAttribute` or a `ShapeGraphicAttribute`, two classes of the `java.awt.font` package. We use the constructors

```
ImageGraphicAttribute(Image image, int alignment)
```

or

```
ShapeGraphicAttribute(Shape shape, int alignment, boolean stroke)
```
Figure 6.8, produced by Example 6.8, shows the use of two fonts in the top line as well as underlining, and foreground and background colors. The bottom line embeds an image at its front.

Figure 6.8 Drawing text

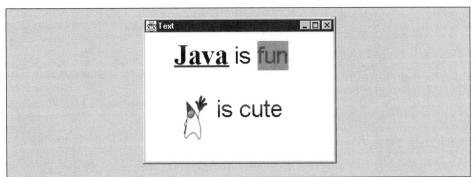

EXAMPLE 6.8   **TextDraw.java**

```
/* Uses text attributes.
 */

import java.awt.*;
import java.awt.event.*;
import java.awt.font.*;
import java.text.*;

public class TextDraw extends Frame {
  private Font lucinda =
            new Font("Lucinda Sans Regular", Font.PLAIN, 36);    // Note 1
  private Font roman = new Font("Times New Roman", Font.BOLD, 42);
  private String s = "Java is fun";
  private String d = "\ufffc is cute";                           // Note 2
  private AttributedString aString = new AttributedString(s);
  private AttributedString dString = new AttributedString(d);
  private Image duke =
          Toolkit.getDefaultToolkit().getImage("duke.gif");      // Note 3
  private ImageGraphicAttribute image;

  public TextDraw(String title) {
    super(title);
    aString.addAttribute(TextAttribute.FONT, lucinda);           // Note 4
    aString.addAttribute(TextAttribute.FONT, roman , 0, 4);      // Note 5
    aString.addAttribute(TextAttribute.UNDERLINE,
                      TextAttribute.UNDERLINE_ON, 0, 4);         // Note 6
    aString.addAttribute(TextAttribute.FOREGROUND, Color.blue, 8, 11);
    aString.addAttribute(TextAttribute.BACKGROUND, Color.red, 8, 11);
    MediaTracker tracker = new MediaTracker(this);
    tracker.addImage(duke,0);
    try {
      tracker.waitForID(0);
    }catch(InterruptedException e) {
      return;
    }
    image = new ImageGraphicAttribute
            (duke, GraphicAttribute.TOP_ALIGNMENT);              // Note 7
    dString.addAttribute(TextAttribute.FONT, lucinda);
    dString.addAttribute
            (TextAttribute.CHAR_REPLACEMENT, image, 0, 1);       // Note 8
    addWindowListener(new WindowAdapter() {
      public void windowClosing(WindowEvent e) {
        System.exit(0);
      }
    });
  }
  public void paint(Graphics g) {
    Graphics2D g2d = (Graphics2D)g;
    g2d.drawString(aString.getIterator(),50,70);                 // Note 9
```

```
      g2d.drawString(dString.getIterator(),50,150);
    }
    public static void main(String[] args) {
      TextDraw t = new TextDraw("Text");
      t.setSize(300,220);
      t.setVisible(true);
    }
}
```

Note 1:   Java 2 documentation recommends using physical font names rather than logical font names such as Serif and Monospaced. Java 2 includes fonts from the Lucinda family, so these fonts will be available wherever the Java 2 platform is installed. The Lucinda Sans Regular font supports the Arabic and Hebrew character sets, in addition to the usual Latin characters.

Note 2:   We can use the CHAR_REPLACEMENT attribute to replace a character in a string. The character to be replaced should be Unicode '\ufffc.'

Note 3:   The image duke.gif comes from the Java2D demo distributed with Java 2 from Sun.

Note 4:   We specify the font for the entire string, aString.

Note 5:   We specify the font for positions 0-3 of aString. The final argument, 4, gives the position just beyond the rightmost position affected by the change.

Note 6:   aString.addAttribute(TextAttribute.UNDERLINE,
    TextAttribute.UNDERLINE_ON, 0, 4);
The first argument specifies the UNDERLINE attribute, the second is its value, UNDERLINE_ON, while the last two give the range of the underline, from position 0 up to but not including position 4.

Note 7:   image = new ImageGraphicAttribute
    (duke, GraphicAttribute.TOP_ALIGNMENT);
We use the GraphicAttribute class when embedding an image in text. The top alignment aligns the top of the graphic to the top of the line. Other choices include bottom alignment. See the documentation for more details.

Note 8:   dString.addAttribute(TextAttribute.CHAR_REPLACEMENT, image, 0, 1);
We replace the first character in dString with an image. The second argument is an ImageGraphicAttribute, but we could also have use a Shape-GraphicAttribute. The third and fourth arguments specify the position of the replacement.

Note 9:   g2d.drawString(aString.getIterator(),50,70);
The getIterator method creates an AttributedCharacterIterator that provides access to the string. The drawString method uses it without any intervention on our part.

Painting and Transforming

We can use the techniques of the last section to transform text, and to paint it using any of the three styles, solid color, gradient, or texture. Figure 6.9, created by Example 6.9, shows two lines of text, both painted with a texture obtained from an image of the Mona Lisa. We transform the second line using a rotation of π/6 radians or 30 degrees.

Figure 6.9 Painting and transforming text

EXAMPLE 6.9 **TextTransPaint.java**

```java
/* Illustrates transforming and painting text.
 */

import java.awt.*;
import java.awt.event.*;
import java.awt.font.*;
import java.awt.geom.*;
import java.awt.image.BufferedImage;

public class TextTransPaint extends Frame {
  private Font lucinda = new Font("Lucinda Sans Regular", Font.PLAIN, 72);
  private String s = "Java is fun";
  private String d = "Duke is cute";
  private AffineTransform affine = new AffineTransform();

  public TextTransPaint(String title) {
    super(title);
    setFont(lucinda);
    affine.rotate(Math.PI/6, 20, 100);
    addWindowListener(new WindowAdapter() {
```

```
      public void windowClosing(WindowEvent e) {
        System.exit(0);
      }
    });
  }
  public void paint(Graphics g) {
    Graphics2D g2d = (Graphics2D)g;
    MediaTracker tracker = new MediaTracker(this);
    Image lisa = Toolkit.getDefaultToolkit().getImage("MonaLisaa.gif");
    tracker.addImage(lisa,0);
    try {
      tracker.waitForID(0);
    }catch(InterruptedException e) {
      return;
    }
    BufferedImage mona = new
    BufferedImage(lisa.getWidth(null),lisa.getHeight(null),
             BufferedImage.TYPE_INT_RGB);
    Graphics2D graphMona = mona.createGraphics();
    graphMona.drawImage(lisa,null,null);
    Rectangle2D anchor = new
    Rectangle2D.Double(0,0,mona.getWidth()/2,mona.getHeight()/2);
    TexturePaint texture = new TexturePaint(mona, anchor);
    g2d.setPaint(texture);
    g2d.drawString(s,20,90);
    g2d.setTransform(affine);                                  // Note 1
    g2d.drawString(d,20,140);
  }
  public static void main(String[] args) {
    TextTransPaint t = new TextTransPaint("Text Transform and Paint");
    t.setSize(400,350);
    t.setVisible(true);
  }
}
```

Note 1:   In contrast to the `transform` method used in Example 6.4, the `setTrans-`
`form` method changes the transform in the graphics context to the transform passed as its argument.

THE BIG PICTURE

By creating an attributed string, we can add attributes to change parts of the string
to use different fonts or colors. We can change the background color, underline,
and even embed graphics within text. All the rendering methods of the last section
apply to text, so that we can transform it, and set paint and stroke properties.

TEST YOUR UNDERSTANDING

TRY IT YOURSELF

10. In Example 6.8, we used `aString.getIterator()` as the first argument in the call to `drawString`. Could we just have used `aString`, as we do with non-attributed strings?

TRY IT YOURSELF

11. In Example 6.9, is it possible to set the stroke to make the text thicker so that the image shows up more?

6.4 Printing

· · · · · · · · · · ·

With Java 2D we can print in the same way that we render, using a `Graphics2D` object. First we show that we can print graphics, and then we print a file which may require more than a single page. The small `java.awt.print` package includes additional facilities for setting up print jobs that we do not discuss.

Graphics

A `PrinterJob` object controls the printing. We use the method

```
public static PrinterJob getPrinterJob()
```

to get a print job. The method

```
public abstract void setPrintable(Printable p)
```

sets a `Printable` object to do the rendering, while

```
public abstract boolean printDialog()
```

pops up a dialog for the user to set properties for the printer job, and

```
public abstract print()
```

prints the pages.

The `Printable` interface has one method

```
public int print(Graphics graphics, PageFormat pageFormat,
                int pageIndex)throws PrinterException
```

which prints each page. The `PrinterJob` print method calls this method to print each page.

In Example 6.10, we show that we can print shapes and text in the same way we displayed them on the screen earlier in the chapter. Printing is very similar to rendering on the screen. To highlight this similarity we have the `print` method call the `paint` method to print the shapes and text displayed on the screen. Figure 6.10 shows the screen. The printed output includes the two joined lines and the message.

Figure 6.10   Printing shapes and text

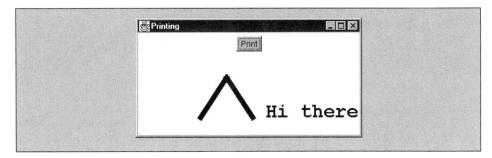

EXAMPLE 6.10   **Printing.java**

```java
/* Prints shapes and text
 */

import java.awt.*;
import java.awt.print.*;                                        // Note 1
import java.awt.geom.*;
import java.awt.event.*;

public class Printing extends Frame {

  public Printing(String title) {
    super(title);
    Button button = new Button("Print");
    Panel panel = new Panel();
    panel.add(button);
    add(panel, "North");
    button.addActionListener(new ActionListener() {             // Note 2
      public void actionPerformed(ActionEvent event) {
        PrinterJob job = PrinterJob.getPrinterJob();
        job.setPrintable(new PrintIt());                        // Note 3
        if (job.printDialog())                                  // Note 4
          try {
            job.print();
          }catch(PrinterException e) {                          // Note 5
            e.printStackTrace();
          }
      }
    });
    addWindowListener(new WindowAdapter() {
      public void windowClosing(WindowEvent event) {
        System.exit(0);
      }
    });
  }
```

```
public void paint(Graphics g) {
  Stroke sqMi = new BasicStroke(8);
  Graphics2D g2d = (Graphics2D)g;
  g2d.setStroke(sqMi);
  g2d.setFont(new Font("Monospaced", Font.BOLD, 30));
  g2d.drawString("Hi there", 200, 150);
  g2d.draw(new Line2D.Double(100,150,140,90));
  g2d.draw(new Line2D.Double(180,150,140,90));
}
class PrintIt implements Printable {
  public int print(Graphics g, PageFormat f, int i) {        // Note 6
    if (i != 0)
      return NO_SUCH_PAGE;                                    // Note 7
    paint(g);
    return PAGE_EXISTS;                                       // Note 8
  }
}
public static void main(String[] args) {
  Printing p = new Printing("Printing");
  p.setSize(350,180);
  p.setVisible(true);
}
}
```

....

Note 1:   The `java.awt.print` package contains the classes and interfaces needed to print.

Note 2:   We use an anonymous inner class to provide an action listener which implements the printing when the user presses the *Print* button.

Note 3:   The `PrintIt` class implements the `Printable` interface, and its `print` method which prints the page.

Note 4:   The `printDialog` method pops up a dialog to allow the user to configure the print job. It also gives the user an opportunity to cancel which is a desirable option when printing. We prefer to include the call to `printDialog`, but it could be omitted if desired.

Note 5:   `PrinterException` is checked, so we must catch it.

Note 6:   `public int print(Graphics g, PageFormat f, int i)`
The `PageFormat` argument allows us to format the page for printing. We do not use it in this example. The `setPrintable` method has another version with a second argument of type `PageFormat` which would allow us to use our own `PageFormat` object. Because we used the `setPrintable` method with one argument, Java will pass a default `PageFormat` object. This `print` method will be called to print each page. The third argument represents the page number.

Note 7:   `if (i != 0) return NO_SUCH_PAGE`
Because we only have one page, we return `NO_SUCH_PAGE` if i has any value other than 0 that denotes the first page.

Note 8: `return PAGE_EXISTS`

We return `PAGE_EXISTS` when a page is printed.

Printing a File

We print a file that may extend over multiple pages. We use the default PageFormat to find the imageable part of the page. Useful `PageFormat` methods include:

`double getImageableHeight()` Height, in points, of the imageable area of the page.

`double getImageableWidth()` Width, in points, of the imageable area of the page.

`double getImageableX()` X-coordinate of the upper left point of the imageable area.

`double getImageableY()` Y-coordinate of the upper left point of the imageable area.

A `LineMetrics` object provides information about a `Font`. The `Font` class has the method

`LineMetrics getLineMetrics(String str, FontRenderContext frc)`

that returns a `LineMetrics` object. The first argument is a string, and the `LineMetrics` methods help to display that string. We only use the `getHeight` method to find the height of the font. The second argument has type `FontRenderContext`, and contains the information for rendering the font. The `Graphics2D` class includes the `getFontRenderContext` method that returns a `FontRenderContext`.

In Example 6.11, we use the `getHeight` method of the `LineMetrics` class to get the height of the font. We create a `Vector` to hold the lines that fit on each page, using the height of the font, and the size of the imageable page to make that determination, at the same time reading the lines from the external file into the vector. In the `print` method, for each page we display each line of the corresponding vector. We choose not to display the file on the screen, but only print it.

EXAMPLE 6.11   **PrintFile.java**

```
/* Prints a file which extends over
 * multiple pages
 */

import java.awt.*;
import java.awt.print.*;
import java.io.*;
import java.awt.font.LineMetrics;
import java.util.Vector;

public class PrintFile extends Frame implements Printable{
  private String filename;
  private int size = 0;                    // number of pages
  private float height;                    // font height
  private Vector pages = new Vector();     // holds page vectors   // Note 1

  public void setup(PageFormat f) {
    Graphics2D g2d = (Graphics2D)getGraphics();
```

```
      Font font = new Font("Times New Roman", Font.PLAIN, 12);
      g2d.setFont(font);
      LineMetrics metrics =
          font.getLineMetrics("Test", g2d.getFontRenderContext());      // Note 2
      height = metrics.getHeight();
      float oldh = (float)f.getImageableY();                            // Note 3
      float h = oldh;                                                   // Note 4
      float end = h + (float)f.getImageableHeight();                    // Note 5
      try {
        BufferedReader reader =
              new BufferedReader(new FileReader(filename));
        String line;
        do {
          Vector nextPage = new Vector();                               // Note 6
          while(((line = reader.readLine()) != null) && h < end) {
            if (line.equals(""))
                    line = " ";                                        // Note 7
            nextPage.addElement(line);
            h += height;
          }
          if (!nextPage.isEmpty())
            pages.addElement(nextPage);                                // Note 8
          h = oldh;
        } while (line != null);
        reader.close();
      }catch(IOException e) {
        System.exit(1);
      }
      size = pages.size();                                             // Note 9
  }
  public int print(Graphics g, PageFormat f, int i) {
    if (i >= size)
      return NO_SUCH_PAGE;                                             // Note 10
    Graphics2D g2d = (Graphics2D)g;
    float h = (float)f.getImageableY();
    float begin = (float)f.getImageableX();
    Vector current = (Vector)pages.elementAt(i);
    for(int k = 0; k < current.size(); k++)
      g2d.drawString((String)current.elementAt(k), begin, h += height);
    return PAGE_EXISTS;
  }
  public static void main(String[] args) {
    PrintFile p = new PrintFile();
    p.pack();                                                          // Note 11
    p.setVisible(true);
    p.filename = args[0];                                              // Note 12
    p.addWindowListener(new WindowAdapter() {
      public void windowClosing(WindowEvent event) {
        System.exit(0);
      }
    });
```

```
      PrinterJob job = PrinterJob.getPrinterJob();
      p.setup(job.defaultPage());
      job.setPrintable(p);
      if (job.printDialog())
      try {
        job.print();
      }catch(PrinterException e) {
        e.printStackTrace();
      }
    }
  }
}
```

Note 1:   We use a vector rather than an array because it grows dynamically so we do not have to specify its size in advance.

Note 2:   We pass an arbitrary string "Test" as the first argument because we only need the height of the font, which does not depend on the string used.

Note 3:   Because the drawString method, called in the print method, has float arguments for the drawing position, we cast to a float.

Note 4:   The variable h represents the y-coordinate of the current line of text.

Note 5:   The variable end represents the y-coordinate of the bottom of the imageable region.

Note 6:   `Vector nextPage = new Vector();`
This vector hold the lines of text for the current page.

Note 7:   `if (line.equals("")) line = " ";`
The renderer does not like blank lines, so we convert them to contain some blanks.

Note 8:   `if (!nextPage.isEmpty())pages.addElement(nextPage);`
We only add a page to the vector of pages if it is not empty.

Note 9:   `size = pages.size();`
The size variable holds the number of pages. The pages vector contain a vector of lines for each page. Its size gives the total number of pages.

Note 10:   `if (i >= size) return NO_SUCH_PAGE;`
The print method numbers pages starting with 0, so the last page will have number size-1.

Note 11:   `p.pack();`
Packing makes the frame just large enough to hold all its components. Because we added no components to this frame, it will display as a thin title bar.

Note 12:   `p.filename = args[0];`
We pass the name of the file to print as a program argument.

THE BIG PICTURE

To print, we get a `PrinterJob` object and implement the `print` method of the `Printable` interface which uses `Graphics2D` and `PageFormat` objects to format the pages. We can use the rendering techniques used to display to the screen, so we can print graphics as well as text.

TEST YOUR UNDERSTANDING

TRY IT YOURSELF   12. Omit the call to `printDialog` in Example 6.10. Does the example still work as before?

TRY IT YOURSELF   13. Omit the test for an empty line in Example 6.11. Does the example still work as before?

SUMMARY

- Java2D provides methods for professional design. The `Shape` interface includes general methods that apply to standard shapes and to custom shapes created by the programmer (See Exercises 6.10 and 6.11 below for custom shapes). A path iterator traverses the segments that make up a shape, classifying each as a move, line, quadratic, cubic, or close. A quadratic segment has two endpoints and one control point, while a cubic segment has two endpoints and two control points.

- Rectangular shapes include 2D rectangles, ellipses, and arcs, defined either with float or double coordinates. Arcs may have one of three types, `OPEN`, `PIE`, and `CHORD`. An `Area` allows us to combine shapes using `add`, `subtract`, `intersect`, and `exclusiveOr` operations.

- Rendering a figure displays it on an output device. We customize the rendering by applying transformations and setting paint styles, stroke styles, and clipping regions. The transformation operations include `rotate`, `scale`, `shear`, and `translate`. We can create a new shape using a transformation, or we can apply the transform to the graphics context so all figures drawn from then on will be transformed.

- We can paint with a solid color, a gradient, or a texture. A gradient varies the colors between two points from the color at the first point to the color at the second. `acyclic` gradients continue the endpoint colors in their respective directions in the remainder of the shape. `cyclic` gradients repeat the traversal from one color to other. Textures tile with an anchor rectangle filled with a buffered image.

- Before Java2D, lines had a one-pixel thickness. Using Java2D, we can set many properties of the drawing lines. Line segment end styles can be `CAP_BUTT`, `CAP_ROUND`, or `CAP_SQUARE`. Line segment join styles can be `JOIN_BEVEL`, `JOIN_MITER`, or `JOIN_ROUND`. We can set the thickness and set the style for dashed lines. The `Graphics2D` class inherits the `setClip` method from the `Graphics` class.

- With Java2D we can embed graphics or shapes within text, and associate attributes for fonts, foreground and background colors, and underlining with different portions of a string to style it. We can paint and transform text using the same rendering techniques we apply to shapes.

- Printing uses a Graphics2D object to render shapes, images, and text for a printer. We can format individual pages, and interact with the user to set properties for the printer job.

Program Modification Exercises
· · · · · · · · · · ·

1. In Example 6.1, we drew a rectangle with upper-left corner at (50,50), width 340, and height 200. Modify Example 6.1 to use a path iterator to display the segments of this path.

2. Modify Example 6.5 to use a Swing ImageIcon for the Mona Lisa image.

3. Modify Example 6.3 to add an ellipse that overlaps with all four rectangles on the left, and fill the intersection of it with the top two rectangles and with the bottom two.

4. Modify Example 6.4 to do all the transformations using graphics context methods rather than creating new shapes.

5. Modify Example 6.4 to do all the transformations by creating new shapes rather than using graphics context transformation methods.

6. Modify Example 6.8 to insert a shape at the beginning of the second line rather than an image. Draw a little happy face.

7. Modify Example 6.9 to display "Java is fun" vertically at the left and "Duke is cute" vertically at the right.

8. Modify Example 6.11 to add a *Print* button to the frame so the printing occurs in response to a button press.

Program Design Exercises
· · · · · · · · · · ·

9. To better understand the representation of a cubic curve, draw a rounded 2d rectangle of half the size of its containing frame, and centered in the middle. Find the array of points representing the upper left curve. Draw lines from the control points to the corresponding endpoints. These lines should be tangent, just touching at one point. Use the method

```
CubicCurve2D.Double(double x1, double y1, double ctrlx1,
double ctrly1, double ctrlx2, double ctrly2,
double x2, double y2)
```

to construct a replacement for the upper left curve, keeping the same endpoints, but changing the control points. Draw the new curve to see how close it is to the rounded corner of the rectangle.

10. Use Area methods to create a pear shape and draw it.

11. Java provides the `GeneralPath` class to construct a curve from segments. Methods include:

```
public GeneralPath()
public void moveTo(float x, float y)
public void lineTo(float x, float y)
public void quadTo(float x1, float y1, float x2,
    float y2)
public void curveTo(float x1, float y1, float x2,
    float y2, float x3, float y3) // cubic
public void closePath()
```

Use these methods to create a general path in the shape of a bow tie and draw it.

12. Use the `GeneralPath` methods of Exercise 6.11 to create a general path from two quadratic curves. Draw the lines from the control point for each quadratic segment to the two endpoints of that segment. These lines should be tangent to the path.

13. Write a program that allows the user to enter total sales in one text field and sales for division A in another. The program displays a pie-shaped arc representing the percentage of sales made by division A.

14. Write a graphical interface for the user to choose the type of transformation, rotate, scale, shear, or translate, and to provide the necessary parameters. Display a rectangle in its original position and then show it after applying the chosen transformation.

15. Make a simple design of an X followed by an O. Draw the design in a `Buffered-Image` and make a `TexturePaint` from it. Fill an ellipse with this texture.

16. Write a graphical interface for the user to choose and end style and a join style for a line segment, and an angle. Draw two line segments with the chosen styles and intersecting in the chosen angle.

17. Use the `GeneralPath` methods of Exercise 11 to make a general path in the shape of a heart. Then draw the image of the Mona Lisa clipped to the shape of the heart.

18. Use attributed strings to design a special license plate for Java lovers with three digits followed by a drawing of a coffee cup followed by three letters.

PUTTING IT ALL TOGETHER 19. Write a program using Swing which has a *Print* menu item. When the user presses *Print*, pop up a file dialog for the user to select a file to print, and print the selected file.

20. Design a brochure of two to four pages for your favorite college using the Java2D techniques of this chapter.

7

Internationalization

Introduction

Using Java we can internationalize our programs so the numbers, dates, and currency appear in the format customary at the user's location. Collation can be done according to the rules for the user's language. We can customize user interface labels and messages to appear in the user's language.

OBJECTIVES

- Experiment with different locales and encodings.

- Format numbers, currency, dates, and times to reflect the user's locale.

- Collate according to the customs of the user's locale.

- Provide user interfaces that conform to the language of the user's locale.

- Format messages to conform to the language of the user's locale.

7.1   Locales and Encodings

· · · · · · · · · · ·

Locales define the location environment our programs will operate in, and encodings define mappings from characters to numbers.

Locales

Java uses locales to customize code to reflect differences in language and location. A locale represents a distinct area with its own language and style for representing numbers, date, and currency. We use a two-letter language code, a two-letter country code, and sometimes add a variant string to construct a Java locale.[*] Some locales are:

en_US	English in the United States
en_GB	English in the United Kingdom
es_ES	Spanish in Spain
es_MX	Spanish in Mexico
fr_FR	French in France
fr_CA	French in Canada
fr_FR_EURO	French in France with the Euro variant

The simple Java program of Example 7.1 lists the locales Java supports.[†] Typically one does not set a locale explicitly. The program gets the default locale setting on the user's platform.

EXAMPLE 7.1   **Locales.java**

```java
/* Lists supported locales.
 */

import java.text.DateFormat;
import java.util.Locale;

public class Locales {
  public static void main(String[] args) {
    System.out.println("Default locale is " + Locale.getDefault());  // Note 1
    Locale[] locales = DateFormat.getAvailableLocales();             // Note 2
    String spaces = "    ";
    for (int i = 0; i < locales.length; i++)
      if (locales[i].getCountry() != "")                             // Note 3
        System.out.println(locales[i] + spaces.substring
          (locales[i].toString().length())
                           + locales[i].getDisplayName());           // Note 4
  }
}
```

---

[*] ISO-639 lists language codes, while ISO-3166 lists country codes.

[†] More locales will be supported in future releases.

Output (The command java Locales >out directs output to the file out.)

```
Default locale is en_US
en_US          English (United States)
ar_AE          Arabic (United Arab Emirates)
ar_BH          Arabic (Bahrain)
ar_DZ          Arabic (Algeria)
ar_EG          Arabic (Egypt)
ar_IQ          Arabic (Iraq)
ar_JO          Arabic (Jordan)
ar_KW          Arabic (Kuwait)
ar_LB          Arabic (Lebanon)
ar_LY          Arabic (Libya)
ar_MA          Arabic (Morocco)
ar_OM          Arabic (Oman)
ar_QA          Arabic (Qatar)
ar_SA          Arabic (Saudi Arabia)
ar_SD          Arabic (Sudan)
ar_SY          Arabic (Syria)
ar_TN          Arabic (Tunisia)
ar_YE          Arabic (Yemen)
be_BY          Byelorussian (Belarus)
bg_BG          Bulgarian (Bulgaria)
ca_ES          Catalan (Spain)
cs_CZ          Czech (Czech Republic)
da_DK          Danish (Denmark)
de_AT          German (Austria)
de_AT_EURO     German (Austria,Euro)
de_CH          German (Switzerland)
de_DE          German (Germany)
de_DE_EURO     German (Germany,Euro)
de_LU          German (Luxembourg)
de_LU_EURO     German (Luxembourg,Euro)
el_GR          Greek (Greece)
en_AU          English (Australia)
en_CA          English (Canada)
en_GB          English (United Kingdom)
en_IE          English (Ireland)
en_IE_EURO     English (Ireland,Euro)
en_NZ          English (New Zealand)
en_ZA          English (South Africa)
es_AR          Spanish (Argentina)
es_BO          Spanish (Bolivia)
es_CL          Spanish (Chile)
es_CO          Spanish (Colombia)
es_CR          Spanish (Costa Rica)
es_DO          Spanish (Dominican Republic)
es_EC          Spanish (Ecuador)
es_ES          Spanish (Spain)
es_ES_EURO     Spanish (Spain,Euro)
es_GT          Spanish (Guatemala)
```

es_HN	Spanish (Honduras)
es_MX	Spanish (Mexico)
es_NI	Spanish (Nicaragua)
es_PA	Spanish (Panama)
es_PE	Spanish (Peru)
es_PR	Spanish (Puerto Rico)
es_PY	Spanish (Paraguay)
es_SV	Spanish (El Salvador)
es_UY	Spanish (Uruguay)
es_VE	Spanish (Venezuela)
et_EE	Estonian (Estonia)
fi_FI	Finnish (Finland)
fi_FI_EURO	Finnish (Finland,Euro)
fr_BE	French (Belgium)
fr_BE_EURO	French (Belgium,Euro)
fr_CA	French (Canada)
fr_CH	French (Switzerland)
fr_FR	French (France)
fr_FR_EURO	French (France,Euro)
fr_LU	French (Luxembourg)
fr_LU_EURO	French (Luxembourg,Euro)
hr_HR	Croatian (Croatia)
hu_HU	Hungarian (Hungary)
is_IS	Icelandic (Iceland)
it_CH	Italian (Switzerland)
it_IT	Italian (Italy)
it_IT_EURO	Italian (Italy,Euro)
iw_IL	Hebrew (Israel)
ja_JP	Japanese (Japan)
ko_KR	Korean (South Korea)
lt_LT	Lithuanian (Lithuania)
lv_LV	Latvian (Lettish) (Latvia)
mk_MK	Macedonian (Macedonia)
nl_BE	Dutch (Belgium)
nl_BE_EURO	Dutch (Belgium,Euro)
nl_NL	Dutch (Netherlands)
nl_NL_EURO	Dutch (Netherlands,Euro)
no_NO	Norwegian (Norway)
no_NO_NY	Norwegian (Norway,Nynorsk)
pl_PL	Polish (Poland)
pt_BR	Portuguese (Brazil)
pt_PT	Portuguese (Portugal)
pt_PT_EURO	Portuguese (Portugal,Euro)
ro_RO	Romanian (Romania)
ru_RU	Russian (Russia)
sh_YU	Serbo-Croatian (Yugoslavia)
sk_SK	Slovak (Slovakia)
sl_SI	Slovenian (Slovenia)
sq_AL	Albanian (Albania)
sr_YU	Serbian (Yugoslavia)
sv_SE	Swedish (Sweden)

```
th_TH          Thai (Thailand)
tr_TR          Turkish (Turkey)
uk_UA          Ukrainian (Ukraine)
zh_CN          Chinese (China)
zh_HK          Chinese (Hong Kong)
zh_TW          Chinese (Taiwan)
```

Note 1:   The `getDefault` method of the `Locale` class returns the default locale.

Note 2:   The `DateFormat` class, which we will use later, has a static method which returns the available locales in an array.

Note 3:   Each language has a locale without any country. For example `en` for English and `fr` for French. We use the **if** statement to omit those general locales which consist of a language only.

Note 4:   The second column of the output contains the display name for the locale. To keep that column aligned, we add as many blank spaces as we need to fill out the first column. We obtain the blanks by taking a substring of the `spaces` array starting from the end of the first column to the end of the `spaces` array. Thus a longer locale string results in a shorter string of blank spaces to fill out the first column.

Encodings

The world's languages use many different characters. Internally, Java uses **Unicode** which has codes for characters used by many of the major languages. People in different countries use a variety of encodings to convert bytes to characters when inputting characters and to convert characters to bytes when outputting them. The encodings we discuss are:

Cp437   MS_DOS United States, Australia, New Zealand, South Africa

Cp1252   Windows Latin-1

ISO8859-1   International Standards Organization Latin 1

Each of these encodings uses one byte for each character, ranging from 0 to 255. The first 128 characters are the same and correspond to the ASCII codes.

The DOS encoding, Cp437, contains characters for drawing boxes, and various other special characters. The Latin character sets agree except at positions 128-159, which are reserved for control characters in ISO8859-1. Characters numbered from 160-255 help in writing Western European languages. Figure 7.1 shows the Latin-1 encoding for the range 160-255, while Figure 7.2 shows Cp437.

Keyboards are configured for a particular language. Using Windows, one can change the keyboard mapping to reflect a language other than English, but this is awkward without relabeling the keys. Using the `Alt` key and the numeric keypad we can enter special characters used in foreign languages.

In a DOS command window, entering three digit numbers on the keypad, while holding down the `Alt` key, will cause the corresponding letter of the Cp437 encoding

Figure 7.1 Latin-1 character encoding for the range 160–255

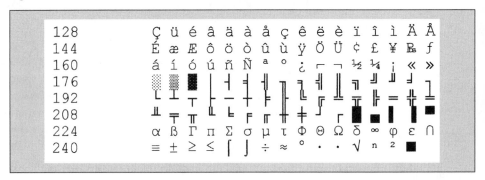

Figure 7.2 Cp437 character encoding for the range 128–255

to appear. For example, Alt+160 gives á. Entering four digits, the three-digit code preceded by a zero, will cause the corresponding Latin 1 character to appear. For example, Alt+0160 gives a space. Figure 7.3 shows some characters useful in Spanish text.

Figure 7.3

Character	Cp437 code	Latin 1 code
á	Alt 160	Alt 0225
é	Alt 130	Alt 0233
í	Alt 161	Alt 0237
ó	Alt 162	Alt 0243
ú	Alt 163	Alt 0250
ñ	Alt 164	Alt 0241
ç	Alt 135	Alt 0231
¡	Alt 173	Alt 0161
¿	Alt 168	Alt 0191

Within our program, we use Unicode to represent special characters. The Spanish word for more, "más," would be m\u00E1s in Unicode. To enter it from the keyboard we can use either Alt+160 or Alt+0225 to enter á. The value 0225 is the decimal equivalent of the hexadecimal value 00E1. Since the DOS command window uses the Cp437 encoding, we should read from the keyboard using that encoding. To output to a DOS window we use the Cp437 encoding for output. But to output to a Windows screen, we should use the Cp1252 or the ISO8859_1 encoding.

We can specify the encoding to be used with an `InputStreamReader` or an `Output-StreamWriter`. Example 2 shows how this is done. Java translates from the specified input encoding to Unicode, used internally, and translates from Unicode to the specified output encoding.

EXAMPLE 7.2   **Encodings.java**

```java
/* Uses encodings for input and output
 * entered as program arguments.
 */

import java.io.*;

public class Encodings {
  public static void main(String[] args) {
    try {
      BufferedReader in = new BufferedReader
              (new InputStreamReader(System.in,args[0]));        // Note 1
      System.out.println("Enter a character string");
      String s = in.readLine();
      for (int i = 0; i < s.length(); i++)
        System.out.println((int)s.charAt(i));                   // Note 2
      OutputStreamWriter o = new OutputStreamWriter
              (new FileOutputStream("out"),args[1]);            // Note 3
      PrintWriter out = new PrintWriter(o,true);                // Note 4
      out.println(s);
    }catch (IOException e) {
      e.printStackTrace();
    }
  }
}
```

....

Output (from `java Encodings Cp437 Cp1252`**)**

```
Enter a character string
más                                                            // Note 5
109
225                                                            // Note 6
115
```

Listing the file `out` in the DOS command window (using `type out`) gives

mßs   // Note 7

Opening the file `out` in a Notepad window (using `notepad out`) gives

más   // Note 8

....

Output (from `java Encodings Cp437 Cp437`**)**

```
Enter a character string
más
109
225
115
```

Listing out in a DOS command window gives

más   // Note 9

Opening out in Notepad gives

m s   // Note 10

....

Note 1:   The second argument to the `InputStreamReader` constructor specifies a character encoding. This constructor will throw `UnsupportedCodingExcep-tion`, a subclass of `IOException`, if the string passed in does not represent a valid encoding.

Note 2:   We show the internal Unicode values for the string we enter.

Note 3:   The second argument of the `OutputStreamWriter` constructor specifies the character encoding. This constructor will throw `UnsupportedEncodingEx-ception` if that argument string does not represent a valid encoding.

Note 4:   Setting the second argument of the `PrintWriter` constructor to **true** insures that the output buffer is flushed at each call to the `println` method.

Note 5:   We entered á by holding the `Alt` key while entering `160` on the numeric keypad, its code in the Cp437 encoding.

Note 6:   The `InputStreamReader` translates the 160 internally to 225, the Unicode code for á.

Note 7:   The `OutputStreamWriter` leaves the output code for á at 225, since the Cp1252 encoding is the same as Unicode in the range 160–255. Display-ing the output file in the DOS command window, which uses the Cp437 encoding, shows the character 225 as the German letter ß. The problem is that the DOS command window does not use the same encoding that Java used to write the file.

Note 8:   Displaying the output file in Notepad uses the Windows Cp1252 encod-ing in which 225 is the letter á.

Note 9:   Using the Cp437 encoding for the output file causes the internal 225 code to be written as 160, the Cp437 code for á. When we display the file in the DOS command window we see the letter á.

Note 10: Opening the output file in Notepad causes the character 160 to be displayed as a blank space, since 160 is the code for a blank space in the Cp1252 encoding. The problem is that this window does not use the same encoding in which the output file was written.

THE BIG PICTURE

Java supports a number of locales, defined by a language code, a country code, and, optionally, a variant. Locales let us configure programs to reflect the customs of the user's location. A number of character encodings convert bytes to characters. A DOS window uses Cp437, while Windows uses Cp1252 a variant of ISO8859-1 for Latin characters for Western European languages.

In Windows, we can enter characters using the Alt key. Java, in Windows, uses Cp1252 as the default encoding, but we can change it by specifying another argument in the reader and writer constructors.

TEST YOUR UNDERSTANDING

TRY IT YOURSELF 1. Run Example 7.2 with the input señor. Use the Cp437 encoding for input and the Cp1252 encoding for output. Explain the result when the output is displayed on the console, and when it is sent to a file opened in an editor such as Notepad.

TRY IT YOURSELF 2. Run Example 7.2 with the input señor. Use the Cp437 encoding for both input and output. Explain the result when the output is displayed on the console, and when it is sent to a file opened in an editor such as Notepad.

TRY IT YOURSELF 3. Run Example 7.2 with the input señor. Use the Cp437 encoding for input and the ISO8859-1 encoding for output. Explain the result when the output is displayed on the console, and when it is sent to a file opened in an editor such as Notepad.

7.2 Number, Currency, Percent, Date, and Time Formatting

Different locales use surprisingly different ways of formatting numbers and dates. For example, in the US we write 1,234.567, while in France the same number would be written as 1 234,567, and as 1'234.567 in Switzerland. Java lets us express numbers and dates using local customs.

Numbers

We use the NumberFormat class to display numbers, currency, and percents in the manner preferred in a given locale. Typically, programs will use the default locale set on the user's machine, and get NumberFormat instances without specifying a locale, as in

```
NumberFormat numDefault = NumberFormat.getNumberInstance();
```

To illustrate different formats, we can set the locale by passing a locale as an argument, as in

```
NumberFormat numDefault = NumberFormat.getNumberInstance(new Locale(fr,CA));
```

With a number format instance we use the `format` method to display numbers according the style of the locale chosen.

Customs vary for displaying monetary amounts. In the US, we write $1,234.56, with the dollar sign preceding the amount, but it France an amount would be written as 1 234,56 F in French francs. Percents may also vary depending on locale.

Example 7.3 shows how to format numbers to use locale information. It uses the default encoding, Cp1252, which is not suitable for displaying results in the DOS command window. We can either redirect the output to a file using the command

```
java Numbers fr FR >out
```

and open `out` in Notepad, or we can specify another encoding on the command line using

```
java -Dfile.encoding="Cp437" Numbers fr FR
```

We use the -D option to specify system properties, in this case the `file.encoding` property.

EXAMPLE 7.3   **Numbers.java**

```java
/* Formats numbers, currency, and percents, first in the
 * default locale, then using a language and country passed
 * as program arguments.
 */

import java.text.NumberFormat;
import java.util.Locale;

public class Numbers {
  public static void main(String[] args) {
    NumberFormat numDefault = NumberFormat.getNumberInstance();
    NumberFormat curDefault = NumberFormat.getCurrencyInstance();    // Note 1
    NumberFormat perDefault = NumberFormat.getPercentInstance();     // Note 2
    System.out.println("Max fraction digits: " +
                            numDefault.getMaximumFractionDigits()); // Note 3
    double d = 12345.67899;
    System.out.println(numDefault.format(d));                        // Note 4
    System.out.println(curDefault.format(d));
    System.out.println("Min fraction digits: " +
                    numDefault.getMinimumFractionDigits());          // Note 5
    System.out.println(perDefault.format(d));
    perDefault.setMinimumFractionDigits(2);                          // Note 6
    System.out.println(perDefault.format(d));
    Locale locale = new Locale(args[0], args[1]);
```

```
    NumberFormat number = NumberFormat.getNumberInstance(locale);     // Note 7
    NumberFormat currency = NumberFormat.getCurrencyInstance(locale);
    NumberFormat percent = NumberFormat.getPercentInstance(locale);
    System.out.println
              ("Encoding: " + System.getProperty("file.encoding"));// Note 8
    System.out.println(number.format(d));                            // Note 9
    System.out.println(currency.format(d));
    percent.setMinimumFractionDigits(2);
    System.out.println(percent.format(d));
  }
}
```

....

Output (using java Numbers fr FR**)**

```
Max fraction digits: 3
12,345.679
$12,345.68
Min fraction digits: 0
1,234,568%
1,234,567.90%
Encoding: Cp1252
12á345,679                                                          // Note 10
12á345,68 F
1á234á567,90%
```

....

Output (using java Numbers fr FR >out**, and opening** out **in Notepad)**

```
Max fraction digits: 3
12,345.679
$12,345.68
Min fraction digits: 0
1,234,568%
1,234,567.90%
Encoding: Cp1252
12 345,679
12 345,68 F
1 234 567,90%
```

....

Note 1:   The getCurrencyInstance method will return a NumberFormat object for currency values, localizing the number and the currency sign and position. Passing no arguments, we use the default locale, en_US in this example.

Note 2:   The getPercentInstance method returns a NumberFormat object that we use to format percents.

Note 3:   The number format instance has a default maximum of 3 digits after the decimal point. We could change the default by calling the setMaximumFractionDigits method.

Note 4: The format method displays the number according to the customs of the given locale.

Note 5: The default minimum fraction digits for this number format instance is 0, so the percent is rounded to the nearest integer.

Note 6: `perDefault.setMinimumFractionDigits(2);`
We set the minimum fraction digits to 2 to format percents with two places after the decimal point.

Note 7: `NumberFormat.getNumberInstance(locale)`
To experiment with other locales, we pass in a locale constructed from a language and country passed as program arguments.

Note 8: `("Encoding: " + System.getProperty("file.encoding"))`
We list the `file.encoding` property which specifies the encoding to use if none in used explicitly in the program as in Example 7.2, or on the command as an alternative way to run this example. The default encoding, Cp1252, is not suitable for displaying in the DOS command window.

Note 9: `System.out.println(number.format(d));`
Formats now will reflect the locale created from the language and country entered as program arguments.

Note 10: `12á345,679`
The correct output, shown in the second run, is `12 345,679`. The space used in the formatting is the non-breaking space, '\u0160.' The DOS command window uses encoding Cp437 which displays '\u0160' as á.

Dates

The Java classes for dates and times can be confusing to use. Many methods of the `Date` class were deprecated in Java 1.1 in favor of the `Calendar` class to better handle internationalization. However the `DateFormat.format` method requires a `Date` as an argument. `Calendar` is abstract, so we create an object of `GregorianCalendar`, a concrete subclass, and use the `getTime` method to return a `Date`.

```
Calendar calendar = new GregorianCalendar(2000,6,4,14,10,5);
Date theFourth = calendar.getTime();
```

The arguments to the `GregorianCalendar` constructor are the year, month, day, hour, minute, and second in that order. Another constructor uses on the year, month, and day. Java numbers the months from 0 through 11, with 0 for January, and 11 for December, however the correct month numbers appear in the output.

Date and time formats have four styles. From the most complete to the least they are:

Format	Example
DateFormat.FULL	Tuesday, July 4, 2000 2:10:05 PM PDT
DateFormat.LONG	July 4, 2000 2:10:05 PM PDT
DateFormat.MEDIUM	Jul 4, 2000 2:10:05 PM
DateFormat.SHORT	7/4/00 2:10 PM

The getDateTimeInstance method returns a DateFormat for both date and time. We use getDateInstance for dates only and getTimeInstance for times. Each of these methods has a version for the default locale and another in which the locale is specified.

EXAMPLE 7.4 **DateTime.java**

```java
/* Formats dates and times, first in the default locale,
 * then using a language and country passed as program arguments.
 */

import java.text.DateFormat;
import java.util.Locale;
import java.util.Calendar;
import java.util.GregorianCalendar;
import java.util.Date;

public class DateTime {
  public static void main(String[] args) {
    Calendar calendar = new GregorianCalendar(2000,6,4,14,10,5);
    Date theFourth = calendar.getTime();
    DateFormat fullDefault = DateFormat.getDateTimeInstance
                (DateFormat.FULL, DateFormat.FULL);           // Note 1
    DateFormat longDefault = DateFormat.getDateTimeInstance
                (DateFormat.LONG, DateFormat.LONG);
    DateFormat mediumDefault = DateFormat.getDateTimeInstance
                (DateFormat.MEDIUM, DateFormat.MEDIUM);
    DateFormat shortDefault = DateFormat.getDateTimeInstance
                (DateFormat.SHORT, DateFormat.SHORT);
    DateFormat justDate = DateFormat.getDateInstance();       // Note 2
    DateFormat justTime = DateFormat.getTimeInstance();
    System.out.println(fullDefault.format(theFourth));        // Note 3
    System.out.println(longDefault.format(theFourth));
    System.out.println(mediumDefault.format(theFourth));
    System.out.println(shortDefault.format(theFourth));
    System.out.println(justDate.format(theFourth));
    System.out.println(justTime.format(theFourth));
    Locale locale = new Locale(args[0], args[1]);
    DateFormat fullDT = DateFormat.getDateTimeInstance
                (DateFormat.FULL, DateFormat.FULL, locale);   // Note 4
    DateFormat longDT = DateFormat.getDateTimeInstance
                (DateFormat.LONG, DateFormat.LONG, locale);
    DateFormat mediumDT = DateFormat.getDateTimeInstance
                (DateFormat.MEDIUM, DateFormat.MEDIUM, locale);
```

```
      DateFormat shortDT = DateFormat.getDateTimeInstance
                  (DateFormat.SHORT, DateFormat.SHORT, locale);
   System.out.println(fullDT.format(theFourth));
   System.out.println(longDT.format(theFourth));
   System.out.println(mediumDT.format(theFourth));
   System.out.println(shortDT.format(theFourth));
  }
}
```

Output (using java DateTime fr FR**)**
Tuesday, July 4, 2000 2:10:05 PM PDT
July 4, 2000 2:10:05 PM PDT
Jul 4, 2000 2:10:05 PM
7/4/00 2:10 PM
Jul 4, 2000
2:10:05 PM

mardi 4 juillet 2000 14 h 10 GMT-07:00
4 juillet 2000 14:10:05 GMT-07:00
4 juil. 00 14:10:05
04/07/00 14:10

Note 1: The first argument specifies the style for the date, while the second indicates the time style. This method returns a DateFormat instance for the default locale. We used the same styles for the date and the time, but could have chosen different ones for each.

Note 2: The getDateInstance method will handle just the date, not the time. By omitting a style argument we accept the default style, which is MEDIUM.

Note 3: The format method returns a string formatted for the desired style and locale.

Note 4: We pass the locale as a third argument so that the date and time will be formatted for that locale.

THE BIG PICTURE

Using locales, we can format numbers, percents, currency, dates, and times in the style of the user's location. Typically, the locale is set on the user's machine and Java methods can use the default locale. For testing, we set a locale in the format objects. When using special characters, we must be aware of the character encoding used in order to view the output correctly.

TEST YOUR UNDERSTANDING

TRY IT YOURSELF   4.   Run Example 7.3 setting the file.encoding property to Cp437 on the command line. Is the output in a DOS window is the same as that of Example 7.3?

TRY IT YOURSELF   5.   Run Examples 7.3 and 7.4 for the French language in Switzerland. How do the outputs differ from those of Examples 7.3 and 7.4?

TRY IT YOURSELF   6.   Run Examples 7.3 and 7.4 for the Spanish language in Mexico. How do the outputs differ from those of Examples 7.3 and 7.4?

7.3   Collation

Rules for comparing strings vary according to the locale. For example, in traditional Spanish ch is a single letter which is alphabetized after all the other words starting with 'c' and before those starting with 'd.'* Thus in English "chocar" comes before "comprar," but in traditional Spanish the order is reversed. European languages use accented characters and other special characters such as á, ñ, and ß. Middle Eastern, Asian and other languages have many character variants.

The Collation class allows us to arrange strings according to the rules used in a given locale. The getInstance method returns a Collator object for the locale passed as its argument. The abstract Collation class has the RuleBasedCollator subclass that specifies collation rules for each supported locale.

The Collator class for the (Spanish,Spain) locale that comes with the JDK uses the revised Spanish which does not include the 'ch' character, but it does order accented characters. For example, comparing strings without a collator would order "más" after "mes" because the Unicode value for á is 225 which is greater than the value 101 for e. With the collator, "más" comes before "mes."

We can modify the Spanish collator to add rules to handle the 'ch' and 'll' characters found in traditional Spanish. The format for rules is tricky because they have to deal with the myriad of variations found in the world's languages. At the simplest level they look like

< a, A < b, B < c, C

and so on through the alphabet, indicating that 'a' comes before 'b,' which comes before 'c' and so on. To handle 'ch,' we just concatenate the rule

& c < ch, cH, Ch, CH

to the default Spanish rules. The new rule means that any variant of 'ch' should immediately follow 'c.'†

---

* In 1994 the Spanish language was modernized to omit ch and ll as separate letters.

† The commas in ch, cH, Ch, CH are significant, meaning that these variants differ only at the TERTIARY strength.

We can set the strength of a collator to one of four integer values, PRIMARY, SEC-ONDARY, TERTIARY, and IDENTICAL. In Spanish these strengths can be summarized as

least discriminating

```
PRIMARY      á == a, a == A,    \u0001 == \u0002
SECONDARY    á != a, a == A,    \u0001 == \u0002
TERTIARY     á != a, a != A,    \u0001 == \u0002
IDENTICAL    á != a, a != A,    \u0001 != \u0002
```

most discriminating

We can also set a decomposition property for a collator that could be used to handle accented characters or languages which elide characters together in other ways. We do not use decomposition in this text.

EXAMPLE 7.5   Alphabetize.java

```
/* Uses a Collator to compare Spanish strings. Customizes a
 * Collator by adding rules. Sets the collator strength. Uses
 * the compare package to hide the details of the comparison method.
 */

import java.text.Collator;
import java.text.RuleBasedCollator;
import java.text.ParseException;
import java.util.Locale;
import compare.Test;                                            // Note 1
import compare.TestCollator;


public class Alphabetize {
  public static void sort(String[] item, Test t) {
    for (int i = 1; i < item.length; i++) {
      String current = item[i];
      int j = 0;
      while (t.test(item[i],item[j]) > 0) j++;                  // Note 2


      for (int k = i; k > j; k--)
        item[k] = item[k-1];
      item[j] = current;
    }
  }
  public static void comparisons(Collator collator, int strength) {  // Note 3
    System.out.println("Level " + strength);
    collator.setStrength(strength);
    System.out.println
      ("\t Detects accents? " + collator.compare("m\u00e1s","mas")); // Note 4
```

```
    System.out.println
      ("\t Case sensitive? " + collator.compare("POT","pot"));        // Note 5
    System.out.println
      ("\t Detects controls? " + collator.compare("\u0001","\u0002"));// Note 6
    System.out.println();
  }
  public static void main(String[] args) {
    String[] item = {"m\u00e1s", "a\u00f1o", "comprar", "chocar",
          "luchar", "mes", "menudo", "arriba", "men\u00fa",
          "antes", "llegar"};                                          // Note 7
    System.out.println("String comparison");
    sort(item, new Test());                                            // Note 8
    display(item);
    Locale locale = new Locale("es","ES");
    Collator spanishDefault = Collator.getInstance(locale);            // Note 9
    System.out.println();
    System.out.println
      ("Rules: " + (spanishDefault instanceof RuleBasedCollator));     // Note 10
    System.out.println("Default Spanish collator");
    sort(item, new TestCollator(spanishDefault));
    display(item);
    String ruleText =
            ((RuleBasedCollator)spanishDefault).getRules();            // Note 11
    String newRules =
      ruleText + "& c < ch, cH, Ch, CH & 1 < ll, lL, Ll, LL";          // Note 12
    Collator spanishPlus = spanishDefault;
    try {
      spanishPlus = new RuleBasedCollator(newRules);
    } catch(ParseException e) {                                        // Note 13
      e.printStackTrace();
    }
    System.out.println("Augmented Spanish collator");
    sort(item, new TestCollator(spanishPlus));
    display(item);
    System.out.println();
    System.out.println
      ("Default Strength: " + spanishDefault.getStrength() + '\n');    // Note 14
    comparisons(spanishDefault, Collator.PRIMARY);                     // Note 15
    comparisons(spanishDefault, Collator.SECONDARY);
    comparisons(spanishDefault, Collator.TERTIARY);
    comparisons(spanishDefault, Collator.IDENTICAL);
  }
  public static void display(String [] anArray) {
    System.out.print("{");
    for (int i=0; i<anArray.length; i++) {
    if (i!=0) System.out.print(",");
      System.out.print(anArray[i]);
    }
    System.out.println("}");
  }
}
```

Output

String comparison
{antes,arriba,año,chocar,comprar,llegar,luchar,menudo,menú,mes,más}

Rules: true
Default Spanish collator
{antes,año,arriba,chocar,comprar,llegar,luchar,más,menú,menudo,mes}
Augmented Spanish collator
{antes,año,arriba,comprar,chocar,luchar,llegar,más,menú,menudo,mes}

Default Strength: 2
Level 0
    Detects accents? 0
    Case sensitive? 0
    Detects controls? 0

Level 1
    Detects accents? 1
    Case sensitive? 0
    Detects controls? 0

Level 2
    Detects accents? 1
    Case sensitive? 1
    Detects controls? 0
Level 3
    Detects accents? 1
    Case sensitive? 1
    Detects controls? -1

....

Note 1: The package `compare` shown below hides the compare method used in sorting so we avoid repeating code for each method.

Note 2: The `test` method of the `compare.Test` class returns a negative number if the first argument is less than the second, 0 if equal, and a positive number if greater.

Note 3: The `comparisons` method contains some tests to show how collators of differing strengths behave.

Note 4: Compares *más* with *mas*, outputting a non-zero value if the collator distinguishes accented characters from non-accented ones.

Note 5: Outputs a non-zero value if the collator is case sensitive.

Note 6:

```
System.out.println("\t Detects controls? " +
                   collator.compare("\u0001","\u0002"));
```

Outputs a non-zero value if the collator distinguishes control characters.

Note 7: The words with special characters are más, año, and menú.

Note 8:

```
sort(item, new Test());
```

We sort the `item` array using the default `test` method that does not use a `Collator`. The `compareTo` method used in the default test does not sort Spanish words properly. *año* comes after *arriba* because the Unicode value for 'ñ' is greater than that for 'r.' *chocar* comes before *comprar* and *llegar* comes before *luchar* because `ch` and `11` are not treated as single letters. *más* comes after *mes* and *menú* comes after *menudo* because the `compareTo` method does not handle accents properly, and uses the Unicode values to order strings. This would remain the case if we set the default locale to Spanish using `Locale.setDefault(new Locale(es,ES))`

Note 9:

```
Collator spanishDefault = Collator.getInstance(locale);
```

We get a collator for the locale es_ES. This collator from the Java SDK uses the revised Spanish which does not recognize the letters `ch` and `11`. Converting this program to an applet and using the corresponding collator in a browser will show that the browser collators do recognize the `ch` and `11` characters found in traditional Spanish.

Note 10:

```
spanishDefault instanceof RuleBasedCollator
```

Collator is an abstract class, so that collator objects are instances of a subclass, in this case `RuleBasedCollator` which uses ordering rules.

Note 11:

```
((RuleBasedCollator)spanishDefault).getRules();
```

The `getRules` method returns the rules as a `String`, but because the string contains many Unicode characters it is difficult to display. Fortunately we do not need to display the rules, but merely to augment them to handle the `ch` and `11`.

Note 12:

```
String newRules = ruleText
          + "& c < ch, cH, Ch, CH & 1 < 11, 1L, L1, LL";
```

Rules follow a specific intricate syntax. The `&` character indicate a reset to the position of the next letter, c. The following expression, `ch, cH, Ch, CH,` after the `<` sign, representing a primary difference, indicates that all variants of `ch` should be ordered immediately after c. The commas between the `ch` variants indicates that these are tertiary differences only taken into account if the collator has TERTIARY strength. A PRIMARY or SECONDARY strength iterator would treat `ch` as equal to `Ch`, but a TERTIARY strength iterator would find `ch` less than `Ch`. The semicolon separator, `;`, indicates a secondary difference, while the equality sign, `=`, denotes equality.

Note 13: `catch(ParseException e)`
Java will throw a `ParseException` if the collator rules are not correctly formed.

Note 14: `spanishDefault.getStrength()`
The four collator strength levels are:

```
primary 0
secondary 1
tertiary 2
identical 3
```

The default strength is 2, or tertiary.

Note 15: `comparisons(spanishDefault, Collator.PRIMARY);`
We execute the `comparisons` method for each of the four strength levels to see how collators of different strengths order accented characters and control characters, and whether or not they are case sensitive.

The package `compare` lets us hide the details of the comparison method used. The superclass `Test` has a `test` method that uses the `String compareTo` method which does no localization. The `TestCollator` class overrides the `test` method to use a collator for a specific locale. When making comparisons in Example 7.5, we used the `test` method each time, but with three different instances of the Test class or a subclass. Example 7.6 contains the code for the classes in the compare package.

EXAMPLE 7.6 **Test.java and TestCollator.java**

```java
/* The class Test hides the comparison method.
 * This superclass uses the String compareTo
 * method with no internationalization.
 */

package compare;

public class Test {
  public int test(String s1, String s2) {
    return s1.compareTo(s2);
  }
}

/* Extends Test to use the Collator
 * compare method.
 */

package compare;

import java.text.Collator;
public class TestCollator extends Test {
  Collator collator;
```

```
public TestCollator(Collator c) {
  collator = c;
}
public int test(String s1, String s2) {
  return collator.compare(s1, s2);                        // Note 1
}
}
```

Note 1:   The `compare` method uses the ordering rules of its collator.

THE BIG PICTURE

Comparing strings with the `String` `compareTo` method uses Unicode values to compare individual characters, which treat accented characters and other special characters incorrectly. The `Collation` class allows us to arrange strings according to the rules used in a given locale. By setting the collator's strength appropriately, we can choose to distinguish accented characters, special characters (perhaps represented by multiple regular characters), control characters, and upper- and lower-case.

TEST YOUR UNDERSTANDING

7. Which of the following does the default Spanish collator distinguish? Upper- from lower-case? Accented characters from the corresponding unaccented letter? One control character from another?

TRY IT YOURSELF   8. How does á compare to a using the collators in Example 7.5? To find out, add the word *mas* to the item array of Example 7.5, and interpret the results.

7.4   Localizing User Interfaces

Users from all over the world can download our applets or use programs we have written. Java allows us to localize user interfaces so that the labels, button names, display strings and other locale dependent items can be displayed in the language variant found on the user's platform. To illustrate this localization, we use the interface shown in Figure 7.4 viewed in the default en_US locale.

Figure 7.4   A user interface in the en_US locale

The title, "Growth," the labels, "Rate," "Balance," and "Years," the button name, "Amount," and the "Press Button" instruction need to appear in the language of each supported locale, rather than always in English. The output message shown in Figure 7.5 appears when we use the interface, and it should be localized also.

Figure 7.5   Another view of the user interface of Example 7.7

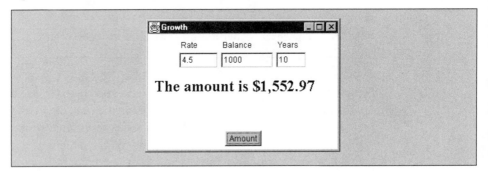

We name a property for each item we wish to localize. For this user interface we define the title, rate, balance, years, button, message, and result properties. The ResourceBundle class makes properties available to a Java program. We use the getBundle method to create a resource bundle

```
bundle = ResourceBundle.getBundle("Labels")
```

and then use the getString method to get the value of each property

```
bundle.getString("rate")
```

Rather than hardcoding a label value as

```
Label rate = new Label("Rate");
```

for English, or

```
Label rate = new Label("Tipo");
```

for Spanish, we use the property value returned by the getString method

```
Label rate = new Label(bundle.getString("rate"));
```

One way to define a property list uses text files while another uses Java classes. In either case we group properties in hierarchies with each group name reflecting a locale. When the program is run, it uses the locale to find the appropriate group of properties.

Property files

Using property files, we group properties in text files with the .properties extension. For our example we create two files, Labels.properties and Labels_es.properties. In the Spanish properties file we use '\u00f3' for ó and '\uoof1' for ñ.

Labels.properties
```
title = Growth
result = The amount is
rate = Rate
message = Press Button
balance = Balance
years = Years
button = Amount
```

Labels_es.properties
```
title=Crecimiento
result=La cantidad es
rate=Tipo
message=Pulsa el Bot\u00f3n
years=A\u00f1os
button=Cantidad
```

These two property files localize our program for Spanish or English. We would need additional files to use other languages correctly, or to add variants of English or Spanish for different countries.

When we call getBundle("Labels"), Java uses the locale to find properties. If the locale is en_US, Java first looks for a file Labels_en_US.properties containing properties localized for English in the United States. We did not provide this file, so it next looks for Labels_en.properties, which would define properties for English. Since this is not found, our program uses the properties from the Labels file that is at the highest level of the hierarchy.

If the locale is es_MX, Spanish in Mexico, Java looks for a Labels_es_MX.properties file, and not finding such a file it gets properties from the Labels_es.properties file. If it does not find a property name from this file, it looks for it in the Labels.properties file. Thus our program will find the rate property value, Tipo, in Labels_es.properties, but will find the balance property value, Balance, in the Labels.properties file. To localize for French would need to define a Labels_fr.properties file, and perhaps files for specific countries such as Labels_fr_CA.properties.

Running Example 7.7 with any of the commands

```
java GrowthProperty
java GrowthProperty en US
java GrowthProperty fr FR
```

gives the interface of Figure 7.4 and a result like Figure 7.5. We do not provide properties to localize the interface for French.

Running Example 7.7 with any of the commands

```
java GrowthProperty es ES
java GrowthProperty es MX
```

gives the interface of Figure 7.6, and the result appears as in Figure 7.7 with the amount localized for Mexican pesos for the command

```
java GrowthProperty es MX
```

Figure 7.6 `GrowthProperty` **localized for Spanish**

Figure 7.7 `GrowthProperty` **with** `es_MX` **localized currency**

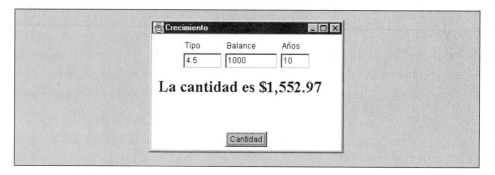

EXAMPLE 7.7 **GrowthProperty.java**

```java
/* Localizes a user interface with a resource
 * bundle and property files.
 */

import java.awt.*;
import java.awt.event.*;
import java.text.NumberFormat;
import java.util.ResourceBundle;
import java.util.Locale;

public class GrowthProperty extends Frame
                            implements ActionListener {
  private TextField getRate = new TextField(5);
  private TextField getBalance = new TextField(8);
  private TextField getYears = new TextField(3);
  private Label rate;
  private Label balance;
```

```
private Label years;
private MyCanvas canvas = new MyCanvas();
private Button button;
private String amount;
private NumberFormat nf;
private ResourceBundle bundle;

public GrowthProperty(String language, String country) {
  Locale.setDefault(new Locale(language, country));              // Note 1
  bundle = ResourceBundle.getBundle("Labels");                   // Note 2
  setTitle(bundle.getString("title"));
  rate = new Label(bundle.getString("rate"));
  balance = new Label(bundle.getString("balance"));
  years = new Label(bundle.getString("years"));
  button = new Button(bundle.getString("button"));               // Note 3
  message = bundle.getString("message");                         // Note 4
  Panel p1 = new Panel();
  p1.setLayout(new GridLayout(2,1));
  p1.add(rate);
  p1.add(getRate);
  Panel p2 = new Panel();
  p2.setLayout(new GridLayout(2,1));
  p2.add(balance);
  p2.add(getBalance);
  Panel p3 = new Panel();
  p3.setLayout(new GridLayout(2,1));
  p3.add(years);
  p3.add(getYears);
  Panel p = new Panel();
  p.add(p1);
  p.add(p2);
  p.add(p3);
  Panel p4 = new Panel();
  p4.add(button);
  add(p,"North");
  add(canvas,"Center");
  add(p4,"South");
  addWindowListener(new CloseWindow());
  button.addActionListener(this);
  nf = NumberFormat.getCurrencyInstance();
}
public String computeGrowth() {
  double rate = new Double(getRate.getText()).doubleValue();
  double balance = new Double(getBalance.getText()).doubleValue();
  int years = new Integer(getYears.getText()).intValue();
  for (int i = 1; i <= years; i++)
    balance += balance * rate/100;
  return nf.format(balance);
}
```

```
        public void actionPerformed(ActionEvent event) {
          String result = bundle.getString("result");          // Note 5
          message = result + computeGrowth();
          canvas.repaint();
        }
        public static void main(String [] args) {
          String language = "en";
          String country = "US";
          if (args.length == 2) {
          language = args[0];
          country = args[1];
        }
        GrowthProperty f = new GrowthProperty(language, country);   // Note 6
          f.setSize(300,200);
          f.show();
        }
        class CloseWindow extends WindowAdapter {
          public void windowClosing(WindowEvent event) {
            System.exit(0);
          }
        }
        class MyCanvas extends Canvas {
          public MyCanvas() {
            Font f = new Font("Serif",Font.BOLD,24);
            setFont(f);
          }
          public void paint(Graphics g) {
            g.drawString(message,10,30);
          }
        }
}
```

Note 1:   We set the locale to allow experimentation with different locales. Normally the program would just use the default locale.

Note 2:   The getBundle method finds the appropriate .properties file based on the locale. The argument, Labels, specifies the property file prefix, so for the locale es_MX, the files Labels_es_MX.properties, Labels_es.properties, and Labels.properties will be searched for in that order when seeking a property value in a resource bundle.

Note 3:   Instead of hardcoding the button's label we read the button property from the resource file to localize the label.

Note 4:   The value of the message property is the message displayed when the program starts.

Note 5:   The value of the result property is the description of the result.

Note 6:   GrowthProperty f = new GrowthProperty(language, country);
If the user does not specify a language and a country as program arguments, we use en_US.

Property classes

Using property files is convenient when all the properties have string values, but when properties may have `Object` values that are not strings, we use property classes. When using property files, Java creates a `PropertyResourceBundle` subclass of `ResourceBundle`, but when using property classes the subclass is `ListResourceBundle`.

To specify property values we create a hierarchy of Java classes. For this example we create `LabelList`, `LabelList_en_CA`, `LabelList_es`, and `LabelList_es_MX` classes. Each class extends `ListResourceBundle` and overrides the `getContents` method to return an array of properties and their values. We illustrate with the same interface used in Example 7.7, but add `background`, `foreground`, and `color` properties whose values are of type `Color` rather than `String`. The interface appears in the colors of the national flag of the locale. Example 7.8 includes the various `LabelList` classes. The class that creates the interface would be exactly the same as that of Example 7.7, except that we add the extra color properties.

EXAMPLE 7.8

LabelList.java, LabelList_en_CA.java, LabelList_es.java, LabelList_es_MX.java, GrowthList.java

LabelList.java

```java
/* Creates a property class which include properties
 * whose values are colors. Values are set for en_US.
 */

import java.util.ListResourceBundle;
import java.awt.Color;

public class LabelList extends ListResourceBundle {
  public Object[][] getContents() {
    return contents;
  }
  static final Object[][] contents = {                    // Note 1
    {"title", "Growth"},
    {"result", "The amount is "},
    {"rate", "Rate"},
    {"message", "Press Button"},
    {"balance", "Balance"},
    {"years", "Years"},
    {"button", "Amount"},
    {"foreground", Color.blue},                           // Note 2
    {"background", Color.red},
    {"color", Color.white}
  };
}
```

LabelList_en_CA.java

```
/* Overrides properties for en_CA.
 */

import java.util.ListResourceBundle;
import java.awt.Color;

public class LabelList_en_CA extends ListResourceBundle {
  public Object[][] getContents() {
    return contents;
  }
  static final Object[][] contents = {
    {"foreground", Color.red},                              // Note 3
    {"background", Color.white}
  };
}
```

LabelList_es.java

```
/* Overrides properties for es.
 */

import java.util.ListResourceBundle;
import java.awt.Color;

public class LabelList_es extends ListResourceBundle {
  public Object[][] getContents() {
    return contents;
  }
  static final Object[][] contents = {
    {"title", "Crecimiento"},
    {"result", "La cantidad es "},
    {"rate", "Tipo"},
    {"message", "Pulsa el Bot\u00f3n"},
    {"years", "A\u00f1os"},
    {"button", "Cantidad"},
    {"background", Color.yellow},
    {"foreground", Color.red}
  };
}
```

LabelList_es_MX.java

```
/* Overrides properties for es_MX.
 */

import java.util.ListResourceBundle;
import java.awt.Color;
```

```
public class LabelList_es_MX extends ListResourceBundle {
  public Object[][] getContents() {
    return contents;
  }
  static final Object[][] contents = {
    {"background", Color.green},
  };
}
```

GrowthList.java

```
// The only changes from GrowthProperty.java involve adding colors.

public GrowthList(String language, String country) {
  ...
  bundle = ResourceBundle.getBundle("LabelList");              // Note 4
  ...
  Color color = (Color)bundle.getObject("color");             // Note 5
  getRate.setBackground(color);
  getBalance.setBackground(color);
  getYears.setBackground(color);
  button.setBackground(color);
  ...
  setBackground((Color)bundle.getObject("background"));
  setForeground((Color)bundle.getObject("foreground"));
  ...
}
```

Note 1: The contents array of arrays has one element for each property. The first component of each element is the name of the property, while the second is its value which can be any subclass of `Object`. We would need to wrap primitive types in wrapper classes such as Integer.

Note 2: The foreground property has a value of type `Color`.

Note 3: We override the foreground property to change it to red for the Canadian flag. Java searches the most specific class first, so `LabelList_en_CA` will be searched before the `LabelList`.

Note 4: We change the top-level name to `LabelsList`. We could have used these `LabelList` classes in Example 7.7 by changing the top level name there from `Labels` to `LabelList`. The `getBundle` method first looks for property classes for the desired locales, and if they are not found it then looks for property files with the `.properties` extension.

Note 5: We use the `color` property to set colors for the interface.

Running Example 7.8 with the command

```
java GrowthList es ES
```

produces the interface of Figure 7.8. The yellow background and red writing use the colors of the Spanish flag. There is no LabelList_es_ES class or properties file, so Java uses the LabelList_es class to get the property values, and would look in the Label-List class after that for any values not yet found.

Figure 7.8 GrowthList **for Spain**

Running Example 7.8 with the command

```
java GrowthList es MX
```

produces an interface like that of Figure 7.8, but with a green background and red writing representing the colors of the Mexican flag.

THE BIG PICTURE

In a Java program we use a resource bundle to localize user interface labels and strings. We can either use property files or Java classes to hold the localized values. Java classes permit Object values as well as strings. Java searches for resources looking for the most specific locale first, using language and country code, then using just the language code, and finally the resource name.

TEST YOUR UNDERSTANDING

9. When running Example 7.7, both locales es_ES and es_MX use the Labels_es and Labels property files. Nevertheless in Figure 7.7, for the locale es_MX, the amount appears in pesos, while running Example 7.7 for the locale es_ES the amount appears in pesetas. Why the difference?

10. The top-level property file usually specifies values for the default locale. How would we write the Example 7.7 Label property files for a Spanish language default locale?

TRY IT YOURSELF   11. Modify Example 7.7 to pass the top-level name of the resource bundle as a program argument. Run, passing LabelList as the top-level name to show that we can execute the example using property files or Java classes.

7.5   Message Formatting

Some parts of a message are static and some are dynamic. For example, in

```
The time is 2:52 pm.
```

we can write the text "The time is " in advance, but we need to wait until the program is run to get the correct time to display. The MessageFormat class lets us create strings with patterns that are filled at runtime with the correct values.

In our program, we add argument numbers in curly brackets to indicate where dynamic content should be substituted. To display the current date we create the pattern

```
String s = "The date is {0}."
```

create an array of objects to specify how to fill in the arguments

```
Object [] arguments = { new Date() };
```

and format the string

```
String formatted = MessageFormat.format(s,arguments);
```

which will display as

```
The date is 11/4/99 4:33 PM.
```

If we want just the date and not the time, we can be more specific about the format, to override the format method's use of a default date format. Specifying the string as

```
String s = "The date is {0, date}.";
```

will display s as

```
The date is Nov 4, 1999.
```

To control the date style, we can add one the styles, full, long, medium (the default), or short to the argument. The result would be

Figure 7.9

Format	Output
{0, date, full}	The date is Thursday, November 4, 1999.
{0, date, long}	The date is November 4, 1999.
{0, date, short}	The date is 11/4/99.

We can use several arguments in one string. In the string

```
The due date for assignment {0} is {1}, before {2}.
```

argument 0 is the assignment number, argument 1 is the due date, and argument 2 is the time.

Message formatting helps in internationalizing programs. We can use property files to localize message strings. Date, time, number and percent arguments will appear correctly for the user's locale and in the correct position in the localized string. In Example 7.9 we use the file `Patterns.properties` which contains the strings

```
pattern1 = The date today is {0}, the time is {0}, and my name is {1}.
pattern2 = The date today is {0,date,long}, and the time is {0,time,short}.
```

and, for Spanish, the file `Patterns_es.properties`

```
pattern1 = Me llamo {1}, la fecha de hoy es {0}, y el tiempo es {0}.
pattern2 = El tiempo es {0,time,short}, y la fecha de hoy es el {0,date,long}.
```

Note that the arguments appear in different places in the corresponding Spanish patterns, which is not a word for word translation of the English.

EXAMPLE 7.9   **MessageBundles.java**

```
/* Uses message formatting to localize
 * messages which include dynamic content.
 */

import java.text.MessageFormat;
import java.util.Date;
import java.util.Locale;
import java.util.ResourceBundle;

public class MessageBundles {
  public static void main(String[] args) {
    if (args.length == 3)
        Locale.setDefault(new Locale(args[1],args[2]));       // Note 1
    ResourceBundle bundle = ResourceBundle.getBundle("Patterns");
    String pattern1 = bundle.getString("pattern1");           // Note 2
    MessageFormat mf1 = new MessageFormat(pattern1);          // Note 3
    Object[] arguments = { new Date(), args[0] };             // Note 4
    System.out.println(mf1.format(arguments));
    String pattern2 = bundle.getString("pattern2");           // Note 5
    MessageFormat mf2 = new MessageFormat(pattern2);
    System.out.println(mf2.format(arguments));
  }
}
```

Output (Using the command java MessageBundles Art**)**

```
The date today is 12/4/99 4:30 PM, the time is 12/4/99 4:30 PM,
                                            and my name is Art.
The date today is December 4, 1999, and the time is 4:30 PM.
```

Output `java -Dfile.encoding=Cp437 MessageBundles Arturo es ES`

> We specify the correct encoding for the DOS command window, in case
> we use any special characters.)

```
Me llamo Arturo, la fecha de hoy es 4/12/99 16:49, y el tiempo es 4/12/99 16:49.
El tiempo es 16:49 16:49, y la fecha de hoy es el 4 de diciembre de 1999.
```

....

Note 1:   We set the locale for testing purposes, to try other locales. The deployed
program would accept the user's default locale.

Note 2:   The `pattern1` string uses the default format for dates which is not ideal
here.

Note 3:   We create a `MessageFormat` object and use its `format` method. This is more
appropriate when we have several messages to format. We could have used
the static `MessageFormat.format` method to format this one message.

Note 4:   The arguments must be objects so we would have to wrap primitive types
in wrapper classes such as `Integer` and `Double`.

Note 5:   The `pattern2` arguments include `date` and `time` modifiers and `long` and
`short` styles to better format the date and time.

We can use choice formats to further customize our strings. For example, we can distinguish between singular and plural forms of words, outputting

```
You have one missing assignment
```

for a singular value, but

```
You have 7 missing assignments
```

for a plural value.
    The choice pattern

```
{0, choice, 0#s|1#|2#s}
```

states that argument 0 is a choice. For values of argument 0 from 0 up to but not
including 1, the choice is "s." For values from 1 up to 2 the choice is " ", while for values 2 and greater the choice is "s." Concatenating this pattern onto the word "*assignment*" will make the form used correct. The full string is

```
"You have {0,number,integer} missing assignment" +"{0,choice,0#s|1#|2#s} "
```
Example 7.10 demonstrates this use of the choice format.

EXAMPLE 7.10   **Messages.java**

```
/* Illustrates the choice format
 */

import java.text.MessageFormat;
```

```
public class Messages {
  public static void main(String[] args) {
    String pattern1 = "You have {0,number,integer} missing assignment"
                      +"{0,choice,0#s|1#|2#s} ";
    Object[] missing = {new Integer(Integer.parseInt(args[0]))};
    System.out.println(MessageFormat.format(pattern1, missing));
    String pattern2 = "You have {0,choice,0#no|1#{0}} missing assignment"
                      +"{0,choice,0#s|1#|2#s} ";                    // Note 1
    System.out.println(MessageFormat.format(pattern2, missing));
  }
}
```

Output (Using java Messages 7**)**

```
You have 7 missing assignments
You have 7 missing assignments
```

Output (Using java Messages 1**)**

```
You have 1 missing assignment
You have 1 missing assignment
```

Output (Using java Messages 0**)**

```
You have 0 missing assignments
You have no missing assignments
```

Note 1:   We further customize the string to display "*no*" instead of "0."

THE BIG PICTURE

We add dynamic content to messages using patterns. We mark the spots to insert content with curly braces enclosing an array index to an array of values to be substituted in the message. At run time, the `format` method inserts the values from the array into the message. By including modifiers in the arguments we can select the style for numbers, dates, and times. Using property files or Java classes, we can customize the messages for the user's locale.

TEST YOUR UNDERSTANDING

12. In Example 7.9, what would the output for `pattern2` in English be if we change the date style to *short* and the time style to *long*?

SUMMARY

- Java operates globally. Our programs can customize user interfaces and output to appear in the style of the language and country in which the program is run. Two letter language codes, combined with a two-letter country code, and an optional variant, specify a locale. For example, `en_US` denoted English in the United States, while `fr_CA` represent French in Canada. Java internationalizes based on the user's locale.

- Java uses Unicode internally to represent characters. Various encodings translate bytes input by the user to Unicode characters and from Unicode to bytes output to the user. Encoding typically preserve the ASCII characters at their usual values from byte 32 to 127. DOS command windows use the Cp437 encoding which differs in bytes 160-255 from Cp1252 used by Windows, and the very similar ISO standard 8859-1 containing characters for Western European languages. In Windows we can use the `Alt` key to enter characters using byte numbers or Unicode values.

- Numbers and dates have a surprising number of different formats common around the world. The `NumberFormat` class has methods to get number, currency, and percent instances with which to format. These methods have one version that uses the default locale read from the user's machine, and another in which we pass the locale as an argument. Using these format methods, numbers, dates, and percents will appear appropriately whenever the program is run in one of the many supported locales.

- By default, the `compareTo` method uses Unicode values to compare strings. This only works well when using the basic ASCII characters. Languages with additional characters and accented characters use different rules for collating. Fortunately, Java has a `Collation` class which implements rules based on the user's locale. We can set the strength of the collator to determine how precise we wish it to be.

- Resource bundles allow us to customize user interfaces. The program loads values of labels, strings, and other locale dependent data either from property files or Java classes. A given set of resources have a top-level name, say `Stuff`. Java looks for a resource first at the most specific level, `Stuff_en_US` for example. If not found, it tries `Stuff_en`, and if not found, it then tries `Stuff`. The programmer provides the resource files for each locale, and they will be used to localize the program when it is run.

- Messages can include content only available at runtime. The message contains arguments which a format method fills in at runtime with values from an array. We can choose the style for numbers, dates, and percents, and configure messages to choose singular or plural forms as appropriate.

Program Modification Exercises

. . . .

1. Convert Example 7.5 to an applet and execute it in a browser to see how the browser's default collator's work.

2. Modify Example 7.5 to use French collators instead of Spanish. Try the words mèche, pelle, pêche, péché, and meilleur to see how accents are handled.

3. Modify Example 7.7 to use Swing rather than AWT components.

4. Modify Example 7.9 to use the static `format` method from the `MessageFormat` class rather than creating `MessageFormat` objects.

PUTTING IT ALL TOGETHER   5. Internationalize the `ButtonJPanelPink` applet of Example 5.2. For Spanish, use *uno* for *one*, *dos* for *two*, and *Hola* for *Hi there*. Optionally, configure the applet for other languages you know.

PUTTING IT ALL TOGETHER   6. Internationalize the `SelectItem` applet of Example 5.7. For French, use *Rouge* for *Red*, *Vert* for *Green*, *Bleu* for *Blue*, *Cercle* for *Circle*, and *Carré* for *Square*. Optionally, configure the applet for other languages you know.

Program Design Exercises

. . . .

7. Create a collator for the `en_US` locale which does not distinguish between uppercase and lowercase letters. Include test cases to illustrate this behavior.

8. Write a Java program which allows the user to choose a locale from a list, and display a number, a currency amount, and a date according to the chosen locale.

9. Write a Java program that allows the user to choose a locale from a list, and a strength level for a collator for that locale. Provide two text fields for the user to enter two strings. The program should display the lesser string above the greater, or display both on the same line if they are equal.

10. Write a Java program which compares two strings. Use a choice pattern to format the output so that it correctly displays the message that the first string is less than, equal to, or greater than the second. For example, the output might be, "Hat is greater than fat," or "Hat is less than Sat".

8 Multimedia

Introduction

Java facilitates multimedia applications. We discuss animation, sound, the Java Media Framework for playing and capturing audio and video, and Java 3D to work with three-dimensional scenes.

OBJECTIVES

- Animate images, text, and drawings.

- Play sound clips.

- Use Java Media Framework to play video clips.

- Create 3D shapes with lighting, texture, and motion.

8.1 Animation

In animation, we vary the display as time passes. For example, we can display several images in succession to give the appearance of motion. In this section we animate images and text. We use a thread to allow the animation to proceed concurrently with other processing.

Double Buffering

When using AWT components, showing one image after another may cause the screen to flicker. The animation thread repeats these steps:

- Select the new image.

- Request a repainting of the applet.

- Sleep for a fixed duration.

With an AWT component, such as an Applet, the `repaint` method asks for the screen to be redrawn. Window repainting has to be coordinated with the operating system that manages all the windows. The thread that handles paint events calls the `update` method. It clears the screen and calls the `paint` method that we override to specify how we would like the window drawn.

Flickering occurs because of the alternation between the clear screen and the image. Alternating between the white background and the colored image causes an irritating flicker. To avoid the flicker we use double buffering, drawing on an off-screen buffer and copying the buffer to the screen. We clear the buffer before redrawing the new image, but this clearing does not cause flicker because it is off the visible screen. We must also override the update method to eliminate the clearing of the screen, no longer necessary because we clear the buffer off screen.

Swing components automatically incorporate double buffering so this problem did not arise in the animation of Example 5.5. Although we do not use Swing components in Example 5.1, we do use a Swing `ImageIcon`. The `ImageIcon` preloads an image using a `MediaTracker` object, saving us the trouble of using one explicitly to wait for the image to load before using it. To get the different images in Example 8.1, we expand and contract a photo of the author. The thread changes the dimensions of the image, calls for a repainting of the screen, and sleeps for 300 milliseconds.

The `init` method loads the original image, creates an off-screen buffer of the same size as the applet, and gets a `Graphics` object used to draw in the buffer. The `paint` method clears the off-screen buffer, draws the image in its new dimensions in the off-screen buffer, and draws the buffer on the screen.

Figure 8.1 shows the animation of Example 8.1 at an intermediate stage.

Figure 8.1   A frame from the animation of Example 8.1

EXAMPLE 8.1 Animate.java

```
/* Uses double buffering to avoid flicker with AWT
 * components. Animates an image.
 */

import java.awt.*;
import java.applet.Applet;
import java.net.*;
import javax.swing.ImageIcon;

public class Animate extends Applet implements Runnable {
  private boolean done;
  private int imageWidth, imageHeight;
  private Image pic;
  private Image buffer;
  private Graphics bufferGraphics;

  public void init() {
    pic = new ImageIcon("gittleman.gif").getImage();
    buffer = createImage(getSize().width,getSize().height);        // Note 1
    bufferGraphics = buffer.getGraphics();                         // Note 2
  }
  public void start() {                                            // Note 3
    done = false;
    Thread t = new Thread(this);
    t.start();
  }
  public void stop() {                                             // Note 4
    done = true;
  }
  public void update(Graphics g) {                                 // Note 5
    paint(g);
  }
  public void paint(Graphics g) {
    bufferGraphics.
    clearRect(0,0,getSize().width,getSize().height);               // Note 6
    bufferGraphics.
    drawImage(pic,10,10,imageWidth,imageHeight,null);              // Note 7
    g.drawImage(buffer,10,10,null);                                // Note 8
  }
  public void run() {
    imageWidth = pic.getWidth(null);                               // Note 9
    imageHeight = pic.getHeight(null);
    int dx=20, dy=5;                                               // Note 10
    while (true) {
      for(int i=0; i<10; i++) {
        if (done) return;                                          // Note 11
        imageWidth += dx;
        imageHeight += dy;
        repaint();
```

```
          try {
            Thread.sleep(300);
          }catch(InterruptedException e) {
            e.printStackTrace();
          }
        }
      dx = -dx; dy = -dy;
      }
    }
}
```

Note 1: The getSize method returns a Dimension object holding the dimension of the object in public fields, height and width. We create an image the size of the applet to use for our off-screen drawing.

Note 2: The getGraphics methods returns a Graphics object enabling us to draw on the off-screen buffer.

Note 3: The browser calls the applet's start method whenever the user returns to the page containing the applet. We create a new thread and call its start method indicating it is ready to run.

Note 4: The browser calls the applet's stop method whenever the user leaves the page containing the applet. We set the done flag to **true** so the thread will terminate when it checks it in the run method.

Note 5: We override the update method to eliminate the clearing of the screen. Instead of clearing the screen and calling paint, it just calls paint.

Note 6: bufferGraphics. clearRect(0,0,getSize().width,getSize().height); We clear the entire buffer to erase the previous image in preparation for drawing the next image.

Note 7: bufferGraphics.drawImage(pic,10,10,imageWidth,imageHeight,null); This version of the drawImage method scales the image to have size image-Width X imageHeight, and draws the image with upper-left corner at (10,10). The last argument is an ImageObserver, used to track the image loading, which we do not need.

Note 8: g.drawImage(buffer,10,10,null); This version of the drawImage method draws the image, passed as its first argument, at its actual size, without any scaling. Although this method does not scale the image, the buffer contains the image scaled from the original picture by the previous drawImage method.

Note 9: imageWidth = pic.getWidth(null); Again we pass **null** for the ImageObserver argument which we do not use.

Note 10: int dx=20, dy=5; Each time we draw the picture we increase its width by 10 pixels and its height by 5. After drawing it ten times, we decrement the dimensions for 10 more iterations, and repeat in an unending loop.

Note 11: `if (done) return;`

The `stop` method sets the `done` flag to **true**. When the thread returns from the `run` method it terminates.

Animating Text

The animation technique used in Example 8.1 works for other types of drawings. Rather than trying to draw cartoons or other shapes, we animate text. The `ImageIcon` class implements the `Icon` interface, which contains the three methods

```
int getIconHeight()
int getIconWidth()
void paintIcon (Component c, Graphics g, int x, int y)
```

The first argument to `paintIcon` has type `Component`. The method makes a component available to use its methods in drawing. We do not use the component in our `TextIcon` class, designed to draw a string in a given size and color.

The `TextIcon` class implements the `Icon` interface. In the `paintIcon` method, we specify how we would like to draw the text. The `TextIcon` constructor contains arguments to pass the string to display, its color, and its size. It creates a font, and gets its font metrics so the `getIconWidth` and `getIconHeight` methods can determine the size of the text.

The text of Example 8.2 grows larger and larger for ten iterations, and then grows smaller and smaller for another ten, repeating this sequence in an unending loop. Figure 8.2 shows an intermediate stage.

Figure 8.2 A frame from the animation of Example 8.2

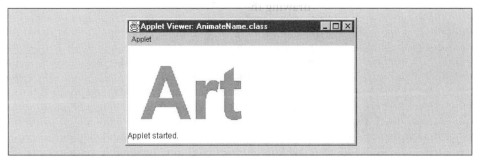

EXAMPLE 8.2 **AnimateName.java**

```java
/* Animates a word. Defines a TextIcon to display the text.
 */

import java.awt.*;
import java.applet.Applet;
import java.net.*;
import javax.swing.Icon;
```

```
public class AnimateName extends Applet implements Runnable {
  private boolean done;
  private int size = 10;
  private TextIcon text;
  private Image buffer;
  private Graphics bufferGraphics;

  public void init() {
    buffer = createImage(getSize().width,getSize().height);
    bufferGraphics = buffer.getGraphics();
  }
  public void start() {
    done = false;
    Thread t = new Thread(this);
    t.start();
  }
  public void stop() {
    done = true;
  }
  public void update(Graphics g) {
    paint(g);
  }
  public void paint(Graphics g) {
    bufferGraphics.clearRect(0,0,getSize().width,getSize().height);
    text = new TextIcon("Art",Color.red,size);            // Note 1
    text.paintIcon(null,bufferGraphics,10,100);           // Note 2
    g.drawImage(buffer,10,10,null);
  }
  public void run() {
    int dx=10;
    while (true) {
      for(int i=0; i<10; i++) {
        if (done) return;
        size += dx;
        repaint();
        try {
          Thread.sleep(300);
        }catch(InterruptedException e) {
          e.printStackTrace();
        }
      }
      dx = -dx;
    }
  }
}
class TextIcon extends Component implements Icon {
  private Color color;
  private String text;
  private Font font;
  private FontMetrics metrics;

    public TextIcon(String t, Color c, int i) {
```

```
        color = c;
        text = t;
        font = new Font("Arial",Font.BOLD,i);
        metrics = getFontMetrics(font);                          // Note 3
      }
    public int getIconWidth() {
      return metrics.stringWidth(text);
    }
    public int getIconHeight() {
      return metrics.getHeight();
    }
    public void paintIcon(Component c, Graphics g, int x, int y) {
      g.setColor(color);
      g.setFont(font);
      g.drawString(text, x, y);
    }
  }
}
```

Note 1: We initialize the size of the text at 10 points, but will change it in the run method.

Note 2: The paintIcon method will draw the string in the off-screen buffer with its lower-left corner at position (10,100).

Note 3: We use the font metrics object to get the height of the font, and the width of the string as displayed in that font.

Using Multiple Images

Examples 8.1 and 8.2 scale an original to obtain additional frames to display. More typically each frame is a different image or drawing. Example 8.3 illustrates this by animating a sequence of words. The words

Have
  A
    Great
      Day

appear one after the other, each in a different color and size.

EXAMPLE 8.3   **AnimateText.java**

```
/* Animates a four word message.
 */

import java.awt.*;
import java.applet.Applet;
import java.net.*;
import javax.swing.Icon;
```

```
public class AnimateText extends Applet implements Runnable {
  private boolean done;
  private int i = 0;
  private TextIcon[] text = new TextIcon[4];
  private Image buffer;
  private Graphics bufferGraphics;

public void init() {
  text[0] = new TextIcon("Have", Color.blue, 30);
  text[1] = new TextIcon("A", Color.green, 40);
  text[2] = new TextIcon("Great", Color.red, 60);
  text[3] = new TextIcon("Day", Color.magenta, 50);
  buffer = createImage(getSize().width,getSize().height);
  bufferGraphics = buffer.getGraphics();
}
public void start() {
  done = false;
  Thread t = new Thread(this);
  t.start();
}
public void stop() {
  done = true;
}
public void update(Graphics g) {
  paint(g);
}
public void paint(Graphics g) {
  bufferGraphics.clearRect(0,0,getSize().width,getSize().height);
  text[i].paintIcon(null,bufferGraphics,10+60*i,100);          // Note 1
  g.drawImage(buffer,10,10,null);
}
public void run() {
  while (true) {
    for(i = 0; i < 4; i++) {                                    // Note 2
      if (done) return;
        repaint();
        try {
          Thread.sleep(1000);
        }catch(InterruptedException e) {
          e.printStackTrace();
        }
      }
    }
  }
// TextIcon is the same as in Example 2
}
```

....

Note 1:   We draw text[i] at a position depending on the index i which changes in
               the run method.

Note 2:   The **for** loop repaints and sleeps for a second. The paint method draws text[i], so as the index i varies, the four words are displayed. The outer **while** loop repeats this animation.

THE BIG PICTURE

We use a thread to animate images and text, displaying sequences of images with a short interval between each frame. Flickering occurs because of the quick alternation between the image and the clear screen. Double buffering eliminates flicker because we clear an off-screen buffer and copy the new image to the screen with clearing it. Swing components implement double buffering automatically, but using AWT components we must do it.

The animation thread sequences the images and sleeps for a short time between frames.

TEST YOUR UNDERSTANDING

TRY IT YOURSELF   1.   Modify Example 8.1 to eliminate the off-screen buffer, and draw the image on the screen with modified dimensions, imageHeight and image Width. Describe the result.

TRY IT YOURSELF   2.   Modify Example 8.1 to remove the overriding of the update method. Describe the result.

TRY IT YOURSELF   3.   Modify Example 8.1 to remove the call to clearRect. Describe the result.

8.2   Sound

· · · · · · · · · ·

Java lets us play sound clips in our applets. Java versions 1.0 and 1.1 support the AU format for audio files, while the Java 2 Platform adds support for MIDI (type 0 and type 1), RMF, WAVE, and AIFF files. Playing audio requires a machine with a sound card.

We can play an audio clip using the play method of the applet class, either with an absolute URL

```
public void play(URL url);
```

or a relative URL

```
public void play(URL url, String name);
```

The java.Applet package contains the AudioClip interface with methods play, loop, and stop. The play method plays an audio clip; the loop method plays an audio clip repeatedly until the stop method is invoked. The Applet class has methods

```
public AudioClip getAudioClip(URL url);
```

and

```
public AudioClip getAudioClip(URL url, String name);
```

enabling us to get an audio clip.

In Example 8.4 we animate a ball. Each time the ball moves we play a spoken word "boom." While the ball moves, we use another thread to loop a whistling rendition of the first few bars of a familiar tune. When the applet stops, we stop the animation and the whistling (mercifully).

We can use a browser or applet viewer to open the URL

```
http://www.engr.csulb.edu/~artg/PlayBall.html
```

If not connected to the Internet, we can test the applet on our own machine.

Figure 8.3   The applet of Example 8.4

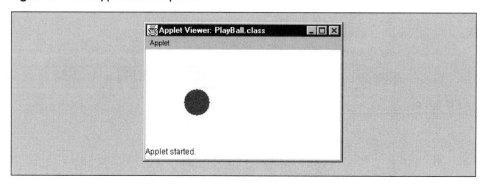

EXAMPLE 8.4   PlayBall.java

```
/* Animates a ball. Plays a boom sound at each frame.
 * Loops a whistle in a separate thread.
 */

import java.awt.*;
import java.applet.*;                                              // Note 1
import java.net.*;

public class PlayBall extends Applet
  implements Runnable {
  private int x, y;
  private boolean done;
  private URL boomURL;
  AudioClip whistle;

public void init() {
  try {
    URL url1 = new URL(getDocumentBase(),"whistle.au");           // Note 2
    boomURL = new URL(getCodeBase(),"boom.au");                   // Note 3
    whistle = getAudioClip(url1);                                 // Note 4
```

```
      setForeground(Color.blue);
    }catch (MalformedURLException e) {
      e.printStackTrace();
    }
  }
  public void start() {                              // Note 5
    x = 50; y = 50;
    done = false;
    Thread t = new Thread(this);
    t.start();
    Sound sound = new Sound(whistle);
    sound.start();
  }
  public void stop() {
    done = true;
    whistle.stop();                                  // Note 6
  }
  public void paint(Graphics g) {
    g.fillOval(x,y,40,40);
  }
  public void run() {
    int dx = 9, dy = 9;
      while (true) {
        for(int i = 0; i < 10; i++) {
          if (done) return;
          x += dx;
          y += dy;
          play(boomURL);                             // Note 7
          repaint();
          try {
            Thread.sleep(1000);                      // Note 8
          }catch(InterruptedException e) {
            e.printStackTrace();
          }
        }
        dx = -dx; dy = -dy;
      }
    }
    class Sound extends Thread {                      // Note 9
      AudioClip clip;
      public Sound(AudioClip a) {
        clip = a;
      }
      public void run() {
        clip.loop();                                 // Note 10
      }
    }
  }
```

Note 1: We import `java.applet.*` because we use both the `Applet` class and the `AudioClip` interface from the `java.applet` package.

Note 2: The `whistle.au` file is in the same directory as the document containing the applet, `PlayBall.html`. All versions of Java play the AU format used in this example (the 8000 Hz frequency can be played in all Java versions).

Note 3: The `boom.au` file is in the same directory as the applet code file, `PlayBall.class`.

Note 4: We use an audio clip because we want to loop this sound. The applet itself only includes a `play` method.

Note 5: When the applet starts we start the threads to do the animation and play the whistling.

Note 6: `whistle.stop();`
The `stop` method of the `AudioClip` class stops the looping of that clip.

Note 7: `play(boomURL);`
We use the `play` method of the applet to speak the word boom every time we move the ball.

Note 8: `Thread.sleep(1000);`
The thread sleeps for a full second to give the sound time to play.

Note 9: `class Sound extends Thread {`
We use a thread for the looping sound because we want it to continue concurrently with the animation and the other sound.

Note 10: `clip.loop();`
The `loop` method repeats the clip until the `stop` method is called.

THE BIG PICTURE

The `play` method lets us play a sound clip in an applet. The `getAudioClip` method returns an `AudioClip` class which has `play`, `loop`, and `stop` methods. The `loop` method plays a sound clip until we invoke the `stop` method. We locate a sound clip using a URL. Java 1.1 supports the AU format, while Java 2 supports additional formats.

TEST YOUR UNDERSTANDING

TRY IT YOURSELF 4. Run Example 8.4 with `PlayBall.html` in a different directory from the one containing `PlayBall.java`. In which of these directories should you place `whistle.au`? Which for `boom.au`?

TRY IT YOURSELF 5. What happens if you omit the call to `whistle.stop` from Example 8.4?

TRY IT YOURSELF 6. Modify Example 8.4 to loop the boom sound in the `Sound` thread rather than play it in thread t.

8.3   The Java Media Framework

The Java Media Framework (JMF) allows Java applications and applets to display and capture multimedia data. It supports many media content types including MPEG, QuickTime, AVI, WAV, AU, and MIDI. Various compression methods produce files in these formats. A codec performs media compression and decompression. Each codec has certain formats that it can handle. The Java Media Framework documentation lists the supported formats.

The Java 2 Platform Standard Edition does not include JMF, which may be downloaded from `http://java.sun.com/products/java-media/jmf`. JMF can also be used with Java 1.1. The installation program automatically adjusts the classpath. We introduce JMF, but do not begin to exploit its capabilities.

The JMF classes are a standard extension to core Java. The `javax.media` package contains the basic JMF classes. The JMF distribution comes with a media player, a Java program that plays media files. Our example will create a media player in an applet. A media player processes the data, rendering the sound or images. Timekeeping facilities allow synchronization of several players.

A media player can be in one of several states. For our simple example, we need to know when the player becomes realized so it can provide visual components and controls. The player generates controller events and sends them to controller listeners. We listen for a `RealizeCompleteEvent` subtype of `ControllerEvent` in order to know when to add the visual or control panel components, if they exist. We listen for an `EndOfMediaEvent` subtype to restart the clip when it ends.

The NASA site

`http://www-istp.gsfc.nasa.gov/istp/outreach/movies.html`

has links to interesting clips of astronomical phenomena which we use as illustrations. The site

`http://www.wavsounds.com`

has thousands of sound clips.

Figure 8.4 shows the applet of Example 8.5, which has a text field to enter the URL of a media clip, and a choice box with two preset video and two audio choices. When the user makes a selection a new window pops up to view or hear the clip.

Figure 8.4   The applet of Example 8.5

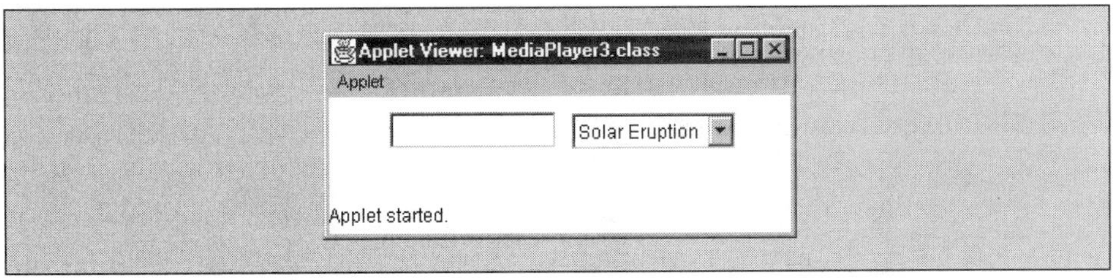

Figure 8.5 shows the media player started in response to the user's request to view a solar eruption.

Figure 8.5 Viewing a solar eruption (Example 8.5)

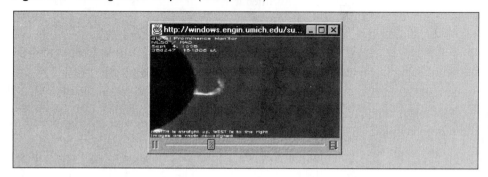

EXAMPLE 8.5 **MediaPlayer3.java**

```java
/* Creates a media player to play
 * video and sound clips.
 */

import javax.media.*;
import java.awt.*;
import java.awt.event.*;
import java.net.URL;
import java.applet.Applet;

public class MediaPlayer3 extends Applet {
  Choice mediaChoice = new Choice();
  TextField mediaText = new TextField(12);
  static int position = 100;
  String[] clip = {
    "http://windows.engin.umich.edu/sun/movies/promerupt495.mpg",
    "/whistle.au",
    "/elephnt3.wav",
    "http://solar.physics.montana.edu/YPOP/Movies/sun_diver.mpg"
  };
  String[] titles = {"Solar Eruption", "Whistle", "Elephant",
                     "Solar Activity"};

  public void init() {
    Panel p = new Panel();
    p.add(mediaText);
    add(p);
    for(int i = 0; i < 4; i++)
      mediaChoice.add(titles[i]);
    add(mediaChoice);
    mediaText.addActionListener(new ActionListener() {          // Note 1
      public void actionPerformed(ActionEvent e) {
        new PlayerFrame(mediaText.getText());
```

```
        }
      });
    mediaChoice.addItemListener(new ItemListener() {        // Note 2
      public void itemStateChanged(ItemEvent e) {
        new PlayerFrame(clip[mediaChoice.getSelectedIndex()]);
      }
    });
}
class PlayerFrame extends Frame implements ControllerListener{    // Note 3
  Player player = null;
  public PlayerFrame(String s) {
    super(s);
    URL url;
    try {
      if (s.substring(0,4).equals("http"))
      url = new URL(s);
      else url = new URL (getCodeBase(),s);
      player = Manager.createPlayer(url);                // Note 4
      player.addControllerListener(this);
      player.start();                                   // Note 5
    }catch (Exception e) {
      e.printStackTrace();
    }
  }
  public void controllerUpdate(ControllerEvent e) {      // Note 6
    Component c;
    if (e instanceof RealizeCompleteEvent) {            // Note 7
      setSize(300,200);
      setLocation(position,0); // Note 8
      position += 100;
      setVisible(true);
      if ((c = player.getVisualComponent()) != null) // Note 9
        add(c,"Center");
      if ((c = player.getControlPanelComponent()) != null) // Note 10
        add(c,"South");
        validate();                                    // Note 11
        addWindowListener(new WindowAdapter() {
          public void windowClosing(WindowEvent e) {   // Note 12
            player.stop();
            player.deallocate();
            dispose();
          }
        });
    }
    else if (e instanceof EndOfMediaEvent) {           // Note 13
      player.setMediaTime(new Time(0));
      player.start();
    }
  }
}
```

Note 1: When the user enters a URL in the text field, we start a media player to play it.

Note 2: When the user selects a URL from the choice box, we start a media player to play it.

Note 3: The `PlayerFrame` creates a media player and implements the controller listener interface to handle controller events the player generates.

Note 4: Java provides the `Manager` class for obtaining system dependent resources such as media players.

Note 5: The `start` method starts the player as soon as possible.

Note 6: `public void controllerUpdate(ControllerEvent e)`
This is the only method of the controller listener interface. It handles controller events generated by the media player.

Note 7: `if (e instanceof RealizeCompleteEvent)`
When a player reaches the realized state, it knows the resources it needs. We can show the window and add the necessary components.

Note 8 : `setLocation(position,0);`
We may have several players active at the same time. We create each at a separate position so it is at least partially visible to the user.

Note 9: `if ((c = player.getVisualComponent()) != null)`
If there is a visual component, we get it and add it in the center region.

Note 10: `if ((c = player.getControlPanelComponent()) != null)`
If there is a control panel component, we get it and add it to the south region.

Note 11: `validate();`
When adding components, we need to have the layout manager redo the layout.

Note 12: `public void windowClosing(WindowEvent e)`
When the user closes the window, we stop the clock, release resources the player is using, and free the window resources.

Note 13: `else if (e instanceof EndOfMediaEvent)`
When the clip finishes, we reset the clock and start the player again to repeat the clip.

THE BIG PICTURE

The Java Media Framework, a separate download, provides classes to play and capture multimedia data. Media players created in Java applets and applications handle many types of media files. They generate controller events that describe the state of the player.

TEST YOUR UNDERSTANDING

TRY IT YOURSELF   7.   Modify Example 8.5 to omit the call to the `validate` method. Describe the result.

TRY IT YOURSELF   8.   Find a multimedia file and enter its URL in the text field of Example 8.5.

8.4 Java 3D Basics

Java 3D provides a programming interface to three-dimensional graphics rendering. A Java 3D program places 3D objects in a scene graph that specifies both content and presentation.

The Java 2 Platform Standard Edition does not include the Java3D classes but they may be downloaded from

`http://java.sun.com/products/java-media/3D/index.html`

The Java 3D documentation and specification require separate downloads via links from the Java 3D site.

The Java 3D API includes the Java 3D core classes in the `javax.media.j3d` package, and core math classes in the `javax.vecmath` package. To make 3D programming easier, Sun also provides utility classes in the packages nested in `com.sun.j3d.utils`.

We introduce some fascinating and powerful Java 3D features, but only scratch the surface of the Java 3D capabilities.

A Scene Graph

The scene graph defines the 3D content and presentation. The `VirtualUniverse` sits at the top of the graph, and may have one or more locales. Each locale has a branch specifying the content and another to specify the viewing perspective. The examples in this text use a `SimpleUniverse` object that provides a default implementation of a locale with a viewing perspective. Thus our scene graphs will start with A `SimpleUniverse` at the top. Figure 8.6 shows the scene graph for Example 8.6.

Figure 8.6 The scene graph for Example 8.6

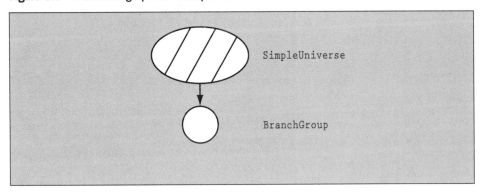

Example 8.6 creates a Canvas3D object, which extends java.awt.Canvas, and adds it in the center of a top-level window. It passes the 3D canvas to the SimpleUniverse as a drawing platform. Creating a BranchGroup to describe the content and adding it to the simple universe complete this simple program. Figure 8.7 shows the blank screen that results because content has not yet been specified.

Figure 8.7   A simple universe with nothing in it

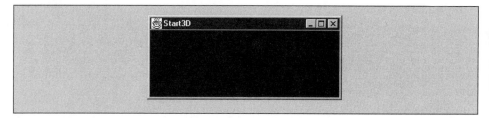

EXAMPLE 8.6   **Start3D.java**

```java
/* Creates a universe with
 * nothing in it.
 */

import java.awt.*;
import java.awt.event.*;
import javax.media.j3d.*;
import com.sun.j3d.utils.universe.*;

public class Start3D extends Frame {
  public static void main(String[] args) {
    Start3D frame = new Start3D("Start3D");
    frame.setSize(300,200);
    frame.setVisible(true);
  }
  public Start3D(String title) {
    super(title);
    addWindowListener(new WindowAdapter() {
      public void windowClosing(WindowEvent e) {
        System.exit(0);
      }
    });
    Canvas3D canvas = new Canvas3D(null);                          // Note 1
    add(canvas, "Center");
    SimpleUniverse universe = new SimpleUniverse(canvas);
    BranchGroup root = new BranchGroup();
    universe.addBranchGraph(root);                                 // Note 2
  }
}
```

Note 1:   The `Canvas3D` constructor takes a graphics configuration as its argument. We do not use it, so we pass **null**.

Note 2:   The `addBranchGraph` method adds a content node to the universe.

A Cube

The basic 3D primitives are vertices and lines. Rather than constructing solids from these primitives, we use the solids provided in the `com.sun.j3d.utils.geometry` package starting with the `ColorCube` in Example 8.7. The scene graph for Example 8.7 adds a leaf node, of type `Shape3D`, representing the color cube.

Figure 8.8   The scene graph for Example 8.7

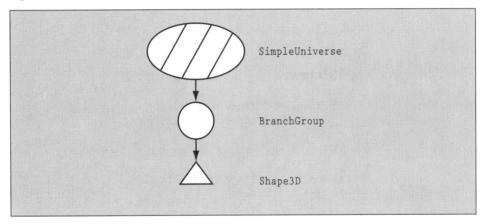

Because we are adding an object to the scene, we get the viewing platform from the simple universe and set a viewing distance. We construct the cube with a scale of .5 so it will not fill the whole canvas. Unfortunately, as Figure 8.9 shows, the default position of the cube has us looking directly at it, so it does not appear three-dimensional. We will fix this in Example 8.8.

Figure 8.9   The cube of Example 8.7

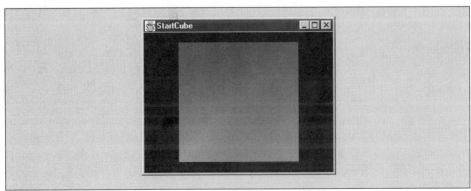

EXAMPLE 8.7   StartCube.java

```java
/* Adds a cube to the scene.
 */

import java.awt.*;
import java.awt.event.*;
import javax.media.j3d.*;
import com.sun.j3d.utils.universe.SimpleUniverse;
import com.sun.j3d.utils.geometry.ColorCube;

public class StartCube extends Frame {
  public static void main(String[] args) {
    StartCube frame = new StartCube("StartCube");
    frame.setSize(300,300);
    frame.setVisible(true);
  }
  public StartCube(String title) {
    super(title);
    addWindowListener(new WindowAdapter() {
      public void windowClosing(WindowEvent e) {
        System.exit(0);
      }
    });
    Canvas3D canvas = new Canvas3D(null);
    add(canvas, "Center");
    SimpleUniverse universe = new SimpleUniverse(canvas);
    universe.getViewingPlatform().setNominalViewingTransform();
    BranchGroup root = new BranchGroup();
    ColorCube cube = new ColorCube(.5);
    root.addChild(cube); // Note 1
    universe.addBranchGraph(root);
  }
}
```

....

Note 1:   BranchGroup inherits the addChild method from Group, which is a superclass of both BranchGroup and TransformGroup.

Transforms

The Transform3D class enables us to apply transforms to orient the objects in space. We add a transform group node to the scene graph to tell the renderer to apply the transform to descendants. To make the cube appear three-dimensional, Example 8.8 rotates it by 30 degrees about the x-axis, and by 60 degrees about the y-axis, as Figure 8.10 shows.

The scene graph of Figure 8.11 contains a transform group node representing these rotations.

Figure 8.10   The rotated cube of Example 8.8

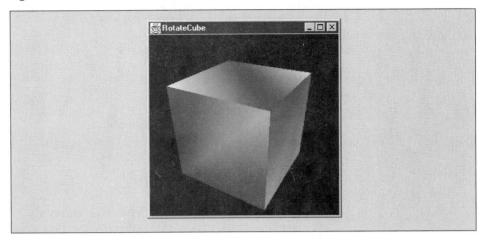

Figure 8.11   The scene graph for Example 8.8

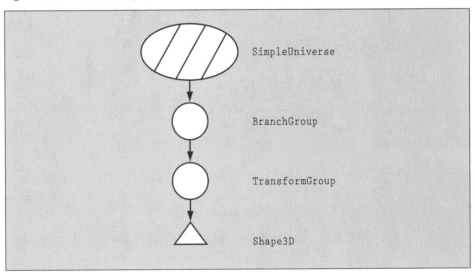

EXAMPLE 8.8   **RotateCube.java**

```
/* Rotates the cube by 30 degrees about the x-axis
 * and 60 degrees about the y-axis.
 */

import java.awt.*;
import java.awt.event.*;
import javax.media.j3d.*;
import com.sun.j3d.utils.universe.SimpleUniverse;
import com.sun.j3d.utils.geometry.ColorCube;
```

```
public class RotateCube extends Frame {
  public static void main(String[] args) {
    RotateCube frame = new RotateCube("RotateCube");
    frame.setSize(300,300);
    frame.setVisible(true);
  }
  public RotateCube(String title) {
    super(title);
    addWindowListener(new WindowAdapter() {
      public void windowClosing(WindowEvent e) {
        System.exit(0);
      }
    });
    Canvas3D canvas = new Canvas3D(null);
    add(canvas, "Center");
    SimpleUniverse universe = new SimpleUniverse(canvas);
    universe.getViewingPlatform().setNominalViewingTransform();
    BranchGroup root = new BranchGroup();
    Transform3D transform = new Transform3D();
    transform.rotX(Math.PI/6.0);                              // Note 1
    Transform3D y60 = new Transform3D();
    y60.rotY(Math.PI/3.0);                                    // Note 2
    transform.mul(y60);                                       // Note 3
    TransformGroup group = new TransformGroup(transform);     // Note 4
    root.addChild(group);                                     // Note 5
    ColorCube cube = new ColorCube(.5);
    group.addChild(cube);
    universe.addBranchGraph(root);
  }
}
```

Note 1:   The rotX method sets the transform to be a rotation about the x-axis, replacing its previous value.

Note 2:   The rotY method sets the transform to be a rotation about the y-axis, replacing its previous value.

Note 3:   The mul method sets the transform to the transform that results from applying the original transform and then the argument transform. The name mul refers to the fact that a matrix represents each transform, and combining the transforms mathematically involves multiplying the matrices.

Note 4:   We create a transform group to represent the desired transform, a composition of rotations in this example.

Note 5:   Adding the transform group to the scene graph will insure that the renderer will apply the transform it represents to its descendants.

Shapes

The `ColorCube` has a predefined appearance. The `com.sun.j3d.utils.geometry` package includes the `Primitive` type with `Box`, `Cone`, `Cylinder`, and `Sphere` subclasses. We need to specify the appearance of these primitive shapes. In Example 8.9 we will create each primitive shape with a default appearance, white in color, with no lighting or texture, and will modify the appearance in subsequent examples.

In Example 8.9, we add four shapes, so we have to translate each to its location in the scene. After translating a shape, we rotate it to make it appear three-dimensional from our viewing point.

The primitive shape constructors include arguments for the dimensions of the shape, and for an `Appearance` object to specify the appearance. Figure 8.12 shows the four shapes of Example 8.9.

Figure 8.12   The shapes of Example 8.9

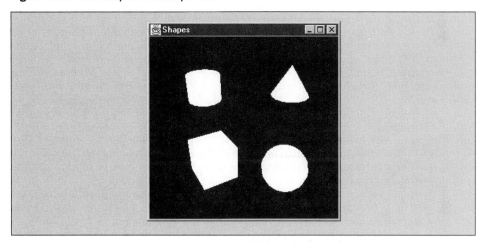

EXAMPLE 8.9   **Shapes.java**

```java
/* Adds a box, cone, cylinder,
 * and sphere to the scene.
 */

import java.awt.*;
import java.awt.event.*;
import javax.media.j3d.*;
import javax.vecmath.Vector3d;
import com.sun.j3d.utils.universe.SimpleUniverse;
import com.sun.j3d.utils.geometry.*;

public class Shapes extends Frame {
  public static void main(String[] args) {
    Shapes frame = new Shapes("Shapes");
    frame.setSize(300,300);
```

```
    frame.setVisible(true);
  }
  public void setShape(BranchGroup parent,
                Vector3d translate, Primitive shape) {          // Note 1
    Transform3D transform = new Transform3D();
    Transform3D t = new Transform3D();
    t.rotX(Math.PI/6);
    transform.set(translate);                                  // Note 2
    transform.mul(t);                                          // Note 3
    t.rotY(Math.PI/6);
    transform.mul(t);
    transform.setScale(.5);                                    // Note 4
    TransformGroup group = new TransformGroup(transform);
    parent.addChild(group);
    group.addChild(shape);
  }
  public Shapes(String title) {
    super(title);
    addWindowListener(new WindowAdapter() {
      public void windowClosing(WindowEvent e) {
        System.exit(0);
      }
    });
    Canvas3D canvas = new Canvas3D(null);
    add(canvas, "Center");
    SimpleUniverse universe = new SimpleUniverse(canvas);
    universe.getViewingPlatform().setNominalViewingTransform();
    BranchGroup root = new BranchGroup();
    setShape(root, new Vector3d(-.6,-.6,-2.0),
                new Box(.7f,.7f,.7f,new Appearance()));         // Note 5
      setShape(root, new Vector3d(-.6,.6,-1.0),
                new Cylinder(.5f,.8f, new Appearance()));       // Note 6
      setShape(root, new Vector3d(.6,.6,-.5),
                new Cone(.5f,.8f, 0, new Appearance()));        // Note 7
      setShape(root, new Vector3d(.6,-.6,-1.0),
                new Sphere(.7f, new Appearance()));             // Note 8
    universe.addBranchGraph(root);
  }
}
```

....

Note 1:   Because we are adding four shapes, we create a method to set the transform for each. The first argument is the scene graph node from which the shape will descend. The second is a `Vector3d` representing a translation, and the third is the primitive shape we are adding. We apply the same rotations about the x- and y-axes to each of the shapes.

Note 2:   The `set` method changes the transform to a translation specified by its vector argument.

Note 3:   We combine the rotation by 30 degrees around the x-axis with the translation.

Note 4:   We use the `setScale` method to reduce the size of the shapes so they do not overlap.

Note 5:   The positive x-axis extends to the right, while the positive y-axis extends upward, and the positive z-axis extends toward the front. Thus the translation of (-.6,-.6,-2.0) moves the box left, down, and back. The box has dimension (.7,.7,.7) where the units are in meters. We specify a default appearance.

Note 6:   `new Cylinder(.5f,.8f, new Appearance())`
The first argument is the radius of the base and the second is the height.

Note 7:   `new Cone(.5f,.8f, 0, new Appearance())`
The first argument is the radius of the base and the second is the height. The third represents flags that we will use in later examples.

Note 8:   `new Sphere(.7f, new Appearance())`
The first argument is the radius.

Colors

We color the shapes of Example 8.9 and change the background to white. To change the background color, we add a `Background` leaf node to the scene graph. We set the application bounds for the background to a large bounding sphere, in effect making it the background color everywhere in the scene. We define a `getAppearance` method that returns an `Appearance` with the color set to the desired color using the `setColoringAttributes` method.

Figure 8.13 Colored shapes on a white background

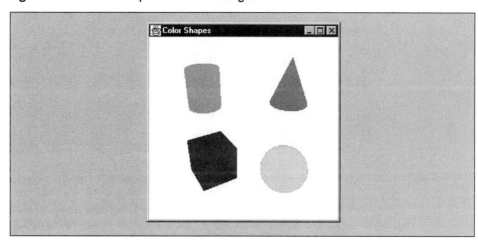

EXAMPLE 8.10 ColorShapes.java

```java
/* Colors the shapes of Example 9, placing
 * them on a white background.
 */

import java.awt.*;
import java.awt.event.*;
import javax.media.j3d.*;
import javax.vecmath.*;
import com.sun.j3d.utils.universe.SimpleUniverse;
import com.sun.j3d.utils.geometry.*;

public class ColorShapes extends Frame {
  public static void main(String[] args) {
    ColorShapes frame = new ColorShapes("Color Shapes");
    frame.setSize(300,300);
    frame.setVisible(true);
  }
  public Appearance getAppearance(float red, float green, float blue) {
    Appearance design = new Appearance();
    ColoringAttributes color = new ColoringAttributes();
    color.setColor(red, green, blue);
    design.setColoringAttributes(color);                        // Note 1
    return design;
  }
  public void setShape(BranchGroup parent,
                            Vector3d translate, Primitive shape) {
    Transform3D transform = new Transform3D();
    Transform3D t = new Transform3D();
    t.rotX(Math.PI/6);
    transform.set(translate);
    transform.mul(t);
    t.rotY(Math.PI/6);
    transform.mul(t);
    transform.setScale(.5);
    TransformGroup group = new TransformGroup(transform);
    parent.addChild(group);
    group.addChild(shape);
  }
  public ColorShapes(String title) {
    super(title);
    addWindowListener(new WindowAdapter() {
      public void windowClosing(WindowEvent e) {
        System.exit(0);
      }
    });
    Canvas3D canvas = new Canvas3D(null);
    add(canvas, "Center");
    SimpleUniverse universe = new SimpleUniverse(canvas);
```

```
universe.getViewingPlatform().setNominalViewingTransform();
Background white = new Background(1,1,1);
BoundingSphere bounds = new BoundingSphere();
white.setApplicationBounds(bounds);                              // Note 2
BranchGroup root = new BranchGroup();
root.addChild(white);                                           // Note 3
setShape(root, new Vector3d(-.6,-.6,-2.0),
              new Box(.7f,.7f,.7f,getAppearance(0,0,1)));        // Note 4
setShape(root, new Vector3d(-.6,.6,-1.0),
              new Cylinder(.5f,1.2f, getAppearance(1,.5f,.3f)));
setShape(root, new Vector3d(.6,.6,-.5),
              new Cone(.5f,1.2f, 0, getAppearance(1,0,0)));
setShape(root, new Vector3d(.6,-.6,-1.0),
              new Sphere(.7f, getAppearance(0,1,0)));
universe.addBranchGraph(root);
  }
}
```

Note 1:   The `Appearance` class has a number of methods that set various attributes.

Note 2:   We need to specify the region over which the background applies.

Note 3:   We add the background leaf node to the scene graph.

Note 4:   The box uses the `Appearance` returned by the `getAppearance` method rather than the default appearance used in earlier examples.

THE BIG PICTURE

A scene graph expresses a scene for the renderer. Java3D provides a simple universe to simplify the viewing branch of the scene graph. A utility package provides a `ColorCube` and the primitive shapes, `Box`, `Cone`, `Cylinder`, and `Sphere`. A transform group node captures transform information. We associate an `Appearance` with a leaf node shape, and set its attributes such as the color of the associated shape.

TEST YOUR UNDERSTANDING

TRY IT YOURSELF   9.   Try removing the scale factor of .5 when constructing the ColorCube in Example 8.7. Describe the result.

TRY IT YOURSELF   10.   We translated the four shapes in Example 8.9 by negative amounts in the z-direction. Try translating them by positive amounts and describe the result.

11.   In Example 8.10, we constructed a white background using (1,1,1) for the RGB values. What RGB values would we use to construct a light blue background?

TRY IT YOURSELF   12.   Omit the call to `setScale` in Example 8.9 and describe the result.

8.5   Java 3D Light, Motion, and Texture

Even when viewed in color, the Java3D examples in the previous section look flat. Lighting the scene gives it a true feeling of depth. We incorporate lighting, motion, and texture in our scene to illustrate some of the many Java3D features.

Light

To light our scene we create light sources and add `Material` objects to the appearance of our shapes. A `Material` defines the appearance of an object under illumination. We include an ambient light that provides light of equal intensity in all directions, and a directional light that models a very distant light source such as the sun. We add leaf nodes for default `AmbientLight` and `DirectionalLight` light sources, and set the bounds of influence of each to a large sphere.

We see objects by means of light reflected from them. The Java3D lighting model considers ambient, emissive, diffuse, and specular light. We see a part of an object not lit by the directional source by means of reflections from the ambient light. The normal reflection from a lit object is diffuse and the brighter highlights are specular reflections. Emissive light enables the object to glow in the dark.

The `Material` constructor

```
public Material(Color3f ambientColor,
                Color3f emissiveColor,
                Color3f diffuseColor,
                Color3f specularColor,
                float shininess)
```

lets us specify the colors for these reflections and a shininess factor which can range from a dull 1.0 to a very shiny 128.0. Figure 8.14 shows the four shapes we used in Figure 8.13, but with lighting added.

Figure 8.14   Lighting in the scene of Example 8.11

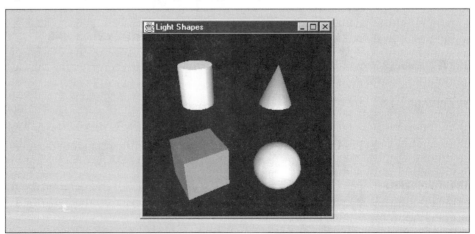

EXAMPLE 8.11   **LightShapes.java**

```java
/* Lights the four shapes of Example 8.10.
 */

import java.awt.*;
import java.awt.event.*;
import javax.media.j3d.*;
import javax.vecmath.*;
import com.sun.j3d.utils.universe.SimpleUniverse;
import com.sun.j3d.utils.geometry.*;

public class LightShapes extends Frame {
  public static void main(String[] args) {
    LightShapes frame = new LightShapes("Light Shapes");
    frame.setSize(300,300);
    frame.setVisible(true);
  }
  public Appearance getAppearance(float red, float green, float blue) {
    Appearance design = new Appearance();
    Color3f ambient = new Color3f(.2f,.2f,.2f);
    Color3f color = new Color3f(red,green,blue);
    Color3f white = new Color3f(1,1,1);
    Color3f black = new Color3f(0,0,0);
    design.setMaterial(new Material(ambient,black,color,white,3.5f)); // Note 1
    return design;
  }
  public void setShape(BranchGroup parent,
                       Vector3d translate, Primitive shape) {
    Transform3D transform = new Transform3D();
    Transform3D t = new Transform3D();
    t.rotX(Math.PI/6);
    transform.set(translate);
    transform.mul(t);
    t.rotY(Math.PI/6);
    transform.mul(t);
    transform.setScale(.5);
    TransformGroup group = new TransformGroup(transform);
    parent.addChild(group);
    group.addChild(shape);
  }
  public LightShapes(String title) {
    super(title);
    addWindowListener(new WindowAdapter() {
      public void windowClosing(WindowEvent e) {
        System.exit(0);
      }
    });
    Canvas3D canvas = new Canvas3D(null);
    add(canvas, "Center");
    SimpleUniverse universe = new SimpleUniverse(canvas);
```

```
      universe.getViewingPlatform().setNominalViewingTransform();
      BranchGroup root = new BranchGroup();
      BoundingSphere bounds = new BoundingSphere();
      AmbientLight ambient = new AmbientLight();
      ambient.setInfluencingBounds(bounds);                          // Note 2
      DirectionalLight directional = new DirectionalLight();
      directional.setInfluencingBounds(bounds);
      root.addChild(ambient);                                        // Note 3
      root.addChild(directional);
      setShape(root, new Vector3d(-.6,-.6,-1.3),
                  new Box(.7f,.7f,.7f,getAppearance(0,0,1)));
      setShape(root, new Vector3d(-.6,.6,-1.0),
                  new Cylinder(.5f,1.2f,getAppearance(1,1,0)));
      setShape(root, new Vector3d(.6,.6,-1.0), new Cone(.5f,1.2f,
         Cone.GENERATE_NORMALS,getAppearance(1,0,0)));               // Note 4
      setShape(root, new Vector3d(.6,-.6,-1.0),
                  new Sphere(.7f, getAppearance(0,1,0)));
      universe.addBranchGraph(root);
   }
}
```

Note 1 :   The color of the reflected ambient light is a very dark gray which shows up most where the object is not illuminated by the directional light source. The black emissive light indicates the object has no light of its own. In the absence of highlights, the object reflects its natural color when lit by the directional light. White is the highlight color. We use 3.5 for the shininess, creating relatively dull objects which are more affected by highlights. When lighting objects use a `Material`, not the `ColoringAttributes` we used to set the color of unlit objects.

Note 2:   We use the `setInfluencingBounds` method to specify the region of influence for ambient and directional light sources.

Note 3:   We add leaf nodes for ambient and directional light.

Note 4:   The Java 3D light model uses the surface normal (a line perpendicular to the surface) in its calculations. We set the flag to generate the normals along with the cone coordinates.

Motion

We spin the objects in Example 8.11. An object rotates 360 degrees in one revolution. At any given point the orientation of the object varies from 0 to 360 degrees. To rotate an object, Java 3D uses a function, `Alpha`, that varies from 0 to 1 over the time taken for one revolution. Multiplying the `Alpha` value by 360 gives an angle that varies from 0 to 360 during that time period.

Motion involves a transformation that is changing over time. To spin, we create a transform group, and use the `setCapability` method to allow it to change dynamically. A `RotationInterpolator` leaf node uses the `Alpha` function and the transform to generate the spinning (a varying rotation) about the y-axis. We set scheduling bounds for the rotation interpolator to be within a bounding sphere. Running Example 8.12 will rotate the shapes shown in Figure 8.14.

EXAMPLE 8.12   **SpinShapes.java**

```java
/* Rotates the shapes of Figure 8.14.
 */

import java.awt.*;
import java.awt.event.*;
import javax.media.j3d.*;
import javax.vecmath.*;
import com.sun.j3d.utils.universe.SimpleUniverse;
import com.sun.j3d.utils.geometry.*;

public class SpinShapes extends Frame {
  public static void main(String[] args) {
    SpinShapes frame = new SpinShapes("Spin Shapes");
    frame.setSize(300,300);
    frame.setVisible(true);
  }
  public Appearance getAppearance(float red, float green, float blue) {
    Appearance design = new Appearance();
    Color3f ambient = new Color3f(.2f,.2f,.2f);
    Color3f color = new Color3f(red,green,blue);
    Color3f white = new Color3f(1,1,1);
    Color3f black = new Color3f(0,0,0);
    design.setMaterial(new Material(ambient,black,color,white,3.5f));
    return design;
  }
  public void setShape(BranchGroup parent,
    Vector3d translate, Primitive shape) {
    Transform3D transform = new Transform3D();
    Transform3D t = new Transform3D();
    t.rotX(Math.PI/6);
    transform.set(translate);
    transform.mul(t);
    t.rotY(Math.PI/6);
    transform.mul(t);
    transform.setScale(.5);
    TransformGroup group = new TransformGroup(transform);
    TransformGroup spin = new TransformGroup();          // Note 1
    spin.setCapability
            (TransformGroup.ALLOW_TRANSFORM_WRITE);      // Note 2
    Alpha alpha = new Alpha(-1,6000);                    // Note 3
    RotationInterpolator interpolator =
            new RotationInterpolator(alpha, spin);       // Note 4
    BoundingSphere bounds = new BoundingSphere();
    interpolator.setSchedulingBounds(bounds);            // Note 5
```

```
      parent.addChild(group);
      group.addChild(interpolator);                           // Note 6
      group.addChild(spin);                                   // Note 7
      spin.addChild(shape);                                   // Note 8
    }
    public SpinShapes(String title) {
      super(title);
      addWindowListener(new WindowAdapter() {
        public void windowClosing(WindowEvent e) {
          System.exit(0);
        }
      });
      Canvas3D canvas = new Canvas3D(null);
      add(canvas, "Center");
      SimpleUniverse universe = new SimpleUniverse(canvas);
      universe.getViewingPlatform().setNominalViewingTransform();
      BranchGroup root = new BranchGroup();
      BoundingSphere bounds = new BoundingSphere();
      AmbientLight ambient = new AmbientLight();
      ambient.setInfluencingBounds(bounds);
      DirectionalLight directional = new DirectionalLight();
      directional.setInfluencingBounds(bounds);
      root.addChild(ambient);
      root.addChild(directional);
      setShape(root, new Vector3d(-.6,-.6,-1.3),
                  new Box(.7f,.7f,.7f,getAppearance(0,0,1)));
      setShape(root, new Vector3d(-.6,.6,-1.0),
                  new Cylinder(.5f,1.2f,getAppearance(1,1,0)));
      setShape(root, new Vector3d(.6,.6,-1.0),
                new Cone(.5f,1.2f,Cone.GENERATE_NORMALS,getAppearance(1,0,0)));
      setShape(root, new Vector3d(.6,-.6,-1.0),
                  new Sphere(.7f, getAppearance(0,1,0)));
      universe.addBranchGraph(root);
    }
}
```

Note 1:   We create the transform group for the spinning.

Note 2:   Because the rotation angle changes, we allow the transform to change by
          setting the ALLOW_TRANSFORM_WRITE capability.

Note 3:   The Alpha object provides a function that varies from 0 to 1. The first
          argument is a repetition count. We pass the value -1 to let the spinning
          continue indefinitely. The second argument is the time taken for the
          function to change from 0 to 1. We pass 6000 to cause one revolution to
          take 6 seconds.

Note 4: The rotation interpolator will adjust the spin transform to cause the objects to rotate around the y-axis in the time, six seconds, specified in `alpha`.

Note 5: The `setSchedulingBounds` method defines the region in which the spin operates. We use a default bounding sphere with center (0,0,0) and radius 1.

Note 6: `group.addChild(interpolator);`
We add the `RotationInterpolator` leaf node to the scene graph as a child of the previous transform group that set the initial orientations of the shapes.

Note 7: `group.addChild(spin);`
We add the `spin` transform group to the scene graph as a child of the previous transform.

Note 8: `spin.addChild(shape);`
We add the `shape` leaf node to the scene graph as a child of the `spin` transform group.

Texture

Texture gives the surface of objects a more realistic appearance. In this section we texture our shapes with an image, and do not light the scene. Since we cover the shapes with the image, we do not use color.

The `com.sun.j3d.utils.image` contains the `TextureLoader` that loads the image and converts it to the proper size. Image dimensions must be powers of 2, as for example 128 by 64. The texture loader has a `getTexture` method that we use to get a `Texture`, which we then set in the `Appearance` that we pass to the constructor for each primitive shape. Figure 8.15 shows the image applied to each of the shapes, which are rotating.

Figure 8.15 Texturing shapes with an image

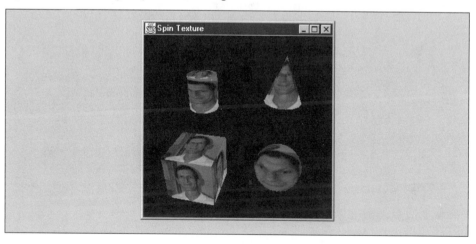

EXAMPLE 8.13   SpinTexture.java

```java
/* Textures shapes with an image.
 */

import java.awt.*;
import java.awt.event.*;
import javax.media.j3d.*;
import javax.vecmath.*;
import com.sun.j3d.utils.universe.SimpleUniverse;
import com.sun.j3d.utils.geometry.*;
import com.sun.j3d.utils.image.TextureLoader;

public class SpinTexture extends Frame {
  public static void main(String[] args) {
    SpinTexture frame = new SpinTexture("Spin Texture");
    frame.setSize(300,300);
    frame.setVisible(true);
  }
  public Appearance getAppearance() {                          // Note 1
    Appearance design = new Appearance();
    TextureLoader loader = new TextureLoader("gittleman.gif",this);  // Note 2
    Texture texture = loader.getTexture();                     // Note 3
    design.setTexture(texture);
    return design;
  }
  public void setShape(BranchGroup parent,
                    Vector3d translate, Primitive shape) {
    Transform3D transform = new Transform3D();
    Transform3D t = new Transform3D();
    t.rotX(Math.PI/6);
    transform.set(translate);
    transform.mul(t);
    t.rotY(Math.PI/6);
    transform.mul(t);
    transform.setScale(.5);
    TransformGroup group = new TransformGroup(transform);
    TransformGroup spin = new TransformGroup();
    spin.setCapability(TransformGroup.ALLOW_TRANSFORM_WRITE);
    Alpha alpha = new Alpha(-1,4000);
    RotationInterpolator interpolator =
                    new RotationInterpolator(alpha, spin);
    BoundingSphere bounds = new BoundingSphere();
    interpolator.setSchedulingBounds(bounds);
    parent.addChild(group);
    group.addChild(interpolator);
    group.addChild(spin);
    spin.addChild(shape);
  }
```

```
public SpinTexture(String title) {
  super(title);
  addWindowListener(new WindowAdapter() {
    public void windowClosing(WindowEvent e) {
      System.exit(0);
    }
  });
  Canvas3D canvas = new Canvas3D(null);
  add(canvas, "Center");
  SimpleUniverse universe = new SimpleUniverse(canvas);
  universe.getViewingPlatform().setNominalViewingTransform();
  BranchGroup root = new BranchGroup();
  setShape(root, new Vector3d(-.6,-.6,-1.0),
  new Box(.7f,.7f,.7f,
      Box.GENERATE_TEXTURE_COORDS, getAppearance()));        // Note 4
  setShape(root, new Vector3d(-.6,.6,-1.5),
  new Cylinder(.5f,1.2f,
      Box.GENERATE_TEXTURE_COORDS, getAppearance()));
  setShape(root, new Vector3d(.6,.6,-.5),
  new Cone(.5f,1.2f,
      Box.GENERATE_TEXTURE_COORDS, getAppearance()));
  setShape(root, new Vector3d(.6,-.6,-1.0),
  new Sphere(.7f,
      Box.GENERATE_TEXTURE_COORDS, getAppearance()));
  root.compile();
  universe.addBranchGraph(root);
  }
}
```

....

Note 1:   Because we are not coloring the objects, we omit the color parameters to the `getAppearance` method.

Note 2:   We use the `TextureLoader` constructor whose first argument is the file name of the image, and whose second is an `ImageObserver` that the loader informs about the progress of the loading.

Note 3:   The `TextureLoader` class provides the `getTexture` method to get the `Texture` derived from the image.

Note 4:   The box, cone, cylinder, and sphere constructors need to generate texture coordinates.

To include lighting and color with textures, we would restore the appropriate parts of Example 8.12, and add texture attributes to modulate between the object color and the image. We would add the following lines to the `getAppearance` method.

```
TextureAttributes mode = new TextureAttributes();
mode.setTextureMode(TextureAttributes.MODULATE);
```

```
design.setTextureAttributes(mode);
```

THE BIG PICTURE

Light, motion, and texture make 3D scenes more realistic. We use coloring attributes to color an unlit scene, but add a `Material` to the appearance to color a lit scene. Ambient and directional lights operate within a sphere of influence. They are leaf nodes in the scene graph. Motion requires a transform that varies. A `Rotation-Interpolator` leaf node enables spinning. A texture loader can load an image to use as a texture, which is part of the object's specified `Appearance`.

TEST YOUR UNDERSTANDING

TRY IT YOURSELF   13. Try different values for the shininess of the material in Example 8.11 and describe the results.

TRY IT YOURSELF   14. Try different colors for the specular color in Example 8.11 and describe the results.

TRY IT YOURSELF   15. In Example 8.12, try different values for the time taken for the `Alpha` function to change from 0 to 1. Describe the results.

SUMMARY

- To animate images or drawings, we use a thread to display successive images or drawings. We clear the screen between frames which causes the animation to flicker due to the alternation of blank screen and image. Double buffering, drawing on an off-screen buffer and copying that buffer to the screen, eliminates flicker. Swing components double buffer automatically. An `ImageIcon` automatically completes loading before we display it.

- Java versions 1.0 and 1.1 support the AU audio format, while versions 2 and higher support additional formats, including Windows WAV files. The applet class has a `play` method that can play a sound file specified by a URL. The applet can also get an audio clip. The `AudioClip` interface has methods to play a sound, to loop it, playing it until the `stop` method is invoked to terminate it. We can add threads to play sounds in the background while animation is in progress. We can also add sounds to the thread in which the animation is running.

- The Java Media Framework allows Java applications and applets to display and capture multimedia data. It supports many media content types including MPEG, QuickTime, AVI, WAV, AU, and MIDI. The documentation indicates which compression formats it supports for each of these types. Using JMF, we can create a media player from within a Java program. The player generates controller events to inform a controller listener of its progress. The listener can add visual and control components to the interface and restart the clip when it finishes.

- Java3D uses a scene graph to represent content and viewing information. Utility packages provides a `SimpleUniverse` which incorporates the viewing details, and color cube, box, cone, cylinder, and sphere shapes to enable us to create scenes without constructing shapes from basic triangles. Transform group nodes allow us to specify transformations to orient shapes. We construct primitive shapes with an `Appearance` which contains color, lighting, and texture information.

■ We set coloring attributes to color an unlit scene, but use a `Material` when we light the scene. The `Material` defines ambient, emissive, diffuse, and specular colors, and a shininess for the object. To spin shapes, we create an `Alpha` function that varies from 0 to 1 in the time it takes for one revolution. A `RotationInterpolator` associates the `Alpha` with a transform group. We add the transform group as a group node and the rotation interpolator as a leaf node to the scene graph. A texture loaders loads an image to use as a texture, which we set as part of the `Appearance`.

Program Modification Exercises

1. Modify Example 8.2 to replace the `TextIcon` class with a `FaceIcon` class that draws a picture of a face.

2. Modify Example 8.3 to replace the `TextIcon` class with a `DesignIcon` class that fills a square with a design using specified colors. Create four design icons, each with different colors, and animate them in a repeating sequence.

3. Modify Example 8.3 to speak the words as they are displayed.

4. Modify Example 8.5 to run as a standalone application rather than an applet.

5. Modify Example 8.8 to run as an applet rather than as a standalone application.

6. Modify Example 8.8 to pass the rotation angles about the x- and y-axes as program arguments. Experiment with different rotations, comparing results.

7. Modify Example 8.13, following the suggestions at the end of Section 8.5, to light the textured scene.

Program Design Exercises

8. Write a Java program that provides a user interface with a list of words. When the user chooses a word, the program should pronounce it.

9. a. Write a Java program that randomly moves a ball around the screen. If you have access to sound, make a sound at each move. If the user clicks the mouse on the ball, increment a score showing in the corner of the screen. If the user reaches a score of 5, make the ball move faster so it is more difficult to catch. If you are including sound, do so in a separate thread so it does not slow the ball down. If the user reaches a score of 10 make the ball smaller.

b. In part a, use an image of your choice instead of a ball.

10. Create an animation with several distinct frames. Start off with a ball. Show the ball at the left. Move it to the center and oscillate it with a slightly larger ball so that it looks agitated. Move it to the right and have it blow up (draw something like a ball in pieces or smoke and fire or whatever looks different.) Put this animation in a thread. Add a button so that when the user presses the button an animation like the above starts in its own thread.

11. (Towers of Hanoi)

    Suppose we have n disks on a peg, each of different sizes, stacked in order of size, with the largest on the bottom, and two other pegs, as shown in Figure 8.16.

Figure 8.16 The Towers of Hanoi puzzle

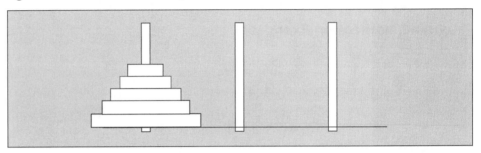

What is the sequence of moves needed to transfer the rings to the second peg, in the same configuration, in order from largest to the smallest, with the largest at the bottom, if we can move only one disk at a time, and we cannot place a larger disk on top of a smaller disk? We may use the last peg to store disks, but the same rules apply. Use a recursive method to provide the solution. To move n disks from peg 1 to peg 2, move n–1 disks to peg 3, move the bottom disk to peg 2, then move n–1 disks from peg 3 to peg 2. Use a thread to animate the solution, using various colors for the disks.

12. Create a 3D graphics program with three rotating color cubes.

13. Create an applet with a spinning 3D clown composed of a sphere with a cone for a hat. Implement the `Icon` interface to draw a clown face and use a texture loader with the constructor

```
public TextureLoader(java.awt.Image image,
                     java.awt.Component observer)
```

to create a texture for the sphere.

14. Create a Java application that displays the word "SUN" in larger and larger letters and then uses a media player to play the clip of solar activity from

    http://solar.physics.montana.edu/YPOP/Movies/sun_diver.mpg

    or another clip chosen from

    http://www-istp.gsfc.nasa.gov/istp/outreach/movies.html/

9

Java Beans

Introduction

Java Beans provide a platform-independent component technology that makes it easier to build Java programs. Hardware designers commonly integrate various components in building a new system. For example, a computer manufacturer uses available memory chips and hard drives, rather than designing them again. Unfortunately many software systems create the whole application from scratch even though many parts of it may be familiar from previously developed systems.

With Java Beans, software developers can integrate components obtained from various sources. For example, a reservation system might want to make a calendar available to the user. The developer might obtain a calendar bean which helps the user make a reservation. When the user enters a date in a text field, the calendar for the three months nearest that date appears.

We first show how to use beans to build an application and then show how to write our own beans. Most commonly, developers use a visual tool to create applications using beans, but as we shall see they may also include beans directly in Java programs.

OBJECTIVES

- Use the **BeanBox** to build an applet from `Bean` components.
- Show how to use beans with bound and constrained properties.
- Write a simple Java Bean.
- Package a Java Bean in a JAR (Java Archive) file.
- Write beans that have bound properties.
- Introduce anonymous inner classes.
- Use `BeanInfo` to make beans more user friendly.
- Use beans in a Java program.

9.1   Building with Beans

Typically developers use a visual tool to build applets from Java Bean **components**. Our example demonstrates this process, using beans from the `demo` directory included with the Bean Development Kit.

Several vendors provide visual tools with which to develop applications using Java Beans. Sun offers the Beans Development Kit (BDK) as a free download from its web site, `java.sun.com`. The **BDK** contains a simple development environment, the **BeanBox**, which is available for learning and testing, much as the applet viewer is a simple tool for testing applets, rather than a full browser.

Figure 9.1   Running the **BeanBox**

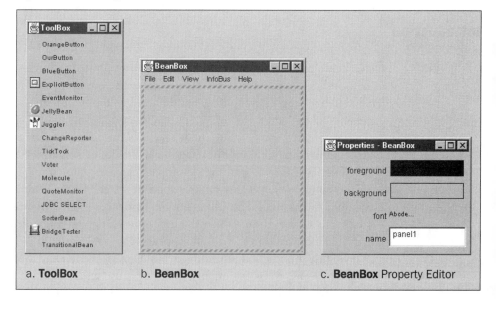

a. **ToolBox**   b. **BeanBox**   c. **BeanBox** Property Editor

Starting the BeanBox

Once the BDK has been installed, we can start the **BeanBox** by executing the `run` command from the command prompt in the `C:\BDK\beanbox` directory on Windows systems, where `C:\BDK` is the directory in which the BDK is installed. The three windows shown in Figure 9.1 will pop up. Figure 9.1a, the **ToolBox**, contains a list of beans we can drag into the **BeanBox**, Figure 9.1b. The border inside the **BeanBox** surrounds the currently selected bean, in this case the **BeanBox** itself. Every bean is configurable, meaning that we can change its properties.

Figure 9.1c shows the four properties of the **BeanBox** that we can change, its foreground and background colors, font, and name. Clicking on the gray rectangle, showing the current light-gray background, will pop up the color editor shown in Figure 9.2, in which the rectangle on the left shows the current background, the numbers 192,192,192 in the center text field are the red, green, and blue components of light gray, and the Choice box lists other colors from which to select. We can either enter new RGB values or select another color, such as yellow, from the Choice box. Doing so will immediately change the **BeanBox** to have the chosen background color.

Figure 9.2 The color editor for the **BeanBox** background

Figure 9.3 The `Juggler` and `ExplicitButton` beans

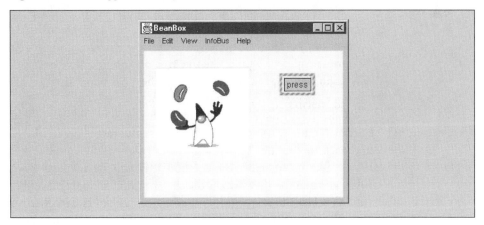

Building an Applet with Beans

To use the **BeanBox** to build an applet, we drag beans from the **ToolBox** to the **BeanBox**, customize the beans using the property editors from the **Properties** window, and connect the beans using hookup classes generated by the **BeanBox**.

For example, we drag the `Juggler` bean and the `ExplicitButton` bean into the **BeanBox**, each time clicking the mouse where we want to position the bean. Figure 9.3 shows the **BeanBox**, with the `ExplicitButton` selected. In color, the **BeanBox** background would appear yellow, and when run on the computer the `Juggler` is actually juggling the beans. Because we selected `ExplicitButton`, the **Properties** window in Figure 9.4 shows its properties that we can change. By typing `Stop` instead of press in the text field for the label property and pressing the `Enter` key, the button will have "Stop" as its label.

Figure 9.4   Changeable properties of an `ExplicitButton`

When the user presses the *Stop* button, Java generates an `ActionEvent`, passing it to the `actionPerformed` method of an object registered with the button as an `ActionListener`. The code inside the `actionPerformed` method implements the behavior desired when the user presses the button. We might call the class containing the `actionPerformed` method the **hookup** (or **adapter**) **class** because it connects the source of the action event with the target.

When we write our own applets we implement all these steps to make button presses have the desired effects. Using Java Beans, the **BeanBox** (or other bean development tool) creates the hookup class for us, generating the `actionPerformed` method. In our example, we would like the `Stop` button to cause the `Juggler` to stop juggling. We highlight the *Stop* button, click on the *Edit* menu, then *Events*, then *button push*, then *actionPerformed*, as Figure 9.5 shows.

Clicking on the `actionPerformed` item causes a red line to emanate from the *Stop* button (Figure 9.6). We drag the line to the target object, Juggler in this example, and click the mouse. The mouse click brings up the `EventTargetDialog` (Figure 9.7), which asks us to select the method that will be invoked by the `actionPerformed` method when the user presses the *Stop* button.

We select the `stopJuggling` method and click OK, receiving the message that the **BeanBox** is generating and compiling an adapter class to hookup the *Stop* button source to the `Juggler` target. Now, pressing the *Stop* button will cause the `Juggler` to stop juggling.

Figure 9.5   Connecting the `Stop` button

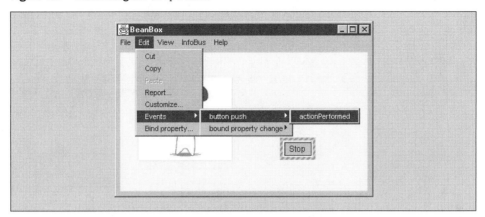

Figure 9.6   Connecting the source to the target

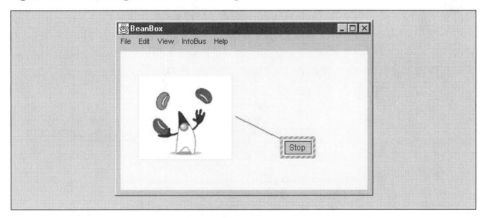

Figure 9.7   The target methods

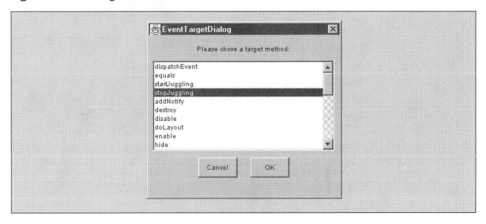

To be able to start the `Juggler` juggling again we add another button to the **Bean-Box**. This time we drag an `OurButton` rather than an `ExplicitButton` to the **BeanBox**, changing its label to `Start` (See Figure 9.8).

Figure 9.8 Adding a Start button

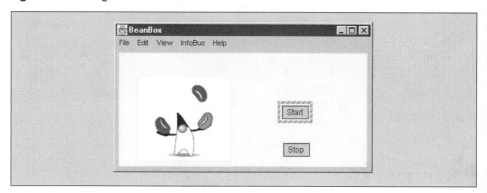

When we select the `Start` button, click on `Edit`, and click on `Events`, we get a different list of events, shown in Figure 9.9, than we got for the *Stop* button. We will explain the reason for this difference later in the chapter.

Figure 9.9 Connecting the `Start` button

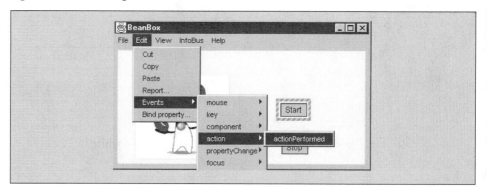

Continuing, we connect the `Start` button to the Juggler. The **BeanBox** then generates the hookup class that will cause the `startJuggling` method of the `Juggler` to execute when the user presses the `Start` button.

The **BeanBox** is a tool we can use to build an applet from beans. We have customized the **BeanBox** to have a yellow background and the buttons to have `Start` and `Stop` labels. We let the **BeanBox** create hookup classes which implement the actions for the events the buttons generate. Now we click on `File, Make Applet` to let the **BeanBox** make this creation into an applet.

We will discuss JAR (Java Archive) files later in this chapter. In the Make an Applet window we change the default `myApplet` name to `ButtonJuggle` in both text

Figure 9.10 Making an applet

fields and click OK. We get a sequence of messages listing the steps the **BeanBox** is taking to create the applet. The **BeanBox** puts all the files for the ButtonJuggle applet in the directory c:\BDK\beanbox\tmp\ButtonJuggle. We can test the applet using the applet viewer with the ButtonJuggle.html file or we can run it using the Internet Explorer browser.

THE BIG PICTURE

The JavaBean component technology allows us to build applets by customizing and connecting bean components, without doing any programming. The **BeanBox** is a simple visual tool for building with beans. Each bean has a property list providing editors to change each property. We can connect a source event in one bean to a target method in another. The **BeanBox** will create the hookup class which will call the target method when the source event occurs. The bean developer writes beans which the applet designer uses to make an applet run by the end user.

TEST YOUR UNDERSTANDING

TRY IT YOURSELF 1. Start the **BeanBox**. Change its background color to orange.

TRY IT YOURSELF 2. Following the steps in the text, use the **BeanBox** to create the ButtonJuggle applet, additionally changing the background color of the Start and Stop buttons to blue and the foreground color to white.

9.2 Bound and Constrained Properties

With **bound properties**, beans can use Java events to notify other components of changes in property values. **Constrained properties** allow those components to veto the changes.

In building the ButtonJuggle applet, we used the **BeanBox** to hookup the Start button source of an ActionEvent with the Juggler target, so the Juggler will start juggling when the user presses the Start button. In this section, we show how the **Bean-Box** can hookup sources and targets of property changes and vetoable changes.

Simple Properties

Java objects may have various properties that we can change. For example, every component, such as a `Button`, has foreground and background properties that we can change using the `setForeground` or `setBackground` methods in a Java program. When using a tool such as the **BeanBox**, we often want to change some properties of beans before we incorporate them into an applet. In building the `ButtonJuggle` applet, we changed the labels on the buttons, for example.

By using the **BeanBox** we avoid the details of calling the `setLabel` method in a program, using instead the property editor for the label in the **Properties** window. The **Properties** window, shown in Figure 9.4, lets us change the `foreground`, `label`, `background`, and `font` properties of an `ExplicitButton`.

Bound Properties

A bound property lets other components know when it is changed. We can use the **BeanBox** to connect beans so changing the color, for example, of the source bean will notify the target bean to change its color also. If a bean has any bound properties there will be a `Bind Property` item in its `Edit` menu. Not all beans have any bound properties; the `Juggler` has no `Bind Property` item on its `Edit` menu.

For example, let us drag an `ExplicitButton` and a `JellyBean` into the **BeanBox**. Selecting the `Explicit Button` and clicking `Edit, Bind Property` pops up the window of Figure 9.11a to let us choose the property whose changes we want to transmit to other beans. If we choose the background property and click OK a red line will appear which we can drag, clicking on the JellyBean, popping up the list of properties shown in Figure 9.11b.

Figure 9.11 Bound Properties

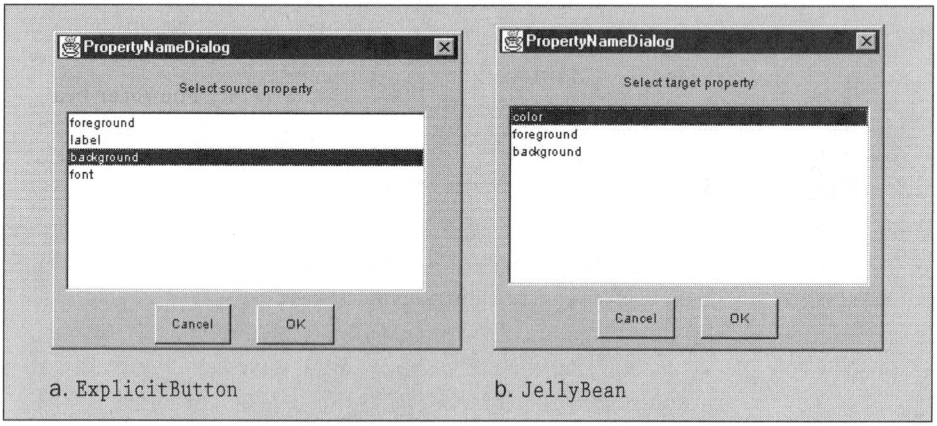

a. `ExplicitButton`   b. `JellyBean`

Selecting color and clicking OK, binds the background of the `ExplicitButton` to the color of the `JellyBean`. Before binding the two beans in this way, changing the background of the `ExplicitButton` to red leaves the `JellyBean` orange (Figure 9.12a).

After binding, changing the background of the ExplicitButton to red also changes the color of the JellyBean to red (Figure 9.12b).

Figure 9.12

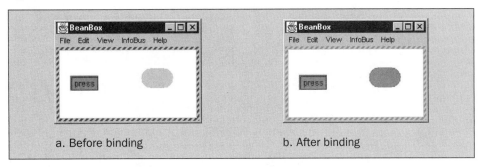

| a. Before binding | b. After binding |

We must distinguish between the applet designer and the applet user. Using the **BeanBox**, we are functioning as the applet designer. We did not make an applet out of the bound property example above, because the applet user would have no way to change the background color of the button. If the user could change that background color, then the JellyBean's color would also change. As the applet designer we have the property editors in the **Properties** window to use to change the background color of the ExplicitButton, to show how bound properties work. Later we will design an applet that uses bound properties effectively.

Constrained Properties

Simple properties change without affecting properties of other beans. Changes in bound properties may change properties of other beans. Constrained properties give other beans the chance to veto the change before it takes effect. For example, the priceInCents property of the JellyBean is vetoable. The Voter bean, in the **ToolBox**, normally vetoes every change presented to it.

To see how constrained properties work, we drag the JellyBean and the Voter bean into the **BeanBox**. Selecting the JellyBean, we show in Figure 9.13 the Edit, Events, vetoableChange, vetoableChange menu items. The JellyBean can generate a VetoableChange event which is handled by the vetoableChange method. The bean at the right of Figure 9.13 displays a large "**No**" signifying that it will veto every property change presented to it.

Clicking on the vetoableChange item will cause the red line to appear, which we drag and click on the Voter bean popping up the list of Figure 9.14. Selecting vetoableChange and clicking OK will cause the **BeanBox** to hookup the JellyBean source to the Voter target. Highlighting the JellyBean and trying to use the property editor to change its priceInCents to 3 will cause the message

```
WARNING: Vetoed; reason is: NO!
```

Figure 9.13 A vetoable change event

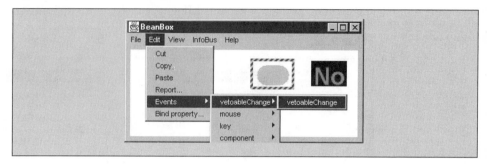

to appear on the console screen. The `priceInCents` remains 2, as the `Voter` bean has vetoed the change. If we change the `vetoAll` property of the `Voter` bean from **true** to **false**, then the `Voter` bean will display a large "**Yes**" instead of "**No**," and will allow the change to `priceInCents` to proceed.

THE BIG PICTURE

In the **BeanBox**, or similar tool, we can bind a bound property of one bean to a property of the same type of another bean. When the source bean's bound property changes value so will the target's. A constrained property is like a bound property with the additional feature that a target bean may veto the change, forcing the source bean to withdraw it.

Figure 9.14 Choosing a target method `vetoableChange`

TEST YOUR UNDERSTANDING

TRY IT YOURSELF 3. Use the **BeanBox** to bind the `priceInCents` of the `JellyBean` to the `animationRate` of the `Juggler`. Enter different values in the **Properties** window editor for the `priceInCents` and observe the change in the `animationRate`.

TRY IT YOURSELF   4.   Use the **BeanBox** to bind the foreground color of an `ExplicitButton` to the color of a `JellyBean` and to the background color of an `OurButton`. Change the foreground color of the `ExplicitButton` several times, using the **Properties** window color editor, and observe the effect.

TRY IT YOURSELF   5.   Use the BeanBox to bind the `priceInCents` of the JellyBean to the `animationRate` of the Juggler. Also hookup the `vetoableChange` event from the JellyBean source to the `vetoableChange` handler method of the Voter bean. Try to change the `priceInCents`, using the **Properties** window editor, and observe what happens.

9.3   Writing and Packaging a Bean

Now that we have used the **BeanBox** to build an applet with the demo beans provided by Sun, we will learn to write our own beans and add them to the **BeanBox**. We package beans in JAR (Java Archive) files that combine individual files to avoid multiple connections when downloading a bean, and compress files to save space and time. We use anonymous inner classes to conveniently define event handlers.

A Simple Bean

A bean is just a Java program. Our first example, `TextBean`, has just a constructor and two methods, `setNumber` and `getNumber`, to set and get a single integer value. It extends `TextField` to provide a display for an integer value. Using the standard prefixes `set` and `get`, followed by the property name, as in `setNumber` and `getNumber`, allows the **BeanBox** to add these properties in the **Properties** window.

Example 9.1 has no `main` method because we will use it in the **BeanBox**, rather than as a standalone program. Adding a `main` method would allow it to run as a standalone application as well as to be used as a bean in the **BeanBox**. All programs to be used as beans should extend the `Serializable` interface, because Java uses object serialization to save the designer's customizations which can be reloaded and used in their customized state.

EXAMPLE 9.1   **TextBean.java**

```
/* A simple program to use
 * as a bean.
 */

import java.awt.*;
import java.awt.event.*;
import java.io.*;

public class TextBean extends TextField
                      implements Serializable {
```

```
          int myNumber = 10; // Value to set and get
          public TextBean() {
            super(5);                                           // Note 1
            setBackground(Color.white);                         // Note 2
          }
          public void setNumber(int x) {
            myNumber = x;
            setText("" + x);                                    // Note 3
          }
          public int getNumber() {
            return myNumber;
          }
        }
```

Note 1:   We call the constructor of the superclass, `TextField`, to set the width of the text field to 5.

Note 2:   Setting the background of the text field to white helps it to standout from the background of the **BeanBox**.

Note 3:   The `setText` method displays the text in the text field. Binding another bean, such as the `JellyBean`, to set the `number` property when its `priceIn-Cents` is changed, will cause the `priceInCents` to be displayed.

JAR Files

JAR (Java Archive) **files** allow us to package several files -- class files, images, and sounds -- together as one file. We will use them here to package our beans, but another important use is to package the files needed for an applet. When we download an applet from a web site, we must make a separate connection to download each of the files used by the applet. Packaging all the files in a JAR file allows the applet to be downloaded with one connection saving much time. The JAR file may also compress the files, further reducing the download time.

We can use the jar utility program to create JAR files. For Java Beans we should always include a **manifest** file which describes the contents of the JAR file, indicating which files are beans. To package our `TextBean`, we first create the manifest file, `Text-Bean.mf`, containing just two lines.

```
Name: TextBean.class
Java-Bean: True
```

The jar command, given at the command prompt, is

```
jar cfm TextBean.jar TextBean.mf TextBean.class
```

where the options are

c   create a new archive

f   archive name is the first file on the list (`TextBean.jar` here)

m   manifest file is the second file on the list (`TextBean.mf` here)

Executing this jar command will create the JAR file `TextBean.jar`. To put this JAR file into the **BeanBox**, we copy it to `c:\BDK\jars` which already contains the Sun demo beans. Starting the **BeanBox** shows the `TextBean` in the **ToolBox** (Figure 9.15a). Dragging the `TextBean` and the `JellyBean` into the **BeanBox** (Figure 9.15b) and selecting the `TextBean` shows the number property appears in the **Properties** window (Figure 9.15c).

Figure 9.15 The **BeanBox** with the `TextBean`

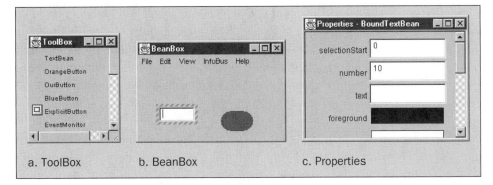

a. ToolBox   b. BeanBox   c. Properties

We will configure these beans so when the `priceInCents` of the `JellyBean` changes the new value will appear in the `TextBean`. Selecting the `JellyBean` and clicking on *Edit*, *Bind property* pops up the *PropertyNameDialog*. Selecting `priceInCents`, and clicking OK produces the red line that we drag to the `TextBean`. Clicking on the `TextBean` pops up the *PropertyNameDialog* for the target property shown in Figure 9.16. Selecting the number property and clicking *OK* will complete the binding.

Figure 9.16 Selecting the target property in the `TextBean`

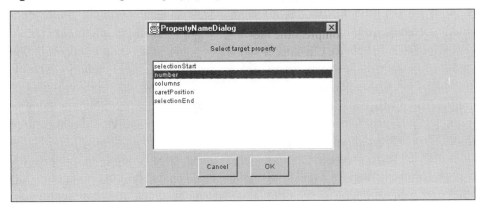

Selecting the `JellyBean` and entering 5 for its `priceInCents` will now cause the value 5 to be displayed in the text field of the `TextBean` (Figure 9.17).

Figure 9.17   TextBean displaying `priceInCents`

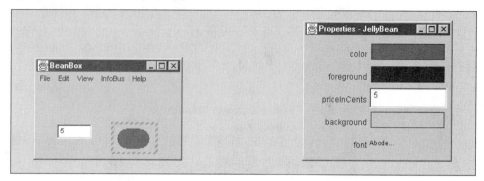

A Bean with a Bound Property

Next we make the number property a bound property with the capability to notify property change listeners when `myNumber` is changed. We will use this `BoundTextBean` later in building an applet.

The `java.beans` package has a `PropertyChangeEvent` class. The `PropertyChangeListener` interface has one method,

```
public void propertyChange(PropertyChangeEvent e)
```

which Java calls when a property value changes. We use the `PropertyChangeSupport` methods to do most of the work implementing bound properties. Instead of managing a vector of `PropertyChangeListeners` ourselves, we delegate that to the `addPropertyChangeListener` and `removePropertyChangeListener` methods. Instead of creating a `PropertyChangeEvent` and sending it to each listener we can just call the `firePropertyChange` method of the `PropertyChangeSupport` class. Example 9.2 shows these additions to Example 9.1.

EXAMPLE 9.2   BoundTextBean.java

```java
/* Makes the number property a bound property.
 * Notifies PropertyChangeListeners when
 * myNumber changes.
 */

import java.awt.*;
import java.awt.event.*;
import java.io.*;
import java.beans.*;

public class BoundTextBean extends TextField
        implements Serializable, ActionListener {
  private int myNumber = 10;
  private PropertyChangeSupport pChange
        = new PropertyChangeSupport(this);               // Note 1
```

```
public BoundTextBean(){
  super(5);
  setBackground(Color.white);
  addActionListener(this);
}
public void setNumber(int x) {
  Integer oldVal = new Integer(myNumber);              // Note 2
  Integer newVal = new Integer(x);
  myNumber = x;
  setText("" + x);
  pChange.firePropertyChange("number",oldVal,newVal);  // Note 3
}
public int getNumber() {
  return myNumber;
}
public void actionPerformed(ActionEvent e) {
  setNumber(Integer.parseInt(getText()));              // Note 4
}
public void addPropertyChangeListener(PropertyChangeListener l) {  // Note 5
  pChange.addPropertyChangeListener(l);
}
public void removePropertyChangeListener(PropertyChangeListener l) {
  pChange.removePropertyChangeListener(l);
}
}
```

Note 1:   We create a PropertyChangeSupport object to manage registering Property-ChangeListener objects, and sending a PropertyChangeEvent to them.

Note 2:   The firePropertyChange method, which notifies property change listeners when a property changes, takes Object arguments for the old and new values of the changing property. Because myNumber is a primitive **int** value we need to wrap it in an Integer object to pass as an argument to firePropertyChange.

Note 3:   Our PropertyChangeSupport object, pChange, notifies each registered PropertyChangeListener of the change to myNumber, using the firePropertyChange method. The three arguments are a string with the name of the property; number is the name we used in the setNumber method, but with lowercase, that is, "number" not "Number." The second argument is the old value of the property, wrapped as an object if necessary, while the third argument is the new value of the property, also wrapped as an object.

Note 4:   We want to enter the value of myNumber in the text field. When the user presses the *Enter* key, Java generates an ActionEvent which we handle in the actionPerformed method by calling the setNumber method to change myNumber to the value entered.

Note 5:   Using the **BeanBox**, we can connect other beans who want to be notified when `myNumber` changes. These beans call the `addPropertyChangeListener` method to register to receive notification of changes. Rather than keep a vector of these listeners ourselves, we let `pChange` keep them for us and inform them of changes using the `firePropertyChange` method.

Smiley Bean

To illustrate a bean with additional features, we create `Smiley` bean with a happy face; pressing its nose generates an `ActionEvent`. `Smiley`'s age is a bound property. Before discussing the code for `Smiley`, we use it in the **BeanBox**. Figure 9.18 shows the **BeanBox** containing our `BoundTextBean` from Example 9.2, an `Explicit Button`, `Smiley`, and a `Juggler`.

Figure 9.18   Using `Smiley` in an applet

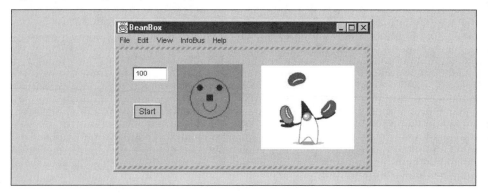

We customized the `ExplicitButton` to have the label "Start" and the `Smiley` bean to have a red background color. We bound the number property of the `BoundTextBean` to the `Smiley`'s age, so when we enter a value in the `BoundTextBean`, `Smiley`'s age will also have that value. We bound `Smiley`'s age to the animation rate of the `Juggler`, so entering a value in the `BoundTextBean` will actually change the `Juggler`'s animation rate.

Using the **BeanBox**, we hooked up `Smiley` to the `Juggler`, so when the user clicks on `Smiley`'s nose, generating an `ActionEvent`, the `Juggler` stops juggling. The `Start` button starts the `Juggler` juggling. Figure 9.19 shows Internet Explorer running the `SmileApplet` applet made in the **BeanBox** by clicking on the `File, Make Applet` menu item.

Now that we have used `Smiley` as part of `SmileApplet`, we discuss its implementation. Implementing the age property follows the same steps used for the number property in Example 9.2. `Smiley` generates an `ActionEvent` when the user presses its nose. We use the `mousePressed` method to detect when the mouse is over `Smiley`'s nose. We are making `Smiley`'s nose function like a button, and like a button we generate an `Action-Event` and call the `actionPerformed` method of all listeners.

`Smiley` implements the `addActionListener` and `removeActionListener` methods to allow objects to register to be notified when the user presses `Smiley`'s nose. A vector

Figure 9.19   Running `SmileApplet`

holds these listeners. When the user presses `Smiley`'s nose, the `fireAction` method calls the `actionPerformed` method of all the registered listeners.

Anonymous Inner Classes

Sometimes we use an inner class just once, perhaps to define an event handler. Our `Smiley` example uses an inner class that overrides `MouseAdapter` to handle the `MOUSE_PRESSED` event. We could have named it, for example, as

```
class MousePress extends MouseAdapter {
  public void mousePressed(MouseEvent e) {
    // code to handle mouse press goes here
  }
}
```

and registered it using

```
addMouseListener(new MousePress());
```

Because we only use the `MousePress` class once, we do not need to give it a name. Java lets us use it anonymously, as in

```
addMouseListener(new MouseAdapter() {
  public void mousePressed(MouseEvent e) {
    // code to handle mouse press goes here
  }
} );
```

which uses an extension of the **new** operator for the syntax. Writing 'new Mouse-Adapter()' signifies an anonymous inner class that extends MouseAdapter. The class definition follows, as usual, between curly braces. An **anonymous inner class** is an unnamed class defined within a block of code.

While we do not name an anonymous class, Java does name it. Looking in the package smiley, after compiling Smiley.java, we find the class file, Smiley$1.class, containing the byte code for the anonymous extension to MouseAdapter. We include the Smiley$1.class file in the manifest with an entry

```
Name: smiley/Smiley$1.class
```

and add it to the list of files to include in the JAR file for Smiley.

EXAMPLE 9.3   **Smiley.java**

```
/* A bean with a smiley face. Pressing its nose
 * generates an ActionEvent. Smiley's age is a
 * bound property.
 */

package smiley;                                          // Note 1
import java.awt.*;
import java.awt.event.*;
import java.beans.*;
import java.io.Serializable;
import java.util.Vector;

public class Smiley extends Canvas
  implements Serializable {
  private int age = 10;
  private PropertyChangeSupport changes = new PropertyChangeSupport(this);
  private Vector listeners = new Vector();
  public Smiley() {
    setSize(new Dimension(100,100));
    addMouseListener(new MouseAdapter () {               // Note 2
      public void mousePressed(MouseEvent evt) {
        int x = evt.getX();
        int y = evt.getY();
        if( x >= 45 && x <= 55 && y >= 45 && y <= 55)
          if(listeners != null) fireAction();           // Note 3
      }
    } );
  }
  public void paint(Graphics g) {
    g.drawOval(20,20,60,60);
    g.fillOval(30,30,10,10);
    g.fillOval(60,30,10,10);
    g.fillRect(45,45,10,10);
    g.drawArc(40,50,20,20,170,200);
  }
```

```
public void fireAction() {
    ActionEvent e = new ActionEvent(this, 0, null);              // Note 4
    for (int i = 0; i < listeners.size(); i++)
      ((ActionListener)listeners.elementAt(i)).actionPerformed(e);  // Note 5
}
public void setAge(int a) {
    Integer oldage = new Integer(age);
    age = a;
    Integer newage = new Integer(a);
    changes.firePropertyChange("age", oldage, newage);
  }
  public int getAge() {
    return age;
  }
  public void addActionListener(ActionListener l) {              // Note 6
    listeners.addElement(l);
  }
  public void removeActionListener(ActionListener l) {
    listeners.removeElement(l);
  }
  public void addPropertyChangeListener(PropertyChangeListener l) {
    changes.addPropertyChangeListener(l);
  }
  public void removePropertyChangeListener(PropertyChangeListener l) {
    changes.removePropertyChangeListener(l);
  }
}
```

....

Note 1:   We put Smiley in a package to keep all its files together. In the manifest file we use the forward slash, /, to name files, as in

smiley/Smiley.class

even on Windows systems. Executing the jar command from the command prompt in the directory containing the smiley package directory, we include the package name when naming files, as in

jar cfm smiley\Smiley.jar smiley\Smiley.mf
smiley\Smiley.class smiley\Smiley$1.class

on Windows systems.

Note 2:   This is an anonymous inner class. We define it right where it is used. Defining a named class MousePress would be fine too, but anonymous inner classes are often used to provide adapter classes for event handling as we do here.

Note 3:   If the coordinates where the user pressed the mouse are within the rectangle defining Smiley's nose, and if there are any listeners waiting to be notified, we call the fireAction method to notify them.

Note 4:   We create an `ActionEvent` to send to registered listeners. The first argument is the source of the event; we pass this representing `Smiley`. The second argument, of type **int**, is an ID for the type of event. We do not use the ID and arbitrarily pass 0. The AWT passes `ActionEvent.ACTION_PERFORMED` when it generates an `ActionEvent`, and we could alternatively have passed that value. The third argument, of type `String`, is the command; for example, a label for a button. We do not use this argument and pass **null** instead.

Note 5:   We cast each listener in the listener's vector to an `ActionListener` (we added only action listeners to listeners so this cast is valid), and call its `actionPerformed` method which specifies how that listener wants to handle the nose press. In the `SmileApplet`, the **BeanBox** has hooked up the `Juggler` to respond to this action by stopping juggling.

Note 6:   `public void addActionListener(ActionListener 1)`
We implement the `addActionListener` method to save listeners in a vector. They will be notified when the user presses `Smiley`'s nose.

A LITTLE EXTRA
⇨

The `SmileApplet` uses four beans, each with its own JAR file composed of files needed to implement that bean. The `archive` attribute allows us to list JAR files in the applet tag of an HTML file. The browser or applet viewer will search these JAR files for the classes needed to load an applet. We use the `archive` attribute in addition to the `code` attribute which still specifies the applet's class file. For example the **BeanBox** generated the applet tag

```
<applet
  archive="./SmileApplet.jar,./support.jar
    ,./juggler.jar,./Smiley.jar,./buttons.jar
    ,./BoundTextBean.jar"
  code="SmileApplet" width=382 height=173>
```

for `SmileApplet`.

THE BIG PICTURE
In writing a bean we include `set` and `get` methods for each property. The `PropertyChangeSupport` object helps us manage property change listeners, but we still need to include `addPropertyChangeListener` and `removePropertyChangeListener` methods if we have bound properties. We call the `firePropertyChange` method when the property value changes. If our bean generates an `ActionEvent` we call the `actionPerformed` method for all listeners, and include `addActionListener` and `removeActionListener` methods. We use the `jar` command to package our bean in a JAR file; the manifest indicates which files are beans.

TEST YOUR UNDERSTANDING

TRY IT YOURSELF   6.   Modify `TextBean` by changing the name of the `setNumber` method to `numberSet` and `getNumber` to `numberGet`. Create the JAR file and add it to the **BeanBox**. When you drag the modified `TextBean` into the **BeanBox** does the number property appear in the **Properties** window?

TRY IT YOURSELF   7.   Using the **BeanBox**, bind the number property of the `BoundTextBean` to the `priceInCents` of the `JellyBean`. In the **BeanBox**, change the number and check the **Properties** window of the `JellyBean` to see that its `priceInCents` changes to that same value.

8.   An anonymous inner class can implement an interface as well as extend a class. Write the argument to the `addActionListener` method, called in the `BoundTextBean` of Example 9.2, as an anonymous inner class. Its start is `new ActionListener() {`

TRY IT YOURSELF   9.   Modify Example 9.3 not to implement `Serializable`. Follow the steps to create the `SmileApplet`. What happens?

9.4   Using BeanInfo

· · · · · · · · · ·

In the absence of a **BeanInfo class** for a bean, Java uses its reflection facility to inspect the bean's code and determine its characteristics. By adding a `BeanInfo` class, the bean creator can configure the bean to present its properties in a more user friendly form than would result from letting Java figure them out by itself.

What Is `BeanInfo`?

The two **BeanBox** demo beans, `ExplicitButton` and `OurButton`, are very similar. `ExplicitButton` is just an `OurButton` with an `ExplicitButtonBeanInfo` class used to make the `ExplicitButton` more user friendly.[*]

The *Events* menu for the `OurButton`, shown in Figure 9.9, lists six event types, mouse, key, component, action, propertyChange, and focus, some of which are solely used internally by `OurButton` or its superclass, `Component`. By contrast, the *Events* menu for the `ExplicitButton`, shown in Figure 9.5, lists just button push (renamed from action to be more informative) and bound property change (renamed from propertyChange). The other event types, not meant for the end user, have been omitted.

The **Properties** window for an `ExplicitButton` (Figure 9.4) shows four properties; we leave it as an exercise to check that the similar window for an `OurButton` shows seven.

The **BeanBox** uses a `BeanInfo` class, if provided by the bean developer, to determine how to present that bean to the **BeanBox** user. If no `BeanInfo` class is available, the **BeanBox** uses the facilities of the `java.lang.reflect` package to analyze the code for the bean to determine its features to present to the **BeanBox** user. As users of

---

[*] We can read the **BeanBox** demo source files in the directory `c:\BDK\demo\sunw\demo`.

beans, rather than developers of tools such as the **BeanBox**, we do not need to explore Java's reflection facilities in this text.

`BeanInfo` is an interface in the `java.beans` package containing eight methods. The `SimpleBeanInfo` class provides default implementations of the `BeanInfo` interface methods, so by extending `SimpleBeanInfo` we only have to override those methods of interest to us.

To illustrate the use of `BeanInfo`, we will make our `Smiley` bean more user friendly.

Friendly Bean

`Friendly` bean is just a `Smiley` bean with a `BeanInfo` class. Its code is

```
package smiley;
public class Friendly extends Smiley {
}
```

To make `Friendly` more user friendly, we specify that the only properties we want to display in the **Properties** window are background, foreground, and age. Figure 9.20 shows the simplification.

Figure 9.20 Comparing **Properties** windows

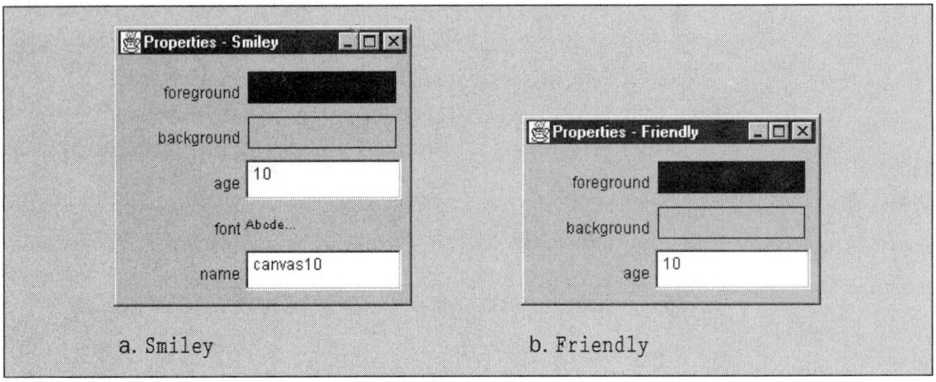

a. Smiley

b. Friendly

We will further specify that the only source events we want to display are nose-Press and ageChange. Figure 9.21 shows the contrast.

The third feature we make more user friendly is the list of target methods that the hookup class can call when handling a source event. When using the **BeanBox** to hookup a `Friendly` nosePress to a `Smiley` target method, Figure 9.22a shows that `Smiley` has many methods with no arguments (20 in all) inherited from its various superclasses. By contrast, when using the **BeanBox** to hookup a `Smiley` action event to a `Friendly` target method, Figure 9.22b shows that `Friendly` has only one method, `fireAction`, available. We have hidden the other 19 inherited methods, for which we have no use.

Figure 9.21   Comparing source events

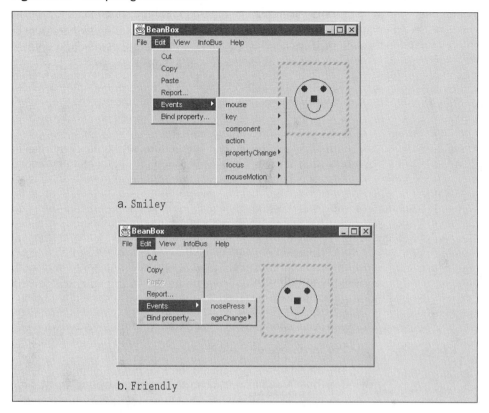

a. Smiley

b. Friendly

Figure 9.22   Comparing target methods

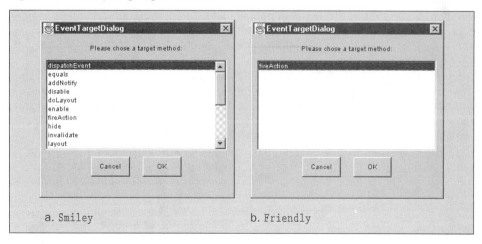

a. Smiley   b. Friendly

BeanInfo for Friendly

The `FriendlyBeanInfo` class makes `Friendly` more user friendly than `Smiley`. By creating `PropertyDescriptor`, `EventSetDescriptor`, and `MethodDescriptor` objects, we can get the **BeanBox** to create the friendlier display in Figures 9.20b, 9.21b, and 9.22b.

To specify the properties to display in the **Properties** window we override the `getPropertyDescriptors` method of `SimpleBeanInfo`. We create a `PropertyDescriptor` for each property we want to display, as, for example

```
PropertyDescriptor age = new PropertyDescriptor("age", Friendly.class);
```

where the first argument, `age`, is the name of the property, and the second argument is the bean class. Writing `Friendly.class` specifies the `Class` object for the `Friendly` class. Because `age` is a bound property we invoke

```
age.setBound(true);
```

so the **BeanBox** will list `age` as an item in the *Edit, Bind Property* menu.

To expose the `background` and `foreground` properties to the designer, we create a `PropertyDescriptor` for each. The return value for the `getPropertyDescriptor` method is a `PropertyDescriptor` array containing, in this case, the three property descriptors we created

```
PropertyDescriptor[] pd = {age,background,foreground};
```

The **Properties** window for `Friendly` displays these three properties in Figure 9.20b.

The `getEventSetDescriptors` method lets us simplify the *Edit, Events* menu in the **BeanBox**, describing the source events available to the designer. We create an `EventSetDescriptor` for each event we want the designer to see. For the `ActionEvent` generated by pressing `Friendly`'s nose, we have

```
EventSetDescriptor nosePress =
    new EventSetDescriptor(Friendly.class, "nosePress",
        ActionListener.class, "actionPerformed");
```

where the arguments are:

Type	Meaning
Class	the bean class
String	the name for our event
Class	the listener type for that event
String	the listener method name to handle the event

In all, we expose two events for `Friendly`, the `nosePress` and the `PropertyChangeEvent`, created in response to age changes. Letting the `getEventSetDescriptors` method return the array

```
EventSetDescriptor[] esd = {ageChange, nosePress};
```

produces the shorter and more informative *Event* menu of Figure 9.21b.

Using BeanInfo can dramatically shorten the list of target methods displayed to the designer. We implement `getMethodDescriptors` to return just one method descriptor so we get the one-item list of Figure 9.22b rather than the 20-item list shown in Figure 9.22a for `Smiley`.

To create a `MethodDescriptor`, we need a `Method` object. `Friendly.class` is a class of type `Class`. We call its `getMethod` method, as

```
Method m = Friendly.class.getMethod("fireAction", null);
```

The first argument names the method. The second is of type `Class[]` which gives the types of the arguments to the method and gives us the `Method` object we need. The `fireAction` method in `Smiley`, which `Friendly` inherits, generates and sends an `ActionEvent`. This event will be handled by the `actionPerformed` method of listeners. We pass **null** for the second arguement since `fireAction` has no arguments.

The **ToolBox** of Figure 9.1a shows some of the buttons with icons at their left. We use the `getIcon` method to return an image of the very friendly author to serve as an icon for `Friendly`.

EXAMPLE 9.4   **FriendlyBeanInfo.java**

```java
/* Uses a BeanInfo class to make a more
 * user friendly version of Smiley.
 */

package smiley;
import java.beans.*;
import java.awt.*;
import java.awt.event.*;
import java.lang.reflect.*;                                  // Note 1

public class FriendlyBeanInfo extends SimpleBeanInfo {
  public PropertyDescriptor[] getPropertyDescriptors() {
    try {
      PropertyDescriptor age =
        new PropertyDescriptor("age", Friendly.class);
      PropertyDescriptor background =
        new PropertyDescriptor("background", Friendly.class);   // Note 2
      PropertyDescriptor foreground =
        new PropertyDescriptor("foreground", Friendly.class);
      age.setBound(true);
      PropertyDescriptor[] pd = {age,background,foreground};
      return pd;
    } catch (IntrospectionException e) {                     // Note 3
      return null;
    }
  }
  public EventSetDescriptor[] getEventSetDescriptors() {
```

```
      try {
        EventSetDescriptor nosePress = new EventSetDescriptor(Friendly.class,
          "nosePress", ActionListener.class, "actionPerformed");
        EventSetDescriptor ageChange = new EventSetDescriptor(Friendly.class,
              "propertyChange", PropertyChangeListener.class,           // Note 4
              "propertyChange");
        EventSetDescriptor[] esd = {ageChange, nosePress};
        ageChange.setDisplayName("ageChange");                          // Note 5
        return esd;
      } catch (IntrospectionException e) {
        return null;
      }
    }
    public MethodDescriptor[] getMethodDescriptors() {
      try {
        Method m = Friendly.class.getMethod("fireAction", null);
        MethodDescriptor fireAction = new MethodDescriptor(m);          // Note 6
        MethodDescriptor[] md = {fireAction};
        return md;
      } catch(Exception e) {                                           // Note 7
        return null;
      }
    }
    public Image getIcon(int iconKind) {                               // Note 8
      return loadImage("gittleman.gif");
    }
  }
}
```

....

Note 1:   The `java.lang.reflect` package lets development tools, such as the **Bean-Box**, find the fields and methods of a class. We use its `Method` class in this program.

Note 2:   Creating a `PropertyDescriptor` for the background will cause the background property to appear in the **Properties** window. The designer will be able to change `Friendly`'s background color. Unlike in the `ExplicitButton`, the background property is not bound.

Note 3:   The `PropertyDescriptor` constructor may throw an `IntrospectionException`, meaning an error occurred when Java was gathering information about a program. Returning **null** tells the **BeanBox** not to use property descriptors, but rather to use reflection to find all the properties as it would if there were no `BeanInfo` class.

Note 4:   For the `nosePress EventSetDescriptor` we were able to choose our own name, `nosePress`, for the event, which we passed as the second argument. For the `ageChange EventDescriptor`, we must use the "propertyChange" name to show the bean generates property change events so the **BeanBox**

will add the *Bind Property* menu item. We use the setDisplayName method to make name propertyChange more user friendly (ageChange).

Note 5:   The setDisplayName method displays its argument, ageChange, in the event list instead of the name in the second argument of the EventSetDescriptor, propertyChange.

Note 6:   MethodDescriptor fireAction = new MethodDescriptor(m);
We only want to make one target method available to the designer, the fireAction method. The MethodDescriptor constructor takes a Method object as its argument.

Note 7:   } catch(Exception e) {
The getMethod method may throw NoSuchMethodException or SecurityException exceptions. We handle them generically with the superclass Exception, again returning **null** to let the **BeanBox** use its default process for finding methods, as if there were no BeanInfo class.

Note 8:   public Image getIcon(int iconKind) {
The BeanInfo class has four constants for different icon types. We ignore this argument, using the loadImage method from the SimpleBeanInfo class to always return the same image.

Packaging Friendly

Because Friendly is just a Smiley bean with BeanInfo, we put it in the smiley package. We package both Smiley and Friendly in the same JAR file so the manifest file, Happy.mf, is

```
Name: smiley/Smiley.class
Java-Bean: True

Name: smiley/Friendly.class
Java-Bean: True

Name: smiley/Smiley$1.class

Name: smiley/FriendlyBeanInfo.class

Name: smiley/gittleman.gif
```

We package all files used in Smiley and Friendly into a JAR file, Happy.jar, using the command

```
jar cfm smiley\Happy.jar smiley\Happy.mf
smiley\Smiley.class smiley\Smiley$1.class
smiley\Friendly.class smiley\FriendlyBeanInfo.class
smiley\gittleman.gif
```

THE BIG PICTURE

We add a `BeanInfo` class for a bean to make it more friendly. The `getPropertyDe-scriptors` method returns a property descriptor for each property we wish to display in the **Properties** window. The `getEventSetDescriptors` method returns an event set descriptor for each source event we wish to display in the menu. The `get-MethodDescriptors` method returns a method descriptor for each target method we wish to display. The `getIcon` method lets us choose an icon to represent the bean. We name our `BeanInfo` class `cnameBeanInfo`, where `cname` is the name of the bean class. By overriding `SimpleBeanInfo` we only have to implement those methods of the `BeanInfo` interface in which we are interested.

TEST YOUR UNDERSTANDING

TRY IT YOURSELF   10. Compare the **Properties** window for the `OurButton`, which does not have a `BeanInfo` class, with that for `ExplicitButton`, which is an `OurButton` with a `BeanInfo` class.

TRY IT YOURSELF   11. Use the **BeanBox** to make an applet using one `Friendly` bean to start the `Juggler` juggling and another to stop the juggling.

TRY IT YOURSELF   12. Modify Example 9.4 to omit the `getEventSetDescriptors` method. How does this effect how `Friendly` is presented in the **BeanBox**?

9.5   Programming with Beans

Java Beans are meant to be used with visual development tools, of which the **Bean-Box** is a rudimentary example. Nevertheless beans are just Java programs, and we are free to use them in hand-coded programs developed without the use of any visual tools. In doing so, we use the event-handling techniques covered earlier in the text.

Using Beans in an Applet

Our example is similar to the `SmileApplet`, developed in Section 9.3 using the **Bean-Box**. We write our program favoring the style of the **BeanBox**, creating a separate hookup class to handle each event. Figure 9.23 shows the `SmileyJug` applet. Pressing `Smiley`'s nose alternately stops and starts the `Juggler` juggling. Entering a value for `Smiley`'s age changes the animation rate of the `Juggler`.

To create beans we use the **new** operator, as in

```
private Smiley smile = new Smiley();
```

The `Juggler` is an applet, so after we construct it we need to call its `init` and `start` methods. Each hookup class handles a single connection from a source of the event to its target.

Bound properties generate a `PropertyChangeEvent` when they are changed. The `PropertyChangeListener` interface specifies the method

```
public void propertyChange(PropertyChangeEvent evt)
```

Figure 9.23 The `SmileyJug` applet

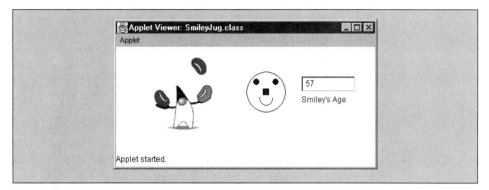

to handle property change events.

EXAMPLE 9.5   **SmileyJug.java**

```
/* Uses Juggler, Smiley, and BoundTextBean in a
 * Java program. Entering Smiley's age changes the
 * Juggler's animation rate. Clicking on Smiley's nose
 * stops and starts the Juggler.
 */

import sunw.demo.juggler.*;                              // Note 1
import smiley.*;
import java.applet.*;
import java.awt.event.*;
import java.awt.*;
import java.beans.*;

public class SmileyJug extends Applet {
  private Juggler jug = new Juggler();
  private Smiley smile = new Smiley();
  private BoundTextBean text = new BoundTextBean();
  private Label label = new Label("Smiley's Age");
  private boolean on = true;              // Is Juggler juggling?
  public void init() {
    add(jug);
    add(smile);
    Panel p = new Panel();
    p.setLayout(new GridLayout(2,1));
    p.add(text);
    p.add(label);
    add(p);
    jug.init();
    jug.start();
    smile.addPropertyChangeListener
          (new HookupAgeToAnimationRate());          // Note 2
    smile.addActionListener(new HookupNosePress());
```

```
      text.addPropertyChangeListener(new HookupNumberToAge());
    }
class HookupNosePress implements ActionListener {
  public void actionPerformed(ActionEvent e) {
    if (on){                                                    // Note 3
      jug.stopJuggling();
      on = false;
    }
    else {
      jug.startJuggling();
      on = true;
    }
  }
}
class HookupNumberToAge implements PropertyChangeListener {      // Note 4
  public void propertyChange(PropertyChangeEvent evt) {
    Object object = evt.getNewValue();
    int a = ((Integer)object).intValue();
    smile.setAge(a);
  }
}
class HookupAgeToAnimationRate
            implements PropertyChangeListener {                  // Note 5
  public void propertyChange(PropertyChangeEvent evt) {
    Object object = evt.getNewValue();
    int a = ((Integer)object).intValue();
    jug.setAnimationRate(a);
  }
 }
}
```

....

Note 1:   The `Juggler` is in the `sunw.demo.juggler` package. We also need to make
sure this directory is on the classpath. In Windows we can add its parent
directory `C:\BDK\demo` to the classpath using the command

```
set classpath=c:\BDK\demo;%classpath%
```

where `%classpath%` is the old classpath, which for the JDK1.1 must include
the current directory, the path to user packages, and the path to the system
packages. When using Java 2 it works best to copy the
`BDK\demo\sunw\demo\juggler` directory to a `sunw\demo\juggler` subdirectory
of the directory containing this program.

Note 2:   We could have let `SmileyJug` implement `ActionListener` and `Property-`
`ChangeListener` to handle these events, but we use hookup classes to more
closely follow the technique of visual tools building applets from components. For simplicity, our hookup classes are inner classes. The **BeanBox**
would make each a public class on a separate file.

Note 3:   The variable on is **true** when the Juggler is juggling and **false** when not. This differs from the SmileApplet of Section 9.3 where Smiley stopped the Juggler and an ExplicitButton started it. The **BeanBox** connects an event, such as a nosePress, unconditionally to a single target method. Here we alternately choose the stopJuggling and startJuggling methods.

Note 4:   When the user enters a desired value for Smiley's age in the BoundTextBean, that bean sets its number property which generates a PropertyChangeEvent that we handle here by calling the setAge method to change Smiley's age to the desired value.

Note 5:   When Smiley's age changes it generates a PropertyChangeEvent which we handle here by changing the Juggler's animation rate.

Customizing Beans

Inside a tool such as the **BeanBox** we use property editors available in the **Properties** window to change properties of our beans as we build an applet with them. We can also write a Java program to change a bean's properties, saving the changed bean which we can use in its new configuration to build applets.

For example, suppose we would like an alternate version of Smiley bean with a red background. We can create a new Smiley in our program, set its background to red,

```
smile.setBackgound(Color.red);
```

and save the red Smiley.

Because Smiley implements Serializable we can save it using the writeObject method. We save it in the file smiley/Smiley.ser, where the .ser extension represents a serialized Java file.

EXAMPLE 9.6   **SaveSmiley.java**

```
/* Saves a red Smiley in the
 * smiley/Smiley.ser file.
 */

import java.awt.*;
import java.io.*;
import smiley.*;

public class SaveSmiley {
  public static void main(String[] args) {
    Smiley smile = new Smiley();
    smile.setBackground(Color.red);
    try {
        FileOutputStream f = new FileOutputStream("smiley/Smiley.ser"); // Note 1
        ObjectOutputStream out = new ObjectOutputStream(f);
        out.writeObject(smile);
        out.flush();
```

```
      }catch(Exception e) {
        e.printStackTrace();
      }
    }
  }
}
```

....

Note 1:   We save `smile` in `smiley/Smiley.ser`, where the `smiley` directory is contained in the directory containing `SaveSmiley.class`. We could have used a
program argument to specify the directory in which to save `smile`.

To use the customized version of `Smiley` in an applet we cannot just call its constructor. Calling `new Smiley()` would give us the original unmodified `Smiley`. The `Beans`
class provides the `instantiate` method to load a class from a `.ser` file. In our `RedSmi-
ley` applet, we use

```
smile=(Smiley)Beans.instantiate(null,"smiley.Smiley");
```

where the first argument specifies the class loader to use to load the class, and the second is the name of the bean. Passing **null** for the first argument lets Java use the standard system loader. The second argument, `smiley.Smiley`, tells Java to look first for a
file `Smiley.ser` in the `smiley` directory (on the classpath) and if it cannot find it to
look for `Smiley.class`, the original `Smiley`. Because `instantiate` returns an object, we
cast the return value to have type `Smiley`.

Example 9.7 shows the changes to Example 9.5 needed to use the red `Smiley`. The
complete code is on the disk included with this text. Running the `RedSmiley` applet
shows a screen like that of Figure 9.23 except `Smiley`'s background is red.

EXAMPLE 9.7   **RedSmiley.java**

```
/* Modifies Example 9.5 to use a serialized
 * red Smiley instead of the original.
 */

// rest of code same as Example 9.5
public class RedSmiley extends Applet {
  public void init() {
    try {
      smile=(Smiley)Beans.instantiate(null,"smiley.Smiley");
    } catch (Exception e) {                                    // Note 1
      e.printStackTrace();
    }
    ....
  }
}
```

....

Note 1:   The `instantiate` method may throw an `IOException` or a `ClassNotFoundEx-
ception`. We catch both with the superclass `Exception`.

THE BIG PICTURE

When using beans in our own Java program, we have to create the hookup classes that the **BeanBox** created. By using `set` methods, we can customize a bean in a program and write it, using object serialization, to a `.ser` file. This assumes that our bean class implements the `Serializable` interface. The `instantiate` method lets us load the customized bean and use it in our program.

TEST YOUR UNDERSTANDING

13. What additional capability does the `instantiate` method give, compared to the **new** operator for loading a bean into a program.

TRY IT YOURSELF   14. Modify Example 9.6 to use the `instantiate` method, instead of the **new** operator, to create the Juggler.

TRY IT YOURSELF   15. Modify Example 9.5 to omit the call `jug.start()`. What is the effect of this change?

SUMMARY

- Java Beans are components we can use to build programs. Typically designers use a visual tool to build with beans. We illustrate this with the simple BeanBox provided by Sun to test beans. The **ToolBox** window contains a list of beans which the designer can drag into the **BeanBox** window. The **Properties** window lists properties of the selected bean, and provides editors for the designer to change these properties, customizing the bean for use in an applet.

- Each bean shows three aspects of itself to interface with the **BeanBox**. In addition to its properties, a bean shows the events it can generate, which can be connected, using the **BeanBox**, to methods in a target bean. The event occurring in the source bean causes the chosen method to execute in the target bean. For example, we connected a button so pressing the button caused the `Juggler` to stop juggling. The **BeanBox** wrote the code to hookup the source event with the target action. The third feature a bean shows is the list of methods it can execute as the target of an event in a source bean.

- Beans use standard syntax for properties, for example using a `getBackground` method to get its background color, and a `setBackground` method to set it. For a custom property such as age, the bean uses `getAge` and `setAge` methods. Properties can be bound or constrained. Using the **BeanBox**, the `Bind Property` menu allows the designer to bind a property of the source bean to a property of the same type in the target bean. When the value of that property changes in the source, it automatically changes in the target also. A constrained property allows the target to veto the change in the value of the source property.

- A bean is a Java program. Our simple `TextBean` has a number property that we can get and set. We package a bean in a JAR file which includes all files needed by the bean so it may be downloaded or otherwise distributed as a component to use in building Java programs. We include a manifest file stating which of the files in the JAR file are beans.

■ A bean with a bound property calls the `firePropertyChange` method when that property is changed. A `PropertyChangeSupport` object handles the details of notifying property change listeners, which register using the `addPropertyChangeListener` method.

■ Our `Smiley` bean creates its own `ActionEvent` when the user presses the nose. This bean uses a vector to keep track of action listeners and notifies them when an action event occurs. It uses an anonymous inner class, defining the unnamed class right where it is used, as a method argument. We often use anonymous inner classes in this way, defining them while registering them as event handlers.

■ By including a `BeanInfo` class with a bean, the bean developer can customize the list of properties, source events, and target methods that the bean designer sees when using a tool such as the **BeanBox**, making that bean easier to use.

■ Although visual tools are the intended way to develop programs using beans, we can use beans in hand-coded programs. Just as the **BeanBox** allows us to customize beans, we can write programs to customize beans and save the modified beans which can be reloaded in their changed state.

■ Component technology will have an increasingly important role in economically producing robust software.

Program Modification Exercises

· · · · · · · · · ·

1. Modify Example 9.2 to use an anonymous inner class to handle the `ActionEvent` generated.

2 . Modify Example 9.3 to generate an `ActionEvent` when the user releases the mouse on `Smiley`'s nose, rather than when the user presses it.

3. Modify Example 9.2 to make the background a bound property.

4. Modify Example 9.2 to catch the `NumberFormatException` thrown when the user enters an invalid value in the text field. Handle the exception by erasing the invalid value and leaving the focus in the text field so the user must enter another value.

5. Modify Example 9.5 to let `SmileyJug` handle the events it generates, rather than using hookup classes.

6. Modify Example 9.6 to save `Smiley` with a red background and an age of `50`.

Program Design Exercises

. . . .

7. Write an `InsertSort` bean which has a value property. When value is set, it should add the new value to an array of integers and display the array in sorted order in a bar chart, using rectangles in alternating colors. Assume the values range from 0 to 100. Package this bean and add it to the **BeanBox**. Add a `BoundTextBean` to the **BeanBox**. Configure the beans so when the user enters a value in the `BoundText-Bean` it is displayed in sorted order in `InsertSort`. Make an applet from this configuration.

8. Write a Java program to make an applet, as described in Exercise 9.7, from a `BoundTextBean` and an `InsertSort` bean.

9. Write a `NewBoundTextBeanBeanInfo` class for the `NewBoundTextBean` which is like the `BoundTextBean` of Example 9.2, but which uses `BeanInfo`. Repackage `NewBound-TextBean` with its `BeanInfo` class and drag it into the **BeanBox** to test it.

10. Write a `Boss` bean that generates an `ActionEvent` when the user clicks its left eye and an `ItemEvent` when the user clicks its right eye. Construct an item event using

    ```
    new ItemEvent (new Choice(),0,null,ItemEvent.ITEM_STATE_CHANGED)
    ```

    Write a `Worker` bean that has methods `payRaised` and `payCut`. The `payRaised` method displays a drawing of a happy face whenever it is called while the `payCut` method displays a sad face. Use the **BeanBox** to create an applet in which clicking the boss's left eye causes a pay raise for the worker, while clicking the right eye causes a pay cut.

11. Using Exercise 9.10, write a Java program to make an applet from a `Boss` bean and a `Worker` bean.

12. Create a `Calculator` bean from various bean components such as button beans and text field beans. You may use beans without any visible representation to hold intermediate values.

13. Create a `Calendar` bean which displays the days of the month which the user enters or selects.

14. Create a `BarChart` bean which displays data entered by the user in a bar chart.

15. Create a `Database` bean that uses JDBC to connect to the database specified by the user, using the driver specified, and execute an SQL query.

10

Enterprise JavaBeans™

Introduction

· · · · · · · · · ·

Enterprise JavaBeans™ (EJB) technology is part of the Java™ 2 Platform, Enterprise Edition (J2EE) for developing distributed applications. A J2EE server handles services such as transaction management, security, and database access so the developer can concentrate on the business logic. The J2EE server resides on a middle-tier in a three-tier architecture, between the client and the database.

EJB components, focusing on the business application, are platform independent. In contrast to the Microsoft COM+ technology that is designed for the Windows operating system, but is language independent, EJB components, written in Java, can run on any platform. Because EJB components will run on any EJB server, the developer is not locked into a proprietary application server.

OBJECTIVES

- Set up a J2EE server.

- Use a tool to deploy enterprise beans.

- Develop and deploy an entity bean.

- Develop and deploy a session bean.

- Use standalone, servlet, and JSP clients.

10.1 Getting Started with EJB

. . . .

We introduce the J2EE architecture, set up an EJB server, and implement a Hello bean as a simple illustration.

The J2EE Architecture

In the middle-tier, a J2EE server includes an EJB container for enterprise beans, and a web container for servlets and JSP (JavaServer Pages) files. The EJB container does not allow clients to communicate directly with enterprise beans. In fact some types of beans may be shared among multiple clients. A client interacts with a bean by means of a remote interface defining the bean's business methods and a home interface defining the bean's life cycle methods.

Enterprise beans come in two varieties, entity beans and session beans. Entity beans model business objects such as a customer or an account. They have a persistent representation, usually in a database. Either the bean can manage the database interaction or the container can do it automatically.

Session beans perform operations on the business objects. They represent the client in the J2EE server, so the client can connect once with a session bean that then interacts with other beans on the server. This minimizes the connections between client and server to improve efficiency. A session bean might place an order, or reserve a flight, for example.

Session beans are not persistent. Each is associated with one client, and when the client terminates, so does the session bean. Session beans can be stateful or stateless. A stateful bean saves information so it can interact with the client. Stateless beans require no continuing interaction with the client and offer the best performance.

Enterprise beans are components, and may be configured as part of the process of deploying them in the EJB container. We can specify the type of transaction processing desired, and the database information for the container to manage persistence.

The steps in developing a simple EJB application are:

1. Create the enterprise bean.
   Write Java programs and compile them to obtain

   `ProgHome.class` for the Home interface
   `ProgRemote.class` for the Remote interface
   `ProgEJB.class` for the bean

2. Start EJB server (if not already started)

3. Deploy the enterprise bean. Use a tool provided by the EJB container vendor to create a JAR file, `ProgEJB.jar`, for the enterprise bean, and create an application file, `Prog.ear`, for deployment in the EJB container. The deployment process will create additional files needed for communication with the clients, and a deployment descriptor.

4. Create a client. `ProgClient.class`

A J2EE Server

In order to use enterprise beans, we need a J2EE server. Sun provides a reference implementation, the J2EE SDK Enterprise Edition. We use version 1.2[*], available from http://java.sun.com/. The documentation requires a second download. We need to set the JAVA_HOME and J2EE_HOME environment variables to the locations where the Java 2 SDK, Standard Edition and J2EE are installed. The J2EE version we use requires the standard edition version 1.2.1. The author's settings on a Windows system are:

```
set java_home=d:\jdk1.2.2
set j2ee_home=d:\j2sdkee1.2
```

The easiest way to start the server is to click on j2ee.bat in the %J2EE_HOME%\bin directory. Clicking on deploytool.bat will execute the batch file that starts the deployment tool, which pops up a GUI that we will use in our examples. One can also start the server and the deployment tool with the commands

```
start %j2ee_home%\bin\j2ee -verbose
start %j2ee_home%\bin\deploytool
```

TIP

When stopping the J2EE server use the command

```
%j2ee_home%\bin\j2ee -stop
```

to allow the server to terminate properly.

Hello Bean

Hello bean will be a stateless session bean that has one method returning a message string. We write the code for the bean and for the home and remote interfaces that allow clients to interact with it.

The remote interface has one method, hello. It extends EJBObject from the package javax.ejb. Packages whose names start with javax are standard extensions, in contrast to core packages that start with java. All methods of the remote interface must declare that they may throw a remote exception. Communication across a network must always allow for the possibility of errors.

EXAMPLE 10.1   HelloRemote.java

```
/* Specifies business methods for Hello EJB.
 * /

import javax.ejb.EJBObject;
import java.rmi.RemoteException;                              // Note 1

public interface HelloRemote extends EJBObject {
  public String hello(String message) throws RemoteException;
}
```

---

[*] See http://www.cecs.csulb.edu/~artg/internet/changes.html for changes needed to use version 1.3.

Note 1:   EJB uses RMI (Remote Method Invocation) for distributed object communication. Methods that invoke a remote object using RMI must include `RemoteException` in their `throws` clauses.

The home interface is also simple. Its purpose is to specify the lifecycle methods that create, find, and remove a bean. Because our bean is stateless, we have no variables to initialize, so our create method has no arguments. It returns a `HelloRemote` object, and declares that it may throw a remote exception and a create exception.

Although we declare the remote and home interfaces, the EJB container implements them. The home interface extends the `EJBHome` interface that has several methods that all will be implemented by the container. Similarly, the container will implement the methods of the remote interface and of `EJBObject` that it extends.

EXAMPLE 10.2   HelloHome.java

```
/* Specifies methods to create, find, and remove a bean.
 */

import java.rmi.RemoteException;
import javax.ejb.CreateException;
import javax.ejb.EJBHome;

public interface HelloHome extends EJBHome {
  HelloRemote create() throws RemoteException, CreateException;     // Note 1
}
```

Note 1:   `CreateException` must be included in the throws clause of all create methods.

A session bean implements the `SessionBean` interface that contains four methods `ejbActivate`, `ejbPassivate`, `ejbRemove`, and `ejbSetSessionContext`. The container uses these methods to notify bean instances about lifecycle events. Our simple Hello bean does not need this information, so we implement these four methods with empty bodies.

In addition, the `Hello` bean implements the `hello` method of the `HelloRemote` interface, but it does not declare that it implements `HelloRemote`. Remember that a client does not interact with a bean directly. The container generates code that implements the `HelloRemote` and `HelloHome` interfaces, and will call the corresponding implementations in our bean class.

EXAMPLE 10.3   HelloEJB.java

```
/* A session bean that returns a message.
 */

import javax.ejb.SessionBean;
import javax.ejb.SessionContext;
```

```
public class HelloEJB implements SessionBean {
  public String hello(String message) {                          // Note 1
    return message;
  }
  public HelloEJB() {}
  public void ejbCreate() {}                                     // Note 2
  public void ejbRemove() {}
  public void ejbActivate() {}
  public void ejbPassivate() {}
  public void setSessionContext(SessionContext sc) {}
}
```

Note 1:   This is the implementation of the business method of the remote interface of Example 10.1. It will be called by the container-generated code.

Note 2:   The `ejbCreate` method corresponds to the `create` method of the home interface of Example 10.2. Each must have the same arguments. It will be called by the container-generated code. Because we have no fields to initialize, we use an empty body.

To compile the bean's file we use the commands

```
javac -classpath .;%j2ee_home%\lib\j2ee.jar HelloRemote.java
javac -classpath .;%j2ee_home%\lib\j2ee.jar HelloHome.java
javac -classpath .;%j2ee_home%\lib\j2ee.jar HelloEJB.java
```

or

```
javac -classpath .;%j2ee_home%\lib\j2ee.jar Hello*.java
```

The `Hello` Application

A J2EE application may contain several beans, and web components such as servlets or JSP files. We do not add enterprise beans directly to the J2EE server, but instead package them in a J2EE application that we deploy on the server.

We use `deploytool`, that comes with the J2EE SDK, to package and deploy the `Hello` bean. First we create the J2EE application. In the `File` menu, we click on *New Application*. In the dialog that pops up, we enter `Hello` in the Application Name field and browse for the directory containing the files for the application. In the file dialog, we select the `D:\book3\ejb` directory, enter `Hello.ear` in the File name field, click on *New Application,* and then on *OK.* A `Hello` entry appears in the Local Applications panel of the deploytool GUI.

Having created a J2EE application to hold our bean, we use `deploytool` to package our three class files composing the enterprise bean in a JAR file. In the File menu, we click on *New Enterprise Bean.* An introductory screen pops up listing the steps involved in packaging a bean.

We click on *Next* to get the EJB JAR dialog, which should show `Hello` as the application in the *Enterprise will go in* field. We enter *HelloJAR* in the *Display name* field, and then add the `HelloRemote.class`, `HelloHome.class`, and `HelloEJB.class` files to the JAR. To add these files, we click on *Add* to the right of the *Contents* field, and enter *D:\book3\ejb* in the *Choose directory* field in the dialog that pops up. We then click *Add*, selecting each of the files `HelloRemote.class`, `HelloHome.class`, and `HelloEJB.class`, and click *OK*.

Clicking *Next* brings us to the *General* screen. We select `HelloEJB` as the class-name, `HelloHome` as the Home interface, `HelloRemote` as the Remote interface, and enter *HelloBean* as the Display name. We check *Session Bean* and *Stateless*, click *Next*, and then click *Finish* because we do not use the remaining screens. This completes the packaging of Hello bean into a JAR and adding the JAR to the `Hello` application.

Deploying the `Hello` Application

The `deploytool` utility assists us in deploying the Hello application on the J2EE server. We click the JNDI tab to give our bean a name that clients will use to look it up. We enter *HiBean* in the JNDI Name field and hit the Enter key. JNDI is the Java Naming and Directory Interface that registers a bean using a name that clients can refer to when looking it up. To deploy `Hello` bean in the EJB container, we click *Deploy Application* in the Tools menu that brings up the *Deploy Hello* screen. We choose `localhost` as the Target Server. Checking *Return Client Jar* displays a field to choose a name and path for the client code. We enter `d:\book3\ejb\HelloClient.jar`. Clicking *Next* allows us to confirm the JNDI name, and clicking *Next* again brings us to the final screen in which we click *Finish*. A Deployment Progress window shows the actions the server takes to deploy our bean. It creates the files in `HelloClient.jar` that allow a client to communicate with the Hello bean. Figure 10.1 shows the final view of the deployment tool GUI, with `Hello` properly installed as a server application.

A client must find the bean in the server. It creates a context in which the lookup proceeds. In the lookup method, the client uses the name *HiBean* that we entered as the JNDI name for the `Hello` bean in the deployment tool. The `lookup` method returns an object that implements the home interface. Calling its `create` method returns an object that implements the remote interface. We call the `hello` method that returns the string `Hello World` that we pass as its argument.

To run the client, we use the command

```
java -classpath .;%J2EE_HOME%\lib\j2ee.jar;HelloClient.jar HelloClient
```

We add `HelloClient.jar` to the classpath because it contains code generated by the container that the client uses to communicate with the bean. The file `j2ee.jar` contains the J2EE classes.

Figure 10.1   The final deployment tool screen

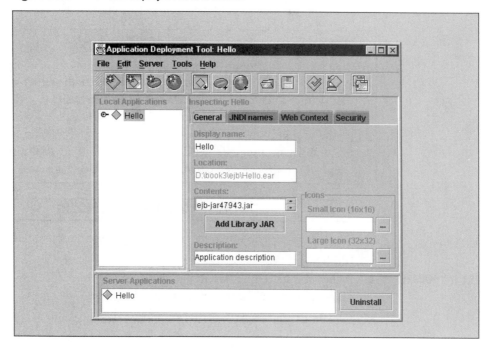

EXAMPLE 10.4   **HelloClient.java**

```java
/* Finds Hello bean and calls its hello method.
 */

import javax.naming.Context;
import javax.naming.InitialContext;

public class HelloClient {
  public static void main(String[] args) {
    try {
      Context context = new InitialContext();
      HelloHome home = (HelloHome)context.lookup("HiBean");
      HelloRemote remote = home.create();
      System.out.println(remote.hello("Hello World"));
    }catch (Exception e) {
      e.printStackTrace();
    }
  }
}
```

Output

```
Hello World
```

The `Hello` bean serves as a simple illustration. Our server and client shared the same machine, but the client could have connected remotely to the server.

THE BIG PICTURE

A J2EE server hosts enterprise beans and web components. Enterprise beans comes in two types, entity and session, and session beans can be either stateless or stateful. A bean defines a remote interface that specifies the business methods, and a home interface that specifies its life cycle methods. It defines a bean class that implements either the session bean or the entity bean interface, and the business methods of the remote interface. Using the J2EE SDK, the `deploytool` utility packages the bean and deploys it on the server. Clients use JNDI to locate a bean.

TEST YOUR UNDERSTANDING

1. Which interface do we extend when defining the remote interface for a bean that specifies the bean's business methods?

TRY IT YOURSELF 2. Follow the steps necessary to deploy the `Hello` bean of Examples 10.1, 10.2, and 10.3 and run the client of Example 10.4.

3. Explain the difference between the `HelloClient.jar` and `HelloClient.java` files.

10.2 Entity Beans

· · · · · · · · · · ·

An entity bean represents a persistent business object, often in a database. Clients may share an entity bean. Persistence means that the entity remains in the database even after the EJB container terminates.

Entity beans can either let the container manage the database accesses needed to load and store the entity (container-managed persistence), or implement the database queries itself (bean-managed persistence). Container-managed persistence requires much less code, and the code is independent of any database. But it may not allow complex representations where a business object's fields are stored in more than one table, and it can be less efficient.

We illustrate with a container-managed `Customer` bean representing a customer as defined in the `Customer` table of the `Sales` database of Section 3.1. The `Customer` table of Figure 3.1 has `CustomerID`, `CustomerName`, `Address`, and `BalanceDue` columns. We define our remote interface to include `get` and `set` methods for the `name`, `address`, and `due` fields.

In this chapter we use the `Cloudscape` database system bundled with the J2EE SDK Enterprise Edition. Using container-managed persistence, `Cloudscape` will create the tables. In our example, in which the bean class has the name `CustomerEJB`, `Cloudscape` will name the table "*CustomerEJBTable*"where the quotes are part of the table name. We will use instance variables id, name, address, and due. Cloudscape adds quotes to make the column names, "id," "name," "address," and "due."

The Remote Interface

The CustomerRemote interface, representing the business operations, has methods to get and set the name, address, and due properties. In this example a column in the database table represents each property, but properties could be derived values instead. We do not include get and set methods for the id field because it is the key which is unique and will not change.

EXAMPLE 10.5   CustomerRemote.java

```
/* Specifies business methods for Customer EJB.
 */

import javax.ejb.EJBObject;
import java.rmi.RemoteException;

public interface CustomerRemote extends EJBObject {
  public String getName() throws RemoteException;
  public void setName(String name) throws RemoteException;
  public String getAddress() throws RemoteException;
  public void setAddress(String address) throws RemoteException;
  public double getDue() throws RemoteException;
  public void setDue(double due) throws RemoteException;
}
```

....

The Home Interface

The CustomerHome interface contains methods to create and find a Customer bean. When creating an entity bean, we need to pass its initial state in the create method. Thus we pass values for the id, name, address, and balance due.

We can find a bean using finder methods. Finder methods start with the word *find* followed by a descriptive phrase. We always include the findByPrimaryKey method and may include others. The CustomerHome interface includes a findByName method that locates all customers with a given name, and a findGreaterDue method that locates all customers whose balance due is greater than a specified amount.

Using container-managed persistence, Java will implement the finder methods for us, but we must specify the appropriate constraint in a WHERE clause in the deployment tool. For example, when using deploytool, we will add the clause

```
WHERE "due" > ?1
```

to the SQL generated for the findGreaterDue method. The ?1 stands for the first argument to findGreaterDue. Calling findGreaterDue(100.00) returns customers whose balance due is greater than $100.

EXAMPLE 10.6   CustomerHome.java

```
/* Specifies methods to create and find a Customer.
 */

import java.rmi.RemoteException;
import javax.ejb.CreateException;
import javax.ejb.FinderException;
import javax.ejb.EJBHome;
import java.util.Enumeration;

public interface CustomerHome extends EJBHome {
  CustomerRemote create(String id, String name, String address,
        double due) throws RemoteException, CreateException;
  CustomerRemote findByPrimaryKey(String id)
        throws FinderException, RemoteException;              // Note 1
  Enumeration findByName(String name)
        throws FinderException, RemoteException;              // Note 2
  Enumeration findGreaterDue(double amount)
        throws FinderException, RemoteException;              // Note 3
}
```

....

Note 1:   `FinderException` must be included in the `throws` clause of every finder method.

Note 2:   Because there may be multiple entries in the database with the same name, we return an `Enumeration`.

Note 3:   Because several customers may have a balance due that is greater than the specified amount we return an `Enumeration`.

The Entity Bean (Container-Managed)

The `CustomerEJB` bean implements the methods of the remote interface, and implements the `EntityBean` interface that contains the `ejbActivate`, `ejbPassivate`, `ejbRemove`, `ejbLoad`, `ejbStore` callback methods that notify the bean of life-cycle events. The container calls `ejbActivate` when the bean instance is taken out of the pool of available instances to be associated with an `EJBObject` that can communicate with a client. It calls `ejbPassivate` before the bean instance disassociates from an `EJBObject`. Using container-managed persistence, the container handles all these details so we can implement the callback methods with empty bodies.

The container calls `ejbLoad` and `ejbStore` to make the bean consistent with the database, and `ejbRemove` before it removes the `EJBObject` associated with the instance. Again, using container-managed persistence, we can implement these methods with empty bodies.

The `EntityBean` interface also contains the `setEntityContext` and `unsetEntityContext` methods. The container calls `setEntityContext` when it creates a bean instance and `unsetEntityContext` when it removes it. When it assigns an instance to an `EJBObject`, it updates its entity context. The `EntityContext` interface contains the `getEjbObject` and `getPrimaryKey` methods that a bean can use to find out about the object it is associated with. The client communicates with the bean via the `EJBObject`. We set the context in our `CustomerEJB` bean but do not use it.

We pass arguments to the `ejbCreate` method of an entity bean to initialize the fields. An entity bean can have more than one `ejbCreate` method, each with different parameters, but `CustomerEJB` has just one. The `ejbCreate` method for entity bean with bean-managed persistence returns the primary key, which in this example has type `String`. For `CustomerEJB`, which uses container-managed persistence, we do not use the return value and return **null**.

After the `ejbCreate` method completes execution and the bean is assigned to an `EJBObject`, the container calls the `ejbPostCreate` method which must have the same parameters as the `ejbCreate` method. The entity context is available in the `ejbPost-Create` method, but not in `ejbCreate`. We implement `ejbPostCreate` with an empty body because the `CustomerEJB` bean does not use the entity context.

EXAMPLE 10.7   **CustomerEJB.java**

```java
/* Entity Bean representing a Customer.
 */

import javax.ejb.EntityBean;
import javax.ejb.EntityContext;
import javax.ejb.CreateException;

public class CustomerEJB implements EntityBean {
  public String id;                                        // Note 1
  public String name;
  public String address;
  public double due;
  private EntityContext context;

  public String getName() {
    return name;
  }
  public void setName(String name) {
    this.name = name;
  }
  public String getAddress() {
    return address;
  }
  public void setAddress(String address) {
    this.address = address;
  }
  public double getDue() {
    return due;
  }
```

```
    public void setDue(double due) {
      this.due = due;
    }
    public String ejbCreate(String id, String name, String        // Note 2
          address, double due) throws CreateException {
      if (id == null) {
        throw new CreateException("id is required");
      }
      this.id = id;
      this.name = name;
      this.address = address;
      this.due = due;
      return null;
    }
    public void ejbPostCreate(String id, String name,
                      String address, double due) { }              // Note 3
    public void setEntityContext(EntityContext context) {         // Note 4
      this.context = context;
    }
    public void unsetEntityContext() { }
    public void ejbActivate() { }
    public void ejbPassivate() { }
    public void ejbRemove() { }
    public void ejbLoad() { }
    public void ejbStore() { }
}
```

Note 1:   We must declare all fields that the container manages as **public**.

Note 2:   Because we are using container-managed persistence, we could declare the return type as **void**. We chose the type String because that would be required if we used bean-managed persistence.

Note 3:   We must include an `ejbPostCreate` method corresponding to each `ejbCreate` method.

Note 4:   Because we do not use the entity context in this example, we could have implemented `setEntityContext` with an empty body, but we chose to show how to implement it to allow for the use of the entity context.

Transactions

Clients may share an entity bean. One client must not change data that another is using. A client may need to execute several methods in order to complete a transaction. For example, transferring funds requires a withdrawal from one account and a deposit to another. In a successful transaction, both the withdrawal and the deposit must complete. Transaction processing deals with these and other issues of consistency and completeness.

Using container-managed transactions, a J2EE server does transaction processing automatically. We declare the desired transaction type for each business method and let the server handle the details. Figure 10.2 shows the six transaction types. The `Required` attribute is a good default choice. We will select it when we use the deployment tool.

Figure 10.2   Transaction types

Transaction	Type Description
Required	Executes within current transaction. If none, starts a new transaction.
RequiresNew	Starts a new transaction, suspending current transaction, if any.
Mandatory	Runs within current transaction, throwing an exception if none.
NotSupported	Suspends current transaction, if any.
Supports	Runs within current transaction, if any.
Never	Throws an exception if asked to run within a transaction.

Deploying an Entity Bean

After compiling the source files using the command

```
javac -classpath .;%j2ee_home%\lib\j2ee.jar Customer*.java
```

we start the deployment tool with

```
start %j2ee_home%\bin\deploytool
```

the J2EE server with

```
start %j2ee_home%\bin\j2ee -verbose
```

and the Cloudscape database with

```
start %j2ee_home%\bin\cloudscape -start
```

TIP
☞

To close the database properly use the command

```
%j2ee_home%\bin\cloudscape -stop
```

By default, the server deletes database tables when we undeploy the application, but that can be changed in the deployment tool.

Using the deployment tool, we

- **Create the Customer application.**
  Click *File, New Application.*
  Enter `Sales` as the Application Display Name.
  Enter `d:\book3\ejb\Sales.ear` as the File Name (the full path).
  Click *OK.*

- **Package the bean.**
  Click *File, New Enterprise Bean.*
  Click *Next.*
  Choose *Sales* as the application the enterprise bean will go in.
  Choose *CustomerJAR* as the display name.
  Click *Add* for the Contents area.
  Enter the Root directory.
  Select the `CustomerEJB`, `CustomerHome`, and `CustomerRemote` class files.
  Click *Add.*
  Click *OK.*
  Click *Next.*
  Choose *CustomerEJB* as the Enterprise Bean class.
  Choose *CustomerHome* as the Home Interface.
  Choose *CustomerRemote* as the Remote Interface.
  Enter `CustomerBean` as the display name.
  Check *Entity* as the Bean type.
  Click *Next.*
  Check *Container managed persistence.*
  Check `id`, `name`, `address`, and `due`.
  Enter `java.lang.String` as the Primary key class.
  Choose `id` as the Primary key field name.
  Click *Next.*
  Click *Next* (for Environment Entities).
  Click *Next* (for Enterprise Bean References).
  Click *Next* (for Resource References).
  Click *Next* (for Security).
  Check *Container-managed transactions.*
  Choose *Required* as the Transaction Type for the business methods,
    `getName, setName, getAddress, setAddress, getDue, setDue`.
  Click *Next.*
  Click *Finish.*

- **Specify Deployment Settings**
  Select *CustomerBean* in the Local Applications area.
  Select the *Entity* tab.
  Click *Deployment Settings.* (Maximize window to see this button.)
  Enter `jdbc/Cloudscape` as the Database JNDI Name, and hit *Enter.*
  Click *Generate SQL now.*
  Click *OK* (for the SQL Generator message).
  Click *OK* in the *Provide finder SQL* information box.
  Select `findByName` in the EJB method area.
  Add `WHERE "name" = ?1` to the SQL statement.
  Select `findGreaterDue` in the EJB method area.

Add *WHERE "due" > ?1* to the SQL statement.
Click *OK.*

■ Deploying the J2EE Application
Click *Tools, Deploy Application.*
Check *Return Client Jar.*
Enter the filename, say d:\book3\ejb\CustomerClient.jar, for the client code.
Click *Next.*
Enter *CustomerHome* (or whatever the client will use) as the JNDI name.
Click *Next.*
Click *Finish.*
Click *OK.*

Figure 10.3 shows the Customer bean in the deployment tool GUI.

Figure 10.3 Customer **bean in the deployment tool GUI**

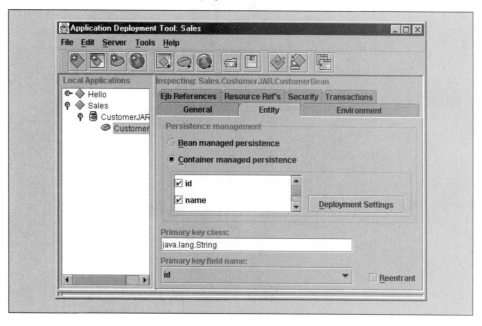

A Customer Client

In Example 10.8, we create the four customers shown in the Customer table in Chapter 3. We use each of the finder methods to locate customers and display the results. The command

```
java -classpath
    .;%j2ee_home%\lib\j2ee.jar;CustomerClient.jar
    CustomerClient
```
will execute the client program.

EXAMPLE 10.8   **CustomerClient.java**

```java
/* Creates four customers. Tests the finder methods.
 */

import java.util.Enumeration;
import javax.naming.Context;
import javax.naming.InitialContext;

public class CustomerClient {
  public static void main(String[] args) {
    try {
      Context initial = new InitialContext();
      CustomerHome home =
              (CustomerHome)initial.lookup("CustomerHome");      // Note 1
      CustomerRemote customer = home.create("1234", "Fred Flynn",
          "22 First St.", 1667.00);                              // Note 2
      customer = home.create("5678", "Darnell Davis",
          "33 Second St.", 130.95);
      customer = home.create("4321", "Marla Martinez",
          "44 Third St.", 0.0);
      customer = home.create("8765", "Carla Kahn",
          "55 Fourth St.", 0.0);
      CustomerRemote id5678 = home.findByPrimaryKey("5678");     // Note 3
      System.out.println(id5678.getName());                     // Note 4
      Enumeration e = home.findByName("Carla Kahn");            // Note 5
        while (e.hasMoreElements()) {
          CustomerRemote carla = (CustomerRemote)e.nextElement();
          String id = (String)carla.getPrimaryKey();            // Note 6
          String name = carla.getName();
          String address = carla.getAddress();
          double due = carla.getDue();
          System.out.println(id + ' ' + name + ' ' +
                address + ' ' + due);
        }
        e = home.findGreaterDue(100.00);                        // Note 7
        while (e.hasMoreElements()) {
          CustomerRemote greater = (CustomerRemote)e.nextElement();
        String id = (String)greater.getPrimaryKey();
        String name = greater.getName();
        String address = greater.getAddress();
        double due = greater.getDue();
        System.out.println(id + ' ' + name + ' ' +
              address + ' ' + due);
        }
    }catch (Exception e) {
      e.printStackTrace();
    }
  }
}
```

Output

```
Darnell Davis

8765 Carla Kahn        55 Fourth St. 0.0

1234 Fred Flynn        22 First St. 1667.0

5678 Darnell Davis     33 Second St. 130.95
```

....

Note 1:   Java 2 provides a specialized method to do the casting. We could have replaced this lookup call with

```
Object o = initial.lookup("CustomerHome");
CustomerHome home = (CustomerHome)javax.rmi.PortableRemoteObject.
                    narrow(o,CustomerHome.class);
```

Note 2:   We create a customer with the given id, name, address, and balance due.

Note 3:   We find the customer with id 5678. Because id is the primary key, there can be at most one customer with that id.

Note 4:   Once we find a customer, we can execute its business methods, such as getName.

Note 5:   We find all customers named Carla Kahn.

Note 6:   ```String id = (String)carla.getPrimaryKey();```
The EJBObject interface contains the getPrimaryKey method.

Note 7:   ```e = home.findGreaterDue(100.00);```
We find all customers whose balance is greater than $100.

THE BIG PICTURE

Entity beans, representing business object, persist in the database. Persistence may be bean-managed or container-managed. Using container-managed persistence, we specify the fields and the transaction types, and the container handles the details of connections and access. The home interface specifies various finder methods to locate entity beans that satisfy a particular constraint. Using container-managed persistence, the container implements the finder methods.

TEST YOUR UNDERSTANDING

4. Which methods of the CustomerEJB class of Example 10.7 are implementing the EntityBean interface?

5. Write a WHERE clause, to use in a deployment tool, for a findBetween(double low, double high) method that finds customers whose balance due is between the low and the high values.

6. What are some advantages and disadvantages of container-managed persistence as compared to bean-managed persistence.

10.3 Session Beans

A session bean represents a client inside the J2EE server. The client calls a coarse-grained method of the session bean, which in turn may call methods of various entity beans to provide the desired service. Rather than have the client, usually on another machine, invoke the business methods of entity beans directly, we let the client make one call to a session bean on the server.

A Stateful Session Bean

We illustrate with an `Agent` session bean containing an `orderItem` method that places an order for a customer. A client invokes the `orderItem` method that makes the changes in the `Customer`, `Orders`, and `OrderItem` tables that use entity beans to represent each row. We leave some of the details of this example as exercises for the reader.

The remote interface contains one method, `orderItem`, with three arguments, the item number, the quantity ordered, and the unit price. It returns a string that describes the action taken.

EXAMPLE 10.9 **AgentRemote.java**

```
/* Specifies business methods for Agent EJB.
 */

import javax.ejb.EJBObject;
import java.rmi.RemoteException;

public interface AgentRemote extends EJBObject {
   public String orderItem(String itemNumber, int quantity,
         double unitPrice) throws RemoteException;
}
```

The `Agent` bean is a stateful session bean. It will save the customer ID and the salesperson ID to use when placing orders. The home interface contains a `create` method in which we pass the customer ID and the salesperson ID.

EXAMPLE 10.10 **AgentHome.java**

```
/* Specifies a method to create an Agent bean.
 */

import java.rmi.RemoteException;
import javax.ejb.CreateException;
import javax.ejb.EJBHome;

public interface AgentHome extends EJBHome {
   AgentRemote create(String cID, String sID)
        throws RemoteException, CreateException;
}
```

The Agent bean places an order by finding the Customer entity bean with the specified primary key, and creating Orders and OrderItem beans with the order information. We use a private getCustomer method to locate the Customer bean. The orderItem method describes what it will do, but does not create the Orders or OrderItem beans, a task we defer to the exercises.

EXAMPLE 10.11   AgentEJB.java

```java
/* A stateful session bean. Uses entity beans
 * to place an order.
 */

import javax.ejb.SessionBean;
import javax.ejb.SessionContext;
import javax.naming.Context;
import javax.naming.InitialContext;

public class AgentEJB implements SessionBean {
  public String customerID;
  public String salespersonID;
  private CustomerRemote customer;

  public String orderItem(String itemNumber, int quantity,
          double unitPrice) {                                  // Note 1
    String message = "";
    if (customer == null) return message;                      // Note 2
    try {
      message = customer.getName() + " is ordering item " +
              itemNumber + " in quantity " + quantity + " at $" +
              unitPrice + " each.";                             // Note 3
      }catch(Exception e) {
        e.printStackTrace();
      }
      return message;
  }
  public AgentEJB() {}
  public void ejbCreate(String cID, String sID) {
    customerID = cID;
    salespersonID = sID;
    customer = getCustomer(customerID);                        // Note 4
  }
  private CustomerRemote getCustomer(String id) {
    try {
      Context initial = new InitialContext();
      CustomerHome home = (CustomerHome)initial.lookup
              ("java:comp/env/CustomerHome");                  // Note 5
      return home.findByPrimaryKey(id);
    }catch (Exception e) {
      System.out.println("Customer not found");
    }
```

```
        return null;
    }
    public void ejbRemove() {}
    public void ejbActivate() {}
    public void ejbPassivate() {}
    public void setSessionContext(SessionContext sc) {}
}
```

Note 1: We implement a simple version of the `orderItem` method because we have not defined the `Orders` or `OrderItem` beans. Using the `Customer getName` method shows how a session bean calls entity bean methods.

Note 2: If the `getCustomer` method fails to find a customer it returns **null**. We alternative would be to throw an exception.

Note 3: We print a message, rather than using entity bean methods to place the order. We use the default formatting for type **double**, leaving the use of a `NumberFormat` object to the exercises.

Note 4: The `getCustomer` method hides the details of looking up an entity bean and finding the customer with the given ID.

Note 5: In the deployment tool, we will us "`CustomerHome`" as the Coded name for the entity bean to which the agent bean refers. The tool adds the `java:comp/env/` prefix to reflect its binding.

Deploying the Agent Bean

We will add the `Agent` bean to the `Sales` application. After compiling the `Agent` files, and with the deployment tool and the J2EE server started, we follow the steps:

- **Package the bean.**
  Click *File, New Enterprise Bean.*
  Click *Next.*
  Choose *Sales* as the application the enterprise bean will go in.
  Choose *AgentJAR* as the display name.
  Click *Add* for the Contents area.
  Enter the Root Directory.
  Select the `AgentEJB`, `AgentHome`, and `AgentRemote` class files.
  Click *Add.*
  Click *OK.*
  Click *Next.*
  Choose *AgentEJB* as the Enterprise Bean class.
  Choose *AgentHome* as the Home Interface.
  Choose *AgentRemote* as the Remote Interface.
  Enter `AgentBean` as the display name.

Check *Session* and *Stateful* as the Bean type.

Click *Next*.

Click *Next* (for Environment Entities).

Click *Add* in the Enterprise Bean References screen.

Enter `CustomerHome` as the Coded name.

Select *Entity* as the Type.

Enter `CustomerHome` as the Home interface.

Enter `CustomerRemote` as the Remote interface.

Click *Finish*

■ **Deploying the J2EE Application**

Select *Sales* in the Server Application area.

Click *Undeploy.*

Click *Yes* in the Confirm dialog.

Select *Sales* in the Local Applications area.

Click *Tools, Deploy Application.*

Check *Return Client Jar.*

Enter the filename, say `d:\book3\ejb\SalesClient.jar`, for the client code.

Click *Next*.

Enter `MyAgent` as the JNDI name for the `AgentBean` Component.

Enter `CustomerHome` as the JNDI name for the `CustomerHome` Component.

Click *Next* (for Deploy Sales).

Click *Finish*.

Click *OK.*

TIP

Because we deployed the `Sales` application when discussing Examples 10.4-10.8, we had to uninstall it before deploying the augmented `Sales` application containing both the `Customer` and the `Agent` beans. Unless we change the default, the server will remove the "`CustomerEJBTable`" table from the database, so we need to run the customer client to create the table again before we run the sales client.

A Sales Client

Our client will create an `Agent` and use it to place two orders. The `Agent`, a session bean, connects to a `Customer` entity bean. We compile the client with the command

```
javac -classpath .;%j2ee_home%\lib\j2ee.jar SalesClient.java
```

and execute it with

```
java -classpath .;%j2ee_home%\lib\j2ee.jar;SalesClient.jar SalesClient
```

EXAMPLE 10.12   SalesClient.java

```
/* Uses Agent bean to place two orders.
 */

import javax.naming.Context;
import javax.naming.InitialContext;

public class SalesClient {
  public static void main(String[] args) {
    try {
      Context initial = new InitialContext();
      AgentHome home =
        (AgentHome)initial.lookup("MyAgent");
      AgentRemote agent = home.create("1234", "98");        // Note 1
      System.out.println(agent.orderItem("222222", 3, 27.00));
      System.out.println(agent.orderItem("333333", 1, 225.95));
    }catch (Exception e) {
        e.printStackTrace();
    }
  }
}
```

Output

Fred Flynn is ordering item 222222 in quantity 3 at $27.0 each.

Fred Flynn is ordering item 333333 in quantity 1 at $225.95 each.

Note 1:   We create an agent to place orders for the customer with ID 1234 and salesperson with ID 98.

THE BIG PICTURE

A session bean performs a task for a client. Session beans can be either stateless or stateful and are not persistent. Stateless session beans can support multiple clients which helps when scaling applications to work with large numbers of clients. Stateful beans can save client information during interactive applications.

TEST YOUR UNDERSTANDING

7. Which methods in Example 10.11 implement the SessionBean interface?

TRY IT YOURSELF   8. Change the customer ID in Example 10.12 to "1111." Rerun the example and describe the result.

9. Both Hello bean, implemented in Example 10.3, and Agent bean, implemented in Example 10.11, are session beans. Describe the differences between them.

10.4   Servlet and JSP clients

So far we have used only standalone clients, but we can include web components in our J2EE application to allow clients to use enterprise beans from the web. First we deploy a servlet to connect to our `Agent` bean to place an order. Then we use a Java server page to connect to the `Customer` bean to update the client's name or address, or get the balance due.

A Servlet Client

The initial web page, shown in Figure 10.4, asks the client for a customer ID and a salesperson ID and uses the POST method when invoking a sales servlet.

Figure 10.4   The initial web page

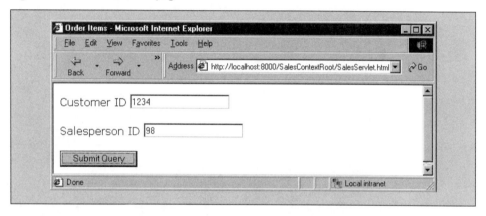

In this J2EE release, we must use the included web server that runs on port 8000. We use the address

```
http://localhost:8000/SalesContextRoot/SalesServlet.html
```

where we specify `SalesContextRoot` using the deployment tool. Figure 10.5 shows the HTML file.

Figure 10.5   `SalesServlet.html`

```html
<html><head>
<title>Order Items</title></head>
<body>
<p>
<form action="SalesAlias" method=POST>
  Customer ID
  <input type=text name="CustomerID"><p>
  Salesperson ID
  <input type=text name="SalespersonID"><p>
  <input type=submit>
</form></body></html>
```

In the servlet, the `init` method looks up the agent bean, and the `doPost` method creates an agent to place an order. It returns the web page of Figure 10.6 to the client to order an item. In this second form, the `GET` method causes the servlet's `doGet` method to invoke the agent and return a message describing the agent's action in placing the order. It also returns another form to allow the client to add an additional item to the order. Figure 10.7 shows the interaction after the client has ordered two items.

Figure 10.6 The form returned by `doPost`

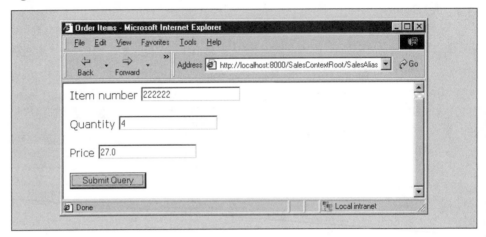

Figure 10.7 The form returned by the `doGet` method

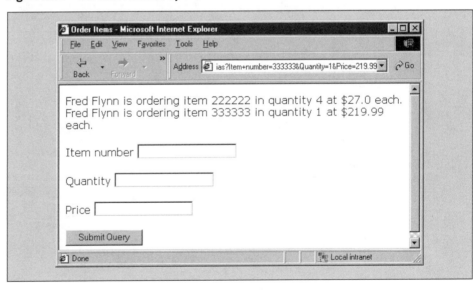

EXAMPLE 10.13 **SalesServlet.java**

```java
/* Connects to the Agent bean to
 * order items.
 */

import java.io.*;
import javax.servlet.*;
import javax.servlet.http.*;
import javax.naming.Context;
import javax.naming.InitialContext;
import javax.ejb.CreateException;
import javax.rmi.PortableRemoteObject;

public class SalesServlet extends HttpServlet {
  AgentRemote agent;
  AgentHome home;
  String message = "";

  public void init() throws ServletException {                // Note 1
    try {
      Context initial = new InitialContext();
      Object o = initial.lookup("MyAgent");
      home =
          (AgentHome)PortableRemoteObject.narrow
                            (o,AgentHome.class);               // Note 2
    } catch(Exception e) {
      e.printStackTrace();
    }
  }
  public void doPost(HttpServletRequest req, HttpServletResponse resp)
              throws ServletException, IOException {          // Note 3
    try {
      agent = home.create(req.getParameter("CustomerID"),
              req.getParameter("SalespersonID"));
      resp.setContentType("text/html");
      PrintWriter out = resp.getWriter();
      out.println("<html><head>");
      out.println("<title>Order Items</title></head>");
      out.println("<body>");
      out.println("<p>");
      out.println("<form action=\"SalesAlias\" method=GET>");  // Note 4
      out.println("Item number");
      out.println("<input type=text name=\"Item number\"><p>");
      out.println("Quantity");
      out.println("<input type=text name=\"Quantity\"><p>");
      out.println("Price");
      out.println("<input type=text name=\"Price\"><p>");
      out.println("<input type=submit>");
      out.println("</form></body></html>");
    }catch (CreateException e) {
```

```
        e.printStackTrace();
    }
}
public void doGet (HttpServletRequest req, HttpServletResponse resp)
            throws ServletException, IOException {
    String itemNumber = req.getParameter("Item number");
    int quantity = Integer.parseInt(req.getParameter("Quantity"));
    double price =
            new Double(req.getParameter("Price")).doubleValue();
    message += agent.orderItem(itemNumber,quantity,price) + "\n";    // Note 5
    resp.setContentType("text/html");
    PrintWriter out = resp.getWriter();
    out.println("<html><head>");
    out.println("<title>Order Items</title></head>");
    out.println("<body>");
    out.println(message);
    out.println("<p>");
    out.println("<form action=\"SalesAlias\" method=GET>");
    out.println("Item number");
    out.println("<input type=text name=\"Item number\"><p>");
    out.println("Quantity");
    out.println("<input type=text name=\"Quantity\"><p>");
    out.println("Price");
    out.println("<input type=text name=\"Price\"><p>");
    out.println("<input type=submit>");
    out.println("</form></body></html>");
  }
}
```

Note 1: In the init method, we look up the Agent bean, which only needs to be done once.

Note 2: The narrow method checks whether its first argument, o, can be cast to the type of its second argument, AgentHome.class. If so it returns an object that can be cast to the desired type, and if not it throws a class cast exception.

Note 3: The client calls the servlet once using the POST method to send the customer ID and the salesperson ID. The doPost method creates an Agent bean and sends the client a form to place an order.

Note 4: We refer to the servlet by a name, SalesAlias, that we specify using the deployment tool.

Note 5: The message concatenates descriptions of each order item.

We use the deployment tool to package the servlet and the HTML file in a .war file and add it to the Sales application using the following steps:

■ **Package the servlet**
Click *File, New Web Component.*
Click *Next.*

Select *Sales* as the WAR file.
Enter *SalesWar* as the Display name.
Click *Add*.
Enter the Root Directory. (Add Content files)
Select *SalesServlet.html*.
Click *Add*.
Click *Next*.
Enter the Root Directory. (Add class files)
Select *SalesServlet.class*
Click *Finish*.
Click *Next* (WAR File General Properties).
Check *Servlet*.
Click *Next*.
Select *SalesServlet* as the Servlet class.
Enter *SalesServlet* as the Display name.
Click *Next*.
Click *Next* (Parameters).
Click *Add*.
Enter *SalesAlias* as a URL Mapping.
Click *Next*.
Click *Next*. (Component Security)
Click *Next*. (WAR file Environment)
Click *Add*. (Enterprise Bean References)
Enter *AgentHome* as the Coded Name
Select *Session* as the Type.
Select *AgentHome* as the Home
Select *AgentRemote* as the Remote.
Click *Finish*.

- **Deploying the Application**
Select *Sales* in the Server Application area.
Click *Undeploy*.
Click *Yes* in the Confirm dialog.
Click *Tools, Deploy Application*.
Do not check *Return Client Jar*.
Click *Next*.
Enter *MyAgent* as the JNDI name.
Click *Next*.
Enter *SalesContextRoot* as the Context Root.
Click *Next*.
Click *Finish*.
Click *OK*.

A JSP Client

We can use a Java server page as a web component to access enterprise beans. The JSP component calls methods of a JavaBean (not an enterprise bean) to separate the content from the HTML presentation. For complex processing the JavaBean would connect to a session bean to handle the processing. For simple processing, as in our example, the JavaBean accesses the entity bean directly.

The JavaBean of Example 10.14 has a `performAction` method that finds a customer and uses its methods to set the name or address or get the balance due. This `CustomerBean` has get and set methods for the `customerID`, `name`, `address`, and `action` properties that the client enters in the HTML form.

We compile `CustomerBean` using the command

```
javac -classpath
    .;%j2ee_home%\lib\j2ee.jar;CustomerClient.jar
    CustomerBean.java
```

We need to include `CustomerClient.jar` in the classpath because `CustomerBean` refers to the `CustomerHome` and `CustomerRemote` classes.

Figure 10.8 shows the JSP page of Example 10.15 that uses the JavaBean of Example 10.14. The URL is

```
http://localhost:8000/CustomerContextRoot/Customer.jsp
```

Figure 10.8   A JSP client

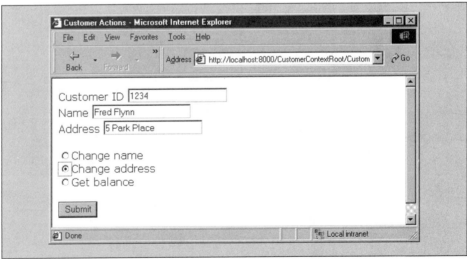

EXAMPLE 10.14   CustomerBean.java

```
/* Connects to the Customer bean to update the name
 * or address or get the balance due.
 */
```

```
import javax.naming.Context;
import javax.naming.InitialContext;
import javax.rmi.PortableRemoteObject;

public class CustomerBean {
  CustomerRemote customer;
  CustomerHome home;
  String message = "";
  String customerID = "";
  String name = "";
  String address = "";
  String action = "";

  public CustomerBean() {
    try {
      Context initial = new InitialContext();
      Object o = initial.lookup("CustomerHome");
      home =
          (CustomerHome)PortableRemoteObject.narrow
                  (o,CustomerHome.class);
    } catch(Exception e) {
      e.printStackTrace();
    }
  }
}
public String performAction() {
  try {
    if (action.equals("name")) {
      customer = home.findByPrimaryKey(customerID);        // Note 1
      customer.setName(name);
      message = "Name changed to " + name;
    }
    else if (action.equals("address")) {
      customer = home.findByPrimaryKey(customerID);
      customer.setAddress(address);
      message = "Address changed to " + address;
    }
    else if (action.equals("balance")) {
      customer = home.findByPrimaryKey(customerID);
      message = "Balance due is " + customer.getDue();
    }
  }catch(Exception e) {
    e.printStackTrace();
  }
    return message;
  }
  public String getCustomerID() {
    return customerID;
  }
  public void setCustomerID(String id) {
    customerID = id;
```

```
      }
      public String getName() {
        return name;
      }
      public void setName(String n) {
        name = n;
      }
      public String getAddress() {
        return address;
      }
      public void setAddress(String a) {
        address = a;
      }
      public String getMessage() {
        return message;
      }
      public void setMessage(String m) {
        message = m;
      }
      public String getAction() {
        return action;
      }
      public void setAction(String a ) {
        action = a;
      }
    }
```

Note 1: The HTML form will have a text field to input the customer ID. The servlet generated from the Java server page will call the `setCustomerID` method
to save the value from the form.

The Java server page focuses on the presentation of the form. The page has text fields
for the client to enter the customer ID, the name, and the address, and radio buttons
for the client to select an action. We allow only one request at a time, leaving it as an
exercise to allow multiple requests.

The Java server page calls the customer JavaBean's `performAction` method to get
the message that describes the action taken. It uses the `<jsp:getProperty>` tag to
retrieve data stored in the JavaBean.

EXAMPLE 10.15 Customer.jsp

```
<html>
<jsp:useBean id="customerBean" class="CustomerBean" />
<jsp:setProperty name="customerBean" property="*" />            // Note 1
<%! String message; %>
<% message = customerBean.performAction(); %>                   // Note 2

<head>
<title>Customer Actions</title>
```

```
</head>
<body>
<p>
<form action="Customer.jsp" method=POST>
Customer ID
<input type=text name="customerID"
  value="<jsp:getProperty name="customerBean"
    property="customerID" />"><br>                                    // Note 3
Name
<input type=text name="name"
  value="<jsp:getProperty name="customerBean"
    property="name" />"><br>
Address
<input type=text name="address"
  value="<jsp:getProperty name="customerBean"
    property="address" />"><p>

<input type=radio name="action" value="name">Change name<br>
<input type=radio name="action" value="address">Change address<br>
<input type=radio name="action" value="balance">Get balance<p>
<input type=submit value="Submit">
</form>

<%= message %>                                                       // Note 4
</body>
</html>
```

....

Note 1:   We use the setProperty tag to have the generated servlet save all the property values we submit in the form.

Note 2:   The performAction method uses the Customer enterprise bean to change the name or address, or to get the balance. We save the return value to display at the end of the form.

Note 3:   We display the form with the values set in the bean. The values are set initially to defaults, and then show the values set by the client in the previous submission.

Note 4:   The message describes the action.

We use the deployment tool to package the servlet and the HTML file in a .war file and add it to the Sales application using the following steps:

- **Package the JSP and JavaBean**
  Click *File, New Web Component*.
  Click *Next*.
  Select Sales as the WAR file.
  Enter CustomerJspWAR as the Display name.
  Click *Add*.
  Enter the Root Directory (Add content files).

Select `Customer.jsp` .
Click *Add*.
Click *Next*.
Enter the Root Directory. (Add class files).
Select `CustomerBean.class`.
Click *Add*.
Click *Finish*.
Click *Next* (WAR File General Properties).
Check *JSP*.
Click *Next*.
Select Customer.jsp as the JSP filename.
Enter `CustomerJsp` as the Display name.
Click *Next*.
Click *Next* (Parameters).
Click *Next* (Componenet Aliases).
Click *Next* (Componenet Security).
Click *Next* (WAR file environment).
Click *Add* (Add Enterprise Bean References).
Enter *CustomerHome* as the Coded Name.
Select *Entity* as the Type.
Enter *CustomerHome* as Home.
Enter *CustomerRemote* as Remote.
Click *Finish*.

- **Deploy the Application**
  Select `Sales` in the Server Application area.
  Click *Undeploy*.
  Click *Yes* in the Confirm dialog.
  Click *Tools, Deploy Application*.
  Do not check *Return Client Jar*.
  Click *Next*.
  Enter *CustomerHome* as the JNDI name.
  Click *Next*.
  Enter `CustomerContextRoot` as the Context Root.
  Click *Next*.
  Click *Finish*.
  Click *OK*.

We do not usually need to uninstall as part of deployment, but do so here because we are adding a component to an existing application.

THE BIG PICTURE

A J2EE application may have web components to allow clients to connect using a browser. An HTML page can specify a servlet to use in processing a form. The servlet, part of a J2EE application, can use enterprise beans to satisfy the client's request. A JSP client can use a JavaBean to separate the business logic from the GUI presentation. The JSP client calls methods of the JavaBean which themselves access enterprise beans.

TEST YOUR UNDERSTANDING

---

10. Example 10.13 processes a `POST` request to create the `Agent` bean. What would be a serious drawback to submitting a `GET` request to create the bean?

TRY IT YOURSELF   11. Will moving the message declaration and assignment in Example 10.15 to a position just before the message is displayed make any difference in the result. Experiment by changing `Customer.jsp` in the `CustomerJspContextRoot` directory and rerunning the client?

SUMMARY

- Enterprise JavaBeans support distributed programming. An EJB server handles the transaction processing, security, and scaling to large numbers of clients. Each enterprise bean has three parts:

  A home interface to create, find, and remove a bean.
  A remote interface to specify the business methods.
  An implementation class.

  Clients do not interact with enterprise beans directly, but rather through methods provided by the container that manages the beans.

- A session bean executes actions for one client, and is not persistent. An entity bean represents a business object, may be shared by many client, and is persistent.

- The remote interface extends the EJBObject interface, while the home interface extends EJBHome. The bean class extends SessionBean for session beans, and EntityBean for entity beans.

- Sun provides a J2EE platform with an EJB server and a deployment tool. We use the deployment tool to create an application, and to package and deploy enterprise beans. A J2EE application, deployed in an EJB server, may have enterpise beans packaged in JAR files, and web components packaged in WAR files.

- Entity beans persist in a database. This persistence may be container or bean managed. The server handles the details of connecting to the database and fetching and storing data when we use container-managed persistence. The bean must implement these details when using bean-managed persistence. Container-managed persistence is easier to implement but may not be suitable for more complex applications.

- Session beans may be stateless or stateful. Stateful beans can hold client information during an interactive session. Stateless beans are more efficient and help in dealing with large numbers of clients.

- Web components can be servlets of Java server pages. They allow clients to access enterprise beans with a browser.

Program Modification Exercises

. . . .

1. Modify the `Hello` bean of Examples 10.1–10.3 to be stateful, rather than stateless. Run a client to test it.

2. Modify Example 10.6 to add a `findBetween(double low, double high)` method, which locates all customers whose balance due is between the low and high values. Modify the client of Example 10.8 to test it.

Program Design Exercises

. . . .

3. Create an `Orders` entity bean to represent an order in the `Orders` table of Figure 3.4. Include finder methods to find orders on a certain date, between two dates, by a certain customer, or using a specific salesperson. Write a standalone client to test it.

4. Write a JSP client to use the `Orders` bean of Exercise 3.

5. Create an `OrderItem` entity bean to represent an entry in the `OrderItem` table of Figure 3.5. Include finder methods to find items with the same order number, and items with the same item number. Write a standalone client to test it. Because the key is compound, create a primary key class that implements the `Serializable` interface. Let it have two public fields for the order number and the item number, and two constructors including a default. It must override the `equals`, `hashCode`, and `toString` methods of the `Object` class.

6. Write a JSP client to use the `OrderItem` bean of Exercise 5.

7. Create an `Item` entity bean to represent an item in the `Item` table of Figure 3.3. Include a finder method to find an item with a given description. Write a standalone client to test it.

8. Write a web client that uses a servlet to display the message of the `Hello` bean of Examples 10.1–10.3.

9. Improve the `orderItem` method of Example 10.11 to use the `Orders`, `OrderItem`, and `Item` entity beans of Exercises 10.3, 10.5, and 10.7 to modify the database appropriately when a customer places an order.

10. Write a servlet client for the `Customer` bean of Examples 10.5–10.7, called from an HTML form, so that the user can get the balance due given a customer name, or get a list of the names and addresses of customers whose balance is greater than a specified amount.

11

Collections

Introduction

Programmers often use collections of data such as lists and sets. The Java 2 release includes a Collection hierarchy in the java.util package, which allows us to use these data structures without having to code them ourselves.

After introducing the overall hierarchy, we look at sets, lists, and maps in detail. Comparing elements of a collection lets us arrange a collection in order. Algorithms implement standard computations so users do not have to implement these basic operations.

OBJECTIVES

- Know the hierarchy of Collection classes.

- Use the methods of the Collection interface.

- Use sets, lists, and maps.

- Compare collection elements to enable sorting.

- Use collection algorithms.

11.1   The Collection Interfaces and Classes

. . . .

Java interfaces provide the framework for the various data structures included in the collection utilities. Figure 11.1 shows that these interfaces occur in two groups.

Figure 11.1 The Collection **interfaces**

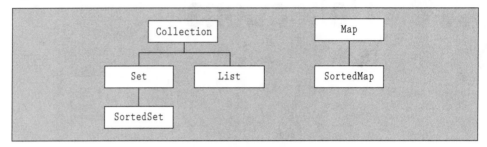

The Collection interface represents a group of objects, known as its elements. It abstracts the behavior common to both sets and lists. The Set interface supports unordered elements; we can determine if an element is in a set but there is no order relation between one element and another in the set. By contrast, the List interface supports a sequence in which elements are ordered from first to last. The SortedSet interface represents a set whose elements can be retrieved in sorted order.

The Map interface represents (key, value) pairs, such as a dictionary in which we look up a word (the key) and obtain its definition (the value). Typically a map does not keep its elements in order, but the SortedMap interface allows us to retrieve map elements in order of their keys. For example, a dictionary is actually a sorted map.

All of these interfaces specify operations in two main groups:

- Accessors that get information, but do not change the collection.

- Mutators that change the collection.

The Collection Interface

The Collection interface specifies the operations common to sets and lists. It contains the following operations:

Accessors:
```
boolean contains(Object o)
boolean containsAll(Collection c)
boolean equals(Object o)
int hashCode()
boolean isEmpty()
Iterator iterator()
int size()
Object[] toArray()
Object[] toArray(Object[] a)
```

Mutators:
```
void clear()
boolean add(Object o)
boolean addAll(Collection c)
boolean remove(Object o)
boolean removeAll(Collection c)
boolean retainAll(Collection c)
```

Interfaces formally just specify the name, parameters, and return value for each method. Informally the documentation states conditions that implementers of the interface are expected to observe. For example, in getting the size of a collection, if it contains more than `Integer.MAX_VALUE` elements, the size method returns `Integer.MAX_VALUE`.

Sets

The `Set` interface has the same methods as the `Collection` interface, but in a few instances the conditions on the methods are more stringent. For example, a `Set` cannot contain duplicates so the `add` method must refuse to add a duplicate. In general, this requirement does not apply to the `add` method for a `Collection`. We will look at each method of the `Set` interface when we present Examples 11.1 and 11.2.

In order to give some examples we need to introduce some implementations of these interfaces,

Interface	Class implementing that interface
Set	HashSet
SortedSet	TreeSet
List	ArrayList, LinkedList
Map	HashMap
SortedMap	TreeMap

The `HashSet` class uses hashing techniques which we will discuss later to implement the `Set` interface. We use a `HashSet` to store the words of the Gettysburg address, keeping count of the duplicates which will be eliminated, and listing the resulting unique words. We will extend this example to illustrate other `Set` methods.

EXAMPLE 11.1   WordsSet.java

```
/* Adds the words of the Gettysburg address to a set, counting
 * the number of duplicates and listing the unique words.
 */

import java.util.*;
import java.io.*;

public class WordsSet {
```

```
public static void main(String[ ] args) {
  try {
    File f = new File(args[0]);
    BufferedReader in = new BufferedReader(new FileReader(f));
    Set set = new HashSet();                                    // Note 1
    String line;
    int duplicates = 0;
    while((line = in.readLine()) != null) {
      StringTokenizer tokens =
                        new StringTokenizer(line,"-,. \n\r\t"); // Note 2
      while(tokens.hasMoreTokens()) {
        String tok = tokens.nextToken().toLowerCase();          // Note 3
        if (!set.add(tok))                                      // Note 4
          duplicates++;
      }
    }
    System.out.println
      (args[0] + " has " + set.size() + " distinct words.");
    System.out.println("There are " + duplicates + " duplicate words.");
    System.out.println("The distinct words are:");
    System.out.println(set);                                    // Note 5
  }catch(IOException e) {
    e.printStackTrace();
  }
}
}
```

....

Output (from java WordsSet gettysburg.txt**)**

gettysburg.txt has 138 distinct words.
There are 129 duplicate words.
The distinct words are:
[live, great, men, add, fitting, under, struggled, did, might, resolve, our, inc
reased, proper, these, remaining, living, government, sense, earth, never, say,
power, do, dead, should, consecrate, created, they, will, full, nobly, devotion,
who, birth, new, forth, battlefield, last, war, task, testing, vain, remember,
world, we, portion, advanced, hallow, seven, it, dedicated, is, note, any, in, b
y, consecrated, continent, shall, the, or, fourscore, on, and, a, honored, ago,
take, which, be, of, forget, field, us, here, endure, what, freedom, final, civi
l, years, highly, poor, their, for, as, but, this, brave, perish, died, gave, be
fore, detract, proposition, now, resting, not, to, nor, fathers, far, conceived,
come, engaged, all, nation, whether, unfinished, above, dedicate, equal, those,
thus, brought, rather, long, fought, ground, people, measure, that, larger, cau
se, little, lives, so, are, work, have, cannot, altogether, liberty, god, from,
place, can, met]

....

Note 1:   We declare our collection as a Set, using only the methods of the Set interface. Java provides a HashSet implementation of the Set interface. We use the
default constructor, but will discuss other constructors later in this section.

Note 2:   We do not want to include punctuation as parts of the words, so we include these characters in the `StringTokenizer` constructor to signal the end of words.

Note 3:   Words such as "`The`" and "`the`" would both appear in the set unless we first convert each word to lower case.

Note 4:   The `add` method returns false if the set already contains the element passed as its argument.

Note 5:   The `HashSet` class inherits the `toString` method from the `AbstractCollection` class which provides a skeletal implementation of the `Collection` interface.

Iterators

Many of the methods of the `Collection` interface have names which clearly describe their behavior. For example, `isEmpty()` returns **true** if the collection has no elements and **false** otherwise. The `iterator` method requires some explanation. It returns an `Iterator` object which is very much like an `Enumeration`, allowing us to iterate through the elements of the `Collection`. An `Iterator` differs from an `Enumeration` in two ways. First we can remove elements from a `Collection` while iterating through it, and second the method names are shorter.

Iterator methods	Enumeration methods
hasNext	hasMoreElements
next	nextElement
remove	

If we just want to list the elements of a `Set` we can use the `toString` method implicitly in a print statement, as for example,

```
System.out.println("The set is " + set);
```

where set is a `Set`. But if we need to process each element then we use a loop such as

```
Iterator i = set.iterator();
while (i.hasNext()) {
// do processing here
  i.next();
}
```

In Example 11.2 we use an iterator to remove all words of less than eight letters from the Gettysburg set and illustrate other methods of the `Set` interface.

EXAMPLE 11.2   SetMethods.java

```
/* Illustrates the methods of the Set interface.
 */

import java.util.*;
```

```java
import java.io.*;

public class SetMethods {
  public static void main(String[ ] args) {
    try {
      File f = new File(args[0]);
      BufferedReader in = new BufferedReader(new FileReader(f));
      Set set = new HashSet();
      String line;
      while((line = in.readLine()) != null) {
        StringTokenizer tokens = new StringTokenizer(line,"-,. \n\r\t");
        while(tokens.hasMoreTokens()) {
          String tok = tokens.nextToken().toLowerCase();
          set.add(tok);
        }
      }
      System.out.println("Contains \"fourscore\"? "
                            + set.contains("fourscore"));
      System.out.println
        ("Contains \"computer\"? " + set.contains("computer"));     // Note 1
      Collection start = new HashSet();                             // Note 2
      start.add("fourscore");
      start.add("and");
      start.add("seven");
      start.add("years");
      System.out.println("Contains \"fourscore, and, seven, years\" ? "
                            + set.containsAll(start));              // Note 3
      Set newStart = new HashSet();
      newStart.addAll(start);                                      // Note 4
      System.out.println("newStart equals start? " + newStart.equals(start));
      newStart.add("computer");                                    // Note 5
      System.out.println
      ("newStart with \"computer\" equals start? " + newStart.equals(start));
      System.out.println("The newStart set is now " + newStart);
      newStart.retainAll(set);                                     // Note 6
      System.out.println
        ("newStart equals start after retainsAll? " + newStart.equals(start));
      Object[] startArray = start.toArray();                       // Note 7
      System.out.print ("The start array is now: " );
      for (int i = 0; i < startArray.length; i++)
        System.out.print(startArray[i] + " ");
      System.out.println();
      start.add(new Integer(5));                                   // Note 8
    start.add(new Double(Math.PI));
    startArray = start.toArray();
    System.out.print("The start array is now: ");
    for (int i = 0; i < startArray.length; i++)
      System.out.print(startArray[i] + " ");
    System.out.println();
    System.out.println("Removing pi worked? "
```

```
                       + start.remove(new Double(Math.PI)));        // Note 9
          System.out.println("The start set is now " + start);
          System.out.println("Removing newStart elements from start worked? "
                       + start.removeAll(newStart));                 // Note 10
          System.out.println("The start set is now " + start);
          Iterator setIterator = set.iterator();                     // Note 11
          while(setIterator.hasNext()) {
            String next = (String)setIterator.next();
            if (next.length() < 8)
              setIterator.remove();                                  // Note 12
          }
          System.out.println("The long words in " + args[0] + " are " + set);
        }catch(IOException e) {
            e.printStackTrace();
        }
      }
    }
```

Output (using the command `java SetMethods gettysburg.txt`**)**

```
Contains "fourscore"? true
Contains "computer"? false
Contains "fourscore, and, seven, years" ? true
newStart equals start? true
newStart with "computer" equals start? false
The newStart set is now [and, seven, fourscore, years, computer]
newStart equals start after retainsAll? true
The start array is now: and seven fourscore years
The start array is now: 3.141592653589793 and seven fourscore years 5
Removing pi worked? true
The start set is now [and, seven, fourscore, years, 5]
Removing newStart elements from start worked? true
The start set is now [5]
The long words of gettysburg.txt are: [struggled, increased, remaining,
government, consecrate, devotion, battlefield, remember, advanced,
dedicated, consecrated, continent, fourscore, proposition, conceived,
unfinished, dedicate, altogether]
```

Note 1:   The `contains` method returns **true** if its argument is in the set and **false** otherwise.

Note 2:   We create a new `Collection`, adding the first four words of the Gettysburg address to it.

Note 3:   The `containsAll` method return **true** if each member of its `Collection` argument is contained in the `Set` and **false** otherwise.

Note 4:   The `addAll` method adds each member of its `Collection` argument to the `Set`, returning **true** if the set is changed and **false** otherwise. A false value will be returned if the argument is empty so there are no elements to add or if all the elements are duplicates. Because we are adding just the elements of start to an empty newStart, the sets start and newStart will be equal.

Note 5: Adding another element to newStart will make start and newStart unequal.

Note 6:   `newStart.retainAll(set);`
The newStart set will retain only those elements contained in set.

Note 7:   `Object[] startArray = start.toArray();`
The toArray method places the elements of the start set into an array, startArray. This is useful when using older API's that expect array input.

Note 8:   `start.add(new Integer(5));`
Sets contain objects, so we need to wrap the integer 5 in an Integer object in order to add it to the start set.

Note 9:   `start.remove(new Double(Math.PI))`
The remove method removes its argument from the start set, returning **true** if start is changed, and **false** otherwise, as for example, when the argument is not in the set.

Note 10:   `start.removeAll(newStart)`
The removeAll method removes all the elements of newStart that are members of start.

Note 11:   `Iterator setIterator = set.iterator();`
The iterator method returns an Iterator object that we use to iterate through each element of the set. When we find an element String with less than eight characters, we remove it from the set. When we exit the loop, setIterator has traversed all set elements. Had we wanted to process the set elements once more, we could have called the iterator method again.

Note 12:   `setIterator.remove();`
The remove method removes the last element returned by the next method. It will throw an IllegalStateException if the next method has not been called or if the remove method has already been called after the last call to next.

TEST YOUR UNDERSTANDING

1. The Collection and Set interfaces have the same methods. What is the difference between them?

2. Why does the Collection interface need an equals method, because Java has the == operator?

3. Can you add a primitive type such as an **int** to a Collection? Why or why not?

THE BIG PICTURE

A group of interfaces specify the methods for `Collection` classes. The `Collection` interface has subinterfaces for `Set`s, which are unordered, and `List`s, which are ordered by position. The `Map` interface describes a collection of keys and the value to which each key is mapped. The `SortedSet` and `SortedMap` interfaces describe collections which keep elements in sorted order. Java provides classes that implement these interfaces. Each collection type has a number of accessor methods to inspect element values and mutator methods to change them.

TRY IT YOURSELF

4. How does the output of Example 11.1 change if we do not change a word to lower-case before adding it to the set?

TRY IT YOURSELF

5. How does the output of Example 11.1 change if we use the default argument for the string tokenizer separator instead of passing the separators explicitly in the second argument?

TRY IT YOURSELF

6. Run Example 11.2 taking input from a file of your choosing and describe the results.

11.2   Lists

. . . .

In contrast to a set, the elements of a list have an order. A list has a first element, a second, and so on until its last element. A list is a sequence of elements. The `List` interface extends the `Collection` interface. The methods it adds are:

Accessors:
```
Object get(int index)
int indexOf(Object o)
int lastIndexOf(Object o)
ListIterator listIterator()
ListIterator listIterator(int index)
List subList(int fromIndex, int toIndex)
```

Mutators:
```
void add(int index, Object element)
boolean addAll(int index, Collection c)
Object remove(int index)
Object set(int index, Object element)
```

The new `List` operations refer to the index to locate a specific position in a list. For example, if `myList` is an object of type `List`,

```
myList.add(3, "Have a good day");
```

would add the string *Have a good day* at position 3 in `myList`. Because a list starts at position 0, this would be the fourth element in the list. Any elements that were at positions 3 and above would be shifted one position higher.

The ListIterator interface extends the Iterator interface with the additional methods

```
void add(Object o)
boolean hasPrevious()
int nextIndex()
Object previous()
int previousIndex()
void set(Object o)
```

With a ListIterator we can traverse the list both forward and backward. We will discuss these methods further when we use them in example programs.

Implementations

Java provides the ArrayList and LinkedList implementations of the List interface. Most often the ArrayList is more efficient. Our examples will compare the efficiency of each and then we will discuss the differences. Example 11.3 uses the ArrayList implementation while Example 11.4 executes the same methods using the LinkedList implementation. We repeat each method 10,000 times to do enough computation to obtain a timing estimate.

EXAMPLE 11.3   **ArrayListTiming.java**

```
/* Checks time needed for list operations
 * using an ArrayList implementation.
 */

import java.util.*;

public class ArrayListTiming {
  public static void main(String[] args) {
    List arrayImp = new ArrayList();
    Date today = new Date();
    long time1, time2;
    time1 = System.currentTimeMillis();                         // Note 1
    for(int i = 0; i < 10000; i++)
      arrayImp.add(today);                                      // Note 2
    time2 = System.currentTimeMillis();
    System.out.println("Time for 10000 adds: " + (time2 - time1));
    time1 = System.currentTimeMillis();
    for(int i = 0; i < 10000; i++)
      arrayImp.add(50, today);                                  // Note 3
    time2 = System.currentTimeMillis();
    System.out.println("Time for 10000 adds at position 50: "
                                         + (time2 - time1));
    time1 = System.currentTimeMillis();
    for(int i = 0; i < 10000; i++)
      arrayImp.get(5000);                                       // Note 4
    time2 = System.currentTimeMillis();
```

```
    System.out.println("Time for 10000 gets at position 5000: "
                                        + (time2 - time1));
    }
}
```

....

Output

```
Time for 10000 adds: 110
Time for 10000 adds at position 50: 3275
Time for 10000 gets at position 5000: 10
```

....

Note 1:   The currentTimeMillis method returns the number of milliseconds since January 1, 1970. We only use the difference between two times in our examples.

Note 2:   Because we are adding at the end of the array, we do not have to move any elements.

Note 3:   Adding at position 50 in this array requires us to move at least 9950 elements one position to the right to make room for the added element.

Note 4:   Using the index we can retrieve the element at position 5000 without accessing any other array elements.

The results show that adding elements to the end of an array is efficient. As Figure 11.2 shows we do not need to move any elements to add at the end.

Figure 11.2   Adding an element at the end of a ArrayList

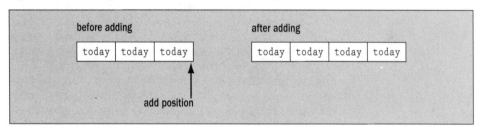

By contrast, adding an element at position 50 to an array that is at least of size 10000 requires moving all the elements one position to the right, as shown in Figure 11.3.

Figure 11.3   Add an element at position 50 in an ArrayList

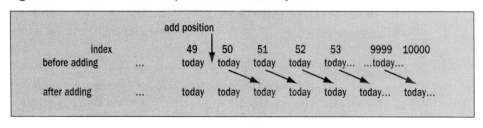

The timing result shows that we can get an element at position 5000 very efficiently using an array because we can retrieve it using the index without accessing any other array elements. Arrays use contiguous storage for their elements, so a simple computation finds the location of a particular element. The results using a linked list implementation will be quite different.

EXAMPLE 11.4   **LinkedListTiming.java**

```java
/* Checks time needed for list operations
 * using a LinkedList implementation.
 */

import java.util.*;

public class LinkedListTiming {
  public static void main(String[] args) {
    List linkImp = new LinkedList();
    Date today = new Date();
    long time1, time2;
    time1 = System.currentTimeMillis();
    for(int i = 0; i < 10000; i++)
      linkImp.add(today);                                      // Note 1
    time2 = System.currentTimeMillis();
    System.out.println("Time for 10000 adds: " + (time2 - time1));
    time1 = System.currentTimeMillis();
    for(int i = 0; i < 10000; i++)
      linkImp.add(5000, today);                                // Note 2
    time2 = System.currentTimeMillis();
    System.out.println("Time for 10000 adds at position 5000: "
                                        + (time2 - time1));
    time1 = System.currentTimeMillis();
    for(int i = 0; i < 10000; i++)
      linkImp.get(5000);                                       // Note 3
    time2 = System.currentTimeMillis();
    System.out.println("Time for 10000 gets at position 5000: "
                                        + (time2 - time1));
  }
}
```

....

Output

```
Time for 10000 adds: 180
Time for 10000 adds at position 5000: 2423
Time for 10000 gets at position 5000: 2447
```

....

Note 1:   Adding at the end of a list can be efficient if the implementation keeps a reference to the end of the list. In that case adding an element does not require traversing other list elements.

Note 2:   To add an element at position 5000, we must traverse the first 5000 list elements to get to position 5000.

Note 3:   To get the element at position 5000, we must traverse the first 5000 list elements to get to position 5000.

The timing results show adding at the end of a list is efficient, but adding or retrieving an item at a specified position is expensive. As Figure 11.4 shows, to get to a position in a linked list, we must start at the head of the list at position 0 and follow the links until we reach element 5000. Linked lists do not use contiguous storage, so the only way to access an element is to follow the links from the head of the list.

Figure 11.4   Finding element 5000 in a linked list

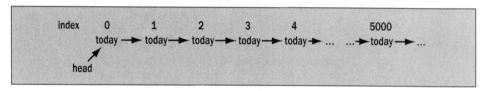

These timing results confirm our understanding of how an array works. We see the get and set operations will be efficient for an ArrayList implementation of a List. In this respect the ArrayList implementation makes the List an improvement over the Vector class which has survived in the Collection class modified from earlier implementations to implement the List interface.

Adding and removing elements from linked lists can be efficient if we are positioned at the element we wish to add or remove, so we do not have the overhead of traversing the links to find the element. Adding and deleting while using a ListIterator to traverse a list should be efficient because we are making changes at the current cursor position.

EXAMPLE 11.5   **LinkedListIterator.java**

```
/* Illustrates List and ListIterator methods.
 */

import java.util.*;
import java.awt.Point;

public class LinkedListIterator {
  public static void main(String[] args) {
    List linkImp = new LinkedList();
    Date today = new Date();
    long time1, time2;
    for(int i = 0; i < 10000; i++)
      linkImp.add(today);
    ListIterator iterator = linkImp.listIterator(50);          // Note 1
```

```
      System.out.println("Previous index is "
                           + iterator.previousIndex());        // Note 2
      time1 = System.currentTimeMillis();
      for(int i = 0; i < 10000; i++)
        iterator.add(today);                                   // Note 3
      time2 = System.currentTimeMillis();
      System.out.println("Time for 10000 adds at position 50: "
                           + (time2 - time1));
      int previousIndex = iterator.previousIndex();
      System.out.println("Previous index is " + previousIndex);
      System.out.println("Previous item is: " + iterator.previous());
      Point point = new Point(5,7);
      iterator.set(point);                                     // Note 4
      System.out.println("The item at the previous index is now: "
                           + linkImp.get(previousIndex));      // Note 5
      System.out.println("Next index is " + iterator.nextIndex());  // Note 6
      List threeItems = linkImp.subList(10048,10051);          // Note 7
      System.out.println("The sublist in reverse is:");
      for (ListIterator i = threeItems.listIterator(threeItems.size());
          i.hasPrevious();)                                    // Note 8
        System.out.println("\t" + i.previous());
      threeItems.set(0, new Point(3,4));                       // Note 9
      System.out.println("Changing threeItems(0) changes linkImp(10048) to:");
      System.out.println("\t" + linkImp.get(10048));
  }
}
```

Output

```
Previous index is 49
Time for 10000 adds at position 50: 100
Previous index is 10049
Previous item is: Mon Aug 23 12:51:04 PDT 1999
The item at the previous index is now: java.awt.Point[x=5,y=7]
Next index is 10049
The sublist in reverse is:
Mon Aug 23 12:51:04 PDT 1999
java.awt.Point[x=5,y=7]
Mon Aug 23 12:51:04 PDT 1999
Changing threeItems(0) changes linkImp(10048) to:
java.awt.Point[x=3,y=4]
```

Note 1: Calling `listIterator(50)` returns a list iterator starting at element 50. Using the default `listIterator()` will return a list iterator which starts at the beginning of the list.

Note 2: The `previousIndex` method returns the index of the element that would be returned by a call to `previous`, or −1 if the iterator is positioned at the beginning of the list.

Note 3:   Using a list iterator to add is efficient, because it adds at the current position. In Example 11.4, using `add(5000, today)` was not efficient because it required a traversal of the first 5000 elements of the list to find the position at which to add.

Note 4:   The `set` method changes the list element returned by the last call to `next` or `previous`. In this case that would be the previous item at index 10049. Java throws an `IllegalStateException` if neither `next` nor `previous` have been called, or `remove` or `add` (from the `ListIterator` interface) have been called after the last call to `next` or `previous`.

Note 5:   Using this `List` method to find the item at index `previousIndex` is less efficient than using the `previous` method of the `ListIterator` class, again because it requires starting at the beginning of the list and traversing element by element to reach the element at index 10049.

Note 6:   `System.out.println ("Next index is " + iterator.nextIndex());`
We displayed the index of the previous element, which was 10049. Calling `previous` moved the iterator one position to the left so the previous index is 10048 and the next index is 10049.

Note 7:   `List threeItems = linkImp.subList(10048,10051);`
The `subList` method creates a view of a portion of the list. Making changes to this list will change the list of which it is a view. The `threeItems` list contains the three items starting at index `10048` and going up to but not including the element at index `10051`.

Note 8:   `for(ListIterator i`
`= threeItems.listIterator(threeItems.size()); i.hasPrevious(); )`
We can process the elements of a list in reverse order by starting a list iterator at the index one greater than the index of the last element in the list. At each iteration of the loop we process the element returned by `previous`, continuing until `hasPrevious` returns **false**. Because we call `previous` in the body of the loop to process the previous element we do not need any code in the `for` loop to decrement the index.

Note 9:   `threeItems.set(0, new Point(3,4));`
Changing element 0 of this view will change element 10048 in the list, `linkImp`, backing this view.

THE BIG PICTURE

The two List implementations, `ArrayList` and `LinkedList`, differ in their performance. In an `ArrayList` finding an element at a fixed position is very efficient while inserting an element there is inefficient. Using a `LinkedList` finding an element at a fixed position is inefficient, but using a list iterator to insert at the current position is efficient.

TEST YOUR UNDERSTANDING

---

7. The List add and set methods have two arguments, while the ListIterator methods have one. Explain the difference.

8. What is the maximum size of the linkImp list of Example 11.4?

TRY IT YOURSELF

9. How much time does it take to get the element at position 9000 in Example 11.4? To get the element at position 1000?

10. Describe the contents of the linkImp list of Example 11.5 just before execution completes.

11.3 Maps

. . . .

A **map** associates a **value** with a **key**. Each key occurs at most once in a map. A key in the map has one value. For example, Figure 11.5 shows the lengths of some of the world's major rivers. The key is the name of the river, while the value is its length.

Figure 11.5 Rivers of the world and their lengths (in miles)

Amazon	4000	Indus	1800
Chang (Yangtze)	3964	Mekong	2600
Colorado	1450	Mississippi	2340
Columbia	1243	Missouri	2315
Congo	2718	Niger	2590
Danube	1776	Nile	4160
Euphrates	1700	Rio Grande	1900
Ganges	1560	Volga	2290
Huang (Yellow)	3395		

The methods of the Map interface are:

```
void clear()
boolean containsKey(Object key).
boolean containsValue(Object value)
Set entrySet()
boolean equals(Object o)
Object get(Object key)
int hashCode()
boolean isEmpty()
Set keySet()
Object put(Object key, Object value)
void putAll(Map t)
Object remove(Object key)
int size()
Collection values()
```

Implementations

The `Map` interface has two implementations, `HashMap` and `TreeMap`. A hash map is more efficient at accessing a single key, but does not easily permit a listing in alphabetical order, whereas a tree map does keep elements in alphabetical order.

A hash map uses a hash function to map each key to a location. In our example we have 17 rivers. We create a hash map with 37 spaces to reduce the chance of collisions. There are thousands of possible river names. A hash function associates a position in a hash table with a name. For example, a simple hash function might add up the ASCII values of the characters in the name and divide by the table size to get the remainder which gives the table position. For Nile that calculation would be

```
N=78, i=105, l=108, e=101
78+105+108+101 = 392
392 = 10*37 + 22
```

So Nile would go in position 22 in the table.

Because Java implements the hashing function, we do not need to know the details, but it helps to see the basic concept to understand the efficiency of the operation. To enter Nile in the table or to search for it requires just a computation of the hash function without traversing other elements in the table except to resolve collisions which arise when another element also hashes to the same value of 22.

The reason an alphabetical listing is difficult is that adjacent elements alphabetically may have totally different hash values. For example to hash Rio Grande

```
R=82, i=105, o=111, blank=32, G=71, r=114, a=97, n=110, d=100, e=101
82+105+111+32+71+114+97+110+100+101 = 923
923 = 24*37+35
```

So Rio Grande would go in position 35 if this hash function were used.

A tree uses two dimensions to arrange data so as to include many data elements without requiring extensive search to find an element. A tree is a compromise between an array and a list which is not as good as either at their best, but not as bad as either at their worst. To get good performance we must keep the tree balanced, making it spread out as much as possible rather than branch unnecessarily deep. For example, the tree of Figure 11.6a is unbalanced, while that of Figure 11.6b is balanced.

Figure 11.6 Examples of trees

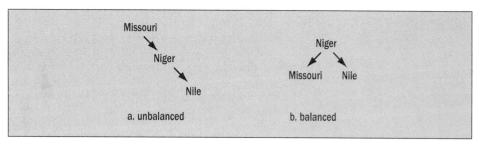

a. unbalanced   b. balanced

The tree map implementation uses a red-black tree which keeps itself balanced so the worst-case search time is of the order of ln n where n is the size of the data in the tree. We will look at efficiency further in Example 11.7. First Example 11.6 illustrates how to use a map.

EXAMPLE 11.6   RiverMap.java

```java
/* Illustrates Map methods
 */

import java.util.*;

public class RiverMap {
  public static void main(String[] args) {
    Map rivers = new HashMap(37);                              // Note 1
    int[] lengths = {4000,3964,1450,1243,2718,1776,1700,1560,3395,
                      1800,2600,2340,2315,2590,4160,1900,2290};
    String[] names = {"Amazon", "Chang", "Colorado", "Columbia", "Congo",
                      "Danube", "Euphrates", "Ganges", "Huang", "Indus",
                      "Mekong", "Mississippi", "Missouri", "Niger", "Nile",
                      "Rio Grande", "Volga"};
    for (int i = 0; i < names.length; i++)
      rivers.put(names[i], new Integer(lengths[i]));           // Note 2
    System.out.println("The size of the rivers map is: "
                  + rivers.size());                            // Note 3
    System.out.println("Rivers map contains key 'Congo': "
                  + rivers.containsKey("Congo"));              // Note 4
    System.out.println("Rivers map contains value 3500: "
    + rivers.containsValue(new Integer(3500)));                // Note 5
    System.out.println();
    System.out.print(rivers.keySet());                         // Note 6
    System.out.println();
    System.out.println();
    System.out.println(rivers);                                // Note 7
    Map riversTree = new TreeMap();
    riversTree.putAll(rivers);                                 // Note 8
    System.out.println();
    System.out.println(riversTree);                            // Note 9
    System.out.println();
    for (Iterator i = rivers.entrySet().iterator(); i.hasNext(); ) { // Note 10
      Map.Entry item = (Map.Entry)i.next();
      int size = ((Integer)item.getValue()).intValue();        // Note 11
      if (size >= 3000)
        System.out.println("\t" + item.getKey() + '\t' + size);
    }
    long starttime = System.currentTimeMillis();
    for (int i = 0; i < 100000; i++)
      rivers.get("Columbia");                                  // Note 12
    long stoptime = System.currentTimeMillis();
    System.out.println("Time for 100000 gets in a hash map is "
```

```
                          + (stoptime-starttime));
        starttime = System.currentTimeMillis();
        for (int i = 0; i < 100000; i++)
          riversTree.get("Columbia");
        stoptime = System.currentTimeMillis();
        System.out.println("Time for 100000 gets in a tree map is "
                          + (stoptime-starttime));
    }
}
```

Output

```
The size of the rivers map is: 17
Rivers map contains key 'Congo': true
Rivers map contains value 3500: false

Mekong Ganges Colorado Euphrates Amazon Mississippi Rio Grande Volga Missouri
Indus Huang Congo Danube Niger Nile Columbia Chang

{Mekong=2600, Ganges=1560, Colorado=1450, Euphrates=1700, Amazon=4000, Missis-
sippi=2340, Rio Grande=1900, Volga=2290, Missouri=2315, Indus=1800, Huang=3395,
Congo=2718, Danube=1776, Niger=2590, Nile=4160, Columbia=1243, Chang=3964}

{Amazon=4000, Chang=3964, Colorado=1450, Columbia=1243, Congo=2718,
Danube=1776, Euphrates=1700, Ganges=1560, Huang=3395, Indus=1800, Mekong=2600,
Mississippi=2340, Missouri=2315, Niger=2590, Nile=4160, Rio Grande=1900,
Volga=2290}

  Amazon 4000
  Huang 3395
  Nile 4160
  Chang 3964
Time for 100000 gets in a hash map is 110
Time for 100000 gets in a tree map is 671
```

Note 1:   We choose a table size of 37 because it is the nearest prime to twice the size of the data. We want the data to be spread as uniformly as possible in the table to minimize the chance of collisions and a prime table size helps spread the values to each possible location using the common hash functions.

Note 2:   The put method enters a key and its associated value in the map. Both the key and value are of type Object. In this example the river name key is a string which inherits from Object, but the river length is an integer that we need to wrap inside an Integer object so it will inherit from Object.

Note 3:   The size method returns the number of elements in the map. Each element is a (key, value) pair.

Note 4:   The containsKey method returns **true** if the key is contained in the map and **false** otherwise.

Note 5: The `containsValue` method returns **true** if the value is associated with some key in the map and **false** otherwise.

Note 6: `System.out.println(rivers.keySet());`
The `keySet` method returns a `Set` of all the keys in the map. Note that the elements do not appear in alphabetical order, but rather in the order they were hashed into the map.

Note 7: `System.out.println(rivers);`
The `Map` implementations inherit the `toString` method in `AbstractMap` so we can list the entire map with a simple println. Note that the elements do not appear in alphabetical order, but rather in the order they were hashed into the map.

Note 8: `riversTree.putAll(rivers);`
The `putAll` method lets us put all the elements of one map into another.

Note 9: `System.out.println(riversTree);`
The `treeMap` elements appear in alphabetical order because they were added to the tree in such a way as to preserve that order.

Note 10: `for (Iterator i = rivers.entrySet().iterator(); i.hasNext(); )`
The `entrySet` method returns a set of elements of type `Entry`, an inner interface of `Map`. The `Entry` interface has three methods:

```
Object getKey();
Object getValue();
Object setValue(Object value);
```

We use this set to iterate through the map, processing each entry in turn. The loop needs no update expression because the `next` method is executed in the loop body to update to the next element.

Note 11: `int size = ((Integer)item.getValue()).intValue();`
In the body of the loop, we get the value from each entry and list all rivers whose length is greater than or equal to 3000 miles.

Note 12: `for (int i = 0; i < 100000; i++) rivers.get("Columbia");`
Executing a `get` in a hash map is more efficient than in a tree map. We will explore this difference further in the next example.

We compare the hash map with the tree map implementation in the next example. We compare searches of maps with different sizes. The search time for a hash map depends on the load factor which is the ratio of the number of items in the table to the table capacity. In our example, the load factor is always .5 because our hash map is constructed with capacity twice the number of elements we add.

As we add more nodes to a tree map, the tree gets deeper, but slowly. The maximum number of comparisons occurs when we search for an item not in the tree. In a balanced tree, the growth in the search time varies as the logarithm of the data size. In running Example 11.7 we use data sets of size 100, 1000, 10,000, and 100,000. Figure 11.7 shows the natural logarithms of these numbers, the ratios compared to the logarithm of 100 as a base, the observed time and the predicted time.

Figure 11.7 Predictions based on $\ln n$ efficiency

Size	Natural logarithm	Ratio	Observed time	Predicted time
100	4.6	1.0	1953	1953
1000	6.9	1.5	2814	2929
10000	9.2	2.0	3685	3906
100000	11.5	2.5	4777	4882

EXAMPLE 11.7 **CompareMaps.java**

```java
/* Compares the efficiency of the hash map
 * implementation with the tree map.
 */

import java.util.*;

public class CompareMaps {
  public static final int MAX = 500000;                       // Note 1
  public static final Integer TEST = new Integer(100000);     // Note 2

  public static String time(Map map, Integer test) {          // Note 3
    Object value = null;
    long starttime = System.currentTimeMillis();
    for (int i = 0; i < MAX; i++) {
    value = map.get(test);
    }
    long stoptime = System.currentTimeMillis();
    return (value + " took " + (stoptime - starttime));
  }
  public static void main(String[] args) {
    int SIZE = Integer.parseInt(args[0]);                     // Note 4
    Map hash = new HashMap(2*SIZE);                            // Note 5
    Map tree = new TreeMap();
    Random random = new Random();                             // Note 6
    for (int j = 0; j < SIZE; j++) {                          // Note 7
      Integer i = new Integer(random.nextInt(5000000));       // Note 8
      hash.put(i, i);                                         // Note 9
      tree.put(i,i);
    }
    System.out.println("Hash for " + time(hash, TEST));
    System.out.println("Tree for " + time(tree, TEST));
  }
}
```

Output

```
C: \book3\collections>java CompareMaps 100
Hash for null took 200
Tree for null took 1953

C:\book3\collections>java CompareMaps 1000
Hash for null took 241
Tree for null took 2814

C:\book3\collections>java CompareMaps 10000
Hash for null took 210
Tree for null took 3685

C:\book3\collections>java CompareMaps 100000
Hash for null took 210
Tree for null took 4777
```

....

Note 1:   MAX is the number of times we repeat the get operation when we estimate the time it takes. One or a few calls would be too quick to time.

Note 2:   We define the key for which we will search as a constant before the search loop so computing the test value does not affect the search time.

Note 3:   The time method returns a string stating the time taken for MAX searches in the map passed as the first argument for the key passed as the second argument.

Note 4:   We pass the number of items in the table as a program argument.

Note 5:   Creating the hash map with a load factor of .5 (fraction of the table that will be filled) gives it good performance. High load factors can degrade the performance.

Note 6:   Random random = new Random();
Java 2 added the Random class in the java.util package.

Note 7:   for (int j = 0; j < SIZE; j++)
We create both the hash map and the tree map with a SIZE which we vary as a program argument. Increasing the number of elements in the hash map will not affect performance as long as the load factor remains the same. Increasing the number of elements in the tree map causes the worst case number of comparisons to increase by one as we double the number of items in the tree. As a balanced tree gets one level deeper the number of items it can hold doubles. This gives the logarithmic performance shown in Figure 11.7.

Note 8:   Integer i = new Integer(random.nextInt(5000000));
The nextInt method returns a random number between 0 and 4,999,999. Because we put at most 100,000 numbers in the map, it is unlikely that the test value of 100,000 will be found in the map and we will be estimat-

ing the worst case behavior when we have search until we determine that the sought for element is not present.

Note 9:   Because we are just comparing the hash map and tree map implementations, we do not use the value associated with the key, and put the key itself as an arbitrary value.

THE BIG PICTURE

A `Map` associates a value with each key. We can get the value associated with a key. The `HashMap` implementation is very efficient but does not keep the keys in sorted order. It uses a hash function computed from the key to find a location in the map. Performance does not depend on the size of the data, but will degrade if the load factor increases because more conflicts will occur with multiple keys hashing to the same location. The search time using the `TreeMap` implementation increases proportional to $\ln n$ where n is the size of the map. It is useful if getting the data in sorted order is important.

TEST YOUR UNDERSTANDING

TRY IT YOURSELF   11. Modify Example 11.7 to make the size of the map five greater than the size of the data. How do the performance figures change?

TRY IT YOURSELF   12. We see from Figure 11.7 that squaring the size from 100 to 10000 doubles the logarithm. Using this rule what is the predicted search time in a `TreeMap` of size 40000 compared to one of size 200? Run Example 11.7 to check your prediction.

13. What advantage would a tree map have over a hash map if used for a spell checker?

11.4   Comparisons and Ordering

Thus far in this chapter we have been adding strings to our collections. Part of the Java library, the `String` class is well-behaved in that comparison between strings work as expected. In this section we learn to make our user classes implement the necessary comparison operations properly, so we can add them to collections and arrange them in order.

Inheriting From Object

Class `Object` provides default implementations of the methods

```
public boolean equals(Object o);
public int hashCode();
public String toString();
```

so every class inherits these methods. However `Object` implements these methods based on a reference to an object, and not based on the state of the object itself. Subclasses normally must override these methods for them to work properly, as the `String` class does. To see why such overriding is necessary we use the `Name` class of Figure 11.8, with the instances of Figure 11.9.

Figure 11.8 A `Name` class

```
/* Groups fields for a name.
 * Uses toString to display.
 */

package personData;

public class Name {
  String first;
  char initial;
  String last;

  public Name(String f, String 1) {
    first = f;
    last = 1;
  }
  public Name(String f, char i, String 1) {
    this(f,1);
    initial = i;
  }
  public String toString() {
    if (initial == '\u0000')
      return first + " " + last;
    else
      return first + " " + initial + " " + last;
  }
}
```

Figure 11.9 Two `Name` instances

```
Name president = new Name ("George", "Washington");
Name first =  new Name ("George", "Washington");
```

president	☐	→ "George","Washington"
first	☐	→ "George","Washington"

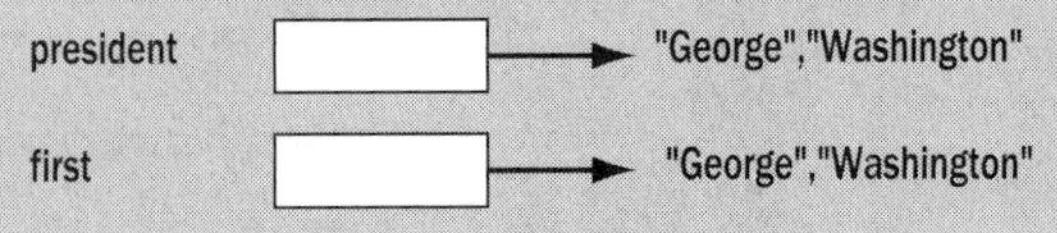

Example 11.8 shows what happens when a class uses the default implementations that it inherits from `Object`.

EXAMPLE 11.8   BadCompare.java

```
/* Shows that the Name class does not behave properly
 * using inherited equals and hashCode methods.
 */

import personData.Name;
import java.util.*;

public class BadCompare {
  public static void main(String[] args) {
    Name president = new Name ("George", "Washington");
    Name first = new Name ("George", "Washington");              // Note 1
    System.out.println("Should be equal, but equals returns: "
                  + first.equals(president));                    // Note 2
    System.out.print("The hash codes for first and president are: ");
    if (president.hashCode() == first.hashCode())
      System.out.println("equal");
    else
      System.out.println("not equal");                          // Note 3
    Set s = new HashSet();
    s.add(president);
    System.out.println("Should contain George Washington, but "
                  + "contains returns: " + s.contains(first));   // Note 4
    Map m = new HashMap();
    m.put(president, "first");
    System.out.println("Should get 'first', but get returns: "
                  + m.get(first));                               // Note 5
    System.out.println("toString overridden so first is: " + first); // Note 6
  }
}
```

Output

```
Should be equal, but equals returns: false
The hash codes for first and president are: not equal
Should contain George Washington, but contains returns: false
Should get 'first', but get returns: null
toString overridden so first is: George Washington
```

Note 1:   Figure 11.9 shows that `first` and `president` refer to different objects.

Note 2:   The `equals` method inherited from `Object` checks the equality of references. The two references, `president` and `first`, are not equal even though
the names they point to are.

Note 3:   The `hashCode` method inherited from `Object` computes a hash value based
on the reference, so the two references, `president` and `first`, have different
hash codes. Any implementation that uses these hash values to find locations for objects will put `first` and `president` in two different locations.

Note 4: The HashSet implementation uses the hashCode method to check whether an object is contained in a set. After adding president the set will contain the name of the first president, but the contains method returns **false** because the hashCode method inherited from Object looks for the object referred to by first in a different location from the one containing the object referred to by president.

Note 5: The HashMap implementation uses the hashCode method to store and retrieve items from the map. Because president and first have different hash codes they will be stored in different locations. Calling m.get(first) will only look in the location found using the hash code of first and thus will not find the name placed using the president reference.

Note 6: System.out.println ("toString overridden so first is: " + first); Because the Name class overrides the toString method, we do obtain the desired result. Had Name not overridden toString, the inherited implementation from object would have been used which displays an empty string.

Overriding Object Methods

To make the Name class function properly we must override the equals and hashCode methods. Example 11.9 shows the rewritten class, where we rename the Name class as NewName to avoid confusion with the incomplete version in Figure 11.8.

EXAMPLE 11.9 **NewName.java**

```java
/* Groups fields for a name. Overrides equals, hashCode,
 * and toString.
 */

package personData;

public class NewName extends Name {

  public NewName(String f, String l) {
    super(f,l);
  }
  public NewName(String f, char i, String l) {
    super(f,i,l);
  }
  public boolean equals(Object object) {
    if (!(object instanceof NewName))                        // Note 1
      return false;
    NewName name = (NewName)object;                          // Note 2
    return first.equals(name.first) && initial == name.initial
          && last.equals(name.last);                         // Note 3
  }
```

```
  public int hashCode() {
    return first.hashCode() + (int)initial + last.hashCode();        // Note 4
  }
}
```

Note 1:   The `equals` method overrides the method inherited from `Object` which of course has a parameter of type `Object`. The actual argument we pass to the `equals` method can be any subclass of `Object`. Because we are checking equality of `NewName` objects, we use the `instanceof` operator to rule out any object which is not of that type.

Note 2:   If execution gets here we know that the object is an instance of `NewName` so we perform this cast to be able to refer to the `first`, `initial`, and `last` fields.

Note 3:   The two objects are equal if they have the same first and last names and middle initial. Because the first and last names are strings, we can use the `equals` method of the `String` class to do these checks.

Note 4:   To compute a hash code for a name we add the hash codes of the first and last names and the ASCII value of the middle initial. The first and last names are strings which implement the `hashCode` method properly. We could have constructed a more complex hash function, for example by shifting the hash code for the first name right by several bits before adding the middle initial and last name hash code. Such a tweaking of the function might make the distribution of hash values more uniform thus reducing the number of collisions and improving the efficiency of the hashing.

Example 11.10 shows that using the `NewName` class the problems encountered in Example 11.8 using the `Name` class are corrected.

EXAMPLE 11.10   **GoodCompare.java**

```
/* Shows that the NewName class behaves properly
 * using overridden equals and hashCode methods.
 */

import personData.NewName;
import java.util.*;

public class GoodCompare {
  public static void main(String[] args) {
    NewName president = new NewName ("George", "Washington");
    NewName first = new NewName ("George", "Washington");
    System.out.println("Should be equal, and equals returns: "
                + first.equals(president));
    System.out.print("The hash codes for first and president are: ");
    if (president.hashCode() == first.hashCode())
      System.out.println("equal");
```

```
          else
            System.out.println("not equal");
          Set s = new HashSet();
          s.add(president);
          System.out.println("Should contain George Washington, "
                        + "and contains returns: " + s.contains(first));
          Map m = new HashMap();
          m.put(president, "first");
          System.out.println("Should get 'first', and get returns: " + m.get(first));
          System.out.println("toString overridden so first is: " + first);
      }
}
```

Output

```
Should be equal, and equals returns: true
The hash codes for first and president are: equal
Should contain George Washington, and contains returns: true
Should get 'first', and get returns: first
toString overridden so first is: George Washington
```

The `Comparable` Interface

Classes implement the `Comparable` interface to allow objects to be ordered. The wrapper classes such as `Integer` and `Double` implement it, as do the `String`, `BigInteger`, and `Date` classes. The `Comparable` interface has one method,

```
public int compareTo(Object object);
```

which returns a negative integer if the result is less, zero if equal, and a positive integer if greater.

The `TreeSet` and `TreeMap` implementations require that their elements implement the `Comparable` interface, because they use the `compareTo` method to arrange them in order. In Examples 11.6 and 11.7 we successfully added strings to a `TreeMap`. In Example 11.8 trying to add a `Name` to a `TreeSet` would have caused a `ClassCastException` to be thrown because `Name` does not implement the `Comparable` interface. Algorithms such as `sort`, which we will consider later, naturally require that elements to be sorted implement the `Comparable` interface.

Names do have a natural alphabetical ordering. In Example 11.11 we revise the `NewName` class to implement the `Comparable` interface.

EXAMPLE 11.11   NewOrderedName.java

```
/* Groups fields for a name. Overrides NewName and
 * implements the Comparable interface.
 */

package personData;
```

```
public class NewOrderedName extends NewName implements Comparable {
  public NewOrderedName(String f, String l) {
    super(f,l);
  }
  public NewOrderedName(String f, char i, String l) {
    super(f,i,l);
  }
  public int compareTo(Object object) {
    NewOrderedName name = (NewOrderedName)object;            // Note 1
    int lastResult = last.compareTo(name.last);
    if (lastResult != 0)
      return lastResult;                                      // Note 2
    else {
      int firstResult = first.compareTo(name.first);
      if (firstResult != 0)
        return firstResult;
      else
        return (int)initial - (int)name.initial;             // Note 3
    }
  }
  public static void main(String[] args) {                   // Note 4
    NewOrderedName jAdams = new NewOrderedName("John", "Adams");
    NewOrderedName jqAdams =
            new NewOrderedName("John", 'Q', "Adams");
    NewOrderedName hAdams = new NewOrderedName("Henry", "Adams");
    System.out.println("jAdams vs. jqAdams " + jAdams.compareTo(jqAdams));
    System.out.println("jAdams vs. hAdams " + jAdams.compareTo(hAdams));
    System.out.println("hAdams vs. hAdams " + hAdams.compareTo(hAdams));
  }
}
```

Output

```
jAdams vs. jqAdams -81
jAdams vs. hAdams 2
hAdams vs. hAdams 0
```

Note 1: The conditions specified in the Comparable interface require the compareTo method to throw a ClassCastException if the object argument cannot be compared to a NewOrderedName. If this cast fails Java will throw such an exception.

Note 2: We first check last names using the compareTo method for strings and return if the last names are unequal.

Note 3: If the first and last names are equal, we return the different of the ASCII values of the middle initials.

Note 4: It is a good idea to include some tests of the class methods in the `main` method.

Sorted Sets and Maps

The `SortedSet` and `SortedMap` interfaces keep the elements in order. Each adds additional operations to make use of the ordering of their elements. Additional method in the `SortedSet` interface include:

```
Object first()
SortedSet headSet(Object toElement)
Object last()
SortedSet subSet(Object fromElement, Object toElement)
SortedSet tailSet(Object fromElement)
```

Additional methods in the `SortedMap` interface include:

```
Object firstKey()
SortedMap headMap(Object toKey)
Object lastKey()
SortedMap subMap(Object fromKey, Object toKey)
SortedMap tailMap(Object fromKey)
```

EXAMPLE 11.12   Ordering.java

```java
/* Illustrates the SortedSet interface
 */

import java.util.*;
import personData.*;

public class Ordering {
  public static void main(String[] args) {
    SortedSet set = new TreeSet();                                    // Note 1
    NewOrderedName jackson, madison;
    set.add(new NewOrderedName("George", "Washington"));
    set.add(new NewOrderedName("John", "Adams"));
    set.add(new NewOrderedName("Thomas", "Jefferson"));
    set.add(madison = new NewOrderedName("James", "Madison"));
    set.add(new NewOrderedName("James", "Monroe"));
    set.add(new NewOrderedName("John", 'Q', "Adams"));
    set.add(jackson = new NewOrderedName("Andrew", "Jackson"));
    set.add(new NewOrderedName("Martin", "Van Buren"));
    set.add(new NewOrderedName("William", 'H', "Harrison"));
    set.add(new NewOrderedName("James", 'K', "Polk"));
    System.out.println("The first element is: " + set.first());       // Note 2
    System.out.println("The last element is: " + set.last());         // Note 3
    System.out.println("The J's are: "
                            + set.subSet(jackson, madison));          // Note 4
    System.out.println("A-I are: " + set.headSet(jackson));           // Note 5
```

```
    System.out.println("M-Z are: " + set.tailSet(madison));        // Note 6
  }
}
```

Output

```
The first element is: John Adams
The last element is: George Washington
The J's are: [Andrew Jackson, Thomas Jefferson]
A-I are: [John Adams, John Q Adams, William H Harrison]
M-Z are: [James Madison, James Monroe, James K Polk, Martin Van Buren,
George Washington]
```

Note 1:   TreeSet implements the SortedSet interface while HashSet does not.

Note 2:   The first method returns the first element according to the natural ordering implemented by the compareTo method.

Note 3:   The last method returns the last element according to the natural ordering implemented by the compareTo method.

Note 4:   The subSet method returns the sorted set starting with the first argument and continuing up to but not including the second argument.

Note 5:   The headSet method returns elements in the sorted set starting with the first element and continuing up to but not including the argument.

Note 6:   System.out.println ("M-Z are: " + set.tailSet(madison));
The tailSet method returns elements in the sorted set starting with the argument and continuing to the end of the set.

THE BIG PICTURE

To add our own object types to containers we need to override the equals, hashCode, and toString method inherited from Object. To be able to sort our own object types, we need to make them implement the Comparable interface and implement the compareTo method. We can add types that implement Comparable to sorted sets and sorted maps, which keep them in order.

TEST YOUR UNDERSTANDING

TRY IT YOURSELF   14. What happens if you change the implementation of the set s in Example 11.10 from a HashSet to a TreeSet? Explain.

TRY IT YOURSELF   15. What happens in Example 11.11 if you try to compare jAdams to the String "John Adams"? Explain.

TRY IT YOURSELF   16. What happens in Example 11.12 if you change the declaration of set to have type Set instead of SortedSet? Explain.

11.5   Algorithms

The Collections class in the java.util package contains static methods including algorithms which operate on certain Collection objects. These algorithms include:

```
static int binarySearch(List list, Object key)
static void copy(List dest, List src)
static void fill(List list, Object o)
static Object max(Collection coll)
static Object min(Collection coll)
static List nCopies(int n, Object o)
static void reverse(List list)
static void shuffle(List list)
static void sort(List list)
```

EXAMPLE 11.13   Algorithms.java

```
/* Illustrates algorithms in the Collections class.
 */

import java.util.*;

public class Algorithms {
  public static void main(String[] args) {
    String[] words = {"sat","tat","hat","fat","vat","cat",
                      "rat","bat","mat","oat","pat"};
    List list = new ArrayList();
    for (int i = 0; i < words.length; i++)
      list.add(words[i]);
    Collections.reverse(list);                                    // Note 1
    System.out.println("Reverse of list is: " + list);
    System.out.println("Max is: " + Collections.max(list));       // Note 2
    System.out.println("Min is: " + Collections.min(list));
    Collections.sort(list);                                       // Note 3
    System.out.println("Sorted list is: " + list);
    System.out.println
      ("Index of rat is: " + Collections.binarySearch(list, "rat")); // Note 4
    System.out.println("Searching for potato returns: "
        + Collections.binarySearch(list, "potato"));              // Note 5
    Collections.shuffle(list);                                    // Note 6
    System.out.println("Shuffled list is: " + list);
    Collections.copy(list,list.subList(5,8));                     // Note 7
    System.out.println("List changed at indices 0-2 is:\n\t " + list);
    Collections.fill(list.subList(0,3),"fill");                   // Note 8
    System.out.println("List filled at indices 0-2 is:\n\t " + list);
    System.out.println
        ("List with 5 fives is: " + Collections.nCopies(5,"five")); // Note 9
  }
}
```

Output

```
Reverse of list is: [pat, oat, mat, bat, rat, cat, vat, fat, hat, tat, sat]
Max is: vat
Min is: bat
Sorted list is: [bat, cat, fat, hat, mat, oat, pat, rat, sat, tat, vat]
Index of rat is: 7
Searching for potato returns: -8
Shuffled list is: [cat, tat, mat, fat, vat, sat, pat, oat, rat, hat, bat]
List changed at indices 0-2 is:
[sat, pat, oat, fat, vat, sat, pat, oat, rat, hat, bat]
List filled at indices 0-2 is:
[fill, fill, fill, fat, vat, sat, pat, oat, rat, hat, bat]
List with 5 fives is: [five, five, five, five, five]
```

Note 1:   The algorithms are static methods of the Collections class. The reverse method reverses the order of the elements in its list argument.

Note 2:   The max method applies to any Collection whose elements implement the Comparable interface. Elements must be mutually comparable. For example a collection could not contain both strings and dates.

Note 3:   The sort method arranges the elements of a list from smallest to largest. The elements must implement the Comparable interface and be mutually comparable.

Note 4:   Uses the binary search algorithm to find an element in a list whose elements must be sorted. It will perform much better for a random access implementation such as an ArrayList.

Note 5:   The search for "potato" returns –8 which equals –7 –1, where 7 is the position at which to insert "potato" in the list (just before "rat").

Note 6:   Collections.shuffle(list);
Permutes the elements of the list randomly.

Note 7:   Collections.copy(list,list.subList(5,8));
Copies the source list to the destination list which must be at least as long as the source. In this example, we copy elements at indices 5, 6 and 7 to indices 0, 1, and 2.

Note 8:   Collections.fill(list.subList(0,3),"fill");
Fills the list with the specified object. In this example we fill the first three positions of the list with the word "fill."

Note 9:   ("List with 5 fives is: " + Collections.nCopies(5,"five"));
The nCopies method returns a list, in this example, with 5 copies of the word "five."

THE BIG PICTURE

A `Collections` class has static methods to implement useful algorithms. These include binary search, sort, reverse, shuffle, max, and min.

TEST YOUR UNDERSTANDING

17. Explain why most `Collections` methods take a `List` as the first argument instead of a `Collection`.

TRY IT YOURSELF   18. What happens in Example 11.13 if you add the line `list.add(new Date());` just after the loop which adds the words?

SUMMARY

- The `Collection` interface abstracts behavior common to both lists and sets. In a `Set`, elements are unordered, while in a list the elements have an order from first to last. A `Set` cannot contain duplicates. Trying to add an element already in the set will leave the set unchanged. A `Map` interface represents (key, value) pairs and allows us to look up the value associated with a key. Each interface includes accessor operations that inspect elements and mutator operations that modify them.

- The `Collection` `iterator` method allows us to process the elements of a collection, and remove elements while iterating, if desired. The `hasNext` method returns **true** when the iterator has not completed traversing the collection, and in that case, the `next` method returns the next element.

- The `List` interface adds methods which refer to the specific position of an element. A list iterator can traverse a list both forward and backward. The `ArrayList` implementation generally is more efficient than the `LinkedList` implementation, but is inefficient when adding at the interior of a list because the elements to the right need to moved to make space. Adding at an interior position is efficient using a `LinkedListIterator` since the iterator is already positioned at the insertion position.

- A `Map` associates a value with a key. We use the `put` method to store a key and value pair, and the `get` method to retrieve the value associated with a key. The `HashMap` implementation is more efficient than the `TreeMap`, but does not keep the elements in sorted order.

- By default the `equals` method compares references and the `hashCode` method computes the hash value of references. Objects that we wish to add to collections must override these methods to check equality of objects, and to compute a hash value based on the object data. A class must implement the `Comparable` interface, providing a `compareTo` method, to allow its objects to be sorted, or placed in a sorted collection which keeps its elements in sorted order.

- The `Collections` class includes `binarySearch`, `copy`, `fill`, `max`, `min`, `reverse`, `shuffle`, `sort`, and `nCopies` methods which perform common operations.

Program Modification Exercises

. . . .

1. Modify Example 11.1 to use a sorted set so that the words will display in alphabetical order.

2. Modify Example 11.3 to also compare times for removing an element.

3. Modify Example 11.4 to also compare times for removing an element.

4. Modify Examples 11.3 and 11.4 to compare the time needed using an iterator to traverse the list.

5. Modify Example 11.6 to display any river names that start with a letter entered by the user.

Program Design Exercises

. . . .

6. Make a Map containing the distinct words of the Gettysburg address as the keys and their frequency of occurrence as the values.

7. Create a list containing 1000 random numbers between 0 and 1,000,000 and sort it. Use binary search to find the index at which 500,000 occurs in the list or the index at which it should be inserted if it does not occur. Repeat for linear search that checks the elements successively beginning at the head of the list.

8. Create a deck of Card objects. Each card has a suit and a value. The suits are Clubs, Diamonds, Hearts, and Spades. The values, which can be characters, are 2, 3, 4, 5, 6, 7, 8, 9, 10, J, Q, K, A. Shuffle the deck and deal 4 hands of 13 cards each. Use suitable collection methods wherever possible.

9. Keep the words macabre, macaco, macadam, macadamia, macaque, macaroni, macaronic, macaroon, macaw, and maccaboy in a list. When the user enters a word alphabetically greater than "mac," but less than "macd," and not in the list, show the nearest four words to it and let the user choose a replacement.

12 Security and the Java Virtual Machine

Introduction

. . . .

Security is crucial when loading applets from remote sites, and whenever we connect to other machines. Java takes precautions when loading classes and before running programs to make sure that they do not accidentally (or intentionally) subvert the rules for safe execution. The Java Virtual Machine verifies code safety before executing it, and a security manager can grant permissions specified in policy files.

OBJECTIVES

- Find system properties.
- Determine the effect of the default security manager.
- Use the Java Plug-in.
- Grant permissions in policy files.
- Use Java tools to sign programs.
- Become familiar with the JVM instruction set.
- Annotate a Java class file.

12.1 Using a Security Manager

The applet viewer and browsers automatically set a security manager when running an applet, but standalone applications do not. We shall see the effect of the security manager regarding access to resources, including local files and system properties. Various properties specify details about the local environment such as the name of the operating system or the directory in which Java is installed.

Properties

Each property represents a local environment setting. For example, in the author's installation, the os.name property has the value *Window NT.* The System class has a getProperties method that returns the system properties. We use the list method of the Properties class to automatically list all the system properties. We shall see that the security manager usually restricts access to some properties.

EXAMPLE 12.1   **ShowProperties.java**

```
/* Displays the system properties.
 */

public class ShowProperties {
  public static void main(String[] args) {
    System.getProperties().list(System.out);
  }
}
```

Output

```
-- listing properties --
java.specification.name=Java Platform API Specification
awt.toolkit=sun.awt.windows.WToolkit
java.version=1.2.2
java.awt.graphicsenv=sun.awt.Win32GraphicsEnvironment
user.timezone=America/Los_Angeles
java.specification.version=1.2
java.vm.vendor=Sun Microsystems Inc.
user.home=C:\WINNT\Profiles\Administrator
java.vm.specification.version=1.0
os.arch=x86
java.awt.fonts=
java.vendor.url=http://java.sun.com/
user.region=US
file.encoding.pkg=sun.io
java.home=d:\jdk1.2.2\jre
java.class.path=d:\jmf\lib\jmf.jar;d:\jmf\lib\sound.j...
line.separator=
```

```
java.ext.dirs=d:\jdk1.2.2\jre\lib\ext
java.io.tmpdir=C:\TEMP\
os.name=Windows NT
java.vendor=Sun Microsystems Inc.
java.awt.printerjob=sun.awt.windows.WPrinterJob
java.library.path=d:\jdk1.2.2\bin;.;C:\WINNT\System32;C...
java.vm.specification.vendor=Sun Microsystems Inc.
sun.io.unicode.encoding=UnicodeLittle
file.encoding=Cp1252
java.specification.vendor=Sun Microsystems Inc.
user.language=en
user.name=Administrator
java.vendor.url.bug=http://java.sun.com/cgi-bin/bugreport...
java.vm.name=Classic VM
java.class.version=46.0
java.vm.specification.name=Java Virtual Machine Specification
sun.boot.library.path=d:\jdk1.2.2\jre\bin
os.version=4.0
java.vm.version=1.2.2
java.vm.info=build JDK-1.2.2-001, native threads, ...
java.compiler=symcjit
path.separator=;
file.separator=\
user.dir=D:\book3\security
sun.boot.class.path=d:\jdk1.2.2\jre\lib\rt.jar;d:\jdk1.2....
```

TIP
☞

We can set system properties when running an applet or a program. For example to set the file encoding to Cp437 we use

```
java -Dfile.encoding=Cp437 Standalone
```

to execute Standalone.class, and

```
appletviewer -J-Djava.encoding=Cp437 CheckSecurity.html
```

to run the CheckSecurity applet.

The Security Manager

The getSecurityManager method of the System class returns the current security manager, if any. The security manager has methods to check if access to a resource is permitted. We will experiment with the following four:

```
public void checkRead(String file);
public void checkWrite(String file);
public void checkPropertyAccess(String key);
public void checkConnect(String host, int port);
```

When a program attempts to construct a FileInputStream, Java calls the checkRead method which throws a SecurityException if access to that file is not permitted by the security policy. Example 12.2 shows the results of the applet viewer's security manager checks for read from a file, connecting to a remote site, writing to a file, and accessing two system properties. We put each check in its own `try` block with its own `catch` clause, because we want to see the results of each check and not terminate the program after the first exception is thrown.

EXAMPLE 12.2   ## CheckSecurity.java

```java
/* Tries security manager checks for reading and
 * writing files, connecting to a remote site, and
 * accessing system properties.
 */

import java.applet.Applet;

public class CheckSecurity extends Applet {
  public void init() {
    SecurityManager security = System.getSecurityManager();
    if (security != null) {                                         // Note 1
      try {
        security.checkRead("out");
        System.out.println("OK to read from file 'out'");
      }catch(SecurityException e) {
        System.out.println(e.getMessage());                         // Note 2
      }
      try {
        security.checkConnect("java.sun.com",80);                   // Note 3
        System.out.println("OK to connect to java.sun.com");
      }catch(SecurityException e) {
        System.out.println(e.getMessage());
      }
      try {
        security.checkWrite("out");
        System.out.println("OK to write to file 'out'");
      }catch(SecurityException e) {
        System.out.println(e.getMessage());
      }
      try {
        security.checkPropertyAccess("java.version");
        System.out.println("Can access java.version");
      }catch(SecurityException e) {
        System.out.println(e.getMessage());
      }
      try {
        security.checkPropertyAccess("file.encoding");
        System.out.println("Can access file.encoding");
      } catch (SecurityException e) {
        System.out.println(e.getMessage());
      }
    }
```

```
    else
      System.out.println("No security manager");
  }
}
```

Output (using the JDK 1.2.2 applet viewer)

```
OK to read from file 'out'
OK to connect to java.sun.com
access denied (java.io.FilePermission out write)
Can access java.version
access denied (java.util.PropertyPermission file.encoding read)
```

Note 1: Because the applet viewer installs a security manager, the value is not **null**.

Note 2: The message method displays the message that the thrower of the exception passed. In this example, we prefer these brief messages to the entire stack trace.

Note 3: The checkConnect method throws a Security Exception if the applet is not permitted to connect to Sun's Java home page.

Had we run the code of Example 12.2 in a standalone application rather than an applet, none of the check methods would have been called because no security manager would have been installed.

The browser installs its own security manager. Figure 12.1 shows the output when running the CheckSecurity applet in Internet Explorer 5 with the default security setting.[*]

Figure 12.1   Running Example 12.2 in Internet Explorer 5 (stack trace omitted)

```
Com.ms.security.SecurityExceptionEx[CheckSecurity.init]:
    cannot access file out
Com.ms.security.SecurityExceptionEx[CheckSecurity.init]:
    cannot access "java.sun.com":80
Com.ms.security.SecurityExceptionEx[CheckSecurity.init]:
              cannot access file out
Can access java.version
Com.ms.security.SecurityExceptionEx[CheckSecurity.init]:
    Unable to access system property: file.encoding
```

We see from Figure 12.1 that the IE5 security manager is more restrictive than the applet viewer's. Browsers use their own Java virtual machines. The IE5 virtual machine implements Java version 1.1. Sun offers the Java Plug-in to use Sun's Java virtual machine with a browser.

---

[*] IE5 has its own Java console accessed from the view menu. Use the *Tools, Internet Options, Advanced* tab to install it if necessary. Use the *Tools, Internet Options, Security* tab to change the security level.

The Java Plug-in

Installing the Java Plug-in, available from java.sun.com, allows us to use the latest JVM with a browser. The Java plug-in does not replace the browser. We must change our HTML files to signal that we wish to use the Java Plug-in rather than the browser's JVM. Sun provides an `HTMLConverter` program that converts HTML files to use the Java Plug-in.

If a user downloads an HTML file that requires the Java Plug-in, the Plug-in will automatically be downloaded if not present in the user's machine. This is time consuming, but useful for intranet sites on a fast local network. Because the plug-in is included with the Java 2 platform, browsing a converted HTML file will immediately cause the browser to use the Java plug-in. The Java plug-in has a GUI control panel with a checkbox to make the Java console visible.

For Example 12.2, we use the HTML file

```
<applet code=CheckSecurity.class width=300 height=200>
</applet>
```

Figure 12.2 shows the converted HTML file that results from using HTMLConverter on the original, and Figure 12.3 shows the GUI obtained when running HTMLConverter.*

Figure 12.2   `CheckSecurity.html` **converted to use the Java plug-in**

```
<!--"CONVERTED_APPLET"-->
<!-- CONVERTER VERSION 1.0 -->
<OBJECT classid="clsid:8AD9C840-044E-11D1-B3E9-00805F499D93"
WIDTH = 300 HEIGHT = 200 codebase="http://java.sun.com/products/plugin/1.2/
        jinstall-12-win32.cab#Version=1,2,0,0">
<PARAM NAME = CODE VALUE = CheckSecurity.class >

<PARAM NAME="type" VALUE="application/x-java-applet;version=1.2">
<COMMENT>
<EMBED type="application/x-java-applet;version=1.2" java_CODE = CheckSecu-
        rity.class WIDTH = 300 HEIGHT = 200 pluginspage="http://java.sun.com/
        products/plugin/1.2/plugin-install.html"><NOEMBED></COMMENT>

</NOEMBED></EMBED>
</OBJECT>

<!--
<APPLET CODE = CheckSecurity.class WIDTH = 300 HEIGHT = 200 >

</APPLET>
-->
<!--"END_CONVERTED_APPLET"-->
```

---

* Sun's Java web site, `http://java.sun.com/`, explains the structure of the HTML file produced by the converter.

Figure 12.3 Using `HTMLConverter`

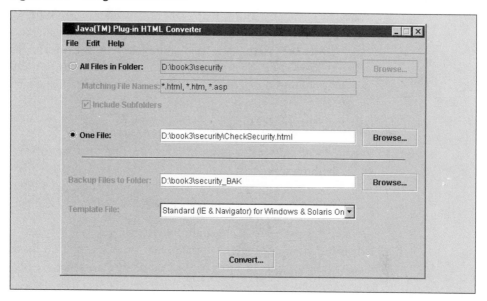

The output when browsing the converted `CheckSecurity.html` with IE5 is the same as that from Example 12.2 because both use the JDK1.2.2 security manager.

THE BIG PICTURE
Browsers and applet viewers install a security manager but standalone applications do not by default. The security manager methods check access to resources such as files and system properties, and throw an exception if access is not permitted. Browsers install their own security managers, but the Java plug-in enables the browser to use the JDK.

TEST YOUR UNDERSTANDING

TRY IT YOURSELF   1.   Run Example 12.1, setting the file encoding property to ISO8859, and notice how the output changes.

TRY IT YOURSELF   2.   Modify Example 12.2 from an applet to a standalone application. What is the output?

3.   What are the differences in the output when running Example 12.2 using the applet viewer and running it with IE5?

12.2   Policies and Permissions
. . . .

Java 2 security managers use security policies to determine which resources a program can access. These policies grant permissions that can be for everyone, or for programs from a certain location, or for programs with signatures we trust.

Policy Files

Policy files contain entries that grant permission to use resources. Each permission refers to a Java class. For example, file permissions refer to the `java.io.FilePermission` class whose constructor takes two arguments, the path to the file and the permitted actions. We do not construct permission objects directly, but rather place them in a policy file. To grant permission to write to the file `out`, we use the policy file of Figure 12.4.

Figure 12.4   A policy file granting write permission

```
grant {
   permission java.io.FilePermission "out", "write";
};
```

To add this policy to the default policies, we set the `java.security.policy` property when running our program. If the policy file of Figure 12.4 is saved in the file `write-permit`, in the same directory as the `CheckSecurity` applet, we run Example 12.2 with the command

```
appletviewer
  -J-Djava.security.policy=writepermit
  CheckSecurity2.html
```

which produces the output

```
OK to read from file 'out'
OK to connect to java.sun.com
OK to write to file 'out'
Can access java.version
access denied
  (java.util.PropertyPermission file.encoding read)
```

This differs from the output of Example 12.2 in that it is now OK to write to the file `out`.

TIP ☞

The `policytool` program that comes with the Java 2 SDK provides a GUI to create policy files. We find them simple enough to write ourselves.[*]

Figure 12.5 shows the policy file `encodingpolicy` that grants permission to read the `file.encoding` property.

Running Example 12.2 with the encoding policy of Figure 12.5 produces the output

```
OK to read from file 'out'
OK to connect to java.sun.com
```

---

[*] See the Java tutorial at `http://java.sun.com/docs/books/tutorial/security1.2/` for policytool examples.

Figure 12.5   Policy to grant a property permission

```
grant {
  permission java.util.PropertyPermission
                        "file.encoding", "read";
};
```

```
access denied (java.io.FilePermission out write)
Can access java.version
Can access file.encoding
```

which differs from the output of Example 12.2 in that the applet can now read the file.encoding property.

We could have combined the permissions of Figures 12.4 and 12.5 into one policy file, to allow writing to file out and reading the file.encoding property. Figure 12.6 lists some additional examples of permission grants.

Figure 12.6   Additional permission examples

Permission Example	Description
permission java.util.PropertyPermission "file.encoding", "read, write";	Allows read and write access to the file encoding property.
permission java.io.FilePermission "c:\\temp*", "write";	Allows writing to any file in the c:\temp directory
permission java.io.FilePermission "c:\\temp\\-", "write";	Allows writing to any file in the c:\temp directory and its subdirectories
permission java.security.AllPermission;	Grants all permissions.

TIP ☞

In Windows, we need to double the backslash character in file name strings, so we write "c:\\temp*" rather than "c:\temp*." In this context, (but not when specifying a codebase later in this section) the backslash is a special escape character and needs to be doubled to be used as a backslash.

By default, standalone applications run without a security manager and have full access to resources. To use the default security manager with a standalone application, we set the java.security.manager property on the command line. Converting Example 12.2 to Standalone.java, we run it with

```
java -Djava.security.manager Standalone
```

which produces the same output shown in Example 12.2.

We add permission files to a standalone application by setting the java.security.policy property, as in

```
java -Djava.security.manager
      -Djava.security.policy=writepermit Standalone
```

which will allow writing to the file out.

Codebase Permissions

A codebase value indicates the location of the source code granted the permission. The policy file, writepermit.Jmf, of Figure 12.7, grants permission to programs in the directory d:\Jmf to write to the file out.

Figure 12.7   Granting permission to a codebase

```
grant codebase "file:/d:/Jmf/" {
    permission java.io.FilePermission "out", "write";
};
```

Running Example 12.2 with the policy file of Figure 12.7 will not change the output because the applet is not in the d:\Jmf directory. Changing the codebase in Figure 12.7 to file:/d:/book3/security/ would permit the applet to write to the file out.

In Figure 12.7, we use a file URL representing a local file. We can also use a URL representing a remote directory, as, for example,

```
codebase "http://www.cecs.csulb.edu/~artg/"
```

TIP   Always use forward slashes in codebase URL's, even on Windows systems.

☛

....

In addition to granting permission to a specific codebase, we can grant permission to code signed by someone we trust. Before doing that we discuss the idea of digital signatures.

Digital Signatures

A digital signature is used for the authentication of digital data. Suppose we want to send a file so the receiver can verify that it came from us and was unchanged. We use an algorithm to compute a hash value, called a digital fingerprint, for our file. This fingerprint may be 20 bytes in length, or 160 bits. We then use public key cryptography to encrypt the fingerprint with our private key.

Using public key cryptography, we generate a private and a public key and distribute the public key publicly. The private and public keys have the properties that

- Applying them in any order, either private then public, or public then private, to a message, produces the original message.

- Practically, it is impossible to find the private key, knowing only the public key.

Thus the sender of a file applies the private key to the fingerprint, producing the digital signature, and sends the file, accompanied by the signature. The receiver uses the same algorithm to compute the fingerprint, call it computed, of the file, then uses the sender's public key to decrypt signature received from the sender into received. If computed equals received then the receiver knows that the file is the one sent by the holder of the private key corresponding to the public key given to the receiver.

Someone could have intercepted the file and computed a new signature, but without the sender's private key it is computationally infeasible to produce a signature that will decrypt to the fingerprint of the file when using the sender's public key.

To use public key cryptography confidently, the receiver must trust that the sender's public key is authentic. In special cases, the sender could personally deliver it to the receiver, but generally the receiver may not personally know the sender. The sender can register with a certificate authority, a trusted third party, which provides a certificate with the sender's public key and signed with its private key. The receiver uses the trusted public key of the certificate authority to authenticate the sender's public key.

Java provides the keytool program to generate keys and jarsigner to create digital signatures. The generated keys go into the keystore, a file protected by a password. We use the command

```
keytool -genkey -keystore profstore
```
which specifies the genkey option to generate public and private keys, and the keystore option to name the keystore file as profstore. keytool then prompts for the remaining information it needs.

```
Enter keystore password: abc123
What is your first and last name?
  [Unknown]: Art Gittleman
What is the name of your organizational unit?
  [Unknown]: Computer Science
What is the name of your organization?
  [Unknown]: CSULB
What is the name of your City or Locality?
  [Unknown]: Long Beach
What is the name of your State or Province?
  [Unknown]: CA
What is the two-letter country code for this unit?
  [Unknown]: US
Is <CN=Art Gittleman, OU=Computer Science, O=CSULB, L=Long Beach,
ST=CA, C=US> correct?
  [no]: y
```

The last question asks for verification of the previously entered data. Once that is verified, keytool prompts for a password for the private key. Each entry in the keystore has an alias by which we refer to it. Because we did not use the alias option on the command line, keytool gave us the default alias, mykey.

```
Enter key password for <mykey>
  (RETURN if same as keystore password): def456
```

This keytool command creates the `profstore` file which contains the generated keys. The public key is in a self-signed certificate, meaning that it is signed with our private key. The default validity for the certificate is 90 days. To authenticate our public key we would need to contact a certificate authority, such as VeriSign, Inc., but we omit this step in this example.

Once we have created our public and private keys, we can sign files using the jar-signer tool. We experiment with the applet of Example 12.2. First we need to place the file we wish to sign in a JAR file, which is a compressed format used by Java for several purposes. We use the command

```
jar cvf CheckSecurity.jar CheckSecurity.class
```

where option c requests the creation of a new archive, option v requests verbose output, and option f specifies the JAR file name.

We use the command

```
jarsigner -keystore profstore -signedjar
          SignedSecurity.jar CheckSecurity.jar mykey
```

where the `signedjar` option gives the name of the signed JAR file, and `mykey` is the alias for our key. The `jarsigner` tool prompts for the passwords.

```
Enter Passphrase for keystore: abc123
Enter key password for mykey: def456
```

The sender can now export the certificate (in this case self-signed) containing the public key to a file, `prof.cert`, using the command

```
keytool -export -keystore profstore -alias mykey
        -file prof.cert
```

`keytool` prompts for the password, and creates the certificate file.

```
Enter keystore password: abc123
Certificate stored in file <prof.cert>
```

The receiver would like to use a policy file to grant certain permissions to trusted files. The sender provides the signed JAR file, `SignedSecurity.jar`, and the certificate file, `prof.cert`. The receiver enters the certificate in a keystore, which will be created if it does not exist, using the command

```
keytool -import -alias profkey -file prof.cert
        -keystore studentstore
```

`keytool` displays the certificate and gives the receiver the opportunity to verify the key, perhaps by contacting the sender, before agreeing to place it as a trusted certificate in the keystore.

```
Enter keystore password: xyz123
Owner:    CN=Art Gittleman, OU=Computer Science, O=CSULB,
          L=Long Beach, ST=CA, C=US
Issuer:   CN=Art Gittleman, OU=Computer Science, O=CSULB,
          L=Long Beach, ST=CA, C=US
Serial number: 3861a242
Valid from: Wed Dec 22 20:17:06 PST 1999
until: Tue Mar 21 20:17:06 PST 2000
Certificate fingerprints:
          MD5:  0B:27:55:D8:A8:6F:5D:AD:EA:E9:98:48:2A:87:95:D5
          SHA1: 2C:13:E0:88:4A:D1:98:C6:A7:79:72
                :67:C1:6F:4F:D6:45:E7:61:C1
Trust this certificate? [no]: y
Certificate was added to keystore
```

Figure 12.8 shows a policy file granting any code signed by profkey write permission to the file out. The entry specifies the keystore containing the profkey certificate.

Figure 12.8 Granting a permission to trusted files

```
keystore "studentstore";
grant signedBy "profkey" {
    permission java.io.FilePermission "out", "write";
};
```

To run the signed applet obtained from the sender we use the HTML file

```
<applet archive="SignedSecurity.jar"
  code="CheckSecurity.class" width=300 height=200>
</applet>
```

where the archive attribute indicates the signed JAR file. The output from the command

```
appletviewer -J-Djava.security.policy=signedpolicy
             SignedSecurity.html
```

Is

```
OK to read from file 'out'
OK to connect to java.sun.com
OK to write to file 'out'
Can access java.version
access denied
    (java.util.PropertyPermission file.encoding read)
```

which shows that permission has been granted to write to file out.

TIP
☞

We could create a policy file which includes both the codebase and the signedBy name/value pairs.

....

THE BIG PICTURE

With policy files, we can grant permissions to all programs, to those that come from a specific location, or to those whose signature we trust. We can include an additional policy file when running an applet to give it additional access beyond the default restrictions. We can run a standalone application using a security manager to restrict the application more than the default, but add a policy file to grant additional permissions.

Signing a certificate uses public key cryptography for senders to provide trusted code to receivers. Java tools support the signing process.

TEST YOUR UNDERSTANDING

4. Write a policy file to grant permission to everyone to read and write the `file.separator` property.

5. Write a policy file to grant permission to code in the c:\test directory to write to the file `results` in the `c:\test` directory.

6. Write a policy file to grant permission to everyone to write to the file `out`, and to read the `file.encoding` property.

TRY IT YOURSELF 7. Write a policy file to grant all permissions to anyone. Run Example 12.2 with this policy file and describe the output.

TRY IT YOURSELF 8. Follow the steps described in this section to sign the applet of Example 12.2, and to run the signed applet, granting it permission to write to the file `out`.

12.3 The Java Virtual Machine

The Java Virtual Machine is an abstract computer. It includes an instruction set for a stack-based machine. An interpreter executes code in a class file which follows a specified structure. These class files may be generated by a Java compiler, but also by compilers written to translate other languages, or by an assembler from one of several available assembly languages. The JVM verifies byte code before executing it to make sure it follows the rules to restrict access to protected memory and will execute safely. The Java security manager, discussed earlier in the chapter, can assume the protection provided by the JVM verification algorithm.

In this section we describe the JVM instruction set. Each opcode is one byte, and there may be one or more arguments. For printing convenience, we show the stack growing toward the right of the page. The instructions fit into several categories. We need to push constants and variable values onto the stack, and store results in variables. We need to perform operations, invoke methods, and branch. Within each category, instructions may simply differ in the type of object they operate on. The JVM used the first letter of an instruction to indicate the type. For example `iload` will load an integer, while `dload` is the corresponding instruction for a double. Figure 12.9 tabulates this use of the first letter.

Figure 12.9   Initial letters

Letter	Type
a	reference
b	byte or boolean
c	char
d	double
f	float
i	int
l	long
s	short

The simplest instruction

```
0 (0x00) nop
```

does nothing. The group in Figure 12.10 loads constants onto the stack.

Figure 12.10   Instructions for loading constants

Opcode	Mnemonic	Arguments	Comment
01 (0x01)	aconst_null		null
02 (0x02)	iconst_m1		-1
03 (0x03)	iconst_0		0
04 (0x04)	iconst_1		1
05 (0x05)	iconst_2		2
06 (0x06)	iconst_3		3
07 (0x07)	iconst_4		4
08 (0x08)	iconst_5		5
09 (0x09)	lconst_0		0L
10 (0x0a)	lconst_1		1L
11 (0x0b)	fconst_0		0.0f
12 (0x0c)	fconst_1		1.0f
13 (0x0d)	fconst_2		2.0f
14 (0x0e)	dconst_0		0.0
15 (0x0f)	dconst_1		1.0
16 (0x10)	bipush	byte	-128 <= byte <= 127
17 (0x11)	sipush	byte1, byte2	-32768 to 32767
18 (0x12)	ldc	index	int, float, or string
19 (0x13)	ldc_w	index1, index2	int, float, or string
20 (0x14)	ldc2_w	index1, index2	long or double

Many of the instructions in Figure 12.10 load small numbers on the stack without using any extra space for arguments. Doubles and longs take two stack entries to hold their 64 bits. The bipush instruction sign extends its byte argument to an int that it pushes on the stack. sipush pushes the sign extended short (byte1 << 8) | byte2 on the stack. In the class file, we would see the instruction 17 0B B8 indicating that 3000(which is 11(256) + 11(16) +8) will be pushed on the stack.

Larger constants can appear as constant table entries in the class file, which we discuss in the next section. The 1dc instruction (load constant) loads the value at the given index in the constant table. If the constant table is large, the instruction set includes 1dc_w that uses a two byte index. These instruction load the value of an **int** or a **float**, or a reference to a string. The 1dc_w instruction loads a **long** or a **double** at the given index. Either uses two stack entries. The instructions

```
08          iconst_5
12          fconst_1
17 0B B8    sipush 3000
```

would change the stack to

… 5 1.0f 3000

The instructions in Figure 12.11 load the values of local variables onto the stack.

Figure 12.11   Instructions to load values of local variables

Opcode	Mnemonic	Arguments	Comment
21 (0x15)	iload	index	variable index
22 (0x16)	lload	index	"
23 (0x17)	fload	index	"
24 (0x18)	dload	index	"
25 (0x19)	aload	index	"
26 (0x1a)	iload_0		
27 (0x1b)	iload_1		
28 (0x1c)	iload_2		
29 (0x1d)	iload_3		
30 (0x1e)	lload_0		
31 (0x1f)	lload_1		
32 (0x20)	lload_2		
33 (0x21)	lload_3		
34 (0x22)	fload_0		
35 (0x23)	fload_1		
36 (0x24)	fload_2		
37 (0x25)	fload_3		
38 (0x26)	dload_0		
39 (0x27)	dload_1		
40 (0x28)	dload_2		
41 (0x29)	dload_3		
42 (0x2a)	aload_0		

Figure 12.11   Instructions to load values of local variables (Continued)

Opcode	Mnemonic	Arguments	Comment
43 (0x2b)	aload_1		
44 (0x2c)	aload_2		
45 (0x2d)	aload_3		
46 (0x2e)	iaload	array value	
47 (0x2f)	laload	"	
48 (0x30)	faload	"	
49 (0x31)	daload	"	
50 (0x32)	aaload	"	
51 (0x33)	baload	"	
52 (0x34)	caload	"	
53 (0x35)	saload	"	

Local variables are untyped and numbers starting with 0. Local variable 0 is always a reference to the this object. For example, iload_2 loads an integer from variable 2. Longs and doubles each use two entries, so lload_3 loads a **long** from variables 3 and 4. Instructions that load array values expect the stack to look like

… arrayref index

They pop the index and the arrayref and push the value of the array element at that index, so the stack changes to

… arrayref[index]

Figure 12.12 shows the store instructions.

Figure 12.12   Shows the store instructions

Opcode	Mnemonic	Arguments	Comment
54 (0x36)	istore	index	variable index
55 (0x37)	lstore	index	"
56 (0x38)	fstore	index	"
57 (0x39)	dstore	index	"
58 (0x3a)	astore	index	"
59 (0x3b)	istore_0		
60 (0x3c)	istore_1		
61 (0x3d)	istore_2		
62 (0x3e)	istore_3		
63 (0x3f)	lstore_0		
64 (0x40)	lstore_1		
65 (0x41)	lstore_2		
66 (0x42)	lstore_3		

(Figure continues)

Figure 12.12 Shows the store instructions (Continued)

Opcode	Mnemonic	Arguments	Comment
67 (0x43)	fstore_0		
68 (0x44)	fstore_1		
69 (0x45)	fstore_2		
70 (0x46)	fstore_3		
71 (0x47)	dstore_0		
72 (0x48)	dstore_1		
73 (0x49)	dstore_2		
74 (0x4a)	dstore_3		
75 (0x4b)	astore_0		
76 (0x4c)	astore_1		
77 (0x4d)	astore_2		
78 (0x4e)	astore_3		
79 (0x4f)	iastore	array value	
80 (0x50)	lastore	"	
81 (0x51)	fastore	"	
82 (0x52)	dastore	"	
83 (0x53)	aastore	"	
84 (0x54)	bastore	"	
85 (0x55)	castore	"	
86 (0x56)	sastore	"	

Store instructions are the opposite of load instructions, taking values from the stack and storing them in local variables. For example, the `bastore` instruction expects the stack to look like

```
..., arrayref, index, value
```

where `arrayref` refers to an array of bytes or booleans, and `index` and `value` are integers. This instruction truncates the value to a **byte** or a **boolean** according to the type of the array and stores the value in the array element at the given index.

Next we have some stack manipulation instructions.

Figure 12.13 Stack manipulation instructions

Opcode	Mnemonic	Stack before	Stack after
87 (0x57)	pop	... x	...
88 (0x58)	pop2	... x y	...
89 (0x59)	dup	... x	... x x
90 (0x5a)	dup_x1	... x y	... y x y
91 (0x5b)	dup_x2	... x y z	... z x y z
92 (0x5c)	dup2	... x y	... x y x y

Figure 12.13   Stack manipulation instructions

Opcode	Mnemonic	Stack before	Stack after
93 (0x5d)	dup2_x1	… x y z	… y z x y z
94 (0x5e)	dup2_x2	… w x y z	… y z w x y z
95 (0x5f)	swap	… x y	… y x

The swap, dup, dup_x1, and dup_x2 instructions can only be used on ints, floats, or references. The dup2, dup2_x1, and dup2_x2 instructions can be used on longs and doubles. Figure 12.14 shows the arithmetic expressions.

Figure 12.14   Arithmetic instructions

Opcode	Mnemonic	Stack before	Stack after
96 (0x60)	iadd	… i j	… i + j
97 (0x61)	ladd	… l m	… l + m
98 (0x62)	fadd	etc.	etc.
99 (0x63)	dadd		
100 (0x64)	isub		
101 (0x65)	lsub		
102 (0x66)	fsub		
103 (0x67)	dsub		
104 (0x68)	imul		
105 (0x69)	lmul		
106 (0x6a)	fmul		
107 (0x6b)	dmul		
108 (0x6c)	idiv		
109 (0x6d)	ldiv		
110 (0x6e)	fdiv		
111 (0x6f)	ddiv		
112 (0x70)	irem		
113 (0x71)	lrem		
114 (0x72)	frem		
115 (0x73)	drem		
116 (0x74)	ineg		
117 (0x75)	lneg		
118 (0x76)	fneg		
119 (0x77)	dneg		

As an example, the following instructions load 4 and 67 on the stack, multiply them and store the result in variable 2.

```
iconst_4
bipush 67
imul
istore_2
```

Bitwise operations, shown in Figure 12.15, apply only to ints and longs.

Figure 12.15 Bitwise instructions

Opcode	Mnemonic	Stack before	Stack after	Comment
120 (0x78)	ishl	… i j	… i << j	int i,j
121 (0x79)	lshl	… l j	… l << j	long l
122 (0x7a)	ishr	… i j	… i >> j	signed
123 (0x7b)	lshr	… l j	… l >> j	signed
124 (0x7c)	iushr	… i j	… i >>> j	unsigned
125 (0x7d)	lushr	… l j	… l >>> j	unsigned
126 (0x7e)	iand	… i j	… i & j	
127 (0x7f)	land	… l m	… l & m	long m
128 (0x80)	ior	… i j	… i | j	
129 (0x81)	lor	… l m	… l | m	
130 (0x82)	ixor	… i j	… i ^ j	
131 (0x83)	lxor	… l m	… l ^ m	

The increment instruction

```
132 (0x84) iinc index const
```

increments the local variable at `index` by the `const` value. Figure 12.16 shows the conversion operations.

Figure 12.16 Converstion instructions

Opcode	Mnemonic	Comment
133 (0x85)	i2l	Increases stack size
134 (0x86)	i2f	
135 (0x87)	i2d	Increases stack size
136 (0x88)	l2i	Decreases stack size
137 (0x89)	l2f	Decreases stack size
138 (0x8a)	l2d	
139 (0x8b)	f2i	
140 (0x8c)	f2l	
141 (0x8d)	f2d	Increases stack size
142 (0x8e)	d2i	Decreases stack size
143 (0x8f)	d2l	
144 (0x90)	d2f	Decreases stack size
145 (0x91)	i2b	Truncates to byte, sign extends to int
146 (0x92)	i2c	Truncates to char, sign extends to int
147 (0x93)	i2s	Truncates to short, sign extends to int

Figure 12.17 shows the control instructions. The branching instructions test ints or references. Additional instructions compare longs, floats, or doubles, leaving 0 on the stack when both are equal, −1 when the first is less than the second, and 1 when the first is greater than the second. The Double class contains the constants Double.NaN, Double.POSITIVE_INFINITY, and Double.NEGATIVE_INFINITY, and the Float class has corresponding values. NaN stands for "not a number," and result from an undefined operation such as 0/0. POSITIVE_INFINITY results from an operation such as 5/0. The dcmpl and dcmpg instructions differ only in the result they provide when either if the numbers is NaN.

One set of instructions compares the stack value to 0 and branches if successful using the offset from the stack. For example, the ifeq instruction

```
153 00 07
```

branches to the instruction seven bytes from its start, if the value on the top of the stack is zero. Another set of instructions compares the two top stack values and branches in the same way if the comparison is true.

The JVM uses a returnAddress type for the jsr and ret instructions. The jsr instruction pushes the address of the instruction following itself on the stack, and branches to the instruction at the offset determined by the bytes b1 and b2 on the stack. The ret instruction has an argument which is a byte representing the number of a local variable which contains a value of type returnAddress. Execution continues from this address.

The various return instructions, except for return itself, pop the value on the stack, pushing it on the stack of the invoker.

Figure 12.17 Control Instructions

Opcode		Mnemonic	Arguments	Stack	Comment
148	(0x94)	lcmp		l,m	0,-1, or 1 on stack
149	(0x95)	fcmpl		f,g	-1 if either is NaN
150	(0x96)	fcmpg		f,g	1 if either is NaN
151	(0x97)	dcmpl		d,e	-1 if either is NaN
152	(0x98)	dcmpg		d,e	1 if either is NaN
153	(0x99)	ifeq	b1,b2	i	Compares stack to 0
154	(0x9a)	ifne	"	"	"
155	(0x9b)	iflt	"	"	"
156	(0x9c)	ifge	"	"	"
157	(0x9d)	ifgt	"	"	"
158	(0x9e)	ifle	"	"	"
159	(0x9f)	if_icmpeq	"	i,j	Branches if i = j
160	(0xa0)	if_icmpne	"	"	!=
161	(0xa1)	if_icmplt	"	"	<

(Figure continues)

Figure 12.17 Control Instructions (Continued)

Opcode		Mnemonic	Arguments	Stack	Comment
162	(0xa2)	if_icmpge	"	"	>=
163	(0xa3)	if_icmpgt	"	"	>
164	(0xa4)	if_icmple	"	"	<=
165	(0xa5)	if_acmpeq	"	r,s	Equal references
166	(0xa6)	if_acmpne	"	r,s	Unequal references
167	(0xa7)	goto	"		Jumps
168	(0xa8)	jsr	"		Pushes return address
169	(0xa9)	ret	b		Local var index b
170	(0xaa)	tableswitch			See the JVM specification*
171	(0xab)	lookupswitch	"		
172	(0xac)	ireturn		i	Returns an integer
173	(0xad)	lreturn		l	
174	(0xae)	freturn		f	
175	(0xaf)	dreturn		d	
176	(0xb0)	areturn		a	
177	(0xb1)	return			
198	(0xc6)	ifnull	b1,b2	r	Checks null reference
199	(0xc7)	ifnonnull	b1,b2	r	Non-null reference
200	(0xc8)	goto_w	b1-b4		Four-byte offset
201	(0xc9)	jsr_w	b1-b4		Four-byte offset

* See `http://java.sun.com/docs/books/vmspec/` for the Java Virtual Machine Specification.

Figure 12.18 shows the object and array instructions. The `getstatic` instruction pushes the value of the static field in the constant pool given by the index with bytes b1 and b2. For example, `178 00 05` would push the value of the static at index five in the constant pool. We will discuss the format for these constant pool entries in the next section when we explain the structure of class files. The `getfield` instruction is similar, but finds the field of the object reference on the stack. The `putstatic` and `putfield` instructions store field values.

Four instructions invoke methods. The JVM uses `invokevirtual` to call instance methods, so it can dynamically find the proper code. For example, a reference, declared as type `BankAccount`, may actually refer to a `CheckingAccount` subclass. When invoking the `withdraw` method, the JVM will find the overridden checking account withdraw method, rather than the declared bank account withdraw method.

The JVM uses the `invokespecial` instruction for private methods and final methods because these cannot be overridden so there is no need for the more complicated search procedure used by `invokevirtual`. The `invokespecial` method is also used for constructors. As their names suggest, `invokestatic` calls static methods and `invokeinterface` calls methods declared with an interface type.

Figure 12.18   Object and array instructions

Opcode	Mnemonic	Arguments	Stack	Comment
178 (0xb2)	getstatic		b1,b2	pushes value
179 (0xb3)	putstatic	b1,b2	value	stores value
180 (0xb4)	getfield	b1,b2	obref	pushes value
181 (0xb5)	putfield	b1,b2	r,val	stores value
182 (0xb6)	invokevirtual			See the JVM specification*
183 (0xb7)	invokespecial			"
184 (0xb8)	invokestatic			"
185 (0xb9)	invokeinterface			"
187 (0xbb)	new	b1,b2		pushes reference
188 (0xbc)	newarray	atype	count	pushes aref
189 (0xbd)	anewarray	b1,b2	count	pushes aref
190 (0xbe)	arraylength		aref	pushes length
191 (0xbf)	athrow		obref	exception
192 (0xc0)	checkcast	b1,b2	ref	checks type
193 (0xc1)	instanceof	b1,b2	obref	1 or 0 result
194 (0xc2)	monitorenter		obref	for threads
195 (0xc3)	monitorexit		obref	for threads
196 (0xc4)	wide			See the JVM specification
197 (0xc5)	multianewarray			See the JVM specification

* See `http://java.sun.com/docs/books/vmspec/` for the Java Virtual Machine Specification.

The new instruction pushes a reference to the object whose symbolic type is given in the constant pool at the index specified by the byte arguments. The newarray instruction for creating a numerical array has one argument to specify the array type.

Argument	Type
boolean	4
char	5
float	6
double	7
byte	8
short	9
int	10
long	11

The integer stack value specifies the number of components for the array. newarray creates the array and pushes a reference to it on the stack. The anewarray instruction creates an object array using the symbolic type descriptor in the constant pool at the entry given by bytes b1 and b2. The stack contains the size of the array. Anewarray pops the size entry and pushes a reference to the newly created array of objects that are initialized to **null**. The arraylength instruction pops an array reference form the stack and pushes its length. The multinewarray instruction allocates an array of arrays.

The athrow instruction pops the stack, which must be a reference to an instance of Throwable, searches for a handler to which it jumps, and pushes the reference back on the stack, after possibly making other stack changes necessitated by the jump.

The checkcast instruction checks that the stack reference is **null** or can be cast to the type given symbolically by constant pool entry at index given by bytes b1 and b2. If so the stack is unchanged, but if not the JVM throws an exception. The instanceof instruction pops the object reference, pushes a 1 on the stack if it is an instance of the type given symbolically in the constant pool, or pushes a 0 if it is not. The thread that executes the monitorenter instruction locks the object whose reference is on the stack, or waits until is unlocks and tries again. If it already has a lock it increases the count of the times it has entered the monitor for that object. The monitorexit instruction decreases the count and releases the lock if the count becomes zero. The wide instruction modifies other instructions to use a larger index.

THE BIG PICTURE

The Java Virtual Machines verifies that bytecode is safe before executing it. It includes an instruction set for a stack machine. Each opcode is one byte, and may be followed by additional bytes representing arguments. There are JVM instructions for loading constants and local variable values, storing values in local variables, manipulating the stack, performing arithmetic and bitwise operations, type conversions, control, and working with objects and arrays.

TEST YOUR UNDERSTANDING

9. Write JVM instructions to add 17 to the integer value in local variable 3 and store the result in local variable 4.

10. Write JVM instructions to set local variable 2 to 4 if value of local variable 1 is greater than 2, and to 3 if not.

11. Write JVM instructions to set local variable 3 to 2 if the double local variable 2 is less than or equal to 1.0.

12.4   The Structure of a Class File

Each time we compile a Java program, we get a class file. In this section, we describe the structure of these class files, studying the class file compiled from a Java program to see how the elements of the class file are derived from it.

Using A Disassembler

The Java SDK comes with a disassembler, `javap`, that takes a class file and produces a listing of the JVM instructions, in symbolic form, that correspond to the Java program that compiled to the given class file. Figure 12.19 shows the simple Java program we use.

Figure 12.19 A simple Java program

```
public class AssignIt {
  public static void main(String [] args) {
    int number1 = 25;
    int number2 = 12;
    number2 = number1 + 15;
    System.out.print("number2 is now ");
    System.out.println(number2);
  }
}
```

Compiling `AssignIt.java` and using the `javap` program with the command

```
javap -c AssignIt
```

produces the listing of Figure 12.20

The option, `-c`, lists the Java virtual machine instructions along with the class names. The `javap` program reads the `AssignIt.class` file to produce this listing of machine instructions in symbolic form.

To begin to understand this listing let us start with the beginning of the main method. The first statement in the Java source

```
int number1 = 25;
```

corresponds to the two machine instructions

```
bipush 25
istore_1
```

The first pushes an integer byte onto the stack, while the second pops the stack and stores the values in variable 1. Java refers to local variables internally using numbers, so the source code variable `number1` becomes variable 1 in the JVM.

The symbolic listing produced by the `javap` disassembler makes the bytecode easier to read. The `AssignIt.class` file contains numerical codes for each instruction. For example the bytecode for the above two instructions is

```
16 25
60
```

because 16 is the code for the bipush instruction and 60 is the code for istore_1. This explains the numbers to the left of the instructions, which are byte numbers. Starting with

Figure 12.20   Symbolic JVM instructions from `AssignIt.class`

```
Compiled from AssignIt.java
public class AssignIt extends java.lang.Object {
  public AssignIt();
  public static void main(java.lang.String[]);
}

Method AssignIt()
  0 aload_0
  1 invokespecial #6 <Method java.lang.Object()>
  4 return

Method void main(java.lang.String[])
  0 bipush 25
  2 istore_1
  3 bipush 12
  5 istore_2
  6 iload_1
  7 bipush 15
  9 iadd
  10 istore_2
  11 getstatic #7 <Field java.io.PrintStream out>
  14 ldc #1 <String "number2 is now ">
  16 invokevirtual #8 <Method void print(java.lang.String)>
  19 getstatic #7 <Field java.io.PrintStream out>
  22 iload_2
  23 invokevirtual #9 <Method void println(int)>
  26 return
```

the first instruction of the method at byte 0, we see that the second instruction will be at byte 2, and, because it is one byte in length, the third instruction will be at byte 3.

After completing the assignments to both variables, the code continues with

```
iload_1
bipush 15
iadd
istore_2
```

which loads variable 1 onto the stack, pushes 15, pops and add these two values, storing the result in variable 2.

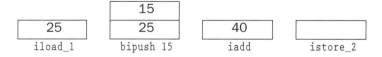

To understand the remaining instructions we need to discuss the constant pool, which contains numerical values, class names, field names, method names—the various names and values occurring in the Java source. We will look later carefully at the class file structure including the format of the constant pool table. For now we just need to know that the bytecode refers to each constant pool entry by a number. The next instruction

```
getstatic #7 <Field java.io.PrintStream out>
```

in bytecode, 178 0 7, pushes the reference to the static field, out, of the PrintStream class, onto the stack. The assembly listing conveniently includes the field name in a comment, but the actual bytecode just refers to entry number 7 in the constant pool table, which as we shall see, describes this field.

The next instruction

```
ldc #1 <String "number2 is now ">
```

loads the constant referred to in constant pool table entry 1. Because the constant, in this case, is a string, a reference to that string is pushed onto the stack. The ldc instruction could also push an integer or float value.

The next step is to execute the print method of the out object with the argument "number2 is now," which is the function of the

```
invokevirtual #8 <Method void print(java.lang.String)>
```

instruction. The name invokevirtual signifies that the method to be invoked is an instance method which may be overridden in subclasses. The JVM will find the correct version to invoke, referring in this case to constant pool table entry 8. Because there is no return value, it does not push a result on the stack, but it does pop the one argument and the method object reference.

Although our Java source only contains one method, the bytecode shows two. If we do not include a constructor for our AssignIt class, Java creates one for us. The code for AssignIt() is very simple. The JVM uses variable 0 to represent this, a reference to the object itself. The first instruction

```
aload_0
```

loads the object reference, this, onto the stack and uses the instruction

```
invokespecial #6 <Method java.lang.Object()>
```

to call the superclass constructor, Object(), referred to in the constant pool table entry 6. We use the invokespecial instruction to invoke constructors, private methods, and superclass methods.

Reading the Class File

We shall look carefully at the structure of the class file. In order to do that we need to be able to read it. Each operation code (opcode) uses one byte to hold an unsigned value from 0 to 255. Some instructions use additional bytes. We also need to read the constant pool table and the other parts of the class file. The Hex program below reads a byte file and outputs it in a form appropriate for a class file.

EXAMPLE 12.3   Hex.java

```java
/* Displays a class file
 */

import java.io.*;
public class Hex {
  public static void main(String[] args) {
    try {
      File f = new File(args[0]);
      FileInputStream fis = new FileInputStream(f);
      PrintWriter pw = new PrintWriter(System.out,true);
      int length = (int)f.length();
      for (int i=0; i<length; i++){
        int b = fis.read();
        if (i%28==0)
          pw.println();                                      // Note 1
        if ((b>=48 && b<=57) || (b>=65 && b<=90)
          || (b>=97 && b<=122) || b==40 || b==41 || b==47
          || b==60 || b==62 || b==91 || b==46 || b==59)      // Note 2
          pw.print((char)b);
        else
          pw.print(b + " ");                                 // Note 3
      }
      pw.println();
    } catch (IOException e){
      e.printStackTrace();
    }
  }
}
```

....

Output—`java Hex AssignIt.class` (Using Java 2 virtual machine)

```
202 254 186 190 0 3 0 45 0 33 8 0 29 7 0 19 7 0 25 7 0 26 7 0 27 10 0 4
0 10 9 0 5 0 11 10 0 3 0 12 10 0 3 0 13 12 0 18 0 14 12 0 30 0 23 12
0 31 0 16 12 0 32 0 15 1 0 3 ()V1 0 4 (I)V1 0 21 (Lj
ava/lang/String;)V1 0 22 ([Ljava
/lang/String;)V1 0 6 <init>1 0 8 A
ssignIt1 0 13 AssignIt.java1 0 4 Co
de1 0 15 LineNumberTable1 0 21 Ljava
/io/PrintStream;1 0 10 SourceFil
e1 0 19 java/io/PrintStream1 0 16 ja
va/lang/Object1 0 16 java/lang/S
ystem1 0 4 main1 0 15 number232 is32 no
w32 1 0 3 out1 0 5 print1 0 7 println0 33
0 2 0 4 0 0 0 0 2 0 1 0 18 0 14 0 1 0 21 0 0 0 29 0 1 0 1
0 0 0 5 42 183 0 6 177 0 0 0 1 0 22 0 0 0 6 0 1 0 0 0 1 0 9 0
28 0 17 0 1 0 21 0 0 0 G0 2 0 3 0 0 0 27 16 25 <16 12 61 27 16 15
96 61 178 0 7 18 1 182 0 8 178 0 7 28 182 0 9 177 0 0 0 1 0 22 0 0 0 26
0 6 0 0 0 3 0 3 0 4 0 6 0 5 0 11 0 6 0 19 0 7 0 26 0 2 0 1
0 24 0 0 2 0 20
```

Note 1: After displaying 28 bytes, we go to the next line. The number 28 is arbitrary.

Note 2: It would be very difficult to display each byte in the best format for a class file. Rather than displaying only numbers we show the bytes that are typically used as characters as letters and symbols rather than numbers. The numerical values in the conditions represent ASCII values. Thus 48 through 57 represent the digits 0 through 9, 65 through 90 the upper-case letters, 97 through 122 the lower-case letters, and 40, 41, 46, 47, 59, 60, 62, and 91 the symbols (,), ., /, ;, <, >, and [. Occasionally this is not the format we want. For example, in the fourth line from the bottom in the output, the letter G would be better written as the number 71, and the symbol < as the number 60.

Note 3: We display the remaining values as bytes. Occasionally this is not what we want. For example, the output "number232 is32 now32" is actually "number2 is now ," because 32 is the ASCII for the blank space. Leaving it as 32 lets us see the value 32 when it is really used as a number.

In order to see the structure of the class file we need to arrange the output more informatively. Figure 12.21 shows the output from Example 12.3 annotated to show the structure of `AssignIt.class`.

The boldface comments are the main sections of the class file, which starts with the four byte magic number, `0xCAFEBABE`, or `202 254 186 190` in decimal, identifying it as a class file. The minor version, 3, and the major version, 45 indicate the Java Virtual Machine specification version. The constant pool count, 33, gives the number of items in the constant pool, except that the first, item 0, is reserved and not used by the application. Thus the entries range from 1 through 32.

Before going further, let us explain the structure of the constant pool entries. Each entry start with a one-byte tag giving its type. These tags are

```
CONSTANT_Utf8                 1
CONSTANT_Integer              3
CONSTANT_Float                4
CONSTANT_Long                 5
CONSTANT_Double               6
CONSTANT_Class                7
CONSTANT_String               8
CONSTANT_Fieldref             9
CONSTANT_Methodref            10
CONSTANT_InterfaceMethodref   11
CONSTANT_NameAndType          12
```

The first type, `CONSTANT_Utf8`, handles strings. The Utf8 format (Utf stands for Unicode Text Format) writes Unicode strings in which most characters are ASCII in a compact way. ASCII characters use one byte so it would be wasteful to always use the full two-byte Unicode format for each character.

Using Utf8, the first two bytes give the length of a string s. We write each character in s using one, two, or three bytes. Characters from \u0001 through \u007f take

Figure 12.21 The annotated `AssignIt.class` file

```
202 254 186 190                    ; the magic number, 0xCAFEBABE
0 3                                ; minor version, 3
0 45                               ; major version, 45
0 33                               ; constant pool count, 33
                                   ; constant pool, entry 0 reserved so only 32 in pool
8 0 29                             ; 1. 8=String entry 29
7 0 19                             ; 2. 7=Class  entry 19
7 0 25                             ; 3. 7            25
7 0 26                             ; 4. 7            26
7 0 27                             ; 5. 7            27
10 0 4 0 10                        ; 6. 10=Methodref class=4 name_and_type=10
9 0 5 0 11                         ; 7. 9=Fieldref   class=5 name_and_type=11
10 0 3 0 12                        ; 8. 10          3           12
10 0 3 0 13                        ; 9. 10          3           13
12 0 18 0 14                       ; 10. 12=Name_and_type name=18 type=14
12 0 30 0 23                       ; 11. 12               30      23
12 0 31 0 16                       ; 12. 12               31      16
12 0 32 0 15                       ; 13. 12               32      15
1 0 3 ()V                          ; 14. 1=Utf8 length=3 method--no args returns void
1 0 4 (I)V                         ; 15. 1         4 int arg returns void
1 0 21 (Ljava/lang/String;)V       ; 16. 1        21 String arg returns void
1 0 22 ([Ljava/lang/String;)V      ; 17. 1        22 String array arg returns void
1 0 6 <init>                       ; 18. 1         6 Constructor
1 0 8 AssignIt                     ; 19. 1         8 class name (this class)
1 0 13 AssignIt.java               ; 20. 1        13
1 0 4 Code                         ; 21. 1         4
1 0 15 LineNumberTable             ; 22. 1        15
1 0 21 Ljava/io/PrintStream;       ; 23. 1        21 Class type
1 0 10 SourceFile                  ; 24. 1        10
1 0 19 java/io/PrintStream         ; 25. 1        19 class name
1 0 16 java/lang/Object            ; 26. 1        16 class name
1 0 16 java/lang/System            ; 27. 1        16 class name
1 0 4 main                         ; 28. 1         4
1 0 15 number2 is now              ; 29. 1        15 String
1 0 3 out                          ; 30. 1         3 field
1 0 5 print                        ; 31. 1         5 method
1 0 7 println                      ; 32. 1         7 method
0 33                               ; access flags, 33 1=public 32=super(compatibility)
0 2                                ; this class, 2 AssignIt
0 4                                ; super class, 4 Object
0 0                                ; interfaces count, 0
                                   ; interfaces, none in this example
0 0                                ; fields count, 0
                                   ; fields, none in this example
0 2                                ; methods count, 2
                                   ; first method
0 1                                ; access flags, 1 public
0 18                               ; name index, 18 <init>( AssignIt() generated for us)
0 14                               ; type index, 14
0 1                                ; attributes count, 1
                                   ; first attribute
0 21                               ; first attribute name, 21 Code
0 0 0 29                           ; attribute length, 29
0 1                                ; max stack, 1
0 1                                ; max locals, 1
```

(Figure continues)

Figure 12.21   The annotated `AssignIt.class` file (Continued)

```
0 0 0 5              ; code length = 5
42                   ; aload_0
183 0 6              ; invokespecial #6
177                  ; return
0 0                  ; handlers_count, 0
                     ; handlers
0 1                  ; code attributes count, 1
                     ; code attributes
0 22                 ; attribute name index, 22 LineNumberTable
0 0 0 6              ; bytes_count, 6
0 1                  ; lines_count,1
0 0 0 1              ; start_pc bytecode 0, line_number source 1

                     ; second method
0 9                  ; access_flags, 9 1=public, 8=static
0 28                 ; name index, 28 main
0 17                 ; type index, 17
0 1                  ; attributes_ count, 1
                     ; first attribute
0 21                 ; attribute name, 21 Code
0 0 0 G              ; attribute length, 71
0 2                  ; max stack = 2
0 3                  ; max locals = 3
0 0 0 27             ; code length = 27
16 25                ; bipush 25
<                    ; istore_1 (< is 60)
16 12                ; bipush 12
61                   ; istore_2
27                   ; iload_1
16 15                ; bipush 15
96                   ; iadd
61                   ; istore_2
178 0 7              ; getstatic #7
18 1                 ; ldc 1
182 0 8              ; invokevirtual #8
178 0 7              ; getstatic #7
28                   ; iload_2
182 0 9              ; invokevirtual #9
177                  ; return
0 0                  ; handlers_count
                     ; handlers
0 1                  ; code attribute count = 1
                     ; code attributes
0 22                 ; attribute name index, 22 LineNumberTable
0 0 0 26             ; bytes_count, 26
0 6                  ; lines_count, 6
0 0 0 3              ; start_pc 0 line_number 3
0 3 0 4              ;              3              4
0 6 0 5              ;              6              5
0 11 0 6             ;             11              6
0 19 0 7             ;             19              7
0 26 0 2             ;             26              2
0 1                  ; attributes_count, 1
                     ; attributes
0 24                 ; attribute_name_index, 24, Source File
0 0 0 2              ; bytes_count, 2
0 20                 ; source_file_index, 20, AssignIt.java
```

one byte, so \u0063 would be 01100011. Characters from \u0080 through \u07ff take two bytes, with 110 starting the first byte and 10 starting the second byte, so \u06ab would be 11011010 10101011. Characters from \u0800 through \uffff take three bytes, with a 1110 starting the first byte and 10 starting the second and third bytes, so \u749c would be **11100111 10010010 10011100**.

Because we use only ASCII characters in AssignIt, no multibyte characters will appear in the class file, but the format handles them when they occur. Entries 14 through 32 use the Utf8 format. Other entries in the class file refer to these strings by their constant pool table numbers.

Some of these Utf8 constant pool entries describe types of fields, local variables, method arguments or return values using a special format, using a single letter for primitive type names

```
B    byte
C    char
D    double
F    float
I    int
J    long
S    short
Z    boolean.
```

The letter L precedes an object type, the semicolon, ;, follows an object type, the left bracket, [, precedes an array type (one for each dimension), V represents **void**, and parentheses, (), represent a method. Thus (I)V represents a method with an **int** argument which returns **void**, while ([Ljava/lang/String;)V denotes a method with an array of String argument which returns **void**.

In our AssignIt example, we do not have tags 3, 4, 5, or 6. The four-byte values follow Integer and Float tags, while eight-byte values follow Long and Double tags.

Constant pool table entries 2-5 have tag 7 representing a class. The next two bytes give the entry in the constant pool table containing the name of the class. For example, item 3 contains the value 25 that refers to constant pool entry 25, java/io/PrintStream, the name of the PrintStream class.

Entry 1 has tag 8, denoting a String. In this case it refers to entry 29 containing the string "number2 is now ".

Entry 7 has tag 9, denoting a field reference. The next two bytes specify entry 5 that refers to the class name, java/lang/System. The last two bytes of this entry specify entry 11 that is a NameAndType entry with tag 12.

NameAndType entries follow the tag byte with two bytes for the index of the name entry in the constant pool and another two bytes for the index of the type entry in the constant pool. Entry 11, 12 0 30 0 23, specifies entry 30 as the name of the field, out, and entry 23 as its type, Ljava/io/PrintStream;. In all, entry 7 describes the out field of the PrintStream class.

Entries 6, 8, and 9 are method references. Like field references, they follow the tag with two bytes for the index of the class name entry and two bytes for the index of the type entry. For example entry 6, 10 0 4 0 10, specifies the class in entry 4 as entry 26, java/lang/Object, and the name and type as entry 10 which itself refers to entry 18, ⟨init⟩, for the name, and entry 14, ()V, for the type. The name ⟨init⟩ signifies the constructor of the class, while ()V signifies a method with no arguments which returns **void**. In all, entry 6 describes the default constructor for the Object class.

The item in the class file after the constant pool table is the access_flags entry which sets certain bits to indicate the mode of access for the class. In this example, the value 33 = 1 + 32 includes the value 1 to indicate public access. All JVM's except the earliest include 32 to signify the newer semantics of the invokespecial instruction.

The this_class entry gives the constant pool index of the class name, while the super_class entry gives the constant pool index of its super class. The next two bytes count the number of interfaces. Any interfaces would occur here. The next entry counts the fields of the class, and any fields would follow. After the fields, if any, comes the method count, followed by a method table for each method. In the listing, we italicize the main categories of each method table.

The first method has access_flags set to 1 indicating public access. The name index refers to entry 18, ⟨init⟩, while the type index refers to entry 14, ()V. The next two bytes specify attributes_count, the number of attributes for the method. Two supported attributes are Exceptions and Code.

In this example we have a Code attribute. Its first two bytes give the attribute name index to the constant pool entry for the name Code. The next four bytes give the length of this attribute, 29 in this example, starting from the next byte after the count. The two bytes for max_stack give the maximum number of items placed on the stack by this method. The max_locals value tells the number of local variables this method uses. The bytecode for the method follows the two-byte handlers_count value. The handlers_count value indicates the number of exception handlers for this method, and a table describing each would follow. The Code attribute can have attributes, including LineNumberTable and LocalVariableTable.

The attribute_count value for the Code is 1. The Code attribute has four parts, the attribute_name_index giving its name, constant pool entry 22 for LineNumberTable, which will correspond source code line numbers to bytecode. The next four bytes give the bytes_count for the rest of the attribute. The two-byte lines_count specifies the number of entries in the line number table table. Finally, each line in the table uses four bytes, two to give start_pc, and two to give line_number. start_pc is the index in the bytecode corresponding to the source code line whose number is line_number.

The class as a whole may have attributes. After the entries for the two methods, the final part of AssignIt.class contains the two-byte attributes_count of 1. The attribute_name_index shows constant pool entry 24, SourceFile. The four-byte bytes_count gives 2 for the size of the remaining attribute entry, which is source_file_index 20 to the constant pool, AssignIt.java.

We have not covered every facet of the class file structure. The AssignIt example illustrate some of the virtual machine instructions. Example 12.4 includes a loop, and uses an array.

EXAMPLE 12.4   **ReverseArray.java**

```java
/* Reverses an array. Used to study a
 * class file with loops and an array.
 */

public class ReverseArray {
  public static void main(String [] args) {
    int [] score = {56, 91, 22, 87, 49, 89, 65};
    int temp;                         // used to store a value during a swap
    int left = 0;                     // index of the left element to swap
    int right = score.length -1;      // index of the right element to swap

    while (left < right) {
      temp          = score[left];
      score[left]   = score[right];
      score[right]  = temp;
      right--;
      left++;
    }
    System.out.print("{");
    for (int i=0; i<score.length; i++) {
      if (i!=0) System.out.print(",");
      System.out.print(score[i]);
    }
    System.out.println("}");
  }
}
```

Disassembling ReverseArray.class using

`javap -c ReverseArray`

produces Figure 12.22

Figure 12.22   **JVM instructions for** ReverseArray.java

```
Compiled from ReverseArray.java
public class ReverseArray extends java.lang.Object {
public ReverseArray();
public static void main(java.lang.String[]);
}

Method ReverseArray()
0 aload_0
1 invokespecial #8 <Method java.lang.Object()>
4 return
```

Figure 12.22   JVM instructions for `ReverseArray.java` **(Continued)**

```
Method void main(java.lang.String[])
0 bipush 7
2 newarray int
4 dup
5 iconst_0
6 bipush 56
8 iastore
9 dup
10 iconst_1
11 bipush 91
13 iastore
14 dup
15 iconst_2
16 bipush 22
18 iastore
19 dup
20 iconst_3
21 bipush 87
23 iastore
24 dup
25 iconst_4
26 bipush 49
28 iastore
29 dup
30 iconst_5
31 bipush 89
33 iastore
34 dup
35 bipush 6
37 bipush 65
39 iastore
40 astore_1
41 iconst_0
42 istore_3
43 aload_1
44 arraylength
45 iconst_1
46 isub
47 istore 4
49 goto 74
52 aload_1
53 iload_3
54 iaload
55 istore_2
56 aload_1
57 iload_3
58 aload_1
59 iload 4
61 iaload
62 iastore
63 aload_1
64 iload 4
66 iload_2
67 iastore
68 iinc 4 -1
71 iinc 3 1
74 iload_3
75 iload 4
77 if_icmplt 52
```

(Figure Continues)

Figure 12.22 JVM instructions for `ReverseArray.java` (Continued)

```
80 getstatic #9 <Field java.io.PrintStream out>
83 ldc #2 <String "{">
85 invokevirtual #11 <Method void print(java.lang.String)>
88 iconst_0
89 istore 5
91 goto 120
94 iload 5
96 ifeq 107
99 getstatic #9 <Field java.io.PrintStream out>
102 ldc #1 <String ",">
104 invokevirtual #11 <Method void print(java.lang.String)>
107 getstatic #9 <Field java.io.PrintStream out>
110 aload_1
111 iload 5
113 iaload
114 invokevirtual #10 <Method void print(int)>
117 iinc 5 1
120 iload 5
122 aload_1
123 arraylength
124 if_icmplt 94
127 getstatic #9 <Field java.io.PrintStream out>
130 ldc #3 <String "]">
132 invokevirtual #12 <Method void println(java.lang.String)>
135 return
```

Figure 12.23 shows the class file produced by

`java Hex ReverseArray.class`

Figure 12.23 `ReverseArray.class`

```
202 254 186 190 0 3 0 45 0 39 8 0 22 8 0 37 8 0 38 7 0 27 7 0 30 7 0 31
7 0 32 10 0 6 0 13 9 0 7 0 14 10 0 5 0 15 10 0 5 0 16 10 0 5 0 17
12 0 23 0 18 12 0 34 0 26 12 0 35 0 19 12 0 35 0 20 12 0 36 0 20 1 0 3
()V1 0 4 (I)V1 0 21 (Ljava/lang/Str
ing;)V1 0 22 ([Ljava/lang/String
;)V1 0 1 44 1 0 6 <init>1 0 4 Code1 0 15 Li
neNumberTable1 0 21 Ljava/io/Pri
ntStream;1 0 12 ReverseArray1 0 17 R
everseArray.java1 0 10 SourceFil
e1 0 19 java/io/PrintStream1 0 16 ja
va/lang/Object1 0 16 java/lang/S
ystem1 0 4 main1 0 3 out1 0 5 print1 0
7 println1 0 1 123 1 0 1 125 0 33 0 4 0 6 0 0 0 0 2
0 1 0 23 0 18 0 1 0 24 0 0 0 29 0 1 0 1 0 0 0 5 42 183 0 8 177 0
0 0 1 0 25 0 0 0 6 0 1 0 0 0 8 0 9 0 33 0 21 0 1 0 24 0 0 0
224 0 4 0 6 0 0 0 136 16 7 188 10 Y3 16 80Y4 16 [OY5 16 22 0
Y6 16 WOY7 16 1OY8 16 YOYO16 6 16 A0L3 >43 190 4 d
64 167 0 25 43 29 .61 43 29 43 21 4 .043 21 4 28 0132 4 255 132 3 1 29
21 4 161 255 231 178 0 9 18 2 182 0 11 3 65 167 0 29 21 5 153 0 11 178 0 9 18
1 182 0 11 178 0 9 43 21 5 .182 0 10 132 5 1 21 5 43 190 161 255 226 178 0 9 18
3 182 0 12 177 0 0 1 0 25 0 0 0 F0 17 0 0 0 10 0 )0 12 0 43 0
13 0 10 15 0 40 16 0 80 17 0 63 0 18 0 D0 19 0 G0 20 0 J0
15 0 P0 22 0 X0 23 0 94 0 24 0 k0 25 0 u0 23 0 127 0 27 0 135 0
9 0 1 0 29 0 0 0 2 0 28
```

We leave it as an exercise to annotate this class file.

THE BIG PICTURE
The javap utility lets us disassemble a class file into symbolic bytecode, showing the JVM instructions used to implement the Java source (or source from another language). The class file contains all the information need to execute the bytecode. The main sections of the class file are the magic number, minor version, constant pool count, constant pool, access flags, this class, super class, interfaces count, interfaces, fields count, fields, methods count, first method, second method, etc., attributes count, and attributes. Some of these sections have substructures.

TEST YOUR UNDERSTANDING

12. Annotate the class file, `ReverseArray.class`, shown in Figure 12.23, and available in the file `ra.byte` on the disk included with this text. The output should appear like that of Figure 12.21.

13. The instructions in Figure 12.20, produced by the `javap` disassembler, are in symbolic form. Rewrite them using numerical bytes only.

14. In Figure 12.20, what does the "#7" represent in the instruction `getstatic   #7`?

15. In Figure 12.21, trace through all the constant pool entries that occur when starting from the line

    ```
    182 0 9 ;invokevirtual #9
    ```

16. In Figure 12.21, trace through all the constant pool entries that occur when starting from the line

    ```
    178 0 7 ;getstatic #7
    ```

SUMMARY

- Java enforces security to ensure that code runs safely. The Java Virtual Machine verifies bytecode before execution. Browsers and applet viewers implement security managers that restrict access to local resources. Using the Java Plug-in allows a client to use the latest JVM, and its security manager in place of those provided by the browser. Java uses a number of system properties and can restrict access to these properties.

- When using a security manager, code that accesses local resources, such as a file constructor, calls security manager methods to check whether access is permitted, and throws an exception if it is not. Standalone programs do not use a security manager by default, but can by specifying the `java.security.manager` property on the command line.

- A policy file grants permissions. Each permission represents a Java class, such as `java.io.FilePermission`. A permission entry list the target of the permission, the file `out`, for example, and the specific permission being granted. To use a policy file, we can set the `java.security.policy` property on the command line to have the policy file as its value. Including a codebase value limits the permission to files at that location.

- We can use digital signature to authenticate programs we send to others. We sign the file with our private key and the receiver uses our public key to check that the file has not been corrupted. The receiver must trust that our public key is correct. A trusted signing authority can provide our public key with a certificate to authenticate the public key.

- Java provides the keytool utility to generate keys and the jarsigner utility to create digital signatures. We place the file to be signed in a JAR file before using `jarsigner`. The receiver can grant permissions in a policy file that would only apply to files with a particular trusted signature.

- The Java Virtual Machine verifies code before execution. It is an abstract computer with an instruction set for a stack machine. Each opcode is one byte and may have additional arguments. Local variables use numbers 0, 1, 2, ... Variable 0 represents `this` for instance methods. JVM instructions load constants and variable value onto the stack. Special instruction load small constants, values of low-numbered local variables, and array elements . Another set of instructions stores a stack value in a local variable or in an array element.

- The JVM includes instructions for stack manipulation, arithmetic and bitwise operations, and type conversions. Other instructions manage control flow, invoke methods, create objects and arrays and enter and exit a monitor.

- Using a disassembler, we can see the JVM instructions in a class file. Much of the class file consists of a constant table and other information needed to execute these instructions.

Program Design Exercises

1. Write an applet with a text field to enter the name of a system property. Display a message in the applet indicating whether or not the default security manager permits access to that property.

2. Write an HTML file to run the applet of Exercise 1. Use the `HTMLConverter` program from `http://java.sun.com/` to convert the file to use the Java Plug-in. Compare the output from the Java Plug-in to that obtained when running the applet in a browser using the original HTML page.

3. Write a Java applet that attempts to write the names entered in a text field to a file `Names.txt` on the local machine. Check the result using a browser or an applet viewer. Write a policy file to grant permission to write to this file and rerun the applet to use it.

4. Convert the applet of Exercise 3 to a standalone application and run it with a security manager, and the policy file which allows writing to Names.txt.

5. Change the policy file of Exercise 3 to only permit writes for programs in the directory TestWriter. Compare the results of running the applet of Exercise 3, using this policy file, when the applet is in the TestWriter directory and when it is in another directory.

6. Sign the applet of Exercise 3. Export the certificate. Acting as the receiver of the signed applet and the certificate, import the certificate and grant permission to this signature to write to the file Names.txt. Try the applet using the policy file to grant permission.

7. Write a Java program to average three numbers input in a text field. Compile and use the Hex program of Example 12.3 to display the class. Annotate the display, showing the structure of the class file.

13 XML

Introduction
. . . .

Web pages use HTML to indicate formatting to a browser. The web has become very popular in part because HTML is relatively simple and easy to use. But HTML focuses on presentation making it hard to determine the information on a page. XML (Extensible Markup Language) lets us devise our own tags to reflect the information content. We can pass these standard XML files among various applications to transfer information from one program to another. Java makes programs platform independent and XML makes data platform independent.

OBJECTIVES:
- Learn XML syntax.
- Use a DTD (Document Type Definition) to specify a valid XML type.
- Try a SAX (Simple API for XML) parser for processing XML files.
- Try DOM (Document Object Model) for processing XML files.
- Use XSLT to transform XML to other representations.
- Make SOAP XML remote procedure call requests.

13.1 XML and Information

We first illustrate the limitations of HTML for representing content and then introduce XML.

The Limitations of HTML

With HTML we can easily format data for display, but the content is not easy to retrieve. Figure 13.1 shows the web page displayed by the Internet Explorer browser given the HTML file of Figure 13.2.

Figure 13.1   Listing the author's books

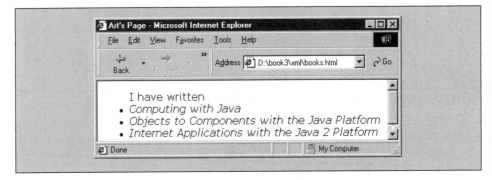

Figure 13.2   The `author.html` file for the web page of Figure 13.1

```
<html>
<title>Art's Page</title>
<ul>I have written
  <li> <em>Computing with Java</em>
  <li> <em>Objects to Components with the Java Platform</em>
  <li> <em>Internet Applications with the Java 2 Platform</em>
</html>
```

Most of the tags in Figure 13.2 refer to the display of the file. `<ul>` indicates and unordered list, while `<li>` specifies a list item. A human reader might deduce quickly that a person name Art is listing books he has written, but the word "books" is never used. A program processing this file would find it very difficult to determine its content.

Moreover browsers accept many variations in HTML syntax. In Figure 13.2 the end tag `</ul>` for the unordered list does not appear, and none of the list items have end tags `</li>`. We could have omitted the `<html>` and `</html>` tags. Permitting such variations in syntax makes it hard for programs to extract information from HTML files.

XML Syntax[*]

We can define our own XML tags to indicate the content. For example we might rewrite (and expand) the HTML file of Figure 13.2 as the XML file of Figure 13.3.

Figure 13.3 The author.xml file

```
<?xml version="1.0"?>
<!-- Books written by an author -->
<author>
  <name>
    <first> Art </first>
    <last> Gittleman </last>
  </name>
  <age> 39+   </age>
  <books>
    <book type="text">
      <title full="false">Computing with Java</title>
      <edition> second </edition>
      <copyright> 1998, 2001 </copyright>
      <isbn> 1-57676-023-5 </isbn>
    </book>
    <book type="text">
      <title>Objects to Components with the Java Platform</title>
      <edition> first </edition>
      <copyright> 2000 </copyright>
      <isbn> 1-57676-035-9 </isbn>
    </book>
    <book type="text">
      <title>Internet Applications with the Java 2 Platform</title>
      <edition> first </edition>
      <copyright> 2001 </copyright>
      <isbn> 1-57676-052-9 </isbn>
    </book>
  </books>
</author>
```

Notice that the author.xml file of Figure 13.3 has content tags such as <author> and <book>, rather than formatting tags such as <li> and <em>. The human reader finds it easy to read, and understandable. More importantly, programs can easily find relevant information such as the copyright date or the ISBN number.

Each XML file starts with an optional prolog, which in Figure 13 is

```
<?xml version="1.0"?>
```

XML comments use the same HTML syntax, as in

```
<!-- Comments go here. -->
```

---

[*] See http://www.w3.org/XML for the XML specification.

Tags may have attributes. For example the `<book>` tag in Figure 13.3 has the `type` attribute with value "text." Attributes may be optional. For example, the `<title>` tag has a `full` attribute that appears in one title, but not in others.

In order for programs to easily process XML the syntax rules are precise.

- Each tag must have an end tag.

  For example, the `<book>` tag must have a `</book>` tag to mark the end of the `<book>` element. We place the content between the start and the end tags. A tag may be empty, meaning it has no content. For example in Figure 13.3 we might have use a `<softcover>` tag to indicate that a book has a soft cover. The correct form would be

  `<softcover></softcover>`

  which may be abbreviated as

  `<softcover/>`

- Tags must be nested.

  For example, If the start tag `<title>` occurs between `<book>` and `</book>` then its end tag `</title>` must occur before `</book>`.
  Correct: `<book>` … `<title>` … `</title>` … `</book>`
  Incorrect: `<book>` … `<title>` … `</book>` … `</title>`

- Attribute values must be enclosed in quotes.
  Correct: `type = "text"`
  Incorrect `type = text`

A Document Type Definition

A well-formed XML document uses correct XML syntax. A document that had an `<author>` tag without an `</author>` tag would not be well-formed. However a well-formed document may not make sense. For example the fragment

```
<name>
  <first> George </first>
  <first> John </first>
  <first> Mary </first>
</name>
```

uses correct syntax, but does not look appropriate. A name has three `first` entries and no `last`.

We can use a Document Type Definition (DTD) to specify the form of a valid type of XML document. A DTD specifies a markup language. Various groups are developing standard markup languages for specialized applications. Examples include Synchronized Multimedia Integration Language (SMIL), Mathematical Markup Language (MathML), and Scalable Vector Graphics (SVG). Figure 13.4 shows a DTD for the author type.

Figure 13.4 The `author.dtd` DTD

```
<!ELEMENT author (name, age?, books)>
<!ELEMENT name (first, last)>
<!ELEMENT first (#PCDATA)>
<!ELEMENT last (#PCDATA)>
<!ELEMENT age (#PCDATA)>
<!ELEMENT books (book+)>
<!ELEMENT book (title, edition?, copyright?, isbn?)>
<!ATTLIST book
   type (text|trade) "text">
<!ELEMENT title (#PCDATA)>
<!ATTLIST title
   full (true|false) "true">
<!ELEMENT edition (#PCDATA)>
<!ELEMENT copyright (#PCDATA)>
<!ELEMENT isbn (#PCDATA)>
```

Before we look at the DTD syntax, we show the tree structure of the author type in Figure 13.5. Because XML tags must nest, we can always diagram XML document structure in tree form.

Figure 13.5 The tree structure of the author document type

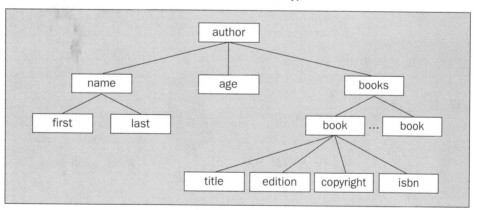

The `ELEMENT` declaration defines the structure of a tag. The `author` type defines the `author`, `name`, `first`, `last`, `age`, `books`, `book`, `title`, `edition`, `copyright`, and `isbn` tags. A tag may have nested tags, which we list, separated by commas, between parentheses. The following symbols may be used

Symbol	Meaning
?	Zero or one occurrence
*	Zero or more occurrences
+	One or more occurrences

The declaration

```
<!ELEMENT name (first, last)>
```

states that the name tag contains a first tag followed by a last tag. The declaration

```
<!ELEMENT author (name, age?, books)>
```

states that the author tag contains a name tag followed optionally by an age tag and then a books tag. The declaration

```
<!ELEMENT books (book+)>
```

states that the books tag contains one or more book tags.

Some tags do not use any of the other tags of the author type. For example,

```
<!ELEMENT first (#PCDATA)>
```

states that the first tag consists of character data.

We used enumerations for the attribute values in the DTD of Figure 13.4. The declaration

```
<!ATTLIST book type (text|trade) "text">
```

specifies an attribute for the book element. We could specify more than one in the same declaration. The attribute name is type and its values must be chosen from text or trade. The default is text. We could have used the declaration

```
<!ATTLIST book type CDATA "text">
```

which states that the attribute values are character data and the default is text, but that would allow any value for the attribute, rather than just text or trade.

Valid Documents

A valid XML documents follows the rules given in its DTD. A document can be well-formed without being valid. For example, the fragment

```
<name>
  <first> George </first>
  <first> John </first>
  <first> Mary </first>
</name>
```

is not valid. The rule for <name> specifies a single <first> followed by a single <last>.

We now turn to the processing of XML documents.

THE BIG PICTURE

XML allows us to define a language to represent data. We define tags and their structure. Well-formed XML follows precise rules to make it easier to transfer XML documents between programs. A DTD defines the language so that we can determine is an XML document is valid, in that it follows the rules of that language.

TEST YOUR UNDERSTANDING

1. Which of the following are well-formed XML documents?

   a. ```
       <author>
         <name>
           <first> Art </first>
           <last> Gittleman </last>
         </name>
       </author>
       ```

   b.  ```
       <author>
         <name/>
           <first> Art </first>
           <last> Gittleman </last>
       </author>
       ```

   c. `<author/>`

2. Which of the following are valid XML documents with respect to the DTD of Figure 13.4?

   a. ```
       <author>
         <name>
           <first> Art </first>
           <last> Gittleman </last>
         </name>
         <books>
           <book>
             <title>Objects to Components with the Java
                    Platform
             </title>
           </book>
         </books>
       </author>
       ```

   b.  ```
       <author>
         <name>
           <last> Gittleman </last>
         </name>
         <age> 39++ </age>
         <books>
           <book>
             <title>Objects to Components with the
                    Java Platform</title>
           </book>
         </books>
       </author>
       ```

3. Write an XML document for a record collection.

4. Write a DTD to define the type used in Exercise 3.

13.2   SAX Processing

. . . .

SAX, Simple API for XML, lets us parse an XML document using an event model. As the parser finds various portions of the document it calls specific methods. In comparison with DOM, which we will study in the next section, it is more efficient because it does not build a memory representation of the document. However, it traverses the document sequentially, not providing random access to elements. The user may have to store earlier results to use when accessing later parts of the document, which can make programming more cumbersome than with DOM.

The `ContentHandler` interface contains the methods that a SAX parser calls as it parses an XML document. The ones we use are

Method name	Description
`startDocument`	signals the start of the document
`endDocument`	signals the end of the document
`startElement`	signals the start of a tag
`endElement`	signals the end of a tag
`characters`	signals the occurrence of text

To avoid having to implement all of the `ContentHandler` methods, we will extend the `DefaultHandler` adapter that implements the `ContentHandler` methods with empty bodies. We only need to override the five methods we use.

Using a SAX Parser

A parser can be validating or non-validating. A non-validating parser checks for well-formed XML, but not for valid XML. It does not need a DTD. A validating parser uses the DTD to determine whether or not the document follows the rules the DTD specifies. Of course, it also checks that the document is well-formed.

For simplicity we shorten the `author.xml` file of Figure 13.3 to `authorSimple.xml` shown in Figure 13.6. The ⟨name⟩ element adds a ⟨gender⟩ attribute to show attribute processing.

Figure 13.6   `authorSimple.xml`

```
<?xml version="1.0"?>
<!-- An author -->
<author>
  <name  gender = "male">
    <first> Art </first>
    <last> Gittleman </last>
  </name>
</author>
```

Example 13.1 will use the SAX parser to identify the parts of an XML file. Later we will use that information in more complex applications. We will allow the user to choose whether to use a validating parser. We use the parser provided by Sun, in the JAXP1.1 release. This release supports SAX 2.0, which adds to SAX 1.0 to allow the use of namespaces.* Java deprecated some of the earlier API so we will use the newer version even though we are not using namespaces.

Because authorSimple.xml does not use a DTD, we will test it with a non-validating parser. When compiling, we must include the XML and parser classes in the classpath. We use the command

```
javac  -classpath
.;%JAXP_HOME%\jaxp.jar;%JAXP_HOME%\crimson.jar  Sax.java
```

to compile, and

```
java  -classpath
.;%JAXP_HOME%\jaxp.jar;%JAXP_HOME%\crimson.jar
Sax authorSimple.xml false
```

to run where the JAXP_HOME is the JAXP installation directory. The argument false selects a non-validating parser. Figure 13.7 shows the result.

Figure 13.7   The output from Example 13.1 on a well-formed XML file

```
Start d:\book3\xml\authorSimple.xml
    Start element author
        Start element name
            Attributes gender male
            Start element first
                Art
            End element first
            Start element last
                Gittleman
            End element last
        End element name
    End element author
End d:\book3\xml\authorSimple.xml
```

To show how the parser checks for a well-formed document, we omit the end tag </first> in the authorSimple.xml file of Figure 13.6 to form the authorSimpleError.xml file. Figure 13.8 shows the result of parsing this file.

EXAMPLE 13.1   **Sax.java**

```
/* Uses a SAX parser to identify the parts of an XML
 * file. The user specifies whether to use a validating parser.
 */
```

---

* See http://www.megginson.com/SAX/index.html for SAX information including the changes from the 1.0 to the 2.0 versions.

Figure 13.8 The output from Example 13.1 on `authorSimpleError.xml`

```
Start d:\book3\xml\authorSimpleError.xml
   Start element author
      Start element name
         Attributes gender male
         Start element first
            Art
            Start element last
               Gittleman
            End element last
org.xml.sax.SAXParseException: Expected "</first>" to terminate element
starting on line 5.
    at org.apache.crimson.parser.Parser2.fatal(Parser2.java:3030)
    at org.apache.crimson.parser.Parser2.fatal(Parser2.java:3024)
    at org.apache.crimson.parser.Parser2.maybeElement(Parser2.java:1467)
    at org.apache.crimson.parser.Parser2.content(Parser2.java:1695)
    at org.apache.crimson.parser.Parser2.maybeElement(Parser2.java:1461)
    at org.apache.crimson.parser.Parser2.content(Parser2.java:1695)
    at org.apache.crimson.parser.Parser2.maybeElement(Parser2.java:1461)
    at org.apache.crimson.parser.Parser2.parseInternal(Parser2.java:499)
    at org.apache.crimson.parser.Parser2.parse(Parser2.java:304)
    at org.apache.crimson.parser.XMLReaderImpl.parse
                                    (XMLReaderImpl.java:433)

    at Sax.main(Sax.java:52)
```

```java
import org.xml.sax.Attributes;                              // Note 1
import org.xml.sax.helpers.DefaultHandler;
import org.xml.sax.XMLReader;
import javax.xml.parsers.SAXParserFactory;
import javax.xml.parsers.SAXParser;
import org.xml.sax.InputSource;
import java.io.FileReader;

public class Sax extends DefaultHandler {
  private int level = 0;                                    // Note 2
  private String spaces = "               ";               // Note 3
  private String docName;

  public void characters(char[] ch, int start, int length){ // Note 4
    String s = new String(ch,start,length);
    s = s.trim();                                           // Note 5
    if (!s.equals(""))
      System.out.println
          (spaces.substring(0,level*3+2) + s);              // Note 6
  }
  public void endDocument() {
    System.out.println("End " + docName);
  }
  public void endElement
      (String uri, String localName, String qName) {        // Note 7
```

```
      System.out.print(spaces.substring(0,level*3));
      level--;
      System.out.println("End element " + localName);
    }
    public void startDocument() {
      System.out.println("Start " + docName);
    }
    public void startElement(String uri, String localName,
                  String qName, Attributes attributes){          // Note 8
      level++;
      System.out.print(spaces.substring(0,level*3));
      System.out.println("Start element " + localName);
      for (int i = 0; i < attributes.getLength(); i++)
        System.out.println(spaces.substring(0,level*3+1)
            + " Attributes " + attributes.getLocalName(i)
            + ' ' + attributes.getValue(i));
    }
    public static void main(String[] args) {
      Sax sax = new Sax();
      sax.docName = args[0];                                     // Note 9
      try {
        SAXParserFactory factory
                = SAXParserFactory.newInstance();                // Note 10
        boolean validate =
                args[1].equals("true")?true:false;               // Note 11
        factory.setValidating(validate);                         // Note 12
        SAXParser parser = factory.newSAXParser();               // Note 13
        XMLReader reader = parser.getXMLReader();                // Note 14
        reader.setContentHandler(sax);                           // Note 15
        reader.parse
                (new InputSource(new FileReader(args[0])));       // Note 16
      }catch (Exception e) {
        e.printStackTrace();
      }
    }
}
```

Output

See Figures 13.7 and 13.8

Note 1:   We use XML related classes from the packages org.xml.sax,
org.xml.sax.helpers, and javax.xml.parsers. We list each class by name to
indicate where each is found.

Note 2:   level represents the level of nesting of tags. We use it to display nicely.

Note 3:   We prefix output with substrings of this string of blanks. We choose the
length of the substring so that the display is indented according to its level
of nesting.

Note 4: The parser calls the `characters` method when it encounters text. We display text that is not whitespace.

Note 5: The `trim` method removes whitespace from either end of the string.

Note 6: `System.out.println`
            `(spaces.substring(0,level*3+2) + s);`
Because we indent the tag by three spaces for each level of nesting, we indent the text by an additional two spaces. The prefix string of blanks has `level*3 + 2` characters.

Note 7 : `public void endElement`
            `(String uri, String localName, String qName) {`
We display a message, indented according to the nesting level. We do not use the first or third arguments. The first gives the Uniform Resource Identifier for the namespace, and the third gives the fully qualified element name relative to that namespace. We only need to use the local name which is the name of the tag. The purpose of namespaces is to keep tag names localized so that they do not conflict with those in other documents.

Note 8: `public void startElement(String uri, String`
            `localName, String qName, Attributes attributes){`
We display the tag, indented according to its level, and then any attributes, indented just under the corresponding tag. The `Attributes` class has methods `getLocalName` and `getValue` to get the name and value of each attribute.

Note 9: `sax.docName = args[0];`
We save the file name of the document to use in the display.

Note 10: `SAXParserFactory factory =`
            `SAXParserFactory.newInstance();`
A parser factory hides the names of the concrete parser classes. We set the desired parser properties in the factory and ask it to produce an appropriate parser.

Note 11: `boolean validate = args[1].equals("true")?true:false;`
The second command line argument, `args[1]` indicates whether to use a validating parser. We use the conditional expression to set a `boolean` flag. Its form is

            `condition ? true-part : false-part`

The value of the expression is `true-part` if the condition is true and `false-part` otherwise.

Note 12: `factory.setValidating(validate);`
We specify validating or non-validating according to the user's choice.

Note 13: `SAXParser parser = factory.newSAXParser();`
`SAXParser` is an abstract class. The factory returns a concrete implementation with the specified properties.

Note 14: `XMLReader reader = parser.getXMLReader();`
XMLReader is an interface for reading an XML document using callbacks as we are doing in this example.

Note 15: `reader.setContentHandler(sax);`
We must pass an argument that implements the ContentHandler interface. Sax extends DefaultHandler which implements ContentHandler. The set-ContentHandler method registers the content handler with the reader.

Note 16: `reader.parse (new InputSource(new FileReader(args[0])));`
The InputSource encapsulates information about the XML source. The reader will accept a character stream or bytes or a URI. A URI (Uniform Resource Identifier) is a name or address used to identify a resource. One example is a URL.

Using a Validating Parser

A validating parser checks that an XML document satisfies the rules in the DTD. Figure 13.9 shows a DTD that we will use with authorSimple.xml of Figure 13.6. The #REQUIRED field indicates that the gender attribute is required.

Figure 13.9 A simple DTD for ⟨author⟩

```
<!ELEMENT author (name)>
<!ELEMENT name (first, last)>
<!ATTLIST name
   gender (male|female) #REQUIRED>
<!ELEMENT first (#PCDATA)>
<!ELEMENT last (#PCDATA)>
```

We can use this DTD either internally, in the same file as the XML document, or externally. Figure 13.10 shows the DTD internal to the XML file.

Figure 13.10 authorSimpleInternal.xml

```
<?xml version="1.0"?>
<!-- An author -->
<!DOCTYPE author [
<!ELEMENT author (name)>
<!ELEMENT name (first, last)>
<!ATTLIST name
   gender (male|female) #REQUIRED>
<!ELEMENT first (#PCDATA)>
<!ELEMENT last (#PCDATA)>
]>
<author>
  <name gender = "male">
    <first> Art </first>
    <last> Gittleman </last>
  </name>
</author>
```

The DTD declaration in Figure 13.10 follows the format

```
<!DOCTYPE author [ DTD ]>
```

Running Example 1 with command line arguments `authorSimpleInternal.xml` and `true` produces the output of Figure 13.7. If we change Figure 13.10 to add an extra line

```
<middle> Paul </middle>
```

between the `<first>` and `<last>` lines to produce the file `authorSimpleInternalError.xml`, the document will be well-formed but invalid. Figure 13.11 shows the result of processing using the command

```
java -classpath
        .;..\..\jaxp.jar;..\..\crimson.jar;d:\book3\xml
        Sax d:\book3\xml\authorSimpleInternalError.xml
        true
```

Figure 13.11 Processing an invalid XML file

```
Start d:\book3\xml\authorSimpleInternalError.xml
   Start element author
      Start element name
         Attributes gender male
         Start element first
            Art
         End element first
org.xml.sax.SAXParseException: Element "name" does not allow "middle" here.
  at org.apache.crimson.parser.Parser2.error(Parser2.java:3008)
  at org.apache.crimson.parser.ValidatingParser$ChildrenValidator

     .consume(ValidatingParser.java:349)
  at org.apache.crimson.parser.Parser2.maybeElement(Parser2.java:1298)
  at org.apache.crimson.parser.Parser2.content(Parser2.java:1695)
  at org.apache.crimson.parser.Parser2.maybeElement(Parser2.java:1461)
  at org.apache.crimson.parser.Parser2.content(Parser2.java:1695)
  at org.apache.crimson.parser.Parser2.maybeElement(Parser2.java:1461)
  at org.apache.crimson.parser.Parser2.parseInternal(Parser2.java:499)
  at org.apache.crimson.parser.Parser2.parse(Parser2.java:304)
  at org.apache.crimson.parser.XMLReaderImpl
                                    .parse(XMLReaderImpl.java:433)
  at Sax.main(Sax.java:57)
```

Figure 13.12 shows how to use the DTD externally. The DTD declaration refers to the file containing the DTD. Figure 13.9 shows `authorSimple.dtd`.

Figure 13.12 `authorSimpleExternal.xml`

```
<?xml version="1.0"?>
<!-- An author -->
<!DOCTYPE author SYSTEM "file:///d:/book3/xml/authorSimple.dtd">
<author>
  <name gender = "male">
    <first> Art </first>
    <last> Gittleman </last>
  </name>
</author>
```

Running Example 13.1 with the arguments `authorSimpleExternal.xml` and `true` produces the output of Figure 13.7.

THE BIG PICTURE

The Simple API for XML (SAX) uses an event handling approach. It calls specific methods to signal the occurrence of particular pieces of the XML document. A non-validating parser will identify XML that is not well-formed. A validating parser will, in addition, identity XML that does not follow the Document Type Definition (DTD).

TEST YOUR UNDERSTANDING

5. Which method should we implement to respond to the occurrence of the `<first>` tag?

6. What is the advantage of extending the `DefaultHandler` class in Example 13.1?

7. Use an `if-else` statement to write code equivalent to the line

   `boolean validate = args[1].equals("true")?true:false;`

   from Example 13.1.

13.3 DOM Processing

The DOM (Document Object Model) API supports the reading of the entire document to make a tree model in memory. We can access nodes of the tree to locate information contained in the XML document. Having the tree facilitates processing compared to a SAX parser, which has to save any information it might need. But the DOM tree requires internal memory. Performance may suffer due to the creation of objects for each node.

We use the following interfaces from the `org.w3c.com` package.

Interface	Description
Document	Represents the entire XML document.
Element	Represents an element in an XML document.
Node	A superinterface for each node of the DOM tree.
NodeList	A collection of nodes.
Attr	An attribute of an element.
Text	The text of an element or attribute.

TIP

Check the documentation for the `org.w3c.com` package to see descriptions of each of the methods of these interfaces, and for the complete list of interfaces.

Building a DOM Tree from an XML File

Example 13.2 produces a DOM tree from an XML file. For example, it will produce a tree with structure like Figure 13.5 from the `author.xml` file of Figure 13.3. We then find all `<title>` elements and read the `full` attribute to determine whether or not each is the full title.

We compile using the command

```
javac -classpath .;%JAXP_HOME%\jaxp.jar;%JAXP_HOME%\crimson.jar Dom.java
```

and run using

```
java -classpath .;%JAXP_HOME%\jaxp.jar;%JAXP_HOME%\crimson.jar
Dom author.xml false
```

EXAMPLE 13.2 **Dom.java**

```
/* Uses a DOM parser to identify the parts of an XML
 * document. The user specifies whether to use a
 * validating parser.
 */

import org.w3c.dom.Document;
import org.w3c.dom.Element;
import org.w3c.dom.NodeList;
import org.w3c.dom.Text;
import javax.xml.parsers.DocumentBuilder;
import javax.xml.parsers.DocumentBuilderFactory;
import java.io.*;

public class Dom {
  public static void main(String[] args) {
```

```
    try {
      DocumentBuilderFactory factory =
             DocumentBuilderFactory.newInstance();                    // Note 1
      boolean validate = args[1].equals("true")?true:false;
      factory.setValidating(validate);
      DocumentBuilder builder = factory.newDocumentBuilder();
      Document document = builder.parse(new File(args[0]));           // Note 2
      Element root = document.getDocumentElement();                   // Note 3
      root.normalize();                                               // Note 4
      NodeList titles = root.getElementsByTagName("title");           // Note 5
      for (int i=0; i < titles.getLength(); i++) {
         Element title = (Element)titles.item(i);                     // Note 6
         String full = title.getAttribute("full");                   // Note 7
         Text text = (Text)title.getFirstChild();                    // Note 8
         String result =
                     full.equals("false") ? : is not" : " is";
         System.out.println(text.getNodeValue()
                + result + " the full title.");                      // Note 9
      }
    }catch (Exception e) {
      e.printStackTrace();
    }
  }
}
```

....

Output

```
Computing with Java is not the full title.
Objects to Components with the Java Platform is the full title.
Internet Applications with the Java 2 Platform is the full title.
```

....

Note 1:   We use `DocumentBuilderFactory` rather than the `SAXParserFactory` we used for SAX processing in Example 13.1.

Note 2:   `args[0]` is the XML file from which we build the DOM tree.

Note 3:   The `getDocumentElement` method returns the `Element` that is the root of the document. It is a child node of the `Document` node that is the root of the DOM tree.

Note 4:   The `normalize` method combines adjacent `Text` nodes into one `Text` node. Otherwise the parser may produce nodes representing whitespace only.

Note 5:   The `getElementsByTagName` method returns a `NodeList` of all descendant elements with the name passed to it.

Note 6:   `Element title = (Element)titles.item(i);`
The item method returns the `Node` with the specified index in the `NodeList`. We cast it to `Element`.

Note 7:   `String full = title.getAttribute("full");`

The `getAttribute` method returns the value of the attribute with the specified name. Attributes are not represented as separate nodes in the DOM tree. They are associated with an `Element` node.

Note 8:   `Text text = (Text)title.getFirstChild();`

The text in an `Element` is a `Text` node that is a child, in the DOM tree, of the containing `Element`.

Note 9:   `System.out.println(text.getNodeValue() + result`
                      `+ " the full title.");`

The `getNodeValue` method returns the text in a `Text` node.

Checking for Well-Formed and Valid Documents

Running Example 13.2 using the command

```
javac -classpath .;%JAXP_HOME%\jaxp.jar;%JAXP_HOME%\crimson.jar
Dom authorSimpleError.xml false
```

with the non well-formed file `authorSimpleError.xml`, which omits the `</first>` tag, produces

```
org.xml.sax.SAXParseException: Expected "</first>" to terminate element
starting on line 5.
  at org.apache.crimson.parser.Parser2.fatal(Parser2.java:3030)
  at org.apache.crimson.parser.Parser2.fatal(Parser2.java:3024)
  at org.apache.crimson.parser.Parser2.maybeElement(Parser2.java:1467)
  at org.apache.crimson.parser.Parser2.content(Parser2.java:1695)
  at org.apache.crimson.parser.Parser2.maybeElement(Parser2.java:1461)
  at org.apache.crimson.parser.Parser2.content(Parser2.java:1695)
  at org.apache.crimson.parser.Parser2.maybeElement(Parser2.java:1461)
  at org.apache.crimson.parser.Parser2.parseInternal(Parser2.java:499)
  at org.apache.crimson.parser.Parser2.parse(Parser2.java:304)
    at org.apache.crimson.parser.XMLReaderImpl

              .parse(XMLReaderImpl.java:433)
  at org.apache.crimson.jaxp.DocumentBuilderImpl
                          .parse(DocumentBuilderImpl.java:171)
  at javax.xml.parsers.DocumentBuilder.parse(DocumentBuilder.java:134)
  at Dom.main(Dom.java:22)
```

We did not need to use a validating parser to detect a document that is not well-formed. Nor is a DTD necessary.

The invalid document `authorSimpleInternalError.xml` includes a DTD which does not specify a `<middle>` tag, yet it uses one. Checking with a nonvalidating parser using the command

```
java -classpath .;%JAXP_HOME%\jaxp.jar;%JAXP_HOME%\crimson.jar
```

```
Dom authorSimpleInternalError.xml false
```

produces no errors. Checking with a validating parser using the command

```
java -classpath .;%JAXP_HOME%\jaxp.jar;%JAXP_HOME%\crimson.jar
Dom authorSimpleInternalError.xml true
```

results in the output

```
org.xml.sax.SAXParseException: Element "name" does not allow "middle" here.
   at org.apache.crimson.parser.Parser2.error(Parser2.java:3008)
   at org.apache.crimson.parser.ValidatingParser$ChildrenValidator
                             .consume(ValidatingParser.java:349)
   at org.apache.crimson.parser.Parser2.maybeElement(Parser2.java:1298)
   at org.apache.crimson.parser.Parser2.content(Parser2.java:1695)
   at org.apache.crimson.parser.Parser2.maybeElement(Parser2.java:1461)
   at org.apache.crimson.parser.Parser2.content(Parser2.java:1695)
   at org.apache.crimson.parser.Parser2.maybeElement(Parser2.java:1461)
   at org.apache.crimson.parser.Parser2.parseInternal(Parser2.java:499)
   at org.apache.crimson.parser.Parser2.parse(Parser2.java:304)
   at org.apache.crimson.parser.XMLReaderImpl
                        .parse(XMLReaderImpl.java:433)
   at org.apache.crimson.jaxp.DocumentBuilderImpl
                        .parse(DocumentBuilderImpl.java:171)
   at javax.xml.parsers.DocumentBuilder.parse(DocumentBuilder.java:134)
   at Dom.main(Dom.java:23)
```

Building a DOM Tree from Data

In Example 13.3 we will build a DOM tree from the customer data in the Sales database we created in Chapter 3. We leave the more interesting problem of representing data from several of the Sales tables in an XML document for the exercises. Figure 13.13 shows the DTD for the XML document we build.

Figure 13.13   A customers DTD

```
<!ELEMENT customers (customer*)>
<!ELEMENT customer (name, address, balance)>
<!ELEMENT name (#PCDATA)>
<!ELEMENT address (#PCDATA)>
<!ELEMENT balance (#PCDATA)>
```

The Document class includes the following methods to create nodes.

```
Attr createAttribute(String name)
Comment createComment(String data)
Element createElement(String tagName)
Text createTextNode(String data)
```

The various subinterfaces of Node inherit the

```
Node appendChild(Node newChild)
```

method to append a new node to the tree.

EXAMPLE 13.3   **MakeXml.java**

```java
/* Uses the DOM API to create an XML document from
 * Sales database information.
 */

import org.w3c.dom.Document;
import org.w3c.dom.Element;
import javax.xml.parsers.DocumentBuilder;
import javax.xml.parsers.DocumentBuilderFactory;
import java.io.*;
import java.sql.*;
import sun.jdbc.odbc.*;
import java.math.BigDecimal;
import java.text.NumberFormat;

public class MakeXml {
  public static void main(String[] args) {
    try{
      new JdbcOdbcDriver();
      String url = "jdbc:odbc:Sales";
      Connection con = DriverManager.getConnection(url);
      Statement stmt = con.createStatement();

      DocumentBuilderFactory factory =
                      DocumentBuilderFactory.newInstance();
      DocumentBuilder builder = factory.newDocumentBuilder();
      Document document = builder.newDocument();            // Note 1
      Element customers = document.createElement("customers");  // Note 2
      document.appendChild(customers);                      // Note 3
      String query = "SELECT * FROM Customer";
      ResultSet rs = stmt.executeQuery(query);              // Note 4
      while (rs.next()) {
        Element customer = document.createElement("customer");
        customers.appendChild(customer);
        Element name = document.createElement("name");
        customer.appendChild(name);
        name.appendChild(document.createTextNode
                    (rs.getString("CustomerName")));        // Note 5
        Element address = document.createElement("address");
        customer.appendChild(address);
        address.appendChild
          (document.createTextNode(rs.getString("Address")));
```

```
      Element balance = document.createElement("balance");
      customer.appendChild(balance);
      BigDecimal b = rs.getBigDecimal("BalanceDue");
      NumberFormat nf = NumberFormat.getCurrencyInstance();
      balance.appendChild
         (document.createTextNode(nf.format(b)));                    // Note 6
    }
    System.out.println(customers);
  }catch (Exception e) {
    e.printStackTrace();
  }
 }
}
```

Output

```
<customers><customer><name>Fred Flynn</name><address>22 First St. </address>
<balance>1667.00</balance></customer> <customer><name>Darnell Davis</name>
<address>33SecondSt. </address><balance>130.95 </balance></customer><customer>
<name>Marla Martinez</name><address>44 Third St.</address> <balance>0.00
</balance></customer><customer> <name>Carla Kahn</name><address>55 FourthSt.
</address><balance> 0.00 </balance></customer></customers>
```

Note 1:   The newDocument method returns the Document to represent the DOM tree.

Note 2:   The customers node represents the <customers> tag.

Note 3:   The customers node will be the only child of the document node.

Note 4:   The result set contains one entry for each row of the Customer table.

Note 5:   We create the Text node and append it without bothering to declare a variable to refer to it.

Note 6:   `balance.appendChild`
　　　　　`(document.createTextNode(nf.format(b)));`
The default BigDecimal format uses four decimal places. We use a currency instance to format the balance due according to the currency format of the default locale.

THE BIG PICTURE

The Document Object Model (DOM) builds a tree representing the XML document. The Node interface represents a single node in the tree. Subinterfaces identify the components of an XML document. Methods allow us random access to nodes. We can create a DOM tree from an XML document or construct it from data.

TEST YOUR UNDERSTANDING

---

8. Draw the tree represented by the DTD of Figure 13.13.

9. Which method, from which class, returns the root element of an XML document?

10. Which is represented as a separate node in the DOM tree, an attribute of an element or the text between the start and end tags of an element?

13.4 XSLT

XSL (Extensible Stylesheet Language) has two parts, one for formatting and the other for transformations. The transformation part, XSLT (Extensible Stylesheet Language for Transformations), has been developed first. It allows us to transform one document to another. We can transform an XML document to another XML document or to HTML for display in a browser.

Stylesheets

We specify the transformations in a stylesheet. The stylesheet follows XML syntax. The transformations use templates that a processor matches against the tags in a XML file. Figure 13.14 shows a stylesheet for the authorSimple.xml file of Figure 13.6.

Figure 13.14   authorSimple.xsl

```
<?xml version="1.0"?>
<xsl:stylesheet version="1.0"
    xmlns:xsl="http://www.w3.org/1999/XSL/Transform">

    <xsl:template match="/">
      <html>
        <head>
          <title> An author </title>
        </head>
        <body>
          <xsl:apply-templates />
        </body>
      </html>
    </xsl:template>

    <xsl:template match="name">
      <h1>
        First: <xsl:value-of select="first"/><br/>
        Last: <xsl:value-of select="last"/><br/>
      </h1>

    </xsl:template>
</xsl:stylesheet>
```

We use the `.xsl` extension for stylesheets. Figure 13.15 shows the HTML file produces when we use Example 13.4 to apply this stylesheet to `authorSimple.xml`, and Figure 13.16 shows the resulting web page.

Figure 13.15 `authorSimple.html`

```
<html>
<head>
<title> An author </title>
</head>
<body>
   <h1>
         First:  Art <br>
         Last:  Gittleman <br>
</h1>
</body>
</html>
```

Figure 13.16 The `authorSimple.html` **web page**

As with other XML files we start the stylesheet with the processing instruction

```
<?xml version="1.0"?>
```

Processing instructions occur between `<?` and `?>`. XSLT stylesheets use the XSLT namespace to provide a context for the XSLT commands. Each command uses a tag with the `xsl` prefix, as in `xsl:template`. The `xsl:stylesheet` tag

```
<xsl:stylesheet version="1.0"
    xmlns:xsl="http://www.w3.org/1999/XSL/Transform">
```

indicates the version, `1.0`. The `xmlns:xsl` attribute states that the namespace name is `xsl` and gives the URL where that namespace is defined. As with all XML tags, the `xsl:stylesheet` tag has a closing tag at the end of the stlyesheet.

The stylesheet of Figure 13.14 uses two `xsl:template` tags. The first

```
<xsl:template match="/">
```

includes a match attribute with the value "/", which matches the root tag of the XML file, <author> in Figure 13.6. We could have used the tag

```
<xsl:template match="author">
```

When the XSLT processor applies the template to authorSimple.xml, it finds a match with the <author> tag and outputs its body

```
<html>
  <head>
    <title> An author </title>
  </head>
  <body>
    <xsl:apply-templates />
  </body>
</html>
```

The <xsl:apply-templates /> tag applies the templates of the stylesheet to tags nested within the <author> tag. Because it is an empty tag, we use the short form, closing it with a forward slash.

Next the XSLT processor finds a match with the <name> tag, so it fills in its body in the output giving

```
<html>
  <head>
    <title> An author </title>
  </head>
  <body>
    <h1>
        First: <xsl:value-of select="first"/><br/>
        Last: <xsl:value-of select="last"/><br/>
    </h1>
  </body>
</html>
```

Finally the <xsl:value-of select="first"/> tag returns the text body of the <first> tag as a String.

Example 13.4 is quite short. The Sun JAXP release includes the Xalan XSLT processor. We add xalan.jar to the classpath, compiling Example 13.4 with

```
javac -classpath .;%JAXP_HOME%\jaxp.jar;%JAXP_HOME%\crimson.jar
;%JAXP_HOME%\xalan.jar XmlToHtml.java
```

and running it using

```
java -classpath .;%JAXP_HOME%\jaxp.jar;%JAXP_HOME%\crimson.jar;
%JAXP_HOME%\xalan.jar XmlToHtml authorSimple.xml authorSimple.xsl authorSimple.html
```

EXAMPLE 13.4   XmlToHtml.java

```java
/* Converts the XML file of args[0] to that of args[2]
 * using the XSL stylesheet of args[1].
 */

import javax.xml.transform.*;
import javax.xml.transform.stream.*;
import java.io.File;

public class XmlToHtml {
  public static void main(String[] args) {
    try {
      TransformerFactory factory
                  = TransformerFactory.newInstance();               // Note 1
      Transformer translate = factory.newTransformer(
                  new StreamSource(new File(args[1])));              // Note 2
      translate.transform(new StreamSource(new File(args[0])),
                  new StreamResult(new File(args[2])));             // Note 3
    }catch (Exception e) {
      e.printStackTrace();
    }
  }
}
```

Output
See Figures 13.15 and 13.16

Note 1:   The `TransformerFactory` provides us with a `Transformer`.

Note 2:   Implements a transform based on the stylesheet passed as its argument. The `StreamSource` handles the input of XML.

Note 3:   Applies the stylesheet transform to the file of `args[0]` outputting to the file of `args[2]`. The `StreamResult` may use instructions in the transformer to handle the output encoding.

A Stylesheet for the Author Document

Now that we have seen how XSLT works, we will process the full `author.xml` document of Figure 13.3. Figure 13.17 shows the stylesheet we will apply. Figure 13.18 shows the resulting HTML file, and Figure 13.19 the web page.

The `author.xsl` stylesheet uses the `<xsl:value-of select="." />` tag inside the age match. The "." in the `select` attribute refers to the tag of the match containing the `value-of` command, which in this case is the age tag. Thus the `value-of` command returns the text of the age tag, which is `39+`.

Figure 13.17   `author.xsl`

```
<?xml version="1.0"?>
<xsl:stylesheet version="1.0"
    xmlns:xsl="http://www.w3.org/1999/XSL/Transform">

  <xsl:template match="/">
    <html>
      <head>
        <title> Book written by an author </title>
      </head>
      <body>
        <xsl:apply-templates />
      </body>
    </html>
  </xsl:template>

  <xsl:template match="name">
    <h3>
        Author: <xsl:value-of select="first"/>
          <xsl:value-of select="last"/><br/>
    </h3>
  </xsl:template>
  <xsl:template match="age">
    <h4>
        Age: <xsl:value-of select="." />
    </h4>
    <hr/>
  </xsl:template>
  <xsl:template match="books">
    <xsl:apply-templates />
  </xsl:template>
  <xsl:template match="book">
    <h4><strong>
        <xsl:value-of select="title"/>
    </strong></h4>
    <table>
      <th>Edition</th>
      <th>Copyright</th>
      <th>ISBN</th>
      <tr>
        <td><xsl:value-of select="edition"/></td>
        <td><xsl:value-of select="copyright"/></td>
        <td><xsl:value-of select="isbn"/></td>
      </tr>
    </table>
    <hr/>
  </xsl:template>
</xsl:stylesheet>
```

Figure 13.18 author1.html

```
<html>
<head>
<title> Book written by an author </title>
</head>
<body>
  <h3>
        Author:  Art  Gittleman <br>
</h3>
  <h4>
       Age:  39+   </h4>
<hr>


    <h4>
      <strong>Computing with Java</strong>
</h4>
<table>
<th>Edition</th><th>Copyright</th><th>ISBN</th>
<tr>
<td> second </td><td> 1998, 2001 </td>
    <td> 1-57676-023-5 </td>
</tr>
</table>
<hr>
    <h4>
      <strong>Objects to Components with the Java Platform
      </strong>
</h4>
<table>
<th>Edition</th><th>Copyright</th><th>ISBN</th>
<tr>
<td> first </td><td> 2000 </td><td> 1-57676-035-9 </td>
</tr>
</table>
<hr>
    <h4>
      <strong>Internet Applications with the Java 2
                Platform
      </strong>
</h4>
<table>
<th>Edition</th><th>Copyright</th><th>ISBN</th>
<tr>
<td> first </td><td> 2001 </td><td> 1-57676-052-9 </td>
</tr>
</table>
<hr>

</body>
</html>
```

Figure 13.19   The `author1.html` web page

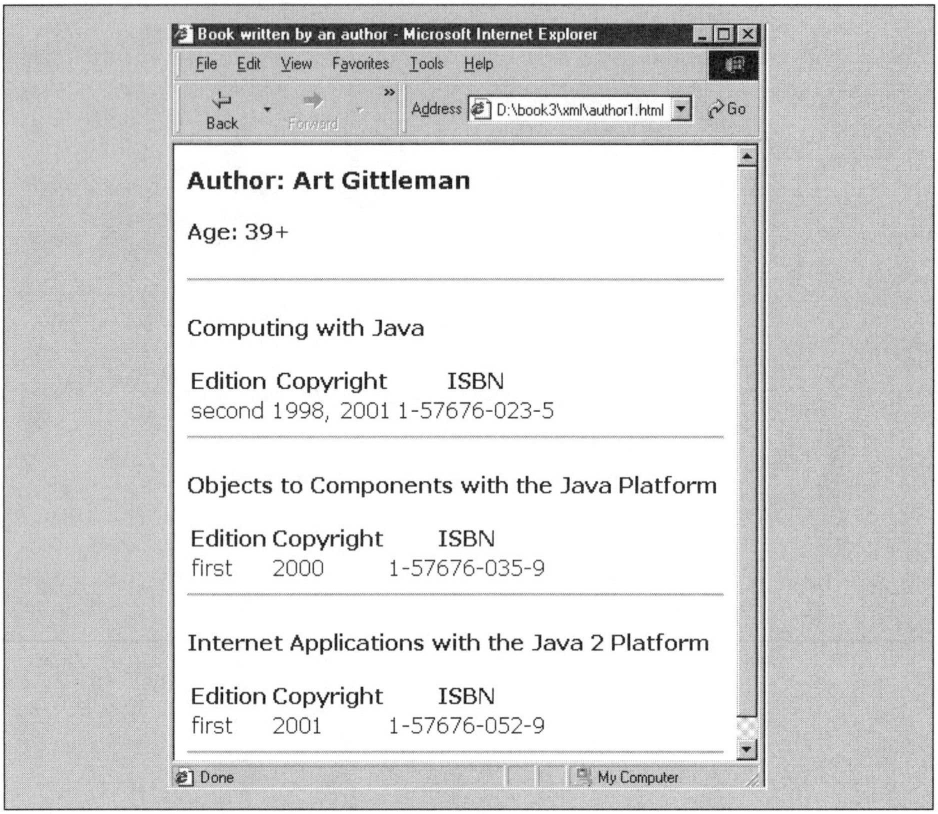

The match for the `<books>` tag does not directly add any new HTML code, but it specifies the `<xsl:apply-templates />` command which causes the XSLT processor to apply the templates to the tags nested within `<books>`. When matching `<book>` we display the title followed by a table containing the book information. The `<th>` tag indicates a table header, while `<tr>` specifies a table row, and `<td>` represents the table data in one cell. We follow each table with the empty `<hr/>` tag to insert a horizontal rule.

We use the command

```
java -classpath .;%JAXP_HOME%\jaxp.jar;%JAXP_HOME%\crimson.jar;
%JAXP_HOME%\xalan.jar XmlToHtml author.xml author.xsl author1.html
```

to run the XSLT processor.

Using a Stylesheet

Example 13.2 created a DOM tree from an XML file and then processed it to the find the book titles and indicated whether each was the full title. We can use a stylesheet to transform the XML file to give the desired information as a web page. Figure 13.20 shows the stylesheet, Figure 13.21 the resulting HTML file, and Figure 13.22 its corresponding web page.

Figure 13.20 `titles.xsl`

```
<?xml version="1.0"?>
<xsl:stylesheet version="1.0"
    xmlns:xsl="http://www.w3.org/1999/XSL/Transform">

  <xsl:template match="/">
    <html>
      <head>
        <title> Book titles </title>
      </head>
      <body>
        <xsl:apply-templates />
      </body>
    </html>
  </xsl:template>
  <xsl:template match="age">
  </xsl:template>
  <xsl:template match="name">
    <h3>
       Author: <xsl:value-of select="first"/>
          <xsl:value-of select="last"/><br/>
    </h3>
  </xsl:template>
  <xsl:template match="books">
    <xsl:apply-templates />
  </xsl:template>

  <xsl:template match="book">
    <xsl:apply-templates select="title"/>
  </xsl:template>

  <xsl:template match="title[@full='false']">
    <h4><strong>
      <xsl:value-of select="."/>
    </strong></h4> is not the full title.
    <hr/>
  </xsl:template>
  <xsl:template match="title">
    <h4><strong>
      <xsl:value-of select="."/>
    </strong></h4> is the full title.
    <hr/>
  </xsl:template>

</xsl:stylesheet>
```

Figure 13.21 `titles.html`

```
<html>
<head>
<title> Book titles </title>
</head>
<body>
  <h3>
          Author:  Art  Gittleman <br>
</h3>



    <h4>
<strong>Computing with Java</strong>
</h4>
 is not the full title.
    <hr>
    <h4>
<strong>Objects to Components with the Java Platform</strong>
</h4>
   is the full title.
    <hr>
    <h4>
<strong>Internet Applications with the Java 2 Platform</strong>
</h4>
   is the full title.
    <hr>

</body>
</html>
```

We use the command

```
java -classpath .;%JAXP_HOME%\jaxp.jar;%JAXP_HOME%\crimson.jar;
%JAXP_HOME%\xalan.jar XmlToHtml author.xml titles.xsl titles.html
```

to do the processing.

We do not want to list the author's age in the output. The `<xsl:apply-templates />` command in the root template will apply to all the nested tags including `<age>`. If we omit an "age" match, the default will be to include the text of the `<age>` tag. To prevent this we include an "age" match with an empty body, so no code will be added to the HTML output.

The `<xsl:apply-templates select="title"/>` command will only apply templates to the `<title>` tag, and will ignore the `<edition>`, `<copyright>`, and `<isbn>` tags. When matching the title we want to distinguish full titles from the others. We use the `full` attribute to indicate which are full titles. It has a default value of "`true`" so it only appears explicitly when its value is "`false`."

We match on titles with the `full` attribute set to `false` using the command

```
<xsl:template match="title[@full='false']">
```

Figure 13.22   The `titles.html` web page

The @ symbol indicates an attribute. We also include a default match for "`title`" that will apply to the `<title>` tags not matched by the previous command when the attribute is `false`. This will cover the cases when the title is the full title.

THE BIG PICTURE

Extensible Stylesheet Language for Transformations (XSLT) allows us to transform an XML document. It is itself an XML file that uses the xsl namespace with stylesheet commands. The `template` command matches document tags, building the transformed document with its included code. One application is to transform an XML document, which expresses content, to an HTML document for presentation.

TEST YOUR UNDERSTANDING

11. Write the unabbreviated equivalent of the `<xsl:apply-templates />` tag.

12. Figure 13.20 includes the

    `<xsl:apply-templates select="title"/>`

    tag. Explain the difference between this tag and the tag

    `<xsl:apply-templates />`

13. How would we have to change the tag

    `<xsl:template match="book">`

    in Figure 13.17 to match only textbooks?

13.5   Simple Object Access Protocol (SOAP)

SOAP provides a simple mechanism for making remote procedure calls and other exchanges using XML.[*] Using SOAP with HTTP makes it readily available. The Apache Software Foundation provides an API for writing SOAP clients and servers in Java.[†] The XMethods site (www.xmethods.com) contains many SOAP servers to which we shall connect.

A SOAP Message

A SOAP message is an XML document that contains a mandatory SOAP envelope, an optional SOAP header, and a mandatory SOAP body. For example the XMethods site has an ITime server which returns the Internet time as defined by Swatch. A day is divided into 1000 beats. Beat 0 starts at midnight in Biel, Switzerland. Everyone in the world uses the same Internet time.

Figure 13.23 shows the SOAP message we use to obtain Internet time.

Figure 13.23   A SOAP message

```
<SOAP-ENV:Envelope
     xmlns:SOAP-ENV="http://schemas.xmlsoap.org/soap/envelope">
  <SOAP-ENV:Body>
   <ns1:getInternetTime xmlns:ns1="urn:lemurlabs-ITimeService"
    SOAP-ENV:encodingStyle="http://schemas.xmlsoap.org/soap/encoding/">
   </ns1:getInternetTime>
  </SOAP-ENV:Body>
</SOAP-ENV:Envelope>
```

The ITime entry on the XMethods site gives us the information we need to write Figure 13.23. We call the `getInternetTime` method. The object on the server is `urn:lemurlabs-TimeService`. We must have the `Envelope` tag. We specify a `SOAP-ENV` namespace with the SOAP URI

```
http://schemas.xmlsoap.org/soap/envelope
```

For the `getInternetTime` tag we declare the `ns1` namespace referring to the object on the server. `getInternetTime` has no arguments.

The ITime service is a servlet that we must connect to with a POST request. Example 13.5 will send the XML SOAP request of Figure 13.23. We find from the ITime entry on the XMethods site that

```
http://www.lemurlabs.com/rpcrouter
```

is the resource we need to connect to on the server. We execute Example 13.5 using the command

```
java TrySoapTime www.lemurlabs.com 80 /rpcrouter
```

---

[*] See http://www.w3c.org/TR/SOAP for the SOAP specification.
[†] See http://xml.apache.org for SOAP and other XML materials.

We ran this program at about 10 am in California. The time of 749 beats shows that three-quarters of the day had passed in Switzerland. Using beats everyone around the world can use the same time. It is 749 beats at the same time everywhere in the world.

EXAMPLE 13.5   **TrySoapTime.java**

```java
/* Connects to an ITime server to get the Internet
 * time (beats).
 */

import java.net.*;
import java.io.*;

public class TrySoapTime {
  public static void main(String [] args) {
    String s;
    if (args.length != 3){
      System.out.println("Usage: java TrySoapTime host port file");
      System.exit(1);
    }
    try {
      int port = Integer.parseInt(args[1]);
      Socket server = new Socket(args[0],port);
      System.out.println("Connected to host "
                            + server.getInetAddress());
      BufferedReader fromServer = new BufferedReader
        (new InputStreamReader(server.getInputStream()));
      PrintWriter toServer = new PrintWriter
                    (server.getOutputStream(),true);
      toServer.println("POST " + args[2] + " HTTP/1.0");      // Note 1
      toServer.println("Host: " + args[0]+ ':' + args[1]);
      toServer.println("Content-Type: text/xml");             // Note 2

      String request =
        "<SOAP-ENV:Envelope xmlns:SOAP-ENV="
          + "\"http://schemas.xmlsoap.org/soap/envelope/\">"
        + " <SOAP-ENV:Body>"
          + " <ns1:getInternetTime "
            + "xmlns:ns1=\"urn:lemurlabs-ITimeService\""
            + " SOAP-ENV:encodingStyle"
            + "=\"http://schemas.xmlsoap.org/soap/encoding/\">"
          + " </ns1:getInternetTime> "
          + " </SOAP-ENV:Body> "
        + "</SOAP-ENV:Envelope>";
      toServer.println("Content-Length: " + request.length());  // Note 3
      toServer.println();                                        // Note 4
      toServer.println(request);                                 // Note 5
      while (!(s=fromServer.readLine()).equals(""))              // Note 6
        System.out.println(s);
```

```
        while ((s=fromServer.readLine()) != null)              // Note 7
          System.out.println(s);
        fromServer.close();
        toServer.close();
        server.close();
      }catch(Exception e) {
        e.printStackTrace();
      }
    }
}
```

Output

```
Connected to host www.lemurlabs.com/208.192.176.221
HTTP/1.1 200 OK
Date: Tue, 10 Apr 2001 16:59:25 GMT
Server: Orion/1.4.7
Content-Length: 438
Set-Cookie: JSESSIONID=DMGJKBIFONLH; Path=/
Cache-Control: private
Connection: Close
Content-Type: text/xml; charset=UTF-8
<SOAP-ENV:Envelope
 xmlns:SOAP-ENV="http://schemas.xmlsoap.org/soap/envelope/"
 xmlns:xsi="http://www.w3.org/1999/XMLSchema-instance"
 xmlns:xsd="http://www.w3.org/1999/XMLSchema">
<SOAP-ENV:Body>
  <ns1:getInternetTimeResponse
     xmlns:ns1="urn:lemurlabs-ITimeService"
     SOAP-ENV:encodingStyle=
             "http://schemas.xmlsoap.org/soap/encoding/">
   <return xsi:type="xsd:int">749</return>
  </ns1:getInternetTimeResponse>
</SOAP-ENV:Body>
</SOAP-ENV:Envelope>
```

Note 1:   We must use a POST request to connect to the `rpcrouter` servlet.

Note 2:   The content type describes the XML message we send.

Note 3:   We must send the length of the message.

Note 4:   The blank line terminates the request headers, according to HTTP.

Note 5:   We send the SOAP request.

Note 6:   `while (!(s=fromServer.readLine()).equals(""))`
We read and display the status line and the response headers.

Note 7:   `while ((s=fromServer.readLine()) != null)`
We read the SOAP response.

Calling a Method with Arguments

The ITime service does not require arguments. The Barnes and Noble Price Quote service on the XMethods site returns the price of a book at BN.com given its ISBN number. Figure 13.24 shows the SOAP XML request.

Figure 13.24   The SOAP request for the Price Quote service

```
<SOAP-ENV:Envelope
    xmlns:SOAP-ENV="http://schemas.xmlsoap.org/soap/envelope/"
    xmlns:xsi="http://www.w3.org/1999/XMLSchema-instance"
    xmlns:xsd="http://www.w3.org/1999/XMLSchema">
 <SOAP-ENV:Body>
   <ns1:getPrice xmlns:ns1="urn:xmethods-BNPriceCheck"
           SOAP-ENV:encodingStyle=
               "http://schemas.xmlsoap.org/soap/encoding/">
     <isbn xsi:type="xsd:string">1576760235</isbn>
   </ns1:getPrice>
 </SOAP-ENV:Body>
</SOAP-ENV:Envelope>
```

We include two extra namespace declarations used in the argument tag.

Example 13.6 sends the SOAP XML request to the server. We execute it using the command

```
java GetPrice services.xmethods.net 80 /soap/servlet/rpcrouter 1576760235
```

EXAMPLE 13.6   GetPrice.java

```java
/* Connects to a SOAP Service to returns the price of a
 * book at BN.com given its ISBN number.
 */

import java.net.*;
import java.io.*;

public class GetPrice {
  public static void main(String [] args) {
    String s;
    if (args.length != 4){
      System.out.println("Usage: java GetPrice host port file ISBN");
      System.exit(1);
    }
    try {
      int port = Integer.parseInt(args[1]);
      Socket server = new Socket(args[0],port);
      System.out.println("Connected to host "
                         + server.getInetAddress());
```

```
            BufferedReader fromServer = new BufferedReader
              (new InputStreamReader(server.getInputStream()));
            PrintWriter toServer = new PrintWriter
                        (server.getOutputStream(),true);
            toServer.println("POST " + args[2] + " HTTP/1.0");
            toServer.println("Host: " + args[0]+ ':' + args[1]);
            toServer.println("Content-Type: text/xml");
            toServer.println
              ("SOAPMethodName: urn:xmethods-BNPriceCheck#getPrice");

            String request =
             "<SOAP-ENV:Envelope"+
                " xmlns:SOAP-ENV="
                    + "\"http://schemas.xmlsoap.org/soap/envelope/\""
                +" xmlns:xsi="
                    + "\"http://www.w3.org/1999/XMLSchema-instance\""
                +" xmlns:xsd="
                    + "\"http://www.w3.org/1999/XMLSchema\">"
            +" <SOAP-ENV:Body>"
              +" <ns1:getPrice xmlns:ns1=\"urn:xmethods-BNPriceCheck\""
                  +" SOAP-ENV:encodingStyle"
                +"=\"http://schemas.xmlsoap.org/soap/encoding/\">"
                +" <isbn xsi:type=\"xsd:string\">args[3]</isbn>"          // Note 1
              +" </ns1:getPrice> "
            + " </SOAP-ENV:Body> "
            + "</SOAP-ENV:Envelope>";
             toServer.println("Content-Length: " + request.length());
             toServer.println();
             toServer.println(request);
             while (!(s=fromServer.readLine()).equals(""))
               System.out.println(s);
             while ((s=fromServer.readLine()) != null)
               System.out.println(s);
             fromServer.close();
             toServer.close();
             server.close();
           }catch(Exception e) {
             e.printStackTrace();
           }
        }
}
```

....

Output

```
Connected to host services.xmethods.net/206.135.115.105
HTTP/1.1 200 OK
Date: Tue, 10 Apr 2001 22:38:49 GMT
Status: 200
```

```
Set-Cookie2: JSESSIONID=To10904mC22528739702399958At;Version=1;Discard;
Path="/soap"
Servlet-Engine: Tomcat Web Server/3.1 (JSP 1.1; Servlet 2.2;
Java 1.3.0; SunOS 5.8 sparc; java.vendor=Sun Microsystems Inc.)
Set-Cookie: JSESSIONID=To10904mC22528739702399958At;Path=/soap
Content-Type: text/xml; charset=utf-8
Content-Length: 469
Content-Language: en
Server: Electric/1.0
Electric-Routing: true
<?xml version='1.0' encoding='UTF-8'?>
<SOAP-ENV:Envelope
    xmlns:SOAP-ENV="http://schemas.xmlsoap.org/soap/envelope/"
    xmlns:xsi="http://www.w3.org/1999/XMLSchema-instance"
    xmlns:xsd="http://www.w3.org/1999/XMLSchema">
  <SOAP-ENV:Body>
    <ns1:getPriceResponse xmlns:ns1="urn:xmethods-BNPriceCheck"
        SOAP-ENV:encodingStyle=
            "http://schemas.xmlsoap.org/soap/encoding/">
      <return xsi:type="xsd:float">62.75</return>
    </ns1:getPriceResponse>
  </SOAP-ENV:Body>
</SOAP-ENV:Envelope>
```

Note 1:   We specify the string type for ISBN argument and give its value.

Using the SOAP API

We can download the SOAP API from the `xml.apache.org` site. These packages allow us to write SOAP clients without having to write the XML request explicitly. We can also write SOAP servers although we do not do that here.[*] Example 13.7 connects to the Barnes and Noble Price Quote service using the SOAP API. We compile it using the command

```
javac -classpath .;%SOAP_HOME%\lib\soap.jar GetJavaPrice.java
```

where SOAP_HOME is the path to the SOAP API, and run using

```
java -classpath .;%SOAP_HOME%\lib\soap.jar;
%JAXP_HOME%\crimson.jar;%JRUN_HOME%\lib\ext\mail.jar;
%JRUN_HOME%\lib\ext\activation.jar
```

EXAMPLE 13.7   **GetJavaPrice.java**

```
/* Uses the SOAP API to connect to the Barnes and Noble
 * Price Quote Service.
 */
```

---

[*] The `RPCRouter` servlet used to manage SOAP services is included with the SOAP API.

```
import java.net.*;
import org.apache.soap.*;
import org.apache.soap.rpc.*;
import java.util.*;

public class GetJavaPrice {
  public static void main(String[] args) {
   try {
    Call call = new Call();                                    // Note 1
    call.setEncodingStyleURI(Constants.NS_URI_SOAP_ENC);       // Note 2
    call.setTargetObjectURI("urn:xmethods-BNPriceCheck");      // Note 3
    call.setMethodName("getPrice");
    Vector params = new Vector();
    params.addElement
      (new Parameter("isbn",String.class,args[0],null));       // Note 4
    call.setParams(params);
    URL url = new URL
      ("http://services.xmethods.com/soap/servlet/rpcrouter");// Note 5
    Response resp = call.invoke(url, "");                      // Note 6
    if (resp.generatedFault()) {
      Fault fault = resp.getFault();
      System.out.println(" Fault code: " + fault.getFaultCode());
      System.out.println(" Fault string: " + fault.getFaultString());
    }
    else{
      Parameter result = resp.getReturnValue();               // Note 7
      System.out.println(result.getValue());
    }
   }catch (Exception e) {
     e.printStackTrace();
   }
  }
 }
}
```

Output

62.75

Note 1: The Call object represents a remote procedure call.

Note 2: We set the encoding style to indicate the serialization rules used in a SOAP message.

Note 3: We specify the target object on the server.

Note 4: The four arguments are the parameter name, the parameter type, the parameter value, and the encoding to use to serialize it. Passing null for the last argument indicates the default encoding.

Note 5: This is the URL for the service.

Note 6: `Response resp = call.invoke(url, "");`
We invoke the method. The last argument is an action that we do not use.

Note 7: `Parameter result = resp.getReturnValue();`
We get the value returned by the `getPrice` method invoked on the server.

TEST YOUR UNDERSTANDING

---

14. What parts of a SOAP message are mandatory?

15. What method will be invoked using the SOAP message of Figure 13.23?

SUMMARY

- HTML tags support the presentation of data. XML tags make it easier to identify the content of a document. The optional prolog `<?xml version="1.0"?>` is a processing instruction tag. Tags may have attributes. XML follows precise syntactical rules to facilitate machine processing of XML files. For example, each tag must have an end tag. Tags must nest properly, and attributes must be enclosed in quotes.

- A Data Type Definition (DTD) defines the valid syntax for a document type. Its rules for elements occur in `<!ELEMENT>` tags and its rules for attributes occur in `<!ATTLIST>` tags. A well-formed document conforms to the XML syntax. In addition, a valid document conforms to its DTD.

- The Simple API for XML (SAX) uses an event handling model. It generates callbacks corresponding to the pieces of the document it encounters. The callback methods are part of the `ContentHandler` interface. We use `startElement`, `endElement`, `startDocument`, `endDocument`, and `characters`. We override the `DefaultHandler` which provides default implementations of `ContentHandler` methods.

- The Document Object Model (DOM) builds a tree representation of the XML document in memory. The parse method builds a DOM tree from an XML file. Methods such as `getElementsByTagName` let us directly access nodes of the tree. Methods such as `createElement` and `appendChild` let us build a DOM tree from data.

- The Extensible Stylesheet Language for Transformations lets us transform XML documents. For example, we can transform an XML document, which focuses on content, to an HTML document for presentation. We could transform the content to an XML document suitable for a different application. The `xsl` namespace includes commands that implement the transformations. A `template` command matches pieces of the XML documents and specifies the transformed code to use when a match is found. Other commands include `apply-templates` and `value-of`.

- The Simple Object Access Protocol allows us to execute remote procedure calls. HTTP provides wide access and ease of use. An XML message specifies the object on the server, the method to call, and any arguments to that method. The server returns a SOAP XML response. The Apache Software Foundation provides a SOAP API to program clients and servers handling the XML details.

Program Modification Exercises

· · · · · · · · · ·

1. Modify Example 13.2 to write the output as an HTML file. Write it to the external file `Dom.html`.

2. Modify Example 13.3 to create an XML document with the customer's name and the dates on which that customer placed orders.

3. Modify Example 13.2 to list those titles that contain a word entered on the command line.

Program Design Exercises

· · · · · · · · · ·

4. a. Using data from the Sales database of Chapter 3, write a program to create a DOM tree which for each salesperson lists the order number and date of each order handled by that salesperson.
   b. Write a stylesheet to transform the XML document of part a to an HTML file to display the results Execute Example 13.4 to obtain the HTML file.

5. Write a stylesheet to produce an HTML file from `author.xml`, using Example 13.4, that displays the title and ISBN of each book.

6. Write a stylesheet to produce an HTML file from `author.xml`, using Example 13.4, that displays the author's name and the copyright date of each book.

7. Write a program that uses a SAX parser on `author.xml` to output the title of each book.

8. Write a program that reads the SOAP XML message from a file and connects to a SOAP server to execute a remote procedure call. Test it with the SOAP messages used in examples 13.5 and 13.6.

9. Write a stylesheet to transform the XML document created by Example 13.3 to an HTML file to display the results Execute Example 13.4 to obtain the HTML file.

10. Pick a service from the www.xmethods.com site and write a SOAP client to access that service. Create the SOAP XML message explicitly.

14

Programming Mobile Devices

Introduction

. . . .

The Java 2 Platform divides into three parts, Enterprise Edition (J2EE), Standard Edition (J2SE), and Micro Edition (J2ME). We look at the Micro Edition in this chapter. J2ME applies to two groups of devices, handheld and those that plug into the wall. The J2ME has configurations for each of these two groups.

The Connected Limited Device Configuration (CLDC) provides the basic classes for devices with 128–512K of memory, such as handheld organizers or cell phones. It uses the KVM, a smaller virtual machine designed for devices with limited memory. The Connected Device Configuration (CDC) applies to devices with over 512K memory such as set top boxes.

Profiles, added to a configuration, provide a complete API for a class of devices. The Mobile Information Device Profile (MIDP), added to the CLDC, applies to cell phones and personal digital assistants.

OBJECTIVES:

- Test MIDP applications on the phone emulator.
- Use the MIDP user interface components.

- Develop MIDP network applications.
- Use the MIDP RecordStore to save data.
- Handle low-level events.

14.1 MIDP Programming Basics

. . . .

We introduce the CLDC and MIDP classes and show how to get started with a first application.

The CLDC Classes

The Connected Limited Device Configuration includes classes from the `java.lang`, `java.io`, and `java.util` packages and adds a `javax.microedition.io` package. `Float` and `Double` are the notable omissions from the `java.lang` package in the CLDC.

The CLDC `java.io` package contains the `InputStream`, `OutputStream`, `Reader`, `Writer`, `DataInput`, `DataOutput`, `DataInputStream`, `DataOutputStream`, `ByteArrayInputStream`, `ByteArrayOutputStream`, `InputStreamReader`, `OutputStreamReader`, and `PrintStream` classes. The `java.util` package contains the `Calendar`, `Date`, `TimeZone`, `Enumeration`, `Vector`, `Stack`, `Hashtable`, and `Random` classes.

The `javax.microedition.io` package enables connections. It contains the `Connector` class, and the `Connection`, `ContentConnection`, `Datagram`, `DatagramConnection`, `InputConnection`, `OutputConnection`, `StreamConnection`, and `StreamConnectionNotifier` interfaces.

The MIDP Classes

The MIDP adds the `Timer` and `TimerTask` classes to the `java.util` package in the CLDC. It adds the `HttpConnection` interface to the CLDC `java.microedition.io` package.

The MIDP adds the following packages.

Package	Description
`javax.microedition.lcdui`	User interface
`javax.microedition.rms`	Persistent storage
`javax.microedition.midlet`	MIDP applications

Installing the J2ME

A MIDlet is a MIDP application. The software of the device it is in controls it. The J2ME distribution has a cell phone emulator so that we can test MIDlets without having to download them to a device. The MIDP API provides commands that have different embodiments on different devices. We cannot assume any particular configuration of keys or other input mechanisms. We illustrate our examples using the cell phone emulator.

Sun provides implementations of the CLDC and MIDP. From the `http://java.sun.com/j2me/` site click on the CLDC and KVM link at the bottom of the page to download the CLDC. Click on the MIDP link to download the MIDP. Update the PATH to include the `midp` and `preverify` programs. That command is

```
SET PATH=%MIDP_HOME%\bin;%MIDP_HOME%\BUILD\WIN32\TOOLS%PATH%.
```

where `MIDP_HOME` is the installation directory. The MIDP specification, which contains the MIDP documentation, requires a separate download.

Hello World on a Cell Phone

Figure 14.1 shows the cell phone emulator running Example 14.1.

Figure 14.1   The Hello World MIDlet

The Hello World MIDlet has a title, `Hello MIDlet`. It displays the message, `Hello World`, in a `TextBox`. The `Exit` command appears at the lower left of the screen. Pressing the button just below it will cause the MIDlet to terminate, simulating the user turning off the phone.

We put the MIDlet of Example 14.1 in the file `Hello.java`. The command

```
javac -classpath .;%MIDP_HOME%\classes Hello.java
```

compiles the MIDlet.

We need to preverify MIDlets. Java strives for robust, secure code. Using the J2SE, the JVM verifies each class as it is loaded to check that it is safe from accidental or malicious operations that can cause errors or damage the user's system. The KVM used on limited devices cannot perform the full verification process, so a preverification step does most of the processing before the class is loaded. The command

```
preverify -classpath .;%MIDP_HOME%\classes Hello
```

places the preverified class file in the output directory.

To run the MIDlet we change to the output directory and execute

```
midp Hello
```

In later examples containing several MIDlets we will need to package them in a JAR file and create a manifest file before running them.

MIDlets extend the MIDlet class, which has three abstract methods that must be overridden. They are startApp, pauseApp, and destroyApp. We can add commands to the display. We implement the Command Listener interface to respond to commands executed by the user. The CommandListener interface has one method, commandAction, which contains the event handling code.

EXAMPLE 14.1   **Hello.java**

```java
/* Displays Hello World!
 */

import javax.microedition.midlet.*;
import javax.microedition.lcdui.*;

public class Hello extends MIDlet
                    implements CommandListener {
  Displayable text = new TextBox
      ("Hello MIDlet", "Hello World!", 50, TextField.ANY);      // Note 1
  Command command = new Command("Exit", Command.EXIT, 1);       // Note 2

  public void startApp() {
    Display display = Display.getDisplay(this);                 // Note 3
    display.setCurrent(text);                                   // Note 4
    text.addCommand(command);                                   // Note 5
    text.setCommandListener(this);                              // Note 6
  }
  public void pauseApp() {
  }
  public void destroyApp(boolean b) {                           // Note 7
  }
  public void commandAction(Command c, Displayable d) {         // Note 8
    destroyApp(false);
    notifyDestroyed();                                          // Note 9
  }
}
```

....

Note 1:   A Displayable object may have commands and listeners associated with it. Two direct subclasses are Canvas and Screen. Canvas provides low-level access for games. Screen provides high-level access to maximize platform independence. `TextBox` subclasses `Screen`. It allows the user to enter and edit text. The four arguments to the `TextBox` constructor are the title, the initial text, the maximum number of stored characters, and the constraints. `TextBox` and `TextField` use the same constraint constants. They are

```
TextField.ANY
TextField.NUMERIC
TextField.PASSWORD
TextField.PHONENUMBER
TextField.URL
TextField.EMAILADDR
TextField.CONSTRAINT_MASK
```

Note 2:   The three arguments to the `Command` constructor are a label, a type, and a priority. Types include BACK, CANCEL, EXIT, HELP, ITEM, OK, SCREEN, and STOP. SCREEN indicates a command that applies to the current screen such as Load or Save. ITEM is intended to be specific to a particular item on the screen. The priority is an integer value with 1 representing the highest priority, 2 next, and so on. The implementation places the command in a manner depending on its type and priority. In Figure 14.1 the Exit command appears over the left button. Pressing that button will cause the application, the simulated phone, to exit.

Note 3:   `Display` represents the manager of the display and input devices. The `getDisplay` method returns the `Display` for the MIDlet passed as its argument.

Note 4:   There is no `Displayable` object when a MIDlet starts. We need to call the `setCurrent` method to provide one.

Note 5:   We add the command to the display.

Note 6:   `text.setCommandListener(this);`
The MIDlet implements the `CommandListener` interface. We register it with the screen, which will be the source of the Exit event.

Note 7:   `public void destroyApp(boolean b)`
The `destroyApp` signals the MIDlet to terminate. It frees any resources used by the application. If the argument is true the MIDlet must terminate unconditionally. If false, it may throw a `MIDletStateChangeException` to indicate that it does not want to be destroyed.

Note 8:   `public void commandAction(Command c, Displayable d)`
The `commandAction` method handles events. It is called when an event occurs. The arguments are the `Command` that occurred and the `Displayable` on which it occurred.

Note 9:   `notifyDestroyed();`
The `notifyDestroyed` method notifies the application management software that the MIDlet has entered the *Destroyed* state.

THE BIG PICTURE

The CLDC provides the basic functionality needed for devices such as cell phones and personal digital assistants. MIDP adds APIs for user interface, data storage and HTTP. We preverify classes to maintain security in devices with limited resources. The cell phone emulator lets us test application without having to load them on a device.

TEST YOUR UNDERSTANDING

1. Check the documentation to determine how the Math class in the java.lang package of the J2ME compares to the Math class in the java.lang package in the J2SE.

2. The pauseApp method in Example 14.1 does not do anything. What would happen if we were to omit it? Would Example 14.1 still compile and run?

TRY IT YOURSELF
3. What would happen if we change ANY to NUMERIC in the TextBox constructor of Example 14.1? Explain.

14.2 User Interfaces

. . . .

Handheld devices have much smaller displays than desktop computers and fewer input devices such as a mouse. The CLDC, a foundation for a range of devices, does not define GUI classes. The MIDP includes the javax.microedition.lcdui package containing user interface classes. It contains a high-level API for business applications that stresses portability, and a low-level API for games. Subclasses of Screen implement the high-level API. We use Graphics and Canvas for the low-level API, which can respond to key events.

Trying a Form

Screen subclasses Displayable, an object that can be displayed. Screen has the Alert, Form, List, and TextBox subclasses. We used a TextBox in Example 14.1.

A Form contains a mixture of items, each of which is a subclass of Item. Subclasses of Item include ChoiceGroup, DateField, Gauge, ImageItem, StringItem, and TextField. In Example 14.2 we add a StringItem and a TextField to a Form. Figure 14.2 shows the initial display.

A horizontal line separates the title "Echo Message" form the two parts of the Form. "Enter Text" is the label of the TextField. "Echo," the label of the StringItem, precedes the initial String, "Input goes here." Uppercase is the default mode for the letter keys. Pressing the up-arrow (and pound sign) key in the lower-left corner changes the input modes. The choices are uppercase, lowercase, numerals, and symbols.

Figure 14.2   The initial display of Example 14.2

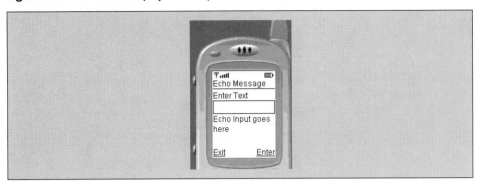

In the default uppercase mode, pressing a key will produce the first letter of the group. Pressing it again will produce the second letter, and so on cycling through the choices on that key. In the symbol mode, we use the four arrow keys to move to the desired symbol, and press the select button with the round circle in the middle to enter that character.

A large text entry area opens when we press the first key. Figure 14.3 shows this screen, where we have omitted the keypad to save space. Pressing the button under the Back label will return to the screen of Figure 14.2. Pressing the key under the Save label produces the screen of Figure 14.4. Pressing the key under the Enter label produces the screen of Figure 14.5 showing the echoing of the text in the StringItem. Pressing the key under the Exit label terminates the application.

Figure 14.3   After pressing the first key in Example 14.2

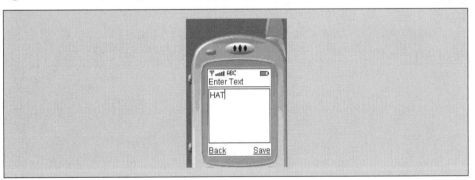

Figure 14.4   After pressing Save Example 14.2

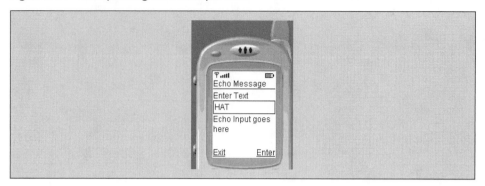

Figure 14.5   Echoing the text in Example 14.2

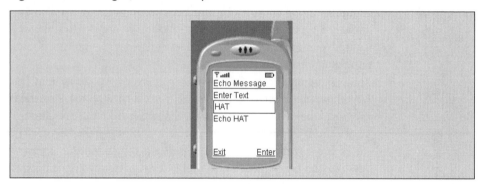

EXAMPLE 14.2   **TryForm.java**

```java
/* Creates a Form containing a TextField and
 * a StringItem.  Echoes the TextField text in
 * the StringItem.
 */

import javax.microedition.midlet.*;
import javax.microedition.lcdui.*;

public class TryForm extends MIDlet
                            implements CommandListener {
  Form form = new Form("Echo Message");
  TextField text =
      new TextField("Enter Text", "", 20, TextField.ANY);      // Note 1
  StringItem echo =
      new StringItem("Echo ", "Input goes here");               // Note 2
  Command exit = new Command("Exit", Command.EXIT, 1);
  Command enter = new Command("Enter", Command.ITEM, 2);       // Note 3
```

```
public void startApp() {
  Display display = Display.getDisplay(this);
  display.setCurrent(form);
  form.append(text);                              // Note 4
  form.append(echo);
  form.addCommand(exit);
  form.addCommand(enter);
  form.setCommandListener(this);
}
public void pauseApp() {
}
public void destroyApp(boolean b) {
}
public void commandAction(Command c, Displayable d) {
  if (c == exit) {
    destroyApp(false);
    notifyDestroyed();
  }
  else if (c == enter)
    echo.setText(text.getString());               // Note 5
  }
}
```

....

Note 1:   The four arguments of the `TextField` constructor are the label, the initial text, the maximum capacity, and the constraints, which are the same as those used for the `TextBox` constructor in Example 14.1, Note 1.

Note 2:   The two arguments to the `StringItem` constructor are the label and the initial text.

Note 3:   We define an `Enter` command which we add to the `Form`. We use it to echo the text that the user enters.

Note 4:   We add the `TextField` to the `Form`.

Note 5:   When responding to the `Enter` command, we use the `getString` method to get the text from the `TextField`, and the `setText` method to place it in the `StringItem`.

Trying a List

A `List` is a `Screen` containing a `List` of choices. We use a `List` as the main screen of Example 14.3. We add an `Alert`, a `DateField`, and a `Gauge` to it. We also include a `Ticker`. Figure 14.6 shows the initial screen for Example 14.3.

The `Ticker` is scrolling across the top. The title "`Try List`" appears followed by a horizontal line. The `List` shows the three items we added. We use the up and down arrow keys to change the selection and the key with the round circle in the center to make the selection. Because we use the `List` constructor

```
new List("Try List", List.IMPLICIT)
```

Figure 14.6   The initial screen for Example 14.3

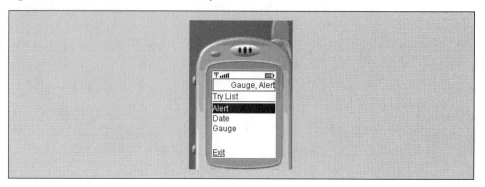

with the second argument specifying the List type of List.IMPLICIT, a selection of a list element will cause notification of the application by calling the commandAction method. We do not need to explicitly add a command, as Java generates one implicitly.

There are five types of Alert: ALARM, CONFIRMATION, ERROR, INFO, and WARNING. An Alert displays a message, and may play a sound. Figure 14.7 show the screen for an ALARM command. It sounds an alarm and appears for five seconds.

Figure 14.7   Selecting the Alert in Example 14.3

A DateField allows the user to select a date. Figure 14.8a shows the screen with the initial selection of the current date. Selecting again produces the screen of Figure 14.8b. Using the arrow keys allows the user to change the date. Pressing the Save key will revert to a screen like Figure 14.8a with the newly selected date.

A Gauge implements a bar graph of a value and may be interactive. We use the constructor

```
new Gauge("Each bar is 3",true,30,0)
```

whose four arguments are the label, a boolean signifying whether the gauge is interactive, the maximum value, and the initial value. The gauge typically shows about 10 bars, so if our range is from 0 to 30, each bar represents 3. Figure 14.9 shows the gauge after the user has pressed the right arrow key nine times.

Figure 14.8 The `DateField` of Example 14.3

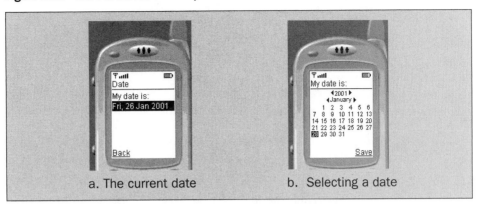

a. The current date   b. Selecting a date

Figure 14.9 The Gauge of Example 14.3

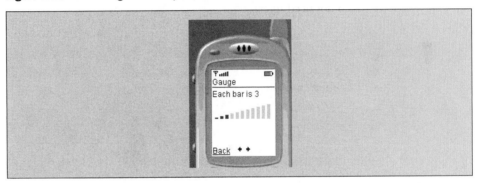

EXAMPLE 14.3   TryList.java

```
/* Displays a List on the main screen.  Includes
 * a Ticker, a Gauge, an Alert, and a DateField.
 */

import javax.microedition.midlet.*;
import javax.microedition.lcdui.*;
import java.util.Date;

public class TryList extends MIDlet
                            implements CommandListener {
  List list = new List("Try List", List.IMPLICIT);
  Ticker ticker = new Ticker("Gauge, Alert, Date --");     // Note 1
  Alert alert = new Alert("This is an Alert");             // Note 2
  Command exit = new Command("Exit", Command.EXIT, 1);
  Command back = new Command("Back", Command.BACK, 2);
  Display display;
```

```
public void startApp() {
  display = Display.getDisplay(this);
  display.setCurrent(list);
  list.setTicker(ticker);                                    // Note 3
  list.append("Alert", null);                                // Note 4
  list.append("Date", null);
  list.append("Gauge", null);
  list.addCommand(exit);
  list.setCommandListener(this);
}
public void pauseApp() {
}
public void destroyApp(boolean b) {
}
public void commandAction(Command c, Displayable d) {
  if (c == exit) {
    destroyApp(false);
    notifyDestroyed();
  }
  else if (c == back)                                        // Note 5
    display.setCurrent(list);
  else {                                                     // Note 6
    List items = (List)display.getCurrent();                 // Note 7
    switch (items.getSelectedIndex()) {                      // Note 8
      case 0:
        alert.setType(AlertType.ALARM);                      // Note 9
        alert.setTimeout(5000);                              // Note 10
        display.setCurrent(alert);                           // Note 11
        alert.getType().playSound(display);                  // Note 12
        break;
      case 1:
        Form f1 = new Form("Date");                          // Note 13
        DateField date =
          new DateField("My date is: ", DateField.DATE);     // Note 14
        date.setDate(new Date());                            // Note 15
        f1.append(date);
        f1.addCommand(back);                                 // Note 16
        f1.setCommandListener(this);
        display.setCurrent(f1);
        break;
      case 2:
        Form f2 = new Form("Gauge");
        Gauge gauge =
          new Gauge("Each bar is 3",true,30,0);
        f2.append(gauge);
        f2.addCommand(back);
        f2.setCommandListener(this);
```

```
            display.setCurrent(f2);
            break;
        }
      }
    }
}
```

....

Note 1: The argument to the `Ticker` constructor is the message that scrolls across the screen.

Note 2: We construct an `Alert` with a title. We could have used a four argument constructor to specify the title, a message `String`, an `Image`, and an `Alert-Type`.

Note 3: We use the `setTicker` method to place the `Ticker` in the `List` screen.

Note 4: The `append` method adds items to a `List`. The second argument is an `Image`, which we do not include.

Note 5: When the user presses the key corresponding to the `Back` command, we revert to the original `List` by setting the current value of the display.

Note 6: `else`
The `else` alternative, with no condition, represents the implicit commands added to respond to selection of the `List` items. We handle the selection of `Alert`, `DateField`, and `Gauge` here.

Note 7: `List items = (List)display.getCurrent();`
We use the `getCurrent` method to return the `List` being displayed.

Note 8: `switch (items.getSelectedIndex())`
The `getSelectedIndex` method return the index of the currently selected `List` item.

Note 9: `alert.setType(AlertType.ALARM);`
The `AlertType` class contains values representing each of the types. Some, like `ALARM`, cause a sound to play when the `Alert` is selected.

Note 10: `alert.setTimeout(5000);`
We set the time for `Alert` to appear as 5000 milleseconds, or 5 seconds.

Note 11: `display.setCurrent(alert);`
We set the current display to make the `Alert` visible.

Note 12: `alert.getType().playSound(display);`
To play a sound we need to refer to the `AlertType` for the appropriate sound. We use the `getType` method to return the `AlertType`, and the `play-Sound` method to play the sound.

Note 13: `Form f1 = new Form("Date");`

We can only display subclasses of `Displayable`, which include subclasses of `Screen`, which includes `Form`, but not `DateField`. We place the `DateField` in a `Form` and add the `Form` to the `List`.

Note 14: `new DateField("My date is: ", DateField.DATE)`

The second argument, for the mode, can be `DATE`, `DATE_TIME`, or `TIME`.

Note 15: `date.setDate(new Date());`

The default `Date` constructor produces the current date.

Note 16: `f1.addCommand(back);`

We add the `Back` command to allow the user to navigate back to the original `List` display.

Packaging MIDlets

We can create an application containing two or more MIDlets. To do that we package the MIDlets in a JAR file and execute using a manifest file. To illustrate we package the `TryForm` and `TryList` MIDlets together as one application. Figure 14.10 shows the initial screen. Selecting the `Form` item will execute the MIDlet of Example 14.2. Selecting the `List` item will execute the MIDlet of Example 14.3.

Figure 14.10 Packaging two MIDlets

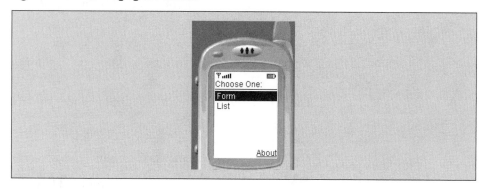

Figure 14.11 shows the manifest file we use.

Figure 14.11 The manifest file `Two.mf`

```
MIDlet-Name: Two
MIDlet-1:  Form,,TryForm
MIDlet-2:  List,,TryList
```

We create the JAR file using the command

`jar cfm Two.jar Two.mf TryForm.class TryList.class`

where the options are the same as we used in Chapter 9 when creating JavaBeans.

TIP
☞

Remember to create the JAR file in the `output` directory, which contains the preverified class files.

....

We execute the application using the command

`midp -descriptor Two.mf`

where `Two.mf` is the manifest file of Figure 14.11. We could have added more information to the manifest file, but had no need to here.

THE BIG PICTURE

The `javax.microedition.lcdui` package contains user interface classes. We display the `Alert`, `Form`, `List`, and `TextBox` subclasses of `Screen`. A `Form` may include subclasses of `Item` such as `DateField`, `Gauge`, `ImageItem`, `StringItem`, and `TextField`. We package an application containing two or more MIDlets in a JAR file.

TEST YOUR UNDERSTANDING
---

4. If a `Gauge` represents values from 1 to 100, about how many units does each bar represent?

5. What do you think is the type of the parameter in the `setCurrent` method?

TRY IT YOURSELF   6. Run Example 14.3 and change the date to July 4, 2010. What day of the week is it?

14.3   Making Connections
· · · · · · · · · ·

MIDP supports HTTP connections. Networking follows an approach in the J2ME different than that of the J2SE. To support a variety of devices the CLDC provides generic connections. The `Connection` interface provides the most basic generic connection. We first use the `StreamConnection` that lets us perform input and output, and then illustrate an `HttpConnection` that lets us control HTTP requests.

A StreamConnection

The `openInputStream` method returns an `InputStream`, while the `openDataInputStream` method returns a `DataInputStream`. The `openOutputStream` method returns an `OutputStream`, while the `openDataOutputStream` method returns a `DataOutputStream`.

The `Connector` class contains the static methods used to create all the connections. We use the `open` method with one `String` argument. This exposes the generic nature of the CLDC approach. The `String` can specify any protocol, but it is up to the implementation to support it. MIDP supports HTTP, which we use in our examples.

Example 14.4 gets a message from the author's web site and displays it in a `TextBox`. Figure 14.12 shows the display of the message. We need to wait a few seconds for it to appear due to the transmission across the network.

Figure 14.12 The message retrieved by Example 14.4

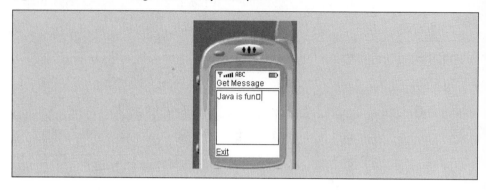

EXAMPLE 14.4 **GetMessage.java**

```java
/* Gets a message and displays it.
 */

import javax.microedition.midlet.*;
import javax.microedition.lcdui.*;
import javax.microedition.io.*;
import java.io.*;

public class GetMessage extends MIDlet
                              implements CommandListener {
  Displayable text;
  Command command = new Command("Exit", Command.EXIT, 1);
  Display display;

  public void startApp() {
    display = Display.getDisplay(this);
    StreamConnection connection;
    try {
      connection = (StreamConnection)Connector.open
        ("http://www.cecs.csulb.edu/~artg/message.txt");       // Note 1
      InputStream input = connection.openInputStream();
      StringBuffer message = new StringBuffer();
      int index = 0;
      int ch;
      while((ch=input.read()) != -1)
        message.append((char)ch);
      text = new TextBox
          ("Get Message",message.toString(),50,TextField.ANY);
      input.close();
      connection.close();
    }catch (Exception e) {
      e.printStackTrace();
    }
```

```
      display.setCurrent(text);
      text.addCommand(command);
      text.setCommandListener(this);
    }
    public void pauseApp() {
    }
    public void destroyApp(boolean b) {
    }
    public void commandAction(Command c, Displayable d) {
      destroyApp(false);
      notifyDestroyed();
    }
}
```

Note 1:   We open a message in a text file on the author's web site.

An HttpConnection

The MIDP adds the `HttpConnection` interface to the `javax.microedition.lcdui` package. It includes a number of methods dealing with an HTTP request and response. These include:

```
long getDate()
long getExpiration()
String getHeaderField(int n)
String getHeaderField(String name)
String getHeaderFieldKey(int n)
String getHost()
long getLastModified()
int getPort()
String getProtocol()
String getRequestMethod()
String getRequestProperty(String key)
int getResponseCode()
String getResponseMessage()
void setRequestMethod(String method)
void setRequestProperty(String key, String value)
```

In Example 14.5 the user enters the name of a `Customer`, from the `Sales` database of Chapter 3, in a `TextField`. When the user presses the `Enter` button, we connect to the `SalesBalance` servlet. It connects to the `Sales` database and retrieves and sends the balance due for that customer. We display the balance due in a `StringItem`. Figure 14.13a shows the entry of a customer name, and Figure 14.13b shows the display of the balance due for that customer.

Figure 14.13   The screens of Example 14.5

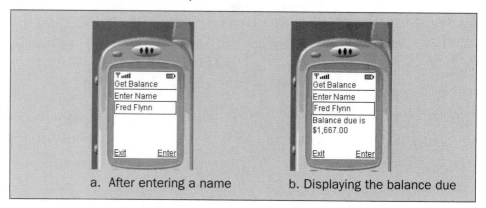

a. After entering a name   b. Displaying the balance due

TIP

To enter text, remember to change the mode between uppercase and lowercase to input the name correctly. When entering consecutive letters using the same key, such as 'e' and 'd,' one needs to wait for the position to change after entering the first character. Otherwise pressing the same key again will just change the letter without changing the position.

A GET request appends any parameters to the URL, prefixed by a question mark. We use a plus sign to join the first name and the last name since the URL cannot contain spaces. In Example 14.5 the complete URL when requesting the balance due for Fred Flynn is

```
http://localhost:8100/servlet/SalesBalance?Name=Fred+Flynn
```

EXAMPLE 14.5   **SalesBalance.java, GetBalance.java**

```
/* Uses a servlet to find the balance due for a customer
 * whose name the user enters.
 */
```

SalesBalance.java

```
/* Reads a customer name and writes the balance
 * due for that customer which it finds from the
 * Sales database of Chapter 3.
 */

import java.io.*;
import javax.servlet.*;
import javax.servlet.http.*;
import java.sql.*;
import java.text.*;
import sun.jdbc.odbc.JdbcOdbcDriver;
```

```java
public class SalesBalance extends HttpServlet {
  Connection con;
  Statement stmt;
  NumberFormat cf = NumberFormat.getCurrencyInstance();

  public void init(ServletConfig sc)
                            throws ServletException {
    super.init(sc);
    try{
      new JdbcOdbcDriver();
      String url = "jdbc:odbc:Sales";
      String user = "";
      String password = "";
      con = DriverManager.getConnection(url, user, password);
      stmt = con.createStatement();
    }catch (Exception e) {
        e.printStackTrace();
        System.exit(1);
    }
  }
  public void doGet(HttpServletRequest req,
                  HttpServletResponse resp)
                        throws ServletException, IOException {
    resp.setContentType("text/html");
    PrintWriter  out = resp.getWriter();
    try {
      String name = req.getParameter("Name");              // Note 1
      String query =  "SELECT BalanceDue FROM Customer "
              + "WHERE CustomerName = '" + name + "'";      // Note 2
      ResultSet rs = stmt.executeQuery(query);
      while(rs.next())
        out.println("Balance due is " + cf.format
          (Double.parseDouble(rs.getString("BalanceDue"))));  // Note 3
    }catch(Exception e) {
      e.printStackTrace();
    }
    out.close();
  }
  public void doPost(HttpServletRequest req,
                  HttpServletResponse resp)
                      throws ServletException, IOException {
    doGet(req,resp);
  }
}
```

GetBalance.java

```java
/* Connects to a servlet to return the balance due
 * for the customer whose name the user enters.
 * Displays the balance due in a StringItem.
 */
```

```
import javax.microedition.midlet.*;
import javax.microedition.lcdui.*;
import javax.microedition.io.*;
import java.io.*;
import java.util.*;

public class GetBalance extends MIDlet implements CommandListener {
  Form form = new Form("Get Balance");
  TextField text = new TextField
                     ("Enter Name", "", 20, TextField.ANY);
  StringItem balance = new StringItem("", "");                    // Note 4
  Command exit = new Command("Exit", Command.EXIT, 1);
  Command enter = new Command("Enter", Command.ITEM, 2);
  Display display;
  HttpConnection connection;
  StringBuffer result = new StringBuffer();

  public void startApp() {
    display = Display.getDisplay(this);
    display.setCurrent(form);
    form.append(text);
    form.append(balance);
    form.addCommand(exit);
    form.addCommand(enter);
    form.setCommandListener(this);
  }
  public void pauseApp() {
  }
  public void destroyApp(boolean b) {
  }
  public void commandAction(Command c, Displayable d) {
    if (c == exit) {
      destroyApp(false);
      notifyDestroyed();
    }
    else if (c == enter) {
      String n = text.getString();
      int i = n.indexOf(' ');                                     // Note 5
      String s = "?Name=" + n.substring(0,i) + '+'
                          + n.substring(i+1);                     // Note 6
      try {
        connection = (HttpConnection)Connector.open
          ("http://localhost:8100/servlet/SalesBalance" + s);
        connection.setRequestMethod(HttpConnection.GET);          // Note 7
        connection.setRequestProperty
                    ("User-Agent", "CLDC/kvm");                   // Note 8
        InputStream input = connection.openInputStream();
        int ch;
```

```
        while((ch=input.read()) != -1)
            result.append((char)ch);                          // Note 9
        input.close();
        connection.close();
    }catch (Exception e) {
        e.printStackTrace();
    }
    balance.setText(result.toString());                       // Note 10
    }
  }
}
```

- -

Note 1: Because we are not using an HTML form to input the Name parameter from the user, we will need to append it to the URL ourselves in the Get-Balance class below.

Note 2: This concatenates the value of name between single quotes in the SQL query.

Note 3: The getString method returns a String with four places after the decimal point. We convert it to a double and then format it as a currency value in the default locale, en_US, in this run.

Note 4: We initialize the label and the text of the StringItem to empty strings because the servlet will respond with the complete message.

Note 5: We find the index of the space between the first and last names.

Note 6:
```
String s = "?Name=" + n.substring(0,i) + '+'
                      + n.substring(i+1);
```
This is the parameter that we need to append to the URL.

Note 7: `connection.setRequestMethod(HttpConnection.GET);`
We use the setRequestMethod to specify the GET method for the HTTP request.

Note 8: `connection.setRequestProperty`
`              ("User-Agent", "CLDC/kvm");`

We use the setRequestProperty method to specify a request header. This is optional. We send it to illustrate its use. Sending request headers helps the server to satisfy the request. The server may have different formats for responses to different user agents.

Note 9:
```
while((ch=input.read()) != -1)
    result.append((char)ch);
```
This loop reads the balance due message sent from the servlet.

Note 10: `balance.setText(result.toString());`
The setText method inserts the response as the StringItem display.

THE BIG PICTURE
To accommodate diverse platforms the CLDC provides a generic Connection with an open method that accepts a String. A StreamConnection allows us to transfer data between client and server. MIDP adds an HttpConnection, which provides methods supporting HTTP requests and responses.

TEST YOUR UNDERSTANDING

7. Which package contains the J2ME classes for generic connections?

8. What methods can one invoke on a StreamConnection?

9. Why might we open a DataInputStream rather than an InputStream?

10. What methods in Example 14.5 require the use of an HttpConnection rather than a StreamConnection?

14.4 Persistent Storage

. . . .

The javax.microedition.rms package provides a record management system to store data on the device for use by an application. This simple API makes use of the limited storage available on MIDP devices.

Using a Byte Array

Each record is a byte array. The easiest way to pack typed data into a byte array is to wrap a ByteArrayOutputStream in a DataOutputStream and use its write methods to write typed values to the stream. The toByteArray method converts the ByteArrayOutputStream to a byte array that we can add to a RecordStore. Example 14.6 illustrates the packing of data in a byte array.

EXAMPLE 14.6   ByteStream.java

```java
/* Uses streams to pack typed data into a byte array.
 */

import java.io.*;

public class ByteStream {
  public static void main(String[] args) {
    try {
      ByteArrayOutputStream byteOut =
                     new ByteArrayOutputStream();
      DataOutputStream dataOut = new DataOutputStream(byteOut);
      dataOut.writeInt(4500);                                  // Note 1
      dataOut.writeUTF("This string has 30 characters.");      // Note 2
      byte[] bytes = byteOut.toByteArray();
      for(int i = 0; i < bytes.length; i++)
```

```
            System.out.print(bytes[i] + " ");                    // Note 3
         System.out.println();
         ByteArrayInputStream byteIn =
                        new ByteArrayInputStream(bytes);
         DataInputStream dataIn = new DataInputStream(byteIn);
         System.out.println(dataIn.readInt());                   // Note 4
         System.out.println(dataIn.readUTF());
         byteOut.close();
         dataOut.close();
         byteIn.close();
         dataIn.close();
      }catch(IOException e) {
         e.printStackTrace();
      }
   }
}
```

Output

```
0 0 17 -108 0 30 84 104 105 115 32 115 116 114 105 110 103 32 104 97 115 32 51
48 32 99 104 97 114 97 99 116 101 114 115 46
4500
This string has 30 characters.
```

Note 1: Using the `writeInt` method of a `DataOutputStream` is much easier than writing each of the four bytes of an integer value directly.

Note 2: The UTF (Unicode Text Format) writes characters in which most are ASCII in a compact way. The `writeUTF` method uses two bytes to give the number of characters followed by the UTF characters.

Note 3: Listing the bytes of the byte array show the four bytes representing 4500 as 0 0 17 -108, because 4500 = 17*256 + 148. Bytes are signed so 148 which equals 256-108 represents -108. The next two bytes, 0 and 30, indicate that 30 characters follow.

Note 4: We use a `DataInputStream` to input the typed values from the byte array we obtained from the `ByteArrayOutputStream`.

A Record Store

The `RecordStore` class stores each record as an array of bytes. It uses an integer key, which we do not use in Example 14.7. The static method

```
open(String name, boolean createIfNecessary)
```

returns a `RecordStore` with the specified name. If the second argument is true it will create one if it does not exist.

The method

```
int addRecord(byte[] data, int offset, int numBytes)
```

adds a record and returns its ID. The second parameter gives the offset in the array at which the record starts, and the third is the number of bytes.

The method

```
enumerateRecords(RecordFilter filter,
              RecordComparator comparator,
              boolean keepUpdated)
```

returns a `RecordEnumeration` which we use to retrieve records. The `RecordFilter`, if used, determines which records to enumerate. The `RecordComparator`, if used, determines in which order the records are enumerated. If the third argument is true, the enumerator will keep its enumeration current with any changes in the records.

See the MIDP documentation for the other methods of the `RecordStore` class.

A RecordFilter

The `RecordFilter` interface contains the method

```
boolean matches(bytes[] candidate)
```

which returns true if the candidate matches according to the implemented criterion. In Example 14.7 we will create a RecordFilter to match records with a given user name.

A RecordComparator

The `RecordComparator` interface contains the fields

```
public static final int PRECEDES
public static final int EQUIVALENT
public static final int FOLLOWS
```

and the method

```
compare(byte[] rec1, byte[] rec2)
```

which returns `PRECEDES` if `rec1` precedes `rec2` in sorted order, `FOLLOWS` if it follows, and `EQUIVALENT` if `rec1` and `rec2` are equivalent in sorted order.

A RecordEnumeration

We use the method

```
bytes[] nextRecord()
```

to return the array of bytes for the next record, and

```
boolean hasNextElement()
```

to determine if more records are available.

In Example 14.7, whenever a user quits running the MIDlet we update the `RecordStore` with a new value, randomly chosen, for that user's score. If the MIDlet provided a game, the score could have been determined by the user's play of the game. Figure 14.14a shows that on entry the user either gets the user's score, or get all scores, or quits. Figure 14.14b shows the screen with the user's score. Figure 14.14c shows the result of the request for all scores.

Figure 14.14   Using a record store

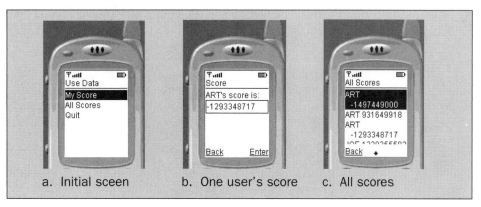

a. Initial sceen   b. One user's score   c. All scores

TIP

When compiling and running Example 14.7 we must preverify the two anonymous inner classes, DataStore$1, and DataStore$2.

EXAMPLE 14.7   **DataStore.java**

```java
/* Uses a RecordStore to save a score for each user.
 * Retrieves the user's score or all scores.
 * Updates the user's score on exit.
 */

import javax.microedition.midlet.*;
import javax.microedition.lcdui.*;
import javax.microedition.rms.*;
import java.io.*;
import java.util.Random;

public class DataStore extends MIDlet implements
        CommandListener, RecordFilter, RecordComparator  {
  List list = new List("Use Data", List.IMPLICIT);            // Note 1
  Command exit = new Command("Exit", Command.EXIT, 1);
  Command back = new Command("Back", Command.BACK, 2);
  Command enter = new Command("Enter", Command.ITEM, 3);
  Display display;
  RecordStore data;
  String nameToMatch = "";                                    // Note 2

  public void startApp() {
    display = Display.getDisplay(this);
```

```
        display.setCurrent(list);
        list.append("My Score", null);
        list.append("All Scores", null);
        list.append("Quit", null);
        list.setCommandListener(this);
        try {
            data = RecordStore.openRecordStore("scores", true);
        }catch(Exception e) {
            e.printStackTrace();
        }
    }
    public void addScore(String name, int score) {                    // Note 3
        try {
            ByteArrayOutputStream byteOut =
                            new ByteArrayOutputStream();
            DataOutputStream dataOut = new DataOutputStream(byteOut);
            dataOut.writeUTF(name);
            dataOut.writeInt(score);
            byte[] bytes = byteOut.toByteArray();
            data.addRecord(bytes, 0, bytes.length);                   // Note 4
        }catch(Exception e) {
            e.printStackTrace();
        }
    }
    public boolean matches(byte[] in) {                               // Note 5
        ByteArrayInputStream byteIn = new ByteArrayInputStream(in);
        DataInputStream dataIn = new DataInputStream(byteIn);
        String name = "";
        try {
            name = dataIn.readUTF();
        }catch(Exception e) {
            e.printStackTrace();
        }
        return nameToMatch.equals(name);
    }
    public int compare(byte[] b1, byte[] b2) {                        // Note 6
        ByteArrayInputStream bIn1 = new ByteArrayInputStream(b1);
        DataInputStream dIn1 = new DataInputStream(bIn1);
        ByteArrayInputStream bIn2 = new ByteArrayInputStream(b2);
        DataInputStream dIn2 = new DataInputStream(bIn2);
        String name1="", name2="";
        try {
            name1 = dIn1.readUTF();
            name2 = dIn2.readUTF();
        }catch(Exception e) {
            e.printStackTrace();
        }
        int result = name1.compareTo(name2);
        if (result < 0)
            return RecordComparator.PRECEDES;
```

```
      else if (result == 0)
        return RecordComparator.EQUIVALENT;
      else
        return RecordComparator.FOLLOWS;
  }

  public int getScore(String n) {                                   // Note 7
    int score = 0;
    try {
      nameToMatch = n;
      RecordEnumeration enum =
                  data.enumerateRecords(this,this,false);           // Note 8
      while (enum.hasNextElement()) {
        ByteArrayInputStream byteIn =
          new ByteArrayInputStream(enum.nextRecord());
        DataInputStream dataIn = new DataInputStream(byteIn);
        String name = "";
        name = dataIn.readUTF();                                    // Note 9
        score =dataIn.readInt();
      }
    }catch(Exception e) {
      e.printStackTrace();
    }
    return score;
  }
  public List getAllScores() {                                      // Note 10
    List scores = new List("All Scores", List.IMPLICIT);
    try {
      RecordEnumeration enum =
                  data.enumerateRecords(null,this,false);           // Note 11
      while (enum.hasNextElement()) {
        ByteArrayInputStream byteIn =
          new ByteArrayInputStream(enum.nextRecord());
        DataInputStream dataIn = new DataInputStream(byteIn);
        int score = 0;
        String name = "";
        name = dataIn.readUTF();
        score =dataIn.readInt();
        scores.append(name + ' ' + score, null);
      }
    }catch(Exception e) {
      e.printStackTrace();
    }
    return scores;
  }
  public void pauseApp() {
  }
  public void destroyApp(boolean b) {
  }
  public void commandAction(Command c, Displayable d) {
    if (c == exit) {
```

```
              destroyApp(false);
              notifyDestroyed();
          }else if (c == back)
            display.setCurrent(list);
          else {
          List items = (List)display.getCurrent();
          switch (items.getSelectedIndex()) {
            case 0:
              final Form f0 = new Form("Name");                      // Note 12
              final TextField text = new TextField
                  ("Enter Name", "", 20, TextField.ANY);
              f0.append(text);
              f0.addCommand(back);
              f0.addCommand(enter);
              f0.setCommandListener(new CommandListener() {          // Note 13
                public void commandAction
                            (Command c, Displayable d) {
                  if (c == back)
                        display.setCurrent(list);
                  else {
                    String n = text.getString();
                    String s = String.valueOf(getScore(n));          // Note 14
                    text.setLabel(n + "'s score is:");               // Note 15
                    text.setString(s);
                    f0.setTitle("Score");                            // Note 16
                  }
                }
              });
              display.setCurrent(f0);
              break;
            case 1:
              List all = getAllScores();                             // Note 17
              all.addCommand(back);
              all.setCommandListener(this);
              display.setCurrent(all);
              break;
            case 2:
              Form f2 = new Form("Name");                            // Note 18
              final TextField t = new TextField
                  ("Enter Name", "", 20, TextField.ANY);
              f2.append(t);
              f2.addCommand(enter);
              f2.setCommandListener(new CommandListener() {
                Random random = new Random();
                public void commandAction
                            (Command c, Displayable d) {
                  addScore(t.getString(), random.nextInt());         // Note 19
                  destroyApp(false);
```

```
            notifyDestroyed();
          }
      });
      display.setCurrent(f2);
      break;
    }
  }
 }
}
```

....

Note 1:   The initial screen is a List.

Note 2:   nameToMatch will hold the name that we use to filter the record store.

Note 3:   The addScore method writes the name and the score to a ByteArrayInput-Stream and then adds the byte array to the data store.

Note 4:   We ignore the return value, which gives the ID of the record.

Note 5:   The matches method, specified in the RecordFilter interface, extracts the name from the record. It returns true if that name equals nameToMatch.

Note 6:   `public int compare(byte[] b1, byte[] b2)`
The compare method, specified in the RecordComparator interface, extracts the names from each record and uses a String comparison of these names to determine the return value.

Note 7:   `public int getScore(String n)`
The getScore method saves its argument as nameToMatch. It creates a RecordEnumeration which filters using the matches method. We include multiple entries for a name so the filter may produce multiple records. We only return the score of the last record enumerated. We could modify the example to save only the highest score for each person, in which case the filter would select at most one record.

Note 8:   `RecordEnumeration enum =`
`             data.enumerateRecords(this,this,false);`
The first argument is a class that implements the RecordFilter interface, while the second implements RecordComparator. We could have passed null for the second argument because we do not need to order the records. We pass false for the third argument because we are not going to change records during the enumeration.

Note 9:   `name = dataIn.readUTF();`
Even though we do not use the name, we need to read it because it appears first in the record.

Note 10: `public List getAllScores()`
The getAllScores method returns a List in which each item is record consisting of a name and a score.

Note 11: `RecordEnumeration enum =`
                          `data.enumerateRecords(null,this,false);`
We do not use a filter, so the enumeration will retrieve all records.

Note 12: `final Form f0 = new Form("Name");`
When the user chooses the `My Score` item from the original `List`, we create a `Form` with a `TextField` to input the user's name. We must declare variables that will be used in an inner class as `final`. Java copies the value of the variable into the inner class. By declaring the variable as `final`, we cannot change its value so that having two copies will not cause an inconsistency.

Note 13: `f0.setCommandListener(new CommandListener() {`
We create an inner class to handle commands in this form. When the user enters a name, we get the score corresponding to the last entry for that name and display it in the text field.

Note 14: `String s = String.valueOf(getScore(n));`
We get the score and convert it to a `String` to display in the `TextField`.

Note 15: `text.setLabel(n + "'s score is:");`
We change the label of the `TextField` to reflect that we will be displaying the score rather than the name.

Note 16: `f0.setTitle("Score");`
We change the title of the `Form` to reflect that we will be displaying the score rather than the name.

Note 17: `List all = getAllScores();`
The `getAllScores` method returns a `List` that we display. We add a `Back` button to return to the original screen.

Note 18: `Form f2 = new Form("Name");`
When the user chooses the `Quit` item, we produce a `Form` with a `TextField` to input the user's name. We then generate a random number to use as the score to associate with this name in the `RecordStore`.

Note 19: `addScore(t.getString(), random.nextInt());`
The `nextInt` methods returns an integer that appears to be randomly generated. It ranges over Java integer values, which are both positive and negative. We could modify the application to use smaller positive values.

THE BIG PICTURE

The MIDP record management system uses a `RecordStore` to store records of byte arrays. A `RecordFilter` can select records based on a criterion implemented in a `match` method. A `RecordComparator` compares records to present them in a particular order. A `RecordEnumeration` enumerates records and may use a filter or a comparator.

TEST YOUR UNDERSTANDING

---

11. What type of data could we enter into a RecordStore easily without using stream classes?

12. What arguments should we pass to the `enumerateRecords` methods to neither filter nor order records?

TRY IT YOURSELF   13. What happens if we omit the call to `readUTF` in the `getScore` method of Example 14.7?

14.5   Low-Level Events

. . . .

The `Canvas` class allows us to draw using a `Graphics` object and to respond to low-level events such as key presses.

Graphics

The `drawArc`, `drawLine`, `drawRect`, `drawRoundRect`, and the corresponding fill methods use the same parameters as the same-named AWT methods. The `drawString` method includes an additional fourth parameter, which is an anchor.

We use anchor points to minimize computation when displaying text. We define an anchor point by combining one of the vertical constants (TOP, BASELINE, BOTTOM) with one of the horizontal constants (LEFT, HCENTER, RIGHT) using the bitwise OR operator. The constants refer to the position, relative to the text, of the point (x,y) used to locate the text. For example, the anchor `Graphics.BOTTOM|Graphics.LEFT` will locate (x,y) at the bottom and to the left of the text. The method

```
drawImage(Image img, int x, int y, int anchor)
```

also uses an anchor.

To set a `Font`, we use the `setFont` method as in the AWT. We specify a color using

```
setColor(int red, int geen, int blue)
```

where `red`, `green`, and `blue` range from 0 to 255. The `getRedComponent`, `getGreenCompo-net`, and `getBlueComponent` methods return color values.

Canvas

We must override the `Canvas` class to use it. We always need to override the abstract `paint` method, and may wish to implement some event handlers.

`Canvas` defines constants for each of the standard telephone keys. They are `KEY_NUM0` through `KEY_NUM9`, `KEY_POUND`, and `KEY_STAR`. The implementation must use negative values for key codes for keys that do not correspond to Unicode characters.

For games that use keys that might vary from platform to platform, `Canvas` defines generic codes DOWN, UP, LEFT, RIGHT, FIRE, GAME_A, GAME_B, GAME_C, and GAME_D. We use the `getGameAction` method to determine if a key code represents a game action. In this way different platforms can execute the same program.

We use the `keyPressed` and `keyReleased` methods to handle key events. MIDP does not use listener interfaces for this purpose.

The `hasPointerEvents` method indicates whether the platform supports the use of a pointer. We emulate the pointer using the mouse. The `pointerPressed` and `pointer-Released` methods handle pointer events.

The `hasPointerMotionEvents` indicates whether the platform supports pointer motion. The `pointerDragged` method handles pointer motion events.

In Example 14.8 we display a red rectangle. We can move it by pressing the arrow keys. Pressing the mouse will gradually alter the color toward white so that eventually the rectangle blends into the background. Figure 14.15 shows the initial screen.

Figure 14.15 The initial screen of Example 14.8

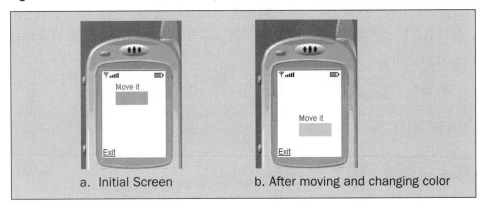

a. Initial Screen   b. After moving and changing color

TIP

Execute the command

```
SET SCREEN_DEPTH=8
```

to see the color display. Preverify the inner class `LowLevel$MyCanvas`.

....

EXAMPLE 14.8   LowLevel.java

```java
/* Displays a red rectangle.  Pressing the arrow
 * keys moves the rectangle.  Pressing the mouse
 * changes the color until it becomes white.
 */

import javax.microedition.midlet.*;
import javax.microedition.lcdui.*;

public class LowLevel extends MIDlet
                      implements CommandListener {
  Command exit = new Command("Exit", Command.EXIT, 1);
  MyCanvas canvas = null;
```

```
public void startApp() {
  Display display = Display.getDisplay(this);
  canvas = new MyCanvas();
  display.setCurrent(canvas);
  canvas.addCommand(exit);
  canvas.setCommandListener(this);
}
public void pauseApp() {
}
public void destroyApp(boolean b) {
}
public void commandAction(Command c, Displayable d) {
  if (c == exit) {
    destroyApp(false);
    notifyDestroyed();
  }
}
public class MyCanvas extends Canvas {
  int x = 20, y = 20;
  int red = 255, green = 0, blue = 0;

  public MyCanvas() {
    System.out.println(hasPointerEvents());                      // Note 1
  }
  public void paint(Graphics g) {
    g.setColor(255,255,255);                                     // Note 2
    g.fillRect(0,0,getWidth(),getHeight());                      // Note 3
    g.setColor(Math.min(red,255),
               Math.min(green,255),
               Math.min(blue,255));                              // Note 4
    g.fillRect(x,y,50,20);
    g.setColor(0,0,255);
    g.drawString("Move it",x,y,
            Graphics.BOTTOM|Graphics.LEFT);                      // Note 5
  }
  protected void pointerPressed(int x, int y) {                  // Note 6
    red += 5;
    green += 5;
    blue += 5;
    repaint();
  }
  protected void keyPressed(int keyCode) {                       // Note 7
    switch (getGameAction(keyCode)) {
      case Canvas.UP :
                      y -= 2;
                      break;
      case Canvas.DOWN :
                      y += 2;
                      break;
      case Canvas.RIGHT :
                      x += 2;
                      break;
```

```
                case Canvas.LEFT :
                            x -= 2;
                            break;
        }
      repaint();
    }
  }
}
```

Note 1:   We inquire if the platform supports pointer events.

Note 2:   We set the color to white to draw over the previous screen.

Note 3:   The getWidth and getHeight methods return the width and height of the Canvas. We fill the entire Canvas with the background color to erase the previous drawing.

Note 4:   Because we keep increasing the color values, we check that they do not increase beyond 255.

Note 5:   We set the anchor point at the bottom and to the left of the string.

Note 6:   protected void pointerPressed(int x, int y)
When the user presses the mouse, we add 5 to each color value and repaint to show the new color.

Note 7:   protected void keyPressed(int keyCode)
When the user presses a key we check if it corresponds to one the game actions UP, DOWN, RIGHT, or LEFT. If so we adjust the position of the rectangle accordingly and repaint to show it in its new position.

THE BIG PICTURE

The Graphics class provides drawing methods. The Canvas class class contains event handlers for key and pointer events. Canvas defines constants for the standard telephone keys and generic constants to represent game actions that might be implemented in different ways on different platforms.

TEST YOUR UNDERSTANDING

TRY IT YOURSELF   14. Try the TOP|HCENTER anchor for the point (x,y) in Example 14.8. Rerun the example and explain the result.

TRY IT YOURSELF   15. What is the sign of the value of keyCode when the key pressed is the up arrow? What is the sign if the 2ABC key is pressed?

TRY IT YOURSELF   16. What value does getGameAction return when we pass it the key code for the up arrow key? What value does it return when we pass it the key code for the 2ABC key?

SUMMARY

- The Connected Limited Device Configuration (CLDC) provides the foundation APIs for devices with 128-512K memory such as cell phones and personal digital assistants. The Mobile Information Device Profile (MIDP) adds APIs for user interfaces, record management, and HTTP connections. A MIDlet is a MIDP application. A MIDlet must override the StartApp, PauseApp, and DestroyApp methods.

- After compiling MIDlet, we preverify it to perform some code checking before loading the code into the device. We can package MIDlets in a JAR file to present several MIDlets in the same application.

- The current screen is a Displayable object. Possibilities include Alert, Form, List, and TextBox. A Form contains a mixture of items, each of which is a subclass of Item. Subclasses of Item include ChoiceGroup, DateField, Gauge, ImageItem, StringItem, and TextField.

- We implement the CommandListener interface to handle commands. The commandAction method has two parameters, the command, and the displayable object containing it.

- StreamConnection has openInputStream and openOutputStream methods to create streams to read and write bytes from a connection. The openDataInputStream and openDataOutputStream methods let us use streams for inputting and outputting typed data.

- A RecordStore stores byte array data. A RecordEnumeration may use a RecordFilter to select records and a RecordComparator to order them. The Canvas class provides handlers for low level events such as key presses. Graphics provides drawing methods.

Program Modification Exercises

· · · · · · · · · · ·

1. Modify Example 14.2 to echo the input in a TextBox rather than a StringItem.

2. Modify Example 14.3 to use an ERROR Alert instead of ALARM. Does it still play a sound?

3. Modify Example 14.5 to use a POST request instead of GET.

4. Modify Example 14.5 to display the number of orders for the product name entered in the TextField.

5. Modify Example 14.7 to create a byte array record directly without using streams.

6. Modify Example 14.7 to only save the highest score for each user.

7. Modify Example 14.7 to order records by the score value rather than the name.

8. Modify Example 14.7 to use random scores between 0 and 100 rather than any integer.

9. Modify Example 14.8 to change the color of the rectangle to blue if the user presses the 2ABC key.

10. Modify Example 14.7 to convert the score to a String before storing it in the RecordStore. When storing and retrieving data use the byte arrays directly without using streams to pack the data.

Program Design Exercises

· · · · · · · · · ·

11. Write a MIDlet in which the user enters a name. The MIDlet connects to a servlet that connects to the Sales database, used in Chapter 3, to determine how many radios a customer with that name has ordered.

12. Write a MIDlet in which the user can select one of three sites from a list. Connect to the site the user selects and display the resource in a TextBox. For this exercise create sites whose content will fit in the limited screen area available.

13. Write a MIDlet in which the user may either enter a new name and address or view the address book. Use a RecordStore to save the names and addresses. Make the entries and retrievals directly using byte arrays without using streams to pack data.

14. Write a MIDlet to play a game of Tick Tac Toe. Let the computer use red squares to mark its moves and let the user use blue squares. Let the user select the position to move using the pointer device. Announce the result of the game at the end.

15. Write a MIDlet in which the user can enter appointment dates in a RecordStore, each identified by a name. Provide a DateField for the user to select a date for the appointment. Give the user a choice of entering an appointment, viewing the list of appointments, or retrieving appointments on a specific day.

15

Jini and JavaSpaces™

Introduction

. . . .

With global computing on a multitude of devices, in addition to personal computers, we need an easier way for a device to connect to the network to add the services it provides and find the services it needs. One device should not need to know in advance the properties of another in order to find and use it.

As with hardware devices, we want software to be able to connect to other software or hardware in this plug and play manner. Jini facilitates distributed computing in which devices and code connect, register their services, and locate other services without knowing where they are or the details of their operation.

OBJECTIVES:

- Introduce datagrams and multicasting.

- Add a lookup service.

- Add a simple Jini service and client.

- Use events to notify a client when a service appears.

- Use RMI to connect to a service.

- Connect to a service with a custom protocol.

- Distribute tasks with a JavaSpace.

15.1 Multicasting and Jini

Jini services and devices form network communities known as djinns. Typically a djinn is a local group rather than a wide-ranging group, because broadcasting to many locations would generate too much network traffic.

Lookup services keep track of services that have joined a djinn. A new service needs to register with lookup services. Clients find services by contacting lookup services. Services or clients wishing to participate in the djinn do not need to know in advance where to locate a lookup service.

Discovery and lookup are basic to Jini. We use discovery to find and join a djinn. Lookup locates services and the code needed to use them. We will illustrate with a simple Hello World service.

Jini Discovery

Our networking in Chapter 2 used the unicast protocol, in which we specified the IP of the server to which we wished to connect. With Jini, the unicast protocol is useful for locating a non-local djinn. More interestingly, the multicast protocol lets us broadcast to multiple receivers. Jini lookup services use the Multicast Announcement Protocol to announce their availability. The Multicast Request Protocol allows a Jini client or service to locate lookup services. Before turning specifically to the Jini use of multicasting we introduce multicasting and the Unreliable Data Protocol (UDP) on which it is based.

UDP

Our networking examples in Chapter 2 made point to point connections, like phone calls in which the parties connect to each other. We used the `java.net` API which deals with the lower-level networking protocols for us. Underneath point to point connections use the Transmission Control Protocol (TCP). Like a phone conversation, messages will arrive in the same order they are sent.

The `java.net` package also supports the Unreliable Data Protocol (UDP) which is more efficient. It operates more like mailing letters. We do not send letters directly to their destination, but deposit them in a mail box for delivery using the given addresses. Mail may not arrive in the same order that it was sent.

Java uses the `DatagramPacket` to implement a connectionless packet delivery service. Each packet contains all the information needed to route it from one machine to another. A `DatagramSocket` sends or receives packets. To illustrate we convert ReverseServer from Example 2.5 and ReverseClient from Example 2.6.

EXAMPLE 15.1 DatagramReverseServer.java

```
/* Revises Example 2.5 to use datagrams.
 */
```

```
import java.net.*;
import java.io.*;

public class DatagramReverseServer {
  public static void main(String [] args) {
    String s;
    int size, port;
    StringBuffer buffer;
    InetAddress address;
    DatagramPacket packet;
    try {
      DatagramSocket socket = new DatagramSocket(9876);           // Note 1
      byte[] data = new byte[1024];
      while(true) {                                                // Note 2
        packet = new DatagramPacket(data,data.length);            // Note 3
        socket.receive(packet);                                   // Note 4
        s = new String(data).trim();                              // Note 5
        buffer = new StringBuffer(s);
        System.out.println(s);
        address = packet.getAddress();                            // Note 6
        port = packet.getPort();
        size = s.length();
        for (int i=0; i<size; i++)
           buffer.setCharAt(i,s.charAt(size-1-i));
        byte[] b = buffer.toString().getBytes();                  // Note 7
        packet = new DatagramPacket(b,b.length,address,port);     // Note 8
        socket.send(packet);
      }
    }catch(Exception e) {
        e.printStackTrace();
    }
  }
}
```

Output

```
hi there
how are you
```

Note 1:   We arbitrarily choose 9876 as the port number.

Note 2:   The server will handle multiple clients. It remains active until we abort it.

Note 3:   This constructor creates a DatagramPacket to receive a packet.

Note 4:   The receive method blocks until a datagram is received. A message longer than the packet's length is truncated.

Note 5:   The trim method removes leading and trailing whitespace.

Note 6:   `address = packet.getAddress();`
The packet contains its address and port used.

Note 7:   `byte[] b = buffer.toString().getBytes();`
We convert the `StringBuffer` to a `String` and use the `getBytes` method to get the byte array to pass to the packet.

Note 8:   `packet = new DatagramPacket(b,b.length,address,port);`
This constructor includes the address and port to create a packet to send.

EXAMPLE 15.2   DatagramReverseClient.java

```java
/* Modifies Example 2.6 to use datagrams.
 */

import java.net.*;
import java.io.*;

public class DatagramReverseClient {
  public static void main(String [] args) {
    String s;
    if (args.length != 1){
      System.out.println("Usage: java DatagramReverseClient host");
      System.exit(1);
    }
    try {
      DatagramSocket socket = new DatagramSocket();              // Note 1
      BufferedReader input = new BufferedReader(
                     new InputStreamReader(System.in));
      DatagramPacket packet;
      byte[] data = new byte[1024];
      while (true) {
        System.out.print("# ");
        System.out.flush();
        if ((s=input.readLine()) == null) break;
        byte[] b = s.getBytes();
        packet= new DatagramPacket(b, b.length,
                  InetAddress.getByName(args[0]),9876);          // Note 2
        socket.send(packet);
        packet = new DatagramPacket(data,data.length);
        socket.receive(packet);
        System.out.println(new String(data).trim());
      }
    }catch(Exception e) {
      e.printStackTrace();
    }
  }
}
```

Output (Using `java DatagramReverseClient localhost`**)**

```
# hi there
ereht ih
# how are you
uoy era woh
# ^Z
```

Note 1:   This constructor creates a socket on any available port. The packet contains the port and address so the server will know where to send the reversed text.

Note 2:   We pass the address of the server to this constructor.

Multicasting

Using multicasting, we can send a packet to multiple recipients. Each receiver must join a group at a specific multicast address which may be chosen from the range 224.0.0.1 to 239.255.255.255. Multicast can greatly reduce the network load. Unicasting a message to many clients require that a separate packet be sent to each. With multicasting we send a single packet which is duplicated only when necessary.

Receivers need to use a `MulticastSocket` to allow them to join groups. To illustrate, we multicast a message every second. Each receiver will display the same message.

EXAMPLE 15.3   MulticastServer.java

```java
/* Multicasts a message every second.
 */

import java.net.*;
import java.io.*;

public class MulticastServer {
  public static void main(String [] args) {
    InetAddress address;
    DatagramPacket packet;
    try {
      DatagramSocket socket = new DatagramSocket(5555);              // Note 1
      int i = 1;
      String s = "";
      byte[] data;
      while(true) {
        s = "Count is " + i++;
        data = s.getBytes();
        address = InetAddress.getByName("229.0.0.7");                // Note 2
        packet = new DatagramPacket(data,data.length,address,5555);
        socket.send(packet);
        Thread.sleep(1000);
      }
```

```
        }catch(Exception e) {
            e.printStackTrace();
        }
    }
}
```

....

Note 1:   We do not need to use a `MulticastSocket` because the server is not receiving any packets.

Note 2:   We choose an address between 224.0.0.1 and 239.255.255.255 to create a multicast address. Receivers join a group at this address to receive messages from this server.

EXAMPLE 15.4   MulticastClient.java

```
/* Joins a group at a multicast address to receive multicasted
 * messages which it displays.
 */

import java.net.*;
import java.io.*;

public class MulticastClient {
  public static void main(String [] args) {
    try {
        MulticastSocket socket = new MulticastSocket(5555);          // Note 1
        InetAddress group = InetAddress.getByName("229.0.0.7");
        socket.joinGroup(group);                                      // Note 2
        DatagramPacket packet;
        byte[] data = new byte[1024];
        while (true) {
          packet = new DatagramPacket(data,data.length);
          socket.receive(packet);
          System.out.println(new String(packet.getData()).trim());
        }
    }catch(Exception e) {
        e.printStackTrace();
    }
  }
}
```

....

Output

```
Count is 32
Count is 33
Count is 34
Count is 35
```

```
Count is 36
Count is 37
Count is 38
...
```

Note 1:   We create a `MulticastSocket` so the client can join a group to receive multi-casted messages.

Note 2:   To receive multicast messages, the client joins a group at the address used by the server.

We can start several Example 15.4 multicast clients and each will produce the output shown. Because the server keeps incrementing the count, the first number outputted will indicate the number of seconds since the server started that the client started.

Notice that the server and the clients all use an arbitrary multicast address. The server has no idea to where the packet it sends will be transmitted. This multicast facility enables Jini to connect entities (software and devices) in this plug and play manner. Plug in the device or start running the software and it makes the connections it needs without knowing where these resources are located.

THE BIG PICTURE

Jini can use multicasting to locate lookup services. Multicasting uses UDP packets which is more like mailing a letter than placing a telephone call. The packet sender uses a special multicast address. Receivers, using a `MulticastSocket`, join a group at that address to receive packets.

TEST YOUR UNDERSTANDING

1. Which Java class provides a method with which to join a multicast group?

2. Which protocol is used when sending a `DatagramPacket`?

3. Explain how multicasting can reduce the network load.

15.2   Starting Jini

We illustrate Jini with a Hello World example. To use Jini we need to start a lookup service. Services will register with the lookup service and clients will lookup services in the lookup service. A lookup service is activatable, meaning that it can sleep between requests and be activated on demand. Moreover, if it crashes it can be automatically restarted. We start an RMI activation daemon to handle activation and deactivation.

Clients use RMI to connect to a lookup service. A client needs the stub to manage the communication with the server. In our examples of Section 2.5, we simply copied the stub to the client. A more flexible procedure is to allow the client to download the stub from the server using HTTP. To enable this we need to start an HTTP server.

In all our Jini examples we use the environment variable JINI_HOME to specify the location of the Jini installation. We use the SET command to set an environment variable. For example, on the author's machine the command is

```
SET JINI_HOME=d:\jini1_1
```

Because some of the commands have many options, we use batch files.

An HTTP Server

The Jini distribution includes a web server. The batch file, `http.bat`, we use to start the server is

```
java -jar %JINI_HOME%\lib\tools.jar -port %1 -dir %2 -verbose
```

The `-jar` option specifies an executable jar. An executable jar packages a class with a `main` method, using a manifest file to specify that class. `tools.jar` contains a web server. We use parameters to specify the port the server will listen on and the directory from which it will serve files. The `%JINI_HOME%\lib` directory contains the Jini files needed to use the lookup service. We start the HTTP server with the command

```
http 8081 %JINI_HOME%\lib
```

The RMI Activation Daemon

A daemon does its work in the background running continuously. An activatable service registers with the daemon (RMID) when it starts up. RMID maintains a log of registered services. Should it fail or be stopped it can be restarted and reactivate all the services using its log. RMID creates a directory name `log` in the directory from which it was activated. RMID manages the activation of services registered with it. We start it using the batch file `rmidStart.bat`

```
rmid -J-Djava.security.policy=%JINI_HOME%\policy\policy.all
```

RMID requires a security policy. We use the `-J` option to pass an option to the JVM. We use the `-D` option to set the security policy. The file `policy.all` that comes with Jini grants all permissions and is useful for development. To stop RMID we use the command

```
rmid -stop
```

A Lookup Service

A lookup service named `reggie` is included with Jini. We use two JVMs when starting an activatable service, one to register it with RMID (startup JVM) and one to run it (server JVM). We start `reggie` using the batch file `reggie.bat`.

```
java -jar %JINI_HOME%\lib\reggie.jar http://%1:8081/reggie-dl.jar
%JINI_HOME%\policy\policy.all c:\tmp\reggie public
```

The -jar option specifies that `reggie.jar` contains the `main` method to start the reggie lookup service. We pass the next arguments to `reggie`. The argument

```
http://%1:8081/reggie-dl.jar
```

specifies the codebase. When Java passes a serialized object containing the object's data it attaches the codebase to indicate from where to download the code for the object. `reggie-dl.jar` contains the files that need to be downloaded to the client. The parameter `%1` specifies the address where `reggie` is running. We could use `localhost` for the address when testing on one machine, but should never use `localhost` if more than one machine is involved.

The argument

```
%JINI_HOME%\policy\policy.all
```

specifies the policy file used when `reggie` is run. The argument

```
c:\tmp\reggie
```

gives the absolute path for the log file `reggie` uses. The directory must exist, but the log file must not exist when we start `reggie`. The argument

```
public
```

names the group used for multicasting. `public` is the default so we could omit it, but include it to remind us that multicasting is used.

We execute the batch file to start `reggie` with the command

```
reggie 192.168.0.1
```

where `192.168.0.1` is the address assigned to the network interface card on the author's machine. Because `reggie` is activatable the JVM that started `reggie` terminates.

A Jini Service

We create a simple service that says Hello World. Example 15.5 contains the interface that a client of this service will use. The interface has one method, `hello`, which returns a `String`.

EXAMPLE 15.5   HelloJiniService.java

```java
/* Clients use this interface to return a
 * hello message.
 */

public interface HelloJiniService {
  public String hello();
}
```

....

Clients will download the code that implements this service from the server containing the service. Clients and servers can communicate using any protocol, as we shall see later. The service could be a hardware device such as a printer, in which case we call the code to use the service a device driver.

Example 15.6 contains the implementation of the service interface of Example 15.5. Clients using `HelloJiniService` will download this implementation.

EXAMPLE 15.6   HelloJiniServiceDriver.java

```
/* Implements HelloJiniServiceInterface.
 */

import java.io.*;

public class HelloJiniServiceDriver
       implements HelloJiniService, Serializable {          // Note 1
  public String hello() {
    return "Hello World!";
  }
}
```

....

Note 1:   We must implement Serializable so clients can receive objects of this
type.

The driver of Example 15.6 is very simple and atypical in that it provides a hello
method that can execute on the client without any further contact with the service.
Later examples will involve continued client-server communication.

To make itself available to clients, a service registers with at least one lookup service. It uses multicasting to discover a lookup service. A LookupDiscovery object
encapsulates the discovery process. The DiscoveryListener interface declares the
methods to be called when a lookup service has been found or discarded. Example
15.7 seeks a lookup service, and if found registers HelloJiniService with it.

We compile Example 15.7 using the batch file compile.bat

```
javac  -classpath .;%JINI_HOME%\lib\jini-core.jar; %JINI_HOME%\lib\jini-ext.jar %1
```

The classpath includes the classes from the Jini library that we need. The parameter is
the file to compile. The command for Example 15.7 is

```
compile HelloDiscoverJoin.java
```

....

TIP
☞

Type batch files with no line breaks. We display them in the text differently to fit on
the page.

....

Example 15.7 registers HelloJiniService with the lookup service. When a client
looks up HelloJiniService it will have to download the driver for it from the service.
Thus the service must have a web server available and must set the codebase to specify the web server port.

We start a web server using http.bat with the command

```
http 8082 driver-directory
```

where *driver-directory* is the directory containing HelloJiniServiceDriver.class.
To execute Example 15.7 we use the batch file runWithBase.bat

```
java -classpath .;%JINI_HOME%\lib\jini-core.jar; %JINI_HOME%\lib\jini-ext.jar
-Djava.security.policy=%JINI_HOME%\policy\policy.all
-Djava.rmi.server.codebase=http://%1:%2/ %3
```

Because HelloDiscoverJoin is not an activatable service, we use the -D option to set
the codebase and the security policy. Parameter 1 is the IP address of the service,
parameter 2 the port number, and parameter 3 the class name. To run Example 15.7
we use

```
runWithBase 192.168.0.1 8082 HelloDiscoverJoin
```

EXAMPLE 15.7   **HelloDiscoverJoin.java**

```
/* Discovers lookup services and
 * joins any found.
 */

import net.jini.core.lookup.*;
import net.jini.discovery.*;
import java.rmi.*;
import java.awt.*;
import java.awt.event.*;
import java.io.*;

public class HelloDiscoverJoin {

  public static void main(String[] args) {
    LookupDiscovery discover = null;

    HelloDiscoverJoin join = new HelloDiscoverJoin();
    System.setSecurityManager(new RMISecurityManager());      // Note 1
    try {
      discover = new LookupDiscovery(null);                   // Note 2
    }catch(IOException e) {
       System.out.println("Discovery error");
       e.printStackTrace();
       System.exit(1);
    }
    System.out.println(discover.getRegistrars());             // Note 3
    discover.addDiscoveryListener(join.new Register());        // Note 4
    Frame f = new Frame("Jini");                              // Note 5
    f.addWindowListener(new WindowAdapter() {
       public void windowClosing(WindowEvent e) {
         System.exit(0);
       }
    });
    f.setSize(100,100);
    f.show();
  }
  public class Register implements DiscoveryListener {        // Note 6
    private ServiceRegistration reg = null;
```

```
      public void discovered(DiscoveryEvent e) {
        System.out.println("discovered");
        ServiceItem item = new ServiceItem
                (null, new HelloJiniServiceDriver(), null);      // Note 7
        ServiceRegistrar[] registrars = e.getRegistrars();       // Note 8
        for (int i =0; i < registrars.length; i++)
          try {
            reg = registrars[i].register(item,600000);           // Note 9
            System.out.println(reg.getServiceID());              // Note 10
          }catch(RemoteException ex) {
            System.out.println("Registration failed");
            ex.printStackTrace();
          }
      }
      public void discarded(DiscoveryEvent e) {                  // Note 11
      }
    }
}
```

Output

```
[Lnet.jini.core.lookup.ServiceRegistrar;@5e3f2d
discovered
79520799-4992-43bd-8c69-ab166298ccc6
```

Note 1: We install a security manager because we will be downloading code from the lookup service.

Note 2: The `LookupDiscovery` object lets us find lookup services. It saves the lookup services found and will notify discovery listeners added later. The argument to this constructor is a `String` array representing the groups sought. Passing `null` will enable a search for lookup services in any group.

Note 3: The `getRegistrars` method returns an array of instances of `ServiceRegistrar`. Each `ServiceRegistrar` is an interface to a lookup service. We display the array reference just to show that we found a lookup service.

Note 4: We add a `DiscoveryListener` be notified about the lookup services found.

Note 5: We create a `Frame` which remains active after main completes. Otherwise the program may terminate before being notified about the lookup services found. We could use the frame to display messages, rather than the console.

Note 6: `public class Register implements DiscoveryListener`
The `DiscoveryListener` interface has two methods, `discovered`, which reports the results of the discovery of lookup services, and `discarded`, which indicates the removal of a lookup service.

Note 7: `new ServiceItem`
`(null, new HelloJiniServiceDriver(), null);`
A service stores a `ServiceItem` in a lookup service. The three arguments are

```
ServiceID serviceID
Object service
Entry[] attributes
```

The `serviceID` can be used when restarting a service. We pass `null` when we first start the service, and do not use the `serviceID` in our examples. The service is the driver that the client needs to use the service. The attributes are features that clients can use when searching for a service. For example, we could specify a color printer for a print service. We only use the `Entry` type in the `JavaSpaces` example.

Note 8: `ServiceRegistrar[] registrars = e.getRegistrars();`
Each `ServiceRegistrar` is the interface to a lookup service. The `getRegistrars` method returns the registrars for the lookup services found.

Note 9: `reg = registrars[i].register(item,600000);`
We register the service item with the lookup service. The second argument, of type `long`, is the lease duration in seconds. When connecting over a network a response may be slow or the service may have crashed. Jini uses leasing to handle such situations. A service requests a lease for a duration, 10 minutes in this example. A service can renew a lease, but if it does not renew it the lookup service can delete it so clients will not be attempting to use a failed service. We do not investigate the details of leasing in this chapter.

Note 10: `System.out.println(reg.getServiceID());`
We display the service ID just to see what it looks like.

Note 11: `public void discarded(DiscoveryEvent e)`
Jini calls the discard method when a lookup service is removed. We do not use it in our examples.

A Jini Client

Figure 15.1 shows the frames created by Examples 15.7 and 15.8. The client of Example 15.8 also has to discover a lookup service. When it does it looks up `HelloJiniService` and invokes its `hello` method.

We compile the client using `compile.bat` and run using `runNoBase.bat`

```
java -classpath .;%JINI_HOME%\lib\jini-core.jar; %JINI_HOME%\lib\jini-ext.jar
-Djava.security.policy=%JINI_HOME%\policy\policy.all %1
```

We do not need to set the codebase for this client because it will not be exporting any code.

Figure 15.1 The service and client frames.

service   client

EXAMPLE 15.8   **HelloClient.java**

```java
/* Looks up HelloJiniService and invokes
 * the Hello method.
 */

import net.jini.core.lookup.*;
import net.jini.discovery.*;
import java.rmi.*;
import java.awt.*;
import java.awt.event.*;
import java.io.*;

public class HelloClient {
  private String message = "";
  Frame f;
  int y = 40;

  public HelloClient() {
    LookupDiscovery discover = null;
    System.setSecurityManager(new RMISecurityManager());
    try {
      discover = new LookupDiscovery(null);
    }catch(IOException e) {
      System.out.println("Client discovery error");
      e.printStackTrace();
      System.exit(1);
    }
    System.out.println(discover.getRegistrars());
    discover.addDiscoveryListener(new Register());
    f = new MyFrame("Jini Client");
    f.addWindowListener(new WindowAdapter() {
      public void windowClosing(WindowEvent e) {
        System.exit(0);
      }
    });
    f.setSize(100,100);
    f.setLocation(100,0);                                    // Note 1
    f.show();
  }
```

```
public static void main(String[] args) {
  HelloClient client = new HelloClient();
}
public class MyFrame extends Frame {
  public MyFrame(String title) {
    super(title);
  }
  public void paint(Graphics g) {
    g.drawString(message,20,y);
  }
}
public class Register implements DiscoveryListener {
  public void discovered(DiscoveryEvent e) {
    ServiceTemplate template;
    ServiceRegistrar[] registrars = e.getRegistrars();
    Class[] serviceTypes = {HelloJiniService.class};                // Note 2
    template =
        new ServiceTemplate(null, serviceTypes, null);              // Note 3
    Object service = null;
    for (int i =0; i < registrars.length; i++){
      try {
        service =registrars[i].lookup(template);                    // Note 4
      }catch(RemoteException ex) {
        System.out.println("Lookup Hello failed");
        ex.printStackTrace();
      }
      if (service != null)
        message = ((HelloJiniService)service).hello();              // Note 5
      else
        message = "No hello service found";
      y += 15;
      f.repaint();                                                  // Note 6
    }
  }
  public void discarded(DiscoveryEvent e) {
  }
}
}
```

....

Output

`[Lnet.jini.core.lookup.ServiceRegistrar;@5d173`

....

Note 1:   We set the location of the client frame so that it does not overlap with the service frame at (0,0).

Note 2:   We create an array of service types that we wish to find. In this example we look up `HelloJiniService`.

Note 3: We use a `ServiceTemplate` to match services in a lookup service. The three arguments are:

```
ServiceID  serviceID
Class[]    serviceTypes
Entry[]    attributes
```

Passing `null` for the attributes will match any attributes of the service.

Note 4: We look up matches for our template with each lookup service found.

Note 5: If we find a service that matches the template we invoke its `hello` method.

Note 6: Repainting will cause the message to be drawn in the frame, 15 pixels below the message from the previous service found, if any.

Using Events

By using events Jini can handle situations in which the client looks up a service that is not found, but is notified when the service becomes available. We need to use remote events and make the connection with RMI because several machines may be involved.

The `RemoteEvent` class is a superclass for remote events. The `ServiceRegistrar` interface has a `notify` method that the client can use to request notification when a requested service becomes available. The client creates a remote object that implements the `RemoteEventListener` interface, which has a `notify` method that will be called when the service becomes available. The client needs to use `rmic` to create the stub and run an HTTP server so the lookup service can load it.

Example 15.9 creates another client for the HelloJiniService. This time we can start the client before starting the service. When we start the service, the client will be notified. We compile this client using `compile.bat` with the command

```
compile HelloClientEvent.java
```

We use the batch file `rmicRemote.bat`

```
rmic  -classpath .;%JINI_HOME%\lib\jini-core.jar;
%JINI_HOME%\lib\jini-ext.jar %1
```

with the command

```
rmicRemote HelloClientEvent.HelloListener
```

to create the RMI stub and skeleton.

We start the web server with `http.bat`, using

```
http 8083 client-directory
```

where *client-directory* is the directory containing the stub

```
HelloClientEvent$HelloListener_Stub.class.
```

We run the client using `runWithBase.bat` with the command

```
runWithBase 192.168.0.1 8083 HelloClientEvent
```

TIP

192.168.0.1 is the address of the master machine on the author's local network. When running on another machine change the IP address. Typically several machines will be used in one application.

To get the intended effect, run this client before starting Example 15.7, HelloDiscoverJoin, which registers HelloJiniService.

EXAMPLE 15.9   **HelloClientEvent.java**

```java
/* Uses events to allow the client to start before
 * HelloJiniService starts.
 */

import net.jini.core.lookup.*;
import net.jini.core.lease.*;
import net.jini.core.event.*;
import net.jini.discovery.*;
import java.rmi.*;
import java.rmi.server.*;
import java.awt.*;
import java.awt.event.*;
import java.io.*;

public class HelloClientEvent{
  private String message = "";
  Frame f;
  int y = 40;

  public HelloClientEvent() {
    LookupDiscovery discover = null;
    System.setSecurityManager(new RMISecurityManager());
    try {
      discover = new LookupDiscovery(null);
    }catch(IOException e) {
      System.out.println("Client discovery error");
      e.printStackTrace();
      System.exit(1);
    }
    discover.addDiscoveryListener(new Register());
    f = new MyFrame("Jini Client");
    f.addWindowListener(new WindowAdapter() {
      public void windowClosing(WindowEvent e) {
        System.exit(0);
      }
    });
    f.setSize(100,100);
    f.setLocation(100,0);
    f.show();
  }
```

```
public static void main(String[] args) {
  HelloClientEvent client = new HelloClientEvent();
}
public class MyFrame extends Frame {
  public MyFrame(String title) {
    super(title);
  }
  public void paint(Graphics g) {
    g.drawString(message,20,y);
  }
}
public class Register implements DiscoveryListener {
  public void discovered(DiscoveryEvent e) {
    ServiceTemplate template;
    ServiceRegistrar[] registrars = e.getRegistrars();
    Class[] serviceTypes = {HelloJiniService.class};
    template = new ServiceTemplate(null, serviceTypes, null);
    Object service = null;;
    for (int i =0; i < registrars.length; i++){
      try {
        service =registrars[i].lookup(template);
        if (service != null)
          message = ((HelloJiniService)service).hello();
        else {
          registrars[i].notify(template,
                  ServiceRegistrar.TRANSITION_NOMATCH_MATCH,
                  new HelloListener(), null, Lease.FOREVER);         // Note 1
          message = "No hello service found";
        }
        y += 15;
        f.repaint();
      }catch(RemoteException ex) {
        System.out.println("Lookup Hello failed");
        ex.printStackTrace();
      }
    }
  }
  public void discarded(DiscoveryEvent e) {
  }
}
public class HelloListener extends UnicastRemoteObject
                      implements RemoteEventListener {              // Note 2
  public HelloListener() throws RemoteException {
  }
  public void notify(RemoteEvent e)
     throws RemoteException, UnknownEventException {                // Note 3
    ServiceItem item = ((ServiceEvent)e).getServiceItem();         // Note 4
    HelloJiniService service =
                    (HelloJiniService)item.service;                // Note 5
```

```
        message = service.hello();
        y= 40;
        f.repaint();
      }
    }
}
```

....

Note 1: The `notify` method registers the client for event notification. The five arguments are:

```
ServiceTemplate template
int transitions
RemoteEventListener listener
MarshalledObject handback
long leaseDuration
```

We ask the lookup service for a service that matches the template. The second argument's choices reflect a change in the lookup service. We can bitwise OR them if desired. The transition values are:

```
TRANSITION_MATCH_NOMATCH
```

A matching value no longer matches, for example when a service becomes unavailable.

```
TRANSITION_NOMATCH _MATCH
```

A matching value appears.

```
TRANSITION_MATCH_MATCH
```

A matching value changes.

The third argument specifies the listener that receives the events. The fourth argument provides for an informational object to be sent to the listener. We do not use this feature. The last argument is the lease duration. We pass the constant `Lease.FOREVER` to request a lease that never expires.

Note 2: We extend `UnicastRemoteObject` so the `notify` method can be called remotely.

Note 3: The method that receives the notification is also called `notify`.

Note 4: The `ServiceEvent` subclass of `RemoteEvent` has a `getServiceItem` method that returns the `ServiceItem` stored in the lookup service.

Note 5: The `service` method returns the service object. In this example the object has type `HelloJiniService` and we invoke its `hello` method.

Figure 15.2 shows the client frame before and after `HelloJiniService` is available.

Figure 15.2 Example 15.9 before and after the Hello service starts

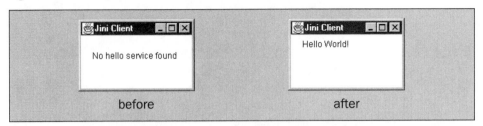

before   after

THE BIG PICTURE

The RMI activation daemon manages activatable services. A lookup service registers other Jini services, which clients can lookup. HTTP servers allow the downloading of Java code. Using remote events allows a client to be notified when desired service appears

---

TEST YOUR UNDERSTANDING

4. What are some advantages of an activatable service?

5. Why do we need to run an HTTP server along with the HelloJiniService?

6. Do Jini services and Jini clients both use a lookup service? Explain why or why not.

7. What advantages does a Jini client get from using events?

15.3 Interacting with a Service

In the last section the service provided a driver that executed on the client and required no further contact with the service. More typically a client will continue to contact the service. Clients may communicate with services uses any protocol. First we make the `ReverseServer` of Section 2.3 into a Jini service. In this case the client communicates over a socket to the service. Next we make the `FortuneServer` of Section 2.5 into a Jini service. In this case the client uses RMI to execute the service's `getFortune` method.

Using Sockets to Connect to a Jini Service

Example 15.10 contains the `ReverseService` interface. The `connect` method returns a socket with which the client connects to the service.

EXAMPLE 15.10   ReverseService.java

```
/* Provides a connect method that returns
 * a socket to connect to the reverse service.
 */

import java.net.*;
```

```
public interface ReverseService {
  public Socket connect();
}
```

....

Example 15.11 provides the driver that implements the `ReverseService` interface. The service will register it with the lookup service and Jini clients will download it. In that way the reverse service can start anywhere and make itself available without clients knowing in advance where it is located.

EXAMPLE 15.11   ReverseDriver.java

```
/* Implements the ReverseService interface.
 */

import java.net.*;
import java.io.*;

public class ReverseDriver
      implements ReverseService, Serializable {
  public Socket connect() {
    Socket s = null;
    try {
      s = new Socket("192.168.0.1", 4444);
    }catch(Exception e) {
      e.printStackTrace();
    }
    return s;
  }
}
```

....

We compile `ReverseService.java` and `ReverseDriver.java`. Then we use `compile.bat` to compile `ReverseDiscoveryJoin` of Example 15.12. We start an HTTP server using the command

`http 8084 reverse-directory`

where `reverse-directory` is the directory containing `ReverseDriver.class`. We run using the command

`runWithBase 192.168.0.1 8084 ReverseDiscoverJoin`

EXAMPLE 15.12   ReverseDiscoverJoin.java

```
/* Registers a reverse service.
 */

import net.jini.core.lookup.*;
import net.jini.discovery.*;
```

```java
import java.rmi.*;
import java.awt.*;
import java.awt.event.*;
import java.io.*;

public class ReverseDiscoverJoin {

  public static void main(String[] args) {
    LookupDiscovery discover = null;

    ReverseDiscoverJoin join = new ReverseDiscoverJoin();
    System.setSecurityManager(new RMISecurityManager());
    try {
      discover = new LookupDiscovery(null);
    }catch(IOException e) {
      System.out.println("Discovery error");
      e.printStackTrace();
      System.exit(1);
    }
    System.out.println(discover.getRegistrars());
    discover.addDiscoveryListener(join.new Register());
    Frame f = new Frame("Reverse");
    f.addWindowListener(new WindowAdapter() {
      public void windowClosing(WindowEvent e) {
        System.exit(0);
      }
    });
    f.setSize(100,100);
    f.show();
  }
  public class Register implements DiscoveryListener {
    private ServiceRegistration reg = null;

    public void discovered(DiscoveryEvent e) {
      System.out.println("discovered");
      ServiceItem item =
        new ServiceItem(null, new ReverseDriver(), null);
      ServiceRegistrar[] registrars = e.getRegistrars();
      for (int i =0; i < registrars.length; i++)
        try {
          reg = registrars[i].register(item,600000);
          System.out.println(reg.getServiceID());
        }catch(RemoteException ex) {
          System.out.println("Registration failed");
          ex.printStackTrace();
        }
    }
```

```
    public void discarded(DiscoveryEvent e) {
    }
  }
}
```

....

Output

```
[Lnet.jini.core.lookup.ServiceRegistrar;@5e3f2d

discovered

a4fbd536-eee8-44be-991e-efce68bd51e7
```

....

We convert ReverseServer of Section 2.3 to run on port 4444 and start it up.
    We compile the client of Example 15.13 and run it using the command

```
runNoBase ReverseJiniClient
```

When we enter *hi there* the frame of Figure 15.3 displays the reversed string.

Figure 15.3   Reversing a string

EXAMPLE 15.13   **ReverseJiniClient.java**

```
/* Looks up a reverse server and sends a string to reverse.
 */

import net.jini.core.lookup.*;
import net.jini.discovery.*;
import java.rmi.*;
import java.awt.*;
import java.awt.event.*;
import java.io.*;
import java.net.*;

public class ReverseJiniClient {
  private String message = "";
  Frame f;
  int y = 40;
```

```java
public ReverseJiniClient() {
  LookupDiscovery discover = null;
  System.setSecurityManager(new RMISecurityManager());
  try {
    discover = new LookupDiscovery(null);
  }catch(IOException e) {
      System.out.println("Client discovery error");
      e.printStackTrace();
      System.exit(1);
  }
  discover.addDiscoveryListener(new Register());
  f = new MyFrame("Reverse Client");
  f.addWindowListener(new WindowAdapter() {
    public void windowClosing(WindowEvent e) {
      System.exit(0);
    }
  });
  f.setSize(200,100);
  f.setLocation(200,0);
  f.show();
}
public static void main(String[] args) {
  ReverseJiniClient client = new ReverseJiniClient();
}
public class MyFrame extends Frame {
  public MyFrame(String title) {
    super(title);
  }
  public void paint(Graphics g) {
    g.drawString(message,20,y);
  }
}
public class Register implements DiscoveryListener {
  public void discovered(DiscoveryEvent e) {
    Socket server = null;
    ServiceTemplate template;
    ServiceRegistrar[] registrars = e.getRegistrars();
    Class[] serviceTypes = {ReverseService.class};
    template = new ServiceTemplate(null, serviceTypes, null);
    Object service = null;;
    for (int i =0; i < registrars.length; i++){
      try {
        service =registrars[i].lookup(template);
      }catch(RemoteException ex) {
        System.out.println("Lookup Reverse failed");
        ex.printStackTrace();
      }
```

```
          if (service != null) {
           try {
             server = ((ReverseService)service).connect();
             BufferedReader fromServer = new BufferedReader
               (new InputStreamReader(server.getInputStream()));
             PrintWriter toServer = new PrintWriter
                        (server.getOutputStream(),true);
             BufferedReader input = new BufferedReader(
                        new InputStreamReader(System.in));
             toServer.println(input.readLine());                    // Note 1
             message = fromServer.readLine();
             fromServer.close();
             toServer.close();
             input.close();
             server.close();
           }catch(Exception ex) {
             ex.printStackTrace();
           }
          }
          else
            message = "No reverse service found";
          y += 15;
          f.repaint();
        }
      }
     public void discarded(DiscoveryEvent e) {
     }
    }
}
```

....

Note 1:   We are able to send only one line to the server.

Using RMI to Execute Service Methods

Example 15.14 contains the Fortune interface which is remote because clients will call the getFortune method. Example 15.15 implements that interface. Clients will download this implementation from the service.

EXAMPLE 15.14   **Fortune.java**

```
/* A remote interface for a Jini service.
 */

import java.rmi.*;
public interface Fortune extends Remote {
  public static final String NOW = "Now";
  public static final String LATER = "Later";
  public String getFortune(String when)throws RemoteException;
}
```

....

EXAMPLE 15.15   FortuneDriver.java

```
/* Implements the Fortune interface.  Extends
 * UnicastRemoteObject to provid remote access.
 */

import java.rmi.*;
import java.rmi.server.UnicastRemoteObject;
import java.util.Vector;
import java.io.Serializable;

public class FortuneDriver extends UnicastRemoteObject
                           implements Fortune, Serializable {
  public static final int SIZE = 3;
  private Vector now = new Vector(SIZE);
  private Vector later = new Vector(SIZE);
  public FortuneDriver()throws RemoteException {
    now.addElement("A friend is near");
    now.addElement("Expect a call");
    now.addElement("Someone misses you");
    later.addElement("Wealth awaits -- if you desire it.");
    later.addElement("Climb the hill of effort for high grades.");
    later.addElement("The door to success is open to you.");
  }
  private Vector find(String when) {
    if (when.equals(Fortune.NOW))
       return now;
    else return later;
  }
  public synchronized String getFortune(String when)
                                  throws RemoteException {
    int number = (int)(3*Math.random());
    Vector fortunes = find(when);
    return (String)fortunes.elementAt(number);
  }
}
```

We compile `Fortune.java` and `FortuneDriver.java`. We generate the stub and skeleton for the driver with the command

```
rmic FortuneDriver
```

Then we use `compile.bat` to compile `FortuneDiscoverJoin.java` of Example 15.16.
   We start an HTTP server with the command

```
http 8085 fortune-directory
```

where *fortune-directory* contains `FortuneDriver_Stub.class`.
   We run using the command

```
runWithBase 192.168.0.1 8085 FortuneDiscoverJoin
```

EXAMPLE 15.16 **FortuneDiscoverJoin.java**

```java
/* Discovers and joins lookup services
 * registering FortuneDriver.
 */

import net.jini.core.lookup.*;
import net.jini.discovery.*;
import java.rmi.*;
import java.awt.*;
import java.awt.event.*;
import java.io.*;

public class FortuneDiscoverJoin {

  public static void main(String[] args) {
    LookupDiscovery discover = null;

    FortuneDiscoverJoin join = new FortuneDiscoverJoin();
    System.setSecurityManager(new RMISecurityManager());
    try {
      discover = new LookupDiscovery(null);
    }catch(IOException e) {
      System.out.println("Discovery error");
      e.printStackTrace();
      System.exit(1);
    }
    discover.addDiscoveryListener(join.new Register());
    Frame f = new Frame("Fortune");
    f.addWindowListener(new WindowAdapter() {
      public void windowClosing(WindowEvent e) {
        System.exit(0);
      }
    });
    f.setSize(200,100);
    f.show();
  }
  public class Register implements DiscoveryListener {
    private ServiceRegistration reg = null;

    public void discovered(DiscoveryEvent e) {
      System.out.println("Discovered a lookup service");
      try {
        ServiceItem item = new ServiceItem
                (null, new Fortune_Driver(), null);      // Note 1
        ServiceRegistrar[] registrars = e.getRegistrars();
        for (int i =0; i < registrars.length; i++) {
          reg = registrars[i].register(item,600000);
          System.out.println(reg.getServiceID());
        }
```

```
        }catch(RemoteException ex) {
          System.out.println("Registration failed");
          ex.printStackTrace();
        }
      }
      public void discarded(DiscoveryEvent e) {
      }
    }
}
```

Output

```
Discovered a lookup service
1dee2529-94bf-46ec-84df-d44255d6874e
```

Note 1:   We register a remote object that implements the Fortune interface.

Example 15.17 contains a client that looks up a Fortune service and calls its getFortune method remotely. We use compile.bat to compile Example 15.17. We generate the stub and skeleton for event notification using the command

rmicRemote FortuneClientEvent.FortuneListener

We start a server with the command

http 8086 *client-directory*

where *client-directory* is the directory that contains

FortuneClientEvent$FortuneListener_Stub.class.

We use the command

runWithBase 192.168.0.1 8086 FortuneClientEvent

to run Example 15.17.

EXAMPLE 15.17   FortuneClientEvent.java

```
/* Look up a Fortune service.  Calls its getFortune
 * method remotely using RMI.
 */

import net.jini.core.lookup.*;
import net.jini.core.lease.*;
import net.jini.core.event.*;
import net.jini.discovery.*;
import java.rmi.*;
import java.rmi.server.*;
import java.awt.*;
import java.awt.event.*;
import java.io.*;
```

```
public class FortuneClientEvent{
  private String message = "";
  Frame f;
  int y = 40;

  public FortuneClientEvent() {
    LookupDiscovery discover = null;
    System.setSecurityManager(new RMISecurityManager());
    try {
      discover = new LookupDiscovery(null);
    }catch(IOException e) {
      System.out.println("Client discovery error");
      e.printStackTrace();
      System.exit(1);
    }
    discover.addDiscoveryListener(new Register());
    f = new MyFrame("Jini Client");
    f.addWindowListener(new WindowAdapter() {
      public void windowClosing(WindowEvent e) {
        System.exit(0);
      }
    });
    f.setSize(200,100);
    f.setLocation(300,0);
    f.show();
  }
  public static void main(String[] args) {
    FortuneClientEvent client = new FortuneClientEvent();
  }
  public class MyFrame extends Frame {
    public MyFrame(String title) {
      super(title);
    }
    public void paint(Graphics g) {
      g.drawString(message,20,y);
    }
  }
  public class Register implements DiscoveryListener {
    public void discovered(DiscoveryEvent e) {
      ServiceTemplate template;
      ServiceRegistrar[] registrars = e.getRegistrars();
      Class[] serviceTypes = {Fortune.class};
      template = new ServiceTemplate(null, serviceTypes, null);
      Object service = null;;
      for (int i =0; i < registrars.length; i++){
        try {
          service =registrars[i].lookup(template);
          if (service != null)
            message =
              ((Fortune)service).getFortune(Fortune.NOW);          // Note 1
```

```
          else {
            registrars[i].notify(template,
                    ServiceRegistrar.TRANSITION_NOMATCH_MATCH,
                  new FortuneListener(), null, Lease.FOREVER);
            message = "No fortune service found";
          }
          y += 15;
          f.repaint();
        }catch(RemoteException ex) {
          System.out.println("Lookup Fortune failed");
          ex.printStackTrace();
        }
      }
    }
    public void discarded(DiscoveryEvent e) {
    }
  }
  public class FortuneListener extends UnicastRemoteObject
                         implements RemoteEventListener {
    public FortuneListener() throws RemoteException {
    }
    public void notify(RemoteEvent e)
       throws RemoteException, UnknownEventException {
      ServiceItem item = ((ServiceEvent)e).getServiceItem();
      Fortune service =
                        (Fortune)item.service;
      message = service.getFortune(Fortune.LATER);
      y= 40;
      f.repaint();
    }
  }
}
```

Note 1:   We invoke the getFortune method remotely using the stub downloaded from the service.

Figure 15.4 shows the client window after the service starts.

THE BIG PICTURE
A Jini client downloads the driver to communicate with a Jini service. The driver can implement any method of communication. Using RMI is one possibility.

Figure 15.4   Using the Fortune service

TEST YOUR UNDERSTANDING

8. How does using Jini make it easier for a client to find a desired service?

9. What choice of protocols does a Jini client have in order to communicate with a Jini service?

15.4 JavaSpaces

JavaSpaces technology, using Jini, provides a tool for building distributed applications. The concept comes from the research-oriented Linda language developed by David Gelernter at Yale University.

Entries

The `JavaSpace` interface from the `net.jini.space` package is very simple. It uses Jini `Entry` objects. We have not used these to specify attribute in our Jini templates, but they are essential in JavaSpaces. An `Entry` may have any methods and constructors. Each field must be an object, not a primitive type.

The three basic `JavaSpace` methods are `read`, `write`, and `take`. A `JavaSpace` works like a communal whiteboard. A client can write an `Entry` to it. Reading an entry provides a copy to the client and leaves it in the space. Taking the entry removes it from the space.

Jini uses leasing and can operate with transactions, although we did not use them in our examples. With the JavaSpaces service we should include transaction processing. A client that updates an entry must take it from the space and write the updated version back to the space. Both of these must succeed for the transaction to be successful.

We illustrate JavaSpaces with a distributed computing example. We will compute the periods of repeating decimals. For example $1/7 = .142857142857...$ where the group of six digits 142857 repeats forever. We say that 1/7 has period 6.

One client will write `Value` entries containing the denominators whose periods we want to compute. It will also take `Result` entries containing the resulting periods. Other clients will take `Value` entries compute the periods and write `Result` entries back to the space.

EXAMPLE 15.18 Value.java

```
/* Encapsulates a denominater for a fraction
 * whose period will be computed.
 */

import net.jini.core.entry.*;

public class Value implements Entry {
  public Integer denominator;                              // Note 1
```

```
      public Value() {                                          // Note 2
      }
      public Value(int d) {
        denominator = new Integer(d);
      }
    }
```

....

Note 1: Fields in an `Entry` must be object references, so we define an `Integer` rather than an `int`. All fields must be public so the templates used to search may access them.

Note 2: Each `Entry` must have a default constructor, which is used when returning it in `read` and `take` operations.

EXAMPLE 15.19 Result.java

```
/* Contains a String used to hold
 * the reulst of a period computation.
 */

import net.jini.core.entry.*;

public class Result implements Entry {
  public String answer;
  public Result() {
  }
  public Result(String a) {
    answer = a;
  }
}
```

....

Starting JavaSpaces

We start a transaction manager even though we do not use it in our example, because it is often important in JavaSpaces applications. Sun provides an activatable transaction manager service called *mahalo*. We start the transaction manger using `mahalo.bat`

```
java -jar %JINI_HOME%\lib\mahalo.jar http://%1:8081/mahalo-dl.jar
%JINI_HOME%\policy\policy.all c:\temp\txn_log public
```

with the command

```
mahalo 192.168.0.1
```

We use the web server already started for `reggie` because the files to download are in the same directory.

Sun's JavaSpaces service is called *outrigger*. We can either start a transient space or a persistent space. The transient space does not maintain data across crashes and restarts of the space, but is easier to use. We start the transient space using `space.bat`

```
java -Djava.security.policy=%JINI_HOME%\policy\policy.all
-Djava.rmi.server.codebase=http://%1:8081/outrigger-dl.jar
-jar %JINI_HOME%\lib\transient-outrigger.jar public
```

The transient service is not activatable so we use the -D option to set the security policy and the codebase in the JVM that starts it.

Distributed Computing with JavaSpaces

Example 15.20 defines the SpaceMaster that writes the Value entries and takes the Result entries. Example 15.21 defines the SpaceTask takes the Value entries, does the computation, and writes the Result entries. We can have various SpaceTask objects doing the computations.

EXAMPLE 15.20   SpaceMaster.java

```
/* Writes Value entries and takes
 * Result entries.
 */

import net.jini.core.lookup.*;
import net.jini.discovery.*;
import net.jini.space.*;
import net.jini.core.lease.*;
import java.rmi.*;
import java.awt.*;
import java.awt.event.*;
import java.io.*;

public class SpaceMaster {
  private String message = "";
  Frame f;
  int y = 40;

  public SpaceMaster() {
    LookupDiscovery discover = null;
    System.setSecurityManager(new RMISecurityManager());
    try {
      discover = new LookupDiscovery(null);
    }catch(IOException e) {
      System.out.println("Client discovery error");
      e.printStackTrace();
      System.exit(1);
    }
    discover.addDiscoveryListener(new Register());
    f = new MyFrame("Jini Client");
```

```
     f.addWindowListener(new WindowAdapter() {
       public void windowClosing(WindowEvent e) {
         System.exit(0);
       }
     });
     f.setSize(100,100);
     f.setLocation(100,0);
     f.show();
   }
   public static void main(String[] args) {
     SpaceMaster client = new SpaceMaster();
   }
   public class MyFrame extends Frame {
     public MyFrame(String title) {
       super(title);
     }
     public void paint(Graphics g) {
       g.drawString(message,20,y);
     }
   }
   public class Register implements DiscoveryListener {
     public void discovered(DiscoveryEvent e) {
       ServiceTemplate template;
       ServiceRegistrar[] registrars = e.getRegistrars();
       Class[] serviceTypes = {JavaSpace.class};                  // Note 1
       template = new ServiceTemplate(null, serviceTypes, null);
       JavaSpace service = null;
       for (int i =0; i < registrars.length; i++){
         try {
           service = (JavaSpace)registrars[i].lookup(template);
         }catch(RemoteException ex) {
           System.out.println("Lookup JavaSpaces failed");
           ex.printStackTrace();
         }
         try {
           if (service != null){
             int digit = 7;
             int test = 0;
             for(int j = 0; j < 8; j++) {
               Value v = new Value(test = 10*test+digit);           // Note 2
               service.write(v, null, Lease.FOREVER);               // Note 3
             }
           }
           while(true) {
             Result result = (Result)service.take
                     (new Result(), null, Long.MAX_VALUE);          // Note 4
             System.out.println(result.answer);
           }
```

```
            }catch(Exception exception) {
                System.out.println("write or take error");
                exception.printStackTrace();
            }
        }
    }
    public void discarded(DiscoveryEvent e) {
    }
  }
}
```

Output

```
6 is the period of 1/7
6 is the period of 1/77
6 is the period of 1/777
12 is the period of 1/7777
30 is the period of 1/77777
42 is the period of 1/777777
42 is the period of 1/7777777
24 is the period of 1/77777777
```

Note 1:   We look up a JavaSpace in the lookup service.

Note 2:   We create `Value` entries from 7, 77, 777, 7777, 77777, 777777, 7777777, and 77777777.

Note 3:   We write each entry into the space. The second argument is a transaction, which we do not use.

Note 4:   We take an entry of type `Result`. The third argument is the time `take` should wait for a matching value to appear before returning. `Long.MAX_VALUE` means to wait indefinitely. The `take` operation will block until a matching entry is available.

EXAMPLE 15.21   SpaceTask.java

```
/* Takes a Value entry, computes the period,
 * writes a Result entry.  Repeats this process.
 */

import net.jini.core.lookup.*;
import net.jini.discovery.*;
import net.jini.space.*;
import net.jini.core.lease.*;
import java.rmi.*;
import java.awt.*;
import java.awt.event.*;
import java.io.*;
```

```java
public class SpaceTask {
  private String message = "";
  Frame f;
  int y = 40;

  public SpaceTask() {
    LookupDiscovery discover = null;
    System.setSecurityManager(new RMISecurityManager());
    try {
      discover = new LookupDiscovery(null);
    }catch(IOException e) {
      System.out.println("Client discovery error");
      e.printStackTrace();
      System.exit(1);
    }
    discover.addDiscoveryListener(new Register());
    f = new MyFrame("Jini Client");
    f.addWindowListener(new WindowAdapter() {
      public void windowClosing(WindowEvent e) {
        System.exit(0);
      }
    });
    f.setSize(100,100);
    f.setLocation(100,0);
    f.show();
  }
  public static void main(String[] args) {
    SpaceTask client = new SpaceTask();
  }
  public class MyFrame extends Frame {
    public MyFrame(String title) {
      super(title);
    }
    public void paint(Graphics g) {
      g.drawString(message,20,y);
    }
  }
  public class Register implements DiscoveryListener {
    public void discovered(DiscoveryEvent e) {
      ServiceTemplate template;
      ServiceRegistrar[] registrars = e.getRegistrars();
      Class[] serviceTypes = {JavaSpace.class};
      template = new ServiceTemplate(null, serviceTypes, null);
      JavaSpace service = null;
      for (int i =0; i < registrars.length; i++){
        try {
          service = (JavaSpace)registrars[i].lookup(template);
        }catch(RemoteException ex) {
          System.out.println("Lookup JavaSpaces failed");
          ex.printStackTrace();
        }
```

```
          try {
            if (service != null)
              while(true) {
                Value value =
                  (Value)service.take(new Value(), null, Long.MAX_VALUE);
                String s= period(value.denominator.intValue())
                        + " is the period of 1/"
                        + value.denominator.intValue();          // Note 1
                service.write(new Result(s), null, Lease.FOREVER);
              }
          }catch(Exception exception) {
            System.out.println("write or take error");
            exception.printStackTrace();
          }
        }
      }
      public void discarded(DiscoveryEvent e) {
      }
      public int period(int number) {                          // Note 2
        int tens = 10;
        int period = 1;
        tens %= number;
        while (tens != 1) {
          tens = 10*tens%number;
          period++;
        }
        return period;
      }
    }
  }
}
```

....

Note 1:   We create a String which describes the result of a period computation.

Note 2:   The `period` method computes the period of the fraction whose denominator is passed to it. Looking at the long division algorithm we can see that the period is the exponent of the smallest power of ten that has a remainder of 1 when divided by the denominator. For example

```
      10 % 7 = 3
     100 % 7 = 2
    1000 % 7 = 6
   10000 % 7 = 4
  100000 % 7 = 5
 1000000 % 7 = 1
```

and the period of 1/7 is 6.

We use `compile.bat` to compile `SpaceMaster.java` and `SpaceTask.java`. We need to start an HTTP server using

```
http 8087 entry-directory
```

where *entry-directory* is the directory containing `Value.class` and `Result.class`. When clients read or take entries they need to know where to download classes for these entries.

We run using the commands

```
runWithBase 192.168.0.1 8087 SpaceMaster
```

and

```
runWithBase 192.168.0.1 8087 SpaceTask
```

THE BIG PICTURE

JavaSpaces is a Jini service that functions like a whiteboard for distributed computation. Clients read entries, or take them from the space. They write entries to the space. A transaction service enables transaction processing. Many clients can combine to solve a problem.

TEST YOUR UNDERSTANDING

10. What Jini services do we need to run to use JavaSpaces?

11. Does the SpaceMaster program of Example 15.20 provide a Jini service or a Jini client? Explain.

SUMMARY

- Jini enables a plug-and-play connectivity for software and hardware services and clients. A lookup service multicasts its presence. A Jini service can use multicast discovery to seek a lookup service. The service registers a driver with the lookup service. A client uses multicast discovery to seek a lookup service. It looks up a service using a template that allows object-oriented matching, returning any class that implements the desired interface and matches the specified attributes. We did not make use of the attribute matching facility in our examples. Nor did we use the leasing or transaction processing capabilities. When a client finds a service it downloads its driver and communicates with the service as needed using that driver.

- The RMI Activation Daemon runs continuously. It restarts activatable services when needed. HTTP servers run to enable the downloading of Java code. Jini services use RMI to connect to lookup services, and download the stubs when needed. Clients that implement `RemoteEventListener` use RMI to enable the lookup service to perform the callback. The lookup service needs to download the stub from the client. Clients download the drivers from the services they wish to use.

- A Jini service provides a JavaSpace which functions like a whiteboard for distributed computing. A JavaSpace contains Entry objects. The simple Entry interface includes the read, take, and write methods. Reading an entry leaves it in the space, while a take operation removes it. Leasing and transaction processing using a Jini service make the system robust. Multiple clients can work on a problem without needing direct connection or even knowledge of one another. They use discovery to find a lookup service and lookup a JavaSpaces service about which they also need no prior knowledge.

Program Modification Exercises

1. Modify Example 15.1 to be a multicast reverse server, and modify Example 15.2 to be a multicast reverse client. Test with at least two clients joining the multicast group. Describe how this system works.

2. Modify the client of Example 15.13 to use remote events to enable it to be notified of a reverse service that becomes available after the client finds the lookup service.

3. Modify Example 15.18 to use BigInteger for the denominator. Modify Example 15.20 to write 1000 Value entries. Denominators must end in 1, 3, 7, or 9. Modify Example 15.21 to calculate with BigInteger values. Test with several Space-Task clients.

Program Design Exercises

4. Write a multicast chat program in which messages sent by one client are received by all others. Identify each message with the name of the client sending it.

5. Write a Jini service that simulates a robot. It should provide a method to move the robot to a new location. Use a simple shape such as a square or a circle to show the robot. Test with clients that move the robot around the service's screen.

6. Use JavaSpaces to create a distributed array. One entry type should define an array element. It will contain the name of the array, the index of the element, and the Object data stored in the element. Another type of entry describes the array. It should have the name of the array and an Integer index. Write a method to add an array element to the space and another to read an element.

7. Use JavaSpaces to implement exchanges. For simplicity we exchange words. Define an entry which contains a word and its size. Have one client write entries with words of various sizes into the space. Have clients look for entries with words of a specific size, or a range of sizes if possible. When a client finds a matching entry it removes it and outputs the word found.

16 JSP Tags

OUTLINE	**16.1 Simple Tags**
	16.2 Body Tags
	16.3 Nested Tags and Script Variables
	16.4 The Jakarta Tag Library

Introduction

. . . .

We introduced JavaServer™ Pages in Section 4.6. HTML uses tags to markup a file for presentation. JSP adds script tags to include dynamic content in the web page. We can design custom tags that allow better separation of Java code and web pages. We illustrate basic tags, attributes, body tags, repeat tags, nested tags, and script variables.

OBJECTIVES:

- Configure tags using JRun.
- Illustrate simple tags and tags with attributes.
- Use body tags, and repeating tags.
- Try nested tags and script variables.

16.1 Simple Tags

. . . .

Simple tags do not have a body. They may have attributes.

Configuring a Tag

We create a `hello` tag that just displays a message. We use that tag in the JSP file `Hello.jsp`

```
<html>
<head>
  <title>Using the hello tag</title>
  <%@ taglib uri="myExamples" prefix="examples" %>
</head>
<body>
  <h1><examples:hello /></h1>
</body>
</html>
```

Figure 16.1 shows the result in a browser.

Figure 16.1 Using the `hello` tag

The JSP file uses the directive

```
<%@ taglib uri="myExamples" prefix="examples" %>
```

to specify the tag library containing the `hello` tag. We can crate any name for the uri as long as it matches the name we use when we configure the library in the `web.xml` file. Here we use `myExamples` as the uri. The prefix, `examples`, indicates that the tag is from the `myExamples` library. We use the tag

```
<examples:hello />
```

which has no body and just displays a message.

Figure 16.2 shows the configuration file `web.xml` that JRun uses with the part we added for our tag library in bold.

Within `<taglib>` we include `<taglib-uri>` which contains the same uri that we use in the JSP file, and `<taglib-location>` that contains the location of the tag library

Figure 16.2 The JRun configuration file

```
<web-app>
 <display-name>Default User Application</display-name>
 <description>
      Default application for getting started</description>
 <session-config>
    <session-timeout>30</session-timeout>
 </session-config>
 <welcome-file-list>
    <welcome-file>index.jsp</welcome-file>
 </welcome-file-list>
 <mime-mapping>
    <extension>jar</extension>
    <mime-type>application/x-java-archive</mime-type>
 </mime-mapping>
 <mime-mapping>
    <extension>jnlp</extension>
    <mime-type>application/x-java-jnlp-file</mime-type>
 </mime-mapping>
 <mime-mapping>
    <extension>txt</extension>
    <mime-type>text/plain</mime-type>
 </mime-mapping>
 <mime-mapping>
    <extension>html</extension>
    <mime-type>text/html</mime-type>
 </mime-mapping>
 <taglib>
    <taglib-uri>
       myExamples
    </taglib-uri>
    <taglib-location>
       /WEB-INF/examples.tld
    </taglib-location>
 </taglib>
</web-app>
```

definition file used to describe the tags in the library. Using JRun we place files according to the table

File	Location
.jsp	JRUN_HOME\servers\default\default-app
web.xml	JRUN_HOME\servers\default\default-app\WEB-INF
.tld	JRUN_HOME\servers\default\default-app\WEB-INF
.class	JRUN_HOME\servers\default\default-app\WEB-INF\classes

Figure 16.3 shows the tag library definition file, examples.tld, we use for our tag library. It includes the tags that we will be developing.

Figure 16.3 The tag library definition file `examples.tld`

```xml
<?xml version="1.0" ?>
<taglib>
  <shortname>examples</shortname>
  <tag>
    <name>hello</name>
    <tagclass>HelloTag</tagclass>
  </tag>
  <tag>
    <name>helloName</name>
    <tagclass>HelloNameTag</tagclass>
    <attribute>
        <name>name</name>
        <required>true</required>
        <rtexprvalue>true</rtexprvalue>
    </attribute>
  </tag>
  <tag>
    <name>helloAndBody</name>
    <tagclass>HelloAndBodyTag</tagclass>
  </tag>
  <tag>
    <name>helloUpper</name>
    <tagclass>HelloUpperTag</tagclass>
    <bodycontent>JSP</bodycontent>
  </tag>
  <tag>
    <name>helloRepeat</name>
    <tagclass>HelloRepeatTag</tagclass>
    <bodycontent>JSP</bodycontent>
    <attribute>
        <name>times</name>
        <required>true</required>
        <rtexprvalue>true</rtexprvalue>
    </attribute>
  </tag>
  <tag>
    <name>helloNested</name>
    <tagclass>HelloNestedTag</tagclass>
  </tag>
  <tag>
    <name>script</name>
    <tagclass>ScriptTag</tagclass>
    <teiclass>ScriptExtra</teiclass>
  </tag>
</taglib>
```

Inside `<taglib>` we provide a `shortname` tag to indicate the tag prefix, and a `<tag>` entry to describe each tag. The `hello` tag has a `<name>` tag to specify its name and a `<tagclass>` tag to specify its class. If we just wanted to define the `hello` tag, we could omit the other tag definitions.

The ⟨tagclass⟩ class handles tag occurrences. It extends TagSupport, which extends the Tag interface. The Tag interface provides various methods that we implement to process the custom tag. Since the hello tag is simple, without a body, we only need to override the doStartTag method that will be executed when the tag is encountered in a JSP file. To compile Example 16.1 we use the command

```
javac -classpath .;%JRUN_HOME%\lib\ext\servlet.jar HelloTag.java
```

EXAMPLE 16.1   HelloTag.java

```
/* Implements the hello tag to display a message.
 */

import java.io.*;
import javax.servlet.jsp.*;
import javax.servlet.jsp.tagext.*;

public class HelloTag extends TagSupport {
  public int doStartTag() {
    JspWriter out = pageContext.getOut();                    // Note 1
    try {
       out.write("Hello World!");
    }catch(IOException e) {
       System.out.println(e.getMessage());
    }
    return SKIP_BODY;                                        // Note 2
  }
}
```

Note 1:   The PageContext contains information about the page available to the tag handler. We use the getOut method to get a writer.

Note 2:   We return SKIP_BODY because this tag has no body. In later examples we will return EVAL_BODY_INCLUDE.

Using an Attribute

The helloName tag has a name attribute that we use to incorporate the user's name into the message. We use a web page, HelloName.html, for the user to input a name and the display size. Figure 16.5 shows the browser request.

The JSP response uses the helloName tag. We get the name attribute from the user's request. We could have added another attribute to hold the size that the user chooses, but instead we get the size inside the tag handler class.

The tag descriptor for the helloName tag in Figure 16.3 contains an attribute tag with the name of the attribute. The ⟨required⟩ tag indicates that we must include the name attribute when we use the helloName tag. The ⟨rtexprvalue⟩ indicates whether we can get the attribute value using a runtime expression. We use such an expression in this example to read the user's request.

Figure 16.4 Providing user input

```
<html>
  <head><title>Try Attributes</title></head>
  <body>
    <form action="http://localhost:8100/HelloName.jsp" method=GET>
      <input type=text  name=name>Name<br>
      <input type=radio name=size value="Large">Large
      <input type=radio name=size value="Small">Small <br>
      <input type=submit>
    </form>
  </body>
</html>
```

Figure 16.5 Inputting in HelloName.html

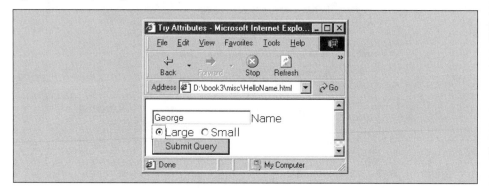

Figure 16.6 `HelloName.jsp`

```
<html>
<head>
  <title>Using the hello tag</title>
  <%@ taglib uri="myExamples" prefix="examples" %>
</head>
<body>
  <examples:helloName name="<%= request.getParameter("name")%>" />
</body>
</html>
```

EXAMPLE 16.2   HelloNameTag.java

```
/* Provides a name attribute. Handles the size request directly.
 */

import java.io.*;
import javax.servlet.*;
import javax.servlet.jsp.*;
import javax.servlet.jsp.tagext.*;
```

Figure 16.7 The JSP response to the request from Figure 16.5

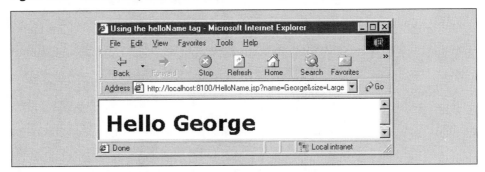

```java
public class HelloNameTag extends TagSupport {
  private String name;

  public int doStartTag() {
    JspWriter out = pageContext.getOut();
    ServletRequest request = pageContext.getRequest();          // Note 1
    String size = request.getParameter("size");
    try {
      if (size.equals("Large"))
        out.write("<h1>Hello " + name + "</h1>");               // Note 2
      else
        out.write("<h5>Hello " + name + "</h5>");
    }catch(IOException e) {
      System.out.println(e.getMessage());
    }
    return SKIP_BODY;
  }
  public void setName(String s) {                               // Note 3
    name = s;
  }
}
```

Note 1: We use the page context to get the user's request.

Note 2: We choose the heading based upon the size that the user indicates.

Note 3: We need to include a set method for every attribute, which will be called to store the attribute's value.

THE BIG PICTURE

JSP tags let a web designer add dynamic content provided by a Java programmer. A simple tag has no body. A JSP tag may have attributes. We reference a tag library in the web.xml configuration file and use a tag library descriptor file to describe the tags. A Java class handles the custom tag.

TEST YOUR UNDERSTANDING

1. What extension do we use for the tag library definition file?

2. Which method of the `Tag` interface will be executed when processing the `<examples:hello />` tag?

3. Change the tag library descriptor file of Figure 16.3 to add a `size` attribute for the `helloName` tag.

4. Which line of the tag library descriptor of Figure 16.3 allows us to use a runtime expression to get the value of the name attribute?

5. If a tag contain an attribute `foo`, what method must the tag handling class include in addition to those needed to handle a tag without attributes?

16.2 Body Tags

. . . .

A tag can pass along its body or it can use it. Tags can use the body repeatedly. Our first example just includes the body, while the second transforms it. The third example in this section uses the body repeatedly.

Including the Body

To illustrate we include a message in the tag body, rather than using an attribute to hold the name.

Figure 16.8 `HelloAndBody.jsp`

```
<html>
<head>
  <title>Using the helloAndBody tag</title>
  <%@ taglib uri="myExamples" prefix="examples" %>
</head>
<body>
  <examples:helloAndBody>
    Hello <%= request.getParameter("name")%>
  </examples:helloAndBody>
  <br>Rest of page
</body>
</html>
```

The HTML file, `HelloAndBody.html`, is similar to Figure 16.4. Figure 16.9 shows the response.

In the tag handler we change the value returned by `doStartTag` to `EVAL_BODY_INCLUDE` to include the body of the tag in the response. We override the `doEndTag` method, which will be called when the processor reaches the end tag, after the body.

Figure 16.9   Including a tag body

EXAMPLE 16.3   HelloAndBodyTag.java

```java
/* Adds heading tags depending on the size chosen
 * by the user.  Includes the tag body.
 */

import java.io.*;
import javax.servlet.*;
import javax.servlet.jsp.*;
import javax.servlet.jsp.tagext.*;

public class HelloAndBodyTag extends TagSupport {

  public int doStartTag() {
    ServletRequest request = pageContext.getRequest();
    String size = request.getParameter("size");
    JspWriter out = pageContext.getOut();
    try {
       if (size.equals("Large"))
         out.write("<h1>");                              // Note 1
       else
         out.write("<h5>");
    }catch(IOException e) {
       System.out.println(e.getMessage());
    }
    return EVAL_BODY_INCLUDE;
  }
  public int doEndTag() {
    ServletRequest request = pageContext.getRequest();
    String size = request.getParameter("size");
    JspWriter out = pageContext.getOut();
    try {
       if (size.equals("Large"))
         out.write("</h1>");                             // Note 2
       else
```

```
            out.write("</h5>");
        }catch(IOException e) {
          System.out.println(e.getMessage());
        }
        return EVAL_PAGE;                                    // Note 3
    }
}
```

....

Note 1: We choose the heading size based on the user's request. The start tag for the heading will precede the body of the `helloAndBody` tag.

Note 2: We output the end tag for the heading after the body has been included.

Note 3: Returning `EVAL_PAGE` causes the rest of the page to be evaluated. Thus the line `Rest of page` appears in Figure 16.9.

Using the Body

The `helloAndBody` tag included its body in the output, but did not modify it. To modify the tag we extend the `BodyTagSupport` class, which extends `TagSupport` and implements the `BodyTag` interface. Its `getBodyContent` method returns a `BodyContent` object that we can use to work with the tag body. The `doAfterBody` method includes actions after the body has been evaluated.

When we evaluate the body we need to add a `<bodycontent>` tag to the `<tag>` entry in the .tld file. Figure 16.3 shows the tag

```
<tag>
  <name>helloUpper</name>
  <tagclass>HelloUpperTag</tagclass>
  <bodycontent>JSP</bodycontent>
</tag>
```

The `<bodycontent>` body can be either `JSP` or `tagdependent`. We use `JSP` because the body includes a JSP tag that needs JSP processing.

Figure 16.10 shows the HTML file for entering a name. We include a message with the name in the body of the `helloUpper` tag in the JSP of Figure 16.11. This tag processes the body to transform it to upper case as shown in Figure 16.12.

EXAMPLE 16.4 **HelloUpperTag.java**

```
/* Transforms the tag body to uppercase.
 */

import java.io.*;
import javax.servlet.*;
import javax.servlet.jsp.*;
import javax.servlet.jsp.tagext.*;

public class HelloUpperTag extends BodyTagSupport {
```

Figure 16.10   Transforming to uppercase

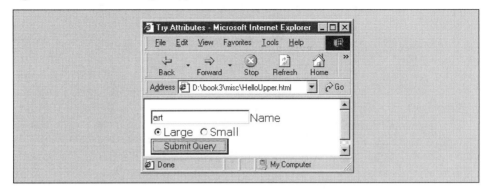

Figure 16.11   `HelloUpper.jsp`

```
<html>
<head>
  <title>Using the helloUpper tag</title>
  <%@ taglib uri="myExamples" prefix="examples" %>
</head>
<body>
  <examples:helloUpper>
    Hello <%= request.getParameter("name")%>
  </examples:helloUpper>
  <br>Rest of page
</body>
</html>
```

Figure 16.12   Transforming a tag body

```
public int doStartTag() {
  ServletRequest request = pageContext.getRequest();
  String size = request.getParameter("size");
  JspWriter out = pageContext.getOut();
  try {
```

```
          if (size.equals("Large"))
            out.write("<h1>");
          else
            out.write("<h5>");
      }catch(IOException e) {
        System.out.println(e.getMessage());
      }
      return EVAL_BODY_TAG;                                      // Note 1
    }
    public int doEndTag() {
      ServletRequest request = pageContext.getRequest();
      String size = request.getParameter("size");
      JspWriter out = pageContext.getOut();
      try {
          if (size.equals("Large"))
            out.write("</h1>");
          else
            out.write("</h5>");
      }catch(IOException e) {
        System.out.println(e.getMessage());
      }
      return EVAL_PAGE;
    }
    public int doAfterBody() {
       try {
        BodyContent body = getBodyContent();
        String s = body.getString().toUpperCase();               // Note 2
        body.getEnclosingWriter().println(s);                     // Note 3
        }catch(IOException e) {
          System.out.println(e.getMessage());
        }
        return SKIP_BODY;                                         // Note 4
    }
}
```

Note 1: We return `EVAL_BODY_TAG` because we will modify the tag body. It requests the creation of new `BodyContent` to evaluate the tag.

Note 2: The `getString` method returns the tag body as a `String`.

Note 3: The `getEnclosingWriter` method returns the writer used by the `doStartTag` and `doEndTag` methods.

Note 4: We return `SKIP_BODY` because we only wish to evaluate the tag body once.

Repeating the Body

The `helloRepeat` tag adds an attribute specifying the number of times to repeat the evaluation of the tag body.

Figure 16.14 show the HTML request, and Figure 16.15 the response.

Figure 16.13 HelloRepeat.jsp

```
<html>
<head>
  <title>Using the helloRepeat tag</title>
  <%@ taglib uri="myExamples" prefix="examples" %>
</head>
<body>
  <examples:helloRepeat times="3">
    Hello <%= request.getParameter("name")%>
  </examples:helloRepeat>
  <br>Rest of page
</body>
</html>
```

Figure 16.14 HelloRepeat.html

Figure 16.15 Repeating a tag body

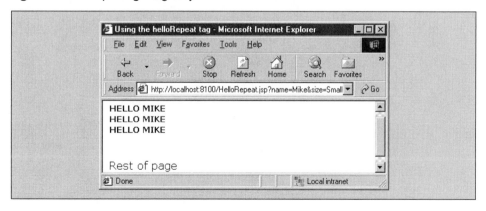

EXAMPLE 16.5   **HelloRepeat.java**

```
/* Repeats the tag body the number of times
 * specified in the times attribute.
 */
```

```java
import java.io.*;
import javax.servlet.*;
import javax.servlet.jsp.*;
import javax.servlet.jsp.tagext.*;

public class HelloRepeatTag extends BodyTagSupport {
  private int times;

  public int doStartTag() {
    ServletRequest request = pageContext.getRequest();
    String size = request.getParameter("size");
    JspWriter out = pageContext.getOut();
    try {
       if (size.equals("Large"))
         out.write("<h1>");
       else
         out.write("<h5>");
    }catch(IOException e) {
       System.out.println(e.getMessage());
    }
    return EVAL_BODY_TAG;
  }
  public int doEndTag() {
    ServletRequest request = pageContext.getRequest();
    String size = request.getParameter("size");
    JspWriter out = pageContext.getOut();
    try {
       if (size.equals("Large"))
         out.write("</h1>");
       else
         out.write("</h5>");
    }catch(IOException e) {
       System.out.println(e.getMessage());
    }
    return EVAL_PAGE;
  }
  public int doAfterBody() {
    BodyContent body = getBodyContent();
    String s = body.getString().toUpperCase();
    if (times-- >= 1) {
     try {
      body.getEnclosingWriter().println(s +"<br>");
      body.clearBody();                                    // Note 1
     }catch(IOException e) {
       System.out.println(e.getMessage());
     }
     return EVAL_BODY_TAG;                                 // Note 2
    }
    else
     return SKIP_BODY;                                     // Note 3
  }
```

```
public void setTimes(String s) {
  times = Integer.parseInt(s);
}
public int getTimes() {                                    // Note 4
  return times;
}
}
```

Note 1:   The `clearBody` method clears the buffer in preparation for the next evaluation of the body.

Note 2:   We return `EVAL_BODY_TAG` because we wish to evaluate the body again.

Note 3:   Returning `SKIP_BODY` prevents the body from being evaluated again.

Note 4:   We include the `getTimes` method to be able to get the value of the `times` attribute. We will use it in a later example.

THE BIG PICTURE
Body tags may include the body, use the body, and repeat the tag body. The tag handler class extends `BodyTagSupport` rather than `TagSupport` when using or repeating the body.

TEST YOUR UNDERSTANDING

6. Which method of the `Tag` interface do we implement to process the end tag `<helloAndBody />`?

7. What value does `doStartTag` return when we wish to include the tag body in the output generated?

8. Which class can the tag handling class extend if the tag uses its body?

9. Which tag handling method will be executed after the tag body has been evaluated?

16.3   Nested Tags and Script Variables

Tags can interact. We show how a nested tag can use an attribute value from its enclosing tag. A tag can define a variable that we can use in a JSP script.

A Nested Tag

We nest a `helloNested` tag inside the `helloRepeat` tag. It calls the `getTimes` method to find out the number of times that the body will be repeated. Figure 16.16 show the JSP file and Figure 16.17 the response in the browser to the `HelloNested.html` request.

Figure 16.16 `HelloNested.jsp`

```
<html>
<head>
  <title>Using the helloNested tag</title>
  <%@ taglib uri="myExamples" prefix="examples" %>
</head>
<body>
  <examples:helloRepeat times="3">
    <examples:helloNested />
    Hello <%= request.getParameter("name")%>
  </examples:helloRepeat>
  <br>Rest of page
</body>
</html>
```

Figure 16.17 Using a nested tag

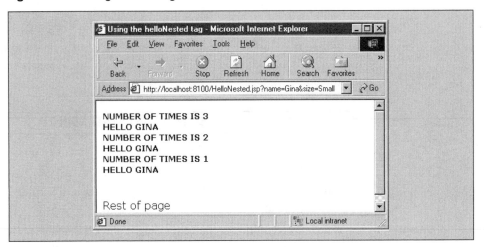

EXAMPLE 16.6 **HelloNested.java**

```java
/* Uses an attribute from its enclosing tag.
 */

import java.io.*;
import javax.servlet.jsp.*;
import javax.servlet.jsp.tagext.*;

public class HelloNestedTag extends TagSupport {
  public int doStartTag() {
    HelloRepeatTag outer =
        (HelloRepeatTag)findAncestorWithClass
                          (this, HelloRepeatTag.class);      // Note 1
    JspWriter out = pageContext.getOut();
```

```
    try {
       out.write("Number of times is "
                            + outer.getTimes() + "<br>");           // Note 2
    }catch(IOException e) {
       System.out.println(e.getMessage());
    }
    return SKIP_BODY;
  }
}
```

Note 1:   The `findAncestorWithClass` method locates the closest enclosing tag of the type specified in the second argument. This method returns a `Tag` that we cast to `HelloRepeatTag`. The first argument is the current tag.

Note 2:   We are able to call the `getTimes` method from the enclosing tag handler.

A Script Variable

Our next example uses a tag to define a script variable that we can include in JSP scripts. The `script` tag contains an `id` attribute. Using the attribute name `id` indicates that the tag is defining a script variable. The JSP file of Figure 16.18 shows that we use the `script` tag and then call the `tossCoin` method of the `toss` variable it defines.

Figure 16.18 `Script.jsp`

```
<html>
<head>
  <title>Using the script tag</title>
  <%@ taglib uri="myExamples" prefix="examples" %>
</head>
<body>
  <examples:script id="toss" />
  The coin is <%= toss.tossCoin() %><br>
  The coin is <%= toss.tossCoin() %><br>
  The coin is <%= toss.tossCoin() %><br>
</body>
</html>
```

Because we want to use the script variable after the script, the tag handler overrides the `doEndTag` method to set the attribute to make an object available. It implements the `tossCoin` method we will invoke to generate a random coin toss. Figure 16.19 shows the response returned by `Script.jsp`. The results may change at each request.

To use a script variable we must override the `TagExtraInfo` class and add its name to the `.tld` file using the `<teiclass>` tag. The `examples.tld` entry for the script tag is

```
<tag>
  <name>script</name>
  <tagclass>ScriptTag</tagclass>
  <teiclass>ScriptExtra</teiclass>
</tag>
```

Figure 16.19 Using a script variable

EXAMPLE 16.7 ScriptTag.java, ScriptExtra.java

ScriptTag.java

```java
/* Make a tag object available in JSP scripts using the
 * id attribute as the variable name.
 */

import java.io.*;
import javax.servlet.jsp.*;
import javax.servlet.jsp.tagext.*;

public class ScriptTag extends TagSupport {
  public int doEndTag() {
    ScriptTag t = new ScriptTag();
    pageContext.setAttribute(getId(), t);            // Note 1
    return EVAL_PAGE;
  }
  public String tossCoin() {                         // Note 2
    if (Math.random() < .5)
      return "Heads";
    else
      return "Tails";
  }
}
```

ScriptExtra.java

```java
/* Defines a script variable from the script tag.
 */

import javax.servlet.jsp.*;
import javax.servlet.jsp.tagext.*;
```

```
public class ScriptExtra extends TagExtraInfo {
  public VariableInfo[] getVariableInfo(TagData data) {          // Note 3
    VariableInfo info =
      new VariableInfo(data.getId(), "ScriptTag",
                       true, VariableInfo.AT_END);               // Note 4
    VariableInfo[] result = {info};
    return result;
  }
}
```

Note 1:   The `setAttribute` method associates a `ScriptTag` object with the name specified as the `id` attribute of the tag.

Note 2:   The `tossCoin` method returns `Heads` half the time and `Tails` the other half.

Note 3:   The `TagData` argument represents the values of the attributes.

Note 4:   The four parameters of the `VariableInfo` constructor are

- The name of the scripting variable.

- The type of the variable.

- Defines a new variable?

- The scope of the variable, which can be `AT_BEGIN`, `NESTED`, or `AT_END`.

THE BIG PICTURE

Nested tags can use methods available to the outer tag. Tags use the `id` attribute to define variables used in JSP scripts.

TEST YOUR UNDERSTANDING

10. Which method allows us to find a tag of a certain type that encloses a given tag?

11. Which attribute should a tag include to define a script variable?

12. Which tag must we add to the tag library descriptor file in order to use a script variable? Which class must we extend to define a script variable?

16.4   The Jakarta Tag Library

The Jakarta project from the Apache Software Foundation provides open source server solutions. The Tomcat servlet engine is the reference implementation for the Java servlet API. The Taglibs project provides open source custom JSP tags. It includes many tags and it expands daily. We can download the tag library from `jakarta.apache.org/taglibs`. We illustrate with database tags.

Using the DBTags Library

To use DBTags with JRun we need to

- Copy `dbtags.tld` to

  `JRUN_HOME\servers\default\default-app\WEB-INF`

- Copy `dbtags.jar` to

  `JRUN_HOME\servers\default\default-app\WEB-INF\lib`

- Add

  ```
  <taglib>
    <taglib-uri>http://jakarta.apache.org/taglibs/dbtags</taglib-uri>
    <taglib-location>/WEB-INF/dbtags.tld</taglib-location>
  </taglib>
  ```
  to web.xml

The tags we use in our example are

Name	Attributes	Description
connection		Opens a JDBC connection
	id	A script variable
	conn	The connection name
url		The JDBC url, used with a connection tag
driver		The JDBC driver, used with a connection tag
statement		A statement
	id	A script variable
	conn	The connection name
query		An SQL query
resultSet		The result set for a query
	id	A script variable
getColumn		A column of the result set.
	position	The position of the column
closeConnection		Closes a JDBC connection
	conn	The connection name

Figure 16.20 shows the `Sales.jsp` file and Figure 16.21 shows the response in the browser.

Figure 16.20 `Sales.jsp`

```
<%@ taglib uri="http://jakarta.apache.org/taglibs/dbtags" prefix="sql" %>

<sql:connection id="con">
  <sql:url>jdbc:odbc:Sales</sql:url>
  <sql:driver>sun.jdbc.odbc.JdbcOdbcDriver</sql:driver>
</sql:connection>

<table>
<sql:statement id="stmt" conn="con">
  <sql:query>
    SELECT CustomerName, Address FROM Customer
    ORDER BY 1
  </sql:query>
  <sql:resultSet id="result">
    <tr>
      <td><sql:getColumn position="1"/></td>
      <td><sql:getColumn position="2"/></td>
    </tr>
  </sql:resultSet>
</sql:statement>
</table>

<sql:closeConnection conn="con"/>
```

Figure 16.21 Using DBTags

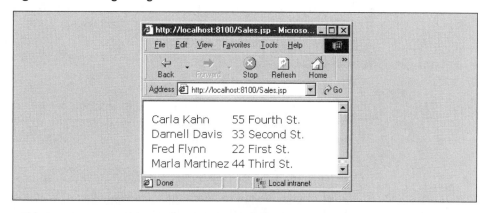

THE BIG PICTURE

The Jakarta project provides a large collection of JSP tag libraries. We illustrated with tags from the DBTags library.

TEST YOUR UNDERSTANDING

---

13. Which of the tags form the DBTags library that we use in Figure 16.20 defined
script variables?

SUMMARY

- JSP tags allow us to separate content and presentation in a web page. The web
designer can use the tag, while the Java programmer implements it. We must add to
the web.xml configuration file used by the servlet engine to locate a tag library. We
need to describe each tag library with a tag library definition XML file. For simple
tags this .tld file includes the name and class for each tag. The class is the Java tag
handler. We need an additional tag to describe each attribute. Within the attribute
tag we give its name, state whether or not it is required, and whether or not it can be
found by a runtime expression.

- We can include the tag body, use it, and repeat it. To include the tag body, we return
EVAL_BODY_INCLUDE from the doStartTag method, and implement the doEndTag
method. To use the tag body the tag handler class extends the TagBodySupport class
and implements the doAfterTagBody method in the tag handler. To repeat the tag
body, the doAftgerTagBody method returns EVAL_BODY_TAG. It returns SKIP_BODY when
it no longer needs to evaluate the tag body.

- A tag handler for a nested tag can call the findAncestorWithClass method to find an
outer tag of a given type. A tag includes an id attribute to define a script variable.

- The Jakarta project provides a large library of custom tags. We used tags from the
DBTags library.

Program Modification Exercises

1. The HelloTag method of Example 16.1 implements the doStartTag method. The
hello tag has no body. Would the tag handler work the same if it implemented
doEndTag instead? Try this modification to Example 16.1. Does Hello.jsp produce the same result?

2. Redefine the helloName tag to have a second attribute, size, giving the desired
point size for the display of the name. Modify Example 16.2 to handle this modified tag. Modify HelloName.jsp to use this modified tag.

3. Redefine the helloAndBody tag to have a size attribute giving the desired point
size for the display of the body. Modify Example 16.3 to handle this modified
tag. Modify HelloAndBody.jsp to use this modified tag.

4. Redefine the helloRepeat tag to have a second attribute, size, giving the desired
point size for the display of the name. Modify Example 16.5 to handle this modified tag. Modify HelloRepeat.jsp to use this modified tag.

5. Redefine the `helloRepeat` tag to eliminate the times attribute. Modify `Hello-Repeat.html` to add a text field to determine the number of times to repeat rather than using an attribute. Modify Example 16.5 to handle this modified tag.

6. Modify Example 16.6 and the `Script.jsp` file so that the `script` tag can be nested within the `helloRepeat` tag to determine the number of repetitions of the coin toss. Do not repeat the call to `coinToss` explicitly in the JSP file.

7. Modify `Sales.jsp` of Figure 16.20 to obtain the query from a text area in an HTML form that the client submits.

Program Design Exercises

8. Implement a simple tag that will return the current time. Write a JSP file that uses this tag.

9. Implement a tag that will specify a font name in an attribute and the user's name in another attribute. Obtain the values of these attributes from an HTML form. Display the user's name using a font with the specified font name. Write a JSP file that uses this tag.

10. Implement a tag that will display the tag body using a font name, style, and size given as tag attributes. Also include a display color as an attribute. Write a JSP file that uses this tag.

11. Implement a tag that repeats its body a number of times given by a number between 1 and 10 selected randomly. Write a JSP file that uses this tag.

12. Write a tag that defines a script variable. Include a method to compute the number of heads obtained when we simulate the toss of a fair coin 100 times. Write a JSP file that uses this script variable.

13. Write a nested tag that defines a script variable. Nest the tag within the `helloRepeat` tag defined in Section 16.2. Include a method to compute the number of heads obtained when we simulate the toss of a fair coin the number of times given in the `times` attribute of the `helloRepeat` tag.. Write a JSP file that uses this script variable.

14. Use the DBTags library to write a JSP file that returns the total quantity of a particular item ordered by a particular customer. The user will enter the customer name and choose the item in an HTML form. Use the Sales database of chapter 3.

17

Messaging and Naming

Introduction

The Java Messaging Service (JMS) provides an interface to message-oriented middleware, just as JDBC provides access to databases. Asynchronous messaging allows systems to communicate without the sender having to wait for a response from the receiver. The message bean adds this messaging capability to Enterprise Java Bean servers. To use JMS we need a JMS provider. We use the JMS server included with the Java 2 Enterprise Edition version 1.3 (See Chapter 10.)

The Java Naming and Directory Interface (JNDI) abstracts the binding and looking up of objects. To use JNDI we need a JNDI service provider. We use Sun's file system service.

OBJECTIVES:

- Use publish-and-subscribe messaging.

- Use point-to-point messaging.

- Introduce the message bean.

- Introduce JNDI.

17.1 Publish-and-Subscribe Messaging

A publisher publishes messages on a topic and subscribers who subscribe to that topic will receive those messages. This is a push technology in which publishers push methods to subscribers. Publishers and subscribers are clients of the JMS server.

Message Types

The five message types are

BytesMessage	Untyped bytes
MapMessage	Name-Value pairs
ObjectMessage	Java objects
StreamMessage	Typed bytes
TextMessage	String

We illustrate JMS using the `TextMessage` type.

Administering a JMS Server

We configure the JMS server with destinations and connection factories that publishers and subscribers will use. The client uses a connection factory to connect to the JMS provider. A destination is the target of messages produced and the source of messages consumed.

To use the JMS provider included with the J2EE we start the server with the command

```
start %j2ee_home%\bin\j2ee -verbose
```

where `j2ee_home` is the directory in which J2EE is installed.

The J2EE provides a default `TopicConnectionFactory` for the publish-and-subscribe approach. We create two topics, `Words` and `Numbers`, using the commands

```
%j2ee_home%\bin\j2eeadmin -addJmsDestination Words topic
```

and

```
%j2ee_home%\bin\j2eeadmin -addJmsDestination Numbers topic
```

We could create a new connection factory using the command

```
%j2ee_home%\bin\j2eeadmin -addJmsFactory jndi_name topic
```

where we replaced `jndi_name` with the name of the factory. We can find the destinations installed using

```
%j2ee_home%\bin\j2eeadmin -listJmsDestination
```

and the installed factories using

```
%j2ee_home%\bin\j2eeadmin -listJmsFactory.
```

JMS clients look up administered objects using the Java Naming and Directory Interface (JNDI). The `InitialContext` method returns the `Context` for the JNDI lookup. Calling `InitialContext` with no arguments will use the JNDI provider specified in the `jndi.properties` file in the classpath. The J2EE includes this configuration file.

Creating a Publisher

We create a publisher that publishes messages on two topics, Words and Numbers. These messages go to the JMS provider, which is responsible for transmitting them to any subscribers.

EXAMPLE 17.1   Publisher.java

```java
/* Publishes messages on the Words and Numbers topics.
 */

import javax.jms.*;
import javax.naming.*;

public class Publisher {
  public static void main(String[] args) {
    Context context = null;
    try {
       context = new InitialContext();
    }catch(NamingException e) {                                    // Note 1
       System.out.println("JNDI failure " + e.getMessage());
       System.exit(0);
    }
    TopicConnectionFactory factory = null;
    Topic topic1 = null;
    Topic topic2 = null;
    try {
      factory = (TopicConnectionFactory)
                context.lookup("TopicConnectionFactory");          // Note 2
      topic1 = (Topic)context.lookup("Words");                     // Note 3
      topic2 = (Topic)context.lookup("Numbers");
    } catch (NamingException e) {
       System.out.println("Lookup failure " +
                e.toString());
       System.exit(1);
    }
    TopicConnection connection = null;
    TopicSession session = null;
    TopicPublisher words = null;
    TopicPublisher numbers = null;
    TextMessage message = null;
    String[] wordMessage = {"Fish", "Tomato", "Cucumber"};
    String[] numberMessage = {"1729", "5050", "123456789"};
    try {
      connection = factory.createTopicConnection();                // Note 4
```

```
          session = connection.createTopicSession
                      (false, Session.AUTO_ACKNOWLEDGE);          // Note 5
          words = session.createPublisher(topic1);               // Note 6
          numbers = session.createPublisher(topic2);
          message = session.createTextMessage();
          int i = 0;
          while(i < 1000000) {                                   // Note 7
            message.setText(wordMessage[i%3]);
            words.publish(message);
            message.setText(numberMessage[i%3]);
            numbers.publish(message);
            Thread.sleep(1000);
            i++;
          }
          connection.close();
        }catch(Exception e) {
          e.printStackTrace();
        }
      }
    }
```

Note 1:   `NamingException` is the superclass of all exceptions thrown by operations in the `Context` interface.

Note 2:   We lookup the `TopicConnectionFactory` configured by the JMS provider.

Note 3:   We lookup the topic that we added to the JMS provider using the `j2eeadmin` utility.

Note 4:   A JMS `Connection` is typically a socket between the client and the JMS provider. A `TopicConnection` is a `Connection` to a JMS publish-and-subscribe provider, used to create one or more topic sessions.

Note 5:   A JMS `Session` is a factory for its message producers and consumers. It provides a transaction capability that we do not use. It retains messages until they have been acknowledged. A `TopicSession` extends `Session`. It provides methods to create a `TopicPublisher` and a `TopicSubscriber`. We set the first argument of `createTopicSession` to `false` because we do not use transactions. The second argument indicates the acknowledgment mode, and is ignored when transactions are used. Message acknowledgment helps to verify that a message has been received. `AUTO_ACKNOWLEDGE` is the most commonly used mode. The other two may give performance improvements in special circumstances. With `AUTO_ACKNOWLEDGE` the server acknowledges reception to the producer and the consumer acknowledges reception to the server.

Note 6:   `words = session.createPublisher(topic1);`
The `createPublisher` method creates a `Publisher` to publish messages on the indicated topic.

Note 7:   `while(i < 1000000)`

We publish 1,000,000 words and 1,000,000 numbers. Because the words and numbers come from arrays of size three, the three words and numbers repeat over and over again.

Creating Subscribers

We create a `TopicSubscriber` who subscribes to a topic passed as a program argument. The `MessageListener` interface provides the `onMessage` method to respond when messages are received.

EXAMPLE 17.2   **Subscriber.java**

```java
/* Subscribes to receive message on a topic passed
 * as a program argument.
 */

import javax.jms.*;
import javax.naming.*;
import java.io.*;

public class Subscriber implements MessageListener {              // Note 1

  public static void main(String[] args) {
    Context context = null;
    try {
       context = new InitialContext();
    }catch(NamingException e) {
       System.out.println("JNDI failure " + e.getMessage());
       System.exit(0);
    }
    TopicConnectionFactory factory = null;
    Topic topic = null;
    try {
      factory = (TopicConnectionFactory)
              context.lookup("TopicConnectionFactory");
      topic = (Topic)context.lookup(args[0]);                    // Note 2
    } catch (NamingException e) {
       System.out.println("Lookup failure " +
               e.toString());
       System.exit(1);
    }
    TopicConnection connection = null;
    TopicSession session = null;
    TopicSubscriber subscriber = null;
    TextMessage message = null;
    try {
      connection = factory.createTopicConnection();
      session = connection.createTopicSession
                  (false, Session.AUTO_ACKNOWLEDGE);
```

```
      subscriber = session.createSubscriber(topic);
      subscriber.setMessageListener(new Subscriber());        // Note 3
      connection.start();                                      // Note 4
      System.in.read();                                        // Note 5
      connection.close();
    }catch(Exception e) {
      e.printStackTrace();
    }
  }
  public void onMessage(Message message) {                     // Note 6
    try {
      TextMessage text = (TextMessage)message;
      System.out.println(text.getText());
    }catch(JMSException e) {
      e.printStackTrace();
    }
  }
}
```

Note 1: Here Subscriber implements the MessageListener interface. We could have used another class.

Note 2: We pass the topic as a program argument.

Note 3: We set a MessageListener handle messages to this consumer.

Note 4: We call the start method, which starts the delivery of messages, after the setup of the connection is complete.

Note 5: When the user hits any key the subscriber will go on to close and terminate.

Note 6: `public void onMessage(Message message)`
onMessage handles a received message. In this example we just echo the message to the console.

Compiling and Running the Clients

We compile using the commands

```
javac -classpath .;%j2ee_home%\lib\j2ee.jar Publisher.java
javac -classpath .;%j2ee_home%\lib\j2ee.jar Subscriber.java
```

Before starting the subscribers and publisher we need to start the J2EE server using

```
start %j2ee_home%\bin\j2ee -verbose
```

We start three subscribers. Two will subscribe to the Words topic and one to Numbers. The commands are

```
start java
-Djms.properties=%J2EE_HOME%\config\jms_client.properties
-classpath .;%j2ee_home%\lib\j2ee.jar Subscriber Words
```

twice, and

```
start java
-Djms.properties=%J2EE_HOME%\config\jms_client.properties
-classpath .;%j2ee_home%\lib\j2ee.jar Subscriber Numbers
```

where we must define `jms.properties`.

We start the publisher using

```
java
-Djms.properties=%J2EE_HOME%\config\jms_client.properties
-classpath .;%j2ee_home%\lib\j2ee.jar Publisher
```

We split the commands on three lines for clarity but type them as one long line at the command prompt. Figure 17.1 shows one of the subscribers receiving the `Words` messages, while Figure 17.2 show the subscriber receiving the `Numbers` messages.

Figure 17.1 Subscribing to Numbers

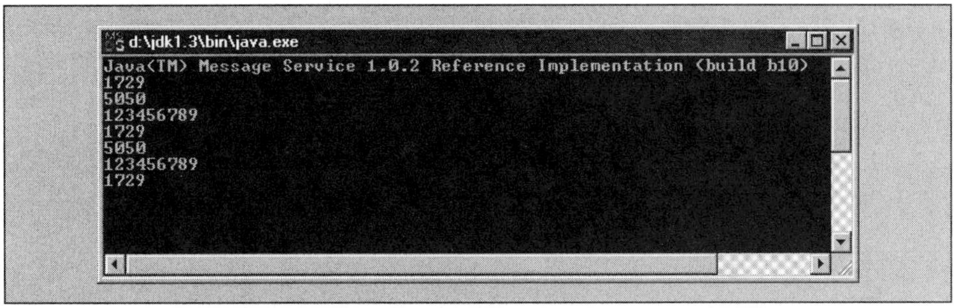

Figure 17.2 Subscribing to Words

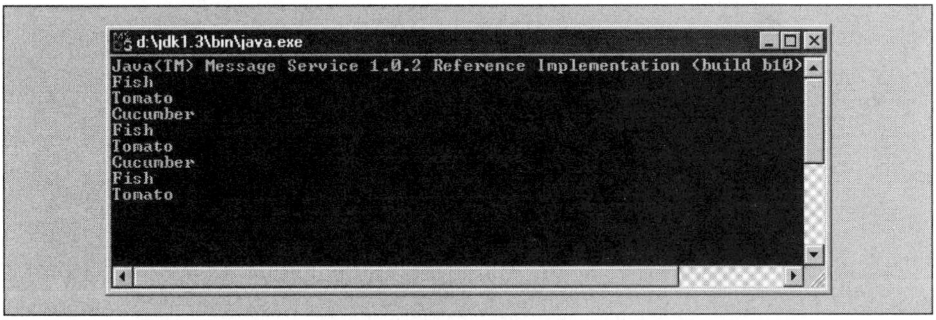

THE BIG PICTURE

The Java Messaging Service adds an asynchronous messaging capability to enterprise applications. The publish-and-subscribe model allows one publisher to reach many subscribers who have indicated they wish to subscribe to the topic of the message.

TEST YOUR UNDERSTANDING

---

1. Where can we find the name of the default JNDI provider.

2. How do we specify that a `TopicSession` not use transactions?

3. What interface do we implement to be notified when a subscriber receives a message?

17.2   Point-to-Point Messaging

· · · · · · · · · · ·

In point-to-point messaging a producer sends a message to a queue, and a consumer receives a message from that queue. JMS supports both publish-and-subscribe and point-to-point messaging in order to be useful with a wide range of providers. Each point-to-point message has only one consumer.

We need to configure the JMS provider to add a queue destination using the command

```
%j2ee_home%\bin\j2eeadmin -addJmsDestination Colors queue
```

A `QueueSender` will send messages containing color names to a queue and a `QueueReceiver` will receive them.

Creating a Receiver

Example 17.3 creates the receiver of point-to-point messages. The steps are similar to those the subscriber used in Example 17.1.

EXAMPLE 17.3   **Receiver.java**

```java
/* Receives messages from a queue.
 */

import javax.jms.*;
import javax.naming.*;
import java.io.*;

public class Receiver implements MessageListener {

  public static void main(String[] args) {
    Context context = null;
    try {
       context = new InitialContext();
    }catch(NamingException e) {
       System.out.println("JNDI failure " + e.getMessage());
       System.exit(0);
    }
    QueueConnectionFactory factory = null;
    Queue queue = null;
```

```
      try {
        factory = (QueueConnectionFactory)
                  context.lookup("QueueConnectionFactory");
        queue = (Queue)context.lookup(args[0]);
      } catch (NamingException e) {
          System.out.println("Lookup failure " +
                  e.toString());
          System.exit(1);
      }
      QueueConnection connection = null;
      QueueSession session = null;
      QueueReceiver receiver = null;
      TextMessage message = null;
      try {
        connection = factory.createQueueConnection();
        session = connection.createQueueSession
                      (false, Session.AUTO_ACKNOWLEDGE);
        receiver = session.createReceiver(queue);
        receiver.setMessageListener(new Receiver());
        connection.start();
        System.in.read();
        connection.close();
      }catch(Exception e) {
        e.printStackTrace();
      }
    }
    public void onMessage(Message message) {
      try {
        TextMessage text = (TextMessage)message;
        System.out.println(text.getText());
      }catch(JMSException e) {
        e.printStackTrace();
      }
    }
  }
```

Creating a Sender

Example 17.4 creates a sender to send messages to the Colors queue. The sender follows steps similar to those used by the publisher in Example 17.2.

EXAMPLE 17.4   Sender.java

```
/* Sends messages to the Colors queue
 */

import javax.jms.*;
import javax.naming.*;
```

```java
public class Sender {
  public static void main(String[] args) {
    Context context = null;
    try {
       context = new InitialContext();
    }catch(NamingException e) {
      System.out.println("JNDI failure " + e.getMessage());
      System.exit(0);
    }
    QueueConnectionFactory factory = null;
    Queue queue = null;
    try {
      factory = (QueueConnectionFactory)
              context.lookup("QueueConnectionFactory");
      queue = (Queue)context.lookup("Colors");
    } catch (NamingException e) {
      System.out.println("Lookup failure " +
              e.toString());
      System.exit(1);
    }
    QueueConnection connection = null;
    QueueSession session = null;
    QueueSender colors = null;
    TextMessage message = null;
    String[] colorMessage = {"Red", "Green", "Blue"};
    try {
      connection = factory.createQueueConnection();
      session = connection.createQueueSession
                  (false, Session.AUTO_ACKNOWLEDGE);
      colors = session.createSender(queue);
      message = session.createTextMessage();
      int i = 0;
      while(i < 1000000) {
        message.setText(colorMessage[i%3]);
        colors.send(message);
        Thread.sleep(1000);
        i++;
      }
      connection.close();
    }catch(Exception e) {
      e.printStackTrace();
    }
  }
}
```

We compile using the commands

```
javac -classpath .;%j2ee_home%\lib\j2ee.jar Sender.java
```

and

```
javac -classpath .;%j2ee_home%\lib\j2ee.jar Receiver.java
```

We run using the commands

```
start java
-Djms.properties=%J2EE_HOME%\config\jms_client.properties
-classpath .;%j2ee_home%\lib\j2ee.jar Receiver Colors
```

and

```
start java
-Djms.properties=%J2EE_HOME%\config\jms_client.properties
-classpath .;%j2ee_home%\lib\j2ee.jar Sender
```

Figure 17.3 shows the receiver receiving messages.

Figure 17.3   Receiving messages from the Colors queue

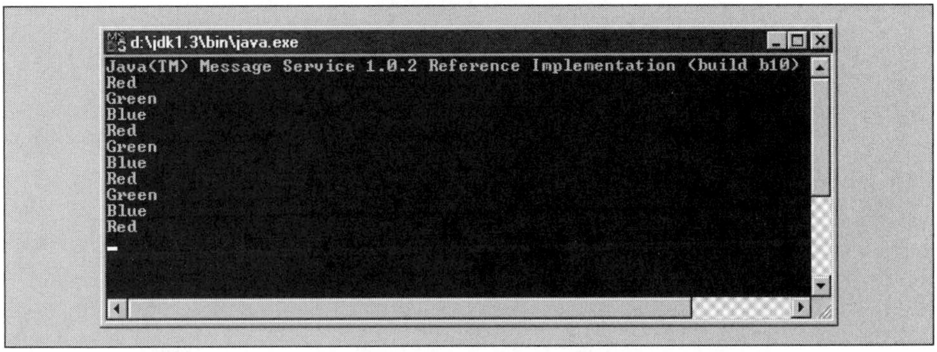

THE BIG PICTURE

In point-to-point messaging, senders send messages to a queue, and receivers remove them. Each message will go to only one consumer.

TEST YOUR UNDERSTANDING

4. Describe the analogies between the objects of Example 17.1 for a publisher and Example 17.4 for a sender.

5. Describe the analogies between the objects of Example 17.2 for a subscriber and Example 17.3 for a receiver.

6. Explain the most important difference between publish-and-subscribe and point-to-point messaging.

17.3 Message-Driven Beans

Enterprise JavaBeans™ version 2.0 includes a new bean type, the message bean. A message bean allows for asynchronous processing, so the invoker of a bean does not have to wait for a response. It can invoke a message bean that can call session bean methods, for example, to complete a transaction for a client.

Creating a Message-Driven Bean

We illustrate message-driven beans with a very simple example of a bean that just echoes the messages it receives rather than contacting session or entity beans to fulfill a client's request.

A message-driven bean implements the `MessageDrivenBean` interface and the `MessageListener` interface. We configure it in the deployment tool to use a particular connection factory and queue, so we do not need to include those steps in the bean.

EXAMPLE 17.5   ReceiverBean.java

```java
/* Echoes the messages it receives.
 */

import javax.ejb.*;
import javax.jms.*;

public class ReceiverBean
        implements MessageDrivenBean, MessageListener  {
  public ReceiverBean() { }                                    // Note 1
  public void ejbCreate() { }
  public void ejbRemove() { }
  public void setMessageDrivenContext
                       (MessageDrivenContext m) { }            // Note 2
  public void onMessage(Message message) {
    try {
      TextMessage text = (TextMessage)message;
      System.out.println(text.getText());
    }catch(JMSException e) {
      e.printStackTrace();
    }
  }
}
```

Note 1:   We must include a no argument constructor.

Note 2:   We do not bother to save the context because we do not use it.

Deployment

We use the deployment tool to create an application and deployed it on the J2EE server. We start the deployment tool using the command

```
start %j2ee_home%\bin\deploytool
```

Using the deployment tool, we

- Create an application

    Choose the `File, New, Application` menu item.
    Enter the application file name (See Figure 17.4) and click `OK`

Figure 17.4 Entering the application file name

- Package the bean

    Choose the `File, New, Enterprise Bean` menu item
    Click `Next` (Introduction)
    Choose `Receiver` as the application the enterprise bean will go in
    Enter `ReceiverJAR` as the JAR Display Name
    Press the `Add` button, choose `ReceiverBean.class`, and press the `Add` button.
    Press `OK`, then press `Next`. (EJB JAR Screen)
    Select `Message-Driven` as the Bean Type.
    Choose `ReceiverBean` as the Bean Class.
    Enter `ReceiverBean` as the Enterprise Bean Name.
    Press `Next`. (General Screen)
    Select `Queue` as the Destination Type.
    Enter `Colors` as the Destination.
    Enter `QueueConnectionFactory` as the ConnectionFactory.
    Choose `Auto-Acknowledge` as the Acknowlegement.
    Press `Next`. (Message-Driven Bean Settings)
    Press `Next`. (Environment Entries)
    Press `Next`. (Enterprise Bean References)
    Press `Next`. (JMS References)
    Press `Next`. (Resource References)
    Press `Next`. (Security)
    Select `Container-Managed Transactions` for Transaction Management.
    Choose `Required` as the Transaction Type.
    Press `Next`. (Transaction Management)
    Press `Finish`.

- Deploy the application.

    Choose the *Tools, Deploy* menu item.
    Choose *Receiver* as the Object to Deploy.
    Press *Next*. (Introduction)
    Press *Next*. (JNDI Names)
    Press *Finish*.
    Press OK (Deployment progress, Figure 17.5)

Figure 17.5   The Deployment Progress Screen

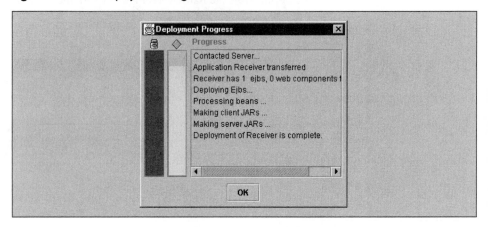

Running the QueueSender of Example 17.4 will cause the bean to echo the messages it receives in the J2EE server window

```
XAResource.start: 1692210095,TMNOFLAGS
Red
XAResource.end: 1692210095,TMSUCCESS
XAResource.commit: 1692210095,true
XAResource.start: 667516174,TMNOFLAGS
Green
XAResource.end: 667516174,TMSUCCESS
XAResource.commit: 667516174,true
XAResource.start: -357177747,TMNOFLAGS
Blue
XAResource.end: -357177747,TMSUCCESS
XAResource.commit: -357177747,true
XAResource.start: -1381871668,TMNOFLAGS
Red
XAResource.end: -1381871668,TMSUCCESS
XAResource.commit: -1381871668,true
XAResource.start: 1888401707,TMNOFLAGS
Green
XAResource.end: 1888401707,TMSUCCESS
XAResource.commit: 1888401707,true
XAResource.start: 863707786,TMNOFLAGS
```

```
Blue
XAResource.end: 863707786,TMSUCCESS
XAResource.commit: 863707786,true
XAResource.start: -160986135,TMNOFLAGS
Red
XAResource.end: -160986135,TMSUCCESS
XAResource.commit: -160986135,true
XAResource.start: -1185680056,TMNOFLAGS
```

and so on until we terminate the sender. The XAResource outputs concern transactions that are managed by the container.

THE BIG PICTURE

The Enterprise JavaBean 2.0 specification includes message-driven beans. These beans allow asynchronous messaging to an EJB container, so the caller does not have to wait for a response. The caller sends a message and returns while the message bean communicates with other enterprise beans.

TEST YOUR UNDERSTANDING

7.   Suppose that ReceiverBean invoked an Agent bean of Section 10.3 to order some items. Explain the difference between a client using an Agent via ReceiverBean and a client using it directly as in Section 10.3.

17.4   The Java Naming and Directory Interface™

· · · · · · · · · ·

The Java Naming and Directory Interface™ (JNDI) provides a common programming interface to many naming and directory services. Programmers can use the same interface with many services. In this text we have used JNDI in Section 2.5 when we used the RMI registry to bind and lookup remote objects. In Chapter 10 we used a naming service included with the reference implementation of the Java 2 Enterprise Edition. In this chapter we used this service when sending messages.

The Java 2 Standard Edition versions 1.3 and higher include the JNDI classes in the javax.naming package. The JNDI code may be downloaded from java.sun.com to use with version 1.2. To use JNDI we need a service provider. The simplest provider to use is the file system provider available from http://java.sun.com/products/jndi/index.html, using the FS Context link after accepting the license. We unzip it into the JAVA_HOME directory in which we installed the Java 2 Standard Edition.

A context provides methods to manage a set of bindings from names to objects. An initial context provides the starting point for the resolution of names. Different service providers will use different naming conventions, but JNDI allows us to access the bindings in the same way.

Using JNDI we create an `InitialContext`, passing it a hash table with properties to specify the environment. The two properties we specify are the service provider's initial context and the base URL for the location of the bindings.

We need use the service provider classes to run Example 17.6. These are not included with the J2SE SDK and require a separate download, as described above. We run using the command

```
java -classpath .;%JAVA_HOME%\lib\fscontext.jar;%JAVA_HOME%\lib\
providerutil.jar FileNaming file://d:/jdk1.3 lib\fscontext.jar
```

EXAMPLE 17.6   FileNaming.java

```
/* Uses a simple file system provider to illustrate JNDI.
 */

import java.util.*;
import javax.naming.*;

public class FileNaming {
  public static void main(String[] args) {
    Context context = null;
    try {
      Hashtable table = new Hashtable();
      table.put(Context.INITIAL_CONTEXT_FACTORY,
             "com.sun.jndi.fscontext.RefFSContextFactory");       // Note 1
      table.put(Context.PROVIDER_URL, args[0]);                   // Note 2
      context = new InitialContext(table);                        // Note 3
    }catch(NamingException e) {
       System.out.println("JNDI failure " + e.getMessage());
       System.exit(0);
    }
    Object object = null;
    NamingEnumeration dir = null;                                 // Note 4
    try {
      object = context.lookup(args[1]);                          // Note 5
      dir = context.list(args[0]);                               // Note 6
      System.out.println
         ("The name " + args[1] + " has the binding " + object);
      System.out.println();
      System.out.println("Directory contents for: " + args[0]);
      while (dir.hasMore()) {
        NameClassPair pair = (NameClassPair)dir.next();          // Note 7
        System.out.println(pair);
      }
    } catch (NamingException e) {
        System.out.println("Lookup failure " +
                e.toString());
```

```
        System.exit(1);
      }
    }
  }
```

....

Output

The name lib\fscontext.jar has the binding D:\jdk1.3\lib\fscontext.jar

```
Directory contents for: file://d:/jdk1.3
bin: javax.naming.Context
COPYRIGHT: java.io.File
demo: javax.naming.Context
doc: javax.naming.Context
docs: javax.naming.Context
include: javax.naming.Context
include-old: javax.naming.Context
jre: javax.naming.Context
lib: javax.naming.Context
LICENSE: java.io.File
plugin: javax.naming.Context
README-FS.txt: java.io.File
readme.html: java.io.File
README.txt: java.io.File
src.jar: java.io.File
Uninst.isu: java.io.File
```

....

Note 1:   We use the INITIAL_CONTEXT_FACTORY constant to set the environment property for specifying the initial context factory to use. Sun provides this file system JNDI implementation.

Note 2:   We use the PROVIDER_URL constant to set the environment property for specifying configuration information to the service provider. For the file system provider we pass the root directory in which to search.

Note 3:   We pass the hash table with the provider and configuration information to this constructor to the naming context.

Note 4:   A NamingEnumeration extends Enumeration. We use the hasMore method to see if another binding is available and the next method to obtain it.

Note 5:   We use the lookup method to lookup a single name and return its binding. The lookup is relative to the provider URL set in the context. In our test run we lookup lib\fscontext.jar, which contains classes for the file service.

Note 6:   dir = context.list(args[0])
The list method returns a NamingEnumeration of the bindings in the specified context.

Note 7:   `NameClassPair pair = (NameClassPair)dir.next()`
`NameClassPair` represents the name and class of the bound object. A directory is itself a context so its class is `javax.naming.Context`.

Other useful service providers are the Internet Domain Name System (DNS) which binds machine names to IP addresses and the Lightweight Directory Access and Protocol (LDAP).

THE BIG PICTURE

The Java Naming and Directory Interface™ provides uniform access from Java to various providers of naming and directory services. We can bind objects to names and lookup bindings. Directories, which we do not consider here, allow us to use attributes to search for objects.

TEST YOUR UNDERSTANDING

8.   The 'I' in JNDI stands for Interface. What do we need to use this interface?

SUMMARY

- Messaging systems allow software systems to communicate with each other. The Java Messaging Service is an API to use various messaging services.

- Publish-and-Subscribe messaging uses topics. Producers publish messages on a topic. Consumers subscribe to topics of interest. Many subscribers may receive the same message.

- Point-to-Point messaging uses queues. Produces send messages to a queue. Consumers receive messages from a queue. Each message goes to only one receiver.

- Message beans add an asynchronous capability to Enterprise JavaBean containers. The message bean can interact with other beans without the sender of the message having to wait for a response.

- The Java Naming and Directory Interface provides a uniform programming interface to various naming and directory services. It refers to a context for binding objects to names and looking up objects by name.

Program Modification Exercises

1.   Modify Example 17.1 to generate words and numbers at random rather than repeating three words and numbers repeatedly.

2.   Modify Example 17.2 to create a subscriber that subscribes to two topics.

3.   Modify Example 17.3 to create a receiver that receives messages from two queues.

PUTTING IT ALL TOGETHER   4.   Modify Example 17.5 to contact an `Agent` (defined in Section 10.3). Send the modified `ReceiverBean` a message containing the IDs of the customer and salesperson the information needed to order several items.

Program Design Exercises

· · · · · · · · · · ·

   5.   Use the JMS to implement a chat room. Use publish-and-subscribe so producers will publish messages on a topic and consumers will subscribe to topics of interest.

   6.   Use JMS to publish stock quotes to interested subscribers. Either find a source for stock quotes or simulate them. Each stock has a current price that changes while the market is open.

PUTTING IT ALL TOGETHER   7.   Use JMS to send messages to a Reverse queue. The receiver will send the message to ReverseServer of Section 2.3 and display the reversed strings.

PUTTING IT ALL TOGETHER   8.   Write a message-driven bean which receives information necessary to update a Customer using a Customer bean of Section 10.2.

Appendix A
Mouse and Key Events

Mouse Events

In the Java event model, a source object generates the event and a handler object handles it. Pressing a button generates a high-level action event. An event handler implementing the `ActionListener` interface has only to implement the `actionPerformed` method. With the mouse, the user can generate seven types of **low-level events** in a component source:

`MOUSE_PRESSED`	user pressed the mouse in a component
`MOUSE_RELEASED`	user released the mouse in a component
`MOUSE_CLICKED`	user clicked the mouse in a component
`MOUSE_ENTERED`	the mouse entered a component
`MOUSE_EXITED`	the mouse exited a component
`MOUSE_MOVED`	the mouse moved (no button down) in a component
`MOUSE_DRAGGED`	the mouse moved (button down) in a component

These are seven types of `MouseEvent`, which is a class in the `java.awt.event` package. The `MOUSE_CLICKED` type refers to a mouse click that consists of a mouse press followed by a mouse release, with no intervening mouse drag.

`MouseListener` and `MouseMotionListener`

Java uses two types of listener interfaces to handle mouse events. An object that wants to be notified of any of the first five mouse events must use the `addMouseListener` method to register as a `MouseListener` with the component that is the event source. It must implement each of the five methods of the `MouseListener` interface:

```
public void mousePressed(MouseEvent e);
public void mouseReleased(MouseEvent e);
public void mouseClicked(MouseEvent e);
public void mouseEntered(MouseEvent e);
public void mouseExited(MouseEvent e);
```

657

An object that wants to be notified of any of the last two mouse events must use the addMouseMotionListener method to register as a MouseMotionListener. It registers with the component that is the event source and must implement each of the two methods of the MouseMotionListener interface:

```
public void mouseMoved(MouseEvent e);
public void mouseDragged(MouseEvent e);
```

We can get the position of any mouse event using the getX and getY methods, as in

```
int x = event.getX();
```

where event is one of the seven types of mouse events. We can use the contains method of the Polygon class to see if the user pressed the mouse inside a polygon, as in

```
boolean inside = p.contains(event.getX(),event.getY());
```

where p is a polygon, and event is a mouse event describing a mouse press.

Moving the Mouse

Java separates the mouse moved and mouse dragged events from the other mouse events. Mouse motion events occur in great numbers and users not interested in them should not have to be bothered by them. As noted above, the MouseMotionListener interface has two methods, mouseMoved and mouseDragged, that need to be implemented by mouse motion listeners interested in these events. A mouse moved event occurs when the user moves the mouse with no buttons pressed, while a mouse dragged event occurs when the user moves the mouse while pressing a button.

Example A.1 enables the user to drag a triangle with the mouse. Figure A.1 shows the triangle when the applet has just started, and then after the user dragged it to the lower-right.

Figure A.1 The applet of Example A.1

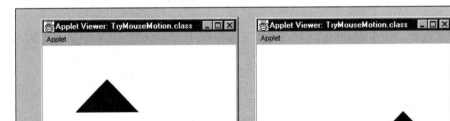

When the user presses the mouse inside the polygon, the mousePressed method saves the x- and y-coordinates of the mouse press for use if the user drags the mouse to a new position.

When the user does drag the mouse to a new position, the mouseDragged method translates the polygon by the amount (x-oldx,y-oldy) where (x,y) is the new location of the mouse, and (oldx,oldy) is its previous location. The `mouseDragged` method then updates the oldx and oldy values to the current position, (x,y), in case the user continues to drag the mouse.

Adapter Classes

An **adapter class** connects the source of an event with its target, implementing the methods of a listener interface. To simplify the handling of low-level events, Java provides adapter classes with default implementations of each method of the appropriate interface. The `MouseAdapter` class implements each of the five methods of the `MouseListener` interface with empty bodies. We can define a subclass of `MouseAdapter` to override just those methods which handle the events we are interested in.

For example, if we just want to handle the mouse pressed event, we can define a class `MousePressListener` which extends the `MouseAdapter` class and just overrides the `mousePressed` method.

TIP
☞

For easier handling of mouse events we use the `MouseAdapter` class from the AWT, but this technique is generally applicable. Whenever we define an interface, say

```
public interface Chores {
  public void washCar(Car aBigCar);
  public void feedDog(Dog iggy);
  public void makeCoffee(Coffee brew);
}
```

we should define an adapter class which implements the interface with empty bodies

```
public abstract class ChoresAdapter
                    implements Chores {
  public void washCar(Car aBigCar) { };
  public void feedDog(Dog iggy) { };
  public void makeCoffee(Coffee brew) { };
}
```

A class that implements the `Chores` interface can override those methods of the `ChoresAdapter` class which handle events of interest to it. For example, a class that just wants to feed the dog could override `ChoresAdapter` to provide an implementation for the `feedDog` method, inheriting the do nothing implementations for the `washCar` and `makeCoffee` methods.

```
public class DogFeeder extends ChoresAdapter {
  public void feedDog(Dog iggy) {
    // routine to feed the dog goes here
  };
}
```

EXAMPLE A.1   TryMouseAdapter.java

```
/* Drags a triangle to a new location using the position of
 * the mouse to determine how to move the polygon.
 */

import java.awt.*;
import java.awt.event.*;
import java.applet.Applet;

public class Mouse extends Applet
      implements MouseMotionListener {                          // Note 1
  private int [ ] x = {50,100,150};
  private int [ ] y = {100,50,100};
  private Polygon p = new Polygon(x,y,3);
  private int oldx; // Saves previous polygon position
  private int oldy;
  public void init() {
    addMouseListener(new MousePressListener());                 // Note 2
    addMouseMotionListener(this);
  }
  public void paint(Graphics g) {
    g.fillPolygon(p);
  }
  public void mouseMoved(MouseEvent event) { }
  public void mouseDragged(MouseEvent event) {
    int x = event.getX();
    int y = event.getY();
    if (p.contains(x,y)){
      p.translate(x - oldx, y - oldy);
      oldx = x;
      oldy = y;
      repaint();
    }
  }

  class MousePressListener extends MouseAdapter {               // Note 3
    public void mousePressed(MouseEvent event) {
      int x = event.getX();
      int y = event.getY();
      if (p.contains(x,y)){
        oldx = x;
        oldy = y;
      }
    }
  }
}
```

Note 1:   The applet implements the MouseMotionListener interface, but uses a
MousePressListener class, which extends the MouseAdapter class, to handle

mouse events. We could have defined another class, extending the Mouse-MotionAdapter class, to handle mouse motion events, instead of having the applet implement the mouse motion listener interface, but we will leave that to the exercises.

Note 2:   We create a new MousePressListener class to listen for mouse press events. MousePressListener extends MouseAdapter so it only has to implement the methods for the events it wants to handle.

Note 3:   MousePressListener is an inner class, defined inside the applet. It implements the mousePressed method to handle mouse pressed events. The MouseAdapter class provides default implementations of all five mouse listeners methods; we only have to override the handlers for the events in which we are interested.

THE BIG PICTURE

Unlike the ActionEvent and ItemEvent classes that represent higher-level events, MouseEvent deals with basic mouse operations. In contrast to the ActionListener interface which needs only one method, the MouseListener interface has five methods and the MouseMotionListener interface has two. The MouseAdapter and MouseMotionAdapter classes provide trivial implementations of these interfaces, in which the methods do nothing. A class can either implement all five methods of the MouseListener interface or extend MouseAdapter and override only those methods needed to handle the mouse events of interest. The choice is similar for events involving mouse motion.

Using the Keyboard

When using the keyboard we have to distinguish between the physical keys pressed and the characters they might represent. For example, we use two keys to represent uppercase letters. With the KeyEvent class and the KeyListener interface Java lets us respond to user generated keyboard events.

Focus

We press the mouse at a specific point, in a specific component. When we press the mouse, the component in which the mouse was pressed receives the mouse event. By contrast, pressing a key has no association with any specific component in the user interface. Java sends key events to the currently selected component, which is said to have the **focus**. A component that wants to receive key events must execute the requestFocus method to get the focus.

Key Events

. . . .

Java defines three key events, KEY_PRESSED, KEY_RELEASED, and KEY_TYPED. Java generates the key pressed or key released events for each physical key that is pressed or released, and generates the key typed event when a Unicode character is typed. The KEY_TYPED event allows Java to give meaning to sequences of key presses used to represent a single Unicode character. We press two keys, the Shift key and a letter key, to represent an uppercase letter. This facility is very useful in adapting keyboards to input characters from diverse languages.

To represent the physical keys, Java uses key codes, (named integer constants), starting with the letters VK_ (for virtual key). Some of these key codes are listed below:

Figure 0.1

Key Code	Physical Key
VK_A, ... , VK_Z	The keys A to Z
VK_0, ... , VK_9	The keys 0 to 9
VK_SHIFT	The shift key
VK_CONTROL	The control key
VK_DOWN, VK_UP	The down and up arrow keys
VK_RIGHT, VK_LEFT	The right and left arrow keys

Pressing the G key will generate a key pressed event and a key released event; it will also generate a key typed event which will indicate a G if the user pressed the Shift key while pressing the G key , or indicate a g otherwise. The key events that occur when the user types the uppercase letter G are:

Figure 0.2

Event	Description
KEY_PRESSED	Press the VK_SHIFT key
KEY_PRESSED	Press the VK_G key
KEY_TYPED	G was typed
KEY_RELEASED	Release the VK_G key
KEY_RELEASED	Release the VK_SHIFT key

KeyListener

An object that wishes to respond to key events must register as a key listener, using the addKeyListener method, with the source of these key events. The KeyListener interface has three methods,

```
public void keyPressed(KeyEvent e);
public void keyReleased(KeyEvent e);
public void keyTyped(KeyEvent e);
```

that a class wanting to listen to key events must implement. The source of a key event passes a `KeyEvent` object to the appropriate method. For example, pressing the G key will cause the component that has the focus to pass a `KeyEvent` object to the `keyPressed` method of any objects registered as key listeners with that component.

To see how we handle key events, consider a simple applet which displays the letter a user types, moving it to the left when the user presses the <- key, and moving it to the right when the use presses the -> key. If we move the letter using the arrow key alone, we change the position of the letter by two pixels, but if we hold down the Ctrl key while we move the letter using an arrow key, then we change the position of the letter by ten pixels. To implement this, the `keyPressed` method changes the increment to ten pixels when the user presses the Ctrl key, and the `keyReleased` method changes the increment back to two pixels when the user releases the Ctrl key.

Figure A.2 shows, on the left, the applet of Example A.2 initially displaying an A, and, on the right, displaying a G that the user typed and moved to the right of the applet.

Figure A.2   The applet of Example A.2

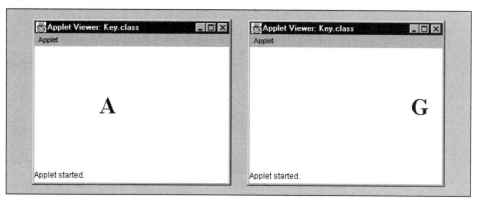

To find the physical key that was pressed or released we can use the `getKeyCode` method, as in:

```
event.getKeyCode();
```

where `event` describes the key event that occurred. The `getKeyCode` method returns a value of type **int** which gives the virtual key code for the key that was pressed or released. For example, it returns VK_G when the user presses or releases the G key, and VK_LEFT when the user presses or releases the left arrow key.

To find the character that was typed we can use the `getKeyChar` method, as in:

```
event.getKeyChar();
```

where `event` describes the key event that occurred. The `getKeyChar` method returns a value of type **char** which gives the character that was typed. For example, it will return g if the user types the G key alone, but will return G if the user presses and releases the G key while pressing the Shift key.

EXAMPLE A.2   Key.java

```
/* Displays a key pressed by the user. Moves the
 * character to the right if the user presses the ->
 * key and to the left if the user presses the <-
 * key. Moves ten pixels if the user holds down the
 * Ctrl key and two pixels otherwise.
 */

import java.awt.*;
import java.awt.event.*;
import java.applet.Applet;

public class Key extends Applet
                implements KeyListener {                        // Note 1
   public static int SLOW = 2;    // pixel change using arrow keys
   public static int FAST = 10;   // pixel change using arrow and Ctrl keys
   private int x = 100,y = 100;   // position of the character displayed
   private char theKey = 'A';
   private Font f = new Font("Serif",Font.BOLD,36);
   private int deltaX = SLOW;
   public void init() {
     setFont(f);
     addKeyListener(this);                                      // Note 2
     requestFocus();                                            // Note 3
   }
   public void paint(Graphics g) {
     g.drawString(String.valueOf(theKey),x,y);                  // Note 4
   }
   public void keyPressed(KeyEvent event){
     int code = event.getKeyCode();                             // Note 5
     if (code == KeyEvent.VK_CONTROL) {                         // Note 6
       deltaX = FAST;
     }
     else if (code == KeyEvent.VK_RIGHT){                       // Note 7
       x += deltaX;
       repaint();
     }
     else if (code == KeyEvent.VK_LEFT) {
       x -= deltaX;
       repaint();
     }
   }
   public void keyReleased(KeyEvent event) {
     if (event.getKeyCode() == KeyEvent.VK_CONTROL)
       deltaX = SLOW;                                           // Note 8
   }
   public void keyTyped(KeyEvent event) {
     theKey = event.getKeyChar();                               // Note 9
```

```
      repaint();
   }
}
```

....

Note 1: To handle key events a class can implement the KeyListener interface
which consists of the methods keyPressed, keyReleased, and keyTyped.

Note 2: The applet registers with itself as a key listener, meaning it wants to be
notified when key events occur. We could have defined another class to
handle the key events.

Note 3: The applet must request the focus to receive key events. Unlike clicking
the mouse, pressing a key does not associate that key press with any specific location in the applet. Any component in the applet could request the
focus, but in this simple example, there are no components other than the
applet itself.

Note 4: We convert the character that the user pressed (or A initially) to a string to
display at the current (x,y) position.

Note 5: The getKeyCode method returns the number of the actual key that the user
pressed. For example, pressing the G key would return VK_G from getKeyCode,
and pressing the Ctrl key would return VK_CONTROL.

Note 6: `if (code == KeyEvent.VK_CONTROL) {`
When the user presses the Ctrl key, we set the increment to 10 pixels, so
that if the user presses a left or right arrow key the letter will move by ten
pixels as long as the user does not release the Ctrl key.

Note 7: `else if (code == KeyEvent.VK_RIGHT){`
If the user presses the -> key, we add the increment to the current value of x
and ask that the applet be repainted. When Java calls the paint method the
character will be drawn deltaX pixels to the right of its current position.

Note 8: `deltaX = SLOW;`
If the user releases the Ctrl key, we set the increment back to two pixels, so
that if the user presses a left or right arrow key the letter will move by two
pixels as long as the user does not press the Ctrl key.

Note 9: `theKey = event.getKeyChar();`
If the user types a Unicode character then the applet will generate a keyTyped
event and the getKeyChar method will return the character typed (not the
key pressed). If the user presses the G key without pressing the Shift key,
then getKeyChar will return g.

Just as there is a MouseAdapter class which provides implementations of the five
methods of the MouseListener interface, there is a KeyAdapter class that provides

implementations, with empty bodies, of the three methods of the KeyListener interface. We did not use the KeyAdapter class in Example A.2.

THE BIG PICTURE

A component that wishes to receive key events can use the requestFocus method to get the focus. To handle key events, a class either implements each of the three methods of the KeyListener interface or extends KeyAdapter, overriding those methods of interest. Two of the key events, KEY_PRESSED and KEY_RELEASED, represent physical key presses, while the third, KEY_TYPED represents a Unicode character typed. The getKeyCode method returns the physical key code, while the getKeyChar method returns the character typed.

TEST YOUR UNDERSTANDING

TRY IT YOURSELF

1. Add a print statement to the mouseDragged method of Example A.1 to see how frequently mouse dragged events are generated. The statement should print the value of a counter which mouseDragged increments each time it handles an event.

2. List the key events that occur if the user presses the G key without holding down the Shift key.

TRY IT YOURSELF

3. Add print statements to the keyPressed, keyReleased, and keyTyped methods of Example A.2 to see in what order these events are generated when the user presses the R key. Try this with and without holding down the Shift key.

TRY IT YOURSELF

4. Remove the requestFocus() from the init method of Example A.2 and note what happens when you run the modified program.

Program Design Exercises

1. Develop a simplified Blackjack game. Create a deck of 51 cards, 17 each of threes, sevens, and tens. Deal two cards face down to the player and two cards to the computer, one face up and one face down. Allow the user to turn over the player's cards by clicking on them. The user will hit the H key to get another card and the S key to stand pat. The player loses if his total is greater than 21. If not, the dealer draws cards until the dealer's total is greater than 16. The dealer loses if her total is over 21. Otherwise the one with the greater score wins.

Appendix B
The ASCII Character Set

The first 32 characters and the last are control characters. We show only the printing characters in the following table.

32	blank	64	@	96	`
33	!	65	A	97	a
34	"	66	B	98	b
35	#	67	C	99	c
36	$	68	D	100	d
37	%	69	E	101	e
38	&	70	F	102	f
39	'	71	G	103	g
40	(	72	H	104	h
41	)	73	I	105	i
42	*	74	J	106	j
43	+	75	K	107	k
44	,	76	L	108	l
45	-	77	M	109	m
46	.	78	N	110	n
47	/	79	O	111	o
48	0	80	P	112	p
49	1	81	Q	113	q
50	2	82	R	114	r
51	3	83	S	115	s
52	4	84	T	116	t
53	5	85	U	117	u
54	6	86	V	118	v
55	7	87	W	119	w
56	8	88	X	120	x
57	9	89	Y	121	y
58	:	90	Z	122	z
59	;	91	[	123	{
60	<	92	\	124		
61	=	93	]	125	}
62	>	94	^	126	~
63	?	95	_		

Note: The ASCII values for the non-printing characters we use are 9 for '\t,' 10 for '\n,' and 13 for '\r.'

Appendix C
Some HTML Tags

` `	Break to the next line.
`<p>`	New paragraph (after a blank line).
`<em> ... </em>`	Emphasize the text.
`<strong>...</strong>`	Strongly emphasize the text.
`<title>... </title>`	Title, displayed separately from text.
`<h1>... </h1>`	Top-level header.
`<h3>... </h3>`	Third-level header, (lowest is sixth).
`<ul> ... </ul>`	An unordered list.
`<li>`	Element of a list.

```
<a                         An anchor, a hypertext link.
    href="URL"> </a>
<img                       An image.
    src="URL">
<applet                    A Java applet.
    codebase="URL"
    code="URL"
    height="integer"
    width="integer"> </applet>
<form                      An input form.
    action ="URL"
    method = ["GET"|"POST"]>
    form elements </form>
```

where form elements include

```
<input                     Various input types.
    name="name"
    size="number"
    type=["text"|"password"|"checkbox"|
    "radio"|"submit"|"reset"|
    "hidden"|"image"]
    value="value">
<select                    A list.
    name="name"
    size="number"
    multiple>
    option tags </select>
```

Appendix D
Javadoc

The `javadoc` utility produced the Java documentation, and we can use it to document our programs. The documentation for the Java 2 Platform Standard Edition may be downloaded from `http://java.sun.com/`. This HTML documentation describes each class, including fields, constructors, and methods.

We download the documentation ZIP file, which unzips in the `docs` directory. To find, for example, the documentation for the String class we go to the `docs\api\java\lang` directory and open `String.html`. Figure D.1 shows part of this file.

Figure D.1 `String.html`

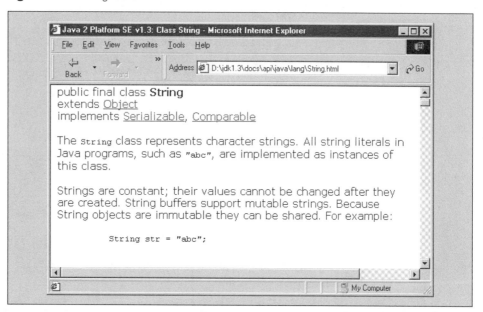

Figure D.2 shows the documentation for the `indexOf(String str)` method. It describes the method, the argument, the return value, and the exception it throws. The `javadoc` utility produced this documentation from a special kind of comment in the source code for the `String` class.

Figure D.2   The documentation for `indexOf(String str)`

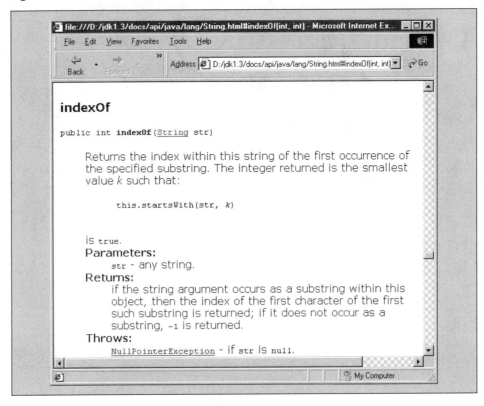

To create comments that javadoc will recognize, use the syntax

```
/**   This is a javadoc comment.
*/
```

with two asterisks after the initial forward slash. Inside the comment use tags that start with the @ character, such as

```
@author       list author here
@param        describe parameters here
@return       describe return value here
```

We illustrate the use of `javadoc` with the program `PassByValue.java`. Example D.1 shows the annotated version.

EXAMPLE D.1   PassByValue.java

```
/**   Illustrates pass by value
      @author   Art Gittleman
 */

public class PassByValue {
```

```
/** Computes the cube of its argument.  Changes the argument.
 *  @param aNumber the number to cube
 *  @return the cube of the argument
 */
public static int cube(int aNumber) {
  int result = aNumber*aNumber*aNumber;
  aNumber += 5;
  return result;
}
/** Test with the input 12.  Shows that the input is unchanged
 *  even though the argument changes inside the cube method.
 *  @param command-line arguments, not used in this example
 */
public static void main(String [ ] args) {
  int x = 12, value = 0;
  value = cube(x);
  System.out.println("The cube of " + x + " is " + value);
  System.out.println("The value of x is still " + x);
}
}
```

We use the command

```
javadoc PassByValue.java
```

to produce the `PassByValue.html` documentation file. Figures D.3 and D.4 show part of it.

Figure D.3 Part of `PassByValue.html`

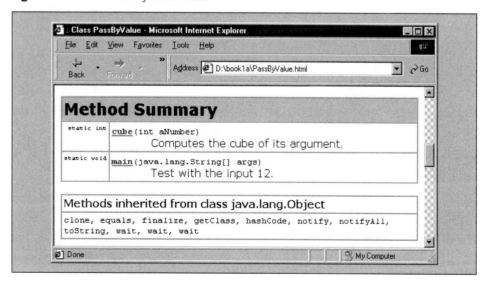

Figure D.4   Another part of `PassByValue.html`

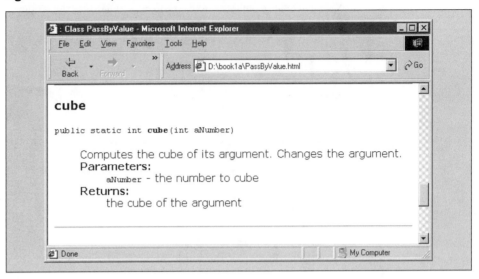

Answers to Odd-Numbered Test Your Understanding Exercises

Chapter 1

1. In Example 1 the output is value=8, the value set in the catch block when an exception occurs. Example 2 also prints the stack trace to show explicitly the error that has occurred.

3. b

5. The program aborts with the exception

```
java.io.NotSerializableException: Person
```

7. The changed part is:

```
for (int i=0; i<10; i++)
    raf.writeDouble(i);
raf.seek(40);
double number = raf.readDouble();
System.out.println("The number starting at byte 40 is " + number);
raf.seek(8);
number = raf.readDouble();
System.out.println("The number starting at byte 8 is " + number);
```

9. import java.awt.*;

```
import java.awt.event.*;
import java.applet.Applet;
public class Separate extends Applet   {
    private Button print = new Button("Print");
    private Button clear = new Button("Clear");
    private Label message = new Label("Message goes here");
    private PrintAdapter printAdapter = new PrintAdapter(message);
    private ClearAdapter clearAdapter = new ClearAdapter(message);
```

```
        public void init() {
            add(message);
            add(print);
            add(clear);
            print.addActionListener(printAdapter);
            clear.addActionListener(clearAdapter);
        }
    }
    class PrintAdapter implements ActionListener {
        private Label message;
        public PrintAdapter(Label 1) {
            message = 1;
        }
        public void actionPerformed(ActionEvent event) {
            message.setText(event.getActionCommand());
        }
    }
    class ClearAdapter implements ActionListener {
        private Label message;
        public ClearAdapter(Label 1) {
            message = 1;
        }
        public void actionPerformed(ActionEvent event) {
            message.setText("");
        }
    }
```

11. main 1, Bonnie 1, Clyde 1, main 2, main 3, main 4, Clyde 2, main 5, Bonnie 2, Clyde 3, Bonnie 3, Clyde 4, Clyde 5, Bonnie 4, Bonnie 5

13. For example, with `java PutGet 100 500`, the buffer becomes full six times, while with `java PutGet 500 100`, the buffer becomes empty ninetimes.

15. The result is the same. The overall row weight is the maximum of the weights for each component in that row, so giving b1 a `weighty` of 1.0 and b2 a `weighty` of 0.0 is the same as the original in which these weights were reversed.

17. Because `gridx` remains equal to 1, the remaining buttons appear in the same column, below b4. Since b6 has a `weightx` of 1.0 and the other buttons have a `weightx` of 0.0, the second column, containing b6, gets all the extra space.

19. `Vector v = new Vector(25,7);`

Chapter 2

1. Using the applet viewer shows a blank screen because the applet viewer does not display HTML documents but only runs applets embedded in those documents.

3. The program displays the HTML file, index.html, with all the HTML tags.

5. The changes are:
```
        URLConnection c = url.openConnection();
        input = new BufferedReader
                        (new InputStreamReader(c.getInputStream()));
```

7. The change is:

```
System.out.println("Content type: " + c.getHeaderField("Content-type"));
```

9. The output includes part of the request headers, which should be informational only to the client.

11. The client receives a message that it is connected, but no data because only headers were requested. We could use this to inspect the headers if we modified the program.

13. Clients will be active simultaneously, and will alternately receive data.

15. The port 3000 overrides the default port of 1099.

Chapter 3

1. The ID is unique, but the name may be duplicated.

3. ```
INSERT INTO Salesperson VALUES ('12', 'Peter Patterson', '66 FifthSt.')
INSERT INTO Salesperson VALUES ('98','Donna Dubarian', '77 Sixth St.')
```

5. ```
DELETE FROM OrderItem
WHERE OrderNumber = '5' AND ItemNumber = '444444'
```

7. ```
SELECT OrderNumber FROM Orders, Salesperson
WHERE Orders.SalesPersonID = Salesperson.SalesPersonID
AND   SalespersonName = 'Peter Patterson'
```

9. Changes are:

```
Class.forName(args[0]); (instead of new JdbcOdbcDriver())
Connection con = DriverManger.getConnection(args[1], user, password);
```

11. ```
SELECT DISTINCT SalespersonName, CustomerName
FROM Salesperson, Customer, Orders
WHERE Orders.CustomerID = Customer.CustomerID
AND   Orders.SalesPersonID = Salesperson.SalesPersonID
```

13. Change `rs.getString("CustomerName")` to `rs.getString(1)` in two places and change `rs.getString("OrderNumber")` to `rs.getString(1)`

15. ```
SELECT DISTINCT CustomerName, CustomerAddress
FROM Customer, Salesperson, Orders
WHERE Customer.CustomerID = Orders.CustomerID
AND   Salesperson.SalesPersonID = Orders.SalesPersonID
AND   SalespersonName = 'Peter Patterson'
```

17. Use `dbMetaData.getTables(null, null, "Order%", tables);`

19. Add

```
displayStrings("Type Info Column Names and Types", colNamesTypes(rs));
  after getTypeInfo().
```

21. java.sql.SQLException: [Microsoft][ODBC Microsoft Access 97 Driver]Invalid cursor state
```

25. After pressing the Display button, the new labels are truncated to have the same size as the generic table labels they are to replace.

27. The `fieldValue` text field remains 12 character wide, centered in its two-column field, rather than expanding to fill the two columns.

Chapter 4

1. Using JRun, `Welcome.class` belongs in the `JRUN_HOME\servers\default\default-app\web-inf\classes` directory. The URL is `http://localhost:8100/servlet/Welcome`. JRun must be started first.

3. Use `Welcome.java` for an entertaining example. Using JRun, put the `Welcome.java` in `JRUN_HOME\servers\default\default-app`.
   Enter the URL http://localhost:8100/Welcome.java. Be sure to start JRun.

5. Change the action to

   `http://localhost:8100/servlet/PostOrGetOrder`.

7. Every time we press the refresh button or use another copy of the browser to connect, the display increases the connection count.

9. The browser cannot display the page.

11. The servlet still functions properly because it has a `doGet` method to respond to GET requests.

13. The order will be updated and the same session ID will be listed for this session.

15. With GET the client appends the data to the URL http://localhost:8100/getOrder.jsp?Order=ice+cream while with POST it is sent separately.

17. We call bean methods inside a <% %> tag. There may be other bean methods besides those that retrieve property values.

Chapter 5

1. There is no difference between the commented and the uncommented version.

3. Use the command `java GrowthFrameSwing 2`.

5. Using `MatteBorder(brightGreen)` makes the border have the thickness needed to draw the icon around the border. The message appears over the icons. Using `MatteBorder(5,5,5,5,brightGreen)` causes only a portion of the icon to be drawn.

7. We can select multiple colors from the list. The selected color with the lowest index becomes the drawing color.

9. We can select both the square and the circle, or neither. The last shape selected or deselected is drawn.

11. The dialog gives the choices Yes or No, which are not appropriate answers for the question, How are your studies progressing?

13. Change the `setSelecteIndex` statement to `tabPane.setSelectedIndex(1);`

15. Add another entry, such as `{"326", "Operating Systems"}`, to the courses array.

Chapter 6

1. The change to the `outcode` method would not be a good idea, because it would limit a point to being in one position only, whereas a point might be both below and to the left. The current `outcode` method returns a flag that encodes this information.

3. The ellipses which replace the rectangles combine in similar patterns to those shown in Figure 3. The combining operations apply to any Area.

5. The shear will transform the original rectangle to {(45,60), (145,110), (170,160), (70,110)} and the translation will transform it to {(165,60), (265,110), (190,110), (290,160)}.

7. Changing the fifth argument in the BasicStroke constructor for `buBeDa` to `new float[] {10,5,5,5}` will create a dashed rectangle with dashes alternating in size between 5 and 10 with a space of 5 between them.

9. The lower CAT only shows when it intersects the ellipse.

11. No

13. No. Java throws an exception,

```
Exception in thread "main" java.lang.IllegalArgumentException:
   Zero length string passed to TextLayout constructor.
```

Chapter 7

1. The Unicode representation for ñ is 241. Because Cp1252 is the same, the value 241 is output. Displaying in Notepad shows señor, because Notepad uses the Cp1252 encoding. Display in DOS shows se±or, because DOS uses the Cp437 encoding in which 241 is ±.

3. The Unicode representation for ñ is 241. Because the output encoding is Cp437, Java ouputs the value 164, which is the Cp437 code for ñ. Displaying in DOS shows señor, but displaying in Notepad shows se or, since   has the code 164 in Cp1252.

5. Using `java Numbers fr FR >out`, the output from Example 3 for the

```
Swiss French locale is
    12'345.679
    SFr. 12'345.68
    1'234'567.90%
```

and, using java DateTime fr FR >out, the output from Example 4 for the Swiss-French locale is

```
    mardi, 4. juillet 2000 14.10. h GMT-07:00
    4. juillet 2000 14:10:05 GMT-07:00
    4 juil. 00 14:10:05
    04.07.00 14:10
```

7. The default Spanish collator distinguishes uppercase from lowercase and accented characters from corresponding unaccented letter, but does not distinguish control characters. Its strength is TERTIARY.

9. The NumberFormat currency instance, nf, formats currency according to the locale.

11. Change the `getBundle` call to

```
bundle = ResourceBundle.getBundle(resources);
```

Include a third parameter, `String resources`, in the GrowthProperty constructor.

Change main to:

```
public static void main(String [] args) {
  String language = "en";
  String country = "US";
  String resources = "Labels";
  if (args.length == 3) {
    language = args[0];
    country  = args[1];
    resources = args[2];
  }
  GrowthProperty f = new GrowthProperty(language, country, resources);
  f.setSize(300,200);
  f.show();
}
```

Chapter 8

1. The screen will flicker and unless you remove the override to update, it will also show extra pieces of the image..

3. The image is not erased between frames, so when the image is shrinking the screen still shows the extra pieces from the larger image.

5. If we stop the applet, the whistle continues to play until we terminate the applet.

7. The frame pops up but does not display the media file.

9. The cube fills the entire window so it does not look like an object in space.

11. (0,0,.8f)

13. Increasing the shininess reduces the highlights.

15. The objects spin faster as the second Alpha argument decreases.

Chapter 9

1. Click on the background entry in the Properties window and choose orange in the color editor that pops up.

3. Bind using the Bind Properties item of the Edit menu. Higher prices make the juggler go slower.

5. The change is vetoed.

7. Bind using the Bind Properties item of the Edit menu.

9. The BeanBox cannot load `Smiley.jar` if `Smiley` does not implement `Serializable`.

11. Use the Events, nosePress item in the Edit menu to hookup one Friendly to the `startJuggling` method of the Juggler, and another to the `stopJuggling` method.

13. The `instantiate` method allows us to load a `.ser` file for a serialized bean whose state we changed by configuring in a tool such as the BeanBox. Using **new** loads only the original version of the bean.

15. The Juggler does not appear in the applet.

Chapter 10

1. We extend the EJBObject interface.

3. HelloClient.java is the client application's source file. HelloClient.jar contains the system-generated files needed for the client to communicate with enterprise beans on the server.

5. `WHERE "due" >= ?1 AND "due" <= ?2`

7. ejbRemove, ejbActivate, ejbPassivate, and setSessionContext.

9. Most importantly, Hello is stateless and Agent is stateful. The Agent bean communicates with the Customer entity bean to satisfy client requests.

11. No.

Chapter 11

1. The conditions on implementations of Set methods may be more stringent. The `add` method must check for duplicates in a Set but not generally in a Collection.

3. Not directly, because the element type is Object. Primitive types need to be wrapped in wrapper classes such as Integer.

5. The punctuation is included, giving words like "detract.," and "us--that."

7. The List methods specify the position at which to insert or update. The ListIterator does not need this argument because it always inserts or updates at the current position of the iteration.

9. Change the argument in the line

   `linkImp.get(5000);`

   to get the time for 10,000 gets. The actual time will vary depending on the system used. Relatively, the time taken increases as the element index increases.

11. The time decreases.

13. It is much easier to find a range of words near the word for which one is searching to provide possible correct spellings.

15. Java throws a `ClassCastException` because the String cannot be cast to a `NewOrderedName`. The `compareTo` method for `NewOrderedName` checks first name, last name, and middle initial and does not work with strings. We could add a constructor to create a NewOrderedName from a String.

17. The algorithms that require the data to be ordered specify a List parameter.

Chapter 12

1. When using the command

   ```
   java -Dfile.encoding=ISO8859 ShowProperties
   ```

   the output shows

   ```
   file.encoding=ISO8859
   ```

3. In IE5,

   ```
   cannot access file out  (to read from out)
   cannot access "java.sun.com":80  (to connect)
   ```

5. ```
   grant codebase "file:/c:/test/" {
      permission java.io.FilePermission "c:\\test\\results", "write";
   };
   ```

7. The policy file is

   ```
   grant {
       permission java.security.AllPermission;
   };
   Running Example 2 with this policy file gives the output
       OK to read from file 'out'
       OK to connect to java.sun.com
       OK to write to file 'out'
       Can access java.version
       Can access file.encoding
   ```

9. ```
   iload_3
   bipush 17
   iadd
   istore 4
   ```

11. ```
    dload_2       // load variable 2
    dconst_1      // load 1.0
    dcmpl         // compare (puts -1 or 0 on stack if variable 2 is <= 1.0)
    ifle  00 06   // jump six bytes ahead to do the assignment
    goto 00 05    // jump five bytes ahead to skip the assignment
    iconst_2      // load 2
    istore_3      // store in variable 3
    ```

13. ```
    42
    183 0 6
    177
    ```

```
16 25
60
16 12
61
27
16 15
96
61
178 0 7
18 1
182 0 8
178 0 7
28
182 0 9
177
```

15. 182 0 9 refers to entry 9 Fieldref 10 class 3 name_and_type 13

Class entry 3 is Class 7 entry 25

Entry 25 is java/io/PrintStream

Name_and_type entry 13 is name 32 type 15

Entry 32 is println

Entry 15 is (I)V

so this instruction invokes the println method of the PrintStream class and the method takes one integer argument and returns void.

Chapter 13

1. They are all well-formed.

3.
```
<cds>
   <cd>
      <title>Beethoven Violin Concerto</title>
      <artist>Itzhak Perlman</artist>
      <artist>Daniel Barenboim</artist>
      <tracks>5</tracks>
   </cd>
   <cd>
      <title>from broken hearts to blue skies</title>
         <artist>Susannah McCorkle</artist>
      <tracks>14</tacks>
   </cd>
</cds>
```

5. `startElement`

7.
```
if (args[1].equals(true))
   validate = true;
else
   validate = false;
```

9. `getDocumentElement()` from the class that implements the Document interface.

11. `<xsl:apply-templates></xsl:apply-templates>`

13. `<xsl:template match="book[@type='text']">`

15. `getInternetTime`

Chapter 14

1. The `Math` class in the J2ME has far fewer methods. It contains `abs`, `max`, and `min` for `long` and `int`.

3. The value entered would be restricted to being a number.

5. `Displayable`

7. `javax.microedition.io`

9. We would open a `DataInputStream` to read typed values. For example `readInt` will read an `int` value.

11. We could enter `byte` or `String` data without using steam classes.

13. We get an erroneous value because we are reading an `int` from bytes entered as a `String`.

15. `getGameAction` returns a negative value when passed the code for the up arrow key, and a positive value when passed the code for the 2ABC key.

Chapter 15

1. `MulticastSocket`

3. With multicasting the entire message is not sent to each recipient. The message only needs to be replicated when a location branches from the common path.

5. We run an HTTP server so the client can download the driver needed to communicate with the service.

7. When a Jini client uses events it can be notified if a service appears after the client has tried to discover it.

9. A Jini client and service can communicate using any mutually agreeable protocol.

11. The SpaceMaster program provides a Jini client. The JavaSpace is the Jini service.

Chapter 16

1. We use the `.tld` extension for tag library definition files.

3. Add

```
<attribute>
  <name>size</name>
  <required>true</required>
  <rtexprvalue>true</rtexprvalue>
</attribute>
```

after the `<attribute>` tag for name.

5. `setFoo`

7. `EVAL_BODY_INCLUDE`

9. `doAfterBody`

11. `id`

13. `connection`, `statement`, and `resultSet`

Chapter 17

1. In the `jndi.properties` file in the classpath.

3. `MessageListener`

5. The analogies are

TopicConnectionFactory and	QueueConnectionFactory
Topic	Queue
TopicSession	QueueSession
TopicSubscriber	QueueReceiver

7. When the client sends a message to `ReceiverBean` it returns immediately and can continue executing. When the client calls an `Agent` directly it waits for its response.

Index

Note: The boldface entries refer to example programs in the text that are also found on the CD included with this text.